THE PROCESS OF PARENTING

EIGHTH EDITION

Jane B. Brooks

Mc Graw Hill

Connect
Learn
Succeed™

The McGraw·Hill Companies

Connect
Learn
Succeed™

Published by McGraw-Hill, an imprint of The McGraw-Hill Companies, Inc., 1221 Avenue of the Americas, New York, NY 10020. Copyright © 2011, 2008, 2004, 1999, 1996, 1991, 1987, 1981. All rights reserved. No part of this publication may be reproduced or distributed in any form or by any means, or stored in a database or retrieval system, without the prior written consent of The McGraw-Hill Companies, Inc., including, but not limited to, in any network or other electronic storage or transmission, or broadcast for distance learning.

This book is printed on acid-free paper.

4 5 6 7 8 9 0 DOC/DOC 1 0 9 8 7 6 5 4 3 2 1

ISBN: 978-0-07-337876-3
MHID: 0-07-337876-3

Vice President Editorial: *Michael Ryan*
Publisher: *David Patterson*
Sponsoring Editor: *Allison McNamara*
Marketing Manager: *Pam Cooper*
Managing Editor: *Meghan Campbell*
Developmental Editor: *Maureen Spada*
Project Manager: *Erika Jordan*
Production Service: *Laserwords Maine*
Manuscript Editor: *Laura Patchkofsky*
Design Manager and Cover Designer: *Laurie Entringer*
Photo Research: *Poyee Oster*
Production Supervisor: *Laura Fuller*
Composition: *10.5/12 Berkeley by Laserwords Private Limited*
Printing: *45# New Era Matte Plus, R.R. Donnelley & Sons*

Cover Image: © *Digital Vision/PunchStock*

Credits: The credits section for this book begins on page C-1 and is considered an extension of the copyright page. (Note: If credits are short and will fit easily, they can be listed on this page.)

Library of Congress Cataloging-in-Publication Data

Brooks, Jane B.
     The process of parenting / Jane B. Brooks.—8th ed.
         p. cm.
     ISBN-13: 978-0-07-337876-3 (alk. paper)
     ISBN-10: 0-07-337876-3
     1. Parenting—United States.   I. Title.
     HQ755.8.B75 2011
649'.1—dc22
                                                                    2009036806

The Internet addresses listed in the text were accurate at the time of publication. The inclusion of a Web site does not indicate an endorsement by the authors or McGraw-Hill, and McGraw-Hill does not guarantee the accuracy of the information presented at these sites.

www.mhhe.com

BRIEF CONTENTS

CONTENTS

CHAPTER **4**

Nurturing Close Family Relationships in a Technological Society 101

CHAPTER **5**

Supporting Children's Growth and Development 133

PART II
Parenting at Developmental Stages 173

CHAPTER 7

Parenting Infants: The Years from Birth to Two 204

CHAPTER **8**

Parenting in Early Childhood: The Years from Two to Five 234

CHAPTER 10
Parenting Early Adolescents 298

CHAPTER **11**

Parenting Late Adolescents 327

CHAPTER 12
Parenting Adults 359

PART III
Parenting in Varying Life Circumstances 385

CHAPTER 13
Parenting and Working 386

A CONCEPTUAL FRAMEWORK FOR UNDERSTANDING THE IMPACTS OF WORK, FAMILY, AND COMMUNITY ON PARENTS AND CHILDREN 387

CHAPTER **15**

Parenting in Complex Family Structures 441

CHAPTER **16**

Parenting in Challenging Times 468

PREFACE

Research advances in many areas have made this revision an exciting one, because we have a greater understanding of the many factors that affect both children's and parents' behavior. First advances in neuroscience have enabled researchers to identify genes and neuroendocrine changes that affect children's behavior and influence the effects of parenting. Conversely, research shows how parenting influences the expression of genes and levels of neuroendocrine hormones.

Second, increasing numbers of longitudinal studies with significant numbers of ethnic minority participants yield more accurate information on how children change over time and the effects of cultural factors on such changes. Third, statistical analyses have enabled researchers to identify the many pathways children and teens take in moving from one stage to another, for example, from high school through young adulthood, or from being single to being in a relationship and being a parent. Such research highlights the variety of developmental patterns and helps us to identify earlier conditions that most frequently are associated with later competence.

Just as research advances inform us about the effects of genes and temperamental qualities on children's behavior, other advances inform us of people's sensitivity to what happens in the environment around them even if they are not directly involved. For example, people engage in more rule-breaking when they are in an environment of order or disorder, reflected in graffiti or litter. Children feel angry and humiliated in an environment in which they witness bullying even though they are not targets and do not know the children involved.

Much new research identifies the powerful ways parents contribute to children's positive growth and development in big and small ways. For example, mothers' positive support (there was no measure of father's support) reduced depressed feelings in adolescent boys and girls of all ethnic groups, and mothers' ability to manage their own frustration and continue to express positive regard and caring for children while helping with mundane homework tasks enabled children to remain confident and learn, whereas mothers' criticism and negative feelings in homework tasks were related to children's feelings of discouragement and helplessness.

Parents' behaviors not only promote healthy development, but they also buffer children from the negative effects of many stressful experiences. Sensitive, responsive parenting buffers children from the effects of negative genes, from the effects of economic downturns, from the effects of discrimination and prejudice, from the effects of divorce, and from the effects of early maturation for girls. So, research documents the many ways in which parents' positive support improves life.

Exciting new interventions teaching parents to use sensitive, responsive behaviors with children have had great success in increasing secure attachments and emotional security in brief periods of time. Based on attachment theory, the interventions, carried out in the home, help parents identify the many ways they connect with their children in synchronized interactions to support children's growth. Parents respond to this approach in which only what goes right is discussed, and they make further changes.

Other new interventions that include teachers and schools in programs to change children's behaviors have had success and illustrate the many partners that play a role in children's growth. For example, training nursery school teachers to carry out the same positive behavioral methods taught to parents has greatly decreased preschoolers' noncompliance, perhaps because the children have the same system of adult responses for all their waking hours. Another school program carried out with parents and early adolescents has proven successful in preventing the increase in depressed feelings often seen in this age period.

Throughout much of the research there is an overriding theme of the power of positive feelings—parents' positive feelings toward children, children's positive confidence in their growing abilities, their positive approach in exploring the world, and the positive approach of other adults and systems in their lives such as teachers and schools. The research also identifies the power of a positive relationship between parents—whether married or not—and the need for a positive support system for a parent. If support does not come from a marital partner or the other parent, then research suggests a parent has to form such a system because all parents need support in child-rearing endeavors.

Although much new research documents the importance of parenting, few parents have had training to succeed in this important activity. Our society requires that people demonstrate competence, for example, to drive a car, or practice a profession. But nowhere does society require systematic parenting education, which may matter most of all.

The aim of the eighth edition of *The Process of Parenting*, like that of earlier editions, is to help parents and caregivers translate their love and concern for their children into effective parenting skills. The book strives to bring to life the child's world and concerns, so parents can better understand what their children may be thinking and feeling. The book also describes myriad thoughts and feelings—positive and negative—that parents have so that they can better understand themselves. Finally, the book highlights the influence of the social context on both parents and children.

APPROACH OF *THE PROCESS OF PARENTING*

I have selected topics and written this book from the points of view of a parent, a clinician, a researcher, and a teacher of parenting skills. I have the firm conviction that anyone who wants to invest attention and effort in becoming a competent, caring parent can do so in his or her own way. The single prerequisite is the desire to succeed along with the willingness to invest time and energy, and the results are well worth the effort. My experience as a clinician has shown me that children face many difficult situations in life; with a loving, supportive caregiver, children can live life fully and happily even if temporarily engulfed by trauma. All the current research supports that view as well.

Children are not the only ones enriched by adults' efforts to be effective parents. Helping children grow is an intense and exciting experience that brings special rewards to us as parents. Our physical stamina, agility, and speed increase as we care for infants and toddlers. Our emotional stamina grows as we deal with our own intense feelings toward our children and help children learn to express and modulate their feelings. Our intellectual skills grow as we answer young children's questions and, later, help them learn school subjects. In helping children grow, we gain for ourselves an inner vitality and richness that affects all our relationships.

ORGANIZATION

Like earlier editions, this edition has three parts. Part I—General Concepts, Goals, and Strategies of Parenting—includes Chapters 1–5. As in the past, Chapter 1 describes the roles and interactions of the three participants in the process of parenting—the child, the parent, and the social system—and the powerful role parents play in children's lives and the ways social forces help or hinder parents and children's growth.

Chapter 3 continues to focus on the cultural influences on parenting, including cultural models of parenting strategies and the ways that values and cultural influences shape what parents do in daily interactions. The chapter focuses on the process by which cultural values exert their influence. The experiences of specific ethnic groups continue to appear throughout the text as they relate to the topic of discussion. For example, ethnic group identity formation and prejudice are discussed in the chapters dealing with identity formation.

As in the past, Chapter 4 focuses on creating close emotional relationships among family members with a special emphasis on how parents and children stay close in a fast-paced technological society. This chapter includes new information on how parents and children apportion their time to include all their activities of school/work, family relationships, and leisure time. Chapter 5 has its same emphasis on all the activities parents undertake to support and stimulate children's growth—ensuring safety and health, guarding against destructive media influences, and providing a collaborative family atmosphere that stimulates children's learning the many competencies needed for independence and adult life.

Part II—Parenting at Developmental Stages—begins with Chapter 6 on how parents make the transition to parenthood. This chapter presents new information on how young adults become parents. It focuses on how the methods and timing of becoming parents influence the process of parenting. Information on teen parenting that appeared here before has been moved to Chapter 14, "Single Parenting," and the material on adoptive parenting has been moved to Chapter 15, "Parenting in Complex Family Structures."

Chapters 7–11 deal with children from birth through the high school years. Each chapter presents updated information on children's physical, intellectual, and personal-social development during the five age periods, emphasizing ways parents can promote positive behaviors. This edition provides new information on neurophysiogical changes in several age periods, includes new information on the development of executive functioning (abilities to plan and organize behavior), and continues to pay particular attention to understanding and promoting children's emotional regulation, especially the regulation of anger and sadness.

Chapter 12 describes theories and tasks of parenting children from age eighteen onward. The chapter presents new information on the many paths teens take to young adulthood and the kinds of high school experiences that facilitate the process of maturing.

Part III—Parenting in Varying Life Circumstances—describes how parents adapt parenting strategies to meet the challenges of everyday life: parenting and working (Chapter 13), parenting in single-parent families including teen parenting and parenting after a divorce or death of a parent (Chapter 14), parenting in families with complex family structures including parenting in stepfamilies, gay/lesbian families, and adoptive families (Chapter 15), and parenting at times of challenge, (Chapter 16). Chapters 13, 14, and 15 emphasize understanding the nature of the circumstances and challenges involved in each situation and discuss how to promote effective functioning in parents and children—in combining working and parenting and parenting in many different family structures.

In Chapter 16, we look at different forms of challenge for children and also for their parents, including physical illness, child maltreatment, community violence, and the current threat of terrorism.

There are several ways in which the chapters can be used together but out of sequential order. For example, before discussing the material in Chapter 6, "Becoming Parents," one might want to summarize material in the beginning of Chapter 12, the transition to young adulthood, because how youth become young adults also sets the stage for how they become parents. Similarly, material in Chapter 4, on families' daily activities, sets the stage for Chapter 13, "Parenting and Working," because most mothers today are working mothers, and most working mothers work full time. Material in Chapter 3 on cultural forces on children's development can be used when it comes to the formation of ethnic identity in the developmental chapters.

CHANGES TO THE EIGHTH EDITION

Chapter 1. New sections or information on

- ways parents' behaviors, children's qualities, and society's resources interact to promote children's growth
- what parents want society to do to help them rear children

Chapter 2. New sections or information on

- insights from genetics, neurobiology, temperament, and study of executive functioning to guide parents' behavior
- intervention with parents titled Video-Feedback Intervention Positive Parenting, used to help parents facing such special challenging situations such as parenting premature infants, parenting when parents feel insecure, parenting adoptive children

Chapter 3. New sections or information on

- ways culture shapes children's development, illustrated with teens' sense of identity related to confidence cultural beliefs give them in dealing with the future
- cultural influences that provide protective or risk factors for parents and children with examples from different ethnic groups and cultures from other parts of the world
- a model of child development that accounts for the experiences that ethnic minority and immigrant children and families experience in terms of discrimination and isolation
- ways research suggests dealing with discrimination
- influence of education as a factor in social class differences among families
- effects of poverty on parents' and children's behavior

Chapter 4. New sections or information on

- rhythms of American family life and ways parents and children combine work/school and family life in comparison with other countries around the world and in ethnic groups within this country
- popular questions raised about parenting and children: Are children overscheduled? Do parents stay too involved in children's lives?

Chapter 5. New sections or information on

- modeling of behavior based on what you think others have done depending on an atmosphere of order and disorder
- sensitive discipline based on attachment theory
- prosocial and moral development
- parenting program designed on the basis of parents' requests

Chapter 6. New sections or information on

- the process of family formation based on recent longitudinal research describing the many paths to parenthood and the personal and social resources that predict these pathways
- birth defects related to assisted reproductive technology
- ways to talk to children about the use of egg and sperm donors
- forming a coparenting alliance with the other parent before the baby is born

Chapter 7. New sections or information on

- maintaining a coparenting alliance in the newborn period and through the first year of life
- programs that help parents deal with a fussy, irritable baby
- interventions with depressed parents

- interventions with parents at risk for abusing young children
- description of Zero to Three, an organization that provides information and guidelines for parents and caregivers

Chapter 8. New sections or information on

- children's mastery orientation to learning
- ways of evaluating self
- parental and environmental factors related to children's anger from birth to age eight
- ways of parenting shy, inhibited children
- development of self-esteem in this period
- development of self-control
- insights from Vygotsky's theory in parenting children this age
- socializing children's gender and ethnic identities
- role of conversations in conveying cultural values
- ways parents stimulate children's competence
- strategies for helping hyperactive preschoolers

Chapter 9. New sections or information on

- parents' views of children's abilities as internal/unchangeable factors or as modifiable/changeable factors
- role of teachers and school culture in children's learning
- immigrant children's experiences in the school system
- interview with mother who homeschooled two of her five children
- forming and socializing ethnic identity
- applying attachment theory to parenting in this stage of development
- how one boy and his family coped with his attention-deficit hyperactivity disorder
- description of five-session parent workshop to reduce parents' stress

Chapter 10. New sections or information on

- process of physical maturation and social and psychological factors that influence it
- relationship between brain development and emotional and sleep patterns
- program teaching children that the brain is like a muscle and improves with use to prevent decrease in grades that occurs at this age
- early teens' emotional ups and downs and patterns of spillover from home to school and from school to home
- cultural differences in children's emotional patterns
- changes in boys' and girls' gender attitudes and relationship of changes to parents' attitudes
- cultural influences on identity formation
- comparison of parent–child relationships in ethnic groups within this country and in countries around the world

- children's reactions to parents' attempts to control them
- sources of conflicts between parents and children
- parenting strategies for encouraging strong sense of ethnic identify
- Internet use and peer relationships and parents' strategies for coping with them

Chapter 11. New sections or information on

- up-to-date survey of sexual behaviors, teens' worries and fears regarding sexual activity, and where they seek advice
- up-to-date survey of substance use following samples from junior high through young adulthood with information regarding developmental factors that promote or protect against drug use
- work patterns of children
- emotional development and growth in self-esteem
- changes in teens' aggression and depression
- self-regulation as related to behaviors in preschool and the early elementary school years, to parents' behavior, to social relationships
- role of religion in teens' lives
- depression scores over the adolescent years in teens from different ethnic groups
- school-based program that works with teachers, parents, and children to prevent rise in depression
- ways to encourage teens' sense of purpose

Chapter 12. New sections or information on

- common trends in those entering young adulthood and parents' role in supporting growth and development
- six paths to young adulthood and the social and personal resources that predict them
- those in need of special support in the transition to adulthood
- pathways to adulthood for those in immigrant groups
- general parenting strategies focusing on issues of growing autonomy and needs for closeness

Chapter 13. New sections or information on

- conceptual framework and research on the impact of work and community resources on parents' and children's functioning as parents integrate work and family life
- effects of community supports on parents and children
- effects of nonstandard work hours on parents and children
- ways the "sandwich" generation rears children and cares for parents and works at the same time
- coping strategies parents use to accomplish all their tasks
- current cost and availability of day care
- marital relationship and work divisions

- children's endocrine changes in response to parents' work
- long-term effects of early child care

Chapter 14. New sections or information on

- changing family structures with many paths within the broad framework of single-parent families
- longitudinal research on teen parenting and its effects on children
- protective and risk factors for teen parents and their offspring
- resilient teen parenting and its origins and effects
- parenting programs for teens and areas they target
- problems unmarried parents face
- developmental patterns of children born to unmarried parents
- evaluation of proposal that genetic differences account for problems of children born to unmarried parents
- research on parenting behaviors of mothers who are single by choice
- patterns of parenting among divorced parents
- expanded section on what helps parents cope
- research following families before and after divorce identifying factors that impact children's development
- research that follows children of divorce into adulthood to describe what helps children function
- new collaborative divorce process
- ways to include unmarried fathers in children's lives
- family functioning when a parent dies

Chapter 15. New sections or information on

- myths about stepfamilies
- fathers and stepmother family patterns
- ways to include stepparents and nonresidential parents in children's lives
- children's feelings about stepparents and nonresidential parents
- gay men's choice of parenthood
- lesbian/gay parents' transition to parenting
- research on national sample of teens of lesbian parents as compared to matched control group showing no differences in developmental competence, romantic relationships, and risk behaviors such as delinquency, victimization, and substance abuse
- psychological adjustment of adolescent adopted children in open adoptions
- longitudinal study of international adoptees as young adults
- talking to children about adoption and children's understanding of it
- parent–child communication patterns in teens who are adopted
- longitudinal study of adopted children searching for biological parents
- three-session intervention that enhances adoptive parents' sensitivity to promote secure attachment with children

Chapter 16. New chapter with sections and information on

- ethnic and cultural influences on maltreatment
- factors that place children at risk for maltreatment
- children's neurobiological responses to maltreatment
- children's behavioral responses to maltreatment
- national longitudinal research on multiple forms of victimization
- activities and experiences that help children cope with victimization
- interventions to help maltreated children
- trauma-focused cognitive behavioral therapy to help individuals and families, as well as groups that experience community violence
- coping styles of victims of Hurricane Katrina
- military families' stress cycles as parents deploy and return from war zones and ways of parenting to promote families' resilience

PROBLEM SOLVING

A portion of each of the chapters in Part II deals with common problems children experience and parents must handle. Because each child is a unique individual, parents require a variety of strategies and techniques for handling problems, depending on the child and the circumstances. A problem-solving approach is presented in Chapter 5 that consists of defining the problem specifically, getting the child's point of view, making certain the problem is the child's and not the parent's, maintaining positive interactions and good times with children, considering possible actions, taking action, evaluating the results, and starting again, if necessary.

THE JOYS OF PARENTING

In addition to describing what parents do, the book describes how parents feel as they raise children. Stages of parenthood are identified, and interviews with parents provide information about what parents wish they had known about parenting before they started. The book also emphasizes the joys that parents experience. In 1948, Arthur Jersild and his colleagues at Columbia University observed that most research on parenting was focused on the problems parents experience and little attention was given to "the cheerful side of the ledger." Because this is still true today, I try in this text to redress the imbalance.

INTEGRATED COVERAGE OF PARENTING CHILDREN WITH SPECIAL NEEDS AND SUPPORTS FOR PARENTS

The eighth edition continues to present a more complete picture of parenting children at specific ages by having material on children with special needs in chapters throughout the book. The discussion of depression has been moved to the chapter on late adolescence. Similarly, material on supports for parents is included in appropriate chapters—such as supports for parents of infants in the chapter on infancy.

SPECIAL FEATURES

New features of the book as discussed at length in the previous section, include sections on insights from neuroscience in Chapter 2 and throughout the developmental chapters, increased focus on the development of cognitive executive skills, increased focus on innovative parenting programs throughout the book, and a new section on parenting in military families in Chapter 16. At the start of each chapter, there is a short outline of important topics and a brief newspaper summary highlighting a topic of contemporary interest relating to the chapter. In many chapters, there are practical questions of interest and significance to parents such as, Is my parenting determined by what my parents did with me? What do parents do if they think their child is not developing according to the usual timetables of growth? When in conflict, should parents stay together for the sake of the children?

SUPPLEMENTAL MATERIALS

Accompanying the book is an *Instructor's Manual and Test Bank*. Please contact McGraw-Hill for more information.

ACKNOWLEDGMENTS

Writing acknowledgments is one of the pleasures of completing a book. As I read the manuscript and page proofs, I am constantly reminded of all the people who have helped make this book a reality.

I wish to thank all of the clinicians and researchers who gave generously of their time not only for the interviews themselves but also to review the excerpts and clarify points: Susan Harter, Jacqueline Lerner, Richard Lerner, James Levine, Paul Mussen, Emily Visher, John Visher, and Emmy Werner.

I thank the following people for a review of the seventh edition of this book, as their comments enabled me to make more insightful revisions:

Kim Brown, California State University Bakersfield

Kathryn Bojczyk, Florida State University

Darbi Haynes-Lawrence, Western Kentucky University

Frankie Rabon, Grambling State University

Susan Reichelt, East Carolina University

Special appreciation goes to Robert Kremers, Chief of the Department of Pediatrics of Kaiser Medical Center, for his willingness to place questionnaires about the joys of parenting in the waiting rooms. I thank the many anonymous parents who completed them there and in parenting classes. Most particularly, I express my gratitude to all those parents I interviewed about the joys of parenting and the ways they changed and grew through the experience. I gained valuable insights about the process of parenting, and their comments enliven the book immeasurably. These parents are Michelle Brown, Steve Brown, Kevin Carmack, Laura Carmack, Mark Clinton, Wendy Clinton, Judy Davis, Douglas Dobson, Linda Dobson, Jill Fernald, Otie Gould, Warren Gould, Caryn Gregg, Robert Gregg, Michael Hoyt, Henrietta Krueger, Richard Krueger, Patricia Landman, Jennifer Lillard, Kathy Malone, Chris McArtor, Robert McArtor, Charles Nathan, Jean Oakley, Paul Opsvig, Susan Opsvig, Sherry Proctor, Stewart Proctor, Robert Rosenbaum, David Schmidt, Nancy Schmidt, Moshe Talmon, Raymond Terwilleger, Anthony Toney, Patricia Toney, Steven Tulkin, Elizabeth Whitney, Julie Whitney, Kenneth Whitney, Leon Whitney, Richard Whitney, Barbara Woolmington-Smith, Craig Woolmington-Smith, and Iris Yotvat-Talmon.

My coworkers at the Kaiser Medical Center at Hayward were supportive and helpful throughout. Becky Hoxsey, our medical librarian, obtained all the books and articles I requested; pediatricians and pediatric advice nurses have given helpful information about parents' concerns. I greatly appreciate the leadership at Kaiser.

Many thanks go to the staff at McGraw-Hill for their tireless work in transforming a typed manuscript into a usable and attractive book. Management Editor Meghan Campbell, Development Editor Maureen Spada, and Project Editor Erika Jordon invariably responded to requests for help immediately and creatively with solutions that fit my every need. Production Editor David Blatty and Sponsoring Editor David Patterson have become treasured colleagues offering invaluable suggestions and help for three editions of the book. It is a pleasure to work with eveyone there.

I am grateful to the late Paul Mussen, who, fifteen years ago, suggested that I use comments from researchers to make material more vivid for students. His concern with the social forces impinging on parenting has continued to influence my thinking.

Finally, I wish to thank my family and friends for their thoughtfulness and company. I want to thank my patients for sharing their lives and experiences with me. I hope they have learned as much about life from me as I have learned from them. Most particularly, I want to thank my children, who are now grown and live away from home. They are very much in my mind as I write, and I relive our experiences together as I explore the different developmental periods. I find that I have learned the most important truths of parenting from our interactions. I believe that when I have paid attention, they have been my best teachers.

F O R E W O R D*

The author of this book, Jane Brooks, has had a wide variety of professional and personal experiences that qualify her as an expert in child development. She is a scholar, researcher, and writer in the discipline of child psychology; a practicing clinician working with parents and children; and a mother. Drawing on the knowledge and insights derived from this rich background of experience, she has produced a wise and balanced book that parents will find valuable in fostering the optimal development of their children—helping them to become secure, happy, competent, self-confident, moral individuals. Dr. Brooks offers guidelines that are explicitly linked to major theorists (e.g., Freud, Piaget, Erikson) and findings of scientific research in child development, so that the reader is also presented with a wealth of information on physical, cognitive, social, and emotional development. Students of human development and all who work with children professionally, as well as parents, will profit greatly from reading this book.

Brooks's approach to parenting incorporates many noteworthy features. Her coverage of the fundamental tasks and issues in child rearing is comprehensive. Included are tasks shared by all parents (e.g., preparing for the birth of the infant, feeding, toilet training, adjusting to nursery school or kindergarten, the adolescent's growing interest in sex) as well as special, although common, problems (such as temper tantrums, delinquency, use of drugs, and physical or mental handicaps). Critical contemporary experiences such as divorce, single parenting, and stepparenting are also treated with insight and sympathy. Brooks's suggestions for ways of dealing with these problems are reasonable, balanced, and practical; her writing is straightforward, clear, and jargon-free.

Authorities in child development generally agree that the principal theories and accumulated findings of scientific investigations are not in themselves adequate to provide a comprehensive basis for directing parents in child rearing. Given the limitations of the present state of knowledge, guidance must be based on established principles of human development *plus* the cumulative wisdom and insights of specialists who have worked systematically and successfully in child-guidance settings. Yet many, perhaps most, academically trained child psychologists pay little attention to the writing of such clinicians as Briggs, Dreikurs, Ginott, Gordon, and Spock, regarding them as unscientific "popular" psychologists. This is not true of Dr. Brooks. After careful and critical reading of their work, she concluded that, as a consequence of their vast clinical experience, these specialists have achieved some profound insights about children and have thus developed invaluable techniques for analyzing and dealing effectively with many problems that parents face.

*This foreword was written by the late Paul Mussen for the third, fourth, and fifth editions. As the book continues to have the features he discusses, the foreword is included in this edition.

Furthermore, Brooks believes that parents themselves can successfully apply some of these techniques to resolve specific problems. Some of the experts' suggestions are therefore incorporated, with appropriate acknowledgment, where they are relevant.

The book is not doctrinaire or prescriptive, however; the author does not advise parents simply to unquestioningly adopt some "system," plan, or set of rules. On the contrary, Brooks stresses the uniqueness of each individual and family, the complex nature of parent–child relations, and the multiple determinants of problem behavior. In Brooks's view, each problem must be placed in its developmental context and evaluated in terms of the child's level of physical, cognitive, and emotional maturity. The processes of parenting are invariably bidirectional: Parents influence children *and* children influence parents. Furthermore, families do not function in isolation; each family unit is embedded in a wider network of social systems that affect its functioning. Successful child rearing depends on parents' accepting these complexities, yet also attempting to understand themselves and their children and maintaining a problem-solving orientation.

It is a pleasure to note the pervasive optimistic, yet realistic, tone of the book. The author has recognized that promotion of children's welfare and happiness is one of the highest parental goals, and she communicates her confidence that most parents *can* achieve this. Underlying this achievement is parents' deep-seated willingness to work hard and to devote thought, time, energy, and attention to their children's development and their problems. Reading this book will increase parental understanding and thus make the difficult tasks of parenting easier.

Paul Mussen
Former Professor Emeritus of Psychology and
Former Director, Institute of Human Development,
University of California, Berkeley

PART

I

General Concepts, Goals, and Strategies of Parenting

1

Parenting Is a Process

CHAPTER TOPICS	IN THE NEWS

CHAPTER TOPICS

In this chapter, you will learn about:

- Reasons parents want children
- Definition of parenting and roles of child, parent, and society in the process
- Society's power to help or hinder parenting
- Parents' importance in children's lives
- Ways children stimulate parents' growth
- Influence of parents' childhood experiences on their parenting today

IN THE NEWS

Wall Street Journal, April 4[1]: Neuroimaging study suggests adults are prewired to respond positively to babies' faces. See page 3.

Test Your Knowledge: Fact or Fiction (True/False)

1. Though we are the wealthiest industrialized country in the world, our rate of infant mortality is far higher than that of other industrialized countries.
2. Because of the many changes in the forms of family life over the past thirty-five years, parents' spend less time with children and adolescents, and so young adults now do not feel as close to their parents as their parents did to their parents in 1970.
3. In a large survey, parents report many more joys and satisfactions than problems in raising children.
4. Parents' behavior toward their children determines the kind of parents their children will be when they grow up.
5. Most parents who were abused as children will abuse their children.

Parenthood transforms people. After a baby comes, a whole new role begins, and parents start a new way of life. What is parenting really all about? Why do people undertake this new and demanding role? How does society help or hinder parents? In this chapter we explore parenting as a cooperative venture among parents, their child, and society.

We define parenting and describe the roles of parents and society in rearing children. The chapter describes parents' important influence on children's lives and the ways children change their parents. Finally, we explore the influence of parents' childhood experiences on their parenting.

WHY DO ADULTS TAKE ON THE JOB OF PARENTING?

Would you apply for this position?

> Wanted: Caregiver to rear one or two children from birth to maturity. The job is a seven-day-a-week, twenty-four-hour-a-day position. No salary or benefits such as sick or holiday pay, no retirement plan. The caregiver must supply all living expenses for self and children, and in the event of any absence, even for a few minutes with younger children, must supply substitute care. There is no opportunity to meet child or children in advance of taking the position to determine compatibility. Motivation for the job and satisfaction in it must come from within the applicant as neither children nor society regularly express gratitude and appreciation.

Although such a newspaper advertisement might get few applicants, in everyday life the parents of more than four million babies accept such a position each year![2] And many exert extraordinary effort and pay thousands of dollars for help in getting pregnant or in locating children to adopt so they can take on this job.

The advertisement describes the time commitment and selfless nature of the job that takes over parents' lives as, at the same time, they continue their roles as spouses and partners, extended family members, friends, and workers. Most parents would say parenting never ends; they feel that as long as they live, they will be trying to help their child grow and be happy. So why take on this daunting role?

People are drawn to parenting for several reasons. First, we appear to be preprogrammed to respond positively to babies.[3] The young of all species have a quality of babyishness—heads are proportionately larger; foreheads and eyes are more prominent; cheeks are fatter; limbs are shorter in relation to the torso; and there is a quality of clumsiness to their movements. Neuroimaging of adults' brains confirms from earlier studies that adults are attracted to babies' and respond positively when they view them. Everyone is not equally attracted to babies, and the fact that there may be a biological contribution to the attraction does not mean that people are required to have children. It suggests only that there may be a biological contribution in addition to the social prescriptions for parenthood.

Second, society's strong encouragement is a major influence in having children. Society needs children to flourish and continue, and so it emphasizes the positive value of having children. More than work or marriage, society describes parenthood as a sign of maturity and adulthood.[4] Social pressure for parenthood has varied over historical time and across cultural groups. Currently, in some European countries and in Japan, pressure is increasing because the population is diminishing.[5] In our society most couples expect to have children, but as we shall see in Chapter 12, many young adults no longer see parenthood as a defining characteristic of adulthood.

Parents say a primary reason to have children is to love and be close to them.

While no one should feel pressured to have children against their will, a little push to have children may be beneficial. And the reason is this. Most parents describe profound joys and satisfactions with their children. One father said, "It is the first time in my life I know what the term 'unconditional love' means. The wonder of this little girl and nature! I have never experienced anything like that. It is 'Yes' without any 'Buts.'"[6] Yet such pleasures are difficult to experience with other people's children and difficult to know in advance of having children. As one father said, he would really have regretted not having children. Society tries to make sure few have that regret.

Reasons Given for Having or Not Having Children

When asked, men and women, parents and nonparents alike, give similar reasons for having children, and the reasons appear in similar order in different ethnic groups.[7] People want children:

- to love and be close to
- to feel excitement at children's growth and development of new skills
- to feel a greater sense of self-growth, of being more sensitive, more caring
- to satisfy society's expectations of being adult and responsible
- to feel a sense of creativity and accomplishment in helping childen grow
- to meet moral or religious expectations
- to feel greater security in times of sickness or old age

Rural residents and African Americans are more likely to list children as providing economic help and security in old age. As we shall see throughout the book, extended families are major bulwarks in stressful times. When people lack close family ties, they must create strong units of support.

Reasons given by couples for not having children center on three broad factors:[8]

- Restrictions (loss of freedom, loss of time for other activities, increase in work load)
- Negative feelings in relation to children (worries concerning their health and well-being, difficulties with discipline, fear of disappointments in children or in self as a parent)
- Concerns about the child being poorly cared for

Joys and Problems with Children

The largest study of joys and problems in child-rearing found that, by and large, parents get what they hope for in parenthood. Arthur Jersild and his colleagues interviewed 544 parents.[9] While the study is fifty years old, it is the only extensive study of parenting joys as well as problems. Parents reported more than twice as many joys, 18,121, as problems, 7,654, in rearing children. The most common joys described are

- Children's special qualities as a person
- Companionship and affection
- Pleasure in watching the child grow in intellectual and social skills
- Feelings of satisfaction in helping them grow and in the general role of parent
- Satisfactions in seeing sibling closeness.

The list shows that parents' joys relate to the everyday life experiences and interactions readily available to all parents and not to children's outstanding or spectacular achievements available to only a few parents.

The problems parents described in Jersild's study centered on:

- The child's difficult personality traits
- Difficulties in getting cooperation in routines
- Concerns about sibling conflicts
- Disappointments in self as a parent

Interestingly, the difficulties did not prevent the closeness that is the main reason parents want children, as only a small percentage of parents (15 percent) reported lack of closeness with the child as a problem. Many parents reported health issues as a problem (18 percent), but few parents (only 2 percent) reported good health as a satisfaction.

As we talk about parents' many activities in helping children grow, and the work and the effort involved, it is wise to recall that there are many more satisfactions than problems in parenting; we just fail to talk about them as much. Special sections in this book draw attention to these joys.

DEFINITION OF PARENTING

We define parents as individuals who nourish, protect, and guide new life to maturity.[10] Parents make "an enduring investment and commitment throughout their children's long period of development"[11] to provide responsible caregiving that includes:

- An ongoing attachment and relationship with the child
- Material resources such as food, clothing, and shelter
- Access to medical and dental care
- Responsible discipline, avoiding injurious and cruel criticism and harmful physical punishment
- Intellectual and moral education
- Preparation for taking on responsibilities of adulthood
- Assuming responsibility for child's actions in the larger society

Parents provide care in **direct** interactions with children (e.g., feeding, teaching, playing with children).[12] They also provide care in **indirect** actions that can take many forms. For example, parents serve as advocates for children in the community by ensuring good schools and education for children as well as libraries and playgrounds for after-school activities.

PARENTING IS A PROCESS

While parents provide care and resources for their children, parenting is not a one-way street in which the parent directs the child to maturity. Parenting is a **process** of action and interaction between parent and child; it is a process in which both parties change each other as children grow to adulthood.[13] Society is a third dynamic force in the process. It provides supports and stresses for parents and children and can change in response to the needs and actions of parents and children.

The child, the parent, and society all influence the process of parenting, and, in turn, are changed by it. Let us look at the contributions of each.

The Role of the Child

Children's physical immaturity at birth and for many years thereafter requires that parents and society care for them and meet their physical and social needs for a long period if children are to survive.

Babies' physical needs for shelter, food, clothing, and warmth are similar around the world, but they can be met in many different ways, depending on the environment and the cultural values of the society in which babies are born. Psychological and social needs are more complex.

Urie Bronfenbrenner and Pamela Morris[14] believe a child has basic psychological needs for:

- An ongoing relationship with at least one adult who has a profound love for the child and a lifetime commitment to provide care
- A secondary adult who joins in the emotional attachment and care and provides emotional support and encouragement for the other caregiving adult
- Stable and consistent interactions with caregivers and objects in the environment that enable the child to develop more complex behaviors and gain greater knowledge of the world

The child need not be biologically related to the caregiver or live in a two-parent family, but the caregivers must have a long-term attachment and love for the child who is seen as special and irreplaceable. And caregivers must have support in their caregiving.

In addition to their basic human needs, children's individual qualities—their gender, temperament, physical health—affect both what parents do and the effects of parents' actions on children. For example, the mother of fraternal twins, a boy and a girl, commented that if she had had either child alone, she would have thought that she was either the best or the worst mother in the world. Her daughter was a quiet, adaptable, easygoing baby, happy with whatever her mother did, and her mother felt she was an excellent mother. Her son was an intense, colicky baby, and nothing his mother did seemed to make him happy in the first few months so she felt very inadequate as his mother. She was the same person with the same skills, but her behavior had a different impact on each child as a result of the child's temperament, and her impact on the babies affected how she felt about herself as a mother.

A child's health influences parenting. Genetic or birth complications can interfere with babies' basic abilities to nurse, to adapt to stimulation, and to sleep. Soothing and caring for babies is more complex, and parents have the added burden of worries about their children's health.

Another factor in the parenting process is the "goodness of fit" between the child's qualities and those of the parent and family.[15] For example, the behavior of a slow-moving, slow-to-adapt child may present a problem in an active, boisterous, on-the-go family, but no problem in a family where most members are quiet and slow-moving.

Children's Importance to Parents and Society   As we noted earlier, children meet parents' basic needs for closeness, sense of accomplishment, and maturity in life. Parents grow as they undertake new activities and become more involved in community activities to meet children's needs.

We do not often think about how children meet critical needs for society, but they do. Children maintain traditions and rituals, and transmit them to the next generation. Very important, they grow into economic producers who support the aging members of society as well as their own children. As Richard Lerner, Elizabeth Sparks, and Laurie McCubbin write, "Children constitute 100 percent of the future human and social capital on which our nation must depend."[16]

The Role of the Parent

Parents' basic role is to provide responsible caregiving, as we described earlier. Society gives parents primary authority in meeting children's needs because parents are assumed to have their dependent children's best interests at heart.[17]

Parents bring a complex set of needs and qualities to the process of parenting. Unlike children who come to the parenting process fresh and inexperienced, parents[18] come with a history of relationships and with many other responsibilities that influence their behavior as parents. They bring:

- Their gender and temperamental qualities just as children do
- Their personal qualities such as sociability and self-esteem
- Their relationships with their parents and siblings
- Their level of physical health and psychological stability
- The relationship they have created with each other
- Their relationships with their broader social network of extended family, friends, and coworkers
- Their problem-solving skills
- Their work skills and satisfaction with their work

Parents' Importance to Children and Society   We explore parents' vital importance to children in an expanded section later in the chapter. Parents meet society's needs as they rear children who will maintain society. They provide around-the-clock care for eighteen years, and they pay all children's expenses. When society is forced to intervene in family life, it is difficult if not impossible, as we shall see, for society to provide the level and continuity of personal care that parents happily give children.

The Role of Society

Children live in families, and families live in neighborhoods and communities in a larger society that provides values and standards of conduct for all three parenting partners—parent, child, and society.[19] Society is a dynamic force that changes in response to economic and social changes that, in turn, affect parents' and children's lives. We first describe society's demands of parents and children and then look at changes that have affected forms of family life.

Legal Definitions of Roles   Although we are a diverse society, the legal system's demands of parents, child, and society apply to all groups and are as follows:[20]

Parent

- A parent is defined as the biological mother of the child and the man to whom she is married, regardless of whether he is the biological father or as a person who, by adoption, has obtained the legal right to take on the responsibility of care for a child in the absence of or with consent of the biological parent.

Box 1-1
DO YOU AGREE WITH THE CALIFORNIA APPELLATE COURT OR THE CALIFORNIA SUPREME COURT?*

The California Supreme Court recently awarded legal custody of a child to the mother's ex-boyfriend over the mother's objections that he was not the biological parent. The State Appellate Court had declared that the ex-boyfriend could not be a legal father because he was not the biological father. The State Supreme Court reversed the ruling and established that the man was the legal father of the child because he had cared for the seven-year-old since birth and no biological father had stepped forward. He was considered the constant in the child's life; without him the child would be fatherless and homeless. The court wrote, "A man who receives a child into his home and openly holds the child out as his natural child is presumed to be the natural father of the child."

If the biological father had been located when the child was seven and was as fit a parent as the boyfriend, should the court have given custody to him rather than the natural father? Why or why not?

*From Michael Janofsky, "Custody Case In California Paves Way for 'Fathers'," *New York Times*, June 6, 2002, A13.

- A foster parent has been given the funds and the responsibility to care for a child for a specific period of time under supervision of the state.

- An unwed biological father's rights vary depending on the state in which he lives; he had no rights until 1972 when the Supreme Court stated his rights depended on his level of involvement in the child's care; states interpret that requirement differently.

- Prebirth figures assisting in the reproductive process—egg donor, sperm donor, surrogate mother—usually relinquish parenting rights prior to birth but the law is vague here.

In cases of conflict about parenthood, the biological tie is the first consideration provided the parent is fit, but it is not the only consideration. See Box 1-1 for an example of a nonbiological "parent" obtaining custody of a child.

Society not only defines a parent, but also the basic requirements of parenting. Because parents are expected to make most of the decisions, society imposes few, but important, requirements. Generally, according to law,[21] parents must provide:

- Childhood immunizations before the age of five
- Ongoing medical care
- Education between the ages of five and eighteen
- Accepted forms of discipline for behavior
- Education so children become law-abiding citizens

Box 1-2
WOULD YOU HAVE SENT THIS MOTHER TO JAIL?*

In 1995, Tabatha Pollock was convicted of first-degree murder and sentenced to thirty-six years in jail because her boyfriend, Mr. English, twice hit, choked, and killed her three-year-old daughter at three in the morning while Ms. Pollock was sleeping. When her boyfriend woke her, and she found the child, she immediately called authorities and sought medical help.

No witnesses testified that the boyfriend was suspected of physical abuse. In his confession, he said Ms. Pollock knew nothing of such behavior, though prosecutors said she should have noticed her children had many scrapes and bruises. She was convicted on a negligence theory that she should have known of potential harm even though she did not. In other cases, parents have been held responsible only when they witnessed or knew of the threat. An appeals court upheld her conviction, and her lawyer at that time said there were no legal grounds to appeal to the State Supreme Court.

After her conviction and incarceration, she lost her parental rights with her other three children, the youngest of whom was the son of Mr. English. After years in jail, Ms. Pollock was able to secure legal help from the Northwestern University law school clinic. Lawyers there were able to persuade the State Supreme Court to hear an appeal even though the deadline had expired. The Supreme Court overturned her conviction, stating that the negligence theory—she should have known what she did not know—had no basis in law. After seven years in prison, she was released.

Mary Becker, Professor of Family and Domestic Violence Law at DePaul University in Chicago, said: "We hold mothers responsible beyond all logic, beyond any possibility that they could stop it. We live in a culture where we want mothers to do everything, and where whenever something goes wrong, it's the mother's fault."

*From Adam Liptak, "Judging a Mother for Someone Else's Crime," *New York Times,* November 27, 2002, p. A 14.

Society acts if it determines parents are being neglectful, abusive, or putting the child at risk. Child protective agencies can remove children from parents' custody and charge parents with crimes if it feels parents have endangered their children. For example, a mother was sent to jail for nine years, not for what she did, but for what her boyfriend did (see Box 1-2). In addition to holding parents responsible for their behavior, society sometimes holds them legally responsible for their children's actions—paying fines, making restitution when children have destroyed property.

Child

- Is considered inexperienced and dependent on parents
- Is expected to follow parents' rules and requests
- Is thought incapable of making informed decisions, and so, prior to a child's eighteenth birthday, parents must give consent for routine medical care, driver's license, entry into the military and marriage.

Most states have made exceptions to this general rule and permit teens to seek treatment for substance abuse, pregnancy, contraception, reproductive health, and mental-health counseling without parental consent. Furthermore, parents cannot obtain information about their teens' medical care in these areas.[22]

Society acts to ensure that children and teens obey parents' rules.[23] Children and teens can go to juvenile detention for repeatedly violating reasonable parental rules or running away. While teens cannot make many decisions, they are increasingly being considered responsible for violent crimes and are charged, sentenced, and jailed as adults would be.

Most often, society looks at family issues from the point of view of the parents, but at the same time tries to keep in mind the best interests of the child. The child's interests are usually the main concern in custody issues.

Although society demands much of parents and children, society provides only limited services to help them meet the demands.[24] See Box 1-3 for parents' descriptions of contradictory expectations.

Society

- Provides free education to children from the age of five to eighteen
- Gives specific tax exemption for each child in the family
- Gives tax credit for child-care expenses
- Any other assistance is given only if a parent or child has a disability or is living in poverty

Although we think of ourselves as a society that cares for children and honors parents, the United States is the only industrialized country in the world that does not provide health care for children and parents, though it does for people over age sixty-five.[25] It is one of only five or six countries that do not provide paid maternity leave at the birth of a child.[26] Many countries provide a family allowance for each child, regardless of income, schooling beginning at age three, and a high percentage of child care expenses. Because our country provides so few benefits, our poverty rates are among the highest in the industrialized world.[27]

Our lack of benefits has consequences. Lack of health care for all children and parents is a factor in this country's having the highest rate of infant mortality among the developed countries. Our rate of infant mortality (the number of deaths of a child under one year of age per 1,000 live births) is twice as high as that of Japan, which has the lowest (6.3 compared to 2.8). Our infant mortality rate is higher than any industrialized European country.[28] These trends continue in the mortality figures for children under the age of five.[29] These rates are of concern because the factors that lead to infant death are the same factors that lead to chronic problems among those infants who live.

This is where we are now. But society is dynamic and changing. Let us look at the changes that have affected family life over the last one hundred and fifty years as they can help us understand how to produce the changes we wish in the future.

Box 1-3
UNREALISTIC EXPECTATIONS FOR CONTEMPORARY PARENTS

Society's roles for parents can be demanding. Here a mother and father identify problems they see in their role expectations.

Judith Warner, author of *Perfect Madness: Motherhood in the Age of Anxiety,*[*] describes the heavy burden society's role prescriptions place on mothers. The "Mommy Mystique," as Warner terms society's demands, makes mothers totally responsible for their children's development and well-being. Mothers are expected to be physically available to children at all times, to meet all their needs for physical care, love, and stimulation, and then, to see that children have access to the best physical, social, and educational programs. Mothers must excel in their role so their children can succeed in our competitive society. Mothers are failures if their children have difficulties or cannot achieve high levels of success. Such total responsibility for children's well-being is especially hard for contemporary mothers who have been raised to have strong commitments to their work as well.

While society demands much of mothers, it gives little help in meeting its expectations. Mothers are often required to work to help support families, but quality, affordable day care is often not available, especially for mothers who work part time; little after-school care is available for older children as well so much of mothers' pay goes for substitute care while they work. More mothers who are financially able have stopped working or have reduced their work hours, but they may still experience anxiety and guilt as they are not fulfilling their career aspirations.

The expectations and lack of help in meeting them create tremendous stress for mothers as they run around frantically trying to accomplish all their tasks. The role demands also arouse intense anxiety in mothers about their children's future performance and guilt whenever children fail to keep up with other children or develop problems. The expectations also affect children as they sense that their mothers feel stress and tension around them.

Warner believes this situation will not change until parents band together and insist on programs that reduce maternal stress, such as affordable quality day care, tax credits and benefits for part-time workers, and a more parent-friendly workplace with flexible hours and work. A *Newsweek* article[**] Warner authored describing mothers' dilemmas drew almost six hundred Letters to the Editor, some disagreeing with her, some offering solutions to the problems. For example, Rob Reiner, Hollywood director and advocate for children's programs, wrote about Parents' Action for Children, a parent group he has formed to exert political pressure for family support programs such as child care and medical care programs. Jennifer Blaske wrote to describe a nongovernmental organization, International MOMS Club, that provides support to stay-at-home mothers with babysitting, play groups, and discussion clubs.[***]

Still other readers believe the stress can be managed when individuals make informed choices as to how to balance work and family commitments. Jennifer Regen Bisbee wrote, "I can relate to the challenges that Judith Warner illuminates, but I was surprised that she only hinted at the one solution available to every harried mom: the power to say no. . . . No, I tell my children, you can't participate in more than one after-school activity, but that keeps our family schedule remotely sane. No, I tell myself, I will not take on another client right now, which would mean more money

Box 1-3

but also more nights away from my children. We are a generation of young women raised to believe we can do it all. We also need the self-discipline and wisdom to understand we can't do it all *right now*."

Joe Ehrmann identifies a misguided role expectation for men.[****] A former NFL football player who became an inner-city minister in Baltimore following the cancer death of a much-loved, younger brother, he has observed that society values and teaches a "false masculinity" that gives boys and men approval for excelling at physical games, attracting and impressing women, and building up financial wealth. Boys are taught to compete and win, to hide their feelings, especially when they feel hurt. But masculinity emphasizing power and dominance prevents men from developing close relationships and becoming loving husbands and fathers. Such masculinity does not bring any lasting sense of worth and happiness in life. Genuine masculinity, he believes, depends on creating close relationships and caring for others and a cause beyond oneself.

Ehrmann believes that in the context of high school football, he and co-coach, businessman Biff Poggi, and eight assistant coaches can encourage adolescents' positive relationships with others by teaching them three basic behaviors: (1) to take responsibility for their actions, (2) to "lead others courageously," and (3) to "enact justice on behalf of others" (p.140). The boys learn responsibility by being on time, following team and school rules, and meeting academic standards. They also take responsibility for finding and developing their skills to the fullest. The boys learn to care about each other and look after each other. They are taught to include people, for example, always asking the person eating alone at school to join the group. Ehrmann terms this program that he carries out at a secular, private high school, "Building Men for Others."

Ehrmann and the coaches give the boys the experience of being nurtured and encouraged. Many of the team practices begin with Poggi asking the boys, "What is our job as coaches?" The boys answer, "To love us." "And what is your job?" "To love each other" (pp. 3, 43). Ehrmann believes that over time and with the coaches' examples, ways of interacting with the boys, and the fun activities of the team, adolescents can learn to take responsibility for what they do and become. The following is an excerpt from an interview with Ehrmann in Jeffrey Marx's book, *Season of Life*.[*****]

> "Nobody grows up in a perfect family, simply does not exist, and we certainly do not live in a perfect society, so we find ourselves with an awful lot of nurturing wounds," Joe said. "And then what we get from that is a tendency to blame others or make an alibi for our own decisions and action."
>
> Joe offered an example. "A father walks out on his wife and kids. The kids struggle without a male role model in the house. Then come the problems.
>
> "But as a kid, Joe said," even though your dad walked away, you've still eventually got to assume responsibility for yourself. And you've got to assume responsibility not to do that to *your* kids the next go-round. . . .

(continued)

Box 1-3
CONTINUED

"It's not so much what your father did, it's more that the responsibility is on what you do with that fact. Everything in our culture
teaches men to either deny or suppress or ignore this kind of pain.
But we have to work through our own woundedness and whatever
happened to us. We simply have to be responsible for what we do
with the stuff that happens to us" (p. 141).

As we shall see in a later section, many adults have done just this—worked through
the hurt feelings of childhood so they do not repeat them with their children.

*Judith Warner, *Perfect Madness: Motherhood in the Age of Anxiety* (New York: Penguin, 2005).
**Judith Warner, "Mommy Madness," *Newsweek,* February 21, 2005, pp. 42–49.
***Letters, *Newsweek,* March 7, 2005, p. 15.
****Jeffrey Marx, *Season of Life* (New York: Simon & Schuster, 2003).
*****Marx, *Season of Life.*

Changes in Family Life

Vern Bengtson points to four major forms of family life in the last two centuries.[30]

- **The extended farm family** of parents, children, and extended family was the
  primary form of family life in this country until the late nineteenth century; it
  was a productive economic and social institution based on law and custom.
- **The nuclear family** of parents and children, based on companionship and
  love, had as its primary purposes socializing children and meeting family
  members' emotional needs; it arose as industrialization and urbanization
  increased and families moved off the farm at the end of the nineteenth
  century; it was the predominant form of family life until the 1970s.
- **Diverse family forms** such as dual-career families, single-parent families,
  and stepfamilies arose in the 1970s as social and economic changes
  requiring more than one parent's income to support families led to women's
  entrance into the workforce and increasing secularism permitted greater
  acceptance of divorce and of childbearing outside marriage.
- **Multigenerational families** relying on two or more generations to sustain
  youth have arisen in the 1990s as young families face greater economic difficulties with unstable employment, increasing housing and child-care costs,
  and reduced incomes in single-parent families, and emotional resources are
  stretched with the demands of work and family. "For many Americans,"
  says Bengston, "multigenerational bonds are becoming more important than
  nuclear ties for well-being and support over the course of their lives."[31]

Demographic changes in the population made this shift possible. In the last
100 years, the lengthening of the lifespan from 49 years for women and 46.4 years
for men in 1900 to an average of 79.4 years for women and 73.6 for men today

"Multigenerational families rely on two or more generations to provide strong emotional ties and resources for children."

has provided an additional thirty years for adults to be involved with younger generations.[32]

In this same period, the average number of children per family has dropped from 4.1 in 1900 to 1.9 in 1990. The age structure of the population now resembles a bean pole, according to Bengtson, with equal proportions of people at all ages. Thus, adults of many ages are available to nourish the small number of children. Grandparents and great-grandparents step in and meet children's emotional needs for closeness. Referred to as "latent kin networks" or the "family national guard," they "muster up and march out when an emergency arises regarding younger generation members' well-being."[33]

Despite all the changes in family structure, adolescents and youth feel as much solidarity with mothers and fathers in 1997 as their parents did with their parents in 1971, according to data from the Longitudinal Study of Generations collected on four generations of working and middle-class families from 1971 to 1997.[34]

Figure 1-1 compares the early life experiences of Generation 3 (termed Baby Boomers) with the life experiences of their children, Generation 4 (termed Gen Xers) including feelings of family solidarity with mothers and fathers. Baby Boomers grew up in families with more siblings, with fathers' and mothers' having less education, with mothers' more likely to be full-time homemakers, and with fewer divorces than their Generation X children. Yet the family solidarity scores of Baby Boomers in 1971 were very similar to the scores of their children with them in 1997.

Children not only feel close to parents, they maintain similar values with regard to achievement as well. Maternal employment has not changed self-esteem or values with the exception that Gen X young women have higher occupational aspirations than did either their mothers or Gen X young men.

Data from a large multinational study of young adults' subjective well-being support Bengtson's view that multigenerational help can compensate for the difficulties

■ **FIGURE 1-1**
HISTORICAL CHANGES IN FAMILY STRUCTURE AND PARENTAL ATTRIBUTES: "GENERATION X" COMPARED WITH THEIR BABY-BOOMER PARENTS AT THE SAME AGE

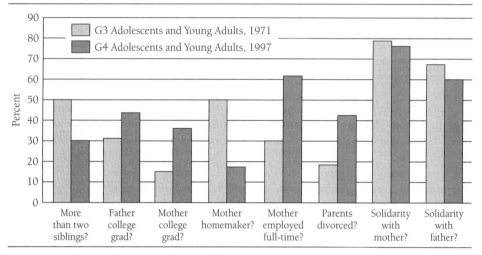

From: Vern L. Bengtson, "Beyond the Nuclear Family: The Increasing Importance of Multigenerational Bonds," *Journal of Marriage and Family 63* (2001): 11. Reprinted with permission.

children experience when nuclear families are under stress.[35] Children of divorced parents in collectivist cultures, which receive more support from extended family members as well as the community, feel greater life satisfaction and more positive moods as adults than do the children of divorced parents living in individualistic cultures where families have fewer resources.

Diversity of Contemporary Social Life in the United States

Many newspaper articles start with phrases like, "Toddlers are. . . ," "Teenagers are . . . ," or "Parents feel . . .". There are no such homogeneous groups in our society. Parents and children live in the many different family constellations listed in Table 1-1. We are a multiracial and multicultural society with 67 percent of our population being non-Hispanic/white, 15 percent Hispanic, 13 percent African American, 4 percent Asian, and 1 percent Native American.[36] Our country adds almost a million immigrants each year to our population, and has done so consistently for the last several years so that currently one in every eight citizens is an immigrant, many of whom bring new cultural traditions and values.[37]

We are economically diverse as well with one of every six children living below the poverty line of $20,600 per year for a family of four, and the top five percent of families having income approximately eight times the income of the lowest twenty percent of families ($174,000 per year compared to less than $20,000 per year in 2006).[38]

So in talking about parents and children, one always has to be more specific— "Teenagers from affluent families . . ." or "Teenagers from working families . . . ,"

■ **TABLE 1-1**
LIVING ARRANGEMENTS OF CHILDREN IN THE UNITED STATES: 2004[*]

Family Form	Percentage of All Children In
Two-parent family	**69.5%**
Two biological/adoptive parents married	60%
Two biological/adoptive parents cohabiting	2%
One biological/adoptive, one stepparent married	7%
One biological/adoptive, one stepparent cohabiting	.05%
One-parent family	**26.5%**
Mother alone	21%
Mother cohabiting	2%
Father alone	3%
Father cohabiting	.05%
Not living with biological/adoptive parent	**3.7%**
Grandparent	2%
Other relative	.07%
Foster care	.04%
Other	.06%

[*]From *www.childstats.gov/americaschildren/famsoc1.asp*. Table Family 1.B: Family Structure and Children's Living Arrangements: Detailed Living Arrangements of Children by Gender, Race, Hispanic Origin, Age, Parent's Education, and Poverty Status, 2004.

"Parents who have many resources . . ." or "Parents who struggle to meet family and work demands . . .". We look at how these diverse racial, cultural, and economic influences affect parenting in Chapter 3.

Economic Changes

The world recently has experienced the sharpest drop in economic security since the Depression of the 1930s. Unemployment has begun to rise, and no one knows how long the economic downturn will last or how many changes it will bring for children and families.

In times of economic uncertainty and psychological anxiety, parents are the main supports for each other and their children. In a study of family life during a period of economic losses for farm families, parents who were cooperative and emotionally supportive with each other felt confident and experienced little distress from the economic pressures.[39] They focused on problem solving and taking specific actions to deal with difficulties. The result was that they felt a sense of mastery over the situation. When parents cope well, children do also.

What Do Parents Want from Society?

In a large national survey of European American, African American, and Latino/a parents, only 6 percent thought government and employers were doing enough to help parents.[40] Eighty-four percent thought the government should do more, and 76 percent thought employers should give more help. Their requests fell into four broad categories:

- Financial help in terms of increasing the tax exemption for each child, the tax credit for child care, and the removal of sales taxes on items necessary for children such as diapers

- Changes that would give them more time with families, for example, tax incentives to employers to encourage part-time and flex-time schedules, requiring employers to give paid maternity and paternity leave, allowing parents to take two extra weeks without pay each year to participate in children's activities

- Laws increasing children's safety and well being, for example, providing health care, requiring safety devices on guns, controlling crimes against children such as kidnapping

- Positive messages that support parents' values[41]

Parents worry that society barrages their children with messages about sexual activity, drugs, and alcohol that undermine parents' goals of rearing responsible, caring children. Forty-seven percent of parents in a 2002 national sample considered protecting children from negative social influences their biggest challenge as parents.[42] Though crimes against children are statistically low, 50 percent of parents worry a lot about this.

Social scientists agree with parents that society presents problems and use terms such as "chaos"[43] and "socially toxic"[44] to refer to social environments with high levels of childhood poverty, abuse, community violence, and family disruption. They point to the rising numbers of children diagnosed with psychosocial problems in pediatric office visits, from 6.8 percent in 1979 to 18.7 in 1996 as an indication that societal changes have a negative impact on children.[45]

We are not doomed to our present culture. We can identify and implement ways to support both children and parents in the growth process.

HOW IMPORTANT ARE PARENTS IN CHILDREN'S LIVES?

Parents invest time, emotional energy, and money in rearing children. They want to think that what they are doing really matters in the lives of children, that the sacrifices they make help children's growth. For most of human history, there has been little question that parents matter most.

Beginning in the 1980s, two strands of research questioned parents' importance. On the one hand, research indicating a major role of genetic influences on children's development challenged the view that parents' behavior was the major influence on children. Popular writer Judith Rich Harris advised parents in 1998 that their role in children's development "had been oversold. You have been led to believe that you have more influence over your child's personality than you really do."[46] She believed that parents nurtured children in the first five years, but parents' genes and children's peer experiences were the major determiners of children's adult personalities and life success. And a number of social scientists agreed with her view.

At the same time that research on genes suggested a reduced role for parents' influence, research concerning the plasticity of the brain at birth led other observers to conclude that parents had a critical role in providing the early stimulation the brain required for proper development. Parental anxieties increased because they feared they were not providing sufficient and appropriate stimulation.

So what does research suggest about parents' role? Overall, it suggests that parents' behavior and efforts are the most important, though not the only, influences regarding children's growth and competence.[47]

It is not a question of either genetic or environmental influences. They are inseparable, and both play a significant role in all behavior. Genes exist only in an environment and from the moment of conception parents have the largest role in providing or monitoring the quality of that environment. Even before birth, the parental environment influences and can dramatically change the genetic potential. While most parents' lifestyles protect intrauterine development, mothers who expose the fetus and growing baby to alcohol or drugs can irreparably damage the genetic contributions to the child.[48] Recent research indicates that a prospective father's work environment, alcohol, smoking, and drug habits can affect the quality of the sperm and the coming baby as well.[49]

Genes provide a baby with a range of potential behaviors that are refined by interactions with people and the environment. Even when a behavior or trait is very much under the control of the genes, as say height is, the environment can affect it. For example, around the world, average heights increased during the twentieth century because of better diets; in our own country, we have examples of Japanese-Americans' being significantly taller than their Japanese grandparents because of enriched diets here.[50]

We look at four areas of parental influence after the child is born: (1) providing an environment of protection as opposed to one of risk, (2) providing experiences that lead to the development of maximum potential, (3) serving as an advocate in the larger community, and (4) being an irreplaceable force in a child's life.

Providing a Protective Environment

Parents' personal characteristics, their forms of interactions with each other and with their children, and their interactions with social institutions create an environment of protection or risk for a child that is more consistent than the child's own characteristics. Researchers at the Rochester Longitudinal Study followed children from birth to adolescence and related the number of protective and risk factors in each child's life to the child's social and emotional functioning.[51] Only maternal qualities were included because few fathers participated in the study.

Protective factors, defined as those factors related to positive changes in intellectual and social-emotional functioning in children between four and thirteen years of age, were:[52]

- The general positive atmosphere of the family—the mothers' feeling good about themselves, their positive comments to children
- Teaching children to think and reflect and make decisions
- Children's feeling the world is predictable and your family has support
- Children's self-esteem

Risk factors were those associated with poor outcomes for children. Risks were

- Mother difficulties—anxiety, lack of emotional stability, lower education, and unskilled occupational status
- Negative family interactions—rigid beliefs about growth, few positive mother–child interactions
- Minority group status, single parenthood
- Stressful events, especially when they occurred in larger families

No one special risk led to a poor outcome for children. It was the accumulation of risks that mattered. Children in a protective environment with no risks scored thirty points higher on intelligence tests than children with eight or more risks who also had more emotional problems.

Family environments greatly expanded or limited children's range of competencies. The least resilient or resourceful child living in a low-risk environment scored higher on measures of competence than did the most resilient or resourceful child living in a high-risk environment. "The negative effects of a disadvantaged environment seem to be more powerful contributors to child achievement at every level than the personality characteristics of the child."[53]

The researchers concluded no one change eliminated risk for children; it was the combination of all the risks "that sap the lives of families."[54]

Other longitudinal research has shown that physical risks (substandard housing, crowding, noise) and psychosocial risks (family turmoil, violence, family separation) experienced in childhood placed a physiological burden detectable three to four years later when adolescents showed changes in endocrine secretions, such as epinephrine, norepinephrine and cortisol, and deposits of fat in the body. These changes were seen only in adolescents whose mothers were low in responsiveness and sensitivity.[55] High-quality mothering appeared to prevent the physiological changes associated with stress.

Providing Experiences That Lead to Maximal Growth and Potential

Like the study of height and diet, many studies point to the nourishing effects of positive parenting in helping children achieve their maximal potential even when genetic influences make offspring susceptible to problems.

Let us look for a moment at animal studies because it is easier to manipulate the environmental experiences of animals with known genetic traits.[56] Both rats and monkeys differ in emotional reactivity at birth. Highly reactive animals in both species tend to be timid in exploring their environment and easily stressed. When nurturant foster mothers rear such reactive rats and monkeys, the animals grow up to be less anxious, more able to explore the environment, and more stress resistant. When highly nurturant foster mothers rear highly reactive monkeys, the monkeys not only decrease in anxiety but show many social competencies and become leaders.[57] They are skilled in avoiding stress and gaining support from other monkeys. If female, the emotionally reactive monkeys reared by nurturant foster mothers become competent mothers, whereas emotionally reactive monkeys reared by control mothers in the average range of nurturance show deficits with their offspring. So, adequate mothering can counteract reactive temperamental traits, and superlative mothering can lead to outstanding competencies.

As a result of his studies, which led to finding the gene contributing to impulsivity and aggressiveness in rhesus monkeys, Stephen Suomi commented that good parenting appeared to buffer offspring against the negative effects of the gene.[58] The gene expression was controlled by environmental influences.

Skilled parenting can stimulate intellectual development.[59] The IQs of adoptive children correlate highly with their biological mothers, though the children have significantly higher average IQs than their biological mothers. Average IQ increases as the socioeconomic status of the adoptive family increases. When adopted in low-status homes, the children gained an average of 8 IQ points, but when adopted into high-status homes, they gained 19 points on average.

The environment adoptive parents provide can influence social development and affect the susceptibility to criminal behavior. A Swedish study examined 862 men born out of wedlock but adopted by nonrelatives on average by eight months.[60] Researchers classified the risk of petty criminality (nonviolent, infrequent, minor crimes, usually property offenses) for both biological and adoptive parents and noted the rate of petty criminality of the adopted men as adults. The men's risk varied with the risk of both adoptive and biological parents. When neither biological nor adoptive parents were at risk, the men's risk of petty criminality was 3 percent; when the adoptive parent was at risk but the biological parent was not, the men's risk was 7 percent; when a biological parent was at risk but an adoptive parent was not, the men's risk was 12 percent; when both the biological and adoptive parents were at risk, the men's risk was 40 percent. When a biological parent was at risk for petty criminality, the risk for the child was reduced two-thirds if that child was reared by parents not at risk. Conversely, the risk for petty criminality increased more than three times when a child at biological risk was reared by an adoptive parent at risk. So effective parenting appeared to buffer the boys against the effects of the genetic risks for criminality.

Parents as Advocates

Parents also influence children's growth indirectly through assembling resources and helping children draw on them to promote growth.

Parents who have children with health or developmental problems have lobbied for improvements so that their children can become more fully integrated into the mainstream. Parents' advocacy has resulted in better educational programs, fewer children living in institutions, and more children living with biological or adoptive families.[61] Community living arrangements and occupational opportunities for adults have increased. In working to expand resources and opportunities so their children can develop their full potential, parents have changed our culture's way of viewing developmental delays.

Parents' efforts at home with children with delays make special contributions to their children's lives. Parents "frequently have expectations that help to elevate the functioning of their children with disabilities in a positive version of a self-fulfilling prophecy. They think their children can learn so they create favorable environments in which to teach them, and thus they do learn more than they would in less favorable environments."[62]

Children of outstanding achievements also benefit from parents' extra efforts and commitment. A detailed study of 120 young men and women who achieved international recognition for high levels of performance in a variety of fields looked at the process by which children achieved such excellence.[63]

Few of the individuals were identified as special in the beginning. A combination of individual commitment, family support, and outstanding instruction led to accomplishment. Parents sought instruction for children, structured practices, and provided support and encouragement, emphasizing the ethic of hard work and doing one's best. As children's skills grew, parents found more advanced teachers and coaches and made further financial and time commitments not only to provide instruction but also to attend recitals, games, and meets.

So whether children have special difficulties or potential talents, parental advocacy organizes resources and support that contribute to accomplishment.

Indispensable Caring Figures in Children's Lives

When families are unable to provide adequate care for children, society attempts to provide such care. Numerous cases in many states illustrate the difficulties society faces in providing a caring adult figure in a child's life when no family member is available.

A recent New Jersey case vividly demonstrated the difficulties state agencies face when they take on the role of parent.[64] In January 2003, the malnourished body of a seven-year-old boy was found in a trunk in a locked cellar, and his twin and four-year-old brothers were found chained nearby, emaciated and scarred with burns. Their mother had been reported to the Division of Youth and Family Services for abuse and neglect eleven times in a ten-year period, but the agency closed the case on the family the year before. At the time there was a report that the mother beat and burned her children, but it was not investigated because the agency could not locate the children.

The governor declared a state of emergency at the agency and the workers were ordered to investigate immediately the 280 outstanding cases of children reported as victims of abuse. Workers could not locate 110 of the possible victims.[65] A review of cases reported to the Division of Youth and Family Services in the previous five years revealed that 82 children had died or were critically injured, despite the report of abuse to the agency.[66]

A Federal survey revealed that not one of the 50 states fully met government standards in providing safe, permanent homes for children who were abused.

"Some of these children are no better off in the care of the state than they were in the hands of abusive and negligent parents,"[67] said Carole Strayhorn, a Texas official reporting on the level of care in that state.

Given parents' importance in children's lives, should we consider licensing parents? See Box 1-4.

HOW PARTNERS IN THE PROCESS OF PARENTING VIEW EACH OTHER

Parents are thrilled to be parents. In a 2002 national survey, 96 percent said they would not trade being parents for the world.[68] But in that same sample, 6 out of 10 parents thought they were doing only a fair or poor job in raising children. These findings echo a similar national sample in 1996 in which nonparents and parents alike thought parents need to improve their performance.[69] Almost two-thirds of those surveyed said parents have children before they are ready for the responsibility and half the sample thought parents spoil children and fail to give them appropriate discipline. Only 22 percent of nonparents and 19 percent of parents felt it was common for parents to be good role models for children.

In 1996, adults, including parents themselves, viewed children negatively. Children and teens are seen as unfriendly and disrespectful, and 30–50 percent of parents describe children as well as teens as wild, disorderly, undisciplined, and uncontrolled in public. These qualities are applied to children of all socioeconomic groups.

The public does not believe parents are failures, but rather that they are overwhelmed with pressures of work and family and need help. Nonparents and parents believe that a parent's job is more difficult than in the past because children face problems with drugs and alcohol, more sex and violence in the media and the world outside the home, and more gangs in school.

The most positive views of parents' effectiveness come from children. About 60 percent of teens between the ages of twelve and seventeen say that parents are doing a good or excellent job in rearing children (only 36 percent of parents say this about parents).[70] These teens say parents are there for them and are affectionate. In another sample, children and teens also reported that both mothers and fathers love, appreciate, and care for them and do a good job of balancing work and family, but these children's main concern is that parents are too stressed and tired.[71]

Jay Belsky and John Kelly, summarizing observations from Belsky's study of new parents, agreed with children's positive assessments of parents:

"As I watched our couples cope with financial concerns and with all the other challenges of the transition, I found myself deeply moved. The quiet dignity and courage of our fathers and mothers—especially our employed mothers—was inspiring to behold. But as I watched them, I also found myself deeply troubled by how little public acknowledgment, how little public support and gratitude they and other new parents receive for their selflessness and devotion.

"In its better moods our society now treats the family with benign neglect; in its darker moods as a source of parody. None of our participants complained about the lack of public support for their family building, but it affected them—in many cases by making the routine sacrifices of the transition that much harder. It is difficult to sacrifice

Box 1-4
SHOULD A PARENTING LICENSE BE REQUIRED?

Given the important influence parents have in children's lives, should we require parents to get a license in order to have children? Although some behavior geneticists minimize parents' role in children's behavior, David Lykken was not among them. Despite the fact that his work has demonstrated high heritability for certain traits, he nevertheless believed that parents have such a profound influence on children's lives that parents should be licensed to have a child. Having studied criminal behavior and its antecedents, he was convinced that immature, impulsive parents doom a child to a life of difficulties.

> Most of the 1,400,000 men currently locked up in American prisons would have become tax-paying neighbors had they been switched in the hospital nursery and sent home with a mature, self-supporting, married couple. The parent with whom they did go home would in most instances not have been fit to adopt someone else's baby. . . . For evolutionary reasons, human beings are reluctant to interfere with the procreational rights of any person, no matter how immature, incompetent, or unsocialized he or she might be. In consequence human beings tend not to think about the rights of a child to a reasonable opportunity for life, liberty, and the pursuit of happiness."[*]

Lykken would require prospective parents to get a license, just as adults have to do to drive a car or operate a truck. Similar to the requirements for adoptive parents, a parenting license would require proof of (1) legal age, (2) marriage, (3) employment or economic independence, and (4) no history of violent criminal behavior. If parenting courses were available, a certificate of completion would be required as well. Proof of marriage was required because Lykken believed the biggest risk factor for adult problems is lack of a biological father. If couples object to marriage, they can sign a legal contract indicating they plan to stay together for twelve years to provide stability in the child's life. Gay or lesbian parents can appeal to a family court for a license. If parents had a child without a license, the child would be removed and placed for permanent adoption. If a divorce occurred after the child was born, the child would remain with the parents.

To critics of licensure, Lykken replied that no system will eliminate all problems, but he insisted, "Parenthood is both a privilege and a responsibility. The privilege of parenthood would not be determined by test scores or family trees, but by behavior. . . . If you wish to have a child, all you have to do is to grow up, keep out of trouble, get a job, and get married."[**]

Few might agree with the specifics of Lykken's plan, but how would *you* go about balancing the needs of the child with the rights of the parent?

[*]David T. Lykken, "Parental Licensure," *American Psychologist 56* (2001): 885–886.
[**]David T. Lykken, "The Causes and Costs of Crime and a Controversial Cure," *Journal of Personality 68* (2000): 598.

oneself when the larger society says the overriding purpose in life is devotion to self, not devotion to others. And in a few cases it made those sacrifices too far to go. . . . Ills that plague the American family are complex and have many sources. But I think one major source is that our society no longer honors what I witnessed every day in the Project—the quiet heroism of everyday parenting."[72]

INTERACTIONS AMONG PARTNERS IN THE PROCESS OF PARENTING

As research becomes more sophisticated with measures of children's genetic makeup and longitudinal samples including previously underrepresented ethnic group participants and improved statistical techniques, we see more clearly the complex ways in which all three partners contribute to children's growth. We illustrate this point with the contributions of the three partners to the development of attention span, an important quality for learning, emotional regulation, and behavioral control. The following example cites just a few of the many factors that influence attention span, but it illustrates that children's qualities, parents' interventions, and actions of the social environment all interact to promote growth.

Children's genetic makeup plays a role. For example, children with attention problems are more likely to have the gene DRD4 7-repeat allele. Parenting behaviors play a role because children with the gene are more reactive to parents' insensitive parenting and are more likely to develop noncompliant and aggressive behaviors, whereas children without the gene do not show such behavioral responses to parents' insensitivity.[73] When, however, parents of toddlers with the DRD4 7-repeat allele learn more sensitive responses to children, their children do not develop the noncompliant and aggressive behaviors that often accompany short attention span.

Nursery school programs too can contribute to increases in preschoolers' attention spans.[74] A nursery school program that emphasized dramatic play to encourage symbolic and imaginative behavior, self-talk to guide behavior, and strategies to facilitate memory and attention increased children's attention spans significantly. A computer-based program for children of the same age also increased children's attention spans and overall intellectual level.[75]

Finally, a school-based intervention using specially designed furniture increases children's attention to schoolwork.[76] A teacher designed desks and stools to permit students to be more physically active because she thought students were expending too much effort to contain their movements and needed an outlet for their physical energy. The desks and stools are adjustable so students can sit or stand, and flexible footrests attached to desks allow them to move their feet at will. Students and teachers believe the desks help students focus attention and get work done, and controlled research is under way to determine if this is so. The principal of the school using the desks believes the results of the controlled study will be positive. "We just know movement is good for kids. We can measure referrals to the office, sick days, whatever it might be. Teachers are seeing positive things."[77]

As we shall see throughout the textbook, in chapter after chapter, positive parental support not only promotes children's competence, but it serves as a buffer against the effects of negative genes, economic downturns, divorce, depressed moods, and discrimination and prejudice.

HOW RAISING CHILDREN HELPS PARENTS GROW

Parents write about their intense love for their children. They write about stress, but less often about the positive changes parents allude to when they talk about how parenting has changed them (see Box 1-5). These parents use such phrases as "a better person," "more patient," "more kind," "more responsible," "more oriented toward the future."

Katherine Ellison's recent book, *The Mommy Brain: How Motherhood Makes Us Smarter,* looks at research showing how mothers especially, but fathers and nonrelated caregivers as well, experience many positive changes in their personalities and behavior as a result of caring for children.[78] After the births of her two boys, Ellison discovered that, "I was complaining a lot more. But I was accomplishing a lot more" (two books in a four-year period while caring for her family and managing a freelance writing career). "Though I often felt frazzled, I was more motivated, excited by all I was learning at work and at home. My children not only had inspired my future-oriented interest in the environment but also had provided me with the 'excuse' to insist on a more flexible work life; this, in turn, allowed me more creativity. The children were also giving me constant lessons in human nature: theirs and my own."[79]

A study finding that the learning and memory abilities of mother rats exceeded those of "bachelorette" rats reinforced her views of positive growth for caregivers. Mother rats caring for young pups were able to locate and recall the location of food more efficiently than the bachelorettes. They retained their improved perceptual and memory abilities into old age. Ellison reviewed many studies, interviewed scientists overseas, and documented the positive changes that occur for mothers and for all who have close contact with and provide care for children. She cautioned that to get the advantages of caregiving, stress levels of caregivers have to be under control.

Ellison identified five areas in which abilities improve:

- Observational skills and sensitivity to others' behaviors
- Efficiency
- Resiliency
- Motivation
- Social skills

Mothers are more sensitive to infants' cries, can identify their own infants' cries from those of other infants in the hospital, can identify their infants' clothes by smell. In one study, they are better able than nonmothers to read the body language and identify the emotional reactions of an adult. Mothers appear more responsible and more understanding of themselves and others in the period after having children.

Ellison believes these changes are most dramatic for mothers because of the numerous hormonal changes during pregnancy, the birth process, and later, during nursing, but clearly hormonal changes are not required for maternal behaviors. When adoptive mothers are matched with first-time mothers with regard to

---

Box 1-5
HOW PARENTING HAS CHANGED ME AS A PERSON

"It has changed my priorities, my perspective. I am much more protective. If I see someone driving like an idiot, I get much more upset. I feel more like a regular person, more grown up." FATHER OF A TODDLER

"Now I'm officially grown up. It's kind of funny because I am a forty-year-old person who is just feeling grown up. For me, it's being less caught up in myself, more unselfish, I don't do everything I want to do all the time, and that's changing and it's okay. I used to resent that. I'm less self-centered, less concerned with myself and how I'm doing, how I'm feeling, what's up. Now I am thinking more about him. For both my husband and me, I don't know whether this is going to change, but we are more oriented toward the future." MOTHER OF A TODDLER

"My own personal sense of the meaningfulness of life in all its aspects has really gone through a dramatic change. It's just been so gratifying and meaningful and important to have this other little life, in a sense, in my hands, to be responsible for it." FATHER OF A TODDLER

"It has changed my sense of the past. I appreciate more of what my parents must have gone through for me. No matter what their problems or shortcomings, gee, they had to do all this for me." FATHER OF A TODDLER

"It's that overused word *maturity*. It happened for both of us, my husband and me. We look back on our lives before our son and afterwards. Our whole lives were what we wanted, every hour of every day. Along came the baby and, by choice, there was a reverse, almost 100 percent. We don't go out like we used to. It seems like an agony sometimes, but we are growing up as a couple and a family. It's very enriching." MOTHER OF A TODDLER

"It has changed me for the better. It matured me, really at the core. I am much more responsible because I want to be a good example for them, provide stability for them. It has helped me to see into myself. I recall things I did as a child, and I understand better what was happening then. It has changed the kind of things I think of as fun." FATHER OF ELEMENTARY SCHOOL–AGE CHILD AND EARLY ADDOLESCENT

"Having children makes you more patient, more humble, better able to roll with the punches because life is not so black and white. You can't just base your life on platitudes. You have the experience of having things go not the way you would have them go, having your children do things you would not have them do, and you have to roll with that. You learn it; it either kills you or you go on, and you have a different view of life. You become more patient, and, I think, more kind." MOTHER OF EARLY AND LATE ADOLESCENTS

"I want to be a good father so it makes me evaluate what I do and say; I look at mistakes as you would in any important and intense relationship, so it certainly makes me more self-examining and more aware of myself and how I an being experienced by the other person. It is also a challenge to be tolerant when I don't feel very tolerant. So in developing certain interpersonal skills, I think being a parent has helped me to become a better person." FATHER OF ELEMENTARY SCHOOL–AGE CHILD

maternal and paternal age and education as well as socioeconomic status, adoptive mothers' attachment to infants is as secure as that of biological mothers. Furthermore, fathers respond to infants' cries in ways similar to those of mothers. They too increase in their ability to read body language and identify emotional reactions. They do not experience the dramatic hormonal changes mothers do.

Mothers, fathers, and teachers identify four similar ways in which children have changed them.[80] First, children have heightened their awareness of environmental issues, and motivated them to change bad habits such as smoking or drinking. One mother said, "It wasn't so much that he [her son] would say anything, it was just how he would look at me, like he was really worried when I smoked. It would kill me. He cared so much. He really helped me to care for myself better. I haven't had a cigarette in over a year."[81]

Second, children have helped them to understand and integrate experiences from their own childhoods. They may hear themselves saying or doing things their parents did and understand their parents better. Or they may use such an experience as a wakeup call for the need to change their behavior with their own children. Parents may recall important childhood experiences they had forgotten so they have greater knowledge of themselves. Third, adults say they have become more knowledgeable and more creative in helping children learn and master tasks. Fourth, children's awe and wonder at life trigger parents' wonder. "Parents and teachers report that children wrestle with life's mysteries, stand awestruck before the most mundane of spectacles, and hunger for meaning and value by which to live their life. When adults interact with children, the familiar categories and concepts adults use to organize the world can be challenged and even cracked open by the child."[82]

So, we grow in many ways as a result of caring for children. As researchers studying the satisfactions and problems of parenting wrote, "Perhaps no other circumstance in life offers so many challenges to an individual's powers, so great an array of opportunities for appreciation, such a varied emotional and intellectual stimulation."[83]

PRACTICAL QUESTION: IS MY PARENTING DETERMINED BY WHAT MY PARENTS DID?

Many parents and prospective parents worry when they read statements in newspapers and magazines that parents who physically abused their children were often abused themselves as children or alcoholic parents grew up in families with an alcoholic parent.

Is parenting limited by genes or what parents experienced as children? The answer, in brief, is "No." Genetic influences in terms of temperamental qualities like irritability or easygoing nature surely influence what we do as parents; they can make certain parenting behaviors involving emotional control harder or easier to carry out. As we shall see, such parenting behaviors can be modified with effort. Childhood experiences with parents influence our development, often in very complex ways we are just beginning to understand, but research indicates parents can come to terms with childhood experiences and develop the behaviors they want to have as parents.

Although it is true, for example, that parents who were physically abused as children have a higher risk of being abusive than a parent who did not experience abuse—between 25 to 35 percent grow up to maltreat their own children—still, the vast majority do not abuse their children.[84] And those parents who feel they are on the verge of hurting a child can learn new behaviors. And this is true in other areas as well. The majority of children who grow up with an alcoholic parent do not, themselves, become alcoholics. The risk is increased, but as adults, parents can decrease the risk through certain actions.[85]

Steven Wolin found that some families with an alcoholic parent acted deliberately to prevent transmission of alcoholic behavior to the next generation by protecting family rituals and routines such as Christmas and birthdays from the alcohol abuse of the parent.[86] Parents who did not transmit alcoholic behavior had healthy patterns of communication; parents talked together about their goals and planned satisfying holidays and routines, sometimes by doing the opposite of what had been done when they were children. Such planning prevented the development of alcoholic behavior in their children who are the grandchildren of alcoholics.[87]

Parents who worry about repeating other negative ways of relating learned in childhood can deal with their feelings about their parents' behavior and adopt new ways of relating. One study found that a group of parents who experienced early hardships and difficulties in their relationships with their parents were able to find new ways of solving problems and relating to other people. With the emotional support of a therapist, spouse, or friend, these parents, as adults, were able to look at their childhood experiences, identify the negative emotional experiences, and accept that their parents could not give them what they needed or wanted. With insights and acceptance of what had been, they were then able to create the kinds of relationships they wanted to have with their sons and daughters. These parents' childhoods were difficult, and they had many sad and depressed feelings about them, but their painful feelings did not limit them. They acknowledged the pain and went on to develop the flexible, warm style of parenting they desired.[88]

Drawing on insights from neurobiology, attachment theory, and parent education classes, child psychiatrist Daniel Siegel and teacher/educator Mary Hartzell's book, *Parenting from the Inside Out: How a Deeper Self-Understanding Can Help You Raise Children Who Thrive,* shows parents how, through awareness of their present feelings and reflections on the sources of these feelings, parents gain self-understanding that allows them to be the parents they want to be. "By freeing ourselves from the constraints of our past, we can offer our children the spontaneous and connecting relationships that enable them to thrive."[89]

They encourage parents

- To live in the present moment with children; focusing on the feelings and perceptions as they occur.

- To look beyond the child's external behaviors to understand the internal ways the child thinks and feels.

- To appreciate what parent and child are experiencing, and then to choose actions that meet children's basic needs.

When parents find themselves reacting to children's behavior with intense feel-ings they do not understand or in ways they do not approve, parents are encouraged to look for the unresolved feelings left over from other situations that interfere with parenting. In such situations, the authors recommend journal writing about the situation because the reflection of writing often gives parents insight and under-standing. Sometimes, others' comments, including the child's, provide insight.

Mary Hartzell illustrates how her feelings from childhood took the joy out of her boys' shoe shopping. The trip would start with the boys excitedly choosing the shoes they wanted. She encouraged them to choose but then criticized the choices—the cost, the color. Finally, the boys would give up in frustration and tell her to choose, and after a great deal of indecision, she would choose. She and the boys, all frustrated, left the store with shoes that nobody really wanted. This scenario was repeated many times until one of the boys asked her, "Didn't you like to get new shoes as a kid?" She immediately answered a heartfelt, "No!"

She then recalled her shoe-buying trips as a child. As one of nine children, she never had a choice of the shoes she really wanted. Her mother had to save money and buy the cheapest shoes on sale. Her older sister, however, had an odd-shaped foot that was hard to fit, and her shoes were never on sale so she always got the choice of shoes she wanted. Mary's foot was easy to fit so there were always some shoes for her on sale, but they were never the ones she wanted. Her mother was often irritated with the shopping trip—the number of shoes to buy and the cost—and ignored Mary's protests about the choice of shoes. So Mary and her mother always left the store angry and resentful. Her son's question made her realize that she was creating the same experience for her children. Insight helped her change.

Siegel and Hartzell conclude,

"We don't need to have had great parents in order to parent our own children well. Being a parent gives us the opportunity to reparent ourselves by making sense of our own early experiences. Our children are not the only ones who will benefit from this making-sense process: we ourselves will come to live a more vital and enriched life because we have integrated our past experiences into a coherent ongoing life story."[90]

Parents can also shift their parenting style under the influence of a partner. When a parent with an insecure attachment to his or her parents in childhood marries someone with a secure history, the insecure partner takes on the parenting style of the more secure partner and becomes warmer, calmer, and more positive.[91]

As you proceed with the book, take the information as guidelines for identifying factors that lead to the effective and satisfying parenting you want to do.

MAIN POINTS

Parenting is
- nourishing, protecting, and guiding new life
- providing resources to meet children's needs for love, attention, and values

Reasons for having children include
- love, affection, and stimulation

- creative outlet, proof of maturity, and sense of achievement
- proof of virtue and economic advantage

Joys of parenting

- arise from everyday experiences
- are generally what parents hope for
- far outweigh the effort and frustrations involved

The process of parenting involves

- ongoing interaction among children, parents, and society
- children who have their own needs and temperaments and at the same time meet important needs of parents
- parents who have responsibilities to rear their children and meet their children's needs while also maintaining marriages, work, and social relationships
- society that defines roles, enforces basic requirements of parents, and serves as a powerful source of support or stress for children and parents

Changes in family life

- involve shift from extended farm family in the nineteenth century to nuclear families that were the primary form for much of the twentieth century
- involve a shift from the primary form of nuclear families to diverse families in the 1970s and more recently a shift to multigenerational families
- are in response to economic and social changes in society
- do not weaken bonds of solidarity between the generations

Parents are

- the single most important influence and resource in a child's life
- not the only influences on children's behaviors, as media, communities, and social events outside the family influence children's behavior and development as well
- stimulators and providers of nourishing environments that enable children to achieve their maximal potential even when genetic factors make special efforts necessary
- advocates who can make social changes to help children
- so influential that some suggest people be required to have a license to become parents
- difficult for state institutions to replace

Raising children changes parents who

- become more observant, sensitive, efficient, resilient, and socially skilled
- are motivated to correct bad habits
- feel a new sense of awe and wonder in the world
- acquire greater understanding of themselves and others

When parents have difficult experiences early in life, they

- are not doomed to repeat them with their children
- can gain self-understanding and reparent themselves

EXERCISES

1. Interview your parent or parents, separately or together, about the joys they anticipated having with you before your birth. Did they experience them or others in addition to them? Were they surprised at any of the joys? If possible, interview a grandparent or grandparents about the joys they anticipated with your parent and ask them the same questions. Were the joys the same for the two generations of parents? Were there differences, and if so, what were they?

2. From the year of your birth, trace the social influences acting on your parents as they raised you. For example, for the 1980s, such influences might have included the increased rate of women's participation in the workforce, the high rate of divorce and remarriage, the drop in skilled-labor jobs. Look for the effects of social change on your daily life and the ways your parents cared for you. For example, if your mother worked, describe the day-care arrangements. If your parents divorced and/or remarried, describe how child care was affected.

3. Suppose that you had to obtain a license in order to have a child, as David Lykken suggests. What would you require for such a license?

4. How do you think an adult's life would be different if he or she never had a child? How would that affect their psychological growth as a person? Where would they seek the joys that children so readily supply to many adults?

5. Read the newspaper for one week and cut out all the articles of interest to parents, including news and feature articles. The articles might cover a broad range of topics—solving children's behavioral problems, laws relating to parents' employment benefits or to the rights of parents in the workplace, laws regarding who is recognized as a parent at times of divorce or death. Describe what these articles tell you about the parenting experience at the beginning of the twenty-first century.

ADDITIONAL READINGS

Ellison, Katherine. *The Mommy Brain: How Motherhood Makes Us Smarter*. New York: Basic Books, 2005.

George, Ben, ed. *The Book of Dads: Essays on the Joys, Perils, and Humiliations of Fatherhood*. New York: HarperCollins, 2009.

Kohl, Susan A. *The Best Things Parents Do*. Boston: Conari Press, 2004.

Siegel, Daniel J., and Hartzell, Mary. *Parenting from the Inside Out: How a Deeper Self-Understanding Can Help You Raise Children Who Thrive*. New York: Penguin, 2003.

Warner, Judith. *Perfect Madness: Motherhood in the Age of Anxiety*. New York: Penguin, 2005.

C H A P T E R

2

Seeking Guidance

<table>
<tr><td>

CHAPTER TOPICS

In this chapter, you will learn about:

- What history tells parents about parenting
- What neuroscience tells parents about their roles
- Theories that describe parents' roles in stimulating cognitive growth
- Theories that describe parents' roles in promoting emotional and social growth
- Theories that incorporate a systems point of view
- What parenting experts tell parents
- Guidance for parents from three extended research programs

</td><td>

IN THE NEWS

New York Times, February 24[1]: Early childhood experience changes gene expression. See page 36.

</td></tr>
</table>

Test Your Knowledge: Fact or Fiction (True/False)

1. Sensitive parenting can buffer children from the effects of negative genes.
2. Video feedback of positive mother–child actions can improve mothers' sensitivity and increase the security of the child's attachment to the parent in just a few sessions.
3. Theories of children's growth and development contradict each other and so are hard to use in dealing with children's day-to-day behavior.
4. There is little stability in children's temperamental qualities over time.
5. Researchers rely on parents' reports of what they do and do not go into the home to see what really happens.

Providing loving care and attention and opportunities for children to develop competence and self-esteem are challenging responsibilities. Where do parents turn for guidance to help them? In this chapter we explore parents' sources of guidance in (1) what history tells us about parents' roles, (2) what science tells us, (3) what current theories about children's growth and development tell us, and (4) what research on parent–child relationships suggests is important.

We have seen the powerful role parents play in children's lives. When families were larger and relatives lived nearby, parents learned their roles from their experiences with their own parents and from their experiences helping to rear younger brothers and sisters, or younger nieces and nephews.

Today, parents turn to other sources because they often do not live near relatives and have not grown up in large families. They turn to what parents have done in the past, what neuroscience, theories, and psychological research tell parents to do to promote children's growth and well-being. Let us review how all these sources can help parents go about their important job of rearing the next generation.

CONSULTING HISTORY

Historical views of parent–child relationships tell us that from the dawn of civilization parents have faced similar challenges in rearing children and by and large have responded with similar levels of care and concern to help their children grow, with similar worries about their own competence in carrying out their task.

Early Egyptians, Israelites, Greeks, and Romans all considered children an important part of family life.[2] Wall paintings showed pictures of happy family times and archaeological remains included balls, dolls, puppets, and games. Egyptians, Greeks, and Romans recognized stages of childhood—infancy, early childhood, youth, and adolescence. They recognized parents had special tasks, first nurturing and protecting children and then teaching and guiding children as they took on adult roles. Both parents were important figures, though mothers were usually nurturers and fathers, teachers. Early societies thought children were eager to learn and believed what they learned early in life would influence their adult behaviors. The early Israelites were the only culture in which ordinary citizens learned to read, write, and do mathematical problems.

All these early societies protected children's health as best they could, and they were aware that children faced special dangers and required special treatments. The Israelites were very concerned about preventive care, urging parents to keep children out of the sun and to encourage healthy diets and careful chewing of food. Parents were concerned about infections and illnesses such as polio. The Romans were the most sophisticated physicians with discussions of obstetrics, care of the newborn, and medical problems according to the age of the child. These early societies had few treatments available for the ailments. They relied on charms, prayers, diuretics, laxatives, and herbal remedies.

Linda Pollock looked at parenting practices as revealed in almost five hundred diaries of parents and children, autobiographies, and newspaper accounts of court cases involving children, all taken from the years 1500 to 1900.[3] She found relationships between parents and children were close. "Parents, although they may have found their offspring troublesome at times, did seem to enjoy the company of their children. . . . It is also clear that the majority of children were not subjected to brutality. Physical punishment was used by a number of parents, usually infrequently and when all else had failed."[4] Restrained discipline was a consistent theme in diaries and in newspaper accounts and so Pollock concluded most parents were not battering their children.

Parents worried about children's health and education and were ready to help them as needed. Children also felt able to come to their parents with their difficulties. Adolescence brought conflicts between the generations, but parents expected children to have independent thoughts and supported them and maintained contact even when there were differences.

Parents in the seventeenth and eighteenth centuries were increasingly concerned with abstract questions about parenting (e.g., the responsibilities of being a parent, the best methods of discipline, worrying whether they were competent enough to be parents).

While variations among parents at a given time and over time existed, Pollock describes a general continuity in parenting practices and concerns over the last five hundred years—given minor changes due to technological advances such as refrigeration as it affected feeding. She believes the limited variation in parenting practices is due to two fundamental features of child rearing: (1) parents' goal to protect and rear children to maturity, and (2) children's state of extended dependency. "Children . . . make demands on their parents and parents are forced to operate within the context of these demands. The parents in every century studied accommodated to the needs of their offspring."[5]

CONSULTING SCIENCE

Scientific advances in the last two decades have provided new insights for parents. Research has shown that both genetic and environmental influences are important in children's growth, and parents provide much of that early environmental input. We look at advances in genetics, neurobiology, cognitive development, and temperament to illustrate what we know about this important partnership.

Genetics

Prior to the mapping of the human genome in 2000, scientists thought that human beings had about 100,000 genes, and each gene had a single, specific function. The complete mapping of the genome, however, revealed human beings have only around 20,000–25,000 genes,[6] and each gene is more versatile than thought, producing several proteins that control brain processes and development depending on messages they receive from other cells, other genes, and hormones triggered by the environment.[7]

Genes not only produce chemical changes in their environment, they also are influenced by the environment. Very early in the prenatal period, before a mother knows she is pregnant, brain development has begun and by day 24 from the last estimated ovulation, the neural tube is formed.[8] Lack of folic acid increases the risk of defects in the tube's closing. Parents' exposure to environmental toxins and drugs can affect genes and change the genetic potential of their child primarily in a negative way. So parents make important contributions to the neurophysiological development of their child.

Genes influence children's reactions to life experiences. For example, maltreated children who have low-activity MAOA genotype were significantly more likely to be described as having a conduct disorder in adolescence and convicted of a violent crime in adulthood than either those low-activity MAOA individuals who did not experience maltreatment or those maltreated children with high-activity MAOA.[9]

Conversely, life experiences can change the expression of genes. Childhood family adversity reflected in childhood abuse and neglect appears to modify the NR3C1 gene expression so that individuals have greater difficulty managing physiological responses to stress and as a result are more vulnerable to stressful situations later in life.[10] In Chapter 16 we describe interventions that reduce physiological responses to neglect and abuse.

Studies carried out by Marian Bakermans-Kranenburg, Marinus van IJzendoorn, and their colleagues illustrate the complex interaction of genes, the environment, and parenting.[11] They found that insensitive parenting was related to increases in preschoolers' aggressive, noncompliant behaviors only when children had a particular form of the gene DRD4 7-repeat allele which is related to an inefficient uptake of the neurotransmitter dopamine. This gene is associated with behaviors like attention problems, state regulation, aggressiveness, and attention-deficit hyperactivity disorder (ADHD) in children.

Researchers undertook a preventive program to increase the sensitivity of parents of 1- to 3-year-olds who were at risk for developing externalizing behaviors such as aggressiveness and noncompliance. Through surveys, they found parents who already described their children as having elevated levels of these traits. Behavioral measures were obtained on all study members at pretest and posttest sessions. Cortisol levels, physiological measures of stress, were obtained at the posttest to determine whether the intervention reduced physiological stress as well as negative behaviors.

Half the families were enrolled in a home intervention program and half were in the control group receiving only six phone calls. In the intervention group's six home visits, each lasting one and a half hours, a home visitor used video feedback to highlight parents' positive behaviors with children in areas such as paying positive attention, responding sensitively to children's signals, and using distraction, persuasion, and explanations to deal with noncompliance. This form of intervention is described in greater detail in the research section.

Those children who had the DRD4 7-repeat allele benefited from the intervention program and showed lower levels of cortisol at the posttest, but the intervention did not have an effect on the cortisol levels of those children who lacked that gene. Furthermore, intervention children with DRD4 7-repeat allele also showed significant decreases in externalizing behavior, and the decreases were the largest for children whose mothers had the greatest increases in sensitive parenting.[12] The study illustrated that those children whose systems were less adequate in regulating neurotransmitters benefited most from increases in mothers' sensitive care. This research confirms several studies with rhesus monkeys showing that nurturant maternal care can buffer offspring from the negative effects of genes.

Neurobiology

In the past, we thought that genetic programming completely controlled brain development and many traits like height. The development of neuroimaging technology has advanced our understanding of the relationship between brain development and behavior because we can look inside the brains of living children and adults to observe the brain's growth, the regions involved as individuals carry out tasks, and changes that occur in the brain over time. Several forms of imaging—PET (Positive Emission Tomography). MRI and fMRI (Magnetic Resonance Imaging and functional Magnetic Resonance Imaging) are used depending on children's age and level of cooperation. Event Related Potential (ERP) technology uses electrical measures of brain activity obtained from numerous electrodes placed on the scalp to tell us about areas of the brain involved in behavioral responses. This method is of use with subjects from the earliest weeks of life.

Neuroimaging techniques indicate that brain development is more plastic, that is, subject to influence from internal and external stimulation, than we had thought, and plasticity is greatest at the most complex levels of functioning.[13]

Neurons and Their Connections
A neuron is a brain cell that processes and transmits information in the brain and to other parts of the body. It consists of a cell body, an axon (an extended branch of the cell that sends messages to other cells) and dendrites (protruding parts of the cell that receive messages from other cells). Cells communicate with each other across a small gap called a synapse. Endings on the axon release a substance termed a neurotransmitter that triggers a change in the dendritic membrane of the receiving cell so the message is received. At the end of the axon are several branching terminals so messages can go to more than one cell. Dendrites too develop branches with numerous endings to receive messages from many cells. In parts of the cortex, one neuron can have as many as 80,000 synapses or connections with other cells, some close by and others more distant. Myelin, a sheath of fatty tissue, covers the axon to increase the speed of conducting messages. Other cells in the brain like glial cells provide support and nutrients to neurons.[14]

In the prenatal period, most all the neurons we will have in life are formed though some new neurons are formed in adulthood in certain parts of the brain like the hippocampus, involved in memory tasks based on new experiences. We discuss neurons further in the next section on brain development.[15]

Human beings are equipped with special neurons termed "mirror neurons" that are found in many areas of the brain.[16] When individuals watch others' actions, mirror neurons in the brain fire in the same way that the neurons in the brain of the person carrying out the action fire. An unknown mechanism prevents the observer from actually making the same physical movements.

So, when observers' watch individuals pick up a pen or throw a ball, observers' brains light up in the same way as that of the person engaged in the action. Actions of the motor area of the brain are thought to trigger emotional reactions so when we see disgusted expressions, the firing of our mirror neurons triggers reactions in the emotional areas of our brain, and we feel the disgust, sadness, or humiliation we witness in another's reaction.

Mirror neurons serve several important functions. They help us understand what others are doing or are about to do, and how they may feel because we are having the same neurophysiological reactions. Scientists think mirror neurons help us have empathy for others because at a very real level, we feel their pain. Mirror neurons may also help us learn language because the movements for language are laid down as we watch others speak and gesture. Difficulties in the functioning of mirror neurons may contribute to developmental disorders such as autism in which children do not seem to understand other people's thinking and intentions.

The existence of mirror neurons has enormous implications for parenting because what children observe, they are also experiencing at the neurological level. Parents' and siblings' behavior and other external influences, such as television, are affecting children's brains. Mirror neurons may account for such phenomena as the negative effects on children of witnessing domestic violence[17] and others' arguing and may account for the negative effects of mothers' depressive behavior as children take on the behaviors they witness. Mirror neurons may help to explain the negative effects of watching violent television shows. A study revealed that when children watched violent television programs, mirror neurons in areas related to aggression fired, and children were more likely to behave in aggressive ways following the show.[18]

One can speculate that motor neurons may also account for the fact that mothers' positive moods and smiles are able to increase the smiles and moods of their infants, and for the fact that toddlers and preschoolers imitate the caring behaviors of their caregivers.

The Developing Brain The architecture of the brain is laid down in the first two trimesters of pregnancy, primarily under genetic control but influenced by negative environmental events.[19] At birth, the neurons are in place, and the connections controlling the most basic processes are formed, again primarily under genetic control. Many of the connections between neurons, however, have not been formed and develop in the first years of life.

At birth, the brain is one quarter of its adult size, but during the first year, there is such an increase in the number of axons, dendrites, and synapses (the connections formed between cells) that by the end of the year, the child's brain has grown to almost its adult size and contains twice as many synapses as exist in the adult brain.[20] In the months following birth, both internal and external stimulation of the brain play a role in the formation of new axons, dendrites, and synapses. Experience stimulates cells and activates them to fire. Cells that fire together are wired together and form strong connections.

Brain development occurs at different rates in different parts of the brain. The overabundance of synapses and increased myelination of the cells indicate that development in the first year occurs most rapidly in the sensory areas like vision and hearing, then later in the motor and sensory integration areas, and then toward the end of the first year and in the second year, in the areas concerned with reasoning and language.

An overabundance of synapses in the brain leads to pruning or eliminating synapses, and close to 50 percent of childhood synaptic contacts are lost by adolescence. Those synapses that are unspecified or inactive are most likely to be pruned. A child's activities and experience strengthen connections between cells and reduce the likelihood of their being pruned. Pruning occurs first in the areas that developed first like the visual cortex, but occurs later in the prefrontal areas where reasoning, planning, and problem-solving develop at a slower rate over a longer period of time.

It was thought that pruning was complete and the brain formed by adolescence, but neuroimaging of the brains of children and adolescents from age 4 to 22 reveals that brain development continues on into the twenties.[21] White matter continues to grow throughout the brain during adolescence, and gray matter increases and decreases in certain areas. Continuing brain development in adolescence provides further opportunities for teens' activities and experiences to contribute to the formation and strengthening of neuronal connections.

Experience affects the brain in several ways.[22] First, the cortex is somewhat malleable, and if there is damage to the child's brain at a young age, other areas of the brain can take on that function. For example, if a child has a brain lesion on the left side of the brain where language is processed, the right side of the brain takes on that function, and the child develops near normal language skills with only minor problems with fluency and complex grammar. Such a lesion in an adult leads to permanent losses in language skills. When children are born blind or deaf, the areas of the brain usually devoted to vision or hearing are taken over for other uses like reading Braille in the blind child or for increased visual processing in the deaf child.

Experience plays a role in shaping the brain's connections in other ways. First, activities and experiences stimulate the growth of axonal and dendritic endings so there are more possible connections with other cells. Throughout the life span, we make and strengthen connections between cells so we continue to develop though at a slower pace. Second, as noted, experiences and activities strengthen the connections between cells so they are less likely to be pruned.

The rapid growth of synapses after birth, the pruning of unused neuronal connections, and continuing development of new brain connections through new experiences point to the contribution of environmental input in shaping the structure and functioning of the brain.

Peter Huttenlocher, who has carried out extensive research on brain development, describes the implications of his work for parents.[23] First, early childhood training that is not continued later has dubious value because the early connections will disappear unless maintained with practice. Practice can be varied so it is not boring, but it must be consistent to maintain the connections. Second, there are no critical periods or closed windows for stimulation or environmental input. There are optimal periods when learning and practice may have the biggest benefits, but stimulation has value at all ages. He uses the example of learning a second language. If children learn before puberty, they can speak without an accent. They can learn languages throughout life, perhaps at a slower rate, but they will most likely have an accent.

Third, he states that the brains of children and adolescents may need time for rest and integration of what has been learned to nourish creativity. He writes, "A proper balance of early exposure to an enriched academic environment and time-off may be important for optimum cortical development. At this point, we do not know where this balance lies."[24]

Neuroendocrine Research   There are now efficient and simple ways to get samples of cortisol, a hormone that tells us about children's levels of alertness and attention throughout the day, their levels of physiological response to stress, and the ripple effects of stress on other areas of behavior like social and intellectual functioning.

Cortisol regulates our daily pattern of arousal, alertness, and attention. In human beings, cortisol is elevated in the morning and gradually declines during the day and early evening as individuals get ready to sleep. Cortisol levels can change over short periods of time when children confront new tasks and new people.[25] Moderate cortisol increase when confronting stimulating experiences, followed by down-regulation of the increase, is associated with flexible problem-solving, self-regulated behavior, and letter knowledge in preschoolers.

Cortisol also helps the body respond to stress. The stress response has two components, a fast-acting component involving the sympathetic nervous system that readies the body for fight or flight, and the hypothalamic-pituitary-adrenal response system (HPA) a slower acting component that involves a cascade of hormones.[26] In the HPA response system, the amygdala perceives danger, triggers the hypothalamus that secretes corticotropin releasing hormone (CRH) that stimulates the pituitary to release adrenocorticotropic hormone (ACTH), which triggers the adrenals to release cortisol as well as epinephrine and norepinephrine. Cortisol is high during stress, and when stress decreases, cortisol binds to receptors to inhibit the stress hormones.

Ongoing stress has negative effects. It disrupts the usual daily pattern of cortisol release, and children show atypical patterns with some children showing low levels in the morning and throughout the day, and some very high.[27] When continuously low, children appear less alert and attentive and perform less well on cognitive tests. Chronic elevated cortisol decreases the immune system creating vulnerability to illness, and it can lead to cell loss in the hippocampus resulting in memory difficulties.[28]

Neuroimaging and findings like those above that moderate cortisol is related to tasks like flexible problem-solving but chronic high cortisol decreases functioning have led to greater attention to the relationship between emotional regulation and problem-solving skills, particularly with regard to children's performance at school. We turn to that topic next.

Executive Functioning

Executive functioning (EF) includes three general skills: (1) the ability to hold and use information in working memory, (2) the ability to inhibit habitual behaviors, and (3) the ability to adjust to change and solve problems flexibly. These skills are related to intelligence but they are more measures of attention and self-control.[29]

They are related to the dimension of effortful control, a dimension of temperament that we discuss in the next section.

Executive functioning skills predict achievement in math and reading throughout the school years.[30] Executive functioning skills depend on developments in the hippocampus, the prefrontal cortex and the surrounding areas where memory, attention, and rudimentary problem-solving skills begin to develop in the first year of life. The ability to control behavior and inhibit responses grows in the second year and improves dramatically in the preschool years.

Children and adults differ in their EF skills, in part because of genetic predispositions that reduce impulsivity, and in part because of parental behaviors that help children develop skills in self regulation. Research indicates these skills can be developed through daily activities and special training.

In a low-income, community-wide study involving 21 preschool classrooms, half the classes used a state curriculum to develop literacy skills and half used what was termed the Tools of the Mind program, carefully developed over many years to increase executive skills.[31] This program, based on Vygotsky's views of intellectual growth (described later in the chapter), developed 40 different skills including self-talk to guide behavior, dramatic play to encourage symbolic and imaginative behavior, and strategies to facilitate memory and attention.

The skills were practiced throughout the day for at least 80 percent of the time during the one or two years that children were in the preschool program. The spring before kindergarten, all children were tested on measures of executive skills. The Tools children performed significantly better on the more complex tasks requiring memory of several directions, flexible problem solving, and the inhibition of habitual responses.

Another strategy has also proved useful in developing executive skills in young children ages four and six.[32] A five-day attention-training program uses computer screens and joy sticks to teach children to track cartoon figures, anticipate movements of a cartoon duck, discriminate between cartoon figures, and make choices among conflicting alternatives in order to conform to specific directions.

Like the nursery-school program, the five-day program, totaling about three and a half hours, led to improvements in EF skills and on measures of intelligence. As yet, reports do not indicate how long the effects might last, the relationship between EF skills and later school performance, and the effects of increased number of training sessions.

Tools of the Mind program contains many useful suggestions for parents to increase children's dramatic play, to involve them in conversations, and model self-talk to guide one's behavior.

Temperament

Some behaviors in infancy and early childhood are part of development and diminish over time without special effort on children's or their parents' part. For example, some babies are irritable and fretful in the first weeks after birth, but most of them develop into happy, outgoing infants at four months of age. However, some irritable babies maintain their negative reactions, and their irritability continues into the preschool years.[33] Again, most toddlers are undercontrolled in their behavior, but they gradually get control of it. A small percentage of children continue to have poor control that continues for years.[34] Behaviors that easily decrease in most children linger and create problems for a small group of children. For this small group, we think of their behaviors as especially engrained in their physiology, part of their temperament.

Researchers come to the area of temperament as a way of describing and eventually explaining how biological factors affect emotional and personality development. Jerome Kagan describes his study of high and low reactive temperaments as a way of relating actions in the brain—for example, in the reactivity of the amygdala—to children's behavior in everyday life.[35]

Temperament is defined as, "Constitutionally based individual differences in reactivity and self-regulation in the domains of affect, activity, and attention."[36] The definition refers to biologically based differences in how children react to experiences and how well they regulate their reactions. A child's temperament is important because it refers to behaviors that (1) are biologically based, arise spontaneously, and require effort to change; (2) influence children's reactions in many situations; (3) trigger reactions in parents, peers, and others in the environment; (4) shape the effects of parents' behavior on the child; and (5) can put a child at risk for certain problems.

Three broad dimensions of temperament are identified in infancy and childhood: (1) negative emotional reactivity, (2) extraversion/surgency, and (3) effortful control/self-regulation.[37] Negative emotionality includes reacting to experiences with fear, sadness, frustration, anger, or discomfort. Extraversion/surgency includes reactions of smiling, spontaneity, positive approach to stimulation, and high activity. Effortful control includes inhibiting behavior, focusing attention, and low-intensity pleasure.

In general, there is modest stability in these broad behavioral categories over time. Where there is change, it is often not from one category to another or from one end of the scale to the other, but from marked characteristics of a dimension to intermediate behaviors.

A careful study of the stability of high reactivity and low reactivity has followed children from four months of age to mid-adolescence.[38] General consistency in behavior is seen in those highly reactive four-month-old infants who cried and squirmed and had strong physiological reactions when confronted with new, unfamiliar stimuli and those who were low reactors. In early childhood and school years, high reactives were fearful, shy, and inhibited, and as teens, they were more emotionally subdued, quiet, cautious, religious, and worried about the future. Those four-month-old infants who reacted little to unfamiliar stimuli were sociable, outgoing, and eager to approach new situations and make friends.

There were different risks for psychological problems in adolescence for these two groups. Five high-reactive girls were being treated for depression, in contrast to only one low-reactive girl, and one high reactive boy was being treated for social anxiety.

Parents' behavior, when children were infants, had different impacts in these two groups depending on the child's temperament. When mothers of high-reactive infants were protective and nurturant, rocking and holding their crying baby, the child remained fearful and inhibited in the toddler years.[39] When, however, mothers were supportive but firm that the child had to soothe him- or herself, children were much less reactive as toddlers. Other studies have obtained similar results. Parents' nurturant protection did not affect low-reactive children's low level of inhibition. As inhibited children develop a conscience and learn prosocial behavior, they are so responsive to parents' rules and regulations that parents have to use only requests and explanations because children are fearful of not following them.[40]

Another group that has negative emotional reactivity is the irritable, fussy infant who is demanding. Though early crying and distress did not persist, irritability at six and seven months tended to last for the next year or two and was related to behavior problems at age three.[41] In Chapter 7, we describe a brief intervention with irritable babies and their mothers at six to nine months of life (p. 218) that increased mothers' sensitivity to their babies and increased infants' secure attachments to mothers at one year and children's cooperative and sociable behavior with peers in the preschool years.[42] So, irritable, fussy behavior can change with sensitive parenting.

Several longitudinal studies have identified three groups of children—overcontrolled (similar to high-reactive, inhibited children), undercontrolled, and resilient/well-adjusted—and found consistency in behavior over time. A New Zealand study followed children from age three to young adulthood and looked at their behavior in significant areas of life—work, romantic relationships, friendships, and social networks.[43] Children identified as having confident, well-adjusted, or reserved temperaments at age three were doing well in all areas. Those who were inhibited, cautious, and fearful at age three had good relationships at work and were satisfied with their romantic relationships, but they had fewer friends, fewer interests, and less social support.

Those who were poorly controlled at age three had the greatest number of difficulties as young adults. They were highly impulsive, aggressive, risk-taking people who irritated others. Other studies too have found undercontrolled children face a growing number of problems with peer relationships and poor schoolwork.[44]

Parenting of undercontrolled children requires adaptation just as parenting of inhibited children does. When children are relatively active and fearless and have little response to their own wrongdoing, they do not benefit from gentle, persuasive techniques nor do they benefit from punishments that arouse their anger.[45] Instead, they learn rules most easily when parents establish a positive, initially cooperative partnership based on a secure attachment. More securely attached, fearless children comply with what the mother wants because of the relationship, not the specific disciplinary techniques used.

Temperament research indicates then that no one set of interventions will help all children. Rather, parents must be sensitive, flexible caregivers who target their behavior to be a good fit with their child's temperamental qualities, recognizing that their child's biological inheritance may present special vulnerabilities for them in development. We come back to this topic in chapters on development, especially Chapter 8 (p. 240), and show the influence of culture—the American culture, for example, is more accepting of the extraverted, active, positive person and less accepting of the timid, fearful, inhibited person—on a child's behavior and the ways temperamental qualities modify children's development.[46]

Advances in science help us to see parents' important role in their children's growth in all areas. Parents' lifestyles can influence the expression of genes; the experiences parents provide can buffer children against the expression of negative genetic characteristics and help the brain realize its full potential. Parents' daily interactions can promote children's executive functioning that influences all learning. Finally, sensitive parenting directed to the child's specific qualities can help children live comfortably with their unique physiology.

We now look at what theories tell us about how children incorporate biological, emotional, psychological, and social influences in their lives.

CONSULTING THEORIES OF GROWTH AND DEVELOPMENT

Theories describe children's growth and development and the factors thought to stimulate healthy growth. Although theories do not provide step-by-step directions for parents, they do help parents understand children's needs and the many ways parents meet them and contribute to children's growth. In most instances, theories are complimentary, each contributing important information on different facets of children's growth.

We describe major theories of development and their usefulness to parents. Box 2-1 shows how each theory views and responds to a common problem parents confront with children: a child's difficulty in adjusting to the academic and social demands of first grade. The child may be a boy who is overly active, won't stay in his seat, and doesn't do his work or it may be a girl who is overly sociable, talking to others, getting out of her seat to help others, but not doing her own work. Such children may have done well in preschool, are healthy and intellectually capable, but they are not completing challenging work, not following class rules, and not making expected academic progress.

Theories are grouped according to the area of development of central concern. We first take up theories of cognitive development, then theories concerning emotional and social development.

Learning Theories

Learning theorists identify the specific forms of environmental stimulation that promote children's growth and provide a very important and active role to parents. Children's role may vary from blank slates who learn all behavior from external rewards and punishments to more active learners who interpret the environment around them and select goals and models to imitate. Still, the major force for development is seen as coming from outside forces that teach and produce behavior change.

Learning theories trace their origins to the work of Ivan Pavlov in the late nineteenth and early twentieth centuries.[47] His classical conditioning studies showed that animals could learn new behaviors when new signals were repeatedly linked to already existing responses—when a buzzer was linked with salivation at the sight of food, the buzzer alone came to trigger salivation.

We see the process of classical conditioning in everyday life when people who experience a strong emotional feeling attach that feeling to other stimuli present at

Box 2-1
THEORIES' VIEWS OF SCHOOL PROBLEMS

This box contains what each theory's view might be of a boy or girl who is having difficulty in the first grade staying in his or her seat, settling down, and completing classwork. The child has always been an active participant in school programs and has many friends. There are no medical or family problems.

Learning theory would focus on the external environment of the classroom, the teacher's behavior, and the system of rewards given at school and at home by parents. It is possible that the teacher or the parents only attend to the child when he or she is having problems so the difficulties gain attention; even though it is not positive attention, the child might accept it rather than no attention at all. Remedies would also involve teacher or parent changes that would change the child's behavior.

Vygotsky's approach would also focus on what teacher and parents might do but would focus on joint interactions with the child, engaging and supporting the child's behavior at the high end of the zone of proximal development. Language would be emphasized to help the child engage in self-talk to guide his or her behavior and get the work done. Efforts would be made to engage the child with peers in cooperative learning and play to advance thinking and executive skills.

Piaget would emphasize the teacher's role in organizing a classroom in which children can have an active role in constructing knowledge to encourage greater participation and completion of the work. Objects and materials would be available for manipulation and exploration, and the child would be encouraged to interact with them. The child's ways of reasoning about the materials would be elicited in discussions. The child would be given projects and small experiments to carry out in class to promote a greater understanding of the world through action.

Freud would identify the child's emotional difficulties in coping as the source of school difficulties. The child may have been indulged and is immature, and, unused to exerting independent effort, he or she does not complete the work. The child may have anxiety that can come from many sources—anxiety about separation from the family for an extended day, anxiety about his or her performance in relation to other children in the class, fear of criticism of the schoolwork from the teacher or parents, fear of bullying or rejection from peers. Perhaps anxiety comes from worry about a parent's health or family conflict. The aim would be to help the child to identify and cope more effectively with the source of the anxiety.

Erikson, like Freud, would look at the child's inner qualities but focus on whether the child had opportunities to develop initiative, confidence, and a sense of purpose about activities. He would look at parents' responses to their child's increasing mastery of skills and wonder whether they were encouraging their child to grow. But like a systems theorist, he would also look at qualities of the teacher. Was the teacher stimulating the child to work hard and gain a sense of industry or was the teacher arousing feelings of inferiority, leading the child to withdraw from class work and engage, instead, in restless activity? He would also wonder whether the teacher and the school were valuing the child's growing skills and sense of cultural identity that begins to develop in these early elementary school years. For example, are girls' scientific and math skills encouraged? Do boys receive praise when they make up stories to express feelings?

(continued)

Box 2-1
CONTINUED

Attachment theorists would consider whether the child's problem-solving abilities and self-control are related to the quality of attachment relationships in the present and in the past. Children with secure attachments would have an internal model of supportive, responsive adults and a history of confident, curious, problem-solving behavior.

They would explore the history of attachments wondering whether a child has an insecure-avoidant or resistant attachment relationship with parents, thus making it difficult to become attached to the teacher, settle down, and follow his or her requests. Most particularly, they would expect difficulties when children have disorganized/ disoriented attachment relationships. Children would find it difficult to sustain attention, focus, and organize to learn and complete work.

In addition, however, to looking at past and present attachment relationships outside the classroom, they would look at the teacher's behavior. They would note whether he or she interacts with this particular child in a warm, sensitive, responsive way that establishes a secure attachment to the teacher so the child will see him or her as an available, reliable source of help, a secure base from which one can move forward independently.

Evolutionary theorists would not be surprised at the problem because they would say that the child's genetic nature is not built to sit long hours carrying out culturally invented activities such as reading and writing. The young child's nature is to engage in rough-and-tumble play and motoric activity. They would see the solution as more time in recess and active play during the day, and more rest from the effort of doing "unnatural" kinds of work. Such practices are already in place in Japan and Taiwan where there is a rest or recess of 10 minutes for every 50 minutes of work. Research suggests that frequent breaks throughout the day, most important for the younger students, increase learning even if the breaks do not involve active physical exercise.

Bioecological theorists would look at the process of the child's interactions with teachers, peers, and parents. Are the interactions between the child and adult figures helpful in promoting learning and new, more complex behaviors?

More than most theorists, bioecological theorists would look at the context of the inattention and overactivity. What is the general culture of the school and its personnel regarding physical activity and attention to the requests of others? What is the attitude of the particular teacher in the classroom? Are a large proportion of students living at the poverty level and coming to school hungry and restless? What is the culture of the community surrounding the school? Is there community disorganization due to special stresses, such as violence, that promote inattentiveness and inability to concentrate on work? Does the community provide recreational places and activities for youth?

Bioecological theorists would look at the mesosystem—the relationship between the parent and the teacher. Can they communicate and understand each other? Do they share common values about what is most important for students to learn, so they can work together to help the child adjust? Parents may feel that the teacher is unreasonable in his or her demands of the child or does not understand their culture.

Bioecological theorists would also look at the macrosystem—the general cultural milieu of the child. They might point to the problems of less time with activities and parents and too much time with electronic games, videos, and TV, which provide instant gratification and discourage the daily effort that much learning involves.

Box 2-1

Just as one would look in many places for the sources of the difficulties, one would look at several ways to address them. In addition to all the individual interventions parents and teachers could carry out with the child, bioecological theorists would encourage parents to get involved in parent–teacher–community organizations to provide resources that enable children to engage in many physical activities in a safe atmosphere.

*Anthony D. Pellegrini and David F. Bjorkland, "The Role of Recess in Children's Cognitive Performance," *Educational Psychologist 32* (1997): 35–40.

the time. Later, these stimuli alone may trigger an emotional response. For example, a child, frightened by a dog that chased him, may become frightened the next time the child sees a dog running near him. A running dog alone triggers the fear the child felt when a dog actually chased him.

American learning theorists focused on what happened after the behavior of interest. They looked at how behavior changed as a result of the positive or negative consequences that followed the behavior. They noted that behaviors increased when positive consequences followed consistently and decreased with consistent negative consequences. They identified kinds of rewards—such as food or a toy, extra privileges such as staying up, and social rewards such as attention or physical affection. They found personal attention to be a most important reward for children and adults alike. If children do not get attention for positive behaviors, they will seek attention through irritating behaviors such as whining and arguing.

Social learning theorists found that children learn even when there is no reward at all. They observe people around them and imitate them. For example, babies will not play with a toy if the mother has looked at it with disgust. Observation of behavior alone is enough to stimulate imitation. Children are most likely to imitate models who are warm, nurturing, and powerful. In extreme circumstances when there is no model of warmth to copy, children will imitate a hostile, cold model.

Social learning theorists such as Albert Bandura focus on the active nature of the learner who chooses goals to pursue and reflects on performance. In understanding the process of learning, the learner's thoughts and interpretations of the environment are as important as environmental rewards and punishments.[48]

What Learning Theories Help Parents Understand (1) Their important role in modeling appropriate behaviors for children and structuring the consequences that teach children new behaviors; (2) children copy parents whether parents are carrying out approved or disapproved behaviors, (3) children want parental attention and will seek it by negative means if they do not get it for positive behaviors, and (4) the conditions under which children learn best.

Lev Vygotsky's Theory

Lev Vygotsky, a Russian psychologist born in the late nineteenth century, gives parents a central role in supporting children's growth, but one that differs from the role given by learning theorists.[49] Every culture, he believes, has a view of the world and the way to solve problems. Language, art, and everyday routines all reflect the cultural worldview that children learn from parents and daily experiences. He believes that knowledge, thought, and mental processes such as memory all rest on social interactions with knowledgeable partners.

Whatever children learn, Vygotsky believes, they first experience in a social interaction with someone, usually a parent, teacher, or peer, and then internalize the social interaction at the individual and psychological level. For example, preschoolers learn about their culture from taking on society's roles in dramatic play with their peers. They learn what mothers, fathers, and policemen do, and their language and knowledge grow as they take on these roles.

Vygotsky describes a unique concept called the *zone of proximal development*. There is a range of actions a child can perform alone, demonstrating a capacity that is clearly internal. This is what we consider the child's level of ability. But Vygotsky points out that when a more experienced person guides or prompts the child with questions, hints, or demonstrations, the child can respond in a more mature level not achieved when the child acts alone.

So, a child has potential that emerges in social interaction guided by an experienced partner. That area of potential development is termed the *zone of proximal development*. For example, a child learning to talk may use a particular number of words spontaneously. That would be the child's verbal ability. A mother, however, might increase the number of words or the length of the sentence by prompting the child to use more words, saying "The doggie?" and waiting for "runs" or "goes bow-wow." Adults' teaching has the greatest impact, Vygotsky believes, when it is directed to the child's learning potential at the high end of the zone of proximal development.

Language plays an important role in mental development in Vygotsky's theory. Language develops in social interaction and serves several functions. It influences others' behavior. Adults and children talk to each other and say what they need or want or what is upsetting them.

Language also serves as a guide to what to do. Parents can use language to help children remember sequences of actions in terms of steps. Children initially guide their own behavior with external language similar to the words they hear from others. They then talk aloud to themselves as others have talked to them and guide their behavior with their speech when they are alone. A toddler will say, "No, no," to herself as a way of stopping forbidden action, and gradually the speech becomes internal or inner speech. Such inner speech becomes thought in the older child. So language is the forerunner of thinking and a means of self-regulation.

Dramatic symbolic play also helps children to grow because they are interacting with their peers and have to play by rules and adjust to others' actions, developing imagination and self-control in relationships with others. Peers play an important role because in cooperating with each other to achieve a goal, children learn the give and take of social relationships as well as gain knowledge.

What Vygotsky's Theory Helps Parents Understand   (1) Their important role in conveying their culture's view of the world and how to live in it; (2) their role as experienced partners in guiding children to more advanced behaviors; and (3) the very important role of language both in reflecting the culture's values and in advancing children's ability to think and reason.

Piaget's Theory

Jean Piaget profoundly changed our views of children's intellectual growth by showing that children think about the world differently from adults.[50] Though different, their thinking is understandable as it proceeds through a series of predictable stages. Piaget emphasized the child's active construction of knowledge. Learning about the world is not a passive process of taking in what one sees and hears. Intellectual competence is a dynamic process in which the child explores the world, takes in information, and organizes it into internal structures called schemes. This process of taking in and organizing information is termed *assimilation*.

As children obtain new information, they find their internal schemes inadequate and modify them to account for the new information. The process of changing internal schemes to incorporate new information is called *accommodation*.

Intellectual growth is a constant interplay of taking in new information (assimilation) and modifying internal structures (accommodation) to achieve a balance or equilibrium between the individual's structure of the world and the world itself. *Equilibration* is the active process by which the individual achieves this effective balance.

An example of this process is seen in the child's growing understanding of the concept of persons. Initially all adults are "mama" and "dada." Eventually, the child will have an understanding of a world of adults with many different names—grandma, grandpa, auntie, uncle, teacher, coach, principal. Some are family members who will give you special consideration, and some are not.

Piaget described growth in terms of four major periods in which the child takes in and processes information in distinctive ways. In the first eighteen to twenty-four months of life, known as the *sensori-motor period,* the child's own body, perceptions, and actions are the focus of interest, and the schemes consist of action patterns such as kicking legs or opening and closing hands; gradually, actions become more complex and months later, the child acts to achieve a purpose—reaches to grasp a toy. Toward the end of the first year, babies come to understand the permanence of objects—that is, that objects have an independent existence even if the child cannot see them. The concept of permanence leads to exploration of these objects and how they work and where they might be when they are out of sight.

Beginning at about eighteen to twenty-four months, children begin to move from immediate experience of objects, people, and whatever is present at the moment to representations or thoughts of what is not immediately present. At about age two, children enter the *preoperational period,* which lasts until about age seven. They can represent what they see or hear with language that increases in the number of words and in the complexity of sentences to express thoughts.

Although children are curious and ask many questions, Piaget believes their concepts are limited because they pay attention to only a small number of characteristics of objects, usually to sensory features. For example, they may think a tall, thin glass holds more liquid than a short, fat glass because they pay attention only to the the height of the glass.

In the elementary school years, intellectual growth takes two leaps. At age seven, the child enters the *period of concrete operations*. The term "concrete operations" means that children can think more logically and are not so bound by the appearance of objects. They grasp relationships among objects and easily arrange a series of sticks by lengths with little trial and error. Children can think more logically and form classes, because they have a keen interest in understanding how things work.

Between ages twelve to fourteen, children enter the *period of formal operations*, and begin to think more abstractly. Not only can they think logically about tangible objects, they can think more abstractly about possible or hypothetical situations, about what might happen in the future. They can think about their own thoughts and about the thoughts and reactions of others. They become more concerned about abstract concepts such as justice and equality and engage in volunteer activities.

An example of the different ways of thinking in these stages is seen in children's responses to the question, "What do you think with?" Children five or six years old say they think with their mouth or their ears because they speak thoughts with their mouths or hear others' thoughts with their ears. Children age eight or nine will say they think with their heads but they describe thoughts as inner "little voices." Children age twelve will say they think with their heads and describe thoughts as immaterial—they are just there in their heads.[51]

What Piaget's Theory Helps Parents Understand   (1) They must take children's view of the world into account in their interactions with children (e.g., parents will not expect a toddler to understand the abstract concept of danger and future consequences—that if I run in the street or if I pull the pot off the stove, I will be hurt) and (2) that children need opportunities to explore objects and activities and to think their own thoughts about the world in order to grow.

Freudian Theory

Sigmund Freud, the founder of psychoanalysis, revolutionized the way we think about children's experiences in early childhood.[52] In talking to patients, he noticed he could trace many adult symptoms to anxieties about experiences occurring in early childhood. Concluding that what happened in early childhood had lifelong effects on adults' personalities, he set about describing the significant dimensions of childhood. He focused on children's impulses, particularly sexual impulses and their sources of gratification. Children were viewed as pleasure-seeking creatures who had to tame their impulses to conform to parents' and society's demands.

Freud divided childhood into five psychosexual stages that unfolded over time from birth to adolescence. The ways children attempt to gratify each stage's impulses and others' reactions to their attempts shape adult personality. Each stage is named after the area of the body that is the primary source of stimulation and gratification at that time. The stages are: (1) the oral stage, with pleasures of nursing and taking in food; (2) the anal stage at the time of toilet training, with pleasures associated with tightening and releasing the anal musculature; (3) the phallic stage in the preschool years when genital stimulation predominated over oral and anal gratifications; (4) latency in the early elementary school years, when sexual feelings were thought to be dormant; and finally (5) the genital stage in adolescence when sexual development and sexual feelings were thought to mature fully.

Freud believed that the outcome of the Oedipal conflict occurring in the preschool years is a major determiner of personality development. Just as children begin to feel competent and effective, they experience a failure that can permanently damage their self-regard. In these years, the child desires to be romantically involved with the parent of the opposite sex, to marry the parent and have a new family.

While this love flourishes, preschoolers feel very competitive with the same-sex parent. They want to surpass and outperform the adult, and they talk a lot about how grown-up and powerful they are. They are angry at the same-sex parent for standing in the way, and wish that parent would leave or die. They feel guilty and anxious about their anger and seek reassurances that the same-sex parent has not been a victim of their aggressiveness. Eventually, the child deals with the anxiety by giving up the opposite-sex parent as a love object and identifying with the same-sex parent as a model. As the child takes on the behaviors of the same-sex adult, the moral conscience and the commands of society become internalized in the form of what Freud calls the superego and shape the individual's response to authority and society.

Although Freud did not give direct advice to parents, he emphasized the importance of appropriate gratification of children's natural impulses—demand feeding, permissive attitudes about thumb sucking and toilet training, acceptable outlets for aggressive impulses—without criticism or punishment.

What Freud's Theory Helps Parents Understand   (1) Children have internal needs that drive behavior and neither they nor parents have complete control, and (2) parents have a powerful role in understanding children's inner needs and helping them find acceptable ways to gratify their impulses; parents are authoritative guides and supporters on the path to maturity, not generals commanding the course of growth.

Erikson's Lifespan Theory

Erik Erikson, a Freudian psychoanalyst with a strong belief in the importance of cultural and social influences on growth, devised a scheme for understanding lifespan development that focuses attention on the positive and healthy aspects of ego development.[53] Erikson focused more on the positive environmental responses required for healthy growth than Freud did. The experience of parenting is a central feature of adult development so he is an especially relevant theorist.

Erikson describes growth as a series of eight stages, as shown in Table 2-1. In each stage physical and psychological capabilities appear and are the focus of development. A developmental crisis or turning point occurs in each stage, and depending on the balance of positive and negative experiences, leads to the development of the positive or negative basic attitudes of that period (e.g., trust or mistrust, autonomy or doubt/shame). Stages of growth emerge from within the person but require support from the environment for healthy growth to occur.

Individuals have both positive and negative experiences in the process of meeting needs, and both kinds of experience are important for optimal growth. Without some frustrations, we never learn how to cope with difficulties. However, for healthy growth, the balance should favor the positive. When this occurs, a strength or virtue develops.[54] Erikson does not believe that we resolve each crisis once and for all. Later experiences can change earlier resolutions for better or worse. Stress in adulthood, for example, can disrupt mature ways of coping so a person may show immature behaviors. Positive experiences in adulthood can reverse mistrust or doubt developed in childhood.

Let us look briefly at the stages in Table 2-1. We focus on the qualities that develop when the appropriate experiences and positive environmental support occur; if experiences are primarily negative and support is lacking, negative qualities will develop. In the first years of life when all goes well, children develop trust, autonomy, and initiative. In the elementary school years, children attend school and are industrious and productive.

In adolescence, children incorporate sexuality into their expanding sense of self and develop a sense of identity—a feeling of sameness and continuity of self—that is a central concept in Erikson's scheme. Individuals also incorporate society's views of who they are—as men, women, and members of particular religions and ethnic groups. Individuals need to have their identities validated by their parents and society; otherwise, they remain confused, uncertain of who they are and where they are heading. When positive identities are formed and validated, teens develop fidelity—defined as loyalty to one's choices whether they be persons, goals, or ideals. When life events or family members or society are not supportive, individuals may develop a negative identity, a feeling of worthlessness.

■ TABLE 2-1
ERIK ERIKSON'S EIGHT STAGES OF LIFE

Ages	Crisis	Virtue
0–1	Trust versus Mistrust	Hope
1–3	Autonomy versus Shame, Doubt	Will
3–5	Initiative versus Guilt	Purpose
5–12	Industry versus Inferiority	Competence
12–19	Identity versus Identity Diffusion	Fidelity
19+	Intimacy versus Isolation	Love
25+	Generativity versus Stagnation	Care
65+	Integrity versus Despair	Wisdom

Erik H. Erikson, *Childhood and Society,* 2nd ed. (New York: Norton, 1963); Erik H. Erikson, *Insight and Responsibility* (New York: Norton, 1964).

Erikson conceived of three stages in adulthood. In the first, young adults establish intimate personal ties with an agemate. Intimate relationships involve mutuality and surrender of the self to the relationship. The virtue that develops in this period is love and involves transferring the love experienced in the developing years of childhood to adult relationships.

This is followed by a period of creating new life—generativity. In the past women experienced this primarily in the family setting, creating a home and children; men in the past have done so in their work. Now parenting and work are significant creative activities for both sexes. The virtue that develops is care—concern and attention to what has been created even if that requires sacrifice.

In the final life stage, the focus returns to the individual's personal experience. Individuals must come to terms with their lives and be satisfied with who and what they are and what they have done. When this occurs, individuals develop a sense of integrity and wisdom about life. Erikson believes children and grandchildren will be able to face life when parents can face death.

What Erikson's Theory Helps Parents Understand (1) Psychological growth continues in adulthood and resolutions of old conflicts are possible later in life; (2) that children are active, adaptive individuals who go through stages of growth to become independent, giving individuals concerned with other people and the world around them; and (3) parenting is important to both the child who experiences it and the parent who gives it.

Attachment Theory

In 1958, London psychoanalyst John Bowlby used the term *attachment* to describe the parent–infant relationship and defined it as "an enduring affectional tie that unites one person to another, over time and across space."[55] He believed that it implied positive ties leading to healthy development, as opposed to the negative connotations of the term *dependency* that Freudians used to characterize the child's relationship with the parent. Attachment pointed to the positive functions the tie had for survival and preserving life. While attachment initially referred to early parent–child relationships, its use has broadened to apply to parent–child relationships throughout the lifespan and to relationships with significant others such as friends, teachers, caregivers, and marital partners.[56]

Attachment refers to that aspect of the parent–child relationship that gives the infant feelings of safety, security, and protection and provides a safe base from which to explore the world. In infancy and childhood, the relationship is asymmetrical in that the infant derives security from the parents, but not vice versa. In adulthood, attachment involves a mutual, reciprocal relationship in which partners provide security and a safe base for each other.

Initially, attachment was measured in a laboratory situation in which observers noted the quality of mother–child interactions during play (later fathers were observed as well) and noted the child's reactions to the mother's leaving the room, a stranger's entering, and the mother's return.[57] Attachment has usually been measured at twelve months and at varying intervals thereafter. Attachment has also been measured by an attachment Q-sort used by observers, and an attachment interview with teens and adults.

Infants and children differ not in whether attachment takes place—almost all children become attached as part of life—but the quality of the attachment differs depending on the behaviors of the adults.[58] The most common form of attachment is the *secure* one that occurs when parents are accepting, emotionally available, and sensitive in meeting babies' needs. Securely attached infants are happy and secure with mothers, protest when they leave, and are happy and seek closeness when mothers return. About 60 to 70 percent of U.S. babies are described as securely attached.

There are three forms of insecure attachment. When parents are intrusive and overstimulating, infants are likely to form *anxious-avoidant* attachments—being unconcerned when mothers leave and uninterested in their return. About 20 percent of U.S. babies have such attachments. When parents are insensitive to babies' cues and often unavailable, babies are likely to form *anxious-resistant* attachments—strong protests when mothers leave and difficulties establishing closeness when mothers return, alternately seeking the mother and resisting closeness. About 10–20 percent of U. S. babies have such attachments.

A third form of insecure attachment has been identified as *disorganized/disoriented* attachments. These attachments occur in families in which parents appear frightened or traumatized, and as a result may appear frightening to the child. Babies' behavior seems disorganized because at times, they happily approach the mother as a securely attached infant would, and at other times, they avoid the parent. They also appear disoriented because they show signs of confusion as to how to respond, sometimes "freezing" or "stilling" when near the parent. The percentage of such attachments is low in low-risk families (about 13 percent) but the percentage increases in high-risk families—82 percent in families whose members mistreat babies.[59]

Psychologists believe that strong attachments to parents and fear of strangers have survival value for the infant. Secure attachments ensure the infant will stay close to the parent and remain responsive to guidance so the parent can continue to protect the child as the child becomes more independent.

Attachment relationships also provide a framework for babies' understanding of the world.[60] From these relationships, babies build internal models of how people relate to one another. Babies develop expectations of how well others will understand and respond to them, how much influence they will have on others, and what level of satisfaction they can expect from other people. They develop a sense of their own lovability when others respond positively to their overtures, and they anticipate similar responses from adults in new situations. When babies are ignored or rejected, they may develop a sense of unworthiness and helplessness. When interactions make up consistent patterns, babies acquire a sense of order and predictability in experience that generalizes to daily activities and to the world at large.

The benefits of early attachments extend to the future. Securely attached infants are more curious later in childhood than are insecurely attached ones.[61] They attack a problem vigorously and persistently but accept help from others and are not aggressive. Children with early insecure attachments tend later to be more anxious and have tantrums when presented with problems.

Attachment classifications vary in stability over time depending on the sample and length of time. Over short periods of time, say twelve to eighteen months, stability is high[62]; two studies show substantial stability (about 70 percent) for the classification of security from one year to late adolescence and early adulthood.[63] However, two do not show long-term stability.[64] In general, when infants or older children live in families with many changes, especially negative changes (e.g., divorce or loss of emotional support that change the nature of the parent–child relationship), stability of attachment is lower. However, the quality of the attachment can change in a positive direction as well; mothers' increases in confidence and feelings of security improved the quality of their attachment to children.[65]

What Attachment Theory Helps Parents Understand   (1) Attachments are formed with important people throughout the lifespan, (2) the way parents treat babies creates long-lasting expectations about the way the world will treat them, and (3) attachments depend on the quality of the parent–child relationship at the time and will change as circumstances improve or damage the quality of the relationship.

Systems Theory

Systems theory is a broad term that applies to theories in many sciences such as biology, psychology, and sociology. Systems theory emphasizes that the organism of interest—animal, person, family, organization—consists of many parts, all of which influence each other in important ways, and no part is more important than the others. Systems theories in developmental psychology look at several levels of interaction that influence the individual's behavior—genetic, neural, psychological, social, and sociological—and the bidirectional transactions that occur at all levels.[66]

A dynamic relationship exists among all the levels so that the effect of any given event depends on the rest of the system. For example, a child's low birth weight may have a different effect on the course of the child's development, depending on the social status of the family into which the child is born and the resources available to the family to help the child. When families have resources to get services, the effects of low birth weight are minimal or nonexistent; when families have few resources, effects are more marked.[67] As we have seen, recent research in genetics and neuroscience supports a systems perspective.

We now look at two systems theories that illustrate ways of seeing the relationships between the levels of experience and development.

Evolutionary Theory

Evolutionary developmental psychologists look at how our genetic heritage influences our behavior today.[68] As its name suggests, the theory draws on Darwin's concepts of natural selection and reproductive fitness. *Natural selection* is the process whereby adaptive characteristics increase in frequency in a group because those behaviors that enable individuals to survive, grow to maturity, and reproduce—in brief, to adapt to their environment—are passed along to the next generation through the genes. Those who do not fit well in their environment die or reproduce fewer offspring.

Reproductive fitness refers to individuals' success in passing on their genes to the next generation. Contemporary evolutionary psychologists use the term *inclusive fitness* to describe individuals' success in reproducing their genes not only through their own children who share 50 percent of their genes, but also through nurturing relatives such as younger siblings who share 50 percent of the genes or nieces and nephews who share 25 percent of the genes.

Evolutionary developmental psychologists trace the origins of family life back thousands of years to the time we lived in small hunting-gathering tribes that depended on organized, cooperative, social behaviors. Complex social behaviors required a large brain that meant the child had to be born earlier in a less mature state so that the body of the mother could accommodate the size of the child's head in the birth process. Being born in a less mature state required an extended period of dependence on caregivers, and that, in turn, encouraged fathers' ongoing protection and support. Thus, a family system of mother, father, and children was born.

Early conditions of life also fostered the development of heavy parental investment in children. For immature children to survive, mature, and reproduce, caregiving had to extend for the long period of child dependency. The children of parents with minimal investments in caregiving were less likely to survive and reproduce, so natural selection resulted in increasing numbers of parents with heavy investments in rearing their children.

Evolutionary developmental theory provides important insights about contemporary life and suggests social interventions.[69] For example, it helps us understand the necessary conditions for the development of parents who make heavy investments in their children. Research indicates that when children grow up in harmonious families with resources to provide many opportunities for development—lessons, trips, advanced schooling—children postpone sexual activity and mating, produce fewer children, and invest heavily in those they have. Conversely, when children grow up in conflicted families with limited resources and few opportunities for skill development, they reach puberty early, invest heavily in sexual and mating behaviors, and less in parenting behaviors.

Evolutionary developmental theory suggests that one way to increase parental investment for those growing up in families with limited resources is to provide opportunities for growth and development.

What Evolutionary Developmental Psychology Helps Parents Understand

(1) As human beings we have inborn tendencies based on our past history that make certain contemporary adaptations more or less difficult and we must take heritage seriously as we make social interventions; and (2) our strong attachment and closeness to nurturing family members has had and continues to have survival value.

Bioecological Theory

The late Urie Bronfenbrenner developed the most comprehensive system for understanding children's growth and the many factors affecting parents and children. He is a systems theorist who emphasizes the ecological context of development.[70]

Evolutionary theory predicts young children's school performance will improve with frequent opportunities for action and movements.

The term *ecology* refers to the environments that human beings encounter in daily life as they grow and develop.

Bronfenbrenner describes a process–person–context–time (PPCT) framework for understanding development.[71] *Processes* are the daily interactions the child has with people, symbols, and objects in the environment and are the engines of development. A father's feeding a baby, a child's exploring a toy, and a child's learning a skill from a coach are examples of such processes or interactions.

The *person* has many characteristics such as age, gender, ethnicity, temperamental dispositions, abilities, and resources that influence their behavior and responses to others.

Bronfenbrenner's major contribution has been to expand our understanding of the *context* of development, the environment in which processes occur is what makes up the child's environment. He describes several nested systems.[72] The *micro-system* is the pattern of daily activities and interactions the child has with symbols, objects, and people who are primarily parents and siblings in the early period of life and then other caregivers, teachers, coaches, and friends. The *mesosystem* is the pattern of relationships and interactions between two or more settings that a child participates in (e.g., the interrelationships between parents at home and teachers at school, or between parents at home and caregivers at day care). The *exosystem* is a system that influences the child but with which the child does not have direct contact (e.g., parents' work, government agencies). For example, parents' work policies can determine parents' time with children after birth and later their participation in children's school activities.

Finally, the *macrosystem* refers to the broad, culturally shared beliefs about how things are done. It is the cultural context in which microsystems, mesosystems, and exosystems exist.

In addition to processes, persons, and context, Bronfenbrenner's system includes the concept of *time,* to refer to the importance of regularity and stability in interactions and in the systems in the child's life.[73] Children need a sense of stability about where they live and what is expected of them in school. Many moves and changing school policies disrupt children's development.

Time also refers to the timing of an event in a child's development. Poverty or divorce may have very different consequences for a toddler and an adolescent. Finally, time refers to the historical time, which exerts an influence on development. Children growing up in the Depression had a different attitude about work and savings from children who grew up in periods of economic abundance and security. While historical time influences individuals and the contexts of their lives, people and their social lives can produce changes in history as well.

For the last decade of his life, Bronfenbrenner, who died in 2005, expressed concern at what he termed the "growing chaos" in children's and families' lives and the resulting decline in competence of those coming of age in the twenty-first century.[74] Children have less time and involvement with parents because of family disruptions due to divorce and both parents working long hours outside the home. Economic security has decreased and almost 20 percent of children live in poverty. Children are emerging from schools less well educated at a time when a technological economy demands intellectual skills. Youth express decreased trust in authorities. They are committing crimes and an increasing proportion of youth is spending their growing years in prison.

Bronfenbrenner believes that as a society we need to commit more resources to programs such as the G.I. Bill of Rights that helped all families after World War II to get educations and to own homes. He also points to Head Start as a program that strengthens and empowers children and families.

What Bioecological Theory Helps Parents Understand   (1) Forces outside the family—historical events, economic factors, social institutions such as work—impact parents' care of children; (2) importance of regularity and stability in children's lives; and (3) help to improve parenting comes not just from changing what goes on in the home but also what goes on in society.

Systems theories look at the many factors—from genes to governmental institutions to historical time—that shape children's growth and the many factors affecting parents' behavior and their responses to children. While parents do not control these forces, they do take active roles to manage the effects of these forces in their everyday lives.

Summary   Theories help us understand that changes in children's behavior come both from the maturation or an unfolding of internal stages of growth as well as from environmental stimulation. Parents' roles vary from one of authoritative guide and support in the case of maturation to one of active stimulator in the case of theories emphasizing external sources of growth.

All these theories deepen parents' understanding of their role in children's lives and the many factors that affect how parents carry out this role. Parents are not only models of behavior, provider of appropriate consequences for behavior, they are insightful, authoritative guides who understand the pressures children experience as they grow, providing support and direction for them. Parents are influenced by the historical time they live in; the social world they inhabit and bring to the child; the child's experience at the physical, emotional, social, and behavioral levels; the nourishing quality of the environment; and the lessons people outside the family teach children. So parents can rightly consider themselves as the stabilizing and guiding center of a wide array of influences on children's lives.

Looking at the ways the theories would approach a common childhood school problem, we see that each theory has insights on possible causes and remedies and that the insights are complimentary rather than contradictory. While no one child would require the insights of all these theories, still all theories are useful in understanding the many different problems children can have. This illustrates an important point in parenting—there is no one reason and no one remedy for a child behavior of concern.

CONSULTING EXPERTS

It is not surprising that parents consult experts. Parents want to do a good job at what matters most to them, and many experts, books, and television programs are available for advice. In this section, we review what a sampling of experts has recommended. Several are explained in greater detail in later chapters. We then consult three research programs that give parents direction.

Psychologists Haim Ginott[75] and Thomas Gordon[76] focus on children's needs and are similar in emphasizing effective methods of communication to strengthen the parent–child bond and to attend to the child's individuality. Ginott establishes and enforces limits in an impersonal way and Gordon encourages parent–child problem-solving sessions when conflicts arise. We discuss their methods of communicating with children in Chapter 4.

Rudolf Dreikurs, a child psychiatrist and one of the first to organize parents' groups, advises both establishing close relationships and setting limits.[77] Dreikurs believes that children have built-in capacities to develop in healthy ways. Their strongest desire is to belong to a group, and from infancy, they seek acceptance and importance within the family. Each child, however, develops a unique path to family acceptance. Parents influence children by gaining their cooperation, using encouragement to stimulate development of children's inner resources, and applying natural and logical consequences to provide limits for children's behavior. We discuss his concepts in greater detail in Chapters 4 and 5.

Toward the end of the twentieth century, child psychiatrist and psychoanalyst Stanley Greenspan emerged as a major expert.[78] He has been a careful observer who has described children's motor, language, intellectual, social, and particularly their emotional development from birth. Greenspan was one of the founders of the organization Zero to Three, which focuses on the development and needs of children in this period. In addition, he has been concerned with children who have special developmental needs (e.g., children with autism), discussed in greater detail in Chapter 8.

He has written a number of books describing patterns of development and parents' important role in helping children master challenges in each area and developing appropriate skills. He has also turned his attention to advocating for social policies that support parents and children. With T. Berry Brazelton, he coauthored the book, *The Irreducible Needs of Children,* so that parents and public policy experts could lobby for reasonable supports.[79] He and Brazelton want society to pay attention to parents' needs by providing additional resources for families' growth just as they urge parents to support their children's needs and growth. They focus on what society must give parents to help them rear children.

The twenty-first century has brought us parenting experts on television. Dr. Phil,[80] *Nanny 911,*[81] and *Supernanny* all offer parents guidance on child-rearing matters. Dr. Phil is a psychologist, but the nannies are unique among the experts in being individuals whose expertise lies in their having a lot of hands-on experience with many families, living in or spending long days with the children and their parents. In contrast to twentieth-century experts, these experts go into the homes and videotape parents and children interacting prior to the advice and after it. They observe how parents put the advice into practice and fine-tune parental behaviors. Perhaps because these experts go into people's homes and follow up, they are direct with their suggestions.

The nannies are among the most realistic of the experts in knowing the amount of effort change demands. They spend one day observing and drawing up a plan for change and the rest of the week modeling and guiding parents' interactions with children. They also show parents how to organize the home and daily routines.

Nannies Deborah Carroll and Stella Reid describe the "No-nonsense School of Parenting" that teaches parents how to "grow up and be parents"[82] as follows: "We believe that children need lots of love, but they also need lots of House Rules, giving structure to their days. This means strict limits tailored to children's personalities, and lots and lots of positive reinforcement rather than constant nagging and negativity. We'll show you how to confront your family problems head-on with firm but loving discipline, clear and effective communication, and the implementation of family rules. We'll teach you how to stop making excuses, avoid tackling problems that may seem insurmountable, and how to stop giving in when your children are whining and crying."

"Paradoxically, imposing *more* order on children allows them the freedom to thrive and stretch their wings and to grow up to be happy, healthy, and loved."[83]

Dr. Phil sees parenting as a "noble"[84] undertaking that is the center of the meaning of life. Both parents must work together to rear children, and while parents are not the only influences in children's lives, still they create an environment that enables family members "to rise above the noise of the world."[85]

RESEARCH THAT GIVES PARENTS DIRECTION AND SUPPORT

Few parents have heard the names of Diana Baumrind or Gerald Patterson; yet their research work, carried out over decades, has provided a solid base of empirical evidence for experts who believe that love, nurturance, and understanding must be combined with firm, consistent limits if children are to flourish.

In 1961, at a time when psychologists thought permissive, democratic child rearing provided the most benefits for children, and parental control was defined and measured as harsh and rejecting discipline, Diana Baumrind undertook research that has influenced experts for five decades. Her work was groundbreaking in many ways, and we detail her methods here because they account for the solidity of her findings.[86]

Baumrind observed a sample of 150 middle-class, predominantly white preschoolers in several settings—in nursery school; in laboratory sessions, alone and in teaching sessions with mothers; and at home from before dinner until bedtime. She developed measures of their positive behaviors rather than the problematic behaviors, which had so often been the focus of past research. Baumrind did not rely only on parents' verbal reports of how they behaved with children, though she did obtain them via interview as was typical in most parenting research up to that time. She sent observers into the homes to record what occurred between parents and children and she observed parents in the laboratory. Single-handedly, she followed her sample, observing the children again at ages ten, fifteen, and in their early twenties, to determine both the consistency and the long-term effects of her early parenting measures.

Baumrind began her work by first identifying preschoolers who showed positive behaviors such as self-control, approach-avoidance tendency, self-reliance, vitality (mood varying from buoyant to dysphoric), and peer affiliation. Nursery school teachers' quantified observations provided the measures of children's behaviors. From these descriptions, Baumrind identified competent children who had the capacity for socially responsible, independent behavior that included positive, cooperative relationships with parents and peers and purposive, achievement-oriented behavior in the world.

She identified three patterns of parental behaviors associated with varying levels of children's competence: authoritative, authoritarian, and permissive. In all age groups, in all ethnic groups in this country, in all types of family structure, authoritative parenting has had positive benefits for children.

Authoritative parents exercised firm control over the child's behavior but also emphasized independence and individuality in the child. Although the parents had a clear notion of present and future standards of behavior for the child, they were rational, flexible, and attentive to the needs and preferences of the child. Their children were self-reliant and self-confident and explored their worlds with excitement and pleasure.

Authoritarian parents employed similar firm control but in an arbitrary, power-oriented way without regard for the child's individuality. They emphasized control without nurturance or support to achieve it. Children of authoritarian parents, relative to other groups of children, were unhappy, withdrawn, inhibited, and distrustful.

Permissive parents set few limits on the child. They accepted the child's impulses, granting as much freedom as possible while still maintaining safety. They appeared cool and uninvolved. Permissive parents sometimes allowed behavior that angered them, but they did not feel sufficiently comfortable with their anger to express it. As a result, anger built up to unmanageable proportions. They then lashed out and were likely to harm the child more than they wished. Their children were the least independent and self-controlled and could best be classified as immature.

Baumrind described parents' conceptions of children in the three groups of parents. Both authoritarian and permissive parents had unrealistic perceptions of children. "Both Authoritarian and Permissive parents saw their child as dominated by egoistic and primitive forces. Authoritarian parents saw these characteristics in need of constraint, and Permissive parents (many citing Rousseau) tended to glorify these same characteristics. Few parents from either pattern took very much into account, on the one hand, the child's stage-appropriate desire to be good and to conform to parental expectations nor, on the other hand, the child's impulsivity and use of concrete reasoning which often interfered with his efforts to behave maturely. Thus, these parents appeared to construct a fiction about what their child was like and to relate to that fiction. . . . While Authoritarian parents tended to view children as having responsibilities similar to those of adults and Permissive parents tended to view children as having rights similar to those of adults, Authoritative . . . parents saw the balance between the responsibilities and rights of parents and the responsibilities and rights of children as a changing function of stage of development."[87]

Authoritative parents also interpreted the parental role as including the responsibility to teach children that in their relationship, each had to treat the other as they wished to be treated, and children were expected to behave the same way in their relationships with others outside the family.

Baumrind's conclusions about the positive value of firm parental control and parental demands for mature behavior startled psychologists who associated parental control with parental rejection and children's behavior problems. Her findings that firm control and a family atmosphere of nurturance and understanding developed children's competence set her work apart from its predecessors and provided research support for parents who believe understanding and nurturance as well as firm limits and consequences are necessary for rearing children.

With regard to the debate as to whether children's behavior is the result of maturational or learning processes, Baumrind wrote, "Innate and maturational predispositions, present at birth, and mediated by neurophysiological processes, interact throughout the individual's life with environmental factors to determine the course of development. Although maturation of the child's nervous system provides opportunities for development, these opportunities can be realized only in a facilitating environment designed by knowledgeable adults."[88]

Gerald Patterson's research at the Oregon Social Learning Center also encourages parents to give both love and limits. We will refer to his and his colleagues' work in later chapters as well, but here we point to the development of his ideas over decades. His research at the Oregon Social Learning Center, carried out at the same time as that of Baumrind, initially focused on helping families with aggressive children who defied parents at home and teased and bullied children at school.[89] Observers went to the homes to record and understand patterns of family interaction. Parents learned about behavior modification techniques. Then parents and child drew up

To interrupt negative cycles of behavior Gerald Palterin recommends parents create a supportive, consistent positive reinforcement program to establish a warm parent-child relationship.

a contract of rewards and negative consequences to increase positive target behaviors and decrease negative behaviors. Families were followed over time and their progress was noted. The program led to positive behavior change in the family and to fathers' taking more active roles in controlling children's behavior.

Over time, Patterson and his coworkers discerned a family pattern of interactions leading to aggressive behaviors. Several factors contributed to this process over time—children's temperamental qualities, parents' experiences with their own parents, the social conditions of family life such as divorce, cultural factors, as well as parents' personal qualities such as depression.

Combining their observations with insights from attachment research on the importance of sensitive caregiving and maternal warmth, Patterson and his coworkers have sketched a process of development that leads to children's compliance or noncompliance as follows.[90] Sensitive parents, responsive to their children's needs, form secure attachments to their children; they therefore create early in life a climate in which children are willing to comply because parents attend to their needs and wishes. The children act out of the commitment to the relationship with their parents. Throughout the learning process, parents give children the encouragement and support needed to persevere in the often frustrating learning process.

Like mutual responsiveness, the process of coercion begins with the interactions between the mother/caregiver and infant. Either partner can start the process and both keep it going.[91] Typically, the infant is irritable and fussy, and the mother, for whatever reason, is negative and unpredictable in her response. This increases the infant's irritability. The infant comes to see the world as an unrewarding, unsupportive, unpredictable place. Or the mother may be depressed and pay little attention to the infant who becomes irritable and negative and triggers further negativity on the mother's part.

The infant develops into a noncompliant, negative toddler who fails to follow rules. Crying, fussing, and whining give way to hitting, kicking, and breaking things to force parents to do what the toddler wants. Each partner's negative response intensifies the other's response. Eventually other family members are drawn in to the negative cycle. The noncompliant toddler becomes the impulsive, defiant preschooler who then becomes the aggressive, bullying elementary school student.

To counter a negative cycle, Patterson and his colleagues have taught parents to use a supportive, consistent, positive reinforcement program to create a sensitive, caring relationship between parent and child. Once a warm relationship is established, then parents can actively teach desirable habits primarily through the use of positive statements and consistent consequences. Though they believe that temperamental qualities of parent and child affect the interactions between the two, they also believe that behavioral interventions can and do modify parents' and children's behavior.

Both Baumrind and Patterson and coworkers developed parenting recommendations from research based on observations of all family members as they are living life. They have followed their study members over time and have noted the long-term effectiveness of the interventions they recommend. Coming from different perspectives, they have arrived at common ground in recommending both nurturing love and consistent, firm limits.

An extensive series of studies carried out by Dutch researchers Femmie Juffer, Marian Bakermans-Kranenburg, Marinus van IJzendoorn, and their colleagues combine the insights of attachment theory and Patterson's coercion theory and apply them directly to helping parents facing special situations—adoptive parents, parents of preterm children, insecure mothers, and low-income parents.[92]

The aim is to increase parents' sensitivity to children's behavior so that parents and children can form a more secure relationship that serves as a secure base for attachment and continuing exploration. They have also incorporated what they term "sensitive discipline," described in Chapter 5 and especially pertinent to aggressive toddlers, as we saw earlier in this chapter.

The interventions, Video-Feedback Intervention Positive Parenting (VIPP) with the added module VIPP-Sensitive Discipline (VIPP-SD) and a third with an extensive discussion of attachment (VIPP-R), all have a common format of having a clinically trained intervener go into the home for four to eight sessions to videotape the mother and child interacting in play and family routines, identifying positive forms of interaction and highlighting them for parents each week. Building a positive relationship between the intervener and parent is critical to the success of the program.

Each session has a theme. The first two sessions are focused on the child's behavior and learning to read the child's signals, and the next two sessions are focused on the mother's responses (e.g., paying attention to the sensitivity chain—child sends a signal, mother responds, child sends back a positive response that shows mother how important she is for the child's well-being). Each week's video is searched for examples of positive behaviors that illustrate the next week's topic. Explicitly pointing out mother's skill emphasizes mother's competence as a caregiver and her expert knowledge of her child and encourages mother to stay involved in the program.

Because the program directly targets the parent's behavior to increase sensitive responses, the baby's positive reaction provides ongoing reinforcement for the mother and the program can be a short one. Video fragments of mothers' positive behaviors are used to convey to mothers that they are competent and the experts on their child, and they are used because they have found that parents identify more with themselves than with paid model illustrations of the actions.

And the program is effective.[93] Mother's sensitivity and secure attachments increased as a result of the interventions in numerous samples that include around 1,500 families. Interventions were most effective when the child was over six months. The authors believe their program is successful in helping mothers because it communicates and promotes a world in which attachment figures are available, reliable, and trustworthy and the self is worthy of love and care.

Strong support for the importance of parents' sensitivity, warmth, and responsiveness with children comes from an Australian study of 152 children who were born preterm at less than thirty weeks.[94] When the children were two years of age, their neurocognitive and social-emotional growth were assessed. Parents also described their children's social and emotional functioning, and parents' interactions with children were observed as they engaged in play with their toddlers. Parents' positive parenting behaviors—their warmth, their sensitivity, and their ability to coordinate their efforts with children, and support children in their activities—were related not only to children's emotional regulation and positive mood, but also to their toddlers' cognitive skills. When parents laugh and smile and share positive emotions with their children, when they match their behavior to what the child is doing, then children develop optimally in social, emotional, and cognitive areas.

Summary   The history of parent–child relationships over the centuries, much of the theory, and careful research agree that parents' love, nurturance, consistent guidance, and limits are needed to support children's growth that is determined by the maturation of the child's nervous system in a stimulating, supportive environment provided by parents. Following the chapter on the cultural influences on parenting, we explore in greater detail how parents establish close relationships and support growth.

MAIN POINTS

The history of parent–child relationships over the centuries reveals that parenting

- has shown a general continuity with parenting today with closeness and caring between parents and children and parents' concern for children's growth and competence
- continuity is shaped by two factors: (1) parents' goal to help children survive and flourish and (2) children's needs

Science has helped us understand the complex relationship between

- genetic, neurophysiological, psychological, and social factors in children's development

- parents' actions and their effects on children's development and the fact that there is no one way to rear children given the individual's unique makeup

The theories reviewed here

- share many features in common
- deepen parents' understanding of children's development and parents' role in promoting it
- focus on different aspects of development—cognitive, emotional, and social

Theories emphasizing the role of the parent in stimulating cognitive growth

- include learning theories as well as Vygotsky's view of the social nature of knowledge and growth
- view parents as models of curiosity and executive skills, partners in social interactions that stimulate growth, providers of a secure emotional base for exploration and learning, dispensers of rewards that encourage learning
- view parents as knowledgeable guides who provide experiences that help children achieve their maximum potential
- see parents as transmitters of culture

Theories describing parents' role in stimulating emotional development

- describe the importance of parents' love and stability for children's emotional security
- view neither children nor parents as having complete control
- emphasize that both parents and children have active roles as children must satisfy drives in socially acceptable ways and adjust to and integrate new behaviors
- describe parents as authoritative guides who seek to understand children's experiences and support children's growth by providing appropriate experiences

Theories emphasizing the systems approach

- focus on all levels of experience from genes to internal drives to societal organization and historical time
- stress the ways the environment supports internal growth patterns
- include genetic influences from our early human living conditions as well as numerous contemporary social influences such as our economy
- give parents active roles in helping children integrate all the influences impinging on them

Careful researchers of parent–child relationships that are studied in the laboratory as well as at home find

- that authoritative parenting that includes both nurturance and attention to children's individuality and behavioral demands and limit-setting help children achieve social responsibility and competence

- authoritarian parenting that makes many demands of children but gives little support to achieve these demands is associated with unhappiness, inhibition, and distrust in children

- permissive parenting that allows children freedom of impulse expression but does not teach or support self-control and self-regulation is associated with immaturity and dependence in children

- positive and negative cycles of parent–child interactions are established early in life, depend on the qualities of both parents and children, and require the actions of both partners to keep the processes going

Parenting interventions relying on video-feedback of home behaviors have been successful in increasing children's development because they

- focus on parents' skills and existing competencies
- encourage parents' sensitivity and responsiveness to children
- create a positive cycle of interactions between parent and child

EXERCISES

1. Which of the theories of children's development seems most useful to you in understanding children's growth and development and why?

2. As you look at the dimensions of temperament described in the text, do you feel any aspects of temperament have been left out? Which ones?

3. Erikson's theory of lifespan development focuses on the importance of positive experiences and strengths. Review your own life in terms of the positive experiences you have developed. For example, you may have developed a love of the outdoors from camping activities with your family, and feel you have developed independence and a love of the environment.

4. Do you feel the concept of attachment helps you to make sense of your experiences as a young adult?

5. As a parent (or imagining yourself as a parent) how do you think of your role? How responsible do you feel for what children learn and how they function?

ADDITIONAL READINGS

Brazelton, T. Berry, and Greenspan, Stanley I. *The Irreducible Needs of Children.* Cambridge, MA: Perseus, 2000.

Carroll, Deborah, and Reid, Stella with Moline, Karen. *Nanny 911.* New York: Regan Books, 2005.

Hallowell, Edward M. *The Childhood Roots of Adult Happiness.* New York: Ballantine Books, 2002.

Juffer, Femmie, Bakermans-Kranenburg, Marian, and van Ijzendoorn, Marinus H., eds. *Promoting Positive Parenting: An Attachment-Based Intervention.* New York: Lawrence Erlbaum, 2008.

McGraw, Dr. Phil. *Family First.* New York: Free Press, 2004.

CHAPTER

3

Cultural Influences on Parenting

CHAPTER TOPICS

In this chapter, you will learn about:

- Definition of culture and how it influences parenting
- How culture is transmitted from one generation to another
- Cultural influences of race, ethnicity, socioeconomic status, poverty status
- Two cultural models of parent–child relationships
- Cultural diversity and experiences of immigrant and ethnic minority groups
- Ways to reduce discrimination and manage its effects
- The influence of socioeconomic status and economic hardship on parenting

IN THE NEWS

New York Times, May 3[1]: When people of different ethnic groups work together on projects, mutual understanding and respect grow. See page 85.

Test Your Knowledge: Fact or Fiction (True/False)

1. Geneticists agree that the concept of race lacks validity and usefulness.
2. Cultural beliefs and values provide risk and protective factors for individuals and families.
3. Poverty status influences more aspects of children's development than racial or ethnic background.
4. The self-esteem of people in different ethnic groups reflects the general regard their group receives from society at large.
5. Parenting strategies have different effects in different ethnic groups.

Culture provides a nest for all the parent–child interactions we look at throughout the book. In this chapter we look at the many ways cultural forces shape the process of parenting. In discussing the broad trends in parenting within varying ethnic and social groups, we also learn about the great diversity within each group. We examine how socioeconomic status provides a context for the development of all members of our society. Finally, we look at how poverty and the lack of social resources affects parenting and children.

Our country is a diverse society that has grown with waves of immigration that began over twenty thousand years ago when the first Native Americans trudged here from Siberia.[2] Large numbers continue to come to our shores in the present. In this chapter we look at the diverse cultural influences that affect parents and children. We first define culture, look at the many sources of cultural influence, and ways individuals incorporate cultural influences into their lives. We look at two models for understanding diverse cultural forces, and then at the values and behaviors of social groups with special attention to those who have few resources and live under the poverty level.

WHAT IS CULTURE?

Culture is the set of values, beliefs, ways of thinking, rituals, and institutions of a group or population.[3] The group can be as small as a neighborhood, school, or community or as large as racial, ethnic, and social status groups. Culture provides ways of seeing the world and, along with other influences, determines patterns of feelings and behavior in everyday life. As we saw in Chapter 1, it is a dynamic force responding to social, political, and economic events and shaping the meaning of these events for us.

Culture provides a developmental niche[4] that includes (1) the physical and social settings for parents and children, (2) the psychological characteristics valued in parents and children, and (3) recommended behaviors for family members. So, culture shapes a broad range of parental behaviors, from the more general values parents teach to the concrete aspects of daily life such as where children eat and sleep.

The behaviors of U.S. mothers and Italian mothers illustrate the many ways culture influences parents' goals for their children and how the goals influence their care of babies in the first year and a half of life.[5] The mothers and babies age four to sixteen months, all members of nuclear families, were interviewed and observed in their homes.

American mothers wanted their children to grow up to be (1) economically and emotionally independent, (2) happy, no matter what their financial status, and (3) honest and respectful with other people. Mothers' immediate goal was to give babies the proper stimulation for healthy growth, which mothers worried they were not providing.

In line with mothers' goals, babies spent their time in one-on-one interactions with mothers (about one-third of the observation time) or alone in their rooms, sleeping or playing with toys. Although other people came in and out of the home, they, including siblings, did not usually care for the child.

As babies began to get around, American parents baby-proofed the environment and at ten months, taught babies preliminary safety rules because they felt it was important for the child to accept some responsibility for safety. Babies spent 52 percent of observation time crawling on the floor and exploring freely, and mothers felt reassured that their children were developing well because they were active and curious.

American mothers worried about sleep habits and establishing healthy sleep patterns so children got enough sleep even when they resisted nap time or bedtime. By four months of age, most babies slept in their own beds, often in their own rooms, though several shared a room with a sibling but none with their parents. U.S. mothers felt their children could regulate their eating. Infants ate on demand and often at different times from when the family ate, so eating was an activity involving mother and child, with the mother talking while she fed the infant. As children got older, they were encouraged to feed themselves.

Italian mothers' long-term goals focused on (1) good health for their children, (2) financial security, and (3) a good family life that included a spouse and children. These mothers did not worry about being effective; they considered all mothers adequate by virtue of being mothers. They did not feel responsible for the outcome of children's development because they believed that children turn out as they will.

In Italy, infants were social. They had little direct interaction with mothers (10 percent of the observation time) and were almost never alone. They slept in the same room as their parents, often until the second birthday, and were regularly in the company of two or three people. For all but one baby, at least one grandparent lived nearby and visited daily. Italian mothers believed free exploration was too dangerous so their ten-month-old infants spent only 26 percent of observation time crawling on the floor, and when it was time to walk, adults supported and held babies' hands. None of the Italian mothers felt concern that their children were not more independent.

Italian mothers rarely held to any sleeping schedule, and babies often dropped off to sleep in the midst of family activity without bedtime rituals or songs. One mother had no schedule because she felt it was cruel to deprive the child of family time. Eating was much more important. Italian infants were required to eat on four-hour schedules and to come to family meals, even if they had to be awakened to do so. Babies were expected to get used to eating rituals even if they did not like them, because eating was a social activity with the family.

So, cultural goals played a strong role in everyday caregiving activities, with American mothers emphasizing independence—in play, exploration, eating, and sleeping alone at bedtime—and Italian families enveloping their infants in complex social interactions, which required adaptation on the part of the babies and gave few opportunities for independence.

HOW CULTURAL VALUES ARE TRANSMITTED FROM ONE GENERATION TO ANOTHER

Socialization is the term for the process whereby individuals learn the skills necessary for group life.[6] We used to think that parents and other authorities in society taught children and newcomers the beliefs, values, and feelings necessary to function competently in society, and children and newcomers passively absorbed them and lived by them.

More recently, we have seen that children have an active role in the process of socialization.[7] Just as Piaget believes children actively construct a view of the world, social scientists believe individuals actively construct a view of their culture. Based on what parents teach, what children experience, what they see happen to those around them, and what they learn from interactions with individuals outside their own group, children construct a cultural *scheme* of the world. A cultural scheme includes shared meanings and feelings about events or people, and ways to behave.

What role do parents play? William Corsaro and Katherine Brown Rosier describe a process in which the family is at the center of a web of cultural influences originating outside the family but sending strands of influence that end in the family.[8] Children first learn about their culture from interactions in the family, much as American and Italian infants learned about the importance of independence and sociability from the earliest days of life in their daily routines of eating, sleeping, and play, through rituals and stories about the culture. As children begin to move outside the family to the world of other caregivers, teachers, peers, and to other institutions like schools, they learn about different cultures and gain new perspectives on the culture learned at home.

Constructing a cultural scheme is a process of parents or others presenting expectations, children becoming aware of them and evaluating them, sometimes resisting and refusing, and sometimes incorporating them, in part or in whole. Parents initially present cultural expectations in terms of behavioral expectations—sleeping alone,[9] wakening for family meals, playing alone. Children signal their response in their behavior—crying to sleep with parents, following parents and refusing to play alone.

A study with preschoolers illustrates how sensitive children are to adults' signals that something is special.[10] Researchers gave children in preschool classrooms either red or blue T-shirts. In the control classes, the children wore the T-shirts for three weeks with no mentions made of them. In the experimental classes, the T-shirts were used as general identifiers—"Reds and blues, it is time to go to lunch." Or "Reds and blues, it's time to go to recess." There was no positive status or value attached to the shirts or to the groups of children wearing them. Still, at the end of three weeks, children in both groups developed a positive feeling for their group, it was special, with the experimental group showing a stronger in-group bias.

MAJOR CULTURAL INFLUENCES

In rearing children, parents draw on the cultural values and behaviors of their racial, ethnic, social, and religious group.

Race

The term *race* refers to "phenotypic differences that arise from genetic or biological dispositions such as skin color and hair texture."[11] Geneticists identify five racial groups in the world: (1) sub-Saharan Africans; (2) Caucasians, which include

Box 3-1
BLENDING PARENTING STYLES OF TWO ETHNIC GROUPS*

Marriage was not in Steve's plans when he met JoJo at his only friend's wedding. Steve had had a lonely time growing up in his family, and he decided marriage and family were not for him. His parents married quickly after his mother became pregnant with his older brother, but separated shortly after Steve's birth. His father died when Steve was nine so he did not know him.

His mother had two more unsuccessful marriages, and as a single parent, moved a great deal, following her family's tradition of not laying down roots. In one school year, Steve moved three times. His mother did not believe in spending money on babysitters so in the summer, she would drop him off at the movies while she worked, and he watched the same movie three or four times.

As a teen, he saved money and bought a car and at sixteen traveled through the Southwest by himself. He chose to go to college where they lived, earned a degree, and got a management job at K-Mart. He lived alone and had only his college friend whose wedding he attended. He was not close with his mother, but he talked with her on the phone about four times a year. His brother, who had a problem with drugs, had died in a motorcycle accident.

In contrast, JoJo came from a large Filipino family in Chicago. She had fifty-two first cousins and hundreds of relatives dotted around the world. As the oldest daughter, she was very attached to her extended family and its traditions.

Steve felt immediately comfortable with JoJo, and she with him. After a brief courtship, the two decided to get married. JoJo had one condition—that he first meet her family. She wanted their opinion of him because in past relationships, she had failed to detect difficulties that her family sensed from the beginning.

Steve agreed, and when he changed planes on his way to Chicago, relatives appeared to guide him from one plane to the next. While clearly sizing him up as a potential relative, they were warm and accepting and telephoned ahead to Chicago with the news that he seemed a fine person. All the relatives liked him—he was educated, had a good job, was kind and open, and he loved JoJo. They welcomed him with open arms even though he was not Filipino, and Steve responded to their genuine expression of caring for him.

The priest who counseled them before marriage warned Steve, "You are not just marrying JoJo, son. You are marrying this family. They will become *your* family. They will be in your life, in your business, help raise your children, and expect you to care for them when they're in need."

Steve accepted the family. He loved them and considered they "saved him." "I've learned so much from them. They've given me an impression of what family life can be . . . I wish I'd had these ideas in my background. . . . What we have, as a family—despite the problems and rough patches—it's paradise for me. I consider this paradise. . . . They *care*. They genuinely care about each other. So when I walk in a room, they *light up*. They burst out of their chairs, their faces beam, they are enthusiastic. I have never had that in my family."

When their daughter was born, JoJo's parents cared for her while JoJo worked, and a special bond formed between grandfather and granddaughter. Steve never worried

Box 3-1

about what would happen to the family if anything happened to him, as had occurred when he was a child. The extended family would step in and care for JoJo and their daughter.

Just as JoJo helped Steve grow, Steve helped JoJo grow by helping her set limits with her family. In the past, she had always done what they wished—going to Stanford to study medicine, the field her father entered even though she was more interested in music. She left college without finding direction in work, became a clerk in a store, and had not found work she liked.

When her parents were babysitting their daughter, Aubrey, JoJo observed that her parents were very indulgent with her so that Aubrey was becoming a "spoiled princess." When they disciplined her, they used physical punishment. JoJo tried to teach them the things she and Steve learned in parenting classes, but no matter what was said, they insisted on doing it their way.

Finally, Steve stepped in and told his in-laws that they could not visit and be with them until they were willing to follow their rules of child rearing. JoJo was grateful for his firm insistence. Although the families did not speak for a few months, JoJo and her family were there immediately when her father had a heart attack, and the relationships between the families resumed. Steve had asked the parents to telephone before they came to visit, and they followed that rule.

Both Steve and JoJo felt their differences provided strength for their family. Steve's experience in a family stressing independence, self-reliance, and choice enabled him to demonstrate how to make choices and set boundaries. JoJo's warm and loving expressiveness and her commitment to family life provided a bedrock of security for the family. In speaking about their differences as strength, JoJo said, "We've never been able to fall into a pattern, never had a chance to fall asleep at the wheel. Our contrasts have made us conscious, made us pay attention."

As more and more families are blends of different ethnic and racial groups—in 2000, one-third of Latino and Asian American marriages were interracial marriages—combining parenting styles from the families of origins will become more and more common. Steve and JoJo model how blending parenting styles creates a stronger family.

*From Po Bronson, *Why Do I Love These People? Honest and Amazing Stories of Real Families* (New York: Random House, 2005), pp. 79–97.

Europeans, Middle Easterners, and those from the Indian continent; (3) Asians, which include Chinese, Japanese, Filipinos, and peoples from Southeast Asia; (4) Native Americans; and (5) Pacific Islanders.

Scientists debate the usefulness of the concept of race because few genetic differences among races exist and most of us carry genetic markers from more than one race. Even though race is a complex concept, other geneticists and epidemiologists want to maintain the distinction because fine-grained analysis of genetic markers does yield racial differences that can be useful in providing quality medical care to people.[12] Such racial designations are useful in seeking the origins of genetic diseases such as sickle cell anemia, which is more common in African people, and in finding effective treatments for illnesses as is seen in the case in which a medication not useful for Caucasians with congestive heart failure has been found to reduce fatal heart attacks by forty-three percent in African Americans with congestive heart failure.

Ethnicity

The term *ethnicity* refers to "an individual's membership in a group sharing a common ancestral heritage based on nationality, language, and culture. Psychological attachment to the group is also a dimension of ethnicity, referred to as *'ethnic identity.'*"[13] Many ethnic groups exist within each racial group. For example, in the United States Caucasians include people of German, Irish, Eastern European, or Italian descent. Native Americans include members of more than five hundred tribes with their own values. Asian Americans include Hmong, Filipino, Chinese, Japanese, and others. The Latino group includes people from many different countries in Central and South America as well as from the Caribbean Islands. Conversely, an ethnic group may have members in more than one racial group. For example, some Latinos fall in the Caucasian racial group, but others fall in the African racial group. We discuss immigrant groups in a later section.

Social Status

Social status is perhaps the most powerful influence shaping parents' child-rearing behaviors. Belief in the American dream that ability and hard work determine success makes it hard to accept that social position can be such a force in children's experiences growing up, but several studies suggest this is so. Researchers comparing the home environments of four ethnic groups—European Americans, African Americans, Latinos, and Asian Americans—found that while ethnic differences influenced what parents did, social status reflected in families' resources overshadowed ethnic differences in the homes, with parents' providing poor children fewer books, musical instruments, and lessons, but also giving less attention and physical affection. Of the 124 items describing the home and parenting, eighty-eight percent were affected by poverty status, and only fifteen items were unaffected. The effects of having few resources were similar across all ethnic groups.[14]

Annette Lareau, who intensively studied a small sample of European and African American families who differed in social status as well as ethnic background, also found that social position had a stronger influence on the lives of the nine- and ten-year-old children she studied than ethnic background. We discuss this study in greater detail in a later section, but here we highlight her conclusion that while all individuals have both pleasures and difficulties in life, "Class position matters, every step of the way."[15]

Religion

Religions are not discussed in detail because they are so numerous in this country, but it is important to note that religious groups form cultures that provide niches for development and prescribe ways of life—no alcohol, no caffeine, prayers several times a day—that parents pass on to children.

Other Cultural Influences

Other cultural influences include geographical areas with distinct cultures found in areas of the North, South, East, and West, and rural–urban areas of residence also exerting cultural influences.

Personal Identity and Reference Group Orientation

William Cross describes how culture influences self-concept. He distinguishes two aspects of self-concept: *personal identity* (PI), which includes such factors as self-esteem and general personality traits, and *reference group orientation* (RGO), which includes cultural group identities such as gender and ethnic identities, group awareness, and group attitudes (see Figure 3-1).[16] He discusses RGO primarily in terms of racial identity, to explain why people of the same ethnic group with equal commitments to that group may have very different attitudes about ethnic identity—that is, they have very different RGOs.

He states that RGO may be prominent in some groups and not in others—for example, some European Americans think of themselves only as Americans, whereas others have a strong ethnic identity as Italian Americans or Irish Americans. Some people have a strong religious RGO, and others do not. Cross shows the usefulness of these concepts in understanding gender identity. Two women might be similar with regard to self-esteem and self-worth, but one may have a strong RGO as a feminist and interpret much of her experience in light of that group identity, whereas another woman might not and thus perceive situations differently. Or the same person may have a shift in RGO over time as life circumstances change. For example, teenage girls experience what is termed gender intensification (see Chapter 11), and adapt their behavior to meet societal prescriptions regarding gender-related behavior to a greater degree than they did at an earlier age so their RGO of gender would be more prominent in adolescence than elementary school.

A series of Canadian studies illustrate how culture shapes the view of the self, and in turn, behavior.[17] Researchers assessed children's and teens' concepts of themselves as individuals with a sense of self-continuity or personal persistence despite all their developmental changes over time. The research involved interviewing children and teens about their perceptions of consistency in other people and then in themselves. Children and teens described themselves in the present and as they were five years ago. They enumerated all the ways they had changed in that period and interviewers then asked them to explain how they could still be the same person given all these changes.

■ **FIGURE 3-1**
SCHEMATIC OF THE TWO-FACTOR THEORY OF BLACK IDENTITY

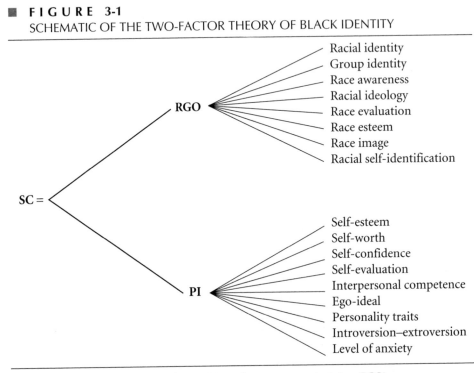

Note: Self-concept (SC) = personal identity (PI) + reference group orientation (RGO)

From William E. Cross, Jr., "A Two Factor Theory of Black Identity," in *Children's Ethnic Socialization,* ed. Jean S. Phinney and Mary Jane Rotheram (Beverly Hills, CA: Sage, 1987); Figure 6.1, p. 122. Copyright © 1987 Sage Publications, Inc. Reprinted by permission of Sage Publications.

Children and adolescents gave two kinds of explanations—termed essentialist and narrativist, each with five levels of complexity and sophistication, related to the individual's age. The explanatory concepts were consistent over time and were applied to changes in others as well as to the self. Essentialist explanations emphasized the person's inner, enduring personality traits that did not change with time despite changes in behavior. "I was competitive in races when I was six, and now I am competitive with grades." Essentialists perceived self-consistency and personal persistence over time. Narrativist explanations focused on people's changes as meaningful developments over time. They gave little attention to what was consistent in the person, but emphasized changing events that related to changes in the person. "Well this happened, and that led to my being here and doing that." Narrativists saw the self as a collection of ongoing experiences that were only loosely connected. Essentialist explanations were given primarily by Canadian youth of EA background, and Narrativist explanations by Native Canadian youth.

Researchers speculated that Narrativists who do not have a strong sense of personal identity connecting past, present, and future might be at high risk for suicide. Because narrativists concentrated on experiences as they occurred and did not have a sense of a personal link to the future, they might not act to ensure their future well-being when confronted with the intense emotional stresses of maturing. The self-consistency explanations of hospitalized suicidal and nonsuicidal adolescents confirmed their speculations. Patients hospitalized for suicidal risk had no understanding of themselves as continuous in time; they could not imagine themselves as existing in the future. Hospitalized teens without a history of suicidal risk were as depressed as those who were at risk for suicide, but they had a view of themselves and others as having a past, present, and a future, and though very unhappy, they did not hurt themselves. The authors commented that when teens do not have a continuous thread connecting their past and present to the future, they do not protect their future lives.

The researchers were able to link a sense of personal continuity with the level of cultural continuity in their communities by examining the suicide rates of 196 Native communities. Those Native communities and tribes that were able to preserve their past and maintain control over their land, their government, and community services conveyed a sense of cultural continuity. These communities and tribes had very low, or zero, rates of suicide in comparison to communities that could not create a sense of continuity between past, present, and future. Using these findings, the researchers are developing interventions that they hope will help communities convey a greater sense of cultural continuity in order to reduce the high rates of suicide among Native youth.

CULTURAL MODELS OF PARENT–CHILD RELATIONSHIPS

Surveys of many ethnic groups' values yield two general cultural models—the independent and the interdependent models—that provide a framework for organizing and understanding what parents think matters and what they do with their children.[18] Table 3-1 outlines these two models, which apply to many different cultural and social groups rather than any one ethnic group in particular.

In the independent model, parents help children become self-sustaining, productive adults who enter into relationships with other adults by choice. The child receives nurturance to develop autonomy, competence, and a freely chosen identity that in adulthood merges with others outside the family.

In the interdependent model, parents help children grow into socially responsible adults who take their place in a strong network of social relationships, often within the family, that place obligations on the adult. Parents indulge the young child, but as children grow older, they are expected to internalize and respect the rules of parents and other authorities. Parents and relatives are respected and obeyed, and family and group needs matter more than individual ones.

The ways dual-earner parents rear their first-born child in Israeli and Palestinian cultures illustrate how cultural patterns can provide risk or protective factors for families. Parents were interviewed and seen with their five-month-old infants, ratings of risk and protective factors were made, and the families were seen again

TABLE 3-1
CONTRASTING CULTURAL MODELS OF PARENT–CHILD RELATIONS

Developmental Goals	Independence	Interdependence
Developmental Trajectory	From dependent to independent self	From asocial to socially responsible self
Communication	Verbal emphasis	Nonverbal emphasis (empathy, observation, participation)
	Autonomous self-expression	Child comprehension, mother speaks for child
	Frequent parental questions to child	Frequent parental directives to child
	Frequent praise	Infrequent praise
	Child negotiation	Frequent parental directives
Collaborative problem solving	Division of labor	Shared multiparty engagement
Parents helping children	A matter of personal choice except under extreme need	A moral obligation under all circumstances

From Patricia M. Greenfield, Lalita K. Suzuki, and Carrie Rothstein-Fisch, "Cultural Pathways through Human Development," in *Handbook of Child Psychology*, 6th ed., eds. William Damon and Richard M. Lerner, vol. 4: *Child Psychology in Practice*, eds. K. Ann Renninger and Irving E. Sigel (Hoboken, NJ: Wiley, 2006), p. 676. Reprinted by permission of John Wiley & Sons, Inc.

when the children were 34 months old.[19] At that time the children's symbolic play and behaviors were assessed.

Israeli families reflect independent values. Parents live in nuclear families, with gender egalitarian roles. Their parental goals focus on rearing children who are autonomous and self-actualized. Palestinian families reflect interdependent and collectivist values. Families live physically close to parents and extended family members; gender roles are traditional, with fathers the head of the household and mothers working primarily to meet the family's needs. Their child-rearing goals are to raise children who defer to authority.

In comparison to Palestinian parents, Israeli parents reported higher marital satisfaction, more work–family interference, and less depression. They scored higher on the measure of parental sensitivity. In comparison to Israeli parents, Palestinian parents reported more social support and less work–family interference, and mothers recovered more quickly from the births. However, they viewed their infants as more irritable and difficult.

Common patterns of risk and protection that occurred in both cultures suggest they may be universal patterns. In both Israeli and Palestinian families, mothers' depression was related to observed and reported infant irritability and difficult temperament and to marital dissatisfaction. Conversely, social support was related to higher parental sensitivity and to greater marital satisfaction. Infant negative emotionality was related to lower parental sensitivity. Certain patterns were specific to each culture. In Israeli culture, mothers' depression correlated with most other risk factors, and in the Palestinian culture perceived infant difficulty was related to lower social support and lower marital satisfaction.

Infants in both cultures had similar levels of symbolic play, but there were different predictors of it in the two cultures—Israeli mothers' sensitivity to children predicted play level and Palestinian mothers' low depression predicted play level. Different qualities in the two cultures predicted children's behavior problems. In the Israeli culture, mothers' depression was related to children's aggressive, noncompliant behaviors and worried mood. In the interdependent Palestinian culture, high levels of social support had a positive effect on promoting children's adaptation. In the independent culture of Israel, mothers' depression had a more widespread effect on children's behavior for two possible reasons. First, the mother was a central caregiving figure and there were few social supports to help if she were having problems. Second, in an independent culture, toddlers are expected to be more autonomous and self-reliant. To achieve independence, they require an active caregiver to support their initiative and autonomy, and depressed mothers may lack the energy to do that. In an interdependent culture, toddlers would need less help to follow directions and conform to requests, and mothers' depression would not, perhaps, have such an impact.

CULTURAL DIVERSITY IN THE UNITED STATES

From our very beginnings, we have been a nation of immigrants. With the exception of Africans forced to come to this country, immigrants up to the mid-twentieth century were primarily from Europe and generally similar to the primarily European resident population here in terms of appearance and religion. Beginning in the 1960s, an increasing number of immigrants have come from South America, the Caribbean, Asia, and Africa. There has been greater diversity in appearance, religion, and values in these later immigrants.[20]

Today 23 percent of children in the United States (nearly one in four) live in immigrant families.[21] These children, however, are rooted in American life. Most were born in the United States and 64 percent live with at least one parent who is a United States citizen. It is estimated that 11 percent of children are undocumented, and 18 percent were born in the United States but have an undocumented parent. Immigrant children join a resident population of ethnic minority children and together constitute about a third of all children in this country. It is estimated that by 2030, this group will make up the majority of children in the United States. Table 3-2 presents basic demographic characteristics of the six major ethnic groups.

■ **T A B L E   3-2**
DEMOGRAPHIC CHARACTERISTICS OF SIX ETHNIC GROUPS*

	Total Population	Native Americans	Whites†	African Americans	Latinas/os	Asian Americans	Middle Eastern Americans‡
Percentage of Total Population: 2007	100%	1%	67%	13%	15%	4%	1%
Median Age: 2007	36%	30%	38%	31%	28%	35%	33%
Education of Population over Age 25: 2006							
High School Graduate	84%	76%	89%	79%	60%	86%	84%
College Degree or Higher	27%	13%	30%	17%	12%	49%	41%
Median Household Income: 2006	58,500	38,800	65,200	38,400	40,100	74,100	52,000§
Families below Poverty Level: 2006	10%	22%	7%	22%	19%	8%	17%
Children under 18 Living: 2007	17%	—	14%	33%	27%	12%	—
in Two-Parent Family	71%	—	77%	42%	69%	87%	85%
in Female-Headed Household	25%	—	19%	53%	28%	10%	8%
in Male-Headed Household	4%	—	5%	5%	3%	2%	7%
Average Number of Children per Household: 2007							
Married Couple	1.87	—	1.84	1.98	2.02	1.71	—
Female-Headed Household	1.71	—	1.65	1.87	1.82	1.54	—
Male-Headed Household	—	—	—	—	—	—	—
Percentage of Children Born 2006							
to Teen mothers	10%	17%	9%	17%	14%	3%	—
to Single mothers	37%	64%	32%	69%	48%	16%	—

*Despite the fact that the years are sometimes different, all statistics unless otherwise noted are from *Statistical Abstract of the United States: 2009*, 128th ed. (Washington, DC: U. S. Government Printing Office, 2008).

†The term white refers to Non-Hispanic whites; not all are European Americans.

‡Data for Middle Eastern Americans come from Census, 2000 Special Report, Augusta Brittingham and G. Patricia de la Cruz, "We the People of Arab Ancestry in the United States, U. S. Census Bureau, March 2005. Available on www.aaiusa.com.

An Integrative Model of the Experiences of Immigrant and Ethnic Minority Groups

Cynthia Garcia Coll and Laura Szalacha present a model of child development that describes the experiences of immigrant and ethnic minority children.[22] They consider these two groups together because they believe both groups are treated as outsiders in the culture. Figure 3-2 presents the model combining an ecological and interactionist approach to describe these children's experiences growing up. Social position, based on social class, race/ethnicity, and gender, triggers a community response. In the case of minority and immigrant children, their social position is associated with racism and discrimination, which lead to inadequate resources reflected in poor schools and violent neighborhoods with few community and economic resources. The disadvantaged environment fails to promote an adaptive cultural community and thus inhibits families' functioning and children's development.

Garcia Coll and Szalacha define racism broadly as any restriction or exclusion or bias that deprives individuals of basic human rights and freedoms in any sphere of life. Racism includes both prejudice, defined as negative thoughts, feelings or

■ **F I G U R E   3-2**
AN INTEGRATIVE MODEL OF CHILD DEVELOPMENT*

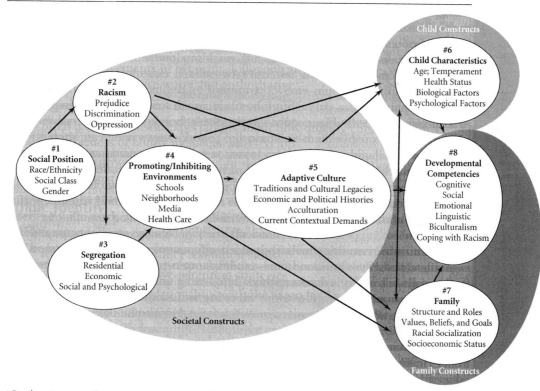

*Cynthia Garcia Coll and Laura A. Szalacha, "The Multiple Contexts of Middle Childhood," *The Future of Children 14*(2)(2004): 83.

judgments about someone based on the person's race, religion, or nationality, and discrimination, defined as unfair treatment because of race, religion, or nationality.

Schools, according to Garcia Coll and Szalacha, are the most important socializing influences on children apart from their families, and are made up of three nested environments: (1) the classroom, with teachers, peers, and learning materials; (2) the school; and (3) the school district. Even if schools are poor and lack many resources, they can promote learning when teachers are warm and focused on helping each child learn. When there are large percentages of children like themselves, children are less worried about discrimination or rejection, but negative school experiences can greatly reduce the positive attitudes and motivation present when children start school.

Neighborhoods can promote development, providing libraries and community centers that offer after-school and vacation care when they have resources. Even when poor and segregated from the rest of the community, they can promote social cohesion by protecting the customs of the culture from the negative reactions they might receive in a more diversified community.

Popular media, they believe, can have positive and negative features. It can increase self-esteem and prosocial behaviors as children see their group positively portrayed in the media and when prosocial behaviors such as empathy and understanding are modeled for children. Media have negative effects when they present models of aggression, discrimination, and prejudice. These issues are discussed in greater detail in Chapter 5.

Diversity can be a risk or protective factor. Garcia Coll and Szalacha believe research has frequently viewed diverse groups through "the lens of deficit." Minority group children are often studied in terms of aggression, delinquency, attention deficits, and hyperactivity. The difficulties are seen as residing in the children rather than in the system that has not made available resources to provide health care, good schools, and safe communities.

"High family cohesion, strong sense of family obligation, strong ethnic pride, and high value of education are some of the characteristics that have been observed in outsider families that can be positive influences on children's development through middle childhood."[23] While some children from these families are overrepresented in high-risk groups, most children are not, even though their families and communities lack the advantages thought necessary for healthy development.

In addition to systemic changes to make more resources routinely available to these families, interventions should be multilevel ones that involve schools, neighborhoods, and families together. Parents can be engaged to target their goals and find ways to work with community agencies to achieve them.

Acculturation

Immigrants to this country experience a process of *acculturation*, defined as a process "of learning about a new culture and deciding what aspects are to be retained or sacrificed from the culture of origin."[24] Because culture is multidimensional, immigrants must attend to many new aspects of experience—language, food, customs, and social attitudes. Adaptation can be difficult.

Similar to the process of learning one's own culture, the process *of acculturation* occurs in stages.[25] Initially, immigrants may feel relief at being here and idolize the new culture, then disillusionment may set in as the process brings frustrations and difficulties, and finally, they come to a realistic acceptance of the new country with its positive and negative features. The host country also changes as it includes groups with new cultural traditions and welcomes them into the mainstream rather than marginalizes them.

When people retain attachment to their culture of origin and still feel comfortable with and attached to the customs of the new culture, they are described, as we noted earlier, as having a *bicultural identity*. Today, members of ethnic groups usually have some form of bicultural identity or attachment to their culture of origin. This stands in contrast to the past, when people coming to this country were expected to give up their previous customs and become assimilated into mainstream culture, becoming "like everyone else."

Child Cultural Brokers

When parents do not speak the language and other adult relatives are not available to serve as interpreters, children of immigrants often interpret for parents in the outside world because they do speak the language.[26] They are termed cultural brokers because they serve as the link between parents' culture and the European American culture. The psychological effects of taking on adult roles are not known. Children can gain in self-esteem and feelings of confidence as they negotiate in adult situations, gaining awareness of, and sensitivity to, parents' needs, promoting closeness to parents.

On the other hand, in acting for parents, children often take on parents' worries about money, living arrangements, job concerns, legal issues, and worries about family members in the country of origin. They have often taken on adult roles in health care situations, reporting symptoms, getting diagnoses of illnesses and directions for treatments and medications. Because children may misunderstand directions and make errors with potentially serious consequences, California has been the first state in the country to consider laws to stop their use as translators except in emergencies.[27] Experts are concerned also about the emotional burden on the child of being the first to learn of a parent's serious medical condition and the one to report it to parents.

Having served as authorities for their parents in public, children sometimes find it difficult to return to the role of inexperienced child at home. This is especially likely true in adolescence when teens want independence and can justify increased freedom with the responsibilities they already have taken on. If parents do not give it to them, teens may challenge and defy them.

Discrimination

Many children fear being excluded and rejected because of their race and/or ethnic background. In a national sample of fifteen- to seventeen-year-olds, 15 percent of white children, 23 percent of African American, and 37 percent of Latinos/as reported that discrimination because of race and ethnic background was a very big concern, and among thirteen- and fourteen-year-olds, the comparable figure was 32 percent of the sample, not broken down by ethnic background.[28] Experience of discrimination was the strongest predictor of poor psychological and social adaptation in a large group of immigrant children.[29]

Feeling discriminated against brings a variety of feelings. A five-year longitudinal study following African American early adolescents from the ages of ten to fifteen enabled researchers to track the feelings that follow perceived discrimination. At each assessment at about ages ten, twelve, and fifteen, early teens reported the frequency of perceived discrimination in the preceding year.[30] Discriminatory events included such experiences as racial slurs and insults, physical threats, and false accusations. Youths also filled out measures of depression and problem behaviors, and both parents and children filled out a measure of the parents' nurturant and involved parenting behaviors.

Latent growth curve modeling revealed that (1) increases in perceived discrimination were positively associated with increases in depressive symptoms and conduct problems, (2) children from higher socioeconomic-status families were more likely to perceive increases in discrimination over time, (3) both boys and girls who perceived discrimination had increases in depressive symptoms but the link between discrimination and conduct problems was stronger for boys than for girls, and (4) effects of perceived discrimination decreased when children had warm relationships with parents, prosocial friends, and school engagement. However, even, with warm parents and good friends, perceiving discrimination was related to increases in depressive feelings and conduct problems.

In African American families followed for two years, mothers reported their experience of discrimination at each yearly assessment as well as their physical problems, depressive symptoms, and their parenting behaviors.[31] Mothers who perceived discrimination reported an increase in stress-related physical problems that, in turn, were related to an increase in depressive symptoms and a decrease in their positive parenting strategies. Parenting interventions with their twelve-year-old children helped to decrease mothers' psychological stress and depressed moods.[32] Mothers focused on paying attention to children's point of view and feelings. They learned communication skills, consistent discipline, and monitoring teens' whereabouts. Early adolescents learned to follow household directions, set goals, complete homework, and avoid risk-taking peers. The program led to improvements in mothers' moods and early adolescents' regulated behaviors.

What can parents do when they worry about their children's experience of discrimination? Having open relationships with children enables them to tell parents what is happening in their lives so they and their parents can problem-solve specific upsetting incidents. Parents' acceptance and support is a main protective factor in insulating children from psychological problems because of others' cruelty and can help in situations of discrimination. In Chapter 10 we discuss a helpful program in greater detail. In general, parents help children feel good about themselves and their group and find ways to achieve their goals despite barriers and discrimination.

Parents and schools want to discourage the prejudice that is so hurtful to the person it is directed against, but is also hurtful to those who observe it. As we will see in later chapters, witnessing bullying and victimization creates stress in the witness as well (see Chapter 9 and 10).

Children begin life with a tendency to view their own group positively. Out-group prejudice develops later in the early elementary school years.[33] Some school programs have been successful in reducing prejudice, and parents can adapt them to family life.[34]

Programs that increase children's social-cognitive skills—their understanding of others' points of view and empathy for their thoughts, feelings, and difficulties—reduce prejudiced attitudes. Working together with other children of diverse cultures on cooperative learning projects to achieve common goals promotes positive behaviors and friendships with their partners and also reduces prejudice.

From early days, parents can read stories to children about the achievements and hardships of other groups of people in the past and present, broadening children's knowledge and understanding of others. In conversations and interactions, parents can model interest, appreciation, and enjoyment of members of all groups. Finally, parents can be sure to engage their children in joint activities with diverse groups of children. That can occur at school, but may not. Then one can seek community activities, interest groups, and summer camps where such cooperative goal-oriented activities can take place.

The Self-Esteem of Ethnic Groups

Researchers, concerned that prejudice and discrimination have led to both low levels of self-esteem and negative self-concepts in ethnic groups that society described negatively, compared the levels of self-esteem of European Americans and African Americans. They found that African American global self-esteem is as high or higher than that of European Americans, despite the negative experiences many African Americans encounter in this society.

"Working together with children of diverse cultures promotes positive behaviors and friendships with partners."

Jean Twenge and Jennifer Crocker carried out a meta-analysis of studies of self-esteem to determine whether other groups also scored as high as African Americans.[35] They looked at 712 comparisons of self-esteem among African Americans, European Americans, Native Americans, Latinos, and Asian Americans and found the rank ordering of these groups on inventories of self-esteem presented in Table 3-3. This table also presents the factors that influence self-esteem scores.

The rank ordering of the groups on self-esteem does not follow the pattern of society's general regard for the group. Despite higher levels of education and income and community respect for their levels of achievement, Asian Americans report the fewest positive self-perceptions. Although they experience great discrimination, African Americans make many positive statements about themselves. Of interest is the fact that the socioeconomic status of the subjects reduced the differences among the groups. High-status individuals of all groups resembled each other in their levels of self-esteem.

With respect to age, the differences in self-esteem among the five groups were smallest in elementary school and grew larger through high school and into the adult years. This suggests that initially, all children tend to make positive statements about themselves, but as they grow older, they become more socialized in their culture's views of what is appropriate to say about oneself. Self-esteem scores decreased with age in those groups, namely Asian Americans and Native Americans, that emphasize an interdependent self and minimize the importance of the self.

Examining self-esteem in relation to the subjects' geographic area of residence and the years of data collection yielded interesting findings. The self-esteem of African Americans and Asian Americans was highest in areas where that group had greater concentrations of population. For example, African Americans' self-esteem was highest in southern states that had the greatest numbers of African Americans. This is similar to the finding that African American students at African American colleges have higher self-esteem than do African Americans at European American colleges. Asian Americans living on the West Coast, where there are higher

■ **TABLE 3-3**
RANK ORDERING OF ETHNIC GROUPS WITH RESPECT TO SELF-ESTEEM
SCORES AND FACTORS INFLUENCING SCORES*

Rank Order of Self-Esteem Scores High Self-Esteem	Self-Esteem Scores Vary Depending on
1. African Americans	1. Age of person
2. European Americans	2. Education
3. Latinos	3. Geographical location
4. Native Americans	4. Year scores obtained
5. Asian Americans	

*From Jean M. Twenge and Jennifer Crocker, "Race and Self-Esteem: Meta-Analyses Comparing Whites, Blacks, Hispanics, Asians, and American Indians, and Comment on Gray-Little and Hafdahl," *Psychological Bulletin 128* (2002): 371–408.

concentrations of Asian Americans, reported higher self-esteem than did Asian Americans in other parts of the country.

The subjects' cohort (year of birth) and the subjects' age at the time the data were collected also related to scores on self-esteem. In 1980, about twenty years after the civil rights movement began in the United States, African American scores on global self-esteem inventories began to rise. Twenge and Crocker speculate that the emphasis on the experiences and contributions of African Americans to this country, and the civil rights movement's emphasis on group pride and self-respect, affected children who absorbed these messages in the 1960s and 1970s. As they got older, they retained the high self-esteem that the data collected after 1980 reflected. Cohort differences are found for other groups as well. The most recently born Asian Americans and Latinos have rising self-esteem scores and differ least from European Americans.

The authors conclude that a variety of cultural factors explain self-esteem in different ethnic groups. First, the cultural influence of the ethnic group itself plays a role. Scores are highest for groups that have an individualistic orientation that emphasizes independence, setting personal goals, taking control to achieve these goals, valuing uniqueness, and seeking to stand out from others. European Americans and African Americans emphasize these beliefs. Having an individualistic orientation does not mean that collectivist goals have to be ignored, although they usually are in the European American group. Asian American, Latino, and Native American groups that stress an interdependent self that seeks harmony with others, not superiority to them, also are less likely to make positive self-statements and therefore score lower on measures of self-esteem.

Social factors also affect the cultural groups' beliefs. First, as ethnic group members reside longer in this country and are exposed to its individualistic orientation, their reports of self-esteem begin to resemble those of European Americans. Second, self-esteem increases when groups receive positive messages from the communities in which they live. When political and social movements emphasize a group's contributions and when groups feel support from large numbers who share their cultural orientation, then self-esteem increases. Since individuals of higher status in all groups make positive comments about themselves, we can speculate that higher education, a major marker of status, brings with it an increasing appreciation of the self.

COMMONALITIES AMONG CULTURAL THEMES

While recognizing cultural differences in parents' behavior, we should not overlook the commonalities among parents in all groups in this country. All cultures place a high value on children and families, and parents want their children to grow up to be effective adults, however they define effectiveness.

The majority of European Americans embrace the independent model of parent–child relationships. The other ethnic groups, including some subgroups of European Americans such as Italian Americans or Greek Americans, use a more interdependent model, emphasizing respect for elders and tradition, the importance of the extended family and family obligations, early indulgence of children followed (usually) by firm expectations, and a strong reliance on spiritual values. Because older European Americans describe these values as the ones they were raised with also, we can assume that large segments of the population endorse an interdependent model. If immigration continues as it has and if ethnic groups continue to have a larger number of children, this model may come to equal or replace the more dominant independent model of today.

While ethnic groups may have special goals and concerns regarding children, parents' behavior has similar effects on children regardless of the ethnic group, family structure, social status, or gender of parents and children.[36] For example, parental support, monitoring children, and avoidance of harsh punishment have been linked to children's positive growth and well-being in European American samples of parents and children. In national samples that include African American and Mexican American parents as well as European American parents of all educational and financial backgrounds, the same factors of parental support and avoidance of harsh punishment are associated with good grades, psychological adjustment, and rule-following behaviors in boys and girls from five to eighteen in all groups.

In the adolescent years, parents' acceptance and involvement were related to teens' reports of academic achievement and general feeling of well-being in four ethnic groups—European Americans, African Americans, Latinos, and Asian Americans.[37] The greater the parents' involvement, supervision, and autonomy granting, the more teens reported competence and well-being.

A finding that initially emerged in African American samples has been found in European American and Latino samples as well. Nonabusive spanking that occurs in the context of warm family relationships is not related to an increase in children's behavior problems and aggression over time from ages four to eleven.[38] Spanking in the context of little emotional support is associated with increases in problem behaviors over time in the three ethnic groups.

We have now looked at differences in parenting goals and strategies among members of different ethnic groups and also looked at similarities in the effects of their strategies despite having different goals. As Mary Kay DeGenova wrote in *Families in Cultural Context,*

> No matter how many differences there may be, beneath the surface there are even more similarities. It is important to try to identify the similarities among various cultures. Stripping away surface differences will uncover a multiplicity of similarities: people's hopes, aspirations, desire to survive, search for love, and need for family—to name just a few. While superficially we may be dissimilar, the essence of being human is very much the same for all of us. Experience the paradox of diversity, that "we are the same but in different ways."[39]

THE INFLUENCE OF SOCIOECONOMIC STATUS

Socioeconomic status (SES) provides a developmental niche for parent–child relations just as racial and ethnic backgrounds do.[40] Three factors—parents' occupation, education, and level of income—make up SES. Although income at or below the poverty level affects parenting (see the next section), income closer to the average appears less influential in shaping parenting beliefs than do education and occupational status.

The influence of social status, like that of culture, is not fixed. For example, parents' occupations may change as the result of increased education, or a family may find great success in some endeavor and their income may rise sharply. Conversely, income and social status may drop as a result of unemployment. Furthermore, parents can change their ideas about parenting as a result of new information rather than a change in educational level.

Summarizing the research on the influence of SES on parenting, Erika Hoff, Brett Laursen, and Twila Tardif state that higher SES parents are more likely than lower SES parents to have a child-centered orientation to parenting. They seek to understand children's thoughts and feelings and to make them important partners in the process of parenting. They elicit opinions and encourage children's participation in making rules. Lower SES parents are more parent-centered than are higher status parents. They see themselves as authorities and want children to comply. When children do not obey, such parents may be harsh and punitive.

A second major finding is that differences in SES correlate with more differences in verbal than nonverbal interactions between parents and children. Higher-status parents talk more to children and elicit more speech from them. They also show more responsiveness when children do speak, and they encourage the development of verbal skills by supplying more labels that describe what children see and do.

Such differences may seem uninteresting and unimportant, but an unusual study has documented the profound impact of these verbal differences on young children's lives. Betty Hart and Todd Risley recorded the words spoken to and by children in their homes from the ages of one to three years.[41] For an hour each month, researchers visited the homes of forty-two European American and African American families of professional, working-class, and welfare backgrounds. Results indicated no gender or racial differences in language acquisition, but they did reveal large differences based on social group. All children in the study experienced quality interactions with their parents; all heard diverse forms of language spoken to and around them; all learned to speak by the age of three. However, the differing amounts and kinds of language heard in the homes surprised the investigators. First, professional parents spoke about three times as much to their children as did welfare parents and about one and a half times as much as did working-class parents. Children in professional families heard about 487 utterances per hour; children in working-class families, 301; children in welfare families, 178.

The emotional tone of the conversations also reflected startling differences. In professional families, children received affirmative feedback (confirming, elaborating, and giving explicit approval for what the child said) about thirty times an hour, or every other minute. In working-class families, children received affirmative feedback fifteen times an hour, or once every four minutes. In welfare families, children received positive feedback six times an hour, or once every ten minutes. Professional parents gave prohibitions about five times an hour, and welfare parents about eleven. Children in welfare families heard twice as many negative comments as positive ones, whereas children in professional families heard primarily positive comments and rarely any negative ones.

These findings have important implications for the development of self-concept and general mood as well as for language development. Language differences in the home at ages one to three strongly predicted vocabulary growth and intellectual development when the child was about nine years of age. The most important predictors of vocabulary and intellectual competence were the emotional tone of the feedback and the amount of linguistic diversity the child heard.

Encouragingly, the study shows that all parents have the capacity to promote language and intellectual development, because they already have the ability to speak and interact with children effectively. Increasing verbal interactions with children and providing more positive feedback to them will help language development and intellectual growth in homes where parents are inclined to say less and what they do say is negative.

Annette Lareau went into the homes of middle-class (those with managerial jobs or complex jobs requiring college level skills), working-class (those with unskilled, lower-level, white-collar jobs with little or no managerial responsibility), and poor parents (those receiving public assistance) of European- and African-American background.[42] She and her research assistants observed interactions occurring over many hours on about twenty occasions with each family, following the children and families at school events and doctor visits as well. Like Hart and Risley, Lareau found many elements of family life common to all social groups and found too that socioeconomic differences overshadowed the influence of ethnic background.

Table 3-4 presents the features common to families of all social levels. Table 3-5 describes the features of a parental philosophy of "concerted cultivation," which Lareau believes is characteristic of middle-class families, and features of a parental philosophy of "accomplishment of natural growth," characteristic of working-class and poor families.

The children of all families had positive experiences and all parents worked hard rearing children, but parents in different classes exerted energy in different ways.

■ **T A B L E 3-4**
CHARACTERISTICS OF ALL FAMILIES REGARDLESS OF SOCIOECONOMIC STATUS*

1. Enormous time and effort expended by parents
2. Challenges children face in process of growing up
3. Times of fun, laughter, happiness, emotional closeness, and comfort
4. Rituals regarding favorite meals, television shows, toys, games, and outings
5. Large percentage of time spent in routines such as eating, dressing, daily chores, homework
6. Tragedies such as premature deaths, auto accidents
7. Differing temperaments among family members
8. Differing levels of messiness and neatness among families
9. Atmosphere of safety, security, and hominess

*Adapted from Annette Lareau, *Unequal Childhoods: Class, Race, and Family Life* (Berkeley: University of California Press, 2003), pp. 237–238 and 274.

■ **TABLE 3-5**
TYPOLOGIES OF DIFFERENCES IN CHILD REARING*

	Child-Rearing Approach	
	Concerted Cultivation	*Accomplishment of Natural Growth*
Key Elements	Parent actively fosters and assesses child's talents, opinions, and skills	Parent cares for child and allows child to grow
Organization of Daily Life	Multiple child leisure activities orchestrated by adults	"Hanging out," particularly with kin, by child
Language Use	Reasoning/directives	Directives
	Child contestation of adult statements	Rare questioning or challenging of adults by child
	Extended negotiations between parents and child	General acceptance by child of directives
Interventions in Institutions	Criticisms and interventions on behalf of child	Dependence on institutions
	Training of child to take on this role	Sense of powerlessness and frustration
		Conflict between child-rearing practices at home and at school
Consequences	Emerging sense of entitlement on the part of the child	Emerging sense of constraint on the part of the child

*Reprinted with permission. Annette Lareau, *Unequal Childhoods: Class, Race, and Family Life* (Berkeley: University of California Press, 2003), p. 31.

Middle-class parents stimulated children with lessons, trips, and group activities. They helped children develop verbal and social skills; they encouraged children's sense of individuality. They taught their children how to interact with adults outside the home, how to present their own needs, and to persist in an assertive but polite way until adults attended to these needs. They conveyed to children a sense of ease and confidence that the world would treat them well.

Children in working-class and poor families had advantages at home in the sense they were less pressured and scheduled to attend lessons and activities. These children had more time for free play and often had much closer relationships with family members and cousins than children of the middle class. Still, these children longed to have lessons and trips. The real disadvantages of working-class and poor families came in their decrease in self-confidence as they moved outside the home.

Many parents felt they did not meet the expectations of middle-class teachers and doctors, and some feared more severe criticism that might remove children from the home for failure to meet middle-class standards of discipline and punishment. Their children did not have the view that all would go well.

The parents in the two social groups had different conceptions of both childhood and adulthood. Middle-class parents wanted children to have some fun in childhood, but childhood was seen as a period of preparation and development of skills that would enable children to get good educations and good jobs in adulthood. Then, as adults, they could have fun and pleasure at work and with their families. The orientation was toward a future full of good experiences. Parents in working-class and poor families saw adulthood as a stressful time with uncertain jobs and little control of one's work and income. Childhood was the period of pleasure and freedom from stress.

Lareau believes the middle-class pressure for lessons and stimulating activities to develop each child's potential to the fullest comes from the changing nature of the country's economy in which only outstanding performance will qualify a child for the shrinking number of well-paid jobs in the economy. This is what Judith Warner described in *The Perfect Madness*, discussed in Chapter 1.

Lareau also believes that well-funded community recreational programs can provide working-class and poor children with the athletic and musical lessons and the enriching experiences that middle-class parents provide so that these children too can look forward to a bright future.

Sandra Hofferth believes that the family patterns and child-rearing strategies Lareau attributes to social class are really the result of mothers' education, just one of the components of social class.[43] She and her colleagues observed middle-class and working-class children and families and found that within both groups, it was mothers' education that determined what children did. Even when resources were more limited in working-class families, mothers with education enrolled children in community and church activities that provided the benefits that middle-class children gained from private lessons and country club activities. Hofferth believes it is more useful to consider that it is mothers' education that is the pivotal element because it can be increased.

Recent research suggests that when working-class families adopt the daily family routines of the middle class reflected[44] in valuing reading activities, having regular routines of reading to children, dinner-time conversations, special homework times, and getting extended sleep at night,[45] working-class children's cognitive performance and school achievement resemble that of the middle class.

THE INFLUENCE OF ECONOMIC HARDSHIP

The previous section included some families who received public assistance, but here we focus exclusively on what happens to families when income falls to the lowest levels.

Parents who lack resources to care for their children experience increased stress in meeting the challenges of daily life. When experiencing economic hardship, parents become more irritable, depressed, and more easily frustrated, and their psychological tension decreases their parenting skills that in turn affects their children.[46] Parents and children get caught in a vicious cycle of anger. Parents are angry and worried, and children respond to anger with anger of their own. The relationships between economic strain and parent–child conflicts are seen in African American families[47] and Latino/a families[48] as well as in European American families.

When parents who are experiencing economic hardship can support each other, avoid angry conflicts, and maintain nurturant and involved parenting, the whole family benefits.[49] Parents have happier marriages, and their children feel confident and perform well in school. Children have good relationships with peers and siblings; they avoid relationships with children who engage in high-risk activities. Parents' nurturant parenting in adolescence predicts their children's stable romantic relationships in young adulthood.

Who Are the Poor?

The official federal index of poverty developed in the 1960s is the most common measure of poverty; it is based on pretax, cash income and the number of people in the family.[50] The index is determined by the estimated cost of food multiplied by three, as food was found in surveys in the 1960s to absorb about one-third of the family income. The index is considered inadequate because food now is less than one-third of the budget, and other costs such as transportation to work and day care are not considered. Despite criticisms for over a decade, it is still the official figure. Because the official index is too low, some consider poverty 200 percent of the official Poverty Index.

Children are the poorest individuals in the United States. In 2006, the official poverty rate for children under eighteen was 17 percent (compared with a poverty rate of 6 percent for those aged 65 and older).[51] Rates of poverty are higher for children in certain ethnic groups. In 2006, 33 percent of African American and 27 percent of Hispanic children were living in poverty, compared with 14 percent of European American and 12 percent of Asian American children.

Many factors influence rates of poverty. Poverty decreases when parental education increases and when the number of children in the family decreases.[52] Poverty increases when children live in single-parent families, although living in a two-parent family is not a complete protection because in one study, almost half the years children spent in poverty occurred when they were living with two parents.

Three factors seem to push families into poverty: (1) decreases in the number of skilled jobs that can support families, (2) increases in the number of single-parent families, and (3) reductions in government benefits to families.[53]

Jeanne Brooks-Gunn and Greg Duncan refute the argument that the problems of the poor result from parents' genetic endowment or their work ethic.[54] They report that siblings reared in the same family with the same parental attitudes can differ in the age and duration of poverty in their lives and thus serve to control for the effects of parental characteristics on poverty. They found that sibling differences in income during childhood were related to siblings' years of completed schooling, suggesting that income does matter even when genes and work ethic are controlled for.

The Effects of Poverty on Children's Development

Poor children are at higher risk for many problems that include:[55]

- Physical health risks like higher infant mortality, low birth weight, greater exposure to lead poisoning, toxic wastes, poor air quality
- Neighborhoods with poorer day care and schools, greater risks for violence, aggressive peers
- Fewer toys, less verbal stimulation; cognitive delays appear as early as age two and persist; children have learning disabilities and are more likely to repeat a grade
- Less family stability with more moves; more divorce; more exposure to domestic violence, neglect, and physical maltreatment; more likely to be separated from parents
- Higher levels of neuroendocrine arousal

Poverty status presents not one risk but a cascade of problems that complicate children's lives at every level.[56] At the level of physiological functioning, poverty status is related to lack of resources such as food, healthy housing, and safe neighborhoods. Even when a resource is free, easy to provide, and beneficial like school recess, poor children are less likely to get it.[57]

Diminished resources place a physical demand on children's bodies that is reflected in changes in blood pressure, neuroendocrine secretions, and self-regulatory behavior. These changes begin in young people in elementary school, and as stress and body changes continue, the body over time is damaged.[58] It is the accumulation of stresses that is important for physical changes, not any particular one. Given all the stresses, it is not surprising poor children are described as more aggressive and more worried.[59]

Children who were chronically poor from birth to age nine experienced lower quality of parental care than those who were never poor in that period.[60] Their mothers were less sensitive caregivers, less stimulating, and more depressed. Over time, the quality of the homes decreased further. Children had lower scores on cognitive and language skills. Their out-of-home caregivers and their teachers rated them as more aggressive, noncompliant, and more anxious and worried.

In this sample, aggressive behaviors decreased when family's income increased, mothers worked, and had a partner.[61] If mothers worked but gained no increase in income, children's behavior worsened. So, financially beneficial employment improved family well-being and children's socioemotional functioning.

Despite all the difficulties poverty creates for poor children and their families in terms of limited resources and parents' high stress levels, children in poor families feel as close to their mothers and fathers as children in affluent families, feel parents pass on moral values, and eat meals with them as often as children in affluent families report about their parents.[62]

In poor and affluent families alike, closeness to parents, particularly to mothers, and parents' positive support predict children's school competence and subjective sense of well-being. In poor and affluent groups of children, there are subgroups of children who are unhappy and detached from parents. In poor families, there are no resources to get help, and in more affluent families, parents are often too reluctant to seek the help that is available to them because of embarrassment about psychological problems.

Interventions can provide the help that poor families need.

Ways to Intervene

Many kinds of intervention help. Interventions to improve children's health also improves their test scores at school.[63] For example, an assistant superintendent of schools in Chula Vista observed several years ago that the schools with the poorest academic progress were those with the greatest absenteeism for health reasons. He approached the director of the local medical clinic, who was also concerned about children's health care. Many of the children lacked health insurance and used expensive emergency room services for routine problems. Such bills went unpaid, and the clinic lost money. The school, the medical center, and the city organized a mobile medical clinic that went from school to school, providing routine care for children. The clinic was linked with a family clinic on the school grounds, and parents were helped to fill out papers for federal health benefits.

Health improved. Children attended school more regularly. In class, they were alert and attentive. Academic performance and test scores improved. Clearly, health played a major role in this change.

Programs to help children initially targeted children's health needs and cognitive delays with such programs as Head Start and Early Head Start that included parenting programs to help parents stimulate children's growth.[64] As ecological systems theories became more prominent and pointed out that parent and child were part of a social system, services expanded to include jobs and income supplements for parents.

But as an individualistic country that adheres to the independent cultural model at the government level we have been reluctant to provide income supplements, health care, and jobs for parents to all families in poverty as most industrialized European countries. Research shows that multifaceted programs have an effect.

Multifaceted Early Head Start programs, targeting low-income parents with infants and toddlers, provide a full array of services to promote child development.[65] The services include health care, home visits, parent education, child care, and family support for twenty months in the first three years of life. In 2004, 62,000 families were enrolled in such programs around the country. In a preliminary study of the effects of the program on 3,000 children, investigators have found that such programs have increased parents' skills in the areas of (1) forming emotionally supportive relationships with children, (2) stimulating children's verbal and learning abilities, and (3) finding alternatives to physical punishment.

Three-year-old children in this program performed better on measures of verbal and intellectual abilities, on measures of attention span, and on ability to emotionally engage parents than control children not enrolled in the program. They were also less aggressive. So, in the areas that parents increased in skills, children increased in performance.

New Hope, a Wisconsin program, provided many services to families with children aged thirteen months to eleven years and yielded improvements in children's functioning.[66] The program provided jobs for parents, financial supplements for the family, health care, and child care. When the children were assessed two years after the three-year program began, boys in the program had higher academic achievement, especially in the area of reading, and better study skills; they were more compliant with rules and more sensitive to others, but at the same time more self-directed than boys in the control group. Girls in the program did not show as many increases in behavior. In comparison to girls in the control group, they had slightly higher academic achievement, but teachers rated them lower on study skills and social behaviors, and higher on fearfulness and social withdrawal. Two years after the program ended, children continued to show academic increases, but boys' social advantages were not seen. The continued achievements even after the three-year program ended may have occurred because families in the program continued to use more center-based child care, and children continued to be more involved in community activities.

Follow-up studies of children attending an intensive, two-year preschool program found that the effects of such programs can last well into adulthood. The High/Scope Perry Project, developed and carried out in Ypsilanti, Michigan, in 1962, enrolled three-year-olds from a very poor neighborhood in a five-day-a-week, three-hour-a-day program that focused on helping children learn active problem-solving skills that included planning activities, doing them, and reviewing what they had done.[67] In weekly home visits, parents got information on how to encourage learning in everyday life situations, such as counting change at the grocery store.

Children in the program and in the control group have been followed into their forties. Although the initial differences between the groups at the ages of seven and eight were not impressive, significant differences have emerged in the quality of the lives of these two groups. Program children got higher grades in high school and were more likely to graduate from high school (66 percent as compared to 45 percent in the control group). Nearly twice as many have completed college. They are more likely to be employed (76 percent as compared to 62 percent), more likely to own a home and a car, and likely to earn more ($20,800 as compared to $15,300).

Social achievements are significant as well. Only 28 percent of the preschool group have been sentenced to jail or prison as compared to 52 percent of the control group. Men were more likely to marry and almost twice as many were involved in raising their own children (50 percent compared to 30 percent).

The exact reasons for the long-lasting impact of the two-year program are not known, but one can speculate that parents increased their skills in relating to children and stimulating their learning, and children gained early problem-solving skills that set in motion a more positive cycle of behavior. Children had greater success in school, became more involved and found it rewarding, and attained more education that enabled them to have greater occupational success and social stability in adulthood.

One can only wonder how well children in all these programs might have done had the stimulation and extra support been provided not for two years but for fifteen to eighteen years as occurs in middle-class families.

PRACTICAL QUESTION: WHAT HAPPENS WHEN PARENT EDUCATORS AND PARENTS HAVE DIFFERENT VALUES?

Knowing that individuals within different ethnic and social groups may have particular values based on both culture and personal experiences makes us aware of the wide variety of beliefs possible about the goals and strategies of parenting. Tammy Mann, a parent educator, questions the effectiveness of parent educators when the mainstream philosophy of parenting they teach differs from the ideas and experiences of the parents whom they seek to influence.[68]

After the birth of her son, Mann became keenly aware of the discomfort parents can feel "when asked to abandon childrearing practices and beliefs that may be intrinsic to their very definitions of themselves."[69] In rearing her own child, she realized how she treasured the authoritarian parenting strategies of her warm and giving parents even though they did not meet the mainstream model of authoritative parenting (described in Chapter 2).

Mann lived in the South in a two-parent family. When she was two, the family moved to Detroit accompanied by many aunts, uncles, and cousins, so she grew up with a large extended family who had frequent gatherings. The extended family periodically returned to the South for vacations, traveling together in "caravans."

Mann's parents shaped and controlled their children's behavior without discussions of their children's preferences or ideas. Children had to obey. Such control was to help children grow into accountable and responsible adults. Her parents expected their children to help in the family from an early age. They emphasized respect for elders, manners, and polite behavior to others. Her mother had a strong religious faith, and the family participated regularly in church activities. Education was very important, and both parents wanted their children to go further in school than they had.

As a parent, Mann finds herself maintaining her son's strong connections to the extended family. Though she, with her husband and son, live far from other relatives, she makes sure he visits the extended family in the summer, and all three travel to the South for family reunions. This does not substitute for the warm cocoon of the extended family Mann experienced as a child in Detroit, but she duplicates those childhood feelings for her son as best she can. Because religion has been so important to her and her parents, she delights in her son's spontaneous and easy reliance on prayers as a way of coping with the stress of waking up in the night alone.

Mann sometimes feels uncomfortable wanting to follow the values that have been such strengths for her and her brother and sisters, because they do not conform to what experts recommend. For example, she does not value independence, individual expressiveness, and achievement above all. Instead, she stresses family connectedness, responsibility to others, a strong religious faith, and educational achievement. Mann suspects that parents she has worked with in the past may have felt as alienated from mainstream parenting beliefs as she has, and she worries that rejecting "aspects of who we are, in an attempt to become something else deemed 'better,' can be more destructive than practitioners sometimes imagine."[70]

She believes parent educators and practitioners must first try to understand families and their values before intervening. Although the particular characteristics defining effective behaviors differ, most parents share the common desires of wanting children to become well-functioning adults. Parents are striving to do their best as they deal with issues of nurturance and setting limits. In rearing children, parents confront their own values regarding the importance of independence, compliance, respect, and achievement. Educators must help parents find the strategies and solutions that both help their children develop and fit with parents' values and earlier experiences.

Vivien Carlson and Robin Harwood describe a four-session program to help parent educators become aware of their own cultural orientations and values with respect to parenting and then to use their increased awareness to better understand and help parents.[71] Carlson and Harwood state that many educators are surprised to discover that cultural beliefs are more than a set of beliefs endorsed by a group. Groups pass on unspoken ways of viewing the world, but individuals interpret these beliefs uniquely in terms of their own experience. Thus, educators have to pay attention to the unique beliefs, socialization goals, and values of the parents they work with. They also have to be sensitive when parents' values differ from their own.

In this program, educators learn to ask questions to discover the long-term goals parents have for children, such as independence, social relatedness, respect and deference, and individual achievement. They also learn to identify parents' expectations about milestones, such as children's feeding themselves, being toilet trained, and sleeping by themselves.

During the course of the training, participants come to realize that knowledge of group history and characteristics is valuable, but not sufficient, for culturally sensitive practice. In particular, they appreciate the training emphasis on specific questioning strategies for use in exploring cultural beliefs and values with families, with 95 percent of participants agreeing or strongly agreeing with the statement, "I will use the information about socialization goal categories and questioning strategies in my work with families."[72]

Such information enables educators to provide more effective and relevant services to parents.

MAIN POINTS

Culture provides
- ways of viewing the world
- goals and strategies for parenting
- a developmental niche for parent–child relations

The cultural models of parent-child relations include
- the independent model, stressing children's independence, initiative, and the capacity for setting and achieving goals

- the interdependent model, stressing children's becoming part of a strong social network that nourishes and supports them

Members of ethnic and immigrant groups in this country

- have often experienced prejudice and rejection
- differ in values and strategies of parenting, with European Americans preferring the independent model and many other groups preferring the interdependent model
- differ in levels of self-esteem, with members of individualistic cultures reporting higher global self-esteem and members of interdependent cultures reporting lower global self-esteem
- report higher self-esteem when they feel supported and appreciated by their community
- are similar to each other in valuing children and wanting them to grow into effective adults
- appear to receive the same positive effects from supportive parenting

Parents of differing socioeconomic status have

- different views of their roles, with higher-status parents being more child-centered in their approach and lower-status parents being more parent-centered in their approach
- different goals and strategies, with higher-status parents valuing verbal interactions with children, eliciting and understanding feelings, and negotiating differences, and lower-status parents valuing obedience and strict discipline for noncompliance.
- similar forms of interactions with children but spend different amounts of time doing them

Poor children

- are more likely to suffer health problems, cognitive delays, abuse, and neglect than are nonpoor children
- lack income that affects the quality of their health care, home environment, and neighborhoods
- tend to experience conflict and tension because their parents face stress from financial pressure yet feel as close to parents as affluent children feel to theirs.
- feel as close to parents as children in affluent families and benefit as much from parents' support and closeness

Parent educators benefit from

- exploring their own values about parenting
- programs that help them to pay attention to parents' goals and preferred strategies

EXERCISES

1. Everyone receives many cultural messages from the groups to which they belong, whether determined by ethnicity, religion, geographic area of residence, age, or gender. What groups most strongly influence your views of the world and your general values?

2. Look at the ethnic influences that are part of your heritage. What values of these groups have you incorporated into your own life?

3. Recall the independent and interdependent models of parent–child relations. What are the advantages of each? Which of the two is more appealing to you? Why?

4. What are your short- and long-term goals for parenting?

5. If you were a parent educator working with a parent with a set of values that differed greatly from yours, how would you handle it?

ADDITIONAL READINGS

DeGenova, M. K., ed. *Families in Cultural Context: Strengths and Challenges in Diversity.* Mountain View, CA: Mayfield, 1997.

Demo, D. H., Alien, K. R., and Fine, M. A., eds. *Handbook of Family Diversity.* New York: Oxford University Press, 2000.

Hart, B., and Risley, T. R. *Meaningful Differences in the Every Day Experiences of Young American Children.* Baltimore: Brookes, 1995.

Illick, J. E. *American Childhoods.* Philadelphia: University of Pennsylvania Press, 2002.

Lareau, Annette. *Unequal Childhoods: Class, Race and Family Life.* Berkeley: University of California Press, 2003.

McAdoo, H. P., ed. *Black Children.* 2nd ed. Thousand Oaks, CA: Sage, 2002.

4

Nurturing Close Family Relationships in a Technological Society

<table>
<tr><td>

CHAPTER TOPICS

In this chapter, you will learn about:

- Family systems and coparenting
- Ways contemporary parents and children spend time together
- Multinational comparisons of family time use
- Popular questions about family life
- The power of positive feelings, physical touch, and closeness
- Emotional closeness and communication of feelings
- Family routines, rituals, and storytelling
- Identifying and managing negative feelings
- Developing support systems
- Maintaining positive feelings under stress
- Children's definitions of a good parent

</td><td>

IN THE NEWS

Wall Street Journal, March 11[1]: Sharing family stories increases children's confidence. See pages 121–122.

</td></tr>
</table>

Test Your Knowledge: Fact or Fiction (True/False)

1. When parents have unhappy marriages, children function poorly even if parents develop good parenting skills.
2. Positive feelings such as joy and happiness are pleasurable in the moment, and they also contribute to the development of physical and psychological health.
3. Coaching children in understanding and expressing feelings helps children develop effective social skills and maintain physical health.

4. Children become distressed when parents fight, even if parents find a compromise and are happy about it.

5. Parents today put in more hours of work on the job and at home but find more time for child care.

Parents in all ethnic groups give the same primary reason for wanting children—to love them and feel close to them.[2] Parenting experts agree that a primary task of parenting is nurturing close ties with children. How do parents do this? How do they create close bonds with children and at the same time manage the hassles and frustrations of everyday life so children feel loved and cherished?

In a 2002 national survey of 1,600 parents, 92 percent said it was crucial for parents to give children love and encouragement.[3] In this chapter we look at how a parent or parents give children love and nurture close ties among family members while managing the daily frustrations that can interfere with closeness. We first look at patterns of family interactions from a systems point of view to identify those patterns that foster children's development and well-being, and then look at more specific ways to increase emotional closeness and to manage negative feelings.

FAMILY SYSTEMS

Parenting occurs in families. Whether families are small with one parent and one child or large with several generations living together, family members form a system that cares for its members. The systems view emphasizes that a family, regardless of its structure, is a system made up of interdependent members who affect each other in a mutually responsive way. An event in one family member's life has a ripple effect, touching all members, and their reactions, in turn, affect the person who initially experienced the event. Thus, a parent's losing hours and pay at a job, or losing a job completely, affects the couple's relationship and children, as we saw in the last chapter when we looked at the effects of economic hardship. An illness of a child or a parent touches everyone in the family. Or brothers' and sisters' fighting affects parents, perhaps in different ways, and they react. Events touch everyone in the system, and everyone's reactions affect all the members in the system.

Philip Cowan, Douglas Powell, and Carolyn Pape Cowan identify six dimensions of the family system.[4] We have added a seventh to include all those individuals who play a role in bringing the child to life for parents who adopt or use assisted reproductive technology because in many instances they are part of the family system that parents and child inhabit. The family system includes:

1. Each parent and already existing child with his or her individual traits

2. The quality of each parent's relationships—both now and in the past—with members of the family of origin

3. Parents' relationship with each other and their abilities to communicate with each other and solve problems together, whether single or married, together or separated

4. The quality of the relationships between brothers and sisters, if they exist

5. Relationships between parents and other important people in their lives—coworkers, work supervisors, friends

6. The relationship between each parent and each child in the family

7. Individuals such as birth parents who give birth to children and give them to adopting parents and those who donate eggs, sperm, or a surrogate womb to help bring the child to life; they can be a part of the parenting process, as occurs in open adoptions or ongoing relations with donors

The Centrality of the Parental Relationship

The family system begins with the relationship between the parents, and that relationship is the basic support for each parent as he or she deals with the challenges of life—working, rearing children, and caring for older parents all at the same time (see Chapter 13), economic downturns (see Chapters 3 and 13), illness of a child (see Chapter 16), and problems with an adult child (see Chapter 12). Even if parents are not together and had only a fleeting relationship at the time of conception, that coparenting relationship is an important support in rearing the child born of the relationship.

Parenting behaviors and children's well-being depend on the quality of parents' relationship to each other. When psychologists studied family interactions in representative samples of families, they found that parents in happy marriages generally had effective parenting skills and their children functioned well.[5] Mothers and fathers who were warm and sensitive marital partners were also warm and sensitive parents, and their children then functioned well. When conflicts arose and parents resolved them with compromises and expressed positive emotions, children felt secure because the parental relationship appeared stable and reliable.[6]

When, however, parents were in conflict with each other and could not resolve their disagreements and were unhappy, angry, or sad, children felt emotionally insecure. Children's stress increased as measured in cortisol changes, and over time, children developed aggressive behaviors.[7] Researchers speculated that living with parental hostility, tensions, and difficulties decreased children's emotional security; they felt more vulnerable in the world and, as a result, had symptoms of nervousness.

One study carried out on a large, national sample of eight hundred families was able to identify a small cluster of families in which the quality of parenting and marital relationships differed.[8] Although 75 percent of the families had patterns of parenting skills mirroring marital satisfactions, with children's functioning reflecting the parents' effectiveness in these areas, 20 percent of the parents were described as having good parenting skills but unsatisfying marriages.

Their children were less socially skilled and more aggressive than children whose parents had good marriages in addition to good parenting skills, but they performed better on language and cognitive tests than children whose parents lacked parenting skills, even if marriages were good. The children from families in which parents had good parenting skills but poor marriages were most similar in functioning to those children from families in which parents had moderately satisfying marriages and moderate parenting skills. So, good parenting skills enabled children to function at an average level even though marriages were poor.

Box 4-1
INGREDIENTS IN EFFECTIVE COPARENTING*

- Cooperation
- Clear communication
- Coordination of effort
- Agreed-upon standards for children
- Clear boundaries of authority within the household
- Emotional closeness
- Connection

*Adapted from James McHale et al., "Coparenting in Diverse Family Systems," in *Handbook of Parenting*, 2nd ed., ed. Marc H Bornstein, vol. 3: *Being and Becoming a Parent* (Mahwah, NJ: Erlbaum, 2002), pp. 75–107.

Coparenting

Coparenting focuses not on the marital relationship but on how two or more parenting figures relate to each other as they work together to rear children.[9] The concept is useful because it describes a relationship that is independent of the marital status of the parents and the family structure—whether parenting figures are married, separated, divorced, or remarried, or whether extended family members are active parenting figures with or without the biological parent and whether parenting occurs in periods of transition or periods of stability—coparenting occurs.

The principles of effective coparenting provide guidelines for parents in establishing a stable family atmosphere so children can enjoy loving relationships with parents and with other family members and feel secure.

"Effectively functioning coparenting units are those in which the significant adult figures collaborate to provide a family context that communicates to children solidarity and support between parenting figures, a consistent and predictable set of rules and standards (regardless of whether the child lives in a single household or in multiple ones) and a safe and secure home base."[10]

Research shows that parents' patterns of relating to each other as coparents are observable even before the child's birth in their role playing of their anticipated reactions to each other as they include a baby into their family. Follow-ups of the parents' behaviors during the first year of the baby's life show patterns consistent with their role playing before the birth.[11]

Box 4-1 presents the basic ingredients of effective coparenting. The qualities suggest that just as sensitive, responsive behavior with young children promotes emotional closeness and children's development, sensitive, responsive interactions between coparenting figures build a strong alliance that promotes children's growth. The parental qualities of clear communication and cooperative and coordinated working together to help children achieve agreed-upon goals, within definite boundaries of authority, create a calm, predictable family system. Within such a system parents can then concentrate on nurturing emotional closeness and connections with children.

Sibling Subsystem

Families also include brothers and sisters, and parenting changes as the family grows larger. Parents want very much for their children to feel close and loving with each other as well as with them.

Parents first need to solidify their own relationship. Just as the quality of parents' marriages influences individual children's well-being, it also influences sibling relationships. When parents get along with each other and relate positively to each child, brothers and sisters get along well. Conversely, when parents are angry with each other or are overwhelmed with stress, siblings are more likely to have negative relationships with each other.[12]

You might say that all brothers and sisters fight and dislike each other, and it doesn't matter. It is part of life. It does matter because children learn social skills and patterns of negotiating with brothers and sisters that they may carry over into friendships with peers. Poor relationships between siblings can lead to sibling assaults. When brothers and sisters do not get along, older ones are more likely to lead younger ones into rule-breaking activity when they are both adolescents. When siblings do get along with each other and have positive relationships, both siblings have more positive moods.[13]

When parents relate directly to children, the most important guideline is to avoid favoritism of one child over another. Parents do not always treat each child identically, as children of different ages and different temperaments have differing needs and rules, but parents must avoid making children feel one child is more special or valued than the others.[14]

Parents can also help children relate to new brothers and sisters by helping them form good relationships with other children prior to the birth of a new baby. When children can relate positively to other children, they bring these skills to the relationship with the new baby.[15]

So, positive relationships between the parents and having peer relationship where social skills are learned and practiced improve sibling relationships. We discuss this topic in later chapters as well, but highlight it here to emphasize that family interactions among siblings affect everyone's development.

PATTERNS OF CONTEMPORARY FAMILY LIFE

In their book, *Changing Rhythms of American Family Life*, Suzanne Bianchi, John Robinson, and Melissa Milkie describe changes in family life in the last fifty years and paint a picture of how American families spend their time together and apart.[16] Relying on statistics from the Current Population Survey and from parents' daily time diaries from 1965 to 2000 and from the Panel Study of Income Dynamics Child Development Supplement (PSID-CDS), these researchers describe work and family activities of mothers and fathers and single mothers from 1965 to 2000, as well as children's activities in 2002. Data were not presented for single fathers.

Before proceeding, it is important to emphasize that the statistics represent averages for broad samples, and as such may obscure significant differences between subgroups of parents and children. As we will see in later chapters, for example in Chapter 12, being able to look at the paths of change in subgroups of individuals is more informative than looking at averages over periods of time, but such data are not available here. When other studies describe subgroups of individuals, we will describe them.

Parents' Activities, Satisfactions, and Stresses

Researchers found that in 2000 mothers spent six hours more in paid and unpaid work (paid employment and work at home), and fathers spent four hours more than they did in 1965. While 78 percent of mothers with children under age 18 were currently employed and 77 percent worked full time for an average of 47 weeks a year in 2000, there was still great variability; 22 percent were not employed because they had young children, and of the employed, 25 percent worked less than full time. Thus, the average number of hours mothers worked in a year was 1,200 hours rather than 2,000 hours that equal full-time employment.

Mothers and fathers have combined paid and unpaid work of 9.0 to 9.5 hours per day, seven days a week or 64 hours a week, and employed mothers have 10.5 hours a day, seven days a week or about 72 hours a week. So both men and women were working harder in 2000 than in 1965.

Even though men and women are spending more time in work, direct time spent in child care such as feeding and taking a child to the doctor and in interactive care such as reading increased from 1965 to 2000. Fathers' time in all child-care activities increased from 3 hours weekly in 1965 to 6.5 hours in 2000; married mothers' time, from 11 to 13 hours weekly; and single mothers' time, from 8 to 12 hours weekly. Total parental time spent each week in the presence of children, in giving care and in other pursuits such as recreational activities, increased in the 1975–2000 period from 21 to 33 hours for married fathers and 47 to 51 hours for married mothers, but decreased for single mothers from 50 to 44 hours.

Time spent in direct care of children has increased for several reasons. First, in dual-earner families fathers have increased the amount of time they spend in chores and child care. While they engage slightly more in teaching and recreational activities with children than mothers, they are more engaged with children than in the past. Single mothers frequently lack this support.

Second, parents allocate their time at home differently in 2000 from the way they did in 1965. Time spent in housework and household chores decreased, and time spent multitasking increased. Parents watch TV with children while they fold laundry, or they listen to reports about school while they prepare dinner. Third, parents have included children in their leisure activities so parents and children are together much of the time parents are not at work. Fourth, parents have decreased the time they spend with each other, with friends, in civic activities, and time spent alone.

The quality of parent–child time is high, with parents' expressing great satisfaction in playing and talking with children and taking them places. Single mothers spend less time going places with children, but they enjoy the time together when they have it. Parents also report enjoying physical affection and hugs with children.

"Fathers spend more time in child care, and both parents spend more time multitasking."

While they are spending more time with children than parents did in 1965 and enjoying that time, parents still, have worries and concerns. Almost half the parents in 2000 felt they did not have enough time with children, but more, around 60 percent, said they did not have enough time with their spouse, and about 50 percent of fathers and 75 percent of mothers felt they did not have enough time for themselves.

Despite their worries and stresses, only 20 percent of men and women believed they were sacrificing their family life for their work, and a larger number, between 30 and 40 percent, believed they were sacrificing their work life for their family. Although mothers and fathers worked longer hours in 2000, they made children the center of family life and sacrificed adult relationships and adult activities in order to give children more time than parents had given in the past when they were working fewer hours.

Differences among Parents

While men and women have similar overall workloads each week, there are gender differences in work patterns. Men spend two-thirds of their work time at paid employment and one-third at home, whereas women spend two-thirds of their work time at home and one-third at paid employment. Recall that these numbers represent averages, so many mothers, especially single mothers, who work full time have employment schedules like men and also home work schedules that exceed those of men. Women may feel more rushed than men because they have long hours at work and the major responsibility of family activities. It also may be the reason that 67 percent of married mothers and 72 percent of single mothers but only 42 percent of fathers felt they were multitasking most of the time.

The factor making the largest difference in the time spent with children in 2000 was mothers' employment status. Unemployed mothers spent more time in all categories of child care and in overall amount of time—65 hours per week compared to 42 hours for employed mothers—a difference of about three hours a day. This is the reason that many mothers do not work or work limited hours per week when children are young.

While total time with children is less, employed mothers reported similar levels of enjoyment in caring for children and similar amounts of positive interactions such as praising and hugging and kissing children, as unemployed mothers. There were larger differences among mothers in satisfaction with how well children were doing and with amount of family time. Employed mothers were more worried about how well children were doing and how much time they spent with children.

There were differences between married and single mothers in how much total time they spent with children. Single mothers spent less time in all activities than married mothers and fathers, but they rated their activities as slightly more enjoyable and satisfying. Educated mothers were more likely to spend time reading and stimulating children, and their children's activities differed. Children of educated mothers watched less television, read more, and studied more.

Children's Activities, Satisfactions, and Stresses

Combining data from a variety of surveys and time diaries, Bianchi, Robinson, and Milkie reported that after allotting time for personal care such as eating and sleeping and educational activities of school and homework, children between the ages of 5 and 18 had about 41 hours of free time per week in 2002. This compared to 35 hours for fathers and 32 hours for married and single mothers. Children spent more free time in unstructured leisure activities such as watching television or going on the computer (averaging about 19 hours a week) than in structured activities such as sports, artistic activities, and organizational clubs (about 8 hours a week).

In general, children's activities paralleled those of their mothers' participation. Children who engaged in sports, fitness activities, housework, and television had mothers who reported increased participation in these activities. Children's activities were positively related to fathers' participation, but not as strongly as to that of mothers. There were few differences in the activities of children of employed and unemployed mothers and in the activities of children of married and single mothers.

In a 2006 survey of children's activities between the ages of 8 and 18, children reported hanging out with parents two and a quarter hours a day and about the same amount of time hanging out with friends.[17] This sample reported a greater amount of time in a variety of media activities per day (discussed in Chapter 5), but media use did not seem to displace more active pursuits such as physical play, reading, and hobbies.

While parents wanted more time with children, that was not children's major request. Most children were satisfied with the amount of time parents gave them, and felt parents, especially mothers, were there for them.[18] Children's most important request was that parents earn more money and have less stress. About two-thirds of children expressed some worry about parents' work stress. While parents felt they controlled their temper, about 20 percent of children gave parents failing grades in that area. So children are more concerned about parents' happiness and stress levels than parents recognize. We discuss children's feelings about parents work in greater detail in Chapter 13.

Children's satisfaction with their time with parents testifies to parents' success in making children the central priority of life.

Multinational Comparisons of Parents' and Children's Time Use

To understand American data better, Bianchi, Robinson, and Milkie compared trends in parental time allocation in the United Kingdom, Canada, Australia, France, the Netherlands, and 16 other Western countries with data on American families.[19] They found that in all the countries, mothers and fathers increased the amount of time spent in child care over the last thirty to forty years, except in France where mothers showed a decrease in the amount of time in child care.

The biggest factor in how much time parents spent caring for children was having a preschool child in the family. The other factors were similar to those in the United States. Employment reduced the amount of time both mothers and fathers spent in child care with children; parental educational level increased the amount of time spent, and married parents spent more time in child care than single parents. So there seems to be an international trend in parents to spend more time in caring for their children.

The biggest factor in how children around the world spend time is the country's level of industrialization.[20] In nonindustrialized countries, children spent more time in chores and paid work, often done in the company of parents and family members. When countries were industrialized, children's major block of time was spent in school and in doing homework, so there is a growing percentage of time spent out of the company of parents as children go through adolescence.

Around the industrialized world, television watching consumes about the same amount of time with similar gender and social differences. Boys watched more TV, and children in higher social groups watched less.

Leisure time can be categorized into structured and unstructured leisure activities. Sports, artistic activities, clubs, and civic activities are structured activities. Americans exceeded all countries in the amount of time spent in sports; this too related to gender and social status, with boys engaging in more sports and children in higher social groups more involved in sports.

Asian countries, freed from work, encouraged children to spend long hours at school and in schoolwork that would lead to productive work and economic gain. American youth were permitted to spend time in leisure activities that were structured, such as sports or artistic activities, or unstructured activities such as free play and getting together to talk with friends. The value of structured activities may be that they help children develop initiative and self-regulation.

There are more cultural similarities than differences in the people children spend time with. In most industrialized countries, time spent with families decreased as children went off to school. While Asian youth spend most of their out-of-school time at home studying, American children spend more time with peers and adults outside the home as they go through adolescence.

So the trends we see in parents' and in children's activities are similar to those seen in other Western industrialized countries. We do differ from Asian countries in the amount and emphasis placed on schoolwork.

Popular Questions about Contemporary Family Life

A frequently asked question in the popular press is, "Are today's parents over-scheduling children and pressuring them to the point of creating psychological problems?" A study of affluent, middle-class early adolescents provided insights on the topic.[21] These children had about 7–8 hours of activities a week of sports, artistic activities, civic activities, and extra academic activities. Children engaged in about 5 hours of these activities because they enjoyed them, about 2 hours for future benefit, and about an hour a week to meet school requirements.

There was little suggestion that parents pressured children to pursue activities except in the area of added academic work, and researchers believed it was possible that children were not doing well in school subjects and parents arranged tutors. In general, children's levels of anxiety and depression, poor grades, and substance use were related to parents' qualities in the relationships. When parents were critical and did not provide after-school supervision, then boys and girls were more likely to have psychological difficulties. For girls, close relationships with parents, reflected in having dinner together, was related to positive feelings and few problems, and for boys, parents' having high expectations for their behavior was related to effective functioning.

The authors concluded that for suburban early adolescents, "High extracurricular involvement in itself is not necessarily destructive. It is much more damaging when children feel that their failures render them unworthy in their parents' eyes or when they believe that their parents are uninvolved and uninvested in their activities and pursuits."[22] The positive value of these activities is discussed in Chapter 11.

Other questions include, "Do parents hover over their children like helicopters and make it hard for children to develop independence?" and a related question, "Does parents' constant care for children give them an exaggerated sense of how others will treat them?"

We have just seen that parents devote more time to children, spend their leisure time with them, and reduce commitments to other people and activities during the child-rearing years. Parents have fewer children and so their energy is focused on one or two children with whom they are close. In the age of electronic devices such as cell phones and personal digital assistants that increase the amount of contact parents and children can have, it is not surprising that parents would be available for quick consultations about issues in ways that were not possible a decade ago. Also, parents want the contact because they worry about safety issues.

Research has not yet told us how increasingly close relationships and electronic means to stay in touch will change parent–child relationships. One suspects there will be only slight modifications for several reasons. First, as the above study on scheduled activities illustrated, children definitely develop problems from lack of support, lack of contact, and lack of supervision. Children need warm, close relationships with parents who monitor and know what children are doing.

Second, as children mature, they use parents as consultants in making decisions. A cell phone call or a text message may be a quick way to get that consultation rather than from a phone call.

Third, granting autonomy as children mature has always been a parental task. Children need opportunities to make decisions on their own.[23] As we saw in Chapter 2, parents' overprotection of shy, inhibited children is not helpful to children, and parents have to monitor their behavior to see they do not fall into the category of overprotective parent. But children arrive at maturity in the adult years, when the process of gaining independence has occurred in the context of warm relationships with parents.

The habits of shared time and frequent contact may simply make the autonomy-granting process a little harder. We can count on children to push for independence, and if they do not, parents will have to be more active in creating independence. But that is a far preferable problem to have than angry, argumentative, or distant relationships with children. Parents may just have to work harder at an age-old problem that has never been easy.

Another question raised is whether American children are becoming couch potatoes who watch television or playing athletes sports, but are not developing the intellectual knowledge or work habits to compete with students who come from countries where academic work takes 10 or more hours a day, and is seen as a measure of the child's commitment to family values. The American school system has been criticized for not teaching as much information and for not demanding as much homework as other countries do. Recall, however, Peter Huttenlocher's comment in Chapter 2, that for creative activity at which this country has excelled, the brain may need rest periods from an enriched academic environment.[24] We do not yet know how to balance those two features. It is certain, though, that everyone needs exercise, and as we take up in the next chapter, television viewing requires limits.

Another question is, "Are parents wise to subordinate their marriage relationship to their parenting tasks?" The answer is generally no, unless there are some special circumstances in which a parent is abusive or a child has special needs. The two relationships form the core of family life. As we have seen, parents reduce their time with each other to meet children's needs. Yet as we have also seen, parents are happier and more effective parents when they have a supportive relationship with each other, and this requires time with each other. Third, parents will weather all family crises with fewer difficulties when they can count on each other.

A primary reason for giving time to the marital relationship is that more than anything in life, most children want their parents together.[25] So even if parents' first concern is making a good life for their children, having a happy marriage is a most important factor in meeting that goal.

Researchers are discovering that an important reason unmarried parents have unstable relationships is not that they do not care for each other, but they lack the skills to maintain relationships.[26] Thus, some policymakers now consider teaching couple relationship skills as a public health initiative to support families and to reduce children's emotional insecurity.[27] As we have emphasized, even if parents never marry, they need to be able to resolve issues so each has a role in their child's care.

THE POWER OF POSITIVE FEELINGS AND THOUGHTS

We have seen that when there is a positive emotional tone in the family—between parents and siblings—children develop in healthy ways. Recent research documents numerous benefits positive feelings have for people.

Researcher Barbara Fredrickson believes each positive emotion broadens individuals' behavioral responses.[28] Joy stimulates play and creativity; interest encourages exploration and learning; contentment fosters appreciating experiences and understanding their importance to individuals' growth; pride builds connections with others to share what has been achieved; and love, described as an amalgam of all the positive emotions shared in relationship with others, stimulates play, creativity, exploration, and learning together. So, positive feelings broaden people's interactions and connect people more closely in activities.

Furthermore, positive emotions appear to undo the effects of negative feelings by calming cardiovascular arousal triggered by negative feelings such as anger, sadness, or fear. The arousal of positive feelings following negative experiences appears also to enable individuals to put negative experiences in a broader perspective, minimizing their impact on the person. The person is able to make plans and take action and does not become immobilized by negative reactions.

Positive emotions also contribute to the important psychological quality of resilience, defined as functioning effectively and achieving good outcomes when confronted by adversity and situations that decrease adaptation.[29]

Positive feelings are important in children's development as well. If children simply think of some pleasant event for a short time, they resist temptation more successfully and respond to unfair treatment with fairness and generosity.[30] In addition, happy feelings inoculate children against the effects of negative events.

Because so many benefits flow from positive feelings, we focus attention on how to nurture these feelings in our homes with family members and in our daily lives.

Physical Touch and Closeness

Physical closeness brings feelings of pleasure and relaxation. We have learned about the importance of physical contact from studies with animals and newborn infants. Rats whose caretakers handled and gentled them had great resistance to stress and survived surgeries that killed rats without such handling.[31] Preterm infants who received deep-pressure massages several times a day in the hospital gained weight faster, were awake and more active during the day, were more alert and responsive during a developmental assessment, and were discharged from the hospital sooner than infants who did not receive massages.[32]

Close physical contact with mothers serves to regulate infants' hormonal levels, sleeping patterns, eating patterns, heart rate, and vagal tone. (Vagal tone refers to the neural control of increases and decreases in the heartbeat and is considered a measure of individual differences in the expression and regulation of emotion.) The close contact of nursing appears to serve as a protective factor against maltreatment over a fifteen-year period.[33] In the first few weeks of life, infants who receive extra carrying and physical closeness cry less than babies who are not carried so much, and they are more visually and aurally alert.[34] When mothers are away or unavailable because of hospitalizations or trips, babies do not eat, sleep, or function physically and socially as well as they did before mothers' absence.[35]

The parents of colicky babies who were having trouble sleeping at three to six months of age were taught to massage their babies for fifteen minutes before bedtime.[36] Massaged babies, when compared to nonmassaged colicky babies, were less irritable, fell asleep faster, and awoke fewer times during the night. During the day, they were more alert.

There is much less research on the importance of physical touch for older children and adults.[37] Neuroscientists recently used magnetic resonance imaging scanning machines to document that holding their husbands' hands, as opposed to strangers' hands, decreased stress from anticipated mild shocks and produced changes deep in the brains of married women. Those women in extremely close marriages experienced the greatest relief from stress.

Adults who have given infant massages have benefited from them as well.[38] Depressed mothers who gave massages to their infants were more alert and responsive in face-to-face interactions with their children. Older adult volunteers who were taught to give infant massages reported that they felt less anxious and depressed, slept better, and were more socially active, and benefits increased over a month.

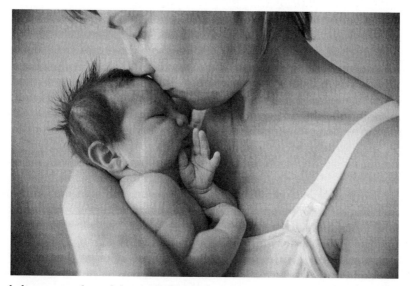

Physical closeness and touch brings feelings of relaxation and emotional closeness for both participants.

INTERVIEW
with Emmy E. Werner

Emmy E. Werner is Research Professor of Human Development at the University of California, Davis. For three decades, she and her colleagues, Jessie Bierman and Fern French at the University of California, Berkeley, and Ruth Smith, a clinical psychologist on the Hawaiian island of Kauai, have conducted the Kauai Longitudinal Study, resulting in books such as Vulnerable but Invincible, The Children of Kauai, Kauai's Children Come of Age, *and* Overcoming the Odds.

From your experience watching children at risk grow up on Kauai, what would you say parents can do to support children, to help maximize their child's potential? From your work with children at risk, what helps children survive and flourish even when faced with severe problems?

Let me say that, in our study, we studied the offspring of women whom we began to see at the end of the first trimester of pregnancy. We followed them during the pregnancy and delivery. We saw the children at ages one, two, and ten, late adolescence, and again at thirty-two and forty years. We have test scores, teachers' observations, and interview material at different times on these people. We have a group of children who were at high risk because of four or more factors. They were children who (1) experienced prenatal or perinatal complications, (2) grew up in poverty, (3) lived in a dysfunctional family with one or more problems, and (4) had a parent with alcohol or mental health problems.

You ask me to comment on parenting and what parents can do, but first I would like to urge that we redefine and extend the definition of parenting to cast a wider net and include people who provide love in the lives of children. I like to talk about alloparenting, the parenting of children by alternate people who are not the biological parents—they can be relatives, neighbors, siblings.

In our study of vulnerable but invincible children, we found that a major protective factor was that at least one person, perhaps a biological parent, or a grandparent, or an older sibling, accepted them unconditionally. That one person made the child feel special—very, very special. These parent figures made the child feel special through acts. They conveyed their love through deeds. They acted as models for the child. They didn't pretend the child had no handicap or problem, but what they conveyed was, "You matter to me, and you are special."

Now, another theme in our findings is that the parent figure, whoever he or she was, encouraged the child to reach out to others beyond the family—to seek out a friendly neighbor, a parent of one of their boy or girl friends, and, thus, learn about normal parenting from other families.

So, physical touch is important and can be maintained with toddlers and older children with nighttime massages, hugs, physical play that fathers often engage in, and a pat on the shoulder.

Emotional Closeness

Parents form a close relationship when they love the child as a special person. Dorothy Briggs describes the psychological climate that enables children to feel

The resilient child was temperamentally engaging. He or she encouraged interaction with others outside the home and was given the opportunity to relate to others.

I had no preconceptions about this protective factor, but what came through was that, somewhere along the line, in the face of poverty, in the face of a handicap, faith has an abiding power. I'm not referring to faith in a narrow, denominational sense, but having someone in the family or outside of it who was saying, "Hey, you are having ups and downs, this will pass, you will get through this, and things will get better."

Another thing was that these children had an opportunity to care for themselves or others. They became nurturant and concerned, perhaps about a parent or a sibling. They practiced "required helpfulness."

Now, another protective factor is whether the children were able to develop a hobby that was a refuge and gave them respect among their peers. One of our study members said later, "If I had any doubts about whether I could make it, that hobby turned me around." The hobby was especially important as a buffer between the person and the chaos in the family. But it was not a hobby that isolated you from others; it nourished something you could share with other people.

As many of the children looked back, they describe how a positive relationship with a sibling was enduring and important. As adults, they commented with surprise on how supportive the relationship was and how these relationships were maintained despite great distances and despite dissimilarities in life and interests.

What did adults say they wanted to pass on to their own children?

Looking back as adults, they felt that some sort of structure in their lives was very important. Even though the family life was chaotic, if a parent imposed some reasonable rules and regulations, it was helpful.

They emphasized faith as something to hang on to and make this clear to their children. As parents now they are quite achievement-motivated. They graduated from high school, and some went back and got additional training. They encourage their children to do well in school.

The main theme that runs through our data is the importance of a parent figure who says "you matter" and the child's ability to create his or her own environment. The children believed they could do it, someone gave them hope, and they succeeded against the odds.

---

their parents' love: "Nurturing love is tender caring—valuing a child just because he exists. It comes when you see your youngster as special and dear—even though you may not approve of all that he does."[39] Children are loved simply because they exist—no strings attached, no standards to meet. This is the "unconditional support" that Susan Harter refers to in her interview in Chapter 5 and Emmy Werner suggests in hers.

Parents form close relationships with children of all ages in two basic ways: by providing sensitive, responsive care that meets the child's individual needs and by becoming an interactive social partner. Sensitive care and forming a social partnership take many forms, depending on the age and unique qualities of the child, as we discuss in subsequent chapters.

UNDERSTANDING AND EXPRESSING FEELINGS

Babies come into the world with emotions and feelings that serve as signals to others of what the infant needs. Long before they have language, children express their feelings through smiles, laughs, cries, and frowns.

A series of studies by John Gottman and his associates indicate that parents differ in their attitudes and thoughts about how important feelings are in life.[40] Some parents have a heightened awareness of their own and their children's feelings and believe feelings signal that change is required. Anger serves to initiate action in frustrating situations, and sadness slows a person down to have time to cope with loss. These parents feel comfortable with their feelings, and they coach children to manage their feelings.

Other parents feel uncomfortable with feelings and seek one of three ways to handle the discomfort:[41] dismissing the importance of feelings and making light of or ignoring them; disapproving and punishing the expression of feelings; and finally accepting all feelings. Children of dismissive and disapproving parents have a hard time trusting their own judgment. By learning that their feelings are wrong, they come to believe there is something basically wrong with *them* for having the feelings. Because they have little experience in acknowledging and dealing with their feelings, they often have difficulty controlling them and solving problems.

Finally, parents who accept all feelings and often comfort the child when the child experiences a negative emotional reaction do little to teach or guide the child in how to express feelings appropriately. These parents seem to believe that expressing feelings in any form—whether appropriate or inappropriate—will take care of the problem. Their children do not learn to cope with feelings constructively and have difficulty concentrating and learning in school and in making friends.

So, the three types of response—ignoring or criticizing feelings so they occur as little as possible and accepting all expressions of feeling without providing guidance for expression—lead to similar kinds of problems for children, such as the inability to regulate feelings and to feel comfortable with themselves and others.

Gottman and his coworkers found that when parents coach their five-year-old children in how to deal with feelings, the children function better physically and psychologically when they are eight years old. They perform better academically and are socially more competent with peers. They are physically healthier as well, perhaps because coaching helps children modulate their emotional reactions that, in turn, helps their physiological system function better. Coaching consists of five key steps:[42]

> Step 1: Parents recognize when they are having a feeling, what that feeling is, and when others are having feelings.

Step 2: Parents consider feelings as opportunities for intimacy or teaching. When the child is upset, happy, or excited, parents see this as an opportunity to be close to the child and to teach the child how to express feelings appropriately.

Step 3: Parents listen empathically and validate the child's feelings. They use active listening skills and validate what the child feels feels without trying to argue the child out of the feeling (see "Active Listening," below).

Step 4: Parents help the child verbally label the feeling. The child may be confused about what he or she is feeling. Labeling the feeling is identifying the feeling, giving the child a word for the strong emotion; it is not telling the child how to feel. Labeling a feeling while the child is experiencing it appears to have a soothing effect on the child's nervous system. Labeling feelings also helps a child see that he or she can have two feelings at the same time.

Step 5: Parents set limits while helping a child solve a problem. Parents limit the way feelings are expressed; they do not, however, limit the child's having the feeling itself. Anger, for example, is acceptable, but hitting a sibling is not. Parents help the child think of possible actions to express feelings and ways to achieve his or her goals in the situation.

Gottman speculates that talking about emotional reactions has positive benefits for children because the verbal expression of feelings helps children plan appropriate actions and eliminates the consequences of inhibiting negative emotional reactions.[43]

Active Listening

Active listening, a specific tool parents use in coaching, is Thomas Gordon's term for what parents do when they reflect their children's feelings.[44] Parents listen to children's statements, pay careful attention to the feelings expressed, and then frame a response similar to the child's statement. If a child says she feels too dumb to learn a school subject, the parent might feed back that she feels she is not smart enough. Here is one of Gordon's examples of active listening:

> CHILD: I don't want to go to Bobby's birthday party tomorrow.
> PARENT: Sounds like you and Bobby have had a problem maybe.
> CHILD: I hate him, that's what. He's not fair.
> PARENT: You really hate him because you feel he's been unfair somehow.
> CHILD: Yeah. He never plays what I want to play.[45]

If the parent's response is accurate, the child confirms the feedback with a positive response. If the parent's interpretation is wrong, the child indicates that and can correct the misinterpretation by expanding on his feelings. The parent can continue active listening to understand what is happening to the child.

Active listening has many advantages. First, it helps children express feelings in a direct, effective way. As feelings are expressed and parents accept them, children feel understood and learn that they are like everyone else.[46] Second, as feelings are expressed, parents and children together learn that the obvious problem is not necessarily the real or basic problem. Like the rest of us, children use defenses and sometimes start by blaming a friend, a parent, or circumstances for what they are feeling. As parents focus on the feelings, children gradually come to identify the underlying problem and discover what they can do about it. Third, listening to children's feelings is sometimes all that is needed to resolve the problem. Often when we are upset, sad, or angry, we simply want to express the feeling and have someone respond, "It is really painful when a friend walks off with someone else and leaves you behind." The response validates the feeling as being justified and important, and frequently that is all we want.

Active listening requires persistence, patience, and a strong commitment to attend to both the child's words and accompanying behavioral clues. Furthermore, there are times when active listening is not appropriate. If a child asks for information, give the information. If a child does not want to talk about his feelings, respect the child's privacy and do not probe. Similarly, if active listening and the dialogue have gone as far as the child is willing to go, then a parent needs to recognize that it is time to stop.

One of the mothers in Haim Ginott's parenting group raised the question of reflecting back feelings of great sadness over a loss.[47] Is this wise? Does it help children? Ginott responded that parents must learn that suffering can strengthen a child's character. When a child is sad in response to a real loss, a parent need only empathize, "You are sad. I understand." The child learns that the parent is a person who understands and sympathizes.

I-Messages

When a parent is angry, frustrated, or irritated with a child's behavior, the parent can communicate his or her feelings constructively with an I-message rather than nagging, yelling, or criticizing. The I-message contains three parts: (1) a clear statement of how the parent feels, (2) a statement of the behavior that has caused the parent to feel that way, and (3) a statement describing why the behavior is upsetting to the parent. For example, a parent frustrated with a teenager's messy room might say, "I feel upset and frustrated when I look at your messy room, because the family works hard to keep the house clean and neat and your room spoils our efforts."

Parents need to spend time analyzing their feelings and becoming more aware of exactly how they feel. Gordon points out that, often, when a parent communicates anger at a child, the parent may actually be feeling disappointment, fear, frustration, or hurt. When a child comes home an hour late, the parent may launch into a tirade. The worry that grew into fear during the hour of waiting is transformed into relief that the child is safe, and that relief is then translated into angry words intended to prevent a recurrence of this irresponsible behavior. The parent who has learned to use accurate I-messages is less likely to misplace anger and to use a child as a scapegoat.

What should a parent do if a child pays no attention to I-messages? First, be sure the child can pay attention to the I-message. Do not try to communicate feelings when the child is rushing out of the house or is already deeply immersed in some other activity. If an I-message is then ignored, send another, more forceful message, in a firm tone of voice.

Sometimes, a child responds to an I-message with an I-message. For example, when a parent expresses distress because the lawn is not mowed, the daughter may reply that she feels annoyed because mowing interferes with her after-school activities. At that point, the parent must "shift gears," as Gordon puts it, and reflect back the child's frustration by using active listening.

I-messages have several benefits. First, when parents use I-messages, they begin to take their own needs seriously. This process benefits all family relationships because parents feel freer—more themselves—in all areas of life. Second, children learn about the parents' reaction, which they may not have understood until the I-message. Third, children have an opportunity to solve problems in response to I-messages. Even toddlers and preschoolers have ideas, not only for themselves but also for others. Siblings often have good ideas about what might be bothering another child in the family. They think of things that might have escaped the attention of parents.

I-messages can convey appreciation—"I feel pleased when you help me with the dishes because then we have time to go to the store for your school supplies." I-messages are also useful in heading off problems and in helping children see that their parents have needs, too. These messages, termed *preventive I-messages*, express parents' future wants or needs and give children an opportunity to respond positively. For example, if a parent says, "I need quiet so I can drive the car," the child learns what to do to be helpful.

Although closeness is enjoyable for and helpful to children, some parents do not feel good about themselves or some of their own qualities, causing them to wonder if their children might not be better off remaining distant from them. They fear that their children will pick up their bad qualities. Research on close and non-close relationships among adolescents and their parents reveals that children who feel close to their parents are less likely to take on the parents' negative qualities than are children who feel distant. Parents' negative behaviors are a more potent influence on children when parents and children are not close.[48] Thus, even when parents have many self-doubts and self-criticism, closeness with them and all their failings is still a positive experience for their children.

FAMILY ROUTINES AND RITUALS

Family rituals and routines bring family members closer together. Family rituals were first studied to shed light on how troubled families preserved stability at times of stress. Steven Wolin and Linda Bennett found that rituals provided continuity to life that increases children's feelings of security.[49] Children who grew up in alcoholic families who nevertheless maintained their family celebrations and rituals were less likely to develop problems with alcohol as adults than those who grow up with an alcoholic parent who did not maintain traditions.[50]

Routines are defined as patterned interactions occurring regularly on a daily/ weekly/monthly basis that accomplish a practical goal—eating, sleeping, doing chores.[51] Routines may not have symbolic or emotional investment for families, but they structure family life, and are especially important at times of transition (e.g., to parenthood or to single parenthood). Single parents who maintained

---

Box 4-2
MAJOR PRINCIPLES FOR ESTABLISHING REWARDING FAMILY RITUALS*

- Get agreement between adults in the family
- Have as much participation as possible from all family members in planning and deciding what to do
- Expect that cooperation from children will emerge slowly
- Have clear expectations of what will happen and who will do what
- Reduce conflict through open communication and respect for others' feelings
- Protect rituals from the demands of other activities
- Be willing to change or modify the rituals as needed

*Adapted from William J. Doherty, *The Intentional Family* (New York: Avon, 1997), pp. 198–199.

---

routines around eating, bedtime, and doing things together felt more successful as single parents, and their children functioned better.[52]

Organized routines also increase children's academic competence.[53] For example, routines of dinnertime meals, reading aloud, and homework routines made up what was termed the "intimate family culture" and significantly predicted children's reading skills in grade 3, accounting for most of the variance attributed to family income and ethnicity in predicting the sample's reading scores. When children from families with fewer resources had the intimate culture of families with middle-class resources, children with limited resources improved in reading at the same rate as middle-class children.

Rituals are defined as repeated patterns of behavior that have symbolic meaning for the family.[54] Members invest emotion in them and feel a sense of belonging when they carry them out. Rituals are major ways that cultural and ethnic groups pass their values on to the next generation. Rituals include family celebrations of major secular or religious holidays and special family traditions such as vacations or birthday celebrations.

Family therapist William Doherty categorizes rituals in terms of their purpose.[55] There are (1) connection rituals that promote bonding between family members (family outings and vacations); (2) love rituals for showing love to each member (birthdays, Mother's Day, Grandparent's Day), and (3) community rituals that connect family members to the larger community (weddings, baptisms, other spiritual and ethnic celebrations). Box 4-2 includes Doherty's suggestions for creating rewarding family rituals.

Many routines, such as bedtime or dinner, can become family rituals. For example, bedtime routines can take on symbolic meaning and emotional investment when children are young—bath, a story the child chooses, talking and cuddling, prayers and being tucked in and kissed—may be a routine parents and children cherish.

STORYTELLING

Telling stories draws family members close to each other. As Susan Engel writes, "We all want to know who we are and how we came into our world. We all want to know that we were recognized, that we are singular and special. And we each learn this, in part, through the stories we are told about our beginnings."[56]

Storytelling begins at birth. "Babies are surrounded by the stories parents, siblings, and friends tell one another, and to them, a captive audience. By the time children are two and three years old, they begin adding their own voices to the stories that surround them."[57] Stories initially consist of only a few words about an event (e.g.,"Played house. I was baby.").

Observations reveal that mothers and toddlers tell about nine stories each hour. In addition to telling stories to others, young children, as they play, often construct ongoing stories of what they are doing.[58] By the time children grow up and are in college, they tell as many as five to thirty-eight stories each day.

Engel gives parents tips for encouraging children to participate in storytelling. Children tell stories when they feel "confidence and joyousness in telling stories,"[59] and parents give that confidence when they listen attentively and express interest with smiles, gasps, facial expressions, and repetitions. Parents collaborate in the stories by asking open-ended questions that encourage elaboration, and they expose children to a variety of stories and poems that stimulate children's stories.

Stories serve several purposes.[60] They shape our views of ourselves, other people, and events in our lives. Stories tell us about the world and our culture and the values that hold our families together.

Stories reflect important family themes that are expressed in other behaviors as well.[61] Mothers and fathers who told stories at dinner about rewarding, fulfilling relationships in their families of origin reported satisfactions in their marriages, and showed more positive feelings at dinnertimes. They perceived their children as functioning well. Continuity of positive and negative affect flowed across generations, with parents' reporting affective relationships in their childhoods, mirrored in their relationships with spouses, and children expressing similar affect to parents.

In attempting to tell stories about their personal experiences, family members sometimes struggled to make sense of the experiences, and the effort was worth it because "Families that are able to make sense of their experiences, pleasant or challenging, however, provide their children with a meaning-making system that can better prepare them for an unpredictable world."[62]

IDENTIFYING AND MANAGING NEGATIVE FEELINGS

Preventing stress is a major way to decrease negative feelings. Strategies to minimize hassles and negative feelings in the family include (1) creating family time, (2) developing a support system, and (3) learning ways to manage negative feelings.

Sources of Negative Feelings

We are aware that strong emotional reactions such as anger or depression affect children's behavior, but we may not be so aware that even negative moods in the course of daily life—such as those caused by the overall challenges of parenting—can also adversely affect parents' interactions with children and children's behavior.

Lack of Time   As we noted earlier in the chapter, many parents feel rushed for time even though they have about 32–35 hours of free time a week.[63] John Robinson and Geoffrey Godbey believe that the accelerated pace of life contributes to feelings of "time-famine." Robinson and Godbey write,

> Speed and brevity are more widely admired, whether in serving food, in the length of magazine articles, or in conversation. As the pace of life has speeded up, there has been a natural tendency to assume that other time elements have been reshaped as well. Primary among these assumptions is the notion that hours of work (duration) are increasing and that those who feel most rushed must work the longest hours.[64]

Feelings of lack of time may also come from the fact that Americans spend about 40 percent of their free time in an activity that gives them less satisfaction than most other leisure activities—namely, watching television. Thus, they do not take the time they have for more satisfying social activities and pursuits with family and friends.

Suggestions for Dealing with the Problem   First, Robinson and Godbey suggest that parents might feel less pressured if they realized that their feelings of time-famine, although genuine, are not related to the actual number of free-time hours available.[65] Free time is available in small chunks during the week and larger ones during the weekend, but parents must plan carefully to make good use of it.

Second, they advise parents to spend free time in activities that give them satisfaction. Television absorbs 40 percent of people's free time because it is easy to do, requires no planning, and costs little.

Third, Robinson and Godbey voice concern about what they term *time-deepening activities*—that is, multitasking to maximize one's use of time. Instead of time-saving efforts, Robinson and Godbey recommend cultivating time-savoring skills in order to appreciate

> ...the simpler delights of life as they are occurring: the taste of good food, the presence of good company, and the delights of fun and silliness. To be happier and wiser, it is easier to increase appreciation levels more than efficiency levels. Only by appreciating more can we hope to have a sustainable society. While efficiency, at least as envisioned in American society, always starts with wanting more, appreciating may start both with valuing more what is already here and with wanting less.[66]

Everyday Negative Moods

Minor daily hassles at work or with children contribute to parents' negative moods, which in turn affect parenting and children's behavior. Negative moods bias what parents recall about children's past behaviors, shape parents' interpretations of current behavior, and cause parents to discipline children more harshly.[67]

Hassles do not have to be intense or prolonged. In one study, even a briefly induced negative mood reduced mothers' positive comments and verbal interactions with their children during play and laboratory tasks.[68] In another study, being distracted by a simple task involving anagrams resulted in parents' being less positive, more irritable, and more critical of and interfering with their preschoolers.[69]

The hassles that generally trigger a negative mood stem from the daily challenges of parenting rather than major difficulties with children.[70] Hassles fall into two broad categories: (1) the effort required to rear children—continually cleaning up messes, changing family plans, running errands to meet children's needs—and (2) the challenge of dealing with irritating behaviors such as whining, sibling fights, and constant demands.

Parents' personality characteristics, their coping styles, and the amount of support available to them can intensify or decrease stress.[71] Outgoing, sociable, optimistic parents are less likely to respond to hassles with negative moods. Parents who use avoidant coping styles, who wish stress would go away so they wouldn't have to deal with it, experience increased stress. Parents who use positive reappraisal of the situation, who feel they are learning from the situation and becoming more skilled, experience decreased stress and retain their self-confidence.

Everyday Anger   Even when there is no particular distress, family members, both parents and children aged five to fifteen, see themselves as major causes of angry feelings in others.[72] Children accurately perceive that they cause mothers' anger; mothers' diaries confirm that children's noncompliance and demandingness cause their anger.

Mothers, however, do not realize that they are the major source of children's anger. Mothers believe that children's anger comes from events outside the home and that happiness comes from within the home, but children report the opposite. They see their happiness coming from friends and personal accomplishments, and irritations and anger from the family.

In short, all family members see anger as very much a part of family life. Children appear the most accurate in seeing their behavior as a major cause of family anger—although on any given occasion they can be mistaken—and the family routines and demands as the main source of their own irritations.

Parents' arguments and angry fights with each other affect their parenting skills so they are more overcontrolling and less warm with children.[73] The fighting also affects children's physiological functioning—their heart rates and cortisol levels—their emotional distress and insecurity, and their behavioral and emotional control over time.[74] Some children seem to have built-in physiological reactions of high vagal suppression that calms the child's system so behavioral and emotional control problems do not develop, but other children do not have this inner protective mechanism and are more vulnerable to the effects of their parents' fighting.

When distressed, some children are spurred to action and they intervene to remind parents not to argue, or present a solution to the problem, or at the least, try to cheer parents up after an argument.[75] Their actions tend to decrease parents' arguing over time, perhaps because parents become more keenly aware of how upsetting the fighting is to children. Those children who take action are less likely to develop adjustment problems over time. In contrast, those distressed children who respond to parents' arguing with yelling and uncontrolled behavior have an increase in adjustment problems, and parents' arguing increases over time as well.

Does this mean that parents should never fight or disagree in front of children? No. Conflict is a natural part of life when people live together, and children may need to observe how conflicts are settled in order to learn these skills themselves. When angry adults compromise and seem pleased with the solution, children were not distressed and seemed to have greater feelings of security, knowing that parents could resolve problems.[76]

Managing Negative Feelings

Because anger, stress, frustration, and guilt are all part of rearing children, parents need to find their own strategies for controlling the expression of these feelings. When these feelings lead to criticism, nagging, yelling, and hitting, both parents and children suffer. Children are hurt and discouraged; parents feel guilty and inadequate.

Nancy Samalin, who runs parent groups on dealing with anger, suggests that families compile lists of acceptable and unacceptable ways for parents and children to express anger.[77] Acceptable ways include such actions as crying, going for a walk, and yelling, "I'm mad." Unacceptable ways include destroying property, hitting, spitting, and swearing.

Of course, I-messages are the most direct way to express anger, but sometimes people want physical outlets such as work or exercise. Table 4-1 lists a variety of ways to deal with anger.

■ **TABLE 4-1**
EIGHT WAYS TO DEAL WITH PARENTAL ANGER

1. Exit or wait—taking time out is a way to maintain and model self-control.

2. Make "I," not "you," statements to help the child understand your point of view.

3. Stay in the present—avoid talking about the past or future.

4. Avoid physical force and threats.

5. Be brief and to the point.

6. Put it in writing—a note or letter can express feelings in a way that the other person can understand.

7. Focus on the essential—ask yourself whether what you are arguing about is really important and worth the energy involved.

8. Restore good feelings—calmly talk over what happened or give hugs or other indications that the fight is over.

Adapted from Nancy Samalin with Catherine Whitney, *Love and Anger: The Parental Dilemma* (New York: Penguin Books, 1992).

To parents who feel guilty about or frustrated with the mistakes they have made, Jane Nelson, using Rudolf Dreikurs's guidelines, suggests following a three-step program: (1) recognize the mistake, (2) reconcile with the child by apologizing, and (3) resolve the problem with a mutually agreed-upon solution.[78] Nelson advises parents to view mistakes as opportunities for learning. Seeing mistakes in that way reduces parents' self-criticism and their resistance to recognizing them. Apologizing is a behavior children can emulate when they have made a mistake. It also enables parents to experience children's quickness to forgive.

Dreikurs emphasizes that, like children, parents must develop the courage to be imperfect. He writes,

> The importance of courage in parents cannot be overemphasized. Whenever you feel dismayed or find yourselves thinking, "My gosh, I did it all wrong," be quick to recognize this symptom of your own discouragement; turn your attention to an academic and impersonal consideration of what can be done to make matters better. When you try a new technique and it works, be glad. When you fall back into old habits, don't reproach yourself. You need to constantly reinforce your own courage, and to do so, you need the "courage to be imperfect." Recall to your mind the times that you have succeeded, and try again. Dwelling on your mistakes saps your courage. Remember, one cannot build on weakness—only on strength. Admit humbly that you are bound to make mistakes and acknowledge them without a sense of loss in your personal value. This will do much to keep your own courage up. Above all, remember that we are not working for perfection, but only for improvement. Watch for the little improvements, and when you find them relax and have faith in your ability to improve further.[79]

DEVELOPING A SUPPORT SYSTEM

When parents receive support from friends, relatives, and each other, they experience less stress and fewer negative moods. The support may come from organized parenting groups, which we discuss in the next chapter. Or support may come from family members such as grandparents.

Grandparents as Supports

Outside the child's nuclear family, grandparents are the most important figures in most families. Grandparents influence grandchildren directly when they serve as caregivers, playmates, and family historians who pass on information that solidifies a sense of generational continuity. They are a direct influence when they act as mentors to their grandchildren and when they negotiate between parent and child. They influence grandchildren indirectly when they provide both psychological and material support to parents, who then have more resources for parenting.

Because minority families interact more with extended family members, more information on the role of grandparents in such families is available than for other families. The extended family often includes one or both grandparents. Grandmothers help families nurture and care for children in a less structured, more spontaneous way than is possible when only two generations are present. The grandparents' role depends on whether one or both parents live in the home.[80]

In general, contacts between grandparents and grandchildren vary, depending on the age, health, and proximity of the grandparents.[81] Grandparents typically see their grandchildren once or a few times a month. Although a few studies suggest that only a small percentage of grandparents enjoy close, satisfying relationships with their grandchildren, many other studies indicate that young adults generally feel close to grandparents (averaging 4 on a 5-point scale of emotional closeness) and that "the grandchild–grandparent bond continues with surprising strength into adulthood."[82]

Geographic proximity is the most important predictor of the nature of the relationship.[83] When grandparents live close by, contact naturally increases. When grandparents are young and healthy enough to share activities, grandchildren feel close because of the shared fun. At the same time, when grandparents are older and in poorer health, grandchildren feel close because they can help them.

Gender plays a role in such relationships. Grandmothers are more likely to be involved with grandchildren than are grandfathers, and they appear to play a powerful role in children's well-being.[84] Anthropological research presented at an international conference on grandmothers indicates that the involvement of grandmothers and older female kin enhance the lives of their grandchildren.[85] In one study, the presence of the maternal grandmother increased childhood survival at age six to 96 percent; the survival figure for homes without grandmothers was 83 percent. The presence of the paternal grandmother did not change the childhood survival rates.

When grandchildren are very young, they see grandparents as sources of treats and gifts. When grandchildren are in elementary school, they look to grandparents to share fun activities with them, and in early adolescence, they also take pleasure in sharing a variety of activities with them. Grandchildren often see grandparents as more patient and understanding than their parents, and contemporary grandparents try to live up to this expectation.[86] They seek to be supportive to grandchildren rather than intrusive and critical. A grandparent can become particularly close at times of family change and serve as confidant and advocate for the child who could become lost in the chaos of events (see Chapter 14).

Community Supports for Parents

Most people in the community realize that raising children in today's world is a hard job. Over 70 percent of a national sample of 1,400 adults reported that adults in the community can play an important role by forming relationships with children, conversing with them, encouraging them to do well in school, and commenting on their positive behaviors. Only 5 percent, however, take any actions like this in their community.[87]

Parents have to organize their own community support network for their children. Suggestions for how to do this are presented in Box 4-3. We discuss community support for parents in Chapters 9, 10, and 13 as well.

🌳 **Box 4-3**
BUILDING COMMUNITY SUPPORT FOR CHILDREN*

Parents and children profit when adults in the community take an interest in children and take actions to engage in relationships with them and support them in their activities. When such support is not immediately available, parents can take the following actions to create it for children.

- Encourage extended family members to take an interest in your children. Invite them to your children's special events—birthdays, school, and athletic events. Invite them to join you and your family for events of mutual interest.
- Take an active role in supporting the friends of your children. Tell their parents about their special qualities or positive actions that you have observed. Ask the children about their interests and views about things.
- In your neighborhood, set an example of how you want adults to relate to your children by relating in that way to other children and their parents. Get to know children's names, their special interests—hire teenagers to do extra chores, organize and participate in block parties that include all generations. Organize families to accomplish a needed neighborhood chore such as cleaning up debris after a storm or shoveling snow on sidewalks.
- As appropriate, encourage older children to ask parents of friends about career satisfactions, advice about specific colleges or graduate schools, or part-time jobs.
- Get to know your neighbors. Help them get to know your children and have your children get to know them (e.g., speaking politely to them, offering to do favors for them). As appropriate, involve neighbors in your children's lives. Invite them to events in your home such as a dinner or watching a sporting event of interest. Invite them to school events of interest.

*Adapted from Peter C. Scales, Peter L. Benson, and Eugne C. Roehlkepartain, *Grading Grown-Ups: American Adults Report on Their Real Relationships with Kids* (Minneapolis, MN: Lutheran Brotherhood and Search Institute, 2001), p. 57.

PRACTICAL QUESTION: HOW DO YOU INCREASE POSITIVE FEELINGS WHEN PARENTS HAVE ECONOMIC STRESSES?

Experiencing positive feelings helps family members not only enjoy life and function more effectively but also to handle problems. A program designed in the Netherlands to reinforce potential family strengths focused on eight areas of positive parent–child communication, is highlighted in Table 4-2.[88]

Increasing these positive forms of communication enabled families to improve their behaviors in all areas. For three to four months, social workers in Israel went into the homes of welfare families in which parents were having difficulties with

■ **T A B L E 4-2**
EIGHT FORMS OF POSITIVE PARENT–CHILD COMMUNICATION

1. *Positive naming with approval* of what is occurring when the parent and child interact, so that the child understands the significance of the interaction.

2. *Taking turns* so all family members have an opportunity to express themselves and gain the appropriate attention

3. *Strengthening the weak link.* Any family member who is less interactive and assertive, whether child or adult, is encouraged to be more active.

4. *Following.* The parent makes verbal and nonverbal responses following an interaction with the child. The parent both comments on the interaction and looks at the child.

5. *Saying yes.* The parent phrases all directions to the child in terms of what the child is to do—"Carry your coat," not "Don't drag your coat on the floor."

6. *Supporting initiative.* Any initiative the child makes to learn something receives a positive response from the parent.

7. *Taking the lead.* The parent takes action and guides the child's behavior so that the child knows what is expected and that the parent is in charge.

8. *Sharing pleasant moments.* The parent takes time to enjoy the child and share in pleasurable moments.

These eight activities are broad enough to be adapted to interactions with children of any age.
Adapted from Anita Weiner, Haggai Kuppermintz, and David Guttmann, "Video Home Training (The Orion Project): A Short-Term Preventive and Treatment Intervention for Families of Young Children," *Family Process* 33 (1994): 441–453.

preschool children. For the first ten or twenty minutes of the weekly hour-and-a-half visit, they videotaped family interactions. At the next visit, the workers and the family members watched the tape that workers had already reviewed for positive interactions. Workers identified and reinforced one form of positive parent–child interaction at each visit. Occasionally, the workers modeled a positive interaction not yet observed in the family.

Prior to the intervention, few of the families interacted positively with their children, rarely making positive comments to children about their behaviors or sharing pleasurable times with them. The families receiving the intervention went from a mean of 1.83 on an index of positive parent–child communication at the start of the program to a mean of 8.04 at the end of the visits, and they maintained these changes six months after the program ended. The mean index of a group of control families who did not receive visits remained unchanged over a comparable period.

The intervention concentrated on increasing positive behaviors, but an index of negative interactions—shouting at children, hitting them, and ignoring their attempts to get close—declined also. When children cried or sought attention for a problem, parents were more likely to pick them up or give them some other form of attention. So, focusing on the positive increased the family closeness that was maintained over time and helped to decrease negative behavior as well.

How Do Children Define a Good Parent?

Thus far we have looked at close relationships from the point of view of how a parent promotes them. Let us look at the qualities children of different ages say they want in the "good parent" or "good mother."

Preschoolers interviewed about the qualities of a good and a bad mother and father suggest that good parents are physically affectionate and nurturant, especially in providing food for children. In addition, good parents like to play games with their children and read to them, and they discipline them—that is, they keep children from doing things they should not, but they do not spank them or slap them in the face. Bad parents have the opposite qualities. They do not hug or kiss, do not fix food, do not play games. They hit and do not let children go outside. Bad parents are also described as irresponsible—they go through red lights, throw chairs at people, and do not read the newspaper.[89]

As children grow older, they continue to value physical nurturing and affection, but they also appreciate qualities reflecting psychological nurturing. Mothers' good qualities include "understanding feelings and moods," "being there when I need her," and "sticking up for me." Children continue to emphasize the limit-setting behaviors in a good mother—"She makes us eat fruit and vegetables," "She yells at me when I need it"—but they want their mother to consider their needs and wishes in setting the rules. Older children still enjoy mutual recreational time—playing, joking, building things together. Finally, as children get older, they appreciate the teaching activities of the good mother.[90]

When early adolescents and their parents talked in a group about their definitions of a good parent, they agreed on several qualities. Early adolescents' definitions touched on three main themes: attention to the child's feelings and individuality, spending time together, and parents' self-control. For early teens, the good parent is one who "listens," "respects you for who you are," "gives you a hug when you are sad." These teens emphasized spending time together, going places together, and having a parent who "knows when to be silly, not always serious." They saw the good parent as one who "manages their temper," "doesn't bark at you," "knows when to stop talking," and "tells you what they want you to do before you have to do it."

In sum, children's descriptions of the good parent point to three main areas: being a sensitive caregiver, a social partner, and a person with self-control. The very qualities research suggests are essential.

MAIN POINTS

Family systems theories emphasize that

- family members form a system and are affected by events in each others' lives
- marital tie strongly influences family well-being and children's development
- good parenting skills have positive effects on children's behavior even when parents have marital difficulties
- siblings form a subsystem that influence each others' social skills

Coparenting involves

- cooperation between caregiving, parenting figures whether married or not
- communication and coordination of effort
- agreed-upon rules and standards of behavior and clear demarcation of power

In 2000, parents

- worked harder but still spent more time in child care than in 1965
- made children center of activities, reducing time with spouses and others

In 2000, children

- divided bulk of time between school and leisure activities
- leisure included structured activities and unstructured activities such as TV viewing
- felt they had enough time with parents but wanted parents to be stress-free

Positive feelings

- help people be more understanding and sympathetic
- contribute to later psychological health and physical health
- contribute to problem-solving skills and social skills

Physical touch and closeness

- help infants stabilize their functioning after birth
- help colicky babies with sleep problems develop longer sleep periods at night and greater alertness during the day
- help adults reduce anxiety, depression, and stress

Close emotional ties rest on the parent's love for the child

- as a unique person
- as expressed in sensitive daily care and in becoming a social partner
- in the sharing of feelings and thoughts

Understanding and expressing feelings

- involves listening to children's feelings and expressing one's own
- is avoided by parents who are dismissive, disapproving, or laissez-faire
- involves five steps of identifying, labeling, and validating feelings and helping the child find appropriate ways to express them

Family rituals and routines

- differ from each other in that rituals have symbolic and emotional meaning and give a sense of identity and routines are practical solutions to everyday tasks
- provide stability by ensuring predictability in family life
- encourage communication among family members
- link family members with the past and the future
- serve as a protective factor in times of difficulty

Storytelling
- begins at birth and helps children discover who they are
- reinforces close relationships as parents and children share experiences

Disruptive negative feelings include
- stress from lack of time with family members
- daily hassles
- family anger

When parents have angry arguments, children
- have negative physical and emotional reactions
- feel distress and emotional insecurity that are associated with adjustment problems
- feel emotionally strengthened when parents compromise and feel good about it
- sometimes try to intervene and stop arguing

Strategies for dealing with negative feelings include
- using family time for satisfying activities
- using communication skills to express feelings appropriately
- developing a support system
- learning to deal with negative feelings

Positive forms of parenting can be encouraged in families experiencing economic hardship by
- focusing on the positive behaviors the family shows
- helping parents take turns with children and listen to children's comments
- helping parents guide the child's behavior
- sharing pleasurable times together

Children see the good parent as
- a sensitive caregiver
- a social partner
- a person with self-control

EXERCISES

1. Imagine a time when you were a child and felt very close to one of your parents (if you like, you can do the exercise for each of your parents), and describe your parent's behavior with you. What qualities of your parent created the closeness? Share these qualities with class members. Is there a common core? If you do this exercise with each of your parents, note gender differences. Have your mother and father at times shown different qualities of closeness with you? Have your classmates experienced differences in their mothers' and fathers' behavior toward sons and daughters?

2. Imagine a time when you were a child and felt distant from one of your parents (again, you can do this for each of your parents), and describe your parent's behavior with you. What qualities of your parent created the distance? Again, share these qualities with class members and find the common core. Are these qualities the opposite of qualities that lead to closeness, or do they represent a variety of dimensions? Do the qualities you discovered in Exercises 1 and 2 support what clinicians and researchers say is important?

3. Take turns practicing active listening with a classmate. Have a partner active-listen as you describe one or several of the following situations, and then you active-listen as your partner does the same: (a) Describe a time when you were frustrated as a child, (b) describe scenes you have witnessed between parents and children in stores or restaurants, (c) follow the directions your instructor hands out for what one child in a problem situation might say.

4. With a classmate, practice sending I-messages. Again, choose from a variety of situations: (a) Recall a situation when a parent was frustrated at you when you were growing up and describe I-messages your parent might have sent, (b) describe public parent–child confrontations you have witnessed and devise appropriate I-messages for the parents, (c) devise I-messages for problem situations presented by your instructor.

5. Think back to the family rituals from your childhood. Which ones were most meaningful to you? The most enjoyable? Which ones do you want to pass on to your children? Which ones do you not want to pass on to your children? Is there a common theme to those you liked and disliked?

ADDITIONAL READINGS

Bianchi, Suzanne M., Robinson, John P., and Milkie, Melissa A. *Changing Rhythms of American Family Life*. New York: Russell Sage Foundation, 2006.

Doherty, William J. *The Intentional Family*. New York: Avon, 1997.

Engel, Susan. *The Stories Children Tell*. New York: Freeman, 1999.

Gottman, John M., and DeClaire, Joan. *The Heart of Parenting: Raising an Emotionally Intelligent Child*. New York: Simon & Schuster, 1997.

Honore, Carl. *Under Pressure: Rescuing Our Children from the Culture of Hyper-Parenting*. New York: HarperCollins, 2008.

5

Supporting Children's Growth and Development

<table>
<tr><td>

CHAPTER TOPICS

In this chapter, you will learn about:

- ■ Parents' modeling
- ■ Ways parents establish healthy lifestyles
- ■ Children's media use and parents' rules and actions to get positive benefits and reduce negative effects of media
- ■ Creating a collaborative family atmosphere through conversations, encouragement, and sensitive discipline
- ■ Ways parents promote prosocial and moral development
- ■ Tool chest for dealing with problem behaviors

</td><td>

IN THE NEWS

San Francisco Chronicle, May 2[1]: Parents wonder about toddlers' and preschoolers' iPhone use for games. See pages 146–147.

</td></tr>
</table>

Test Your Knowledge: Fact or Fiction (True/False)

1. Parents believe they are doing as good a job raising their children as their parents did with them.
2. When people see signs that others do not follow rules, they are less likely to follow rules.
3. Most parents who spank their children do it because they believe it works.
4. Children who watch the most television have time for few other activities.
5. Children as young as age two do kind acts for others.

Parents want children to be healthy, responsible individuals, caring of others and themselves, and believe it is their responsibility to help children develop these qualities. With the hectic pressures of life today, however, parents report they are not doing as good a job as their parents did.[2] They would like more skills to do the job and to control outside influences, such as television, that interfere with what they are trying to teach children. This chapter focuses on how parents can accomplish their goals.

Parents believe it is their responsibility to (1) ensure the physical health and safety of their child, (2) prepare the child to become an economically independent adult, and (3) encourage positive personal and social behaviors such as psychological adjustment and moral responsibility.[3] In this chapter we look at how parents support children's growth and contribute to the development of their children's positive qualities. Table 5-1 provides a useful framework of parenting tasks for children of different ages.

MODELING

Folk wisdom has long advised parents to be what they want their children to become. As we saw in Chapter 2, mirror neurons make it likely that children will copy parents' behavior. New research suggests that not only do people copy what they see others do, they also copy what they think others have done based on seeing the results of their actions.[4] In a series of carefully controlled studies in the community, Dutch researchers demonstrated that people are more likely to litter or steal when they see signs other people have broken community rules. For example, 33 percent of people threw flyers they received on the ground when no graffiti appeared on a building wall, but 69 percent of people littered when graffiti appeared on a wall next to a sign saying "No Graffiti." People were twice as likely to steal an envelope sticking out of a mailbox showing a 5 Euro note when graffiti covered the mailbox or when papers littered the ground as when there was no graffiti or littering (27 percent compared to 13 percent). While these studies were done with adults, there is no reason to think that children are more controlled and disciplined and less influenced by signs of disorder than adults.

So children copy what they see others do and, one suspects, they copy what they think others have done based on signs of order or disorder.

HEALTHY LIFESTYLES

In the United States, life expectancy increased from forty-five years in 1900 to seventy-five years in 1999. The gain of thirty years resulted primarily from the prevention of illnesses rather than from increasingly successful treatments of illnesses such as heart disease. Immunizations, improved nutrition, increased exercise, and better housing and drinking water all contributed to the gains.[5]

Establishing physically healthy environments and health-promoting behaviors are major parental tasks although parents do not place them as high on their list of parental responsibilities as teaching social behaviors. For example, while 84 percent of parents say it is absolutely essential to teach courtesy and politeness, only 68 percent think it is essential to teach healthy eating habits, and 51 percent think it essential to teach good exercise habits.[6] Yet establishing healthy eating, sleeping, and exercise habits promotes competent functioning in childhood and prepares children for a lifetime of health.

■ **T A B L E 5-1**
DEVELOPMENTAL CHALLENGES FACED BY CHILDREN AND CAREGIVERS
FROM INFANCY THROUGH ADOLESCENCE*

Developmental Level	Children's Issues	Caregivers' Role
Infant	Physiological regulation	Sensitivity
	Attachment	Responsiveness
	Interactional synchrony	Availability
Toddler	Exploration of the world	Secure base
	Sense of mastery	Clear, realistic expectations
	Individuation	Consistent discipline
	Autonomous self	Direct, persistent supervision
	Sense of right and wrong	Use of internal-state language
		Emotion regulation
Preschooler	Self-control	Clear roles and values
	Cooperation	Organize/support peer relations
	Sex-role identification	
	Peer relations	Flexible management
School-age child	Self-confidence	Open communication
	Peer group membership	Acceptance
	Close friendship	Indirect monitoring
	School adaptation	
Adolescent	Heterosexual peer relations	Psychological autonomy granting
	Dating	
	Autonomy	Indirect monitoring (especially early)
	Occupational plans	
	Identity formation	Involvement and support
	Romantic relationships	

*From E. Mark Cummings, Patrick T. Davies, and Susan B. Campbell, *Developmental Psychopathology and Family Process: Theory, Research, and Clinical Implications* (New York: Guilford Press, 2000), p. 207. Reprinted with permission.

Safety

Safety measures are the first concern because injuries are the leading cause of death in children and teens. In the United States injuries kill more children than all other diseases combined.[7] Not only do children die from injuries, they also suffer physical trauma requiring hospitalizations, extensive medical care, lengthy recuperations, and lifelong impairments. Initially people thought injuries were the result of random accidents. About forty years ago, however, safety experts realized that like illnesses, injuries could be prevented.

Figure 5-1 describes the major health hazards to children and teens, and actions parents take to reduce injuries. A recent survey of parenting books found that injury prevention was stressed for parents of young children, but books for parents of teens did not emphasize all areas of concern for teen safety, such as wearing bike helmets and safe driving.[8]

To provide a safe home, parents must monitor their own behavior so that their cigarette, alcohol, and drug use do not present a risk to children as well as to their caregiving abilities.[9]

Eating

Parents' tasks here are to (1) provide healthy food and nutrition to children, and (2) help children develop healthy eating habits. These tasks are vitally important because good nutrition in early childhood promotes motor and cognitive development.[10] Poorly nourished children are less physically active and they perform more poorly on measures of attention span and short-term memory. While nutrient-rich diets can improve performance, adults who were poorly nourished over long periods of time in childhood continue to show lower performance on cognitive tests than well-nourished adults.

Good nutrition and eating habits are important also because the number of overweight children has tripled, from 5 percent in 1980 to almost 16 percent today.[11] Being overweight and the intake of fatty foods are related to the development of many physical problems, such as heart disease and diabetes, that compromise the quality of children's lives in adulthood. Parents get guidance from medical and health personnel regarding nutrition, recommended foods, and sizes of portions, as these recommendations change from time to time.

Parents establish regular mealtimes and routines so that eating becomes a happy social occasion.[12] Sitting down and eating dinner together each day, with pleasant conversation and no television, benefits children physically and psychologically. People eat more sensible portions, and children feel more emotionally secure. As we shall see when we discuss sleep, eating together brings a sense of stability and the absence of that routine can result in feelings of isolation and insecurity. Discussions of conflicts or problems should be postponed for another time.

It is especially important to discourage eating in front of the television because watching television while eating encourages eating high-calorie and fatty snacks. Children who reduced television time did not exercise more, but they reduced their eating in front of the television and that led to slower weight gain.[13]

■ **FIGURE 5-1**
WAYS TO PREVENT ACCIDENTS AND INJURIES*

Bedroom

1. Install devices that prevent windows from opening and child from getting out or falling out.
2. Cover electrical outlets.
3. Inspect toys for broken and jagged edges.

Bathroom

1. Keep safety caps on all bottles.
2. Keep medicines, aspirin, rubbing alcohol in locked cabinets.
3. Adjust water heater so water is not scalding hot.
4. Use rubber mats in bath and shower.
5. Keep bathmat next to tub and shower.
6. Do not allow young child alone in bath.

Living Room

1. Cover electrical outlets.
2. Check safety of plants.
3. Put rubber-backed pad under small scatter rugs.
4. Pad sharp edges of tables.
5. Have screen for fireplace.

Have lock for door.

Stairs

1. With young child, block off tops and bottoms of stairs.
2. If necessary, mark top and bottom steps.

Kitchen

1. Keep vomit-inducing syrup on hand.
2. Store soaps, cleaners, all poisonous chemicals in locked cabinet.
3. Have guard around burners or use back burners on stove so child cannot pull contents onto self.
4. Unplug all appliances when not in use.
5. Store sharp knives in safe place.
6. Store matches out of child's reach.

Dining Room

1. Cover electrical outlets.

Garage-Workroom

1. Keep tools out of child's reach.
2. Keep poisons locked up.
3. Store paints and other toxic materials out of child's reach.
4. Store nails and screws in safe place.

General

1. Install smoke alarms in house.
2. Have fire extinguishers in kitchen, most rooms in house, and garage.
3. Keep firearms out of home; if in the home, keep ammunition and unloaded guns in separate locked cabinets; become aware of firearms in homes the child visits and be sure they have same precautions.
4. Keep poison control, fire, and police department telephone numbers by the telephone.
5. Learn infant, child, and adult cardiopulmonary resuscitation and how to access 911.
6. Never allow buckets of water to remain after use when infants and young children are in home, as children can drown in them.
7. Discourage use of infant walkers.
8. Use currently approved automobile safety restraints for children of all ages and parents.
9. For all children and adolescents, use helmets for bicycling, skate boarding, and in-line skating; use appropriate padding and safety equipment for all sports.
10. Teach children pedestrian safety in parking lots, street corners; do not let children under six or seven cross the streets by themselves.
11. Have fire escape routes planned from home in event of fire, and make sure children know them well.
12. Never believe that children under five can be water safe, even if they have had lessons; be sure that children over five have swim lessons; but no child should swim alone, and even adults should always be encouraged to swim with another person present.
13. Discuss the role of alcohol in car and water accidents with early and late adolescents.

*From: The American Academy of Pediatrics Committee on Injury and Poison Prevention, "Office-Based Counseling for Injury Prevention," *Pediatrics* 94 (1994): 566–567.

Parents model moderate intake of healthy foods as children prefer the foods parents eat. In introducing new foods, parents cannot expect children to like them the first time, but must introduce them as many as eight or ten times before children accept them.[14] Parents can also work with schools to eliminate high-fat, high-sugar foods in the cafeteria and in vending machines. While recent studies indicate that school changes by themselves do not control children's weight, they can still contribute to the healthy eating habits established at home.[15]

There is no one simple change that will encourage healthy eating, but many small changes can help, most of which are under parents' control.

Exercise

Physical activity contributes not only to children's physical fitness and skill, but also to increases in children's self-esteem and self-image and to decreases in anxiety and stress.[16] Physical well-being in childhood predicts overall long-term physical health, reducing the risk of heart disease, osteoporosis, and in women, breast cancer.

Our increasingly sedentary habits have resulted in decreasing levels of physical fitness. In 2001, 77 percent of California's fifth-, seventh-, and ninth-graders failed six aerobic strength tests, and performance levels decreased with age.[17] While physical fitness was lowest in urban and poor areas of the state, even in wealthy Marin County 28 percent of children were described as physically unfit. Mark Dessauer, communications director of the organization Active Living by Design, commented, "Kids today are better at running a software program than running a mile. They have stronger thumbs than legs."[18]

Many influences, both physical and social, contribute to physical activity. Genetic factors such as gender—boys are more active than girls—play a role.[19] Social factors, such as the safety of the neighborhood, school policies regarding recess, and resources for physical activity, play a role. Having friends who are physically active can encourage sports and outdoor activities.

Again, however, parents play a major role as models, and their influence is critically important. Physically active mothers tend to have children who are physically active. Parental inactivity is a strong predictor of child inactivity. Families are strongly advised to begin exercising together to get the benefits of exercise and reduce the problems brought on by being sedentary.

Sleep

Sleep is necessary for life. Rats deprived of sleep die faster than rats deprived of food.[20] Sleep is so important that newborns spend sixteen to twenty hours a day sleeping, and by the time children are two years of age, more than half their life—fourteen months—has been spent sleeping. Similarly, throughout childhood and adolescence, adequate, good-quality sleep is related to physical, cognitive, and emotional well-being.

Yet we are becoming a nation of sleep-deprived individuals. A recent headline in the *New York Times* stated, "Poll Finds Even Babies Don't Get Enough Rest."[21]

It reported the result of a survey by the National Sleep Foundation that toddlers get on average two hours less than the minimum amount of sleep recommended and preschoolers get four hours less on average. Furthermore, 18–21 percent of schoolchildren report feeling tired during the day, and 63–87 percent of adolescents report they do not get as much sleep as they need.[22]

Even though sleep is essential, its function is not well understood. Several theories exist.[23] First, it is thought that, during sleep, the brain repairs itself, restoring depleted energy levels, repairing damaged cells, and growing new brain connections. Sleep is also thought to consolidate recent learning in long-term memory. Sleep is related to the regulation of metabolic processes related to obesity. Finally, healthy sleep is related to daily alertness and reduced accidents (e.g., while driving).

Research demonstrates the importance of sleep for healthy cognitive growth. When children add one hour of sleep to their nightly pattern, whatever that pattern is, their improvement on cognitive measures is the equivalent of two years of growth.[24] Other work demonstrates that adequate amounts of sleep reduce racial and social differences on cognitive tests.[25] When schoolchildren from different ethnic and social groups get adequate amounts of sleep, their performance on assessment tests is similar. When sleep is disrupted, traditional performance differences between racial and social status groups appear on these cognitive tasks. The performance of European Americans and high social status groups is less affected by decreased sleep than that of African American and lower social status children.

Helping children develop healthy sleep habits is a critical task for parents not only because poor sleep patterns are associated with lack of alertness, poor attention span, and poor memory as well as learning problems,[26] but because sleep problems are also associated with emotional problems such as aggressiveness and depression.[27]

Sleep is a family affair. Parents' warmth, stability,[28] and marital harmony influence amount and quality of children's,[29] teens', and young adults' sleep.[30] In order to sleep well, children seem to need to feel emotionally secure and relaxed and not vigilant. Because parents' actions differ depending on the age of the child and parents' values, we take up the topic of sleep in the appropriate age-related chapter. Here we simply emphasize parents' critical role in ensuring that their children develop healthy sleep habits to prevent the behavioral, learning, and emotional problems associated with sleep deprivation, which is becoming increasingly common in our society.

Play

Every child's day should include some time to play and part of that time should be play with parents. A longitudinal study of children's activities and behavior in the first six years of life found that those children who in infancy and early childhood had opportunities to engage in productive play developed greater self-control and were less likely to have behavior problems in first grade.[31] The exact reasons for the positive effects of play are not known. It may be that play creates feelings of pleasure and joy that enable children to adjust to demands more easily, as we saw in Chapter 4. It may be play drains off tension so there is less negative emotion to control. Furthermore, it may give children feelings of relaxation that increase ease of adjustment to others' requests.

Play with parents may only be 20 minutes, but it should be a time in which parents do not make demands on children or insist on some behavior, a time during which parents follow children's leads and engage with children under their direction. Children spend so much time in the day doing what parents or other caregivers request that it is important to have a time simply to play and interact for fun. The exact nature of the play will depend on the age of the child and the child's interests. With older children, play time may be just conversation, but it is nevertheless time set aside for pleasurable activity. Within safety limits, children can do what they want, and parents engage without giving corrections or criticisms.

INCLUDING MEDIA IN FAMILY LIFE

Families live in a media-rich world that includes books, magazines, television, ipods, and computers. The average home with children from age eight to eighteen has three to four televisions, two to three VCRs/DVD players, two video game consoles, and one to two computers. Two-thirds of the children this age have televisions in their bedrooms, and 30 percent have computers there as well.[32] Thirty-three percent of children under age six have televisions in their bedrooms, 23 percent a VCR/DVD player, and 5 percent a computer.[33] Children spend more time with media than in any other activity except sleeping.

Parents' behaviors powerfully shape children's media use, but many parents feel uncertain about how to use their power to manage media use. In this section we look at family media use, then on media's impact on children's lives, and finally at specific actions parents can take to control media's influence on their families.

Media Use

Children under Age Six   Media use starts early and grows through the toddler years, according to a national survey of one thousand parents of children under age six.[34] Although the American Academy of Pediatrics recommends no screen time for children under age two,[35] the average child that age has about an hour of screen time per day, rising to two hours per day at age two and remaining there. Screen activities are the most frequent activity of young children and twice as much time is spent in them as in reading activities.

Children between Age Eight and Eighteen   In 2005, a representative national sample of 2,032 children answered detailed questionnaires about the availability and daily recreational use of media.[36] Children in this sample report that they devote an average of six and a half hours a day, seven days a week, to recreational media use, primarily television and listening to music. Table 5-2. presents the amount of recreational time per day spent with each form of media. Since children use more than one media at a time, they put the equivalent of eight and a half hours of media use into six and a half hours a day—about the equivalent of a full-time job with some overtime.

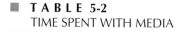

TABLE 5-2
TIME SPENT WITH MEDIA

Average Amount of Time 8- to 18-Year-Olds Spend per Day

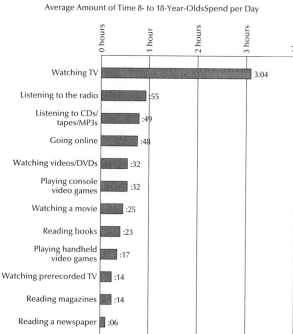

From Victoria Rideout, Donald F. Roberts, and Ulla G. Foehr, "Generation M: Media in the Lives of 8–18-year-olds" (#7251), Henry J. Kaiser Family Foundation, March 2005, www.kff.org. p. 7.

TABLE 5-3
TIME SPENT IN NON-MEDIA ACTIVITIES

Average Amount of Time Young People Spend per Day

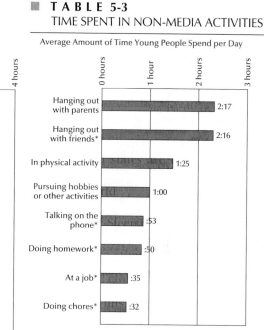

*Data collected among 7th- to 12th-graders only. All other results are among all 8- to 18-year-olds.

From Victoria Rideout, Donald F. Roberts, and Ulla G. Foehr, "Generation M: Media in the Lives of 8–18-Year-Olds" (#7251), Henry J. Kaiser Family Foundation, March 2005, www.kff.org. p. 8.

Table 5-3 presents the percentage of time children spend in non-media activities to understand how media use fits into their overall pattern of activities. Children who report extensive media use also report spending a significant amount of time hanging out with parents and friends, pursuing hobbies, and reading for pleasure, so media use does not appear to displace these activities. However, media use may affect amount of time spent doing homework and chores, as children spend a small amount of time in these activities. Media use is three to six times more frequent than any other activity in their lives.

There are gender, age, and ethnic differences. Teens spend more time listening to music and using the computer than younger children, who spend more time watching television. Boys spend more time playing video games, an average of seventy-two minutes each day compared to twenty-five minutes for girls. Girls listen to music more than boys do. African American children watch more television and movies and play more video games than Latino or European American children do. European American children watch less television and fewer movies and play fewer video games, and Latino children fall between these two groups.[37] Children of higher social status read more, use the computer more, and watch less television.[38]

Multimedia Use About 20 percent of the time is spent using two media. Television and video games have the highest percentage of time as the sole focus of attention—55 percent of the time.[39] Children, however, spend almost half their TV time in secondary activities such as eating (14 percent), doing homework (6 percent), and chores and talking on the phone (both 4 percent). Computers were the most likely media to be used with other forms of media.

Research suggests there is a limit to the amount of information that the brain can take in at one time, and when we do two things, we devote decreased resources to each. Fewer facts were recalled about news stories, for example, when they were presented in the CNN format, with other information crawling along the bottom of the screen, than when stories were presented one at a time in a simple visual format.[40] Similarly, more facts were recalled from a lecture when students had their laptops closed than when they were open and students were encouraged to get more information from the Internet during the lecture.

Parents' Media Use Parents of young children report an average of two and a quarter hours of screen use per day.[41] Thirty percent report none or less than an hour per day, and 42 percent report more than two hours per day. Children whose parents have more than two hours a day of screen time also have increased screen use (30 minutes more) compared to children whose parents have less than an hour of screen time.

Parents of children under age six also report encouraging children's media use for several reasons. It gives parents free time to do chores, relax, and watch television themselves. Media use also provides a way to interrupt children's bickering and rule breaking. And some parents use media to calm children down and help them sleep. Some believe that playing video games is a way for fathers and sons to bond and have fun together.

In many homes, parents have the television on even if no one is watching. In almost one-third of children's homes, the television is on all the time, and in an additional 30 percent of homes, television is on during mealtimes. Children with background television watch more television and are less likely to read and be read to.

Parents' Attitudes about Media Parents' attitudes about media vary.[42] They view computers as generally helpful to children (69 percent) and view video games rather negatively, with 49 percent believing they mostly hurt children. About television, parents appear ambivalent. Although 70 percent believe children have learned information and positive behaviors from television, about a third of parents have seen children imitate negative, mostly aggressive behaviors from it.[43]

Media's Impact on Children's Activities and Development

When children read more, especially when they read for pleasure, they develop literacy skills that are related to school success. The concern is that children do not do enough reading because other activities displace it.[44] When television is a constant presence in family life, reading occurs less frequently.

Of audiovisual media, television has been the focus of research on the effect of children's media use on growth and development. Television affects viewers powerfully. For example, one-year-old infants reacted to TV actresses' emotional preferences for toys just as they had copied a mother's emotional responses, avoiding toys actresses did not like and playing with toys she viewed positively.[45]

Positive Impact of Educational Programs   Watching educational television programs can increase children's literacy and number skills and their knowledge of science and history. Studies that followed children whose viewing habits were first recorded in the preschool years and noted their behavior, interests, and viewing habits when they were teens found that children who viewed educational and informative programs as preschoolers reported higher grades, reading more books, greater creativity, valuing achievement more, and less aggression than students who watched the general entertainment fare available.[46]

The amount of time preschoolers watched was not predictive of adolescent qualities, but the content of what they watched was. The results were more consistent for boys than for girls and appeared when intelligence, family variables, and adolescent media use were controlled.

The positive impact of video games and computer programs has not been extensively explored as it will be in the future. We do know that video games increase visual processing abilities and visual motor skills.[47] However, we do know that preschoolers can be trained briefly with computer games to increase attention skills, which are reflected in better scores on cognitive tests and overall cognitive capacity,[48] much as the Tools of the Mind program did (described in Chapter 2). Science, math, and writing skills are only a few of the areas that can be explored with the wise use of technology that is in the process of development.[49]

Children's Sleep and Attention Span   Television viewing in children under three years of age is related to irregular nap and bedtime schedules in a sample of 2,000 families, independent of the family's social status, mother's health, family's functioning, and parenting behavior in getting the child to bed.[50] As noted earlier, poor sleep has negative consequences for children.

Second, in a large sample of 2,500 children, amount of television exposure when children were ages one to three was related to mothers' reports of poor concentration, impulsivity, and restlessness at age seven.[51] Even when controlling for the child's gestational age and characteristics of the family, such as social status, parents' substance use, maternal mental health, and social status, the findings remained: The more television the child watched, the more likely the mother was to describe the child as having attention problems.

Third, television viewing before age three was also associated with poorer performance on tests of reading and math achievement when children were six and seven[52]; television viewing between ages three and five did not have similar negative consequences. It is possible that watching television at very young ages displaces other activities.

The placement of the TV set matters. Children with bedroom sets scored less well on tests of achievement in math, reading, and language arts than children without bedroom sets.[53]

Television viewing has an indirect effect on weight. Television viewing appears to stimulate intake of high-calorie snacks; decreasing school-age children's viewing time was related to decreases in body mass index.[54]

Aggression   The first concern regarding television use thirty-five years ago centered on its effects in producing aggressive behavior in young children who witnessed aggression on television. Reviews of the most careful studies "indicate that the effects of television violence-viewing accounts for about 10 percent of the variance in child aggression, which approximately equals the magnitude of effect of cigarette smoking on lung cancer."[55]

Viewing violent television is not only related to childhood aggression, but also to adult aggression for both boys and girls. Longitudinal follow-up of two hundred children whose viewing habits were studied when they were in elementary school found that both boys and girls who watched violent television programs as children showed serious adult anger and violence as adults with spouses and other individuals.[56] For example, 40 percent of men and 35 percent of women who were high TV-violence watchers had pushed or shoved a spouse, and almost two-thirds of men and half the women self-reported a crime in the last year. Controlling for the child's initial level of aggression, intellectual level, family social status, and parenting style did not change the results.

Recently the American Psychological Association (APA) has called for more research on the effects of violence in video games. The APA believes video games may be more harmful than other media because of the interactive nature of the games and has adopted "a resolution calling for the reduction of all violence in video games and other interactive media marketed to children and youth."[57]

Sexual Attitudes and Behavior   Accumulating research suggests that teens who are exposed to media with high sexual content initiate sexual activity at younger ages.

Sexual content occurs on 83 percent of the most popular adolescent TV shows, about seven times per hour. Sexual intercourse is implicitly or explicitly depicted in 20 percent of the encounters.[58] It is rare that serious negative consequences of sexual behavior (pregnancy or sexually transmitted diseases) are shown. Teens who view more television with sexual content tend to overestimate the occurrence of sexual behaviors in everyday life and to develop more permissive attitudes about premarital sex than teens who watch shows with less sexual content.

A longitudinal study relating teen viewing to teen behavior over the course of the next year found that teens who watched more shows with sexual content were more likely to initiate sexual intercourse during the course of the year than those who watched fewer shows.[59] Hearing talk about sexual actions had the same effects on behavior as witnessing a scene. An adolescent who was at the 90th percentile in viewing shows with sexual content had twice the probability of initiating sexual intercourse in the next year as someone at the 10th percentile.

Sexual activity naturally increases in the course of adolescence, but viewing shows with sexual content in a sense seemed to "age" teens because they took on the sexual behaviors of teens one to two years older than they. For example, a twelve-year-old who watched the most sexual content on television behaved like a fourteen- or fifteen-year-old who saw the least. This study needs to be replicated, but it does suggest that viewing sexual behavior influences adolescent behavior.

Similar findings occurred when the sexual content of several media—music, movies, television, and magazines—was related to teens' sexual behavior over a two-year period.[60] Teens with the highest sexual diet were twice as likely to initiate sexual intercourse in the next two years as teens with the lowest exposure. The results were significant for European American teens when other factors were controlled, but were not significant for African American teens because other control variables such as parent and peer attitudes were more powerful.

The Internet poses another challenge for parents. It contains images with sexual content and the possibility of sexual solicitations. Twenty percent of teens reported having stumbled onto explicit sexual images accidentally in the last year, and 19 percent reported having received an unwanted sexual solicitation in the last year. Most of these instances (73 percent) occurred while the teen was surfing the Net at home.[61]

Rules about Media Use

In general, parents have fewer rules about media use than might be expected. Parents of younger children under six years of age are more likely to have rules about media use than parents of older children. Sixty percent of parents with children under six have rules about how much their children can watch and 85 percent have rules about the content of programming.[62] These rules seem to have an effect as children in households with rules watch thirty minutes less of television a day than children in homes with no rules.

Fewer than half the children age eight to eighteen (46 percent) report they have rules about television watching, and of those who do, only half report that the rules are usually enforced—the other half report they are enforced some, a little, or none of the time.[63] Yet for children age twelve to eighteen, rules reduced television viewing one hour per day.

When it comes to computers and video games, only a small percentage of children report they have rules—about 20 percent for computer use and about 17 percent for video games, and having rules makes little difference in the amount of time children spend with these media.

Whereas about 25 percent of parents use some form of filter or control on computer use, about 30 percent of teens say they have claimed to be older to get into websites and have succeeded.[64]

Parents' interactions with children around media use have effects.[65] Reading with children and talking about what is being read increase children's reading and comprehension. Parents' discussions with children about TV and movies influence children's interpretations of what they see. School programs that increase children's awareness of media use and encourage reductions in their use have reduced use in elementary school children, in turn reducing their aggressiveness and weight gain.[66] So interactions with children around media use are effective.

Parents can talk about the rules and the reasons for them so children understand why they are important.

Parental Actions to Control Media

Parents can take many actions to get the positive benefits of media use and reduce the negative ones.

1. Parents can limit the number of media in the home and locate them in places to reduce their use. For example, televisions and computers should be removed from the bedroom and placed in family living areas.

2. Turn media off during all mealtimes and when no one is watching and avoid eating while watching television.

3. Interact with children around media use. Watch programs with them, talk about shows or video games and surf the Net together. Use these interactions

as opportunities to learn about your child's thinking and interests and have the child learn about yours; have media used as family entertainment.

4. Use V-chips, video game ratings, and computer filters to control programming.

5. Set media rules for children and enforce them. The American Academy of Pediatrics discourages any media for children until they are two years of age, and for children and teens recommends no more than one or two hours of quality programming per day.[67]

6. Model appropriate media use.

7. Use media most often for learning and family interaction rather than relaxation, and use board games and reading together to relax.

When parents and children bond together around media use, children can understand parents' concerns about the media and may be more willing to follow rules and share upsetting experiences they have had with other people on the Internet.

Parents can also take community action with other parents and community organizations to get the kinds of programs they want for their children on television or to find ways to block unacceptable sites or solicitations on the Internet.

Patricia Greenfield points out that no one medium—be it books, television, video games, or computers—can provide all the cognitive skills a person needs. Special video games may play a role in developing visual processing skills and visual motor skills and in increasing attention span. Reading excels in developing thoughtfulness, reflection, and critical analysis of material, qualities society requires in accumulating and evaluating information and knowledge. Reading also helps to develop imagination and creativity. She concludes that, "The developing mind still needs a balanced media diet."[68]

A Healthy Lifestyle Is a Simple Lifestyle

In Chapter 2 we discussed that we live with a genetic inheritance that developed tens of thousands of years ago when we lived a physically active life in small bands of closely attached people who ate simple foods and slept long hours. Our fast-paced, multitasking society that stimulates us as many of the 24 hours in a day as we choose makes it hard to meet our needs for physical activity, simple foods, good-quality sleep, and close, emotionally secure contact with our relatives.

As we saw in Chapter 4, parents have focused intently on meeting the needs of their children so it is possible to have those close ties. But for food, physical activity, and sleep, we have to plan carefully so our needs are met. This means managing the technological devices that crowd into our homes so we get the best of what they can offer us, and barring the negative influences from entering.

CREATING A COLLABORATIVE FAMILY ATMOSPHERE

Psychologists have identified a family atmosphere of collaboration that enhances children's growth and enables them to learn the lessons parents most want to teach.

An Emotional Climate of Mutual Responsiveness

Parents create a family culture of cooperation and mutual responsiveness from the earliest days of a child's life. Sensitive parents provide responsive care that meets children's individual needs. Such care creates harmonious parent–child relationships and helps to establish a secure attachment between parent and child.[69] That attachment, in turn, encourages cooperation and a willingness to attend to parents' requests since parents attend to children's.

When children have secure attachments to parents, they respond to such gentle parenting techniques as reasoning, so parents need not rely on assertive strategies such as threatening and spanking. Reasoning with children helps children develop internal moral standards that then determine their conduct. Children with insecure attachments are not responsive to gentle discipline.

For several reasons, secure attachments may create a climate of receptive compliance.[70] First, when children feel secure with caregivers, they may be better able to understand and remember parents' messages because they are not anxious about their parents' acceptance of them. Second, when children feel secure with parents, they are happy and enjoy carrying out parents' requests. Third, secure attachments may increase children's attention and orientation to their parents' presence and what they want.

Although it is easier to establish an atmosphere of receptive compliance when children are infants, it is possible to create such an atmosphere when children are elementary-school students and teenagers.[71] Recall the discussion of Gerald Patterson's work in Chapter 2, which indicated that parents can create a positive atmosphere of collaboration with school-age children by paying positive attention to their behavior, spending time in enjoyable activities, encouraging them in their activities, and engaging in problem solving when problems arise. All these actions increase children's willingness to listen and comply with rules.

Making children partners in routines as soon as they can participate contributes to a collaborative atmosphere.[72] Parents can show infants how to cooperate in dressing by guiding them through the actions in a playful way and letting them push their arm through a sleeve or stick their head out of the top of a shirt. Toddlers like to help, and many parents discourage their participation because everything takes longer, but finding small tasks to include young children in routines helps them develop a clearer idea or a script of the behaviors that make up the family routines around eating, picking up, and cleaning.

Conversations

A second step in establishing a collaborative family atmosphere is to talk—about what people are doing, what they are thinking or feeling, whatever is happening.[73] In a world in which communication is becoming increasingly electronic, direct talking time is decreasing. As we noted in Chapter 4, storytelling is important because it talks about what has happened and creates closeness. Conversations as we talk about them here are about routine events and are more informational, concerning what is happening now and in the future. For example, a mother can have a conversation about what she and other family members will be doing on a Saturday morning. "We have to stop at the store to pick up the snacks for the picnic that we are all going to after Jimmy's soccer game." Such conversations help children see how different activities fit into the whole family's needs and schedule.

Parents can talk about the rules and the reasons for them so children can understand why they are important. Even when children are young and cannot understand the exact words, the tone of voice indicates there is a routine to follow.[74] As children gain greater verbal understanding, clarity about the purpose of the rules and the effects on others when rules are not followed help children remember the rules and follow them. Talking when everyone's emotions are calm increases the likelihood children will hear and take in what parents are saying. Conversation in the midst of conflict is not as useful.

Talking about rules in a telegraphic fashion, saying only a few words, does not have as great an impact on children. When conversations describe how rules help everyone, children gain a richer understanding of how people relate to one another in a caring and considerate way.

At times of actual misbehavior and rule-breaking, verbal strategies of discipline have many benefits. Children's social and emotional competence grows and they are able to internalize the rules when mothers remain calm, use reasoning, and avoid threats and physical force. Forcing children with yelling and angry gestures increases children's frustration and defiance. In a later section, we discuss mutual problem solving that helps parents verbally express themselves in positive ways at times of frustration and irritation.

Reading stories illustrating the behaviors you want to see in your children reinforces your values in a way that appeals to children. For example, *The Little Engine That Could* illustrates for young children the value of courage and persistence in meeting a challenge.[75] For older children, stories about adventure or historical events can serve as springboards for longer discussions about approved behaviors.

Encouragement

Drawing on the insights of Alfred Adler—the first of Freud's followers to modify psychoanalytic theory and focus on individuals' healthy, purposive, and social behavior—Rudolf Dreikurs proposed positive child-rearing strategies that rely on encouragement to stimulate children's built-in capacities to develop healthy, effective behaviors.[76] Because children naturally seek to develop their abilities and become competent and important members in the family, parents' main tasks are to provide an environment for growth and to avoid the use of parental power to force or punish children.

A central feature in the growth-promoting environment is encouragement, which Dreikurs defined as "a continuous process aimed at giving the child a sense of self-respect and a sense of accomplishment."[77] Parents' tone of voice in speaking to children, their gestures, their affection, their willingness to play with children all communicate to children that they are valued and well-loved family members.

Parents provide encouragement when they (1) give children independence to act on their own—even babies can have opportunities to amuse themselves,

INTERVIEW
with Susan Harter

Susan Harter, a professor of psychology at the University of Denver, has spent forty years studying the development of the self and self-esteem and has written numerous articles and chapters on the subject.

You have done a great deal of research on self-esteem. More than any other quality, I would say, parents hope to help children develop self-esteem. What can they do to promote it in their children?
We have identified two broad themes that impact children's self-esteem. First, the unconditional support and positive regard of parents and others in the child's world are particularly critical during the early years. What do we mean by support? It is communicating to children that you like them as people for who or what they are.

That sounds relatively easy but is in fact extremely difficult. Most of us as parents are far more skilled at providing conditional regard or support for children even though we are unaware we are doing it. We approve of our child if he cleans up his room or shares or doesn't hit his brother. So our support is conditional on his conduct. However, it isn't perceived by children as supportive at all. Basically it specifies how the child can please the parents. That does not feel good to children.

Unconditional regard validates children as worthy people and lets them know they are appreciated for who they are, for their strengths and weaknesses. It also involves listening to them, which is very validating to children as well as adults. So many well-meaning parents, and I make the same mistake, preach at their kids because we think we have a lot to say. We think we're teaching when we are really preaching. We don't refrain from talking; we don't shut up, listen well, and take the child's point of view seriously.

With unconditional support early on, children internalize positive regard so that when they are older, they can approve of themselves, pat themselves on the back, give themselves psychological hugs—all of which contribute to high self-esteem.

Another major part of self-esteem, beginning at about age eight, is feeling competent and adequate across the various domains of life. One does not have to feel competent in every domain in order to experience high self-esteem. Rather, one needs to feel competent in those domains that he or she judges to be *important*. Profiles of competence for two children in the different areas of athletic, social, and intellectual competence can look very similar, but one child can have high self-esteem while the other can have low self-esteem. They both can feel competent in the same areas and feel inadequate in the same other areas. What distinguishes the low-self-esteem child is the fact that areas of incompetence are very important to his or her feeling of being worthwhile; thus the child doesn't feel good about him- or herself. The high-self-esteem child feels the low areas are very unimportant and so still feels good about him- or herself.

feed themselves, and as toddlers, share in family chores so they learn their own capabilities; (2) identify the child's positive contributions and help—"It's a real help when you empty the trash," or "Thank you for taking the napkins to the table"; and (3) teach children to ask for what they need so parents can better meet their needs—"Tell me what is upsetting you so we can see what can be done."

Parents encourage children by teaching them how to do basic self-care routines and chores—like dressing themselves or making their bed. Parents anticipate that children will need time to develop skills, and they do not criticize or tear down children's confidence with statements like, "I can do it for you faster" or "You are too little to set the table." When children are frustrated with the process of learning, parents call attention to the challenge of the task and to the gains the child is making. "Practicing the piano is hard in the beginning, but you are learning all the scales, and you are able to play more pieces."

In all families, children make mistakes. Dreikurs describes parents' tendencies to overemphasize these errors by pointing out every minor mistake and continually telling children what they must do to improve. Under such a regime, children may feel they have to be perfect in order to gain acceptance and such a fear can keep children from trying activities because mistakes are so painful. As Dreikurs observed,

> We all make mistakes. Very few are disastrous. Many times we won't even know that a given action is a mistake until after it is done and we see the results! Sometimes we even have to make the mistake in order to find out that it is a mistake. *We must have the courage to be imperfect*—and to allow our children to be imperfect. Only in this way can we function, progress, and grow. Our children will maintain their courage and learn more readily if we minimize the mistakes and direct their attention toward the positive. What is to be done now that the mistake is made leads to progress forward and stimulates courage. Making a mistake is not nearly as important as what we do about it afterwards.[78]

According to Dreikurs, mistakes are incompletions, not failures. They are signs that the child is trying to do something, exerting effort, but is not quite ready to do the task completely. The child may need more time to learn or practice a skill. Though unfortunate in that they take up time and sometimes cost money, mistakes are valuable because a child learns what is not effective. In addition, many warm family memories center on mistakes that were overcome. So parents help children figure out what the next step is.

Sensitive Discipline

Femmie Juffer, Marian Bakermans-Kranenburg, and Marinus van IJzendoorn have combined concepts of attachment theory with the learning concepts of Gerald Patterson, described in Chapter 2, to help parents and children gain control of impulsive, aggressive, inhibited behaviors. While designed for parents of toddlers, the program's positive emphasis in discipline can be adapted for parents of older children. The program emphasizes the following basic guidelines for parents:[79]

1. Use reasoning to help children understand the need for rules and routines and the benefits for all that come from following the rules, saying, for example, "We all need to go to bed at our bedtime, even Mom and Dad, so we will get enough sleep and have energy to play and work tomorrow."

2. Help children refocus attention on positive alternatives when they are frustrated (e.g., when children are hungry and insist on eating cookies just before dinner, parents can say, "Why not help me set the table so we can eat sooner" or "You can clean a carrot and eat that").

3. Pay attention to the many times that children follow rules and engage in positive actions, and express appreciation for their behavior.

4. Empathize with children's feelings, desires, and stage of life and verbalize what you think they might be feeling. "I know it's hard to have your little brother grab your cars and play with them, then forget where he left them so you can't find them." Or, "I know it's hard to have to do chores before you leave the house on Saturday morning. Maybe we can find a different time."

5. Help children withdraw from a tantrum or angry confrontation by taking a time out in the living room or hallway. Parents must stay calm and say they will be available for talk or play when the time out is finished. When they are young, children spend one minute for each year of children's age in time out. With older children, parents and children can take a time out to cool down and discuss the problem later.

6. Talk to children during routines, explaining them and answering questions, especially if the routine is not a happy one, such as going to the dentist.

7. Give children advance warnings when it is time to shift activities and give choices when possible.

8. Be available for play and fun.

PROMOTING PROSOCIAL AND MORAL DEVELOPMENT

Parents want to know how to help children grow into responsible and moral individuals—91 percent of parents say it is absolutely essential that they teach their children to be honest and truthful, and 83 percent say it is absolutely essential to teach children self-control and self-discipline.[80] This area of research and theory provides useful guidelines for doing that.

Prosocial and moral development integrate research and theory from the areas of cognitive, social, and emotional development to understand how helping, sharing, and moral behavior develop. Here we discuss the area broadly and take up more detailed topics in the developmental chapters (Chapters 7–12) in sections on emotional growth and self-regulation. We focus first on prosocial behavior because it appears early in children's lives.

The Development of Prosocial Behavior and Reasoning

Prosocial behavior, defined as "voluntary behavior intended to benefit another,"[81] includes such actions as comforting, helping others, and sharing with others. In its most advanced form, prosocial behavior involves a desire to help others without any concrete benefit to oneself, and in fact, sometimes at a cost to the self. Prosocial behavior is thought to rest on feelings of empathy, defined as awareness of others' distress and a desire to help. Young children progress from global, diffuse empathy to more refined feelings of empathy.[82]

Newborns show the beginnings of prosocial behavior in the form of crying empathically in response to the crying of other newborns. Newborns' diffuse empathy becomes refined as infants and toddlers gain a clearer sense of themselves and others. Sometime in the second year of life, toddlers have sufficient awareness of others' needs and feelings as separate from their own to engage in prosocial behaviors. Initially, toddlers may respond to the distress of others in a self-centered way—by seeking comfort from others when they see another is upset. When they are a little older, they help others by giving or doing what they would like in the situation—such as giving their security blanket or a favorite toy to a child.

As children grow, develop language, and have greater social awareness and understanding, they are better able to recognize and respond empathically to others' needs, giving what the other person would like. In the school years, children's social understanding is greater and they are able to empathize with a broader range of people and with groups of people as well. In adolescence, helping behaviors expand as teens get involved in volunteer activities and help others on an ongoing basis.

Those children who are most helpful at young ages continue to be the most helpful when they are older. Those children who become overwhelmed at others' distress may not to be helpful as they are caught up in their personal reactions to others' distress.

Like helping behavior, sharing shows a similar increase over time. William Damon found stages in children's reasons for sharing and dividing property fairly.[83] At the first level at about age four, children share on the basis of their own personal desires—they give what they feel like giving and keep the entire amount if they want. At the second level, children in early elementary school share on the basis of equality; all children should get the same amount. At level 3, children share on the basis of a more abstract principle of equity—what is fair and takes account of each person's effort and contribution to a task so some get more than

Young children can engage in helping behavior when parents give them opportunities.

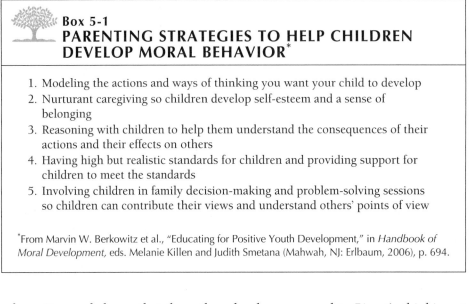

Box 5-1
PARENTING STRATEGIES TO HELP CHILDREN DEVELOP MORAL BEHAVIOR*

1. Modeling the actions and ways of thinking you want your child to develop
2. Nurturant caregiving so children develop self-esteem and a sense of belonging
3. Reasoning with children to help them understand the consequences of their actions and their effects on others
4. Having high but realistic standards for children and providing support for children to meet the standards
5. Involving children in family decision-making and problem-solving sessions so children can contribute their views and understand others' points of view

*From Marvin W. Berkowitz et al., "Educating for Positive Youth Development," in *Handbook of Moral Development,* eds. Melanie Killen and Judith Smetana (Mahwah, NJ: Erlbaum, 2006), p. 694.

others. Damon believes that these three levels correspond to Piaget's thinking at the preoperational level (level 1), concrete operations level (level 2), and formal operations level (level 3).

As children think more abstractly in late childhood and early adolescence, prosocial behavior reflects the expression of internalized codes of values and principles. Also, as they gain greater emotional regulation, children's behavior becomes more focused on others' feelings and experiences.

Parents promote prosocial behaviors by establishing warm, nurturant relationships with children and by modeling helpful and sharing behavior.[84] (See Box 5-1.) Parents also take more active measures as well, prompting children to engage in helping behaviors, "preaching" about the good that comes from prosocial actions for those who receive them and those who do them. In adolescence, parents engage in dialogues with children to draw out their thinking and reasoning about moral actions. Parents listen and ask questions so children have an opportunity to think about their own reasoning in these situations. Parents also encourage kind and generous behavior by helping children learn to control their own emotional reactions so they can perceive others' needs and take action.

While parents play an important role in encouraging prosocial behavior, interactions with siblings and friends are also very important, but in different ways. Children interact with peers and siblings as equals and ready partners for sharing and comforting. While older brothers and sisters are more likely to be the caregivers and helpers, younger siblings often like to give help.

The helpful actions that children take with peers are different from compliance to parents' rules and requests. There is a greater sense of obligation expressed in helping parents whereas with peers, sharing and helping are given more freely on the basis of friendship and kindness. Peers' helping behaviors may be powerful models for age-mates. Preschoolers who had contact with prosocial peers at the beginning of the school year showed more prosocial behavior themselves later in the school year, and the effect was still evident a year later.

Prosocial behavior would also be considered moral behavior when it involves altruism and putting aside one's own needs to help others, but it would not fall under the rubric of moral behavior when it involves doing a routine task in the course of an everyday activity such as returning a friend's book to the library.

Moral Development and Theories

Moral behaviors are those that reflect the ideal behaviors, values, and standards of one's society. The individual has internalized society's core values and voluntarily lives up to them as a matter of conscience.

Most developmental theorists have had views on how moral behavior develops. Learning theorists believe that children gradually learn moral behaviors through parental rewards and punishments for approved actions. As noted in Chapter 2, Freud believed that children develop control of their self-centered impulses through identification with parents and internalization of their values and standards at about age four or five. Social learning theorists adopted the concept of identification to account for children's following the rules and values of adults they observe.

Like Freud, Piaget believed that young children are egocentric.[85] Children have a subservient relationship with parents whose values and standards of conduct they wholeheartedly and unquestioningly embrace and consider inviolable. Piaget termed this the heteronomous stage because children take in authority's views and treat them as their own. Through childhood games and egalitarian relationships with peers in the school years, children develop concepts of fairness, justice, and individuals' rights. Through arguing and negotiating conflicts, children become more independent in their thinking about rules and responsibilities. By late childhood or early adolescence, children have entered what Piaget terms the autonomous stage. Advances in cognitive thinking contribute children's reasoning more abstractly and objectively about behavior.

Psychologist Lawrence Kohlberg expanded Piaget's two stages of moral development into six stages organized into three levels: preconventional, conventional, and postconventional.[86] The second stage at each level is a more advanced elaboration of the first stage. Kohlberg constructed his stages from interviews, largely with boys, about hypothetical moral dilemmas such as whether one should steal an otherwise unobtainable drug to save a life. At the preconventional level, when children are about age five, their moral judgments reflect their own interests: At stage 1 they choose actions to avoid punishment, and at stage 2, at about ages seven or eight, they seek to get their own needs met, like justifying actions to get others' support. At the conventional level, children make judgments in terms of social obligations. At stage 3, at about ages ten to eleven, they seek to please an authority figure such as a parent or teacher by being the good child, and at stage 4 in late adolescence, they seek to follow the system's rules and regulations and be part of the larger group. In the postconventional level, children and adults reason in terms of abstract principles and codes. At stage 5, they justify actions as fulfilling a social contract, and at stage 6, almost never observed in people, they justify actions in terms of following an inner moral code and set of principles that directs actions.

Observation and research do not support several aspects of Freud's, Piaget's, and Kohlberg's theories. First, children are not passive recipients of parents' rules. They resist, defy, argue, and negotiate with parents from the early years of life. Many are not afraid of parents' power and punishment, and they struggle to get their way. Second, children from very early years also express concern for others' feelings and show helping, giving behaviors.[87] In the preschool years, they draw a clear distinction between rules that prevent harm to others and should be obeyed, and conventional rules that are changeable. Although preschoolers respect authorities and believe they should always be obeyed, by ages five or six, children do not believe they should obey a parent or authority figure who tells them to hit another child.

Kohlberg's stages have had enormous influence on research and thinking in the areas of moral development because of the attention to the way children think and to the emphasis on the way children actively construct a system of moral thought that changes with time. He revised his scoring of moral reasoning when problems were found with the first system, and his stages have generally been supported with research. The progression through them has not always been in the invariant manner he predicted—older adolescents and adults sometimes shift back to an earlier stage and then go ahead—and the pace may be slower.[88]

Gender Differences

Carol Gilligan believes that Kohlberg's emphasis on moral reasoning in terms of justice, rights, and obligations has ignored the morality of care that focuses on responding to others' needs and giving care without exploitation of others.[89] The morality of care views people as embedded in relationships with others and moral issues rest on how people treat each other. A justice morality rests on a view of the individual as an autonomous entity divorced from social ties. Women, Gilligan asserts, are more concerned with the morality of care. Empirical research shows that both genders reason in terms of justice and care orientations, and in the preschool years there are no differences between boys and girls. Adolescents and adults of both genders rely more on a justice orientation, but girls and women judge more in terms of a care orientation, and boys or men rely on a justice orientation more than girls or women.

Gender differences have been found in prosocial behavior as well. Both peers and teachers describe girls as more helpful, kind, comforting, and considerate of others' feelings than boys, and girls report more prosocial behaviors than boys do.[90] The findings, although consistent from the school years on, vary in the degree of difference depending on the kind of prosocial behavior—there are fewer gender differences in giving instrumental help.

No gender differences were found in the prosocial reasoning in young children, but as children grow, girls tend to have more complex and advanced prosocial and moral reasoning than boys, and, as noted, to rely on a care orientation and boys on a justice orientation.[91]

Cultural Differences

Culture plays a role in the moral values that individuals internalize and the sanctions or punishments that result from violations. Many other cultures emphasize helping and sharing behaviors more than the American culture, and children in other cultures are frequently found to show more helping behavior than American children.[92]

Elliot Turiel emphasizes that although a culture may present a set of values and approved ways of behaving, individuals within that society may struggle against the values even though they abide by them in their behavior.[93] He cites studies of Bedouin women who occupy a subservient position in a traditional, patriarchal society, yet who, nevertheless, find ways to resist husbands' and society's demands and are able to get an education and avoid arranged marriages. Within our own society, inequalities exist between men and women, different racial groups and social classes, but some individuals refuse to accept these inequalities and seek to change them. Turiel states, "Distinctions need to be made between cultures as publicly conveyed ideologies or as social practices and the ways individuals interpret and make judgments about social experiences. Social and cultural practices embody multiple messages and are carried out in multiple ways."[94]

Connecting Children with Spiritual and Religious Values

A value system provides children with a framework for understanding life experiences. Children who feel that there is an order to the world and that they have a definite place in that order feel more secure. If parents participate regularly in a church program, it is easy to incorporate children in services and activities that present a worldview that is meaningful to all family members. If parents do not belong to any spiritual or religious group, they can have discussions with children as they get older about what they believe and how they translate beliefs into actions. It is important to include children in the activities that parents carry out to make their community a better place. Children learn social responsibility in this way. It is important that actions mirror values; otherwise, children feel values are just so much talk if not backed up by action.

TOOL CHEST FOR DEALING WITH PROBLEM BEHAVIORS

No matter how skilled the parent or how good the parent–child relationship, problems arise, and parents must deal with them. Verbal strategies of dealing with problems are preferred because they enable children to learn the reasons behind consequences and to understand principles that can be used in other situations. For example, if parents talk about why it is important for children to be ready to go to school in the morning, they can then generalize the importance of promptness to other situations in school or with friends.

We give a number of strategies for parents' use depending on the situation and their values. These tools should all be used in a family atmosphere in which good behavior receives attention and appreciation. Attention alone is enough reward for some children to increase the positive behaviors you want. Sometimes in the rush of everyday life, parents rush from one problem to another and pay attention only when the child is not doing what is requested. Thus, the child hears only what requires changing. Parents must be sure they are giving attention to the many ways their child follows their requests.

When actions are required, the following choices exist. We begin with natural and logical consequences because it requires primarily that parents let children learn from the consequences of their actions.

Natural and Logical Consequences

Rudolf Dreikurs described the method of natural and logical consequences as an alternative to parents' use of power and punishment. The terms *natural consequences*[95] and *logical consequences* are used jointly and interchangeably but have slightly different meanings. Natural consequences are the direct result of a physical act. For example, if you do not eat dinner, you experience hunger. If you do not get your dirty clothes in the laundry, they are not washed. Parents mainly have to stand aside and let the natural consequences occur—let the child remain hungry until the next meal or wear dirty clothes.

Logical consequences are events that follow a social act. For example, if you lie, other people will not believe you. If you misuse the family car, your parents will not trust you with it. Natural and logical consequences are directly related to the act itself and are not usually imposed by others. Exceptions exist, however. If a natural consequence presents a risk to a child—for example, running out into a busy street could result in being hit by a car—parents generally use a logical consequence. If a child starts toward the street, the child is restricted to playing in the house.

Logical consequences differ from punishment in several ways. Logical consequences are directly related to what the child has done—no clothes in the laundry basket results in having no clean clothes. A punishment may have no logical relationship to what the child has done—a spanking is not the direct result of being late for a meal but is the result of the parent's authority. The method of logical consequences does not place moral blame or pass moral judgment on the child. The child has made a mistake and pays the price. The parent stands by as an adviser rather than a judge.

When a parent establishes a logical consequence, it has to be one that he or she can accept when the child experiences it. For example, if a teen is told that the logical consequence of not getting homework turned in on time is that she will have to stay in on the weekend and complete it all even though there is a desirable party on Friday night, then the parent has to stand by the consequence even though the child is sad and angry, and the parent would like to see the child go to the party.

Mutual Problem Solving

Thomas Gordon describes mutual problem solving as a useful technique when parents feel a situation must change.[96] Using an I-message, described in Chapter 4, parents describe their feelings of frustration or worry and identify the problem behavior from their point of view. A mother may say, "I get frustrated on weekday mornings when I am driving the children to school and they are not ready to go on time, because I am late for work and my supervisor yells at me. What do you think can be done to solve the problem?" Children can then give their suggestions—one might say he cannot get in the bathroom because his sister stays in there so long blow-drying her hair so he is always late and even if he gets up earlier, he won't be able to get in the bathroom. His sister may agree that it is she who slows things down for him, and she volunteers to shower and then eat breakfast so he can get in the bathroom before she dries her hair. They all agree to try this solution for a week and see what happens. The aim of problem solving is to find a win–win solution agreeable to all concerned. There are six steps to the problem-solving process:

1. defining the problem, both parents and children send I-messages
2. generating possible solutions
3. evaluating possible solutions
4. deciding on the best solution
5. implementing the decision
6. doing a follow-up evaluation

When an agreed-upon solution is not followed, parents must send a strong I-message of disappointment and surprise as soon as possible. Perhaps the child can be helped to keep the agreement. Or perhaps another problem-solving session is needed. Gordon advises against the use of penalties to enforce agreements. Parents should assume children will cooperate instead of starting with a negative expectation expressed in the threat of punishment. Children frequently respond well to trust.

Parents can also use a behavioral contracting system. Just as parents want children to perform certain behaviors, so children want to attain certain objects, activities, and privileges. Parents offer desired rewards in exchange for the performance of certain activities. For example, if a child does his chores (making his bed, clearing the table) without reminders, he earns an extra 15 minutes of time for playing. Likewise, an older child may be given use of the family car on the weekends if she maintains acceptable school grades and arrives home at the prescribed times. Contracting is similar to mutual problem solving but differs in that parents are more authorities who agree to dispense privileges and rewards in exchange for actions rather than joint problem-solvers.

Negative Consequences

Recall our discussion of learning theories in Chapter 2. Negative consequences are used to decrease behaviors that are not desired. If attention to positive behaviors and the preceding methods have not worked, parents can institute a negative consequence to decrease the likelihood of the behavior's recurrence. There are six general principles for using negative consequences:

1. Intervene early. Do not let the situation get out of control. As soon as the rule is violated, begin to take action.

2. Stay as calm and objective as possible. Sometimes parents' anger and frustration are rewarding to the child. Parents' emotions can also distract the child from thinking about the rule violation.

3. State the rule that was violated. State it simply and do not argue about it.

4. Use a *mild* negative consequence. A mild consequence has the advantage that the child often devalues the activity itself and seems more likely to resist temptation and follow the rule in the future.

5. Use negative consequences consistently. Misbehaviors continue when they are sometimes punished and sometimes not.

6. Reinforce positive social behaviors as they occur afterward; parents do not want children to receive more negative than positive consequences.

The following negative consequences range from mild to severe. First, ignoring might seem the easiest in that the parent simply pays no attention to what the child says or does. It requires effort, however, because the parent must keep a neutral facial expression, look away, move away from the child, and give no verbal response or attention to what the child says or does. Ignoring is best for behaviors that are not harmful to anyone. For example, children's whining, sulking, or pouting can be ignored.

A second is *social disapproval*. Parents express in a few words, spoken in a firm voice with a disapproving facial expression, that they do not like the behavior. When children continue disapproved behavior, parents can institute a consequence—removing a privilege, using the time-out strategy, or imposing extra work. When families have contracts, children agree to carry out specified chores or behaviors in exchange for privileges. When certain behaviors do not occur, children lose privileges.

Finally, *time out* is the method best reserved for aggressive, destructive, or dangerous behaviors. It serves to stop the disapproved behavior and to give the child a chance to cool off and think about the rule violation. The time-out method has many variations. The child can be requested to sit in a chair in the corner, but many children get up. If the child is required to face the corner, parents can keep a young child in the corner for the stated time. With older children, parents may want to add the rule that if the child does not comply with time out for one parent during the day, making the presence of both parents necessary, then the child will spend twice the amount of time in time out. The time need not be long. For young children, the number of minutes in time out should equal the number of years in age. It is best to have only two or three behaviors requiring time out at any one time. Otherwise, a child may spend a great deal of time in the corner for too many different things. Furthermore, both parents and all caregivers need to agree on the two or three things that will lead to time out so the child receives punishment consistently.

When children get older and have many toys and recreational pleasures in their rooms, such as stereos and computers, restriction to their room is not an effective punishment. For these children, it is better to substitute extra work or chores that have a constructive outcome such as cleaning the garage or devoting time to a community activity.

Ineffective Forms of Discipline

A review of over three hundred studies[97] identifies four kinds of problems in disciplining children: (1) inconsistent discipline, referring to inconsistency both on the part of one parent and between two parents; (2) irritable, harsh, explosive discipline (frequent hitting and threatening); (3) low supervision and low involvement on the part of the parent with the child; and (4) inflexible, rigid discipline (use of a single form of discipline for all transgressions regardless of seriousness). All four forms of ineffective discipline are related to increases in children's aggressive, rule-breaking behavior that then frequently leads to social difficulties with peers.

The Use of Physical Discipline

Parents do not like to spank, and they do not consider it effective discipline.[98] Children believe parents have a right to spank, but they do not like it; it hurts their feelings and makes them feel angry and upset.[99] Health-care professionals and social scientists recommend against it.[100] Yet, the majority of parents have spanked children at one time or another.[101] How can we decrease or eliminate this behavior that no one wants to continue?

Definition of Levels of Physical Discipline First, we must distinguish among forms of physical discipline. Physical discipline is often divided into two categories: (1) mild spanking, defined as a slap or two with the flat of the hand on the buttocks or extremities without causing any physical injury to the child and normatively used with young children between ages two and six, and (2) abuse, including beating, kicking, and punching that results in injury to the child.[102]

Even though these two categories seem clear-cut, researchers face difficulties in classifying parents with regard to their use of physical discipline, and therefore, understanding of its use is more difficult than we would like.[103] First, as self-reporters of physical discipline, parents may not be accurate. Second, parents are often asked only whether and how often they spank within a specified period of time, such as the preceding week, and the behavior that week may not have been typical. Although researchers think that these errors cancel each other out, they do not know for sure. Third, parents are rarely asked how severely they spank their child, so whether the physical punishment is mild, harsh, or abusive remains unclear.

Prevalence and Frequency of Physical Discipline When asked whether they have ever spanked their child, between 63 percent and 94 percent of parents say they have.[104] While spanking has decreased over the past three decades, the vast majority have still spanked a child.[105] In two large-scale studies, about two-thirds of parents of preschoolers aged three to five had spanked their child in the previous week, with an average of one to three spankings, depending on the sample and subgroup.[106]

In a survey of parents of children five to fifteen years of age, 63 percent said they had used physical punishment. In a telephone survey, caregivers for 60 percent of children reported that they used physical punishment and minor physical violence (pushing, grabbing, shoving, and slapping), and 10 percent reported one or more instances of physical abuse or severe violence, consisting of kicking, biting, or hitting with a fist.[107]

Spanking starts early in life. About 50 percent of parents report that they had spanked their child of under one year of age one or more times in the preceding week.[108] Spanking increases in the years from two to five, when between 60 and 65 percent of parents report having spanked a child. Beginning at age five, spanking decreases, so only about one-third of parents report having spanked their child in the previous week; by ages nine or ten, that number drops to about 20 percent. Parents also report giving preschoolers, on average, more spankings per week (three) than they give older children (two).[109]

Characteristics of Parents Who Use Physical Discipline

Parents who are young, single, and under financial stress are more likely to spank than are older, married parents who have financial resources.[110] Parents who experience daily frustrations with children and have psychological problems report more spanking, and, as noted, 83 percent of middle-class parents in one study and 94 percent of middle-class parents in another used physical punishment.[111]

Mothers are more likely to use physical means of discipline than are fathers, perhaps because they do more of the daily child care.[112] African American parents are more likely to use physical punishment than are European American or Latino parents.[113] People who live in rural areas and in the southern part of the United States are more likely to use physical means of discipline than are parents in urban areas and the northern part of the United States.[114] Parents who identify themselves as religiously conservative report more frequent physical discipline than do those who do not identify themselves as religious conservatives,[115] and Catholics report less spanking than do Protestants.[116] Physical discipline is more likely, then, when parents are under stress or when they hold more traditional or conservative values.

Characteristics of Children Who Receive Physical Discipline

As noted, preschool children are more likely to receive physical discipline than are elementary and high school students. Boys are more likely to be spanked than girls—in one study, 67 percent of boys received spankings, compared with 57 percent of girls.[117] Children described as having difficult temperaments and being noncompliant received more spankings than did other children. Spankings also occurred more frequently in families in which parents and children argued and in which parents had fewer supports.

Reasons Given for Spanking   Parents were most likely to use spanking and hitting when children were out of control, disobedient, or disrespectful.[118] Four factors related to parents' use: (1) parents' belief in its usefulness, (2) parents' own experience with it as a child, (3) an authoritarian style of parenting, and (4) children's problems of aggressiveness and acting out. Although 93 percent justified its use,

85 percent of those who used it said they would rather not. They felt they were angry when they did it and that it upset the children; they wished they had alternatives.

Of concern to the researchers was the fact that parents continued its use despite their discomfort with it and its doubtful value. Parents seemed to rely on it as a continuation of their own childhood experience of physical punishment rather than to institute change and learn new methods. The investigators were concerned that the children in the sample would continue the practice for the same reason.

Effects of Physical Discipline   There is no doubt that physical abuse is related to many difficulties for children (see Chapter 16). Here we focus on the effects of mild physical discipline.

Diana Baumrind believes that the effects of a spanking, which she defines as a slap or two with the flat of the hand on the buttocks or the extremities, depends on the context of the parent–child relationship.[119] Much research supports this position. The most recent study involved data collected from 1,990 children over a six-year period as part of the National Longitudinal Survey of Youth. It included a sizable number of African American and Latino parents as well as European American parents.[120]

In this study, mothers were categorized into three groups—no spanking in the last week, spanking once in the last week, and spanking more than once in the last week—when their children were four years of age and at two-year intervals over the next six years. When children were four, there was no relationship between the use and frequency of spanking and the child's behavior problems. Some children with few behavioral problems received many spankings, and some children with many behavioral difficulties received no spankings.

Spanking, however, increased behavioral difficulties over time. Although the behavior problems of all children increased from age four to ten, those whose mothers continued to spank had more behavior problems than those who had not been spanked, unless moderating influences were present. When parents increased their spanking in these years, the increase in problems was greater than when spanking decreased or stayed the same. The findings were the same for all groups, so the effects of spanking did not differ as a result of ethnicity.

Children's mothers were also described in terms of their emotional warmth and supportiveness. Children with warm and supportive mothers had fewer behavior problems. Furthermore, as the authors concluded,

> Although spanking can have a negative impact on children's socioemotional functioning over time, this effect is moderated by the emotional context in which such spanking occurs. When spanking occurs in the context of strong overall emotional support for the child, it does not appear to contribute to a significant increase in behavior problems.[121]

Although a large review of studies in 2002 revealed difficulties with aggressive behavior and social relationships, that review included moderate and abusive physical discipline that led to more serious concerns.[122] When that review focused on mild physical punishment, the connection with difficulties disappeared. We can conclude then that parents who have positive, warm relationships with their children and use reasoning and mild physical discipline with young children from ages eighteen months to about five years do not appear to be placing these children at risk of long-term harm. Physical punishment in the absence of a warm relationship appears to contribute to an increase in children's behavior problems. Beyond age five, parents are well advised to find other disciplinary strategies.

Should We Ban or Outlaw Physical Discipline? Social scientist Murray Straus wishes to ban physical discipline in schools and at home because of the potential for abuse and because it is related to aggressiveness among children and to a more violent society.[123] He cites statistics from a national, representative sample of children revealing that the more corporal punishment a child receives in middle childhood and early adolescence, the greater the probability of the child's being a delinquent. Other social scientists such as Baumrind believe that research does not support a blanket injunction against spanking, as there are "no documented harmful long-term effects."[124] Furthermore, she points out that in Sweden, where physical punishment was outlawed at home and at school in 1979, both parental physical abuse of children and violent acts by teenagers increased.

How Can We Decrease Physical Discipline? Gerald Patterson and Philip Fisher describe a vicious behavioral cycle that physical discipline reinforces.[125] When children do not comply, parents argue and then use physical discipline. When children comply, parents see that such discipline "works" and are therefore encouraged to use it again. Sometimes though, during arguments, parents threaten physical punishment but do not carry it out because of children's loud protests. Thus, children are encouraged to protest loudly in the next encounter. In this way, parents and children train each other to escalate to a maximal level of protests and punishments. So, ending physical punishment relies on changes in both parents' and children's behavior.

Parents start the process of change by using positive disciplinary techniques that create a collaborative family atmosphere, as described in Chapter 2 and earlier in this chapter. Parents pay attention to children's positive behaviors and devote time to playing games. When parents discipline children, they use nonphysical means of contracting, earning privileges, and time outs for behaviors that must be stopped. They use these techniques consistently, without anger or criticism or belittling the child, and they supervise children to make sure children follow through with behaviors. Even if children protest loudly, parents persist with nonphysical discipline. Gradually, parents and children emerge from their vicious cycle of escalating conflict and physical discipline.

Discouraging the use of physical discipline, while a useful first step, does not automatically put in place the strategies of supportive parenting unless parents follow Patterson and Fisher's suggestions. Pediatrician Robert Chamberlin identifies the use of physical punishment as just one risk factor related to poor outcome for children. Because the accumulation of risk factors is what causes the most damage, he believes that communities and professionals need to join with parents to promote the "affectionate and cognitively stimulating types of parenting behavior that appear more directly related to positive developmental outcomes rather than focus on whether or not parents use physical punishment."[126] Baumrind also cautions professionals,

> It should be the concern of professionals who work with parents to respectfully offer them alternative disciplinary strategies, using carefully evaluated intervention programs, rather than to condemn parents for using methods consonant with their own, but not with the counselor's, beliefs and values. Parents who choose to use punishment often seek guidance in using it efficaciously. Efficacious punishment is contingent upon the child's misbehavior, as well as upon the parents' responding in a prompt, rational, nonexplosive manner and with knowledge and consideration of the child's developmental level and temperament.[127]

PRACTICAL QUESTION: HOW CAN WE KEEP CHILDREN SAFE?

Parents become concerned about their safety as children spend more time away from parents and home, going to and from school or to friends' homes. They want to help children be independent and safe in the world, yet they do not want to frighten them and make them afraid of strangers and new experiences.

Fostering children's awareness of danger, sense of caution, and preparedness for unsafe situations does not mean making children live in fear. Children can learn that even though most people in the world are good and helpful and many situations are safe, some people and experiences are not, and everyone must learn to protect him- or herself from dangers that arise. Parents can help by putting this knowledge in perspective for children. Life has always involved danger of some sort, and many objects or experiences that are positive also have dangerous aspects. Cars are useful—they get us to work, to stores, to hospitals—but they can be dangerous if they hit us while we are crossing the street. The answer lies not in eliminating cars, because before we had cars, there were dangers from horses and horse-drawn vehicles. The solution is to take precautions to minimize the dangers and enjoy the benefits.

Families need to develop a set of instructions, to be discussed and revised as necessary, regarding certain dangerous situations. A one-time discussion is not enough; parents must periodically review instructions with children. Children can learn these safety rules gradually—for example, when and where they may go alone or what they should do if bothered by someone on the street or in a store, even when parents are nearby. Learning safety rules can become as natural to children as learning to brush their teeth. Parents emphasize teaching children the skills to deal with the environment, to make them competent and independent.

Although parents worry that talk of possible fearful events will damage the child, the risks that come with ignorance are much greater. Parents can begin with simple discussions of traffic safety—where, when, and how to cross the street. They can move from that topic to others of importance for the child. Television may prompt some discussion. Grace Hechinger recommends playing the game "What If?"[128] Parents ask a variety of questions and give children chances to develop solutions to difficult situations. "What if someone takes your backpack?" "What if a stranger threatens you on the street?" Parents should not be upset if their children's initial answers are impractical, because they can guide their children in learning more reasonable responses.

Parents should have clear safety rules on (1) behavior if there is a fire at home; (2) traffic behavior, whether on foot or on a bicycle; (3) boundaries within which the child can come and go freely and outside of which an adult or parent must be present; (4) behavior in public with strangers; (5) behavior at home if strangers telephone or come to the house; (6) behavior when the child is a victim or witness of muggings by peers or adults; and (7) behavior when sexual misconduct occurs. Home behaviors at the time of fires, for example, should be practiced just as they are in schools or workplaces.

If children are victimized—their bike is stolen, their money is taken, a stranger approaches them—parents' reactions can help speed the healing process. When parents listen to children's reactions and help children take constructive action, such as notifying the police, they help children cope. When parents' responses are exaggerated ("This is horrible!") or detached ("I cannot deal with this"), children get no help in coping with their feelings. If they cannot talk about how they feel, they will find it difficult to work out their feelings. Active listening and simple I-messages ("If that happened to me, I'd be really upset") give children a chance to say what the experience meant to them. Sometimes children need to describe the event several times. Each time, more details emerge, as do more feelings. Gradually, after the incident, children regain their self-confidence. If a child's eating, sleeping, or play habits change or if marked changes in schoolwork or personality continue for some time, professional help should be sought.

An important step in promoting children's safety is working with people in the community. Developing community awareness and programs gives everyone a positive feeling of working together, which does much to banish fear. Promoting public safety programs with school and police officials and organizing block-parent programs to help children in the neighborhood are useful steps. In block-parent programs, one house in the neighborhood is designated as a house where children can come if they need help or reassurance when no one is home.

Family members grow stronger when they face problems and work together to deal with them. Sense of community grows when families and agencies cooperate to make the environment safe for children.

PARENTING PROGRAMS

Just as people take courses in driving to get a license or cooking to master basic skills, parents seek to learn skills in parenting programs. Parenting programs can be divided into those targeted for the general population of parents and those directed to parents with special needs, such as parents of multiples, parents of premature children, or parents of children with attention-deficit hyperactivity disorder. We discuss parenting programs throughout the book, and here we focus on three programs that target parents with children of different ages.

The first is a program organized for young, low-income African American parents with children under the age of three,[129] titled Parenting in the Real

World: Kids Don't Come with Instructions (abbreviated PRW). Organized on the basis of parents' requests in focus groups, the program aimed to give parents knowledge of children's development, skills to manage their behavior, and tools to deal with their own stress levels. Parents wanted opportunities to talk with other parents to discuss real-life problems, to see videos with real parents not celebrities or professional experts, and they wanted to have discussions that respected their cultural values and their knowledge.

PRW consists of seven 90-minute sessions, with a video for each. With an introductory and closing session, the five remaining sessions focus on knowledge of child development; discipline; attachment; juggling work, school, and family; and taking care of yourself. Parents meet with a coordinator and discuss the topic. Parents receive a handbook and message reinforcement objects such as key rings. Each week the parent chooses a topic to work on and discusses progress the next week. Parents and instructors rate the materials highly, and parents rated the groups as effective. They were able to form groups for babysitting and support.

Based on their own work, university researchers Philip Cowan and Carolyn Cowan have organized parent groups that do not seek so much to develop specific skills as to give parents opportunities to discuss their own parenting experiences.[130] The Cowans first organized discussion groups for parents who were expecting their first child. The groups, consisting of four couples and two professionals, began in the last trimester of pregnancy and continued for six months to provide support for parents as they created their families. Parents talked about sources of stress and well-being, and ways to increase closeness between the couple. Following the couples over five years, the Cowans found that those who participated in the couples groups were still together at the end of three years when those in the control group experienced a divorce rate of 15 percent. At the end of five years, the divorce rate was similar for the two groups.

Impressed with the effects of the six-month groups, the Cowans began another intervention study at the time of the child's entrance into elementary school. Groups began when the child was four years old and about to enter school within a year.[131] The groups met for two hours, and lasted for sixteen weeks. Although the parents were well-functioning volunteers who had not sought mental health services, their scores on measures of depression and marital satisfaction still suggested they were experiencing stress in their daily lives.

Parent groups consisted of four couples and two mental health professionals and focused on five topics central to parents' and children's adjustment: (1) parents' sense of self and their relationships (2) with each another, (3) with their parents, and (4) with their children, and (5) the life stresses and supports they experienced. In each session, parents had time to raise questions or problems. Researchers devised two forms of the parenting groups. In one group, leaders were told to focus on marital issues and parents' relationship as a couple in the open-ended discussion periods; in the other group, leaders emphasized parents' relationships with their children.

The control group consisted of parents who were offered a consultation with the staff couple who did their initial interview once a year for three years—the year before children entered kindergarten, during kindergarten, and then during first grade. Compared to children whose parents were in the control group, children of the parents who were in the intervention groups were more competent in kindergarten and first grade. They had higher academic achievement, fewer behavior problems, and more positive self-concepts. Both forms of the intervention groups were related to positive behaviors in children in kindergarten and first grade.

Gene Brody and his coworkers at the University of Georgia surveyed rural African American families' concerns.[132] The families identified two areas—early sexual activity and adolescent substance use—of great concern to them. Researchers set up a training program to help parents and their eleven-year-old, early adolescent children develop skills to avoid these behaviors. Titled the Strong African American Family Program, the program consisted of two-hour sessions for seven weeks. Parents and children met separately for an hour and then jointly for an hour to practice the skills learned.

Parents learned nurturing parenting skills, ways of monitoring and controlling children's behavior, adaptive strategies of racial socialization, and strategies for communicating information about sex and substances as well as parents' expectations in these areas. Children learned the value of following household rules and doing chores, adaptive ways to counter racism, the importance of having a future orientation of setting and achieving goals, ways to counter and resist the temptations of substance abuse and early sexual activity, and ways that those who did not engage in these activities differed from those who did. Families in the control group received three pamphlets in the mail on early adolescent development, ways to manage stress, and ways to encourage exercise.

Seven months after the parenting program, parents and children who received training demonstrated more behaviors associated with protective factors against substance use and early sexual activity than did those in the control group. Parents were more communicative of general information on the topics of early sexual activity and substance abuse as well as of their own expectations of children in these areas, and were more positive and supportive with children in this age period. Compared to youths in the control group, youths in the program had greater acceptance of parents' rules, a greater orientation to the future and to setting goals, and a more negative view of those who use substances and engaged in early sexual activity. The future behavior of these early adolescents will be tracked to see whether parents' and children's attendance at the programs and development of protective factors against substance use and early sexual activity reduced the rates of these behaviors in children as they progress through adolescence. In Chapter 10, we describe the adaptive ways researchers taught early adolescents to combat racism.

The evidence from parenting programs is that they help to develop useful skills. The Cowans' programs have been highly successful in impacting children's behaviors when other programs have been less successful at doing this. It may be that practice in communication skills and setting limits is most useful in a group where there is extended time for talking about one's own frustrations and needs in marital and extended family relationships as well as in interactions with children.

Camille Smith, Ruth Perou, and Catherine Lesesne reviewed the history and present state of parent education and concluded that,

Parenting is open to change, but it is not easy to change. . . . What has become clear from the research over many years is that the fundamental principle that parenting education programs (both universal and targeted) must stress is the importance of relationships. Relationships are among the most significant influences on healthy growth and psychological well being. The quality of the parent–child relationship has long been acknowledged to be one of the most powerful predictors of optimal child development. Warm, responsive parenting is associated with later child language development, cognitive development, school success, and behavioral adjustment. Conversely, parents who are less involved and affectionate with their children are more likely to experience many more academic and behavioral problems with those children as they grow in years. . . . It is imperative that we stress the key component that should be a part of every parent education program: the importance and significance of the parent–child relationship.

Even when parents and children have good relationships, problems arise, and parents often wish they had a single solution to each kind of problem they encounter in child rearing—one way to handle temper tantrums, one way to deal with teens' rebelliousness. Unfortunately, there is no one formula that all parents can use to raise all children. Each child, as well as each parent, is a unique individual.

When parents have difficulties, a seven-step problem-solving approach seems most useful. This approach allows parents to choose interventions that take into account the child's age and temperament as well as the family's social values and living circumstances. It also enables parents to encourage the qualities that they and their ethnic group value. Here are the seven steps:

1. Spend pleasurable time daily with the child
2. Specifically identify any problem; observe when and how often it occurs
3. Question yourself on the reality of the problem, is it the child or your own expectation that creates a problem
4. Get your child's point of view
5. Carry out an intervention
6. Evaluate the results of the intervention
7. Start over again if necessary

As we conclude this chapter on supporting children's growth, it is good to keep in mind the words of Arnold Gesell and Frances Ilg:

When asked to give the shortest definition of life, Claude Bernard, a great physiologist, answered, "Life is creation." A newborn baby is the consummate product of such creation. And he in turn is endowed with capacities for continuing creation. These capacities are expressed not only in the growth of his physique, but in the simultaneous growth of a psychological self. From the sheer standpoint of creation this psychological self must be regarded as his masterpiece. It will take a lifetime to finish, and in the first ten years he will need a great deal of help, but it will be his own product.[134]

Parents have the privilege of serving as guide and resource as their child creates a unique "psychological self."

MAIN POINTS

Modeling
- is natural to us as we have mirror neurons built into our nervous system
- is an important behavior in all aspects of parenting

Healthy lifestyles
- prevent injuries and illnesses
- require parents' efforts to model and structure daily routines for eating, exercise, and sleeping
- influence intellectual performance and psychological adjustment

A collaborative family atmosphere
- rests on responsive, sensitive parental care of children
- rests on secure attachment of child to parents
- is never too late to establish
- includes children as partners in routines
- includes conversations about rules and future events
- includes the process of encouragement

Promoting competencies includes helping children develop
- emotional regulation through sensitive care, soothing/modulating negative moods, structuring routines, and coaching children in expressing emotions, as described in Chapter 4
- problem-solving skills of identifying the problem, developing strategies to reach goals, and evaluating results of actions
- moral competence through modeling, nurturing care, reasoning with children, having high but realistic standards for children, involving them in family decision making, and connecting to parents' value system

Children's media use
- occupies six and a half hours a day for children between the ages of eight and eighteen, and up to four hours for children under age six
- does not prevent their enjoying and participating in other activities
- when it includes quality programming, has positive benefits of teaching children, giving them literacy and number skills, modeling examples of positive actions
- can be related to negative consequences such as increased aggression in childhood and adulthood and early initiation of sexual behaviors; irregular sleep and reduced attention span when children use too much media or media of poor quality
- can be shared with parents who regulate use

Tool chest for dealing with problem behaviors includes

- natural and logical consequences
- mutual problem solving and contracting
- using negative consequences such as ignoring, loss of privileges, social disapproval, and time out

Nonabusive spanking

- is not approved by parents, children, or professionals
- is used by most parents at one time or another but most often by young parents under stress
- may or may not have detrimental effects, depending on the context of the parent–child relationship
- is best supplanted by other forms of negative consequence

Ineffective forms of discipline

- inconsistent discipline
- harsh, explosive discipline
- low supervision of the child
- rigid, inflexible discipline

Keeping children safe requires that parents

- teach children about potential dangers, ways to minimize them, and ways to respond if they occur
- work with other agencies and people in the community to provide a safer community for everyone

Parenting programs

- can provide support groups for parents and reduce the stress of parenting
- teach specific skills to parents
- enable parents to reduce children's behavioral difficulties
- increase parents' self-confidence and feelings of competence
- whatever else they include must focus on the importance of the quality of the parent–child relationship and ways to improve and nourish it

EXERCISES

1. Observe parents and children together in a grocery store or at a playground or other public place. Try to find parents and children of different ages to observe. Are parents on a cell phone? Are parents and children talking to each other? If they are not, are they still having a good time being together? What is the nature of their conversation? Is it about dos and don'ts? Is it about something they will be doing in the future? What theories of growth do

parents seem to be using? What conclusions do you come to after observing three or four pairs of parents and children?

2. Write a description of the disciplinary techniques you recall your parents used with you in the elementary school years. How would you characterize your parents' methods of child-rearing and your response to them?

3. Watch the television show *American Idol* or any other popular show of your choosing. What messages does that show convey about the meaning of life, values of daily living, moral behaviors? Does that show teach or model positive or negative behaviors, or both? If you have teenagers, would you want them to watch it?

4. The next time you feel frustrated about something, try out the problem-solving process described in this chapter . Did it help you figure out what to do or help you to persist in what you knew you had to do? Why or why not?

5. Investigate the parenting programs available in your area. What is the range of programs in terms of cost, length, content? If possible, attend one meeting and give your evaluation of the class.

ADDITIONAL READINGS

Coles, Robert. *The Moral Intelligence of Children*. New York: Random House, 1997.

Goleman, Daniel. *Emotional Intelligence*. New York: Bantam, 1995.

Gopnik, Alison. *The Philosophical Baby: What Children's Minds Tell Us about Truth, Love, and the Meaning of Life*. New York: Farrar, Straus & Giroux, 2009.

Johnson, Simon. *Keep Your Kids Safe on the Internet*. New York: McGraw-Hill/Osborn, 2004.

Nelson, Jane. *Positive Discipline*. New York: Ballantine, 1987.

PART

II

Parenting at
Developmental Stages

C H A P T E R

6

Becoming Parents

CHAPTER TOPICS	IN THE NEWS
In this chapter, you will learn about:	*New York Times,* July 15[1]: Parents using donor eggs and sperm wonder what to tell their children about their biological origins. See page 184.
▨ How adults form couple relationships and decide to parent	
▨ How age and gender influence conception	
▨ The many forms of assistance in creating new life	
▨ Parents' experiences in the transition to parenthood	

Test Your Knowledge: Fact or Fiction (True/False)

1. About 50 percent of pregnancies in the United States are unintended.
2. Skin-to-skin physical contact between mother and newborn following birth helps to settle the newborn's physiological system.
3. Mothers' age and lifestyle influence the rate of birth defects in their children, but fathers' age and lifestyle do not.
4. Prospective parents talk over their ideas about child rearing before they have children so they can work out their differences.
5. What differences emerge in comparisons of parents using assisted reproductive technology and parents naturally conceiving their child favor parents who have used reproductive technology as they tend to be more emotionally involved and supportive with children.

Each individual who becomes a parent does so within unique circumstances. This chapter describes the many paths to parenthood in our contemporary society. We look at how parents come into parenthood and the many factors in their lives that influence the experiences they have as they make the transition and adjust to parenthood.

The ways parents come into parenthood reflect many of the changes that have occurred in our contemporary society in the last fifty years. Fifty years ago, almost all babies went home from the hospital to married couples who either had reproduced their own child or had adopted a child born to an unmarried mother living in this country. Currently, many persons unable to adopt in the past—lesbians, gays, single parents, disabled parents—are now able to adopt children, who sometimes come from many different countries. In addition, assisted reproductive technology has made it possible for couples, single persons, and gay/lesbian partners to create and bear new life. An ancient and basic desire in life—to have a child—meets the most advanced technological changes in assisted reproductive technology.

As we noted in Chapter 1, parents want children to love and care for, to participate in their growth. Babies who have always connected parents to their extended family and the future, now connect an ever larger number of people to the community devoted to promoting new life.

In this chapter, we look first at factors related to readiness to parent, the pathways to parenthood, then at the transition to parenting and the factors that ease or complicate the adjustment to parenthood.

PROCESS OF FAMILY FORMATION

Currently, parenting has few requirements; even those imposed in the past by such physical characteristics as age are changed with technology, so how do we know parents are ready?

Readiness to Parent

Recall David Lykken's requirements for a parenting license described in Chapter 1.[2] He considered adults ready when they were over eighteen, married, employed, and without a history of violence.

Social characteristics such as parents' education and employment are important because they enable parents to support a child. Parents' psychological characteristics appear the most important of all, as they impact parents' abilities to provide high-quality care once the child is born. Christoph Heinicke identifies three psychological qualities of parents that provide "an optimal parenting environment": (1) parents' feelings of self-esteem; (2) their capacity for positive, mutually satisfying relationships with others, especially with the partner; and (3) their capacity for flexible problem solving.[3]

Research with teen mothers suggests a fourth important quality: cognitive readiness for parenthood.[4] Measured in the last trimester of pregnancy, teen mothers' knowledge of children's growth and major developmental milestones, their realistic expectations of children, and their attitudes about parenting predicted their children's cognitive and socioemotional skills as they moved through childhood. A further qualification for parenthood is a healthy lifestyle because by the time parents know the mother is pregnant, four to eight weeks of important prenatal development have occurred and mother's and father's exposure to drugs and environmental toxins can affect the growing child before the pregnancy is known.

Groups of parents do not differ in why they want children, but they differ in their readiness, their initial resources in providing for children, and the efforts they must make to become parents. The way an individual or family initiates a pregnancy reflects problem-solving and planning skills that set the stage for the child's prenatal development and birth. When children are intended, both parents are more likely to be living healthy lifestyles, mothers are more likely to get prenatal care early, to have fewer pregnancy and delivery complications, and as a result, to have healthier babies.[5]

We wish we knew more about how parents decide to become parents. We do know that half of all pregnancies are unintended, defined as not wanting any child or not wanting a child at this time.[6] Half of unintended pregnancies are terminated through miscarriage or abortion, so that about two-thirds of babies born are from intended pregnancies. You might think that married couples have planned or intended births and unmarried couples have unplanned or unintended births. Not so. About 70–80 percent of births to married couples are intended, and about 45 percent of births to unmarried women are intended.[7] About 15–19 percent of unmarried teens intended to get pregnant. So let us look at how subgroups of prospective parents form families.

Women's and Men's Pathways to Parenthood

The traditional pathway to family formation in the past was self-supporting work, marriage in the early twenties, followed by children one or two years later. Many pathways to family formation have replaced the traditional one because young adults stay in school longer, cohabit more frequently, marry and have children later, and bear more children outside of marriage.[8]

Our information about how young people form families comes in part from large longitudinal studies that follow participants from high school graduation to their early or mid-twenties, chronicling patterns of schooling, work, intimate partner relationships, and parenthood. Using the National Longitudinal Study of Adolescent Health data on study members when they were eighteen and twenty-three, researchers plotted the common pathways young women took as they established stable work patterns and families.[9] Through latent class analysis, they identified seven pathways and the personal and social resources that predicted these pathways.

The most common pathway between eighteen and twenty-three was to continue schooling and then transition to the workforce for an increasing number of hours until full-time participation occurred with no family formation. A second common pathway was to leave school and go directly to full-time work with no family formation, and a third was to enter the workforce on a more part-time basis and cohabit with a partner without children. These three pathways together characterized about 62 percent of the whole sample.

Three other, less frequent pathways characterized mothers who made up about 32 percent of the sample by age twenty-three. One pattern was to work part time, enter marriage by age twenty-one, and then have children. This was the traditional pattern of the past that described about only 14 percent of this sample. Another was to work part time and become a single mother, and a third was to cohabit with a partner and have a child. A final pattern characterized about 6 percent of the sample, those who did not go to school or work, or marry, but instead lived at home, possibly because of a special difficulty.

Data reveal that those young women with many personal and social resources—positive relationships with their parents, high self-esteem, friends, school success—postpone families. Their parents are educated and have prepared them to do well in school, and they are establishing satisfying patterns of work, friendships, and leisure activities. When they marry, they are more likely to rate the relationships as satisfying than those who marry early.[10]

Young women who have children alone or in married or cohabiting relationships are more likely to be those with fewer resources or plans.[11] They value a child as a social resource—someone to love, to care for, provide a grandchild for grandparents, someone to care for them in their old age. These women have reduced abilities to provide for children because they have less education and less extensive work experience. Many obtain further schooling later, but it is more difficult.

A longitudinal study tracking both young men and women from eighteen to twenty-five yielded very similar findings.[12] Most young adults are getting more education or working in their early twenties, and they either live with partners without children or live with friends and date. Those in their early twenties who marry or cohabit and start families represent about a third of men and women. A very small percentage of men and women—about 6 to 8—appear to have difficulty taking on the responsibilities of adulthood. They live at home and have occasional employment. There is a similar pattern of family resources in this sample too. Both young men and women who have the most resources, whose families stressed education, and who have enjoyed school and community activities are those who are going to school, preparing for well-paying jobs, and postponing marriage and children. (See Chapter 12 for greater details about these pathways.)

Although 80 percent of women in 2006 had children by the time they were in the age bracket 40–44, 20 percent were childless.[13] The figure was higher—27 percent—for those women with graduate or professional degrees and lower—18 percent—for those who did not go beyond high school. Women appear more accepting of childlessness then men, especially women with education.[14] In one study, of those who were childless in the age group 40–44, half were voluntarily childless, and half, involuntarily childless.[15] The voluntarily childless are generally of European American backgrounds, employed full time with higher incomes, and not religious. Latinas are underrepresented in this group.

By the time most young adults have turned age thirty, they have finished school, are working, have left home, and are married so they get to the place that their parents achieved at younger ages.[16] Women's and men's paths are similar, and there is greater gender equality in their activities. European Americans participate in schooling and work in greater numbers than African Americans and other minority groups and that gives them greater resources for rearing families. Ways to increase education job levels, and parenting resources for all groups is an important societal task.

Married Parents' Decisions about Parenting

When couples become parents, the most important factor in understanding their decision and its effects is whether the partners agree on the decision. Carolyn Pape Cowan and Philip Cowan identified four decision-making patterns.[17] *Planners* (52 percent) discussed the question and made a definite decision to have or not have a child. *Acceptance of fate* couples (14 percent of those expecting) had unplanned pregnancies that they accepted either quietly or, in many cases, enthusiastically. *Ambivalent* couples (about 26 percent) expressed both positive and negative feelings about being parents, with one parent leaning in one direction and the other parent leaning in the other direction. *Yes–no* couples (about 10 percent) were in marked conflict about having or not having a child.

The couples' decision-making process regarding pregnancy was related to their problem-solving skills in other areas. Yes–no couples were less effective in solving everyday problems, just as they were less effective in deciding about the pregnancy. The decision-making process regarding pregnancy influenced marital satisfaction over time and after the baby's birth. When couples plan the decision, regardless of whether they do or do not have a child, their marital satisfaction remains high following the birth or an equivalent time period. Couples who accept an unplanned pregnancy have a drop in marital satisfaction, but their initial level is so high that they are still as satisfied as the parents who plan the decision.

Marital dissatisfaction is greatest among couples who are ambivalent or in conflict but still have a baby. Ambivalent couples who do not have a child retain a high satisfaction level but these levels drop when they have a baby they do not agree on. The yes–no couples have the least satisfaction. Of nine yes–no couples who had a child, seven divorced by the time the child entered kindergarten. In all seven cases, the husband did not want a child. The two women who did not want to have children seemed better able to adjust, and their marriages continue.

In another longitudinal study, fathers' feelings about the pregnancy—did not want baby or waited too long for a baby—shaped fathers' behavior and his interactions after the baby was born.[18] Fathers who did not want the pregnancy were less warm with infants, and those fathers who wanted babies sooner were more nurturing and caring with their babies. Fathers who were more involved in prebirth activities—going to doctor's visits, seeing a sonogram or ultrasound of the baby—were more involved in all aspects of infant care when babies were three months old. Getting fathers involved in prenatal activities increased their involvement in care after the babies came, regardless of their attitudes about the pregnancy.

Unmarried Parents

Today, parents who have never been married form a heterogeneous group that includes (1) teen parents living at home, (2) cohabiting parents who may or may not marry after the birth of the child, (3) single women who may or may not be in relationships at the time of conception but now live alone and are committed to raising a child alone, (4) unmarried lesbian and gay singles and couples who choose to have children by adoption or by assisted reproductive technology (ART), and (5) single fathers who raise their own child, adopt, or have a child by ART. We discuss all these groups in greater detail in Chapters 14 and 15.

The groups vary in their planning of the pregnancy, with lesbian/gay adults planning very carefully to have children, and some single mothers by choice going to great lengths to have a baby by ART. These two groups often have more resources, but single parents, in particular, have to plan a support system that will help them rear a child, as it is difficult on one's own. Teen parents have a special set of circumstances as they are taking responsibility for a new life just as they themselves are growing up.

Almost 40 percent of babies born to unmarried women are born to women living with the baby's father, almost half of these babies are planned, and the births increase the rate of marriage.[19] Though these unions are more unstable than marriages, research shows that within five years, more than half of these relationships will end in marriage and another 28 percent of the couples will continue living together.

Unintended and Unwanted Parenting

A large study of four thousand mothers found that approximately one-third of all births were *unintended,* meaning births were mistimed or not wanted.[20] Unintended births are of concern because mothers are less likely to seek prenatal care in the first three months and more likely to continue habits such as smoking and drinking alcohol. They are more likely, than mothers who planned babies, to have babies who are premature, low birth weight, or small for gestational age, and they are also less likely to breast-feed their babies. When mothers get appropriate care throughout pregnancy, differences in the two groups of babies disappear.

When mothers have *unwanted* children, defined as the mother's not wanting to have any children or not wanting to have more than she has, mothers are less happy, more prone to depression, and to have greater difficulties rearing not only the unwanted child but also their siblings.[21] Mothers who bear unwanted children are less likely to spend time with them when they are young and more likely to spank them. Difficulties in mother–child relationships continue so that even in adolescence and young adulthood, mothers are less affectionate and less supportive with their children.

In a long-term study carried out in Czechoslovakia, children whose mothers had twice requested but were twice-denied abortions to terminate the pregnancy had significantly more problems and less enjoyment in life than did children whose parents wanted them.[22] In elementary school, the unwanted children had fewer friends, more behavior problems, and poorer school performance even though they had equal intelligence. In adolescence, the differences between the two groups widened, and in young adulthood, individuals unwanted before birth were less happy with their jobs and their marriages. They had more conflict with coworkers and supervisors and less satisfaction with friends. They were discouraged about themselves and their lives, but many took the positive step of getting help for their problems.

At age thirty, there were still differences between unwanted and wanted children, but the gap had narrowed. Women who were unwanted, however, were more likely to be single or divorced, unemployed, and having difficulties in parenting than women who had been wanted. There were few differences between the two groups of men. At age thirty-five, unwanted children continued to seek more psychiatric treatment than wanted children. Adults who were unwanted as children did not develop such problems as alcoholism or criminality, but they were underrepresented on indicators of well-being and excellence.

While an unwanted child may have an increased risk of some difficulties, the following anecdote represents the love many children experience despite their being unwanted initially.

> My twin brother and I were born in postwar Poland, at a time when my parents—both Holocaust survivors whose families were decimated by the Nazis—felt neither emotionally nor financially capable of raising more than the two children they already had. But my mother became pregnant and a doctor told her an abortion might kill her, so here I am. Knowing why I was born has never made me feel insecure or unwanted. My life is so filled with blessings and difficulties like everybody else's, and I have two devoted parents who would move mountains for me.[23]

CONCEPTION

Even though most women have minimal trouble getting pregnant, some individuals and couples have difficulty and feel deeply disappointed. Although the usual estimate of infertility, defined as an inability to get pregnant after twelve months of unprotected sexual relations, is 10–15 percent, a large telephone survey of women, ages 25 to 50, revealed that in the course of their lives, 35 percent of women experienced infertility, most often before the pregnancy with their first child.[24] Infertility was not related to race, age, income, employment, or marriage, although it was related to education. Thirty-seven percent of the women got fertility assistance, and 92 percent of the group eventually conceived. Women experienced long-lasting distress when they were not able to conceive and had no children in adoptive, foster, or stepfamilies. It was infertility combined with childlessness that predicted great distress, not childlessness or infertility alone.

Age and Conception

Increasing age is related to increasing difficulties in conception. Young mothers and fathers in their teens and twenties have few difficulties conceiving. The age of first-time mothers has been increasing. In the past, women over thirty-five having babies were usually having the last of their children; now, many mothers are having their first. In 2004, approximately 600,000 babies were born to women over thirty-five, and 25 percent of the babies were born to first-time mothers.[25] Factors that account for the growing number of older first-time mothers include feminism, a general postponement of childbearing, the large number of Baby Boomers in childbearing age, advances in contraception, better health among women, advances in reproductive technologies, and better obstetrical care.

Still, women over thirty-five more often have difficulties with conception of a first pregnancy. Spontaneous abortions increase from 25 percent at age thirty-five to 50 percent at forty-five,[26] and mothers over thirty-five have greater percentage of genetic abnormalities in the fetus, so screening for such abnormalities are routine for them. Like teenage mothers, older mothers have a greater likelihood of pregnancy complications such as diabetes and low birth weight babies, but these can be treated as they can be with younger women.

Although older mothers face difficulties in conception, they have many advantages as parents. Compared with younger mothers, they have more education, better-paying jobs, and, as a result, greater incomes with more money available to spend on their children.[27] Furthermore, older parents tend to be in more stable marriages and to be more attentive and sensitive parents. Because they are older and have had more experience in life, they find it easier to put children's behavior in perspective and not become frustrated over little things. Yet older parents' work and community responsibilities make incorporating an unpredictable, time-consuming young child into their lives more difficult.

Gender

In the past we have emphasized mothers' role in promoting babies' health, but fathers' behaviors are important too. Just as mothers who smoke, drink alcohol, and use drugs put children at risk for birth defects, these behaviors on fathers' part do the same.[28] Fathers' increasing age at conception may make it more difficult, lead to higher rates of miscarriage,[29] and put children at risk for conditions such as bipolar disorder.[30]

Assisted Conception

Prospective parents seek assistance with conception because they very much want to bear a child. While the procedures were originally developed to help married couples having difficulties with conception, the procedures have made parenthood available to people who could not have had children biologically fifty years ago. Single women without partners and gay and lesbian singles and couples very much want that opportunity now.

There are several levels of assisted conception.[31] The interventions can result in a child that is genetically related to both parents (when the parents' eggs and sperm are used), to one parent (when one parent's egg or sperm is used along with a donor's egg or sperm), or to neither parent (when both donor egg and sperm are used). Initially, assistance takes the form of supporting natural processes by artificial insemination, inserting sperm directly into the woman's reproductive tract with an instrument, and by chemically stimulating the ovaries to produce more eggs, increasing the likelihood of pregnancy.

Assisted Reproductive Technology   The National Center on Birth Defects and Developmental Disabilities uses the term assisted reproductive technology (ART) to refer to the more advanced methods of assistance in which eggs and sperm are handled outside the body.[32] In vitro fertilization (IVF) involves removing eggs from the woman's body, fertilizing them in a petri dish with sperm, and then implanting them back in the uterus. This procedure is used for many reasons, for example, for women who have blocked fallopian tubes. More advanced techniques include introcytoplasmic sperm injection (ICSI), removing an egg and injecting a sperm directly into the egg and then transferring the fertilized egg into the uterus. This has enabled many infertile men to become fathers.

Advances in ART have enabled scientists to make diagnoses of genetic disorders prior to the implantation of the fertilized egg in the uterus.[33] Known as preimplantation genetic diagnosis (PGD), the procedure of taking one cell from the eight-cell embryo and testing it for genetic diseases such as Tay-Sachs disease and implanting only embryos without the genetic defect permits parents to know that the embryo is healthy at the start of the pregnancy. Parents do not have to wait several months to do amniocentesis to determine if the fetus is healthy. Since there can be some error, couples may choose genetic tests later in the pregnancy to increase their confidence that the baby is healthy.

In 2005, there were more than 134,000 ART procedures performed and about 52,000 infants were born as a result.[34] Currently, there is concern that infants born of ART procedures may have a higher risk of birth defects than children conceived naturally. In ART procedures resulting in a single birth, there was an increased number of children born with heart defects, cleft palates, and gastrointestinal defects. Despite the increase, the risk of any birth defect remains very low. Parents considering the procedures should be aware of all possible risks.

Donor Assistance   Donor assistance adds to the possibility of having a baby.[35] There are sperm donations from men and egg donations from women and, more recently, fertilized embryo donations. Furthermore, a surrogate mother (or birth mother) may carry the fertilized embryo to term for the mother. See the interview box with Michelle and Steve, later in the chapter. The surrogate may also, but not necessarily, donate an egg for fertilization.

Sperm donations were the first form of donation; stored in sperm banks, the donations provided healthy sperm that could be matched with the characteristics of the prospective parents. Traditionally, the donors were anonymous, but more recently, banks have asked donors whether they would be willing to be contacted when the child reaches age eighteen. Since the early 1980s, egg donations have also been available through clinics. Because medications are used to stimulate and remove the eggs, egg donation is a more complicated procedure than sperm donation. Perhaps for that reason, egg donors are sometimes friends or relatives of the parents rather than anonymous donors, and they may well sustain an ongoing relationship with the parents.

Donor embryos have raised concerns. These are embryos that couples had frozen, in reserve for their use in the event they did not conceive from the embryos that were implanted. The couples had the children they wanted and no longer needed the embryos. There are approximately 400,000 such embryos in the country, but only about 2 percent have been donated to other couples.[36] Although couples originally felt they would be willing to donate, they decline to do so years later, saying they would feel too uncomfortable knowing they had children being raised by others, and that their children had brothers and sisters they might not know.[37]

A religious organization called Snowflakes has encouraged couples to release these embryos to other parents for adoption and keep some form of contact with the families after the birth as happens in open adoption.[38] The organization insists receiving families get counseling about doing this, and the two families can set criteria for an ongoing relationship. Other organizations have concerns that the term embryo adoption means that the embryo has the same status as a child, and thus far that is not true, as some are donated for research.

PGD has been used to identify embryos with genetic makeup that could, at birth, provide a genetic match to save the life of an existing sibling with an incurable genetic disease. For example, parents of a child with Fanconia anemia, a genetic disorder that leads to the child's early death, can be saved with a perfectly matched bone marrow transplant. Parents have successfully sought help to produce siblings with genetic makeup that saves the life of an existing one.

While most would agree to the use of PGD to prevent or cure illness, there are concerns that it can be used to create designer babies with the preferred sex, height, intelligence, or hair color.[39] Lori Andrews, a lawyer specializing in the legal aspects of reproductive technologies, worries about polls that indicate that 43 percent of responders think it is acceptable for parents to select the physical characteristics of their children, and 42 percent believe it is acceptable to select intellectual traits. She worries that down the road people may shop for a baby like a car. She writes,

> If anything is clear to me as a mother, it is that parenting involves dealing with surprises. Some bring joy: for instance, the discovery of wonderful characteristics you probably never would have thought to program into your child. And yes, other surprises—an illness or accidents—can bring terror.
>
> But, especially where children are concerned, it is the job of the family to provide unconditional love and acceptance, regardless of those surprises. Parents, above all, should not be saddling their babies with admission standards for birth.[40]

Parenting of Parents Relying on ART   Major studies carried out primarily in Europe found that whether parents rely on in vitro fertilization or donor sperm, their parenting behaviors resemble those of parents who naturally conceived their children.[41] Even though parents have experienced numerous anxieties about having children and the numerous medical procedures involved, these difficulties do not detract from their parenting. In fact, when compared with parents who naturally conceived children, mothers in donor insemination families were described as warmer, more sensitive, and more responsive when children were in early elementary school and again at age twelve. Children in these families thought their mothers were as warm as other mothers. Interviewers described fathers in donor insemination families as more detached in matters of discipline when children were twelve, but mothers and children did not perceive any differences in these fathers' behaviors.

Teachers' ratings and psychiatric assessment of the records revealed that the children in all these groups were equally competent and as socially skilled as children reared by parents who had had no difficulties in conceiving.

In studies comparing the parents using sperm and egg donors and parents who naturally conceived their children, the differences between parents favored the parents using egg and sperm donations.[42] These parents had more positive parent–child relationships and were more emotionally involved with the child than parents who naturally conceived their children. Similar findings occurred when parents using surrogate-mother arrangements were compared with parents who naturally conceived their children: Parents using surrogate arrangements were found to have higher psychological well-being and more positive parent–child relationships than parents who naturally conceived their children.[43]

A major hypothesis accounting for the positive differences in families using donor and surrogate arrangements is that those seeking parenthood through those means are highly motivated parents who truly enjoy their children and parent them in a sensitive and effective way.

Telling Children   The American Fertility Society recommends telling children about their origins.[44] Britain and the Netherlands have recently banned anonymous donations of sperm, and any child at age eighteen now has the right to look up and seek the donor father.[45] In Sweden, individuals conceived by donor eggs or donor sperm have the right to identifying information at age eighteen and can contact the donor if they wish. In the United States, the tendency in the past has been not to tell children, but currently there is a move to adopt the policies of Sweden. The Sperm Bank of California, for example, already requests permission from donors to give children identifying information when they are eighteen, and 80 percent of donors have agreed.[46] The first children have recently reached eighteen, so we shall soon see how this works out. The Internet, as we see in Box 6-1, is making some half-sibling and donor–child connections possible.

The desire for greater openness is supported by studies of open adoption that reveal that a lack of secrecy and a better understanding of one's biological parents have improved the adjustment of adoptive children.[47] The situation of children of donor eggs and donor sperm is not exactly comparable to that of adopted children, as a biological parent did not "give them up" but instead helped create them for their rearing parents, but it is similar in that the child's family includes an unknown biological parent. Knowing about a donor and the fact that one can have contact with this person later in life may eliminate the confusion, and a missing biological connection that some children and adults of donor sperm or donor eggs feel. Furthermore, it becomes possible to fill in important gaps in medical history that could be crucial for the child.

The rules for telling children are similar to those in telling children about adoption. See Chapter 15 for further discussion. Parents themselves must first feel fairly comfortable with the facts before talking to children. They then explain them in simplest terms early in children's lives if possible so they grow up hearing about it. Reading books for young children about how families form is helpful and gives children some understanding of the basic concepts. Conversations will occur many times and on many levels as children grow, and parents must be alert to feelings or questions children may have difficulty expressing.

Box 6-1
EXTENDED FAMILIES

Assisted reproductive technologies create new families. Men can donate sperm to a bank many times. Many different women can use batches of the sperm, and sometimes buy and freeze several batches to create full siblings later. While the banks generally keep no records of whether or how many children are born of the sperm, families have organized Internet registries so that siblings and donors can sign up to locate each other by the donor's number. While only a few hundred donors have signed up, seven thousand siblings have signed up. Over a thousand siblings have connected with each other, and a much smaller number of donors and their offspring.*

In one instance, a donor was found to have fathered twenty-one children under the age of three living in very diverse families—four in lesbian couple families, three in heterosexual couple families, and six in single-parent families. These families post pictures of all the children on a website they created and describe children's ongoing development and their response to such demands as toilet training. The families hoped to take a vacation together in the future.

The Donor Siblings Registry enables both older children and mothers to connect and share experiences via e-mail. One sixteen-year-old who had learned only three years before that her parents used donor sperm to conceive her, felt angry at her parents' lying to her for so many years. She shared this with her fifteen-year-old half-sister, who had known for years. Both girls confided that in crowds, they always looked to see if there were a six-foot-tall, blond-haired man with blue eyes present.

When siblings get together, many feel a great sense of familiarity. They introduce them to others as half-brothers or half-sisters, whereas they use the word "donor" to refer to the biological father.

One mother who corresponds with eight other women who used the same man's sperm feels that knowing other children has helped her son feel more connected to a man who has been a very shadowy figure. Knowing the other children has helped him to see his father as a person: "It's not a phantom person out there any more."**

One mother whose daughter is one of the twenty-one siblings feels thrilled as she wants her daughter to have a "family," which she cannot provide. She plans to go on vacation with the other families and hopes to become close to one or two other families so that in the event she dies of high blood pressure, which she developed during the pregnancy, perhaps one of the other mothers or couples would be guardians for her daughter.

As more and more matches are made between siblings and between donors and offspring, we may have the kind of extended family situations created with open adoptions. Desire for a connection to our biological roots is a powerful force drawing people together.

*Jennifer Egan, "Wanted a Few Good Sperm," *New York Times Magazine,* March 19, 2006, p. 44.
**Amy Harmon, "Hello, I'm Your Sister: Our Father is Donor 150," *New York Times,* November 20, 2005, p. A20.

Assisted reproductive technology has created legal and ethical dilemmas that are currently solved on a case-by-case matter in the courts.[48] Who owns eggs, sperm, and fertilized embryos? Can eggs, sperm, or fertilized embryos be used after divorce or death to create children? Should unused fertilized embryos be given to couples seeking to have children? Is it baby selling if models or Harvard students advertise their eggs for $50,000? Should clinics help women in their sixties become pregnant even though they may not live long enough to raise the child? Is it ethical to use PGD to create tall, or smart, or curly-haired children or children of a certain sex to meet parents' requests? At present the United States has few recognized guidelines to resolve these issues. As Debora Spar documents in a recent book, *The Baby Business,* creating babies is a $3 billion industry in this country—and the only one without guidelines.[49]

TRANSITION TO PARENTING

Nine months of pregnancy give parents time to prepare for the baby's arrival even though a month or two of that time may have elapsed before the pregnancy is confirmed.

A Healthy Lifestyle

Parents continue a healthy lifestyle and avoid substances and toxins that can harm the developing child. Pregnancy is described as a critical period of development for the growing fetus because events that affect development at this time may be difficult or impossible to reverse or remedy after birth.[50] Prevention of problems becomes the main aim. Careful screening at birth can identify birth or genetic defects that can be remedied so it is important to have as complete a screening as possible. Some states require little, and some are more thorough.

So, the first act of parenting is to adopt a healthy lifestyle that consists of appropriate levels of exercise, healthy eating habits, and avoidance of damaging substances such as cigarette smoke, alcohol, and environmental toxins. While in many ways mother and child form a symbiotic unit during the pregnancy, it is also important to realize that even in the early months they are two separate organisms and substances that may not harm the mother in any way (e.g., the medication tetracycline) may harm the growing baby.

We cannot address all lifestyle changes as some may depend on the individual parents' health and physical problems, and we cannot go into detail about each. We describe major groups of hazards to mother and child in Table 6-1. In addition to infections and nonprescription drugs, we also list environmental toxins. Numerous prescription drugs affect pregnant women, and pregnant women are advised to check all drugs with their physician, including any herbal or nutritional supplements as they too can have damaging effects on the fetus.

At the same time parents avoid hazardous substances, they take on healthy habits, and chief among them is healthy eating. Good nutrition not only promotes

■ **TABLE 6-1**
RISKS IN PREGNANCY*

Infections	Sexually Transmitted Diseases
Chicken Pox	Chlamydia
Cytomegalovirus	Genital Herpes
German Measles or Rubella	Gonorrhea
Hepatitis B	Human Papillomavirus (HPV)
Human Immunodeficiency Virus	Monilial Vulvovaginitis
Listeriosis	Trichomonal Vaginitis
Toxoplasmosis	
Varicella	

Drugs	Environmental Toxins
Alcohol	Lead
Amphetamines	Mercury
Caffeine	Polychlorinated biphenyls (PCBs)
Cocaine	Glues and solvents
Ecstacy	Pesticides
Marijuana	X-rays
Nicotine	

*Adapted from Glade B. Curtis and Judith Schuler, *Your Pregnancy Week by Week,* 5th ed. (Cambridge, MA: DeCapo, 2004).

a healthy pregnancy for mother and child and growth of the developing fetus, but it affects the child's development after birth.[51] Studies in developing countries and in low-income groups in this country have found that nutritional supplements to mothers during pregnancy have increased birth weights of babies and have also improved performance on cognitive measures after birth.

Maintaining positive emotional moods and managing stress during pregnancy are important as well because high levels of stress have been found to be related to increased fetal motor movements,[52] and later to the child's hyperactivity and irritability.

Experiences in the Transition

Parents who have a committed relationship and plan to become parents more likely come to the experience with the financial and social resources that support family life.[53] When parents—single, partnered, or married—have planned the pregnancy and conception has followed within a matter of months, they come

INTERVIEW
with Michelle and Steve

Michelle and Steve, already the parents of a four-year-old boy, had twins, a boy and a girl, with the help of a gestational surrogate mother. They were delighted to be interviewed about their experiences doing this. Their son had been age three and Michelle had been eight and a half months pregnant with a girl when the placenta ruptured, after which they lost the baby, and the operation to save her life eliminated the possibility of her carrying another child.

Steve: We were devastated, and had grief counseling that gradually transitioned into counseling about how to have another child. We explored adoption and went to seminars about adopting children from China and South America and we also explored surrogacy. We went to two different agencies and had interviews, and decided to try surrogacy, and if that was unworkable, then adoption.

Michelle: We chose an agency in which all the women in charge—the owner, the lawyer who drew up the contract—had children by surrogate parenting. It was a very carefully run place. All the surrogate mothers and their husbands—most were married—had to be screened psychologically. The surrogate mothers had to have given birth to at least one child and had a smooth pregnancy and delivery. They were paid to do it, but if money were the primary goal, then they could not be surrogate mothers. They could not have large debt either. We also were screened for psychological stability.

Steve: We almost balked about the way the owner wanted to choose the mother, but we went along with it. We could look at a book of surrogate mothers and pick a few we definitely liked, and a few we did not want, but the owner would make the final match for the first interview. If we didn't think the person would work, she would choose someone else. The reason she did this was so prospective parents would not be interviewing a number of people trying to decide on a person. When we questioned her about this method, she said, "Trust me," and she hit a home run. She picked Anisa. We all had dinner together—the owner and her husband, Michelle and I, and Anisa and her husband. It was a social occasion, and there was almost no discussion of surrogacy.

Anisa was charming, and she was a dream surrogate. She was from a Seventh Day Adventist family so she was a vegetarian, only occasionally had caffeine, and she had a healthy lifestyle. Also, she was a billing clerk in an obstetrics and gynecology office of a husband and wife team so she had constant access to a medical support network. The woman doctor was her best friend, and she took a great interest in the pregnancy too.

Most surrogates are picky about the couple they do this for, and most want a "virgin" couple. They want to bring the first child into the world for a childless couple, to provide them something they could not have otherwise. We already had a child, but Anisa wanted to help us have a sibling for our son. She has been very close to her sister, and she wanted to provide that kind of relationship for our son. After the dinner, we all felt positive about going ahead, so we had a meeting to settle the parameters of the relationship. We had to decide how many times to try, how many babies she would carry. The cost of one child would be $15,000, with an additional charge of $5,000 for twins. We knew we would be happy with twins as twins run in the family, and Anisa agreed, but we all left more than two children for later discussion.

We also had to decide what kind of relationship we would have afterward. All of us wanted an ongoing relationship. Anisa is an important person in our lives. We see her a few times a year, and every holiday she sends the children gifts, and we always send her flowers or gifts at holidays.

Michelle: We had to go through the process of in vitro fertilization. I had to take fertility drugs to stimulate the ovulation of eggs, but I had done that with our son. Anisa had to take drugs to suppress her cycle so it matched mine, and she had to take drugs so that she could be receptive after my eggs were harvested, fertilized, and ready for the transfer to Anisa. If there are too many embryos that are surviving after the transfer, you have to decide what to do. Three embryos were seen on the first ultrasound, but a week later, there were only two so we were very happy with twins.

During the pregnancy, I talked regularly on the phone with Anisa. She lives about 200 miles from here. I would call and see how things were going. I never had any worry about her taking care of herself as she worked in a medical atmosphere and knew how important diet and sleep were. Sometimes I'd tell her, "Oh, go out and get a new maternity outfit." Her husband was such a low-key guy. I don't know that a lot of guys would go along with her carrying someone else's children. He was an unsung hero. We never worried she would want to keep the children. She had two girls, and the babies were always referred to as "Michelle's babies," and she was carrying them because I could not.

Steve: The labor and delivery were very smooth. About a month before, she had to go to the hospital for a day, but she carried the twins to eight and a half months. She was in the delivery room, our parents were there, our aunt, Anisa's parents were there, and her husband. We drove down, and our son David was with us, but he had been exposed to chicken pox and could not go into the maternity ward. So someone was always with him.

Michelle: With David, I had a painful labor of fifty hours, but Anisa was sitting in the labor room, calm, with an occasional "Ooh." Then the doctor said, "You're ready," and she hadn't moaned or screamed or anything. She was completely calm and casual, like it was nothing. It was so amazing to me how easy it was for her. That first night Anisa and I spent the night with the twins in the hospital. The next morning I went to the motel and got a nap and David and Steve were at the hospital. When I went back, the doctor said, "Everything is perfect. Do you want to take the babies home?" Anisa's daughters came and saw the babies, and we took pictures.

Steve: It was an emotional time for everyone. Anisa was happy because it was so successful. It was a risk to offer someone that. We were thrilled to have the twins, and they slept all the way home.

Michelle: We were on an emotional high for a year because it was such an amazing thing, and we wanted everyone to know about it. And there is more use of surrogacy than you would think. Once you begin to talk about it, you find that many people have been involved. I was talking to someone at work who was visiting here, and he made the comment, "Ever since my wife did surrogacy for a neighbor," and went on to describe something. Friends offered to be surrogate mothers, but we decided to get an objective third party.

(continued)

INTERVIEW with Michelle and Steve

(*continued*)

How do the twins, now five, understand Anisa's role?
Steve: The counselor told us that young children understand helping, and we told them that Mommy made the babies, but she needed help to get them to birth—her tummy could not carry them so Anisa helped us and carried the twins to birth.

---

to pregnancy with great anticipation of what is to come and few stressful feelings from trying to conceive. When the pregnancy is unplanned, the difficulty of making a decision about the pregnancy and conflict that may occur between parents increase the stress of the transition. Such stress makes it hard for the parent or parents to use the time of the transition for psychological preparation for the baby's arrival.

Pregnancy involves many physiological and psychological changes. Physical changes include changes in levels of fatigue, sleep and eating patterns, size, shape, and emotional reactivity, to mention only a few. Parents begin to accommodate to the demands of the life growing within the mother. The changes are easier to adapt to when parents have deliberately taken on the challenges rather than having been forced to adjust to them.

Ellen Galinsky, whose work is discussed in greater detail at the end of the chapter, has interviewed parents regarding their psychological reactions to becoming parents and caring for children.[54] She describes pregnancy as the period of image-making. Parents form ideas of what they will be like as parents and what the baby will be like. In the first three months of pregnancy, parents may feel elated about the coming baby but also fearful about the possibility of miscarriage. Even in the early months their images may clash with reality. Parents may not feel as excited as they anticipated even though they had planned the baby. Maybe there was more morning sickness or tiredness than anticipated. Throughout parenthood, parents have to adjust their images of what they expect to fit the reality of what is happening. That process starts in pregnancy and continues.

In the next three months, Galinsky believes that parents prepare for parenthood. They think of the changes in their roles that will occur after the baby comes. They look at their own childhoods, think how they want their child's life to be similar or different from what they experienced. If they already have a child, they wonder about how a brother or sister will adjust or how they will be able to love more than one child. Parents often look at their relationship with each other and how they as a couple are managing. Are they supportive of each other? What will it be like after the baby comes? They may form new friendships with other parents-to-be, and older friendships may fade into the background.

In the last three months of pregnancy, their thoughts turn to the birth, and they begin to worry about what it might be like. During this time, childbirth classes help parents make realistic preparations for the birth and arrival of the baby and parents in the classes often form an ongoing support group to talk about worries and stresses.

With all the changes occurring inside their bodies, women may become more dependent on help from their partners and their extended family support groups. When relationships among family members have been positive and mothers feel family members are accepting of them, they function more effectively. While prospective fathers may feel excited about the birth, they are beginning to get a taste of feeling on the sidelines as they do not really know what it is like to have a life growing inside them. As noted, they are more likely to be involved after the births when they have been included in prebirth medical visits. With women's preoccupation with the growing child, fathers-to-be have adjustments to make also.

When Parents Are Single

Single parents must begin to build the support group that will sustain them after the birth. They must accept that they will be exhausted with the care of a newborn or young child, and friends or family members must be organized to help.

There are a new group of single parents less studied, and that is single men who have impregnated a woman who wants to give the child up for adoption. The biological father wishes to have custody and raise the child as his, but laws in many states set a very narrow window of time in which fathers can register to claim paternal rights to adopt the child.[55] Currently, fathers have brought suits to obtain custody in several states.

State registries have increased in the last ten years to protect the rights of the child to permanent placement, to protect adoptive parents from having a child taken from them after several years as happened in the early 1990s, and to give fathers rights too. The registries, however, are little publicized and hard to locate, with varying windows of time for registration, some as little as five days from birth, others until the adoption petition is filed. Furthermore, registries may give fathers rights only within a county or state so that if the mother takes the child out of state, the father has no rights. Fathers are at a disadvantage in knowing about registries and registering within the time limit. Senator Mary Landrieu of Louisiana is about to sponsor a law for a national registry for fathers.

One single father in Texas fought for paternal rights after his son had been adopted and arrived at a compromise with the adoptive parents. The adoptive parents are raising the now thirteen-year-old boy, and the noncustodial father has visiting rights.

Another group of fathers being helped to become parents are young men who have fathered children outside of marriage, sometimes having a relationship with the mother and sometimes not. We discuss this in Chapter 14. They are being encouraged to establish paternity and in 1998–2000, 69 percent of fathers established paternity most often in hospital programs.[56] Establishing paternity is related to both formal child support payments for the child and to psychological and social support following the birth.

Summary   Regardless of whether parents naturally conceive their child, use assisted reproductive technology, or adopt, at a young age or older age, it is parents' interactions with children that enable children to flourish and grow, not on how they were created or came into the family.

ADJUSTMENT TO PARENTHOOD

The arrival of a baby changes every aspect of adults' lives, from finances to sex life, sleeping habits, and social life. Although many first-time parents report that nothing could have adequately prepared them for the experience, knowing what to expect can still help parents cope.

The Power of Positive Relationships

Throughout this book, we will see that positive relationships sustain parents as they care for their children. Positive relationships with their own parents and with each other enable parents to be more loving and effective parents.[57] Furthermore, positive relationships with children are related to children's healthy growth.

When mothers and fathers feel support from each other, their competence as parents grows, and interaction with the baby becomes more effective. Father–infant interactions and fathers' competence, particularly, are related to feeling support from mothers (see the interview with James Levine). Even basic activities are influenced by the quality of the marriage. Mothers experience fewer feeding difficulties when their husbands are supportive and view them positively, whereas marital distress is related to inept feeding by the mother.[58]

One of the best predictors of good prenatal care for the mother is whether the partner is involved.

INTERVIEW
with James Levine

James Levine is the director of the Fatherhood Project at the Families and Work Institute. He served as a principal consultant to Vice Present Al Gore in drafting the federal initiative on fatherhood, created by executive order in 1995.

What are the best ways to get men involved in parenting?

There are several issues. I think the absolute key is the couple's expectations of what the father's role will be. If the mom doesn't expect the dad to be involved, and the dad doesn't expect to be involved, that's a prescription for noninvolvement. If Mom doesn't expect Dad to be involved and Dad might want to be involved, he won't be involved. The mother is the gatekeeper in the relationship. Many women say they want husbands to be involved, but in effect, they want them to be involved as a sort of mom's subordinate or assistant. Mom's the manager, telling Dad how to be involved as opposed to assuming Dad will be involved and will learn the skills to be a father. It is important for mothers to back off and be in the background, and let fathers be with children.

So, one key to involvement is the couple's dynamics. I don't mean to blame Mom, but there is a system here—men and women as a system—and one starts here in terms of making a supportive system for fathers' involvement.

Then let's look at men in terms of men and the system outside the couple. All the research we've done shows that men today define success on two dimensions: being a good provider and, equally important, having good relationships with children. So if you look at the values men bring to parenthood, there are generally agreed-upon desires to have close relationships with their children. But, aside from the couple relationship, there are two obstacles. Men sometimes feel incompetent as to how to do this; they need skills. And, second, their work sucks them up in spite of their best intentions to give time to relationships with children. They spend a lot of time working, not to avoid forming relationships with children, but as a way of caring for children.

A key to change is changing the cultural clues men get about being fathers. Looking at this from an ecological and systems point of view, we can ask, "What are the cues that men get about parenting across the life cycle?" The expectations others have about them have a lot to do with shaping their behavior. For example, prenatally if men get expectations from the health-care system that they are expected to be at prenatal visits, they will be there. Mostly, however, they get the message they have no role during the pregnancy. Yet, research has shown that one of the best predictors of good prenatal care for the mother is whether the partner is involved with prenatal care.

We have found in our work with low-income men that when men understand how vital their role is even before the child is born, they can change their level of involvement. Knowing how important their role is with their babies increases the motivation of low-income men to be involved.

So at the time of birth and afterward, if the pediatrician sends messages that he or she wants both parents at visits—"I need to know both of the baby's parents. I want to see you both, not just the mother"—that message shapes the father's behavior. Same thing at preschools or day care. They can also send messages that they want both parents, not just mothers, to be involved.

(continued)

INTERVIEW with James Levine

(continued)

So it is the expectations that are embedded in daily interactions that are the real keys to fathers' involvement. If you look at the face-to-face interactions with maternity nurses and pediatricians, embedded in dialogues with doctors, health-care providers, and teachers are messages about expected involvement. If more messages expect fathers to be involved and daily interactions offer support for fathers' involvement, fathers will be involved.

To give a specific example, West Virginia wanted to increase the rate at which fathers established paternity of children born to single mothers, and the question was how to do that. One could think about a big public-information campaign with messages to encourage involvement, but the key was the maternity nurse, who had the most influence on both the young man and the young woman. The father would come and look at the baby, and if the nurse assumed he was some bad guy and chased him away, if she did not invite him in to be involved with the baby, he would disengage and disappear. They increased the rate of paternity establishment by increasing the dialogue with fathers and also by changing what the nurse said to mothers. The nurse told mothers it is important for children to be involved with their fathers even if mothers decide not to marry the fathers. In two years, the rate of establishing paternity went from 15 percent to 60 percent of fathers who claimed paternity of babies born to single mothers.

The overall message to fathers was we want you here, we want you to establish paternity and be fathers to your children. Changing expectations encoded in daily interactions are the important elements in increasing fathers' involvement with their children.

What constitutes a positive marital relationship? One contributor to marital satisfaction is parents' agreement on role arrangements.[59] It does not matter whether couples are traditional or egalitarian in their division of tasks; satisfaction increases when couples have similar ideologies. A second contributor to marital satisfaction is a couple's ability to communicate with each other—to express thoughts, feelings, and needs in ways each partner can hear and respond to. Communication does not have to be verbal. A look, a gesture, a touch, or an action can communicate support, agreement, or the need for further conversation.

Parents who focus on what is good about the situation or the action of the other person, who avoid negative criticism and angry exchanges, feel less stress and create less stress for each other. These parents discuss different points of view and express themselves forcefully, but they stay focused on how they can make needed changes and improve the situation, and they avoid assigning blame for problems.

These qualities are possible to develop even if parents live separately and care for the child alone. Making agreeable care arrangements, respecting the other parent as a person, and cooperating in coparenting, as we discussed in Chapter 4, can promote parents' effectiveness and babies' growth even when marital satisfaction is not possible.

A single parent develops a support group of extended family or friends who help with the caregiving activities and also share the mother's or father's delight in the baby's growing engagement with her and the world. A support group plays a powerful role in being available when a single parent needs to talk over a problem or needs encouragement when tired or frustrated or lonely.

Changes the Baby Brings

A great deal goes on during the early months. Parents are highly involved in the nurturing stage of parenthood,[60] caring for the child, and accepting their new role as parents. They worry, "Am I doing okay?" "Am I the kind of parent I want to be?" Gradually, parents incorporate other parts of their lives—work, extended family, friends—into their caretaking activities. Parents may find it difficult, however, to give each other the support that is so crucial in coping during this period. New mothers and fathers had similar complaints: (1) tiredness and exhaustion; (2) loss of sleep, especially in the first two months; (3) needing to adjust to new responsibilities; (4) feeling inadequate as a parent; (5) difficulty in keeping up with the amount of work for baby and home; (6) feeling tied down, and (7) worries regarding finances.[61] Neither parent anticipated the many changes that would occur in their lives when their babies arrived, in part because they did not realize how much work is involved in caring for an infant.

Dimensions Underlying the Adjustment

Two longitudinal studies—one carried out by Carolyn Pape Cowan and Philip Cowan[62] and the other by Jay Belsky[63]—have yielded remarkably similar findings on the basic dimensions underlying the adjustment process. See Table 6-2. First, a major determiner of the ease of the adjustment process is parents' ability to balance their needs for autonomy and self-care with the need to be close to other people, particularly their spouse and child. Parents have an easier time when they can

■ **T A B L E   6-2**
DIMENSIONS UNDERLYING THE TRANSITION TO PARENTHOOD

1. Capacity to balance individuality and mutuality

2. Communication skills of both parents

3. Attitude (positive/negative) in confronting situations and people

4. Expectations about what the baby will bring

5. Ability to devise sharing of workload that is compatible with couple's beliefs/ideologies concerning appropriate behavior for men and women

6. Ability to come to terms with patterns of behavior learned in family of origin

7. Ability to manage conflict effectively

Adapted from Jay Belsky and John Kelly, *The Transition to Parenthood* (New York: Delacorte, 1994); Carolyn Pape Cowan and Philip Cowan, *When Partners Become Parents* (New York: Basic Books, 1992).

create an "us" relationship that has priority over individual needs. They put aside immediate individual wants in order to help their partner, because that improves their relationship. A husband may put aside his desire to go visiting as a family because his wife is tired and needs to rest and he wants them both to feel good about the outing. Or a wife may not ask her husband to skip his evening jog to help with the baby, because she feels he needs to unwind from work, and she wants a relaxed family atmosphere when he is with the baby.

Other dimensions are listed in Table 6-3. Those parents most at risk for difficulties are unrealistic about the changes a baby will bring, have negative views of their partner and their marriage, and are pessimistic about solving problems. They take no action to arrive at mutually satisfying solutions to their difficulties.

Both Belsky and the Cowans agree that transitions vary by gender. Although men and women have many common experiences—both find the baby irresistible, both worry about bills and the increased work, and both feel better about themselves as a result of parenthood—they experience the transition in different ways. For one, the experience is much more physical for women than for men. Because women have a biological connection with the child during the pregnancy, labor, and delivery, the child is a greater reality to them, and many maintain the intimate physical connection with the child by breast-feeding. Men experience the pregnancy and the early months after birth from a greater distance and often feel left out. Lacking the close physical connection with the child, fathers often need more time to form a strong attachment with the baby.

In most instances, couples navigate the transition well, not because they have fewer or less serious problems than the couples who experience difficulties, but

■ **TABLE 6-3**
RECOMMENDATIONS TO COUPLES FOR EASING THE TRANSITION TO PARENTHOOD

1. Share expectations.
2. Give yourselves regular checkups on how each is doing.
3. Make time to talk to each other.
4. Negotiate an agenda of important issues; if one partner thinks there is a problem, there is.
5. Adopt an experimental attitude; see how solutions work and make modifications as necessary.
6. Don't ignore sex and intimacy.
7. Line up support for the early stages after the birth.
8. Talk with a friend or coworker.
9. Find the delicate balance between meeting your needs and the baby's needs; children grow best when parents maintain a strong, positive relationship.

Adapted from Carolyn Pape Cowan and Philip Cowan, *When Partners Become Parents* (New York: Basic Books, 1992.

because they have developed effective ways to cope with changes and resolve conflicts.

These domains were identified through studies of couples, but they apply to the transitions of single parents as well. Single parents have to form a supportive network of individuals who can help. Whether their support group is made up of friends or family, single parents have to share with these individuals their expectations and feelings; they must all find ways to divide the workload, manage conflict, and avoid negative outbursts.

Forming a Coparenting Alliance

James McHale and his colleagues observed a group of middle-class, educated families as they made the transition from the last trimester of pregnancy through the first two and a half years of the child's life.[64] Their focus was on the coparenting alliance parents built as they reared their children. Coparenting, as noted in Chapter 4, is parents' ability to work together, to cooperate and coordinate their efforts to provide care for children. The quality of the marriage predicted the coparenting alliance parents would build after the baby came, but coparenting is more than a measure of marital adjustment. It is a measure of the partnership two parents form as they plan and coordinate efforts to care for their children. The researchers did find that some couples were able to build a coparenting alliance even though they were experiencing difficulties in their marriages. They did this by attending to their partners' perceptions, feelings, and desires and tried to coordinate their child-rearing efforts with those of their partners.

In their interviews and assessment measures in the last trimester of pregnancy, McHale and colleagues focused on parents' views of their family of origin and how their parents coparented and on parents' expectations of what their family would be like when the baby came. The researchers were surprised that many of the parents had negative views of their parents' coparenting and were committed to making changes in their own families. In talking about attachments to their parents, many prospective parents expressed feelings of rejection, distance, and detachment from their parents. These negative feelings did not predict their future hopes or behavior when parents were able to gain a broad understanding of their parents and talk about their relationships with them in a coherent way.

When parents could not move beyond these early experiences and handled them by pushing them out of their thoughts or dismissing their importance, or continuing to brood or dwell on them, then these parents were more likely to be distanced and detached about the future they would build. Men and women who felt rejected by fathers were very negative in their expectations of forming a coparenting alliance. McHale and his colleagues emphasized it was not the family of origin or where parents came from that predicted the future but how prospective parents handled their feelings about the early events that predicted the future.

The researchers were also surprised how little parents had talked to each other about their parenting beliefs and values before the birth of the child. Parents did not really know how the other parent felt about letting the child cry or where a child should sleep. Frequently, there were marked discrepancies between parents' actual beliefs and what the other parent predicted they were. It was the discrepancy between what parents thought was the right thing to do with babies and toddlers that produced intense feelings and conflicts.

All parents were a little anxious. It was primarily those parents who struggled with additional issues concerning their parents or difficulties in their marriages that had significant problems. In envisioning the kinds of services most beneficial to parents, McHale suggested that interventions to help parents communicate and discuss issues around caring for children would be the most helpful. While traditional home visiting programs improve parent–child interactions and marriage communication programs improve couples' abilities to talk about their relationship, neither kind of program targets the ability of the couple to coordinate their efforts and work together.

Adjustments of Parents Who Adopt or Who Have Premature Children

In addition to the usual stresses of the birth of a baby, parents who adopt or have premature children face additional challenges. Unlike most parents, who have nine months of preparation for parenthood, parents who adopt or have premature births are often plunged into parenthood in unpredictable ways. Adopting parents may have waited months or even years for a child when suddenly the child arrives with little warning, perhaps ill or stressed at all the changes. Workplaces may be unaccommodating, and friends may ask many questions. Adopting parents may also worry that the birth mother will change her mind.

Fortunately, adopting parents have buffers. These parents tend to be older, with all the advantages of older parents described earlier in this chapter. Compared with younger parents, they are more settled in their work, have greater financial resources, have been married longer, and have developed better coping skills.

Parents of premature children may have little or much to manage. If children are only a few weeks premature, parents may have no problems. If a child is born at twenty-four or twenty-six weeks after conception, however, the child might stay in the hospital for an extended period of time. His or her parents must consider whether the child will survive and whether long-term problems will develop. They also face the ongoing stress of dealing with hospital and medical personnel and the changing medical status of their child. Furthermore, when the child comes home, they may need to make many changes to address his or her special needs.[65]

Parents of premature children are advised to interact with them and to take over as much care of their children as possible in the hospital.[66] A recent hospital intervention, Kangaroo Care (KC), benefited the infant and the whole family. KC consisted of skin-to-skin care between mother and infant; for at least an hour a day for a period of two weeks, the infant, wearing only a diaper, lay between the mothers' breasts. Observations of the families' interaction patterns when infants were three months of age revealed that KC was related to increases in mothers' sensitivity to their infants and in their ability to adjust their stimulation to the babies' needs. KC was also related to increases in affectionate touching between parents and between parents and child. At three months of age, infants were less irritable than infants in a control group who did not receive KC, and there was greater reciprocity in the relationships between parent and child. It is thought that the physical contact helped the mother understand the baby's needs better and give more sensitive care; as a result, she felt more confident and positive toward both the baby and her husband. Mother's positive touching of her husband increased his positive touches with her and the baby.

A very brief version of this intervention has proved useful for full-term infants as well. Infants who received one hour of Kangaroo Care with mothers about twenty minutes after birth were found to have more organized motor movements, to sleep better, and have less crying following KC.[67] The benefits were observed for up to four hours. For full-term infants, KC helped to reduce the stress associated with all the physiological changes at birth and appeared to help newborns achieve greater regulation of their physiological state. More study is needed on the effects of KC during the first postnatal weeks and its effects on mother–infant interactions and babies' focusing skills.

In the special circumstances of adoption and premature birth, all the ways listed for couples to ease the transition to parenthood are important. Support from friends or from those dealing with similar situations and clear communication between parents and between parents and professional workers are especially essential.

PRACTICAL QUESTION: WHAT CHANGES CAN PARENTS ANTICIPATE FOR THEMSELVES?

Ellen Galinsky, a consultant and lecturer on child development, found herself changing after her children were born. Curious about the meaning of her feelings, she consulted books and research reports to see what other parents were describing. Finding little to inform her, she began forming groups of parents of young children. She then interviewed 228 parents with different experiences of parenthood—married, divorced, step-, foster, and adoptive parents. These parents did not represent a random sampling but were a broad cross-section of the population.

Galinsky has divided parenthood into six stages in which parents focus their emotional and intellectual energy on the task of that period.[68] These stages differ from most in that a parent can be in more than one stage at a time with children of different ages. The first stage, occurring in pregnancy, she terms the *image-making* stage. It is a time when parents prepare for changes in themselves and in their relationships to others. The second, *nurturing* stage goes from birth to the time when the child starts to say "no," about eighteen to twenty-four months. As parents become attached to the new baby, they arrange their lives to be caregivers, balancing their own and their child's needs and setting priorities. The third, *authority* stage lasts from the time the child is age two to four or five. Parents become rule givers and enforcers as they learn that love for children goes hand in hand with structure and order. From the child's preschool years through adolescence, parents are in the *interpretive* stage. Children are more skilled and independent, and parents establish a way of life for them, interpret outside authorities such as teachers, and teach values and morals. In brief, they teach children what life is all about.

When their children are adolescents, parents enter the *interdependent* stage. They form new relationships with children, and, though they are still authorities, their power becomes shared with children in ways it was not in past years. In the sixth stage, *departure*, parents evaluate themselves as their children prepare to leave home. They see where they have succeeded and where they might have acted differently.

Galinsky summarizes her views of how parenthood changes adults:

> Taking care of a small, dependent, growing person is transforming, because it brings us in touch with our baser side, it exposes our vulnerabilities as well as our nobility. We lose our sense of self, only to find it and have it change again and again. We learn to nurture and care. We struggle through defining our own rules and our own brand of being an authority. We figure out how we want to interpret the wider world, and we learn to interact with all those who affect our children. When our children are teenagers, we redefine our relationships, and then we launch them into life.
>
> Often our fantasies are laid bare, our dreams are in a constant tug of war with realities. And perhaps we grow. In the end, we have learned more about ourselves, about the cycles of life, and humanity itself. Most parents describe themselves as more responsible, more accepting, more generous than before they had children.[69]

SUPPORT FOR PARENTS

Various kinds of support can help parents adjust to parenting. When parents successfully meet the demands of their new roles, they feel competent and effective. These feelings of self-efficacy can continue, influencing ongoing parenting in beneficial ways. Family and friends provide informal sources of support as well as information, advice, and direct help in the form of shopping, cleaning, and cooking so parents can get some rest. Other, more formal sources of support consist of classes and support groups.

Classes

Most couples are referred to classes at hospitals or in the community prior to the arrival of the baby. Even programs given in hospitals at the time of the birth can provide information that increases parents' competence in caring for their babies. Such information focuses on babies' states and their repertoire of behaviors, the ways they send signals to parents, and how parents learn to understand and respond to the signals. Especially helpful are tips on when to "engage" with babies (when they are fed and alert), when to "disengage" (when babies turn away, fall into a drowsy state), how to feed infants, and how to deal with crying.[70] Brief behavioral parent training[71] enables parents to help their newborn develop healthy sleep patterns.

Support Groups

As we noted in the last chapter, the Cowans have found that couples groups were very helpful to new parents.[72] Couples discussed the stresses of adjusting to

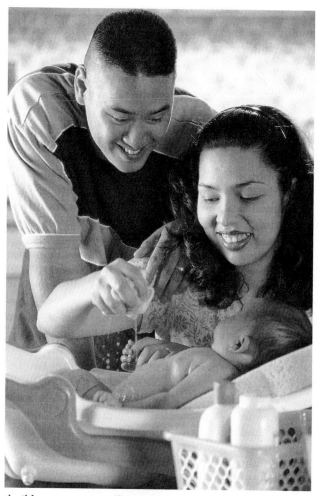

Parents have to build a coparenting alliance as they care for their new baby.

parenting and found reassurance in learning that others have similar problems. The couples discussed activities or attitudes that reduced stress and that produced well-being and closeness between parents.

When parents conceive a child and bring him or her into the world, they embark on possibly the most life-changing experience of their lives. Whether well or poorly planned, the child elicits new behaviors from parents and at the same time brings a host of new pleasures to them. When parents work together with each other or with supportive friends and relatives, when they communicate expectations, experiences, and feelings as they care for the baby, the baby brings parents and friends and relatives closer together to share life experiences in a more intense, meaningful way than previously known. Babies demand a great deal, but they give much in return.

MAIN POINTS

Becoming a parent involves

- assessing parental readiness in terms of time and psychological resources
- couples' planning children and resolving differences
- single adults' planning children
- accepting a child if unplanned
- resolving ambivalence so the child is wanted, not rejected

Changes in adoption policies and assisted reproductive technologies

- mean that people who would have been childless in the past can now have children
- raise questions about children's rights to know their biological roots

Timing of children

- depends on the psychological qualities of parents rather than their age
- affects a child's later adjustment—if parents are not mature, a child may be at risk later problems

The means of becoming parents

- has little effect on parenting strategies
- has no documented effect on children's functioning and competence

Babies bring

- new routines and responsibilities
- great pleasures
- a special appreciation in parents who experienced infertility

Dimensions underlying a parent's transition to parenthood include

- balancing individuality and mutuality
- communication skills
- positive attitudes
- agreed-upon division of labor
- parents coming to terms with their own childhood experiences
- forming a coparenting alliance

Parents experience greater ease in the transition when they

- maintain intimate bonds with their partner or a supportive friend or relative
- share expectations, feelings, and workload with partners
- line up support from friends and relatives
- adopt an experimental attitude toward solutions—trying them and seeing if they work

EXERCISES

1. Imagine that you and your partner were discussing your readiness to have a baby. What factors would make you feel that you are ready? How would you handle a disagreement between the two of you as to whether to have a baby or not? Suppose you both felt strongly about your opinion, what would you do?

2. Describe your expectations of parenthood. What changes will it require of you? Do you think your expectations are realistic? Describe the activities that you do now that might prepare you for being a parent—taking a course in parenting, learning to solve conflicts in a positive way, practicing communication skills with friends, learning about children and their needs. Are there other things you could be doing?

3. Plan out the support system you would organize for yourself and your partner if you were having a baby in three months. Whom would you include? How involved would your relatives be? How much extra expense would such a system create?

4. Imagine you are a fifteen-year-old girl who becomes pregnant and wants to keep her child. Investigate the resources in your community that would enable you to keep the child, remain in school, get a job. Visit the programs or day care center where your child would be cared for. Are the services adequate?

5. Imagine you and your partner required donor insemination or egg donors. Investigate the resources in your area and the requirements for people using them.

ADDITIONAL READINGS

Belsky, Jay, and Kelly, John. *The Transition to Parenthood.* New York: Delacorte, 1994.

Borkowski, John G. et al., eds. *Risk and Resilience: Adolescent Mothers and Their Children Grow Up.* Mahwah, NJ: Erlbaum, 2007.

Cowan, Carolyn Pape, and Cowan, Philip. *When Partners Become Parents.* New York: Basic Books, 1992.

Ehrensaft, Diane. *Mommies, Daddies, Donors, Surrogates.* New York: Guilford Press, 2005.

Spar, Debora. *The Baby Business: How Money, Science, and Politics Drive the Commerce of Conceptions.* Boston: Harvard University Press, 2006.

7

Parenting Infants:
The Years from Birth to Two

<table>
<tr>
<td>

CHAPTER TOPICS

In this chapter, you will learn about:

- Parenting the newborn

- Development in the first two years

- Parent–child relationships

- Promoting children's growth in all areas

- Support for parents

</td>
<td>

IN THE NEWS

New York Times, February 5[1]: Parents are advised to develop skills to cope with toddlers' temper tantrums. See pages 225–227.

</td>
</tr>
</table>

Test Your Knowledge: Fact or Fiction (True/False)

1. Duplicating conditions in the womb helps calm newborns so they can settle into their new world more easily.
2. Though mothers and fathers relate differently to infants they are equally competent caregivers.
3. In the first six months of life, mothers and fathers mainly feed and diaper babies because babies do not yet show social interests.
4. When babies are fussy and irritable, parents need extended help to find positive ways to soothe them.
5. Advantaged middle-class parents with many resources are able to avoid the depression and stress a new baby brings to the home.

What are babies like? How do they relate to parents and shape what parents do? How do parents support children's rapid growth in these first two years of life? Who and what support parents in their important roles as caregivers of the next generation?

After living nine months in warm fluid with necessities automatically provided, babies are thrust into a cold, dry world, required to breathe and eat on their own, and arouse others to provide the necessities of life. In two short years, they develop from newborns struggling to adapt to their new world to assertive toddlers who walk, run, and talk and love their parents but have definite ideas of their own. They know what they want and go get it. This chapter charts how parents become gentle soothers, loving caregivers, active social partners, and persuasive guides who set firm limits.

THE NEWBORN

During the first three months, babies' physiological rhythms and states are not organized and only gradually settle into more organized patterns. Parents feed and help newborns maintain calm states for sleeping and seeing the world.

The average newborn sleeps about sixteen to eighteen hours a day, with some babies sleeping as much as twenty-two hours, some as little as ten.[2] Sleep is of two kinds. Infants spend about 50 percent of their sleep time in active, REM sleep (rapid eye movement sleep, sometimes termed dreaming sleep, thought to stimulate the brain), and 50 percent in non-REM quiet sleep (when the body is relaxed and still). Over the first six to twelve months, sleep becomes organized into a longer period of eight to twelve hours at night, with two naps during the day. Thus, babies are alert and have more time to investigate their new world, even if they initially only use their eyes to do so.

Babies also cry and appear distressed. Again, great individual differences exist. In newborn nurseries, babies cried from one to eleven minutes per hour, with a daily average of about two hours. Hunger and wet diapers were significant causes, but the largest single category of causes was "unknown."[3]

In the first six weeks, infants' crying increases to about three hours per day, mostly concentrated in the late afternoon or evening hours,[4] then decreases to an average of one hour a day at three months. Although hunger seems to be the pre-dominant cause, "unknown" remains the second-highest category for this age.

Ways to soothe babies and help them settle in are described in Box 7-1 and in the section "Parenting Tasks and Concerns."

Early Social Reactions

Babies come into the world preprogrammed to respond to human beings.[5] They see most clearly at a distance of 8–10 inches, the average distance of a parent's face from the baby when being held, hear best in the range of the human voice, and move in rhythm to human speech. They recognize their mother's voice, and quickly show a preference for her face.

Newborns respond to others as well. Babies a few hours old respond to the cries of other newborns and often cry themselves in response.[6] When less than a week old, they can imitate an adult's facial expression of sticking out a tongue, fluttering the eyelids, or opening and closing the mouth, suggesting a rudimentary sense of self as a human being capable of imitating a person and having the motor control to do it.

VOICES OF EXPERIENCE

What I Wish I Had Known about the First Two Years

"I remember when we brought him home from the hospital, and we had him on the changing table for a minute, and I realized, 'I don't know how to keep the engine running.' I wondered how could they let him go home with us, this little package weighing seven or eight pounds. I had no idea what to do. I kind of knew you fed him and you cleaned him and kept him warm; but I didn't have any hands-on experience, anything practical. In a way, I would have liked them to watch me for a day or two in the hospital while I change him, to make sure I knew how to do it. It's kind of like giving me a car without seeing whether I could drive it around the block." FATHER

"I wish we had known a little more about establishing her first habits about sleeping. The way you set it up in the beginning is the way it is going to be. Having enough sleep is so important. We went too long before we decided to let her cry for five minutes. Then she got into good sleep habits." FATHER

"I wish I had known how it would change things between me and my husband. The baby comes first, and by the time the day is over and he is in bed, we have two hours together, but I just want to curl up and take care of myself." MOTHER

"I wish I had known about how much time babies take. It is like he needs twenty-four-hour attention. For an older parent who is used to having his own life and is very set in his ways, it is hard to make the changes and still have some time for your own life." FATHER

"She had this periodic crying at night in the beginning, and you are caught in the raging hormones and somehow I thought if I just read Dr. Spock again or if I read more, I'd understand it better. And we joked about reading the same paragraph in the book over and over. We needed reassurance it would end, and at three months it ended. That was the hardest part." MOTHER

"Someone said, when you have a child, it's like two appointment books—his appointment book and yours. And first you do everything in the kid's appointment book; and then when you're done, you do everything in the kid's appointment book again. I wish I had known they weren't joking. I knew that it would be a challenge, and in some ways I wish I had known more. But in other ways I think if I had really known exactly how hard it would be sometimes, I might have been more reluctant or waited longer, and that I would really have regretted—not doing it." FATHER

"I wasn't prepared for all the decisions. Is it okay if he does this or not? He's trying to do something; shall I step in so he doesn't hurt himself, or shall I let him go? It's making all those choices, making sure what I feel." MOTHER

"I wish I had known what to do about climbing. He climbs all over everything. I have the living room stripped bare, but I wonder if this is the right thing." MOTHER

"I wish I had known how much time they needed between one and two. They are mobile, but they are clueless about judgment. I think it was one of the most difficult times. Even though she did not get into a lot of trouble, sticking her finger in the light sockets, still she takes a lot of time and watching, so the transition to two was great." MOTHER

Box 7-1
WOMB SERVICE*

Pediatrician Dr. Harvey Karp's book, *The Happiest Baby on the Block,* can improve many parents' lives by giving them tools to calm and soothe their newborns. Dr. Karp describes a five-step method that helps newborns settle into their new world more easily, especially those newborns with intense temperaments who find it difficult to soothe themselves.

Dr. Karp believes that newborns would benefit from another trimester in the womb because at birth their neurological systems are still immature and easily overwhelmed with the forms of stimulation they experience. They need the "womb service" they are used to. In the womb, babies are folded up in the tight uterine support surrounding them; they hear the noise of blood coursing through arteries and veins, the sounds of stomachs gurgling, and sometimes background voices. They move in many different ways as mothers go about their daily activities.

When they are born, their little bodies are out in space with arms and legs moving wildly; they miss the enfolding support of the uterine walls, especially when lying on their backs. Often, it is deadly quiet and dark, like a cave. And they can only lie there; they can't move around on their own. So, until the nervous system develops and gives babies greater ability to regulate themselves, as it gradually does in the first three months, babies find it hard to settle in, and many cry.

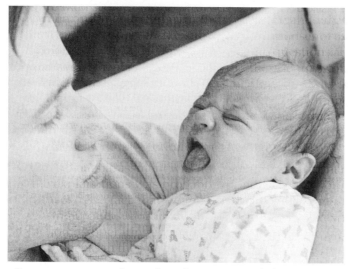

Dr Harvey Korp suggests several steps for calming a crying baby.

Dr. Karp's method is to duplicate as closely as possible the characteristics of life in the womb because reminders of that time trigger a child's powerful calming reflex. This reflex, Dr. Karp believes, is essential to a healthy pregnancy and delivery. If fetuses had tantrums and frenzies of activity and flailed around forcefully, they would increase their risk of having the umbilical cord wrapped around their necks or wedging themselves in odd positions that would be difficult to change in the uterus or birth canal.

(continued)

Box 7-1
CONTINUED

His five-step program is to be done in a specific way:

1. Swaddling—securely wrapping the baby in a receiving blanket (have pediatrician rule out congenital hip problems that swaddling could affect**)
2. Side/stomach position for holding the child—in the stomach position, the child is held against the body so he or she feels pressure on the stomach; the child is always placed on his or her back for sleeping
3. Providing a *shhhh* sound that duplicates noises in the womb helps babies—some parents use a vacuum cleaner or dust buster, but parents can make shushing noises
4. Swinging or some form of rhythmic motion such as jiggling, dancing, rocking, or carrying the child in a sling
5. Sucking on a pacifier or breast or finger

These five steps together makeup what Dr. Karp calls the Cuddle Cure to soothe babies. He believes these steps copy what many other societies do naturally to calm babies.

Innovations in neonatal nurseries have had success in creating more womb-like experiences for premature babies born two to three months early.*** To create an individualized hospital care plan for each baby is a complicated process—training staff and parents to carry it out, and monitoring the child's response—but research indicates great benefits for the baby. The program, begun within seventy-two hours of birth, lasted until the child reached the corrected age of two weeks. (Corrected age is the child's age from the date of expected arrival, not from the date of actual birth.) Parents and staff did everything possible to reduce stress, to physically support the child with much Kangaroo Care time (skin-to-skin contact between mother and child); often two nurses carried out a procedure—one held and supported the baby, while the other did the procedure.

At the corrected age of two weeks, babies receiving experimental treatment had better neurobehavioral functioning and increased coherence between frontal and other brain regions. At the corrected age of nine months, the experimental babies' development was significantly advanced. They scored in the 73 percentile for overall development, and the control babies scored at the 39 percentile. The sample was small, but the results very impressive.

*Adapted from Harvey Karp, *The Happiest Baby on the Block* (New York: Bantam, 2002).
** Susan T. Mahan and James R. Kasser, "Does Swaddling Influence Developmental Dysplasia of the Hip?" *Pediatrics 121* (2008): 177–180.
*** Heideliese Als et al., "Early Experience Alters Brain Function and Structure," *Pediatrics 113* (2004): 846–857.

Early Parent–Child Relationships

In addition to feeding babies, keeping them warm, and getting them to sleep, parents also soothe babies and help them regulate their physical system. As noted in Chapter 4, physical contact with mothers regulates infants' hormonal levels, sleeping and eating patterns, and heart rate.[7] Music and singing to infants also reduce stress and regulate arousal level.[8]

In their early interactions, parents shape infants' emotional reactions, encouraging positive moods and smiling and discouraging negative moods with such phrases as, "Don't cry."[9] Babies copy their parents' emotional reactions, responding with joy and interest to mothers' happy faces, with anger and a form of fear to mothers' angry faces, and with sadness to mothers' sad faces. Over time, mothers' positive expressions are related to increases in babies' smiling and laughter.

As infants' behavior becomes more integrated, parents respond sensitively to babies' rhythms and moods. Parents engage babies in face-to-face interactions, and become social partners, looking for periods of alertness and babies' readiness to respond before playing games. These social interactions stimulate babies' emotional, cognitive, and social growth.

Turn taking involves waiting and adjusting to other people's behavior, and is an early form of self-control predictive of the child's self-control at age two.[10] Babies learn social routines and develop expectations of what others will do.[11] Babies as young as three months become distressed if these expectations are not met. When, for instance, a parent of a three-month-old adopts a still, impassive facial expression, the baby responds negatively and often tries to elicit the anticipated reaction by smiling or vocalizing. If this does not work, the baby turns away.

These interactions as social partners create mutual understanding and a shared state of meaning termed intersubjectivity. In the state of shared meaning, the baby uses the parent as a social reference for responding to experience.[12] For example, babies will not play with a toy if the mother has looked at the toy with disgust.[13]

Coparenting

James McHale's observations of mothers and fathers with their three-month-old babies revealed parents were sensitive and responsive, but cautious in their interactions.[14] Even at this early age, parents already reported differing views about what to do—where the baby should sleep, how long the baby should cry before being picked up, how they should divide the work. Couples who incorporated both parents' points of view in solutions formed a cooperative, supportive, warm alliance. Those parents who were in the process of forming an alliance were not in conflict, but were out of synch with each other, sometimes jumping in at the same time to get the jobs done and sometimes withdrawing at the same time. These parents did not feel they got positive support from the other parent.

In this middle-class sample, 24 percent of mothers and 13 percent of fathers reported clinical levels of depressive symptoms. Some reported decreases in marital satisfaction. Depression and marital distress decreased the warmth and cooperation between the parents and reduced their ability to work together.

When parents anticipated lack of cooperation and support from the other parent before birth, they were less likely to form cooperative relationships after the birth, but only if the baby were irritable and fussy. Negative predictions did not come true when babies were easy and adaptable, possibly because it was easier to provide care and parents received positive feedback from babies and the other parent about their caregiving skills.

McHale believes that if parents are having a hard time working together, they should make every effort to talk to each other about their attitudes and feelings. If they cannot settle their differences, they should seek guidance as the difficulties are likely to continue and eventually will affect the child's behavior.

Managing When Babies Are Born Prematurely

In Chapter 6, we discussed the experiences of parents of premature babies in the hospital; here, we discuss the special challenges of caregiving at home.

Premature babies lack the special "baby" features that draw adults to them—the big heads, broad cheeks, flattened nose, and large eyes.[15] They may make little noise initially, because they may lack the strength to cry; when they do cry, their cries differ from those of healthy babies and are quite arousing. Parents also miss the pleasure of babies' smiles, because smiles appear approximately six weeks after the due date and therefore can occur months after the premature baby is born.

In addition, parenting a "preemie" is more demanding, both physically and emotionally.[16] Because preterm babies left the protective womb early, their systems are not ready for the level of stimulation they experience in the world. They may be unresponsive much of the time, or they may react intensely to stimuli full-term babies can absorb. So, parents have a very narrow range of behaviors that will be intense enough to stimulate but not overwhelm the baby.

Both mothers and fathers naturally adapt their behaviors to meet preterm babies' needs. Compared with other parents, they are more active in holding and touching babies, directing their attention. They may appear overstimulating as they try to compensate for their child's special needs. Over time, preterm babies come to resemble full-term babies in their development, but mothers of preterm babies use different strategies to promote growth. For example, they may hold babies more to encourage mutual gaze and responsiveness, because preterm babies respond with more gazing when being held. Despite all the differences in early experiences and early parent–child interactions, preterm babies are as securely attached to parents at twelve and eighteen months as are full-term babies.[17]

Preterm infants' cognitive development illustrates the powerful effect mother's attitude has on the baby's growth. When mothers felt that their role was important and that they were doing a good job, and when they felt positively about the baby, their husband, and life in general, their babies developed well.[18] The attitudes of mothers of full-term babies were only moderately related to the baby's progress. Parents' responsiveness and social stimulation of preterm babies are related to children's academic and social success through young adulthood.[19]

Parents of premature babies need to understand their strong and important role and the child's capacity for healthy growth, for our culture seems to hold subtle negative beliefs about preterms. When mothers were told an unfamiliar six-month-old baby was premature, they were more likely to rate the child as smaller, less cute, and less likable, even when the child was actually full term.[20] In brief interactions, they touched the child less and offered a more immature toy for play. What is startling is that the babies' behavior changed with these women, and they became less active. College students watching videos of the interactions could tell immediately whether the child was described as full term or preterm.

Such stereotypes may influence friends and relatives who in turn affect the parents.[21] Mothers who do well tend to adopt and nurture an optimistic attitude about the long-term outcome for the child. Professional support that discusses possible difficulties and coping strategies is at times disruptive for these mothers, although such help is useful to women who feel under stress with their infants.[22]

Because preemie babies start life with special problems, parental overprotectiveness is not unusual in the first several months, as the child grows and becomes stronger. If overprotectiveness persists after the first year or exceeds what the pediatrician considers reasonable, however, parents have developed a problem. Parents must learn to grit their teeth and let their initially vulnerable babies take a few tumbles and some hurts. Giving children freedom to grow also gives parents free time to spend with each other. Sometimes they may choose to get a babysitter and go out. This is important. As we have discussed in Chapter 6, parents must make time to nourish the marital relationship if they are to develop a close, satisfying family life.

DEVELOPMENT IN THE FIRST TWO YEARS OF LIFE

In this section, we discuss babies' physical, intellectual, language, and emotional development, as well as development of self, in the first two years. In general, the direction of growth is from broad, diffuse activity to more differentiated and organized behaviors. Keep in mind that all these areas of development are closely intertwined in the early months and years as advances in one area make possible advances in other areas. Growth in physical and motor coordination enables babies to get around and explore more objects in greater detail, thus enhancing intellectual growth.[23] Crawling to people enables babies to initiate more social contacts and to become a more active partner. More social contacts and vocal interactions promote language development.

Observers have identified three periods of major reorganization in babies' development over the first two years of life.[24] They occur at about three months, seven to nine months, and eighteen to twenty months and are related to neural changes that enable babies to become more effective social partners and more efficient learners.

Physical and Neurophysiological Development

On average, the baby grows from 21 inches at birth to about 33 inches at the end of two years, and birth weight increases to about 29 pounds. Growth includes increasing organization of behavior as well.

> Three months: The increased myelination of nerves in cortical and subcortical neural pathways and the increase in the number of neurons at three months of age improve the child's sensory abilities and coordination, bringing greater control of behavior. The nervous system appears more integrated. Voluntary behaviors replace reflexes. Babies are more awake during the day and are more skilled in manipulating and playing with toys and objects.

Eight months: Increased myelination of neurons in the motor area, in areas of the brain controlling coordination of movement, and in areas responsible for organization of behavior enable the child to sit alone. Control of the trunk follows and leads to creeping and crawling. Babies now can move rapidly in all directions. Finally, walking replaces crawling sometime between ten and eighteen months.

Eighteen months: Increased brain myelination is related to rapid advances in language and the development of representational thought.

Intellectual Development

As noted in Chapter 2, Jean Piaget and Lev Vygotsky focus on early development. Piaget emphasizes the child's changing capacities for incorporating stimulation and active exploration of the world.[25] Infants learn from the actions of their own bodies (e.g., learning about spatial relations by working to get fingers to their mouths for sucking). Babies reach for objects in the environment, manipulating them, seeing how they work, and gradually becoming problem-solvers who observe what happens when they drop objects on the floor or throw them in water.

Infants' understanding of the world becomes more differentiated. At first they live very much in the present, but by eight or nine months, they learn that people and objects are separate from them and exist even when they are not seen. Object permanence, the term for this new understanding, is essential to the concept of a coherent world.

As babies move and explore objects, they form intentions and goals (e.g., get a toy, grab the cat). In social play with parents babies learn that others too have goals and intentions. They learn that when a parent looks off at an object or points, they can share the adult's gaze and focus on the object too. They also learn that parents can understand their goals and provide feedback as necessary. So, at about nine to ten months, they seek information and help by referencing parents' facial and emotional expressions. If confronted with what looks like a dangerous cliff, for example, they will not crawl toward it until the mother encourages it.

In the middle of the second year, babies begin to use symbols such as mental images and words to represent their experience so they are not limited to the present and what they see. Toddlers engage in pretend, fantasy play, copying the actions of parents and brothers and sisters. This is the beginning of representational thought.

Vygotsky emphasizes the importance of social interactions.[26] Parents establish routines that draw children into the culture and teach them basic values, as we saw in Chapter 3 with regard to American and Italian families. Parents simplify play so babies can participate, giving toys they can manipulate so skills increase. Vygotsky also emphasizes the importance of language. Words give children tools to communicate with others and enable them to represent their experience in words that are internalized into thoughts.

Both Piaget's focus on active exploration of the world and Vygotsky's focus on social relationships provide parents with guidelines to help children learn and reach their full potential.

Language Development

Infants' emotional reactions—their smiles and cries—are early forms of communication. Gradually, babies develop cooing, babbling, and repetition of syllables, such as *ma-ma* or *da-da-da.*[27] Even before they have words, babies capture adults' attention with sound inflections that express happiness, requests, commands, and questions. A single word, such as *mama,* can be a question, an order, an endearment, or a request.

At about ten months, children attach words to objects that interest them and visually stand out.[28] Parents advance children's language when they label objects children are already focused on. In the second year, children attend to the speaker and what the speaker is looking at or pointing to. Parents can increase children's verbal skills if they have the child's attention and are very clear in communicating the object they are labeling.

The amount, content, and form of parents' language influence what children understand and talk about.[29] Researchers found that the typical parenting routines in all families provide only a very limited vocabulary. Thus, children with the most advanced vocabularies live in families where parents talk a great deal and use a rich variety of words. When mothers are trained to elaborate on what children say and encourage children to talk in more detail about events, then children demonstrate richer memories of events.[30]

Most important is the emotional tone of the language.[31] Thirteen- to eighteen-month-old children whose families directed primarily positive, affirming words to them were observed to use primarily positive words with family members two years later. Conversely, children whose families directed primarily negative, critical words to them used similar words with their family members.

On average, by their first birthday, babies have two or three words and by eighteen months, fifty words.[32] At age two, they have a vocabulary of about three hundred words, but at all these ages, they understand many more words than they themselves use. By age two, toddlers have also made the leap to putting two words together to form a sentence.

Emotional Development

At birth, infants' emotional repertoire consists of three general states: contentment, alert interest, and distress/irritability.[33] In the next three to four months, emotional states develop into more differentiated and specific emotions: contentment into joy, distress into sadness at the loss of pleasure, and anger in response to frustration. Fear develops at seven or eight months, and parents see it most clearly in stranger anxiety, which develops about that time. Babies are able to identify people as newcomers in their environment, and they are fearful of them. This subsides by the end of the first year. By the end of the first year, babies express a range of emotions—interest, surprise, joy, sadness, anger, fear, and disgust.

Anger   Parents most want to know how to handle children's negative feelings. In the second year, toddlers become more self-assertive, and at times defiant. Even when mothers are supportive and offer choices, children refuse to comply with requests and insist on their point of view. Researchers conclude that defiance at this age appears part of healthy development.[34]

Aggressive behavior increases in the years between one and three, and then gradually decreases after the third birthday. Before age two, boys and girls are equally aggressive, but from two years of age, boys are significantly more aggressive than girls.[35] Florence Goodenough asked mothers to keep diaries of young children's anger outbursts and found that many factors influence the occurrence of anger![36]

- Outbursts peak in the second year and are most likely to occur when children are hungry or tired or when they are ill—when reserves are down for physical reasons, tempers flare.
- Outbursts are usually short-lived—most last less than five minutes—and, with young children under two, the aftereffects are minimal; with increasing age, children sulk and hold on to angry feelings.
- From one to two years, outbursts seem caused by conflict with authority, difficulties over the establishment of habits (eating, baths, bedtime), and problems with social relationships (wanting more attention, wanting a possession someone else has).

Parents whose children had the fewest outbursts:

- had a tolerant, positive home atmosphere with realistic expectations that children would be independent, curious, stubborn, and have individual needs.
- anticipated problems and found ways to prevent them.
- helped children conform by preparing them for changes in activities, announcing mealtimes in advance so children had ten minutes or so to get ready.
- had a daily routine and consistent and fair rules.
- were firm when a real conflict arose.

Parents whose children had many outbursts

- were critical and disapproving with children.
- were inconsistent and unpredictable, basing decisions on their own wants rather than the child's needs.
- ignored children's needs until a problem forced them to respond.
- imposed a routine regardless of the child's activity of the moment and forced the child to act quickly in terms of their own desire.

Reducing Negative Feelings   Toddlers find many ways to do this. Toddlers[37] reduce negative feelings in many ways. They look away and soothe themselves or seek aid from parents to fix the situation using words and actions to tell parents what they want. They also use transition objects like a blanket or stuffed toy to comfort themselves. Such use peaks in the middle of the second year when as many as 30 to 60 percent of children have them.

Empathy   Toddlers go beyond crying at others' distress—they take action.[38] They touch, cuddle, or bring the child something he or she would like. Toddlers' concern is most frequently directed to family members, particularly to mothers. Toddlers do not express much concern when they cause distress. They intervene to help or remedy the situation, but they do not feel guilty for causing the problem.

Happiness and Affection   From the start, babies enjoy people and making things happen—getting a parent's attention, kicking a mobile.[39] Exercising their developing skills gives babies' great pleasure in life. They are often unconcerned with failures—recall how hard a child works to master crawling or walking, not getting discouraged or giving up. Unconcerned with others' reactions, they do not appear to make value judgments about their own actions in the first year.[40] Although children begin to develop standards for behavior in the second year, still, their main response is one of delight in what they do.

Although they most enjoy pursuing their own goals, they also enjoy meeting adults' expectations. In one laboratory study, toddlers responded quickly and enthusiastically to adults' requests to arrange toys in a certain way.[41] Later, when allowed to play freely, toddlers happily repeated the tasks. The researchers concluded that the pleasure of accomplishing a goal is a powerful motive for their obeying commands.

Affection also increases in this period. Toddlers pat, stroke, and kiss their parents, particularly mothers. They are also affectionate to animals and younger children.

Development of the Self

The self goes through developmental stages, as described by Susan Harter.[42]

- Birth to four months: the self emerges as infants coordinate visual, sensory, and motor responses and begin to act on the world, for example, by making a mobile move or making a parent laugh.

- Four to ten months: infants have an increasing sense of self as doers and social partners attached to parents. When caregivers react positively to babies' bids for attention, babies have a greater sense of control over events.

- Ten to fifteen months: babies become increasingly differentiated from caregivers and find a greater sense of themselves as agents who make things happen. Although attached to parents, they move off, using parents as secure bases for exploration in the world.

- Fifteen to eighteen months: "me-self" develops. Toddlers begin to internalize how others respond to them—that is, they start to react to themselves as others do. Children at this age recognize themselves in a mirror, identify photographs of themselves, and respond strongly to others' reactions to them.

- Eighteen to thirty months: toddlers develop a greater understanding of what influences others to act; as a result, they gain a greater sense of the separation between the self and others. Their language reflects their feelings of being separate persons. By age two, they use pronouns such as *I, me,* and *mine,* and they describe their physical appearance and actions—"I run," "I play," "I have brown hair." These verbalizations increase self-awareness.

Development of Self-Regulation

As we have seen, self-control too begins to develop in the earliest days of life.[43]

- In the first three months of life, infants regulate arousal states of wake and sleep and the amount of stimulation they get; they also soothe themselves.
- From three to nine months, infants modulate sensory and motor activities and continue to soothe themselves, looking away from what upsets them or sucking on fingers or hands. As they reach out, form intentions, and develop a rudimentary sense of self, their capacity for control begins to emerge.
- From nine to eighteen months, infants show awareness of social or task demands and begin to comply with their parents' requests. As infants act, investigate, and explore, their sense of conscious awareness begins to appear. These trends continue in the second year.

Researchers found that babies in the first year obey their mothers' commands when they accept and are sensitive to babies' needs.[44] Mothers who respect babies as separate individuals and tailor daily routines to harmonize with the children's needs, have babies who are affectionate and independent, able to play alone, and (even at one year) able to follow their mothers' requests. Thus, even at this early age, a system of mutual cooperation between mother and child is established.

Toddlers are most successful in avoiding forbidden activities when they direct their attention away from these objects or activities—looking elsewhere, playing with their hands, finding an acceptable substitute toy.[45] A substantial number of two-year-olds can wait alone as long as four minutes before receiving permission to touch.[46]

Peer Relations

Children pay attention to peers, smiling and glancing at them in the first year.[47] In the second year, children's social skills advance significantly. Toddlers imitate each others' actions, take turns, engage in imaginative play. They also have conflicts. Toddlers argue over toys and activities. Many of the conflicts involve outgoing toddlers who are learning cooperative ways to initiate activities.

Social behaviors of this period may persist into the preschool and early school years. Inhibited children tend to remain shy and fearful; poorly controlled toddlers often continue to have difficulties with peers, and socially skilled children maintain their social competence.

THE PROCESS OF ATTACHMENT

In Chapter 2, we described attachment as an enduring tie that binds the child to the parent, who is a source of security for the child. We also saw that secure attachments promote positive behaviors. How do parents establish such bonds?

Parents provide a secure fare for babies as they begin to explore the world.

An analysis of sixty-six studies on infants' attachments to mothers (as mothers were the focus of most studies) found four important contributors to secure attachment in the first year:[48]

- *Sensitivity* (ability to perceive the infant's signals accurately and respond appropriately and promptly)

- *Mutuality* (positive harmony and mutuality in relationship)

- *Synchronicity* (coordinated social interactions)

- *Positive attitude* (emotional expressiveness, acceptance, and delight in the child)

So, when parents are sensitive, responsive, warm, accepting, and attentive to the rhythms of the child's behavior and individuality, they create a state of mutual understanding that fosters a secure parent–child attachment.

In the toddler years, parents:

- maintain a state of mutual understanding through continuing sensitivity and availability as a secure base for exploration.

- become teachers and guides for children, balancing support and guidance with increasing independence for the child.

- stay one step ahead of the child's level of interaction and when the child confronts a new barrier, the parent steps in to give just the right amount of help so the child solves the problem and moves on. This form of guidance is termed *scaffolding*, or balancing the child's weakness.[49]

Gender Differences in Parents   Research shows that mothers and fathers relate differently to infants in terms of both quantity of time spent and the kinds of

Box 7-2
INTERVENTIONS TO INCREASE SECURE ATTACHMENTS FOR IRRITABLE BABIES AND THEIR MOTHERS

Concerned that irritable temperament puts babies at risk for insecure attachments with their mothers, Dymphna van den Boom recruited a sample of one hundred irritable babies and their mothers to carry out an intervention to decrease that risk. Babies were assessed at the tenth and fifteenth days after birth with Brazelton's Neonatal Behavioral Assessment Scale to identify irritable infants. The babies were all firstborn children in low status, primarily two-parent families (only three families were headed by single mothers) in the Netherlands.

The irritable infants were randomly assigned to a control or experimental group.* When infants were between six and nine months, the experimental group received three home visits in which Dr. van den Boom observed mother–infants' interactions and made suggestions to increase mothers' sensitivity and responsiveness. She increased mothers' attentiveness to infants' signals and appropriate responses to them. She also suggested effective ways for mothers to soothe babies when they cried, and explained why it was important to do so. She encouraged mothers to play with their babies to increase pleasurable interactions and reduce the negative quality of interactions. Each visit lasted two hours, and was focused on the individual behaviors of each mother–infant pair.

After the intervention, experimental group mothers were significantly more sensitive, stimulating, and attentive to their nine-month-old children, and their babies were more sociable and more able to soothe themselves. They cried less and explored more. When infants were twelve months of age, the Strange Situation was administered to determine level of attachment. In the control group, 22 percent of infants had secure attachments, and 78 percent had insecure attachments. In the experimental group, 62 percent had secure attachments, and 38 percent had insecure attachments.

Children and mothers were seen again when children were eighteen, twenty-four, and forty-two months.** Mothers in the experimental group continued to be more attentive, responsive, and supportive, and fathers showed similar behaviors. Their children were more cooperative and involved with peers than children in the control group.

In speculating about the reasons for the long-lasting benefits of the brief intervention, van den Boom attributed the effects to mothers' learning how to attend, interpret, and respond to children's behaviors in sensitive ways. Increases in mothers' sensitivity increased the security of the attachments, and that security also contributed to positive behaviors as children moved outside the immediate family. One suspects that success came partly from the very specific suggestions tailored to each mother–infant pair.

*Dymphna C. van den Boom, "The Influence of Temperament and Mothering on Attachment and Exploration: An Experimental Manipulation of Sensitive Responsiveness among Lower-Class Mothers," *Child Development* 65 (1994): 1457–1477.
**Dymphna C. van den Boom, "Do First-Year Intervention Effects Endure: Follow-up During Toddlerhood of a Sample of Dutch Irritable Infants," *Child Development* 66 (1995): 1798–1816.

activities engaged in with infants.[50] Data collected in the 1980s and 1990s showed that, even though many mothers had jobs, they spent more time with children. In these studies, fathers spent, on average, only 40 percent as much time with children as mothers did.[51]

Data collected from a national representative sample in 1997 reveal that fathers in intact families now spend more time with children.[52] On weekdays, fathers of infants spent 60 percent as much time as mothers in activities and in being available for activities with infants, but on weekends, they spent 80 percent as much time. Fathers do proportionately less caregiving than mothers, but they spend exactly the same amount of time in social activities. In addition to caregiving and play and social activities, fathers also do household chores and teach children.

Although they show different amounts of involvement, mothers and fathers are equally competent as caregivers.[53] Fathers can be as sensitive as mothers in their interactions with infants, reading and responding accurately to babies' cues. Babies drink as much milk in fathers' care as in mothers'. Mothers are more likely to hold babies in caregiving activities and to verbalize than are fathers. Mothers are thought to provide a "holding environment" for infants as they regulate their system and develop increasing skills in interactions with people and objects.[54]

Fathers are more attentive visually and more playful in physically active ways than are mothers.[55] Fathers are most likely to be highly involved in caregiving and playing when the marital relationship is satisfying and their wives are relaxed and outgoing. Both fathers and mothers give mostly care and physical affection in the first three months, when babies are settling in. As babies become less fussy and more alert at three months, both parents become more stimulating and reactive.[56]

TASKS AND CONCERNS FOR PARENTS OF INFANTS

Marc Bornstein describes four main tasks for the parents of infants:[57]

- Nurturant caregiving: providing food, protection, warmth, and affection
- Material caregiving: providing and organizing the babies' world with inanimate objects, stimulation, and opportunities for exploration
- Social caregiving: engaging and interacting with infants—hugging, soothing, comforting, vocalizing, playing
- Didactic caregiving: stimulating infants' interest in and understanding of the world outside the parent–child relationship by introducing objects, interpreting the surrounding world, and giving information

T. Berry Brazelton and Stanley Greenspan add that experiences must be tailored to the individual characteristics of the child and that both parents and children require a community that supports parents' efforts and children's growth.[58]

We look here at two main tasks of parenting: (1) establishing an optimal level of arousal for infants and (2) promoting infants' self-regulation.

VOICES OF EXPERIENCE

The Joys of Parenting Children in the First Two Years

"I love babies. There is something about that bond between mother and baby. I love the way they look and smell and the way they hunker up to your neck. To me it's a magic time. I didn't like to babysit particularly growing up, and I wasn't wild about other people's babies, but there was something about having my own; I just love it. And every one, we used to wonder, how are we going to love another as much as the one before; and that is ridiculous, because you love every one." MOTHER

"There is joy in just watching her change, seeing her individualize. From the beginning it seemed she had her own personality—we see that this is not just a little blob of protoplasm here; this is a little individual already from the beginning. She has always had a real specialness about her. It was exciting to see her change." FATHER

"I think it's wonderful to have a baby in the house, to hear the baby laugh, sitting in the high chair, banging spoons, all the fun things babies do. They seem to me to light up a household. When there's a baby here, a lot of the aggravations in the household somehow disappear. Everyone looks at the baby, plays with the baby, and even if people are in a bad mood, they just light up when the baby comes in the room. I think there is something magical about having a baby in the house." MOTHER

"There is the excitement of baby talk becoming real words." MOTHER

"I enjoy that she directs me more than I could sense. Before, there was a 'yes' or 'no' response, but now there is more back and forth. If I dress her, she shows me she wants to sit or stand—'Do it this way' is what she seems to say. Before, she was tired or not tired, hungry or not hungry, okay or not okay. Now there is much more variation." FATHER

"I've heard of this, and it's true; it's rediscovering the child in yourself. Sometimes, it's the joy that he and I hop around the couch like two frogs on our hands and knees. Or we're in the bathtub pretending we are submarines and alligators. Sometimes he likes to ride around on my shoulders, and I run and make noises like an airplane or a bird. And I am not just doing it for him, but we are doing it together, playing together." FATHER

"I was just blown away by the way he tries to help other children. From a very young age, he has done this. Now, when a little girl he sees everyday cries, he takes her one toy after another and says, 'This is? This is?' meaning, 'Is this what you want?' until he gets her to stop crying by giving her something she wants. He's very people oriented, very affectionate, and seems so secure." MOTHER

"Watching her grow, seeing her grow, seeing the different stages, I just take pleasure in everything she does now, because I know she will be on to a new stage soon." MOTHER

"As he gets older, I relate more, play more. He is more of a joy. Some of the joys are so unexpected. I would stop myself and open up and think, 'Oh, this is my son, he's so joyful. He's smiling for no particular reason.' I am not that joyful, but he's joyful for no reason. He reminds me of joy." FATHER

ESTABLISHING AN OPTIMAL LEVEL OF AROUSAL

Reducing time spent in crying and establishing healthy sleep patterns promote a state of arousal that enables babies to respond to people and to the world around them. Although parents in the United States most often rely on the independent model of caregiving, behaviors characteristic of the interdependent model, such as nursing for a year and carrying babies, have increased.[59] So, let us look at which strategies work best to reduce crying and promote healthy sleep patterns.

Crying

As noted, crying increases from about two hours at birth to three at six weeks and decreases to about one at three months of age. A thorough study of crying in the first year of life found that babies had as many crying episodes at the end of the year as at the beginning, but they spent much less time in each episode.[60] Those mothers who responded immediately to the cries of the baby had babies who cried less at six to twelve months. Conversely, ignoring a baby's cries seemed to increase the amount of crying.

What strategy is most effective in terminating crying? Caregivers around the world follow similar methods—soothing babies by "rocking, patting, cuddling, swaddling, giving suck on breast or pacifier."[61]

Supplemental carrying in a sling for three extra hours per day from three to twelve weeks eliminated the peak of crying that usually occurs at six weeks, reduced crying overall, and modified the daily pattern of the crying so there was less in the evening hours.[62] Equally important, babies who were carried more were more content and more visually and aurally alert. Supplemental carrying provides all the kinds of stimulation that we know soothe babies—rhythmic, repetitive movement with postural changes. Close physical contact also enables mothers to understand and respond to their infants better.

Carrying in a sling not only reduces crying, but increases secure attachments at one year.[63] Low-income, inner-city mothers who from birth carried their babies in slings rather than infant seats were more vocally responsive with infants at three months and at thirteen months and had higher rates of secure attachments (83 percent) than mothers using infant seats (38 percent with secure attachments). Myron Hofer, who has studied the effects of maternal behavior on the infant rat's neurological and regulatory systems, believes that the movements experienced in slings help develop the child's vestibular sense of balance and motion in space, contributing to a child's sense of emotional security.[64]

When healthy babies cry more than three hours a day for more than three days a week for more than three weeks, Jodi Mindell describes them as having colic.[65] No one knows what causes it, and it may be the highest end of normal crying behavior, as it has the same pattern of increasing after birth, peaking at six weeks, and decreasing at three months.

Babies' crying upsets parents as they feel helpless to comfort their babies. Primarily parents are advised to search for patterns of soothing activities, some of which work some of the time. Parents use Dr. Karp's Cuddle Cure (Box 7-1), rock, carry, and soothe babies. We discuss the effects on parents in a later section.

Pediatrician William Sammons has observed that babies gradually have the ability to calm themselves, sucking on fingers and wrists or focusing on objects or walls.[66] Sammons encourages parents to engage in a mutual partnership with babies so that infants can find their own ways to calm themselves. Mindell believes that if parents have tried everything, they should give themselves a rest. It is possible that in the rest, babies may find their own ways to self-calm.

Sleep

In most parts of the world, infants sleep with a parent (cosleeping), and most toddlers and older children sleep with or near a parent. Surveys reveal that, in the United States, infants in middle-class families sleep alone in bassinets, and by six months of age, most sleep in their own rooms.[67] While cosleeping has occurred more frequently in American families with less income and less space, a growing number of more advantaged parents sleep with their babies, perhaps to reduce babies' crying or to stay connected with the child at night.

When babies are expected to sleep in their own cribs—whether in parents' room or their own—the general approach is to help babies develop healthy sleep habits so they get the amount and quality of sleep they need. Drs. Richard Ferber[68] and Jodi Mindell,[69] directors of children's sleep disorder clinics, believe parents have a major role in establishing children's healthy sleep habits.

Since most babies (and adults) awake briefly several times during the night, babies must fall asleep in ways they can duplicate to return to sleep on their own in the middle of the night. If they develop the habit of falling asleep while nursing or being rocked, they will be unable to duplicate those conditions in the middle of the night and will cry.

About six weeks after birth, parents begin a regular bedtime routine that precedes the evening sleep time even if they do not establish a regular bedtime until the child is about three to five months, when sleep patterns have stabilized.[70] The aim is to have a consistent sequence of calming activities that prepare the child for sleep. Since our inner clock is based on a twenty-five-hour cycle, we need a regular schedule to keep to a twenty-four-hour day, and babies must depend on parents to set the schedule.

For the bedtime routine, parents select activities their babies enjoy. It may include a bath, nursing, a song, and brief rocking. While still awake, the child is placed in the crib on his or her back to fall asleep alone. Mindell cites a study from the National Sleep Foundation showing that those babies who go to bed awake take less time to fall asleep, have fewer night wakings, and sleep an hour longer per night than those babies who are put in their cribs when asleep.[71] The American Academy of Pediatrics recommends the Back to Sleep position and giving a child a pacifier to suck on, as these two actions have reduced sudden infant deaths 50 percent since 1992.[72]

Infants and children often cry and object to being left in bed. Both Ferber and Mindell agree that parents should enter the bedroom to reassure the child that everything is okay; parents do not return to previous activities. Mindell says parents can go in as often as they want to reassure the child, and Ferber has a more structured program for entries.

A growing number of families choose cosleeping or bed-sharing to promote physical and psychological closeness. Still, there are risks. The American Academy of Pediatrics does not recommend it because infant deaths are attributed to parents' rolling over on the child or the child's being wedged between the mattress and wall or trapped between the headboard and the mattress.[73] Currently infant beds that can be attached to adult beds lack safety standards.

There are common safety rules regardless of where babies sleep, with some additional ones for cosleeping.[74] All babies should:

- sleep on a firm mattress and not on soft chairs or sofas, waterbeds, or pillows
- have only light coverings; comforters, quilts, or heavy blankets can suffocate or overheat the baby
- sleep in a crib meeting national standards to prevent wedging or entrapment; when put to sleep, their feet should be at the foot of the bed
- be put to sleep on their backs to prevent suffocation; the Back to Sleep rule
- in the first year be put to sleep for naps and at night with a pacifier as research suggests that for unknown reasons a pacifier decreases sudden infant deaths; a pacifier should not be forced or reinserted if it falls out

Cosleeping parents are advised not to sleep with babies when they have physical conditions that decrease their arousal at night (e.g., sleep apnea; extreme fatigue; alcohol, drug, or medication use). Parents are also advised not to put cosleeping babies next to toddlers and older children.

Attachment Parenting

In contemporary society, cosleeping is one facet of a larger system of *attachment parenting,* which incorporates many aspects of the interdependent model of caregiving. Pediatrician William Sears encourages parents to accept their babies' dependency needs and meet them appropriately. He describes the five Bs of attachment parenting in infancy: (1) bonding with the infant at birth, (2) breast-feeding, (3) bed sharing (cosleeping), (4) baby wearing (carrying the baby in a sling), and (5) belief in the baby's cry as an important signal. The five Bs keep baby and parents physically connected so parents can learn who their child is and be able to respond in a sensitive, caring way.[75]

Sears raised his own children this way and has been counseling parents for over three decades. The number of attachment parenting advocates is increasing, perhaps because, as more mothers work outside the home, they want to stay connected to their infants and young children. Advocates of attachment parenting believe it (1) simplifies life (parents have no bottles, cribs, or strollers to manage); (2) increases parents' sensitivity and responsiveness as parents get to know their babies better; (3) promotes gentle discipline, because children's natural tendencies to independence and self-control are allowed to develop slowly and gradually over time; and (4) focuses on the family's needs, not just the needs of the parent or infant.[76]

> With attachment parenting, parents and children find their needs in cooperation with one another, thus creating a family-centered lifestyle. A key benefit of this responsive style of caregiving is that both parents and children feel that they are getting their "cup filled," as some parents say. Children feel whole and secure, while parents feel more relaxed and confident.[77]

Attachment parenting does not require that a caregiver be at home full time, and there is much advice on how to combine attachment parenting and working. Parents are advised to create a community of caregivers who share the parents' values and will behave in the same way toward the baby when the parents are not there. Such caregivers would give breast milk the mothers have pumped, carry the children during the day, and respond quickly and attentively to children's cries.

Advocates believe that "experienced attachment parents who have seen their children through early childhood and beyond describe this gentle nurturing style as a completely fulfilling way of life."[78] Research certainly supports elements of attachment parenting—the importance of sensitive, responsive care and the decrease in crying that comes from increased early carrying—but it is not clear that cosleeping and prolonged carrying of the child are beneficial, nor is it clear that immediate gratification of desires is essential or wise for all babies. Recall that soothed fearful and inhibited children maintained those behaviors when firm support to learn self-soothing appeared more useful in helping them overcome the behaviors (see Chapter 2).

Parents' Responses to Babies' Crying and Sleep Difficulties

Meeting babies' needs successfully makes parents feel confident about themselves as parents. They feel good about their partners, and they love their babies.[79] Fortunately, most parents experience this positive cycle of feelings.

However, as many as 20 percent of parents have irritable, distressed babies who cry more than three hours per day and don't sleep. These parents feel stressed and exhausted, doubt their own skills, and feel others are critical of them. In focus groups, they say more than anything that they want people to listen to their concerns with empathy.[80]

The Fussy Baby Network, an interdisciplinary program in Chicago, has formed to help these parents so they and their babies can get off to a good start.[81] The Network provides many services: preventive education classes to give information and parenting skills, professional assessment of babies' development to identify existing problems, interventions needed to help babies, assessments of parents' mental health, and training and consultation for parents, often in the home.

Three principles guide Network activity. Professionals provide (1) an emotionally safe place for parents to express their concerns and obtain referrals, (2) a collaborative relationship in which parents' insights are sought and parents develop their own strategies, and (3) support in moving forward in small steps. The long-term objectives are to increase parents' confidence, their knowledge and understanding of their baby, and positive relationships among all family members. Their core message to parents is, "You are not alone," "You are a good parent," "You are handling a hard situation well."

Parents report stress drops from an average score of 4.59 (on a scale of five) to .93 when the program ends.

PROMOTING SELF-REGULATION

Now we turn to a task that parents find challenging and demanding: helping children develop the ability to control their own behavior.

Encouraging Compliance

Parents first create an atmosphere of mutual responsiveness and receptive compliance. Secure attachments to children and sensitive caretaking create a climate in which children are more likely to comply.[82] When noncompliance occurs, parents use reasoning and explanations—low-power techniques—that result in a sharing of power. Sharing power with children has a strong impact because it communicates essential respect for the child as a person.

Parents take many other actions to encourage self-control and self-regulation, including:[83]

Modeling—showing the behaviors you want your child to learn

Consistent daily routines that help children learn rules—it is much easier for babies to calm down for sleep if every night a child has a bath, nursing, a song, rocking, and bed in that order rather than an unpredictable rotation of these activities

Preventive actions to head off potential problems—parents divert children's attention from tempting but forbidden activities by suggesting interesting substitutes (e.g., in grocery stores, suggesting children pick out the family items on the shelf when they are bored)

Conversations about rules and reasons for them—when everyone is relaxed and there are no conflicts, conversations about rules and how people feel when rules are broken help children to understand what is expected and why

Establishing Rules

Parents generally introduce rules that dovetail with the toddler's increasing abilities. Research reveals that

- at thirteen months, rules center on safety for the child, for other people (no hitting, kicking, or biting), and for possessions.
- at about eighteen months, the rules expand to include behavior during meals, requests to inhibit behavior and delay activity, and early self-care.
- at about twenty-four months, rules center on polite behavior and helping with family chores (putting toys away) are included.

- at thirty-six months, children are expected to do more self-care, such as dressing themselves.[84] Children's compliance with safety rules is high and increases with age. The time and involvement required for promoting all areas of self-regulation are enormous, and parents of two-year-olds intervene eight to ten times per hour to gain compliance. Such parents need a great deal of energy and support.[85]

Influence of Temperament on Parenting

In the early months of life, babies' reactivity and emotionality strongly influence what parents do and the effects of parents' actions. We discussed this relationship generally in Chapter 2, and here we discuss how temperament affects what parents do in the first two years. We have already described the effects of babies' fussy, irritable behavior on parents' caregiving. When parents lack success in soothing babies, they may withdraw or become harsh and restrictive in discipline, increasing babies' irritability and negative mood. This is especially true when parents have limited economic resources. When parents are older and have more economic resources, parents are more likely to be patient and supportive with babies, the very qualities that are likely to decrease fussiness and irritability.[86]

When young infants are fearful and inhibited in response to new and unfamiliar people and events, sensitive parents are nurturant and protective with their infants, so infants tend to remain fearful and inhibited. The children who decrease in fearfulness and inhibition over time have parents who are both supportive and sensitive, yet expose children to new events, encouraging them to develop coping strategies.[87]

When inhibited, fearful children become toddlers, they are very responsive to parents' instructions and rules.[88] They need only gentle support to internalize the rules. When parents are assertive and directive, using power harshly at times to dictate to children, toddlers become so emotionally stressed they do not learn the rules.

Fearless children who are energetic, curious, self-directed, and independent also fail to respond to power-assertive, restrictive discipline.[89] They learn rules most easily when parents form close, warm, harmonious relationships. Children then follow the rules to maintain the caring and responsive relationship they have with parents.

Parents are most effective in helping children develop self-control and self-regulation when they are warm and sensitive, have harmonious relationships with children, and are gently supportive yet firm in encouraging children to develop coping strategies.

Play, Reading, and Fun

Family fun turns out to be very beneficial for children's growth as well. We know children need toys and objects and opportunities to explore in order to learn about the world. But children benefit also from pretend play, especially with parents. For example, when mothers and fathers engage in imaginary play with their toddlers, toddlers play in a more sophisticated way than they do when playing alone.[90] And they learn from such play. Parents and toddlers talk about what they are doing, and language skills and social understanding increase. Interestingly, research shows that engaging in interactive, productive play in the early years promotes self-control[91] and reduces the risk of behavior problems later in school.[92] As we noted in Chapter 5, it is not exactly clear how play produces positive benefits.

Parents' daily reading to children promotes vocabulary growth and increases intellectual skills.[93] So fun activities, like playing make-believe games, has long-lasting intellectual benefits and important emotional benefits in the form of greater self-control.

PARENTS' EXPERIENCES IN FACING TRANSITIONS

Parents adjust their prebirth images of themselves as parents with the reality of their daily nurturing of their baby.[94] When expectations have been unrealistic, adjustments are painful. Parents of young toddlers face another transition—to Galinsky's authority stage (see Chapter 6). This lasts from the child's second to fourth or fifth year. In dealing with their own feelings about having power, setting rules, and enforcing them, parents have to decide what is reasonable when children mobilize all their energy to oppose them and gain their way. In the nurturing stage, parents were primarily concerned with meeting babies' needs and coordinating their own with caregiving activities. Usually, the appropriate child-care behavior was clear— the baby had to be fed, bathed, and put to bed. Although judgment was required in deciding about letting the child cry or sleep time, the desired aim was clear. In the beginnings of the authority stage, parents are developing clear rules and the confidence not only to enforce them but also to deal with the tantrums that follow. We continue this topic in the next chapter as well.

McHale returned to observe parents' ways of interacting with their one-year-olds and each other.[95] While parents were more confident in interacting with children and all couples had developed some form of coparenting alliance, all parents reported they wanted to improve. All parents wanted more time with the family and for the family to be a major priority. Additionally, fathers wanted mothers to be more relaxed and patient, and mothers wanted fathers to spend more time in child-care and family activities, and to volunteer to help without being asked.

This sample was an advantaged one in which 35 percent of mothers did not work outside the home, an additional 42 percent of mothers had part-time employment, and only 23 percent of mothers were employed full time. Parents had settled into a pattern in which mothers were the primary organizers and managers of family life, and fathers helped out when asked. Rarely were fathers partners in planning and carrying out child care, and as a result about one-third of mothers felt overwhelmed.

When parents disagreed about parenting behaviors, they were more likely to be critical and outspoken than they were when babies were three months old. Beliefs about parenting expressed during pregnancy predicted these behaviors. When parents anticipated disagreements in their interactions, disagreements occurred after the births. Parents who were very unlike in parenting beliefs were most likely to have disagreements when babies were twelve months old.

Warm, cooperative coparenting alliances established at three months tended to continue. Marital distress seemed the main factor in decreasing the collaboration. There were, however, a small group of parents who were unhappy in the marriage but made a strong commitment to work with the other parent for the child's well-being.

PROGRAMS TO HELP PARENTS WITH SPECIAL STRESSORS

Even advantaged parents like those in McHale's study feel stress and depression in meeting babies' needs, especially when babies are irritable and hard to soothe. Some parents are already dealing with stressors such as depression and anger. Existing stresses sap the energy parents require for positive and supportive parenting, and so they become harsh, restrictive, and demanding with children.

Research suggests it is the negative parenting strategies, rather than the existence of stressors, that impact children's development and increase the risk of behavior problems. We look here at programs and interventions for depressed parents and parents who are at risk for child abuse.

Depressed Parents

Studies of depressed parents have focused on mothers, as they are the ones who most frequently care for babies.[96] Fathers' depression no doubt has effects that are not identified at present.

In comparison to nondepressed mothers, depressed mothers interact less frequently and less positively with their infants, looking at and touching them less often and vocalizing less often. They are also less affectionate and playful. They are more critical and see babies in a more negative light.

Infants and young children of depressed mothers develop more problems. Babies of depressed mothers are fussier, more irritable, and less active than are babies of nondepressed mothers. Furthermore, babies of depressed mothers show these behaviors with adult nondepressed strangers, who, in turn, respond with negative affect, setting up a vicious cycle. Babies of depressed mothers show some of the same physiological characteristics that distinguish their mothers from nondepressed mothers. Their EEGs show reduced frontal activity, similar to that of mothers.

Preschool children of mothers who continue to be depressed show the same physiological characteristics as earlier, and depressed mothers continue to report having more behavior problems with their children.[97] The relationship between mothers' depression and children's later behavior problems continues in the first grade.[98] Children whose mothers were depressed over the first six years of life had higher scores on externalizing problems such as noncompliance and impulsivity (measured by parents and teacher reports) and lower scores on measures of social competence than children of nondepressed mothers. Children of depressed mothers also had reduced frontal brain activation that may reduce attention and interest in external events, and higher emotional reactivity in response to emotion-stimulating events.

Difficulties in family functioning appeared to account for the relationship between mothers' depression and children's behavioral difficulties. Children of depressed mothers were more likely to live in families with marital tension, family conflict, and lack of social supports. When exposure to these risks was statistically controlled, the relationship between mothers' depression and children's functional difficulties was no longer significant.

The importance of increasing positive family interactions is highlighted in other research.[99] When depressed mothers of toddlers were able to maintain positive, responsive interactions with their children, guiding them firmly without harshness, their children's behavior problems decreased over the next three years. Depressed mothers most likely to maintain positive parenting were those with nondepressed friends who perhaps served as models for parenting. These depressed mothers also found play dates and friends for their children with children of nondepressed mothers.

Findings on the widespread effects of mothers' depression, particularly its effects on family interactions, underscore the need for effective interventions directed to the mother and the child and their patterns of interactions as well as interactions in the family as a whole as soon as ongoing depression is noted.[100]

In addition to the usual clinical treatments of medication and psychotherapy, interventions to improve mothers' mood include massage therapy and relaxation therapy, which have been found to lower mothers' scores on measures of anxiety and depression. Furthermore, music therapy sessions, during which mothers listen to their preferred music, appear to temporarily reduce right frontal EEG activation.

Massage therapy—provided by mothers and professional therapists—also helps infants of depressed mothers by reducing fussiness, improving sleeping patterns, and increasing self-soothing and activity level, resulting in more positive patterns of interaction with mothers. In one study, just rubbing an infant's legs while the child gazed at the still face of the mother reduced the infant's distress. In another study, rubbing the infant's legs while smiling and cooing increased the infant's eye contact more than did smiling and cooing alone.

Coaching also improved interactions between mothers and children. Withdrawn, depressed mothers were encouraged to keep their infants' attention. When mothers played more games and had more positive facial expressions, their babies responded with more activity and more positive moods.

Interventions that seek to change depressed mothers' lifestyles have also helped decrease depression. Becoming more active and returning to school or work improves mothers' interactions with their babies; they are less negative than depressed mothers who remain at home.

Parents at Risk for Abuse of Infants

Parents at risk for maltreating children benefit from special programs. In one study parents were identified at the child's birth on the basis of two factors:[101] (1) a child's risk for health problems (because of prematurity or low Apgar scores at birth) and (2) parents' risk for poor care (e.g., history of partner violence, substance abuse or mental illness, victim of physical abuse, past involvement with Children's

Protective Services). Parents were assigned to one of three groups: a control group that was given information about community services, a home visit group (HV), or an enhanced home visit (EHV) group. The Home Visit program provided parent education, anger management skills, and establishment of a social support network. The home visits occurred approximately every two weeks for a year and covered such topics as setting and reaching family goals, obtaining health-care and medical services, parenting skills, and managing finances. Parents were trained to support children's healthy development in the areas of physical, language, and socioemotional growth.

In the Enhanced Home Visit program, parents received all the services of the HV program, and at the beginning of each home visit, they also received additional psychological training for dealing with children's behavior. Researchers have found that when parents at risk for child abuse confront problems with children's behavior, they see themselves as helpless in confronting powerful children who are determined to defy them and get their own way. They blame themselves or the child for the problem.

The additional training was designed to empower parents and help them develop confidence in their abilities to care for their children in a competent way. The program had two specific aims: to help parents (1) change their perceptions of their children's behavior and (2) develop problem-solving strategies for coping with children's problem behaviors. At the beginning of every home visit, parents described a recent problem with children, and then the home visitor asked why they thought the behavior occurred. For example, a parent might say that a baby was crying for a long time because she was mad at the parent or because the parent was a bad parent. Home visitors continued to elicit parents' reasons for the child's behavior until parents gave a benign or non-blame interpretation of children's actions—for example, the child is crying because the formula needs adjusting or he needs to eat more often. Home visitors never pointed out parents' misinterpretations.

Home visitors then asked parents to think about actions to reduce the problem. Was there something they could do immediately or did they need more information? Conversation continued until parents came up with a specific action to carry out. At the next visit, parents reviewed the results of the action and fine-tuned the solution as necessary.

At the end of the year the rates of child abuse and harsh parenting (defined as frequency of physically abusive tactics or spanking/slapping) and child health differed in the three groups: Parents in the EHV program were less likely to physically abuse their children (4 percent) than parents in HV (23 percent) and control groups (26 percent). Infant spanking and slapping (legally not abusive) also decreased—only 18 percent of mothers in the EHV program spanked infants, as compared to 42 percent of mothers in the HV and control groups. The rate of spanking in EHV mothers is similar to that of college-educated mothers. The differences between the groups were most striking in the caregiving of medically at-risk infants.

Children's physical health (defined as freedom from physical health problems in the first year) improved with the addition of services to families. Physical health was highest for children in families receiving EHV, then for those with HV, then for those children in the control group. Added services made a difference. Further work is needed to replicate the results of the study and to follow children's well-being for a longer period of time to note the length of the intervention effects.

The intervention programs cited illustrate that it is possible to shift parents' child-rearing attitudes and behaviors, and that changes in the direction of positive, supportive parenting improve children's health and behavior.

WISDOM OF AND FOR PARENTS

The programs reviewed indicate parents have the capacity for positive caregiving, as even brief interventions had profound effects in triggering a positive or benign cycle of interactions between parent and child. For example, when mothers carried babies in slings from birth, the rate of secure attachments at one year was similar to that in advantaged, college-educated samples. When low-income mothers of irritable six-month-old babies received three two-hour visits focusing on positive forms of interaction, mothers and infants had high rates of secure attachment at one year and positive forms of family interactions and social play with peers at age three. These interventions unlock parents' inner capacities for giving loving care.

We have seen that most parents experience stress, and so all families benefit from supportive services. A wise network of family and friends is sometimes sufficient. Parents with financial assets are increasingly hiring baby coaches who come into the home and advise on routines for healthy sleeping, eating, and discipline. Parents of more modest means often rely on community organizations such as Zero to Three.

Zero to Three is a national organization founded by T. Berry Brazelton and Stanley Greenspan to support "the healthy development and well-being of infants, toddlers, and their families."[102] The nonprofit organization seeks to inform and educate parents, professionals who work with parents of infants and young children, and public policymakers regarding young children's needs. The organization holds annual training institutes to bring the latest research to professionals who work with young children and families. It also has developed educational materials for parents that reflect "the belief that parents are the true experts on their children." Thus, each parent must develop his or her own way of promoting a child's growth. Their parent pamphlet, titled "What's Best for My Baby and Me?" presents information on babies' temperament and its effect on behavior, possible interpretations of babies' behavior, and a three-step approach to parenting infants and young toddlers.[103]

All these programs enable parents to learn effective responses for their particular child and contribute to parents' feelings of competency and parental self-efficacy, defined as the belief that one can perform appropriate parental behaviors and influence the child's development.[104] Parental self-efficacy is positively related to parents' satisfaction in the parenting role and to the quality of care parents give children. It also serves as a buffer against stressful factors in the social environment and in the child's development. When difficulties arise, parents believe their behaviors make a difference, and they act.

MAIN POINTS

In the first two years, infants

- gain control over their bodies and learn to sit alone, stand, walk, and run
- take a lively interest in the world around them, reaching out to grasp and explore objects and the world
- develop language gradually from cooing and babbling in the early months, to words at one year and two-word sentences by age two
- develop a wide range of emotional reactions; at the end of the first year, they express anger, fear, joy, pleasure, curiosity, and surprise, and by the end of the second year, they show more affection, more eagerness to please, greater resistance to parents' directives, and great delight in their accomplishments

Effective parents

- are nurturant, material, social, and didactic caregivers
- are available, attentive, sensitive partners who synchronize their behavior with the child's individual needs
- soothe babies and help them regulate their physiological states
- form enduring attachments with their children
- stimulate development when they play and converse with children
- interact with infants in different ways, with mothers holding babies more and doing more caregiving and fathers being more playful and physically stimulating

Parents regulate children's behavior effectively when they

- establish an atmosphere of mutual understanding
- act to prevent problems
- introduce safety rules before other rules
- use low-power techniques such as reasoning and explanation when non-compliance occurs

Parents likely to have trouble establishing secure attachments with infants

- have a negative, critical approach to children
- have difficulty effectively timing responses to children, either withdrawing or overstimulating them
- can be helped with interventions that provide education, opportunities for the parent to get to know the child, and support

Preterm babies

- make special physical and psychological demands on parents
- have a narrow range of optimal stimulation that is neither over- nor understimulating
- receive long-term benefits from parents' attention and stimulation.

As they incorporate infants into family life, parents

- often do not anticipate the stress produced by the number of changes needed
- seek support from each other and their social network
- experience many joys

EXERCISES

1. Recalling the father's comment on page that he knew so little about babies that he should not have been permitted to take one home from the hospital, work in small groups to devise checklist of what parents should know before they take their baby home from the hospital. Compare suggestions among the different groups.

2. Go to a toy store and spend an imaginary $150 on toys for an infant or toddler. Justify your choices.

3. Go to a supermarket or a park on a weekend, and observe parents and infants or parents and toddlers. Note how the children respond to the environment around them, to parents, and to passersby. Try to find children about the same age to see how individual differences among children determine responses to the same environment. Observe parenting behaviors, and describe their effects on the children.

4. Go to local hospitals and agencies to determine what kinds of instruction or hands-on training is given to parents to provide safe environments for infants and toddlers.

5. Interview mothers or fathers about how much time they spend with their infants and toddlers each day. What is the family schedule? Who does what? What do they most enjoy doing with their young child? What do they see as the greatest joys and stresses of having children?

ADDITIONAL READINGS

Brazelton, T. Berry, and Greenspan, Stanley I. *The Irreducible Needs of Children.* Cambridge, MA: Perseus, 2000.

Brott, Armin A. *Father for Life: A Journey of Joy, Challenge, and Change.* New York: Abbeville Press, 2003.

Karp, Harvey. *The Happiest Baby on the Block.* New York: Bantam, 2002.

Karp, Harvey. *The Happiest Toddler on the Block.* New York: Bantam, 2004.

Saarni, Carolyn. *The Development of Emotional Competence.* New York: Guilford Press, 1999.

8

Parenting in Early Childhood: The Years from Two to Five

CHAPTER TOPICS	IN THE NEWS
In this chapter, you will learn about:	*New York Times Magazine*, February 17[1]: Play is a serious business for children and parents have an important role in it. See page 246.
▦ Children's development	
▦ Relationships with parents, siblings, and peers	
▦ Managing sleep, aggression, withdrawal, and developmental delays	
▦ Parents' experiences and supports	

Test Your Knowledge: Fact or Fiction (True/False)

1. Poverty only reduces physical resources such as books and toys in the home, but not the amount of positive attention children receive.
2. Between 10 and 30 percent of children are thought to be sleep-deprived.
3. To help children gain control of aggressive feelings, parents are advised to ignore anger out bursts.
4. The moment with the most potential for causing emotional trauma for a child with special needs is when the child realizes that society views his or her differences as signs of inferiority.
5. Parent–child interactions account for only about 10 percent of the emotional distress preschoolers experience at home.

How do parents help children make sense of the world around them? How do parents support children's growing sense of self and help children learn to regulate their behavior? How do parents promote positive relations with peers and others outside the home? Where do parents get support as they raise their children?

By age two, children have learned the basic skills of walking and talking. They want to understand all that is going on. Their sense of personal identity grows, and they learn to control their emotional reactions and their behavior. Parents help children advance in all these areas and prepare them for the transition to school and learning outside the home.

PHYSICAL AND NEUROPHYSIOLOGICAL DEVELOPMENT

Between ages two and five, children grow more slowly than before, but still, they grow from about 34 inches and 29 pounds at age two to 42 inches and 42–45 pounds at age five. Children's brains are active and primed for learning. Compared with an adult brain, a three-year-old's brain has twice as many synapses (connections among brain cells), is two and a half times more active, requires more glucose, and has more neurotransmitters (chemicals that facilitate the transmission of information from one cell to another).[2] Brain development increases children's motor control, attention, and memory, which underlie advances in motor, cognitive, and personal–social functioning.

INTELLECTUAL DEVELOPMENT

Children are active and verbal. Increased attention span and increased memory enable children to focus on activities for a longer time and recall more detailed sequences, so thinking becomes more complex. Children can distinguish real events from imagined ones and from dreams and nightmares.[3]

Children observe and learn all day long, watching others' reactions to their behavior to see what is acceptable. They are problem-solvers. When children's actions do not achieve their goals, they recall the successful actions of others and use them.[4] As they seek guidance, preschoolers assess the accuracy of what the person has said in the past; they rely on those who have demonstrated knowledge.[5]

Verbal skills, the ability to control attention and effort, and persistence when frustrated all contribute to learning.[6] Neuroendocrine levels too play a role. Moderate cortisol arousal followed by down-regulation was associated with measures of flexible problem solving, self-regulation, and letter knowledge.[7]

By the preschool years, some children have developed what is termed mastery motivation, a strong desire to investigate objects and problems and achieve mastery of them.[8] Children high in this quality persist with challenging tasks and take pride in solving problems, and they learn more in the course of a year in preschool. Children are most likely to develop this motivation when parents are warm, encouraging, and open in conversation with their children.

LANGUAGE DEVELOPMENT

Children progress from having about 50 words at nineteen months to having 10,000 words at age six, in the first grade, learning an average of 5.5 words per day.[9] The

VOICES OF EXPERIENCE

What I Wish I Had Known about the Years from Two to Five

"I wish I'd known how to react when they lied. You know kids lie, but it hurts me terribly. It was a very painful experience even though I know I did it."   MOTHER

"I wish I had known how much frustration comes just because kids are kids and you have to be tolerant. They don't have the attention span for some things. They might want to do something with you, but they can only do it for about fifteen minutes. You have to go places prepared with all his things or with things to keep him entertained. In the car on a trip, we have a lot of things for him to do. When you plan ahead, you can still be spontaneous at times. You learn that if you are prepared, things really don't have to be a hassle."   FATHER

"Everything. I wish I'd known more about communication, how to talk to your children, and the most effective way to help them grow with a strong ego, a good sense of self. We were raised with a lot of 'Do this and don't do that' demands and commands. Trying to get in touch with your child's feelings so you really do understand how they feel about things is really hard to learn. I don't know how you can learn it without the experience of actually having a child. But I'm continually learning how to understand her feelings about things."   MOTHER

"I think it is incredible that we don't teach anything about being a parent. I have to learn it as I go along, because I want things to be different for them than they were for me growing up. I can't use my own experiences as a guide."   FATHER

"I wish I had known how to handle things like believing in Santa Claus. I didn't know whether to encourage it or not or when to tell her there was none. She learned gradually, I think, but she doesn't want to tell her little brother yet."   MOTHER

"[I] wasn't prepared for all the decisions. Is it okay if he does this or not? He's trying to do something; shall I step in so he doesn't hurt himself or shall I let him go? It's making all those choices, making sure what I feel."   MOTHER

"There is anxiety, a feeling of vulnerability I have never felt before. If he gets sick, what are we going to do? If he has a little sickness, we just hope the doctor is doing the right thing. We went through a great deal in the past few weeks choosing a nursery school for him, and we hope we have done the right thing, but is this the one for him?"   FATHER

"I wish we had—because he is our first child—more of a sense of the norms. What is okay versus what is a problem and what is really bad? Is this normal, is this just kids being kids? He pushed someone at school three times; is this par for the course or is this a problem? We don't know when we are reacting and when we are overreacting."   FATHER

length of sentences grows from two words at age two to complex sentences of several words, with clauses.

Parents promote children's vocabulary and intellectual performance when they:[10]

- talk a lot with their children
- refer to many topics
- use a variety of words
- give children positive feedback about their behavior

Children's verbal skills in the preschool years are important because they predict children's verbal IQ and reading skills in the third grade[11] better than vocabulary growth.[12]

Adults' conversations with children not only develop skills, but also convey information about how others think and feel, values about gender and racial matters, and the child's behavior in the past so the child has a sense of autobiographical memory.

EMOTIONAL DEVELOPMENT

Preschoolers' most common form of emotional upset is crying, which accounts for 74 percent of the disruptions at home.[13] Anger represents about 23 percent of these incidents. Parent–child interactions account for 71 percent of the upsets, with sibling conflicts accounting for only 13 percent and peer conflicts for 6 percent of the distress. Parents' usual response to the distress is not to comfort but to give the child a practical, problem-solving response so that the child can deal with the situation. When parents encourage children to take action with problems, children are better able to plan and are more effective in social activities and other areas.

Preschoolers' understanding of people increases.[14] Toddlers' conversations reveal they understand that people's feelings often lead to actions, and conversely, actions lead to feelings—"I give a big hug, Baby be happy." "Grandma mad. I wrote on wall."[15] Toddlers understand that others' feelings determine their actions, but preschoolers go beyond this and see that others' thoughts often determine both feelings and actions.[16]

Preschoolers' greater awareness of others' reactions to their behavior enables them to see how well their behavior meets others' standards. The "self-evaluative" emotions of pride, shame, and guilt develop.[17] Children feel pride and happiness when they accomplish what they set out to, shame when they fail to meet external standards and their weaknesses or inadequacies are exposed, and guilt when they violate the rules of right and wrong. Guilt depends on an internalization of the rules and develops toward the end of the preschool years.

In judging their actions, children, even in these early years, develop one of two approaches—the global performance orientation or the specific learning orientation.[18] When children have a global performance orientation, they believe failure and success reflect their value as a person; they feel great when they succeed or bad when they fail. When children fail, they avoid the activity with reasons like, "I can't draw" or "I'm a terrible runner."

Other children have a specific learning orientation. They look at success or failure as a single action that did or did not succeed. It is not a reflection of their value

Preschoolers know parents will be happy when they help with household chores.

as a person; a failure means they need more information or practice. These children are confident and willing to work hard to learn because they believe they can learn with greater effort or new strategies.

Aggressiveness

A very careful study of physical aggression (hitting, kicking, destroying property) based on mothers' ratings of their children from ages two to nine revealed the majority of children (70 percent) were low or very low on physical aggression for the whole period, and only 3 percent were consistently high.[19] Half of the moderately aggressive two-year-olds learned self-regulatory skills and were at a low level of aggression by age five, and the other half maintained a moderate level of aggression.

Highly aggressive children had early (birth to age 2) stressful lives. Their mothers reported being depressed more often than mothers of low aggressive children. Mothers were coping with significantly more social stressors such as being single parents or having less education and low income. They were less sensitive and responsive parents, and provided less stimulation at home. Children performed less well on an intellectual measure at age two. In contrast, nonaggressive children came from homes where there were emotional support and few stressors. Mothers were educated, psychologically stable women described as responsive and warm caregivers. These family characteristics continued to differentiate the aggressive and nonagressive children from ages two to nine.

The most aggressive children between ages two and five continued to be aggressive at age nine and had many additional problems as well—academic, social, and emotional. Fifty-eight percent of these children were rated below grade level in school performance and a sizeable number had trouble paying attention and complying with mothers' or teachers' requests. Children high on aggression did

The relationships among siblings are emotional, intense, affectionate, and sometimes aggressive. Children are more likely to get along well when parents are sensitive, responsive, and securely attached to each child.

not get along well with peers, teachers, or mothers. In addition, children described themselves as lonely and angry. So these children experienced many early and ongoing deprivations and continued to struggle in several arenas as they grew older. Those children low in aggression at age nine got along well with others, performed well academically, and reported few worries.

Positive parenting strategies reduce aggressiveness in both boys and girls. When parents pay positive attention, reward good behavior, and avoid criticism and harsh punishment, then children decline in aggression.[20] Positive parenting is effective even when the family is under stress and behavior problems have developed, as we discuss later in the section "Parents' Tasks and Concerns."

Fear

Fears are a natural part of life as children grow up. In the early years of infancy, fears of noise and strangers are most evident, but these anxieties gradually fade. In the preschool years, children experience fears of animals, the dark, harm from imaginary creatures, and natural disasters such as fires and storms.

Biological, psychological, and social factors underlie preschoolers' inhibition. Unique patterns of brain activity and physiological reactivity seen in infancy appear to predispose these children to anxiety and fear and the resulting behavioral wariness and withdrawal.[21]

Parents' behavior plays a role as well.[22] Mothers of inhibited two-year-old toddlers responded in a "suffocatingly warm" and overprotective way that prevented their children from becoming independent. When their children's inhibited behavior continued through the preschool years, mothers shifted their behavior and became more power-assertive, directive, and harsh in trying to force children to overcome their fearfulness. Mothers who encouraged their inhibited toddlers to overcome their fearfulness and become more independent were not power-assertive or harsh with their children at age five.

Culture too plays a role. North American culture views inhibition and social withdrawal negatively as children are not conforming to the cultural ideals of independence, self-assertive achievement, and social outgoingness. In Chinese culture, children's wariness and inhibition are viewed positively as signs of sensitivity and cautiousness. Parents are positive and supportive. They are not overprotective or harsh with their children even though Chinese children are far more inhibited than North American children in laboratory situations. Since inhibited children are not rejected by parents or others in Chinese culture, they do not view themselves negatively or feel unloved as happens in North American culture.

As with aggressive children, parents of inhibited children are most helpful to their children when they are positive, supportive, and encourage children as they learn to manage their feelings and develop new behaviors.

Empathy

Children's ability to respond sensitively to others' needs increases as they grow. Toddlers and preschoolers are better able to understand sources of emotional reactions, and use strategies to go more directly to the source of the problem.[23] Children learn empathy from parents' modeling it and from books and stories that have moral themes.[24] Fairy tales, universal favorites of children, present models of kind, caring behavior that triumphs over evil and cruelty.

THE DEVELOPMENT OF THE SELF

In early childhood, children continue to define themselves in terms of their physical characteristics and their actions, but they are beginning to organize their self-perceptions and see themselves in more general though dichotomous terms such as good or bad, smart or dumb.[25] Most children continue to focus on their positive qualities and see themselves as "all good," but preschoolers who have experienced abuse are more likely than other children to consider themselves bad.

Preschoolers need not have experienced extreme stress such as abuse in order to have doubts about their skills. In one study, preschoolers reported negative self-perceptions of their likeability and social acceptance.[26] These self-perceptions were related to mothers' being cold and angry in interactions with their children as well as marital conflict children observed. Children seemed to take negative feedback from mothers very much to heart and believe that since mothers were irritated with them, others would be too. Sadly, preschoolers' self-perceptions predicted their kindergarten teachers' ratings of them as being angry, sad, withdrawn, and unable to get along with others.

Children high on self-esteem show confidence in exploring new situations and adaptability when they meet with frustration and stress.[27] Children low on self-esteem are inhibited in exploring and initiating new activities and unable to manage stress and frustration appropriately. Parents' warmth and sensitive responsiveness promote high self-esteem, as does their modeling adaptable, confident behavior.

Gender Identity

Gender identity is defined as an individual's personal experience of what it means to be a boy or girl, man or woman. Physical, social, and psychological factors contribute to gender differentiation. Physical factors include genes, which, in turn, trigger hormones that lead to the development of internal and external sexual characteristics and also influence behavior.[28] Societies and their subcultures transmit beliefs about what is appropriate for boys and girls through prescriptions of child rearing, and parents contribute their influence as well. Gender identity, however, "is not simply something imposed on children; at all points of development, children are actively constructing for themselves what it means to be female or male."[29]

Even infants of three or four months can distinguish men from women and by one year, they can link men's voices with men's faces and women's voices with women's faces. Between two and two and a half, toddlers announce proudly, "I am a boy" or "I am a girl." They gradually learn, usually between ages three and five, that gender is stable across time—they will always be a boy or a girl. Somewhere between ages five and seven, they also learn gender is consistent—they are girls whether they have short or long hair, wear skirts or pants.[30]

When they identify their gender and see it as an important part of themselves, children begin to develop a gender schema, defined as an organized body of knowledge of what it means to be a boy or a girl. By age two, toddlers have learned to label men, women, boys, and girls and have begun to associate gender labels with objects, activities, tasks, and roles. Conversations with two-year-olds, however, reveal they have little interest in the general qualities of men and women but focus on the activities of specific individuals.[31] Preschoolers, however, make many gender-stereotypic comments.

Up to about eighteen months of age, boys and girls show no differences in such behaviors as aggressiveness, toy play, large motor activity, and communication attempts, all of which exhibit gender differences in the next year.[32] Beginning at age two, boys prefer active pursuits and building activities, and girls prefer arts and crafts and reading. In the third year, boys and girls begin to play in same-gender groups, and this continues into the school years.

On average, boys tend to be more active and aggressive than girls. Girls are found to be more helpful and sometimes more fearful. Caroline Zahn-Waxler refers to the gender issues in problem behaviors as the problems of the warriors and the worriers.[33] We discuss parents' behavior in encouraging gender differences in children's behavior in a later section.

Ethnic Identity

Similar to the stages of gender identity formation, children also go through stages of forming a sense of ethnic identity, defined as a psychological attachment to "a group sharing a common ancestral heritage based on nationality, language, and culture."[34] When the group has an easily noted characteristic such as skin color, children can correctly identify membership in their group by age three. When an ethnic group lacks perceptually distinct characteristics, as for example with ethnic groups from similar geographical areas such as Northern Europe, ethnic group awareness occurs later at age five and reliable self-identification by age seven.

In the process of forming a sense of ethnic identity, children first identify their ethnic group, then see themselves as a member of the ethnic group, gradually learn what is distinctive about their own ethnic group, and finally, by around age seven, realize their ethnic identity is a stable part of them and will not change.[35] Children may develop ethnic identity at an earlier age if ethnic issues are frequently talked about at home.

Children benefit when parents help them form a positive sense of ethnic identity. For example, when children received messages of racial pride, and their homes were rich in Afrocentric items such as books and magazines, then children's problem-solving skills were more advanced, and they had more knowledge on a measure of achievement.[36] Those parents who reported giving strong measures of racial pride also reported fewer behavior problems with their children.

THE DEVELOPMENT OF SELF-REGULATION

Children learn the rules of life from interactions with their parents, their brothers and sisters, and their playmates. They learn about conventions and accepted routines from parents, and they learn about moral actions—sharing, teasing, helping, fighting—from interactions with other children. They want to learn and very early in the preschool years, are aware of the difference between rules that concern kindness and basic consideration of others and rules having to do with social convention.[37] Significantly, they are more impressed with the importance of kindness to others than with social conventions. Still, they feel obligated to do what adults want them to do.[38]

Even though children have a clear idea of right and wrong and want to follow parents' requests, preschoolers evaluate actions by their outcomes. If wrongdoers successfully achieve their ends, preschoolers assume they feel good about that. Preschoolers may know an act is wrong but not necessarily feel wrong or bad for doing it.[39] Children at this age are particularly happy to evade punishment while still getting what they want. Conversely, they get little pleasure out of following the rules when they really want to break them and achieve their ends. It is not until they are older, in elementary school, that children feel good because they have followed the rules.[40]

In an extensive study of children's behavior when children were three to six years of age with follow-up when children were twelve, the behavior of about 20 percent of children was described as undercontrolled.[41] Children failed to cooperate with others, not complying with adults' requests, not collaborating with peers. Instead, they were aggressive and felt unhappy much of the time. They performed less well than self-controlled children on cognitive tests in preschool, and their academic performance declined over the elementary school years. Age was a factor here as the behavior of older children, five and six, was less likely to be described as undercontrolled than that of younger children, and only one-third of three- and four-year-olds described as undercontrolled retained that description two years later.

Children whose behavior was initially adaptable and resilient and became undercontrolled over a two-year period lived in families with external stresses such as loss of family income or family instability. The source of stress was not so important as the number of stresses. As in the case of aggressive children, it is hard to learn self-regulation and self-control when the family is coping with many external stressors.

PARENT–CHILD RELATIONSHIPS

Parents' behavior is central to children's growth and competence. Parents' behavior in the first two years of life influence children's competence in the preschool period, and parents' interactions with children in the preschool years influence how children will fare when they are in elementary school.

Ross Parke and Raymond Buriel believe that parents meet role expectations and socialize children in three ways: (1) as an interactive partner with the child, (2) as a direct instructor, and (3) as a provider of activities and opportunities that stimulate children's growth.[42] Let us look at parents' activities in terms of these three roles.

Attachment

Parents are interactive partners, continuing to provide sensitive parenting to maintain the attachment that gives children a sense of security and trust in relationships with others. Although attachment quality in the first two years influences preschool attachment, preschoolers' present circumstances and the quality of their current relationships with parents are what most influence preschoolers' sense of security and social adaptation.[43]

Positive Parenting

In addition to fostering secure attachments with children, sensitive, responsive parenting (described in Chapter 5) also increases children's willingness and ability to internalize family rules and values and regulate their behavior.[44]

When both parents use positive parenting, they create a family atmosphere of mutual reciprocity and cooperation that benefit not only the parent–child relationship but the relationship between the parents as well. Yet, two-thirds of parents in one sample report that they have concerns about their own and their spouse's anger and irritability with their preschoolers.[45]

Vygotsky's emphasis on working with children at the high end of the zone of proximal development (see Chapter 2) contributes to the positive approach because parents:[46]

1. Adjust the task to challenge but not overwhelm the child (e.g., in the beginning just getting the covers pulled up is considered making the bed; it does not have to be perfect)

2. Problem-solve with the child—raising questions, wondering about possible options

3. Give the amount of help needed until the child gains the skill and then withdraw help

4. Give encouragement to counterbalance the frustration sometimes involved in learning

Vygotsky's suggestions and the guidelines of Positive Parenting contribute to the authoritative parenting Diana Baumrind (see Chapter 2) found so effective in rearing preschoolers.[47] Authoritative parenting, defined as blending warmth with firm control, respect for individuality, and independence, helps children develop competence that enables them to make the transition to kindergarten with few behavior problems.[48]

Parents' use of authoritative parenting depends in part on their relationship with their own parents.[49] Parents who reported anger and little love in their relationships with their parents appeared to have negative views of relationships in general, to be less supportive of their marital partner, and be more critical and authoritarian with their children. When mothers were unhappy with their parents, daughters and sons were more likely to be described in kindergarten as withdrawn, sad, and depressed. When fathers were unhappy with their relationships with their parents, sons and daughters were more likely to be described in kindergarten as angry and noncompliant.

Socializing Gender Roles

Parents teach children about gender roles in many different ways. First, parents model gender behaviors in their direct interactions with children.[50] Mothers carry out more caregiving activities and are more nurturant in everyday activities; fathers are often more direct and assertive. These differences were seen in European American and Latina/o parents and in parents of multiethnic backgrounds.[51]

Second, as interactive partners, parents may stimulate gender-stereotyped behavior indirectly when they respond to boys and girls differently. Although mothers and fathers treat boys and girls alike in many ways—they are equally attached to sons and daughters and use authoritative strategies with both[52]—they also reveal subtle differences in how they respond to boys and girls.[53] For example, mothers are more responsive to irritable infant sons than daughters; they talk more to daughters than to sons and use more supportive speech. Such differences in behavior may indirectly reinforce the gender-related behaviors of assertiveness in boys and verbal skills in girls.

Third, parents may sensitize children to gender issues in conversations. One study found that mothers drew their two-year-old toddler's attention to gender categories, labeling the gender of people, talking about the characteristics of boys and girls and men and women even when children were not particularly interested.[54]

Simply identifying a group has a powerful impact on preschoolers' thinking about membership in the group.[55] Having identified categories and contrasted boys and girls for toddlers, mothers of preschoolers express many egalitarian beliefs and rarely make gender-stereotypic comments, yet by age four, preschoolers make many gender-stereotypic comments in conversations, with the greatest frequency being in the years from five to seven.[56]

Fourth, as educators, parents teach children directly about gender-appropriate behaviors. They have books that show activities for boys and girls, and a variety of toys are available. Such teaching does not always succeed.

Fifth, and most important, parents influence children's gender-appropriate behavior through their encouragement of different activities and interests.[57] Until recently, boys were encouraged to be more active in sports than were girls, and such activities were thought to build boys' skills in teamwork and cooperation. When girls were highly active like boys, they received more negative responses from adults. Today, both boys and girls receive more encouragement for physical activity.

Finally, mothers and fathers seem to elicit different behaviors from boys and girls.[58] Observing preschool boys and girls in playroom interactions with mothers and fathers separately revealed that parents did not reinforce or encourage sex-stereotyped behavior, and boys and girls did not consistently behave in sex-stereotyped ways with both parents, but in play with fathers, both daughters and sons showed more male-stereotyped behavior; they were more boisterous, assertive, aggressive, and noncompliant.

Since children receive gender socialization from peers and teachers in school, parents need to be sure they convey their values to children at home.

Socializing Ethnic Identities

Parents, as we noted, help children form a sense of ethnic identity. In conversations, parents identify the group to which the family belongs, talking about its distinctive qualities and expressing pride in the group's history and accomplishments.[59] Parents also provide books, toys, and pictures that describe the group's values and history. They also introduce children to culturally appropriate ways of doing things such as dressing, cooking food, dancing, and relating to adults. If the group has a distinctive religion, children begin to participate in it.

Even though children are young, parents start to send messages about pride in the group's culture and values, and hearing these messages promotes children's social and academic competence.

Conversations

Conversations convey information directly about values, as we saw in talking about gender or race, and in subtle ways, as seen in a comparison of family conversations with two-year-olds in Taiwanese middle-class families and Irish American middle-class families living in Illinois.[60] Careful analysis revealed common themes and differences in the conversations of the two groups observed at home. All families engaged in personal storytelling with their two-and-a-half-year-olds, talking about pleasurable family events such as trips to the zoo or the market. In both groups, children received attention, affectionate comments, and physical hugs. All families talked about illnesses and physical mishaps such as nosebleeds.

In Taiwanese families, however, conversations were seen as teaching opportunities. Parents corrected grammar and pronunciation. Moral and social misbehavior were the focus of attention in 35 percent of the narrations. The present misdeed triggered discussion of past misdeeds of a similar sort, with an important moral lesson or guideline drawn at the end of the narration.

In Irish American families conversations were sources of entertainment and affirmations of children's positive qualities. Misdeeds were the focus of only 7 percent of narrations. They were described only briefly, presented in the most positive light as signs of curiosity or self-assertion and quickly passed over. Irish American parents were concerned about rules and talked about them, but serious discussions of a child's misbehavior were discussed in private when outsiders were not present and the child would not lose self-esteem.

These conversations illustrate how parents subtly convey attitudes about misdeeds and their consequences, about success and the meaning of failure or mistakes. Parents' conversations create an atmosphere, in the case of the Taiwanese families, one centered on striving to avoid mistakes and improve, and in Irish American families, one centered on self-assertion and success.

Stimulating Growth through Play

In Chapter 4, we talked about the intimate family culture that prepares preschool children to learn in the school setting—involvement in reading activities and having dinnertime conversations.[61] Board games with children can teach factual knowledge (e.g., numbers and basic math concepts) that help prepare children for school.[62]

Parents also stimulate growth when they play with children.[63] Physical play peaks when children are one to four and, for boys, is related to social competence and popularity with peers in the preschool years. Such play, however, is related to abrasive peer relationships for girls. Interactional and object play involve more verbal interactions and more symbolic pretend play as children grow older. In pretend play, children learn the routines of everyday life; as in earlier years, parents emphasize turn-taking and other kinds of reciprocity. In this play, parents also help children take on roles more knowledgeably.

Both interactional and object play help children develop emotional, social, verbal, and intellectual skills. For example, for children between twenty-one months and four years of age, symbolic play with mothers predicted social skills at five and a half years.

RELATIONSHIPS WITH SIBLINGS

In the preschool years, children often experience the birth of a little brother or sister. The birth brings changes not only to the preschooler, but to the parents, who often feel overwhelmed incorporating a second child in the family.

Before the second child arrives, parents are often intensely and positively involved with their first child, forming a tight-knit triangular family unit.[64] The birth of the second child reduces the time and energy parents have for the older child. Furthermore, with increased demands, parents become more directive and controlling with their older child, more parent-centered and sometimes harsh in discipline. Thus, the older child suffers two losses: the loss of exclusive parental attention and the loss of child-centered parenting behaviors.

It is not surprising then that firstborn children often experience anxiety, behavior problems, and conflict with parents and peers following the birth of a sibling. When financial resources are limited, the birth of an additional child further reduces resources for older children, and declines on measures of cognitive achievement and social competence are detectable for these children more than two years after birth.[65] When resources are not limited, children's negative reactions to the birth are usually temporary, and by the end of the first year, 63 percent of preschoolers report wanting another sibling.[66]

Parents use various strategies to integrate a new child into the family.[67] In some families, fathers attend to the needs of the firstborn, and mothers care for the newborn; in others, the father takes on more household tasks, leaving the mother time to care for both children; and in still others, both parents do all tasks. Some families rely on grandparents, aunts, and uncles to give extra time and attention to the older child.

Although many older siblings feel that mothers favor younger siblings, longitudinal studies of mothers' behavior with their two children when each is age one or two reveal that mothers are quite consistent in the amount of affection and verbal responsiveness they direct to each child at that age, but less consistent in their ways of controlling different children at a given age, probably because they have learned from experience.[68]

Parents promote positive sibling relationships in two basic ways.[69] First, parents form positive relationships with each other and with each child because sibling relationships very much reflect the family emotional climate. When parents get along with each other, when they treat each child in a warm, sensitive manner and have secure attachments with each child, then siblings get along with each other.

Second, positive relationships between siblings flourish when parents avoid comparisons and treat children fairly. Hostility and aggression flourish when one child has reason to feel rejected or unfairly treated or valued. For example, preschoolers are more likely to develop anxiety and acting-out behaviors when they are punished more than their sibling.

Therefore, when parents establish a warm, loving home environment and treat children fairly, then brothers and sisters are more likely to have positive relationships.

PEER RELATIONSHIPS

Two-year-olds play with peers, taking turns and sharing. They form stable relationships that can last beyond a year, and such friendships are important emotional attachments that enable them to adapt more easily to changes at preschool or day care.[70]

Preschoolers still spend time watching other children play, engaging in solitary play, drawing, building, and in parallel play.[71] These activities, enjoyable in themselves, help children develop skills for entering play groups of other children. Socially successful children enter groups by first watching what others are doing, playing alongside them, talking to children at play, and then entering play with them. In these years, boys and girls play in gender-segregated groups.

Preschoolers engage in more sociodramatic play that helps their development in many ways. Children talk about the roles they'll play, the actions that will occur; they make up rules they will follow; and they negotiate differences of opinion. From this play children gain a better understanding of others, the usefulness of rules, and negotiating skills. In acting out a variety of roles, they gain a more mature understanding of social behavior.

In the preschool years children form close, stable friendships with children who are like them in age and gender and behave in similar ways. Friends share and cooperate and support each other. They also quarrel and get angry with each other. Although friends have more fights than casual acquaintances because they spend more time with each other, friends handle conflicts differently, disengaging and finding a solution that gives each partner something equal, whereas casual acquaintances fight until someone wins.[72]

Even in early childhood, some children are more socially skilled than others, as they are outgoing and able to regulate their emotional reactions in peer interactions.[73] Secure attachments to parents help children feel trusting and confident in social relationships, whereas insecure attachments increase children's feelings that others are rejecting and neglectful.[74] Parents' monitoring of young children's social interactions and guiding children in how to join in and play with others increase children's social skills.

TASKS AND CONCERNS OF PARENTS

Parents of children aged two to five face new tasks as well as old. Parenting in this age period includes the following:

- Being sensitive, responsive caregivers who foster secure attachments with children
- Helping children learn rules and regulate their behavior
- Helping children manage frustration and challenges so they feel successful
- Stimulating children's growth and competence with books, play, and activities
- Coaching children when they have difficulties in activities and with others
- Providing companionship and guidance in conversation and play
- Accessing and, if not available, advocating for neighborhood services for children and families

The years from two to five can bring frustration for parents and children in the daily routines of sleeping, eating, and tantrums. Problems at home can lead to trouble

VOICES OF EXPERIENCE

The Joys of Parenting Children Ages Two to Five

"When she was four, she was the only girl on an all-boy soccer team. Her mother thought she was signing her up for a coed team, but she was the only girl, and she enjoyed it and liked it even though she is not a natural athlete. She watched and learned and got good at it, and we got a lot of joy out of watching her." FATHER

"Well, every night we have a bedtime ritual of telling a story and singing to her. This is probably beyond the time she needs it, but we need it." MOTHER

"He's very inventive, and it's fun for both of us when he tells stories or figures out ways to communicate something he's learned or heard. When his mother had morning sickness, he heard the baby was in her tummy so he figured out the baby is making the morning sickness, pushing the food out." FATHER

"One of the delights that comes up is reading him stories, telling him the adventure of John Muir, at the four-year-old level. We were talking about places to go, and I said, 'Maybe we could go visit the home of John Muir.' He said, 'Oh, great, then I could go up there and have a cup of tea.' And I remembered I had told him a story about Muir's having tea in a blizzard, and he remembered that. He put that together, and it came out of nowhere. It knocked me over that he remembered that image." FATHER

"I enjoy her because I can talk to her; we have these wonderful conversations, and she can tell me about something that happened to her today at school that was really neat for her, and I just love to hear about it." MOTHER

"It's fun to hear him looking forward to doing things with us. He'll ask how many days until Saturday or Sunday because on those days I wait for him to get up before I have breakfast. Usually I'm up and gone before he gets up. He likes to come out and get up in my lap and share my breakfast, and it's a ritual. He looks forward to that and counts the days." FATHER

"She's really affectionate, always has been, but now out of nowhere, she'll tell you she loves you. She likes to do things with you, and when you give her special attention, one on one, she really likes it. We play games—Candy Land or Cinderella—or just one of us goes with her to the supermarket or to the park. We read stories every night and do some talking. Sometimes I put a record on and we dance." FATHER

"The joy comes from the things we do as a family, the three of us—going to see Santa Claus together or to see miniature trains and take a ride. Early in the morning we have a ritual. When he gets up early, he has a bottle of milk and gets in bed with us; the lights are out, and we are lying in bed, and he tells us his dreams and we watch the light outside and see the trees and see the sun come up. We do that in the morning, and it is a quiet joy." FATHER

"One night at dinner, he was watching his little sister, who's one, and he said, 'Do you think when she gets to be a big girl she'll remember what she did as a baby?' I was amazed at the question." MOTHER

(continued)

VOICES OF EXPERIENCE

The Joys of Parenting Children Ages Two to Five

(continued)

❝I like going for a walk with her, and we went skipping rocks at the reservoir. I was going to show her how to skip rocks because she had never seen that before. Of course, she wanted to try it, and I didn't think she was old enough to do it. I had found the best skipping rock; it was just perfect. I was going to hold her hand and do it with her. She said, 'No, I want to do it myself.' I thought, it is more important to just let it go. So I said, 'Here, let me show you how.' So I showed her, and she said, 'No, I can do it.' She threw it and it skipped three times! The first time she ever threw one! She wanted to stay till she did it again, and we did a little; but it will be a while before she does that again, I think.**❞**   FATHER

---

for children at school or at day care and continue when children enter school. This section emphasizes ways to help children maintain self-regulation through getting optimal amounts of sleep, managing temper outbursts and high activity, and reducing sibling rivalries, aggressiveness, and social inhibition.

Parents' care is nestled in the social context that surrounds families. As we detailed in Chapter 1, resources in neighborhoods can support parents with young children—libraries to go to, parks for children's play and family activities, places for families to meet and talk and get help from each other as needed. When these are not available, parents can perhaps join together, or be involved in groups to advocate for services.

Sleeping

Healthy sleep at night prepares children for active, happy days, as we described in Chapter 5. A consistent, pleasant bedtime routine continues to be important in these years when children between two and five usually need between eleven and twelve hours per night, and children from four to twelve, about ten hours per night.[75] Many do not get enough sleep and between 10 and 30 percent of children are described as sleep deprived.[76]

Night Fears   In the preschool years many children are afraid to go to bed because of monsters or robbers. Richard Ferber believes such fears reflect anxieties about loss of behavior control around issues such as toilet training, anger regarding siblings, and peer aggression.[77] These anxieties are then expressed as fears of monsters. He states,

> She needs to know that nothing bad will happen if she soils, has a temper tantrum, or gets angry at her brother or sister. At such times she can best be reassured by knowing that you are in control of yourself and—to the extent that she needs it—of her, and that

you can and will protect her. . . . The monsters are in your child's mind, and it is there you should focus your efforts.[78]

If the child seems very frightened at night, parents are advised to do whatever is necessary to help the child feel safe and able to sleep, because each night of good sleep makes the next night easier. Parents can spend enjoyable time with the child in his or her bedroom, and move the child's bedtime later so the child will be sleepier. Parents may check in on the child until the child falls asleep to show that they are available. Parents may lie down with the child briefly and may even sleep in the child's room if anxiety is severe. If nighttime fears are the result of a family problem or part of the generalized anxiety seen in many situations, counseling is advised.

Nightmares   Nightmares are scary dreams that occur during light REM (rapid eye movement) sleep, and they result in full awakening, often with the child's having some memory of the dream. The child will call and want comfort. Nightmares are a part of growing up. They peak at about the time children enter school and again at ages nine through eleven. A parent can remain with the child until he or she falls back to sleep, or perhaps can lie down with the child, but it is best not to make the latter practice a habit.

If nightmares occur frequently, parents can begin to examine what in the child's daylight hours is causing the trouble. Adjustment to a new brother or sister or a change to a new daycare may cause stress. Helping the child cope with stress during the day is the surest way to prevent nightmares.

Partial Wakings   As people fall asleep, they move into a deep state of sleep that lasts about ninety minutes, then they transition to a light stage, then return to a deep state of sleep, and gradually during the night, return to longer periods of light-stage sleep in which most dreaming occurs.[79] Children often have difficulty making the transition from deep to light sleep, and sometimes have confusional events in which they are asleep but carry out activities normally associated with the waking state—talking in their sleep, walking in their sleep, screaming and calling for help in a night terror.

It is important not to confuse night terrors with nightmares. In both cases the child awakes in the night, appearing very frightened. The patterns for these two behaviors, however, differ. Night terrors take place during the first few hours of sleep at night—about one and a half to three or four hours after children go to sleep—just as the child enters a light state of sleep; nightmares usually occur much later in the night. In night terrors, the child is not fully awake when he or she calls or cries. The cry may sound like a scream, and so the parents assume the child has had a nightmare. In this case, however, if a parent tries to hold the child, he pushes the parent away; comforting does not help. The child may drop back to sleep automatically and have no memory of the night terror the next day. For night terrors, parents should not attempt to wake the child or offer comfort. They should avoid interacting with the child unless he or she requests it and let the child fall back to sleep. If they believe it was a night terror, parents should not make too much of it with the child, who may be frightened to hear how terrified and out of control he or she appeared. Night terrors disappear as children get older.

Physiological factors are largely at work in confusional events. The best predictor of one is whether the child is sleep deprived. Other factors related to confusional events are inconsistent sleep/wake patterns, sleep disruptions because of
illness or medications, anxiety, and stress. Most confusional events are mild and
are frequently outgrown by ages five to six without treatment, but if they are frequent, severe, and present a safety risk, professional help is advised. In her book,
Sleeping Through the Night, Jodi Mindell gives parents guidelines for ensuring safety
for children who walk in their sleep, such as locking windows, putting up gates,
and bells that can alert parents the child is up.[80]

Since restful sleep is related to children's ability to pay attention and learn, to
their maintaining good moods and getting along with their friends, parents' efforts
at helping children sleep provide many benefits.

Temper Tantrums

Temper tantrums are common responses to parents' requests. Parents take many
actions to increase compliance. They make activities manageable for the child (not
doing six errands on a morning the child has a cold); demands are predictable and
routines are sensitive to children's temperament and needs.[81] Parents observe what
children are doing and step in as frustration begins to increase so they can help the
child problem-solve.

Thomas Gordon recommends mutual problem solving to find a solution agreeable to both parent and child at times of conflict.[82] Even when a compromise is
not possible and a child is still upset, active listening may be useful. He cites the
example of a child who could not go swimming because he had a cold. When the
child's mother commented that it was hard for him to wait until the next day, he
calmed down.

Behaviorists use a method of ignoring. John Krumboltz and Helen Krumboltz
tell of a little boy who learned that, if he cried and whined, his parents would
pick him up instead of paying attention to the new baby.[83] When they realized
that their actions were creating the problems, they agreed to ignore the outbursts.
When the boy learned that he gained nothing by crying and whining, his behavior
improved. Behaviorists insist that parents must be firm and consistent. Otherwise,
outbursts will continue, and each time, children will hold out longer because they
have learned that they can win by outlasting the parents.

Stanley Turecki and Leslie Tonner distinguish between the manipulative tantrum and the temperamental tantrum.[84] Some children use tantrums to manipulate
the parents into getting them what they want, as in the case above. In the case of
a manipulative outburst, Turecki recommends firm refusal to give in. Distracting
the child, ignoring the outburst, and sending the child to his or her room are all
techniques for handling that kind of tantrum.

In the more intense temperamental tantrum, children seem out of control. Some
aspect of their temperament has been violated, and they are reacting to that. For
example, a child sensitive to material may have a tantrum when he or she has to wear
a wool sweater. In these instances, Turecki advises a calm and sympathetic approach;
parents can reflect the child's feelings of irritation or upset ("I know you don't like

this, but it will be okay"). Parents can then put their arms around the child, if permitted. There is no long discussion of what is upsetting the child unless the child wants to talk. If the situation can be corrected, it should be. For example, if the wool sweater feels scratchy, let the child remove it and wear a soft sweatshirt. This is not giving in, but just correcting a mistake. All parents can do then is wait out the tantrum.

Throughout the temperamental tantrum, parents convey the attitude that they will help the child deal with this situation. Though parents change their minds when good reasons are presented, they are generally consistent in waiting out the tantrum and insisting on behavior change.

Sibling Rivalry

We noted earlier the many reactions children have when a younger sibling is born. Parents use many strategies to help children deal with brothers and sisters, depending on the ages of the children.

When a second baby arrives, parents include the child as a helper so that a more adult-like role can compensate a bit for the loss of all the attention. Getting diapers, entertaining the baby, and giving the baby hugs can be done under adult supervision to ensure safety, as a young child may not understand the infant's need for support. Once beyond the newborn stage, infants take an interest in children and their activities so an older child can have a special role with the baby.

Parents can use sociodramatic play with young children. They can get a small doll for preschoolers and encourage their child to feed it. In the course of feeding babies, parents can verbalize the difficulties of being a baby and not being able to get food for yourself or to older children about what their respective babies like to do or what kinds of days they are having. Such play can be fun and informative and also strengthen relationships between parents and older children.

As children get older, the most basic principle is that parents model the warm responses they want children to show to each other.[85] They also model the use of verbal strategies to understand problems, express feelings, and find alternative solutions. When children are very young, parents step in and illustrate how to use words to deal with conflicts and find solutions; they ask children what else they can do in the situation besides hit or bite.

When siblings are older, Gordon's strategies of mutual problem solving create a climate in which children can work out their own problems.[86] One mother whose children were four, six, and eight found that the children, including the four-year-old, devised rules that decreased fighting and name calling. The children were upset by verbal insults and decided they would try to send I-messages. If the situation became too heated, they would go to their rooms to cool off.

Rudolf Dreikurs considers sibling rivalry in detail.[87] He believes that parents can reduce the jealousy among children by making it clear to all that each child in the family is loved for his or her individual qualities and that it is not important whether one child does something better than another. Parents love each child, but a child's trust of that love can be diminished when parents use one sibling's behavior to humiliate another child: "Why can't you be more like Jimmy—he ate everything on his plate."

Dreikurs recommends treating all children the same to reduce sibling fighting. All children should be sent to their rooms if play becomes noisy. If one child complains about another, parents can react so that children feel a responsibility to live in peace. Parents can point out that a child who acts up today may only be trying to retaliate for an incident that happened yesterday. Misbehavior involves all children in the family, and they can learn to take care of each other. Cooperation can be fostered by taking children on family expeditions and having all the children play together. When they see that life is more fun when they cooperate and get along with each other, children learn to settle their differences.

All these techniques are important. Parents must decide which ones will work best in a particular situation.

High Activity Levels

As the brain develops from birth to age three, a child's motor activity increases. As the brain develops further, the child's attention span increases, focusing improves, and motor activity decreases. The inability to inhibit motor behavior is perhaps the biggest single behavior problem in boys and often is identified as a problem in the preschool years. The child may have always been active, but problems arise when a great interest in activity continues after mastery of motor skills occurs in the toddler period and is accompanied by such other qualities as excessive restlessness, short attention span, and demanding behavior that permits no delay in gratification.

A child who experiences these problems in the preschool years is not necessarily hyperactive. Even children with high levels of activity still within the normal range are perceived negatively by preschool teachers, parents, and peers.[88] They are restless, fidgety, poorly controlled, and impulsive. They do not respond well to limits and are often seen as uncooperative and disobedient. With peers, they are outgoing, self-assertive, aggressive, competitive, and dominant. Children described this way at ages three and four are viewed similarly at ages seven and seven and a half.

Both mothers and fathers of highly active children often possess qualities similar to those of their children.[89] They tend to be directive, intrusive, and rather authoritarian. They engage in power struggles and competition with their children. What can parents do? First, parents must get out of the vicious negative cycle that has been created. They must begin to spend some positive time with their children, enjoying them and responding to them in warm, sensitive ways. Using the Positive Parenting strategies, outlined earlier, significantly decreases overactive behavior.[90]

At the same time, parents establish structure and daily routines in which the child takes an active role and puts to constructive use the high energy level that might otherwise be disruptive. The structure need not be rigid, but a general schedule of daily activities will help a child.

As Vygotsky points out, children learn to guide their behavior and achieve greater control by using a form of self-instruction.[91] Parents show the child what they want done and at the same time talk about what they are doing. The child then talks out loud to describe the actions ("First I take off my pajamas, then I hang them up, then I put on my shirt and pants").

Behaviorists advise parents to be alert and consistent in providing rewards for positive behaviors.[92] Highly active children often are rewarded by attention they receive for misdeeds. "Try to catch the child being good," they suggest, and give rewards of attention and social approval.

Leisure activities such as doing puzzles, constructing with Legos, and drawing increase attention and concentration. Limiting electronic games that promote rapid responding and encouraging more active pursuits are helpful. Poorly coordinated, active children benefit from opportunities to develop physical skills. Games that involve running, balancing, and gymnastic movements are helpful.

Aggression

Temper outbursts and hyperactivity reflect anger, lack of control, and noncompliance, but aggression is out-of-control behavior that is destructive and hurts others or their possessions, as we described earlier.[93]

To reduce aggressive, noncompliant behaviors, parents first foster a positive attachment with the child and second, use Positive Parenting principles to teach children new behaviors. When mothers and preschool teachers participated in a program emphasizing positive responses to replace the negative, critical responses such behavior ordinarily arouses, the aggressive behavior of highly aggressive children declined at home.[94] Mothers participated in twelve weekly sessions, and teachers in a six-day training course. Including teachers was more effective in reducing aggression than training mothers and children alone. Changes were greatest for the most aggressive children and were still notable a year later for children whose mothers attended at least six sessions. At the end of the year, the behavior of 80 percent of the aggressive children fell into a category of low risk for conduct problems. Third, parents teach children specific social skills and skills of emotional control, as described in Chapters 4 and 5. Research indicates that aggressive and disruptive preschoolers want to get along, but they need the proper skills.[95]

Social Withdrawal and Inhibition

We described inhibited preschoolers earlier. Even though withdrawal causes significant problems for children, parents are generally more concerned about aggressiveness. Parents of withdrawn children are often surprised and puzzled at their children's behavior, feeling embarrassed and guilty about it. Believing that shyness is an inborn quality, they tend to use high-power, directive strategies with children to change the behavior. These usually do not work. Such parents can, however, take many positive actions that resemble the effective strategies parents of aggressive children use.[96]

First, they can express a positive attitude toward their child as a person. Parents of withdrawn children tend to be negative in their comments about them, expressing the view that parents have to step in and help children function, but this is not a helpful attitude.

Box 8-1
PARENTING BROTHERS AND SISTERS OF CHILDREN WITH SPECIAL NEEDS

When a child has an ongoing health or developmental problem, everyone in the family is touched and reacts. Parents direct their efforts to getting and providing the best possible care for the child, and they organize family and work life to include the additional activities. They get psychological support for the child with special needs and sometimes for themselves from organizations and professionals. In the stress and pressure of all these activities, it is not surprising that the needs of brothers and sisters are often overlooked.

Yet brothers and sisters of children with special needs have their own stresses and needs, and parents can help in many ways. The exact nature of siblings' responses depends on the specific nature and the effects of the special problem confronting the family. In many ways, siblings' reactions are similar to those of parents. Like parents, they too love and often admire the child with a special problem and feel sad at the difficulties or limitations the child experiences; they wish there were something they could do to make things better. Like parents, they share the restrictions or burdens that a physical or developmental problem places on family activities, and they too experience the general public's reactions to unusual behaviors. Sometimes, they feel guilty they are healthy and were spared special problems. And sometimes, they feel angry at the lack of attention and the burdens of intense feelings that appear to have no outlet.

Adult brothers and sisters of children with special needs have several suggestions for parents to ease the stress for siblings.* Easing siblings' stress is important, according to Don Meyer, founder of the Sibling Support Project, because "these brothers and sisters will likely have the longest relationships of anyone, relationships in excess of 65 years. They should be remembered at every turn."**

First, parents should sit down and talk to siblings in age-appropriate terms about the child's special problems—what the problem is, what causes it, what interventions do to help—giving as much information as is appropriate for siblings' ages. Parents should try to see whether brothers and sisters have special fears that they too will develop the problem.

Second, parents should encourage brothers and sisters to express their feelings about what happens in the family and about their relationship with the child with special needs. Parents must be especially accepting of all feelings, giving children permission to express them, especially negative ones, as many children fear burdening their already-stressed parents. One mother of a withdrawing thirteen-year-old sibling asked several times about any upsetting feelings. The girl always denied any, but before giving up, the mother commented, "It must be difficult being the sister to . . . ." Her daughter began to cry, and a host of feelings poured out. Parents can sometimes elicit feelings with their own I-statements: "I wish we didn't have to have all these physical therapy appointments, and I am sure your sister wishes that too. How about you?"***

Third, siblings should be included in discussions and plans for treatments insofar as is possible. Much as one includes even very young children in the plans for a family event such as a new baby or a grandparent's visit, brothers and sisters should be

Box 8-1
PARENTING BROTHERS AND SISTERS OF CHILDREN WITH SPECIAL NEEDS

included in what is happening—a proposed new diagnostic test, new specialist, or new treatment. Siblings' suggestions for helping to care for a child with special needs, as well as their actual help, enable them to feel like important members of the family. Parents need to acknowledge children's help too.

Fourth, give brothers and sisters their special time with parents. It may not be a large amount of time, but regular time that a child can count on indicates that that child is important too. If that is impossible because a child is in the hospital, recruit a family member who can take siblings for special time. Give siblings time, too, when their needs come before those of the child with special problems. Regardless of the problem, at certain points a babysitter can be enlisted to care for that child while brothers and sisters have some special activity with parents.

Fifth, help brothers and sisters develop their own activities and interests that give them pleasure. Again, if parents cannot drive for lessons or sports teams, have a friend or relative who can take siblings. Developing interests helps children increase their skills and make new friends, giving brothers and sisters confidence and a sense that parents care about their development too.

Sixth, model the ways you want brothers and sisters to relate to the child with special needs; think and talk about the problem, explain the situation to others, and accept help from others. One mother reported that, after her daughter had a seizure at a store, she found her four-year-old sister answering shoppers' questions with the same words the mother had used in explaining it to her.

Seventh, involve brothers and sisters in sibling support groups that enable them to talk to other brothers and sisters who live with a child with special needs. Their age-mates can bring special understanding that parents may not have. In Seattle, Washington, Don Meyer has started a support group that gives information and has discussion groups for children around the country.

*Kate Strohm, *Being the Other One* (Boston: Shambala, 2005).
**Gretchen Cook, "Siblings of Disabled Have Troubles of Their Own," New *York Times,* April 4, 2006, p. D5.
***Strohm, *Being the Other One,* p. 170.

Second, they can be supportive in teaching social skills and encouraging play with others. At the same time, they have to stand back and permit the child to act independently. In their zeal to help their physiologically reactive child, they may have become overprotective, too worried about an upsetting interaction, and therefore too controlling. The child does not have a chance to learn that he or she can succeed independently.

Third, parents have to look at their own behaviors. Do they model a fearful, inhibited approach to new situations and people? Do their own problems interfere with their ability to be positive and to support their child? If so, they need to try to change themselves as part of their attempt to help their children.

A PRACTICAL QUESTION: HOW CAN PARENTS HELP WHEN CHILDREN HAVE DISABILITIES OR DEVELOPMENTAL DELAYS?

These early years involve rapid development in children's skills and abilities. Some children show clear signs of developmental delays at birth. Perhaps a genetic disorder or birth difficulties have resulted in significant problems for the child, and services are provided at birth. Sometimes, however, the delay is identified later, when the child fails to develop certain abilities such as hearing or language.

In the last fifteen years, an increasing number of children have been diagnosed with pervasive developmental disorders, a broad category of disorders, the most common among them being autism and Asperger's disorder.[97] Children with autism have qualitative impairments in three areas: (1) language/communication, (2) socioemotional responsiveness and understanding of others, and (3) stereotyped and restricted patterns of behavior, activities, and interests. These impairments appear in the first three years of life and vary in levels of severity. Children with Asperger's disorder have impairments in socioemotional responsiveness and restricted interests, but their language and cognitive skills are average, and sometimes very advanced. Surveys by the National Center for Birth Defects and Developmental Disabilities find that 1 in every 150 eight-year-old children are diagnosed with one of the pervasive developmental disorders. They are found in all ethnic, racial, and social groups but more frequently affect boys, with a ratio of 4 to 1.

In this brief space, we can only present general guidelines for parents to help children with many forms of disabilities and delays. As soon as disabilities or delays are detected, parents must seek professional consultation for diagnosis. If they feel the diagnosis is in error, they should seek additional opinions until they believe all factors have been taken into consideration. Research indicates that, for most disabilities and delays, the earlier the diagnosis and intervention, the greater the child's progress. Accurate diagnosis is sometimes complicated because it is difficult to tell a significant delay from slow growth within the average range.

Once a diagnosis is made, parents must obtain all available services and monitor that the services are effective in meeting the child's needs. This will be an ongoing task during their child's development because children's needs change with age. Each year in school, parents must monitor services and programs, and all the while, keep accurate records of care, treatment, and progress.

Once services are in place, parents focus on the psychological needs of all family members. Box 8-1 presents brothers' and sisters' reactions and needs when a child has a disability. Parents have many profound emotional reactions to their children's difficulties: sadness that their children must work hard to master skills that come so easily to other children, worry about their children's long-term future, stress from finding time and money to provide resources for children, and sadness that their children may not experience some of the typical joys of childhood and adolescence. Sometimes, they struggle with feelings of guilt that in some unknown way they are responsible for the child's difficulties.

Psychological counseling, often provided when services are begun before age three, can help parents and families deal with the stresses that come from a child's having special needs. This includes helping members of the extended family understand a child's special disability and needs so they can participate in bringing about progress.

At all times, parents provide the love, sensitive caregiving and security that are the most valuable aids in helping children achieve their maximum potential. Linda Gilkerson and Frances Stott write,

> Children who have a congenital disability may experience disability as an inherent part of their body and self. Like other aspects of the child, the disability contributes to a sense of identity and is in need of acceptance, appreciation, and affirmation. . . . Infants initially develop unimpeded by an awareness of their disability. However, the moment with the most potential for emotional trauma comes not when the child realizes that he or she is different but when the child discovers that the differences are perceived by society as inferior.[98]

As the child grows and develops, the disability takes on different meanings. At all ages, parents must convey that the child's worth lies in being who he or she is, not in becoming "normal" or like others. Gilkerson and Stott review the "fix-it model of disability" in which the child's value lies in working hard and making progress to become "normal." According to one therapist, children with disabilities must come to see themselves as both intact and disabled at the same time, and to do this they require their families' love and acceptance. Supportive relationships within the family help children develop a sense of themselves as willing, purposive individuals who can act.

A ten-year longitudinal study of children with motor and other disabilities and delays supports the importance of the family emotional atmosphere and parents' sensitive and responsive caretaking.[99] The child's disability predicted growth in intellectual, social, and adaptive skills over this period.

Beyond the disability, however, personal characteristics of the child and the family predicted progress in development. Children's ability to regulate feelings and behavior and express them appropriately, as rated by teachers, and children's ability to remain motivated to learn predicted progress. Sensitive and responsive mother–child interactions predicted growth in social and communication skills.

Parents' stress was related to the extent of the disability and to their child's level of stress as reflected in behavior problems. When children did not develop behavior problems, mothers' stress remained stable and low over the period. Social support and good problem-solving skills reduced parents' stress.

Describing Vygotsky's approach to children's disabilities, Laura Berk writes that it

> is a highly optimistic vision; it accentuates the child's strengths. He underscored the importance of viewing the child not as abnormal or as underdeveloped but rather as having developed differently. . . . To the affected child his or her condition is "normal." Only as a result of social experience does the child come to sense being different and "abnormal"—incomplete and divided from others. Yet social action is equally capable of creating connection and integration if the child is viewed as having altered capacities and positive potential. With the assurance of others, children with disabilities can realize a wealth of possibilities and unique competencies.[100]

PARENTS' EXPERIENCES IN FACING TRANSITIONS

In these years, parents continue in what Ellen Galinsky terms the authority stage.[101] Many parents, bogged down in battle with their young children, find themselves doing and saying things they vowed they never would—the very words they hated to hear from their own parents when they were children. Parents are shaken and upset as their ideal images of themselves as parents collide with the reality of rearing children.

Parents revise their images of themselves in light of their actual behavior. Because it involves change, this can be a painful process. Parents must change either their ideal image or their behavior to come closer to living up to their own standards. Their images of children change as well. Parents discover that children are not always loving, cooperative, and affectionate. Children can be extremely aggressive—breaking things, hitting, pulling hair.

Parents must also deal with each other as authorities. When James McHale followed up with his parents whose children were now two and a half, he found, "Negative emotion had become a feature of family life during the toddler years in a manner seldom seen in infancy."[102] Several factors accounted for the increase in negative tone. First, fathers were more actively engaged in child care so there were more opportunities for conflicts with mothers over caregiving.

Second, parents were in the process of teaching children basic rules and values for functioning in life. When parents disagreed, each parent was likely to feel strongly about basic values and want to have their view the accepted one. Third, at the same time that parents had strong feelings about children's behavior, children experienced strong emotions and wanted their way. They did not give up easily, and they were skilled at going from one parent to the other to get the answer they wanted. So this was a difficult time for all family members.

Researchers were not surprised at parents' concern about discipline issues, but they were surprised that two-thirds of parents reported that they, their spouse, or both needed to learn greater control of their temper and develop more patience and calm in interacting with family members. Parents also worried when they believed the other parent was hampering their child's development by being too indulgent, too overprotective, too lenient, or not encouraging independence.

Despite their difficulties, parents also report wanting to spend more time with each other and with the family as a unit. Those parents who had a warm, cooperative, cohesive alliance when children were twelve months old continued to work together in the toddler years. There was, however, little relationship between parenting at this time and pregnancy attitudes and coparenting at three months, with the exception that fathers' negativity and the discrepancy between mothers' and fathers' ideas about parenting during pregnancy decreased coparenting solidity in the toddler years. Researchers found that parents did not have to agree in order to work together, but they did need to talk to each other and understand the other parent's view.

Parents' ability to work together affected toddlers' functioning. When parents worked together in a warm, cooperative way, supporting each other and not undermining the other parent's efforts with verbal sniping, then toddlers scored well on a test of preacademic skills and were described at home and at day care as emotionally mature and socially competent.

Parents' hostile and competitive interactions affect preschoolers' views of themselves. They view themselves as unlikeable and unable to make friends with others, and their teachers describe them in similar ways when they are in kindergarten. If parents remain warm and caring with each other when they disagree, their conflicts do not affect children's self-perceptions.[103]

SUPPORT FOR PARENTS

Recall from Chapters 5 and 6 the parents' support groups that Philip and Carolyn Cowan organized to help parents cope with the transition to parenting and then with the transition to the child's being in school.[104] Such groups help parents develop realistic expectations for their children and themselves. As one parent stated, in these early years, one is not exactly sure of what the limits or expectations should be, and these groups can provide information and discuss what the range of individual differences are and which strategies work with various children. Parents can then more easily manage problems and enjoy the time with their children. These groups also give parents an opportunity to talk about relationship issues with marital partners and families of origin. Parents get insights and strategies that release tensions so they are more effective partners and parents. When children have special disabilities or needs, parents can often find national groups devoted to helping parents and children with the problem, and many have local groups that provide support and updated and practical information for parents.

MAIN POINTS

As their motor, cognitive, language, and social skills increase, toddlers and preschoolers

- take a great interest in learning about the world
- develop a greater sense of self and independence
- take pleasure and delight in their new accomplishments
- express emotions such as pride, shame, and guilt
- gradually learn control of their behavior through internalization of rules and standards

As they mature in the preschool years, children's behavior

- decreases in aggressiveness, high activity, and undercontrol
- can reveal difficulties in aggressivenss and poor control that persist in the school years
- reflect stressors in family life such as low income and mother's depression
- is competent and resilient when parents form secure attachments and use positive parenting strategies

In these years children's gender and ethnic identities begin to form in stages that

- begin with children's identifying their own group and seeing themselves as a part of the group
- learning about the group and the behavior expected of members
- realizing they will always be part of that group

Parents whose children function well and have secure attachments

- are available and sensitive to children's needs
- grant the child independence within safe limits
- provide models of kind, caring, controlled behavior
- talk with children, answering questions, giving information, getting their views
- play with children to increase closeness and stimulate learning and development

Parents help children learn to regulate their behavior when they

- establish a process of mutual responsiveness
- act to prevent problems
- avoid harsh, critical, directive, and controlling behaviors with children
- introduce rules that dovetail with children's abilities
- use low-power techniques of reasoning and explanations when children do not comply
- work together so children get a consistent set of rules

Problems discussed center on

- sleep
- sibling rivalry
- handling temper tantrums and high activity levels
- dealing with aggression and withdrawal
- helping children with disabilities reach their potential

Joys include the child's

- delight in increasing skills and personal achievements
- helping behaviors
- greater communicativeness

EXERCISES

1. Interview two couples who have preschoolers. Ask them about their children's daily routines and their worries and pleasures regarding their children. What are the sources of stress and support for the parents? Are stresses and supports similar in the two families?

2. In small groups, recall early experiences of gender learning. (a) Did the teachings deal with activities, appearances, behavior, feelings? (b) Who was

teaching you about gender-appropriate behaviors—parents, relatives, siblings, peers, teachers? (c) Were you more likely to accept the teachings of adults or of peers? Make a list of the kinds of experiences members had. (d) Are similar experiences occurring today?

3. In groups, recall early experiences with siblings. Was there much fighting? Did parents teach children how to get along? Did parents punish children for not getting along? What seems to make for the best relationships with siblings? What roles do siblings play in the life of adults?

4. Watch Saturday morning television programs for preschoolers and decide how much time and what specific programs you, if you were parents, would permit your toddlers and preschoolers to watch. Justify your choices.

5. Interview three preschoolers about their joys in life. What do they like to do best? Do they get to do these things as much as they would like to? How can parents make their lives happier? Are their requests reasonable? Do you think parents are aware of what makes their children happy?

ADDITIONAL READINGS

Cohen, Lawrence J. *Playful Parenting*. New York: Ballantine, 2001.

Greenspan, Stanley I., and Wiedner, Serena. *The Child with Special Needs*. Reading, MA: Addison-Wesley, 1998.

Kirp, David L. *The Sandbox Investment: The Preschool Movement and Kids-First Politics*. Cambridge, MA: Harvard University Press, 2007.

Mindell, Jodi A. *Sleeping Through the Night*, rev. ed. New York: HarperCollins, 2005.

Bedrova, Elena and Leong, Deborah J. *Tools of the Mind: The Vygotskian Approach to Early Childhood Education*. Upper Saddle River, NJ: Pearson Prentice-Hall, 2007.

C H A P T E R

9

Parenting Elementary School Children

CHAPTER TOPICS	IN THE NEWS
In this chapter, you will learn about:	*New York Times,* June 9[1]: American Academy of Pediatrics recommends that schools and families adopt program of Dan Olweus to prevent school bullying. See pages 289–290.

In this chapter, you will learn about:

- Children's development
- Social relationships with parents, siblings, and peers
- Promoting healthy lifestyles, emotional control, school success, and social skills
- Helping children with common school difficulties

Test Your Knowledge: Fact or Fiction (True/False)

1. Adding an hour of sleep to a child's nightly schedule increases memory and reaction time on cognitive tests equivalent to two years of chronological age.
2. Elementary school success serves as a protective factor against the development of high-risk behaviors such as delinquency and substance abuse in adolescence.
3. Children around the world, regardless of sex or socioeconomic status, agree with each other on what is upsetting even more than do adults and children within the same culture.
4. Children believe it is okay to violate a moral rule if an adult tells them to do it.
5. Pediatricians see an increase in the number of children they judge need psychological help from 1979 to 1996.

Children's entrance into school marks a new stage in parenthood. Children spend more time away from their parents in school and with peers. They are absorbing new information and are exposed to new challenges and new values. How do parents foster children's success in this new stage of development?

Children have learned the routines of living—eating, dressing, toileting, verbalizing easily, and taking care of many of their own needs. They now adjust to the larger and more demanding world of formal education, and they must create a social place for themselves with new peers as well. This chapter discusses how parents support children's growth and their participation in learning and new activities.

PHYSICAL DEVELOPMENT

From ages five to ten, girls and boys have approximately the same height, weight, and general physical measurements. At five, they are about 42 inches tall and weigh about 40–45 pounds. By age ten, they stand at about 52 inches and weigh about 75–80 pounds. In the elementary school years, children's coordination is well developed. They ride bikes, skate, swim, play team sports, draw, and play musical instruments. Nearly all the basic skills in the area of gross (running, skipping) and fine (cutting with scissors, drawing) motor coordination are laid down by age seven, and further development consists of refining these skills.

Levels of neurobiological arousal and reactivity influence children's abilities to pay attention and focus on learning in school.[2] High levels of emotion can interfere with learning, and parents' role is to help children regulate their feelings. If children go to school with heightened fear and anxiety, they may not be able to focus and learn. If they go to school with heightened impulsivity and emotional arousal, they may have difficulty attending to and learning new material.

INTELLECTUAL DEVELOPMENT

Three major cognitive changes occur in the elementary school years.[3] First, children learn to reason generally. At about age seven, children become less focused on their own perceptions and more involved in the objective properties of what they observe. They organize their perceptions and reason about a broader range of objects and situations. Because they also more easily adopt the other person's point of view, they understand other people and their reactions better. At the end of this age period, around ten to twelve, thinking becomes more abstract and more closely resembles adults' ways of reasoning.

Second, children at this age organize tasks and function more independently than before. In addition to pursuing goals, children observe and think about their own behavior and their thinking processes as well. Third, they acquire knowledge in an organized learning environment—school—that sets standards by which they and others evaluate their performance.

In learning children constantly take in, process, and manipulate information, developing new strategies for handling it.[4] In mastering problems, they try a variety of strategies and select the most effective ways to deal with problems. Parents can help children in their problem solving by giving support as children go through the process of finding effective strategies.

VOICES OF EXPERIENCE

What I Wish I Had Known
about the Elementary School Years

"I wish I'd known how much you need to be an advocate for your child with the school. When we grew up, our parents put us in public school and that was it. Now, you have a lot more options, and the public schools aren't always great; so you realize how active you need to be in order to ensure a good education for your children." MOTHER

"The main thing, I think, is how important temperament is. My daughter was in one school that was very noncompetitive; that's a wonderful philosophy, but it wasn't right for her. She is very competitive, and in that atmosphere she did not do as well. So with the second child, we are going to be more careful to see that there is a good fit between her temperament and what she is doing." FATHER

"I was surprised that, even though the children are older, they take as much time as when they were younger; but you spend the time in different ways. I thought when they started school, I would have a little more time. Instead of giving them baths at night and rocking them, I supervise homework and argue about taking baths. Knowing that things were going to take as much time would have made me less impatient in the beginning, and I would have planned better." MOTHER

"I learned that, especially from five to eight, say, children are not as competent as they look. They really can't do a lot of things that on the surface you think they can. They have language, and they look like they're reasoning, and they look like their motor skills are okay. So you say, 'When you get up in the morning, I want you to make your cereal,' and they can't do it consistently. And so because we didn't know that with the first child, I think we made excessive demands on her, which led to her being a little harsher on herself. Now with the second one, if she can't tie her shoes by herself today, even though she could two weeks ago, we're more likely to say, 'Okay,' instead of 'Well, you can tie your shoes; go ahead and do it.' If you give them a little help, it doesn't mean you are making babies of them; it means they have room to take it from there." FATHER

"I wish I'd known more about their abilities and work readiness. My daughter had some special needs in school. In preschool, I could see there were immaturities in her drawings and writing, but she got lots of happy faces. I thought she was doing better than she was. When she got to school, it came as quite a shock that she was having problems. With my son, I have been more on top, and I ask more questions about how he is really doing, because I want to get any special needs he has addressed. My advice to any parent is that, if at all possible, volunteer in your child's school. I gave up half a day's pay, and in my financial situation that was a real hardship. It is very, very important to keep a handle on not just what is happening educationally, but also who the peers are and what is going on." MOTHER

SCHOOL

School organizes children's daytime hours and much of children's and parents' evening activities as well. Parents must act to remedy difficulties because school achievement has lifelong effects. It determines access to further education, more advanced jobs, and higher incomes. School success has emotional consequences as well.[5] Making friends and developing intellectual skills increase feelings of competence and satisfaction that serve as protective factors against adolescent delinquency and substance abuse. Conversely, school difficulties and peer rejection can be sources of low self-esteem and depression extending into adulthood.

The Process of Learning at School

Many think children's learning and school achievement depend solely on children's ability and the quality of the teaching. But much like parenting, learning in the school setting is a dynamic process. The participants in the process—the child, parents, teachers/school personnel, peers, and sometimes the neighborhood—hinder or facilitate the process, and all interact and change each other in the process.[6]

Children bring their gender, temperament, and skills, and all the experiences they have had in life. Parents contribute resources, intellectual stimulation, and psychological support. They also bring their personal qualities and all the stressors that impact them and their children. Schools and neighborhoods provide educational resources, teachers, social supports, and stressors that vary in quality. Peers encourage and participate in learning, provide pleasurable social time, or conversely, can arouse feelings of rejection and long-lasting depression.

Parents' Role

First, parents' resources enable children to live in safe neighborhoods, attend quality schools, and have stimulating books, toys, lessons, trips, and tutoring as needed.[7]

Parents' conceptions of ability and learning influence their children's views of difficulties and their persistence and effort in remedying them.[8] When parents view ability as an internal and unchangeable quality that children have or lack, termed an "entity view of ability," children adopt the same view and lack confidence that they can improve and remedy their problems. They believe failure means they lack ability. When, however, parents believe ability develops in small steps as one learns skills and practices, termed an "incremental view of ability," children see that learning difficulties can be remedied by developing new skills and exerting effort to master the material. Emphasizing the process of learning—learning new strategies, making gains—also increases children's confidence.

Parents' beliefs in their children's abilities (e.g., to do mathematical work or participate in sports), encourage children's feelings of competence in these areas from first through twelfth grade.[9] Parents' beliefs in children's abilities also encourage boys and girls to participate in activities such as sports and music usually associated with the opposite gender.

Parents' involvement in children's schoolwork promotes children's confidence in their own abilities.

Parents' involvement in children's learning predicts children's achievement.[10] Involvement includes reading to children, helping them problem-solve how to do schoolwork, and participating in classroom activities and school-wide activities. Parents' involvement promotes children's confidence in their own abilities and thus leads to achievement.[11]

Parents' ability to remain calm and positive in helping children with mundane activities such as their homework enables children to maintain confidence about their learning abilities.[12] Most parents feel frustrated when homework requires their aid, but when parents are critical and negative, children feel helpless and discouraged. Parents' remaining positive and loving toward the child even though feeling frustrated at the homework tasks helps children persist and learn. Parents balance structuring learning activities that can create dependence with encouraging children's autonomy that promotes initiative.[13]

Finally, parents are advocates for their children at times of academic or social difficulties. As we will see, parents need to be alert to difficulties so they can work with teachers at the beginning because unaddressed problems continue and exert ongoing effects on learning.

School's Role

Schools are children's homes for up to thirty hours a week, forty weeks a year, and its rules and emotional atmosphere make a difference in children's lives. Children develop strong attachments to teachers and their schools when they are actively involved in the learning process and have opportunities and rewards for developing competencies. Effective teachers, like effective parents, have clear, fair, and realistic expectations of students and emphasize mastery-based learning in a cooperative atmosphere in which students teach each other.[14]

Not only do teachers promote positive learning, they can reduce problems that have already developed. Even when children are identified as being at risk for academic and social problems at the end of kindergarten, having first-grade teachers who offer strong instructional and emotional support enables high-risk students to learn and perform as well as low-risk students.[15] Similarly, first-grade classrooms with a calm, positive, emotional tone reduce the rejection highly anxious boys experience and the depression that highly anxious girls experience in disorganized classrooms with conflict and negative emotional tone.[16]

Knowing that classrooms and teachers can have these impacts empowers parents to insist that schools provide learning environments that help children grow and learn.

Children's Role

Most children start school with positive beliefs about their abilities and capacities to learn. Children in first grade believe that all children can learn and that all they need is effort—those who do best have worked the hardest.[17] When parents encourage an incremental view of learning, children persist when frustrated and improve their work.

School programs too can encourage these children to enjoy the process of learning rather than focusing on the achievements of learning. Such programs reduce feelings of helplessness.[18]

Children's academic and social skills at school entry—in kindergarten and first grade—influence teachers' reactions and set in motion a cascade of events that predict reading achievement in later years.[19] When, for example, children learn to read easily and form positive relationships with teachers, their reading achievement is higher in the third and fifth grades. Conversely, when children experience difficulty and frustration in learning to read, they become aggressive and experience conflict with teachers, and these experiences predict lower reading achievement at the fifth-grade level. Teachers are most likely, in one study, to have conflict with boys and African Americans.

Children's emotional responses decrease learning. Children high in aggression and impulsivity at age five had lower grades in elementary school than those who were low in aggression or impulsivity.[20] Children's feelings of insecurity in their attachments to their mothers and in the parents' marital relationship affected their physiological arousal level, their ability to sleep, and, in turn, their performance on ability and achievement tests.[21]

Peers' Role

Children learn from peers in many ways—through cooperating on classroom projects, observing how others think and reason, and learning negotiating skills in play at recess.[22] Children gain intellectual information, but they also gain social and cultural information on topics such as gender roles. They gain emotional support, and they learn and practice social skills.

When Home and School Cultures Differ

Schools generally reflect middle-class European American values and patterns of behavior, emphasizing independent work habits, verbal interactions and questioning, and competition. Since we are a society of diverse ethnic cultures, many children come to school with interdependent cultural values and ways of interacting with others, and they may feel uncomfortable in what seems a strange environment.[23]

Not only do children struggle with different values at school, but parents may do so as well. Many parents have the following kind of experience. A principal sees a parent bringing a forgotten library book due that day to his child. The principal points out, not for the first time, that the parent is not teaching his son to be responsible for his books. The father points out, not for the first time, that he is teaching his child the family value of looking out for each other, and that value is of lifelong importance.[24]

Studies of three groups of immigrant families in a Northeastern city find that the immigrant families differ with respect to educational level, family constellation, and reasons for coming to the United States. Their children, however, are remarkably similar in (1) having positive attitudes toward school and teachers and (2) having positive patterns of academic achievement over three-year periods of time.[25]

Although family values may differ from school values, children of many ethnic groups are able to blend them. For example, some immigrant children who put family obligations first, nevertheless see excelling at school as a way to please parents.[26] Parents come to the United States so children can have a better life and school achievement satisfies parents' goals.

Children do not have to come from immigrant or culturally different families to feel alienated from school values. As we described in Chapter 3, many children and parents from working-class families feel a similar distance from some values espoused at school.

Parents must be aware that schools may not understand their values and when conflicts occur, talking to teachers and school personnel can help. Teachers and school personnel in some districts are participating in programs such as Bridging Cultures to reduce such problems.[27] To solve conflicts, some parents choose homeschooling. See Box 9-1.

EMOTIONAL DEVELOPMENT

Children's emotional life is more complex. Children realize that feelings depend, in part, on what led up to the event and how the event is interpreted.[28] They now can experience two or more feelings about an event or a person. They can be happy with Mom for baking a birthday cake, but angry at her for not giving permission to open gifts early. Over time, they learn to integrate their feelings.

Children hide their feelings and give four general reasons for doing so: to avoid negative consequences, to protect feelings of self-esteem, to maintain good relations with others and not give offense, and finally, to observe social conventions.[29] By the age of nine or ten, children have rules, such as smile when you get a gift (even one you do not like) and apologize even when you do not want to.

Box 9-1
ONE MOTHER'S EXPERIENCES WITH HOMESCHOOLING

Currently in this country, approximately two percent of children from kindergarten through twelfth grade are homeschooled. Parents report their main reasons: concerns about safety, drugs, and negative peer influences (31 percent), desire to provide religious and moral education (30 percent), and dissatisfaction with school/academic programs (16 percent).[*]

Annie is the mother of Ryan, age nineteen, a second year student at a city college; David, sixteen, a sophomore at a public high school; Adrienne, sixteen, a junior at a public high school; Jimmy, nine, about to enter fourth grade in public school; and Monique, six, entering first grade in public school. Adrienne and Monique have been adopted in the past three years from an orphanage in Haiti. Annie's husband, George, is a public school administrator.

Annie homeschooled Ryan for nine years from the fifth grade through high school, and David for six years, from the fourth grade through the ninth. David wanted very much to return to high school with his friends from public school, and although this has not been easy for him, he has worked hard to succeed and will continue there. Annie would like to homeschool Jimmy as she believes it would help him, but his father is reluctant at this time.

Why did you decide to do homeschooling?
In the fifth grade Ryan was not reading in school, and we could see that there were issues despite our having an Individualized Educational Plan (IEP) in place for him and doing everything we could to help. He wasn't a behavior problem. He was having trouble with reading and so he tuned out in school. The way he explained it was that it was too stressful at school. He is a quiet person, there was noise, and he could not do the work even though he tested at the gifted level.

He began learning at home where it was quiet. In two months, he was reading easily, and it became his favorite activity. He is gifted in math, and I got him a math tutor to teach him as I could not do it. At city college he is a very serious student, wants to get all As. He is not certain what he wants to do, but he has time to decide.

The year after I began homeschooling Ryan, I began to homeschool David. He was social and liked all the interaction with friends at school, but he had ADHD and was dyslexic and learned in different ways. People said you are crazy to try to homeschool a child who is so active, but in my opinion that was just the kind of child to homeschool. He did not want to leave his friends, but he made new ones through homeschooling organizations so he came to like it. He did want to go to high school because he was "tired of hanging out with mom," but he decided to return a year behind his age group. I would have been happy to continue homeschooling but he did not want to do it.

I feel public school ends up taking children away from the family, and every year they take more time from the family and dictate what the family will do in the evenings and with all their time. Parents feel they have to perform like a teacher and see the work is done.

(continued)

Box 9-1
CONTINUED

And the school creates stress. If the child has any problem, the school looks around for who is to blame. Is he having trouble reading? Did you get his eyes tested? Are you making him wear glasses? Parents feel like they really have to perform for the school because if there is any problem, it is your fault. What are you doing or not doing?

And when there are difficulties learning, the school sees the child as lacking, imperfect, not right. The school says to the child and the parent, "Try harder!" and the child feels he is trying as hard as he can, and he still can't do it so he feels like a failure. So the child is defined by his ability to do school work, and when kids feel they can't do it and don't fit in, those feelings spill over to the rest of their lives and can create behavioral issues or depression.

My youngest son has all the academic skills, but he doesn't have focus, and he gets distracted. Also he has trouble writing—dysgraphia—so that slows him down. Everyone in the class is told, "Don't distract Jimmy." When the teacher read a story about a boy who had trouble writing, he came home and was very upset because he thought everyone was thinking about him. We started medication to help him focus for only a couple of weeks because he did not notice any difference, and we did not want to use medication even if lack of attention causes issues at school.

What kind of routine did you have when you were homeschooling?
I got information on curriculum and materials from the Home Schooling Group. Ryan liked workbooks, spelling tests, and we went through those. I tried to find what interested the boys, and then focus all the learning skills around that topic, and we would go from the beginning level to the most advanced. Reading, math, and spelling would be focused on that topic.

David is very active so we were on the go a lot. We went to all the museums, we went to parks and to cultural events. And they remembered what they learned through these activities better than they would have from reading about them. I was careful to find out the educational standards and skill levels for children their age and made sure they met them.

As a result of all the things we did and the places we went, my children feel at ease with others. People who don't know they are homeschooled say, "Oh they talk so easily to adults." They are used to relating to people of all ages.

What qualities do you think a parent has to have to do homeschooling?
I think patience, but I'm not patient. You have to feel you're okay, and your kids are okay, and you become really knowledgeable about how to do whatever it takes to teach your children.

I was involved with three homeschooling groups, and I consulted them and the California code to be sure I was following the laws about homeschooling. Parents in the groups provided support and gave guidance about how to do things. There were also camp outs and social events so kids had other role models for homeschooling and could see that children went on to many different things after homeschooling.

Box 9-1

Parents need initiative. You believe you can do it, and you get the information you need to do it. You also have to have time to be available to be with the children. The more you do homeschooling, the less stress children feel, and everything gets easier.

Your daughters have gone to public school; how has that been?
Well, that works very well for them. Adrienne is in high school in a wonderful English as a Second Language program that includes all kinds of children. That has worked out very well for her because it gives her all kinds of knowledge about the culture as well as the language, and she needs that as she has only been in the country two years. Both she and my younger daughter lived in orphanages—she was there for eight years—and they are used to being with many children in group situations so they feel very comfortable in school settings.

Do you see any down side to homeschooling?
Not really. If they missed some information like a child might get in science, well they can still learn that so I don't see any down side. Knowing how to learn and being life long learners is what homeschooling is about.

Is there anything the public school can do to make it less stressful for students?
Accept students as they are. We all have differences in how we learn. Give them the activities they like to do and the activities they need to do to learn. Focus the schools on the students. Schools have become businesses with budgets, doing what the government wants, directing what teachers must do to get test scores up. What individual children need is not as important as it should be, I believe. In Jimmy's school there is no time for holiday celebrations; every minute is counted as an instructional minute, all geared to passing the tests so schools can be rated by student performance.

Homeschooling made it possible for my kids to feel good about themselves despite learning differences or maybe because of them.

*National Center for Education Statistics, "Homeschooling in the United States: 2003," Retrieved, April, 2008, www.nces.gov/pubs2006/homeschool/index.asp.

Children express their true feelings to parents, adult caregivers, and best friends. Children are most likely to express their inner feelings when they are alone with a person whom they trust to respond in a positive, understanding way.[30] Unfortunately, as children—particularly boys—grow older, they anticipate a less positive response from others, even from parents. Thus, older boys are much less likely to express their feelings than are girls or younger boys.

Stressful Life Events

The way children ages nine to eleven around the world rank twenty stressful situations demonstrates that children share perspectives on life that are quite different from those of their parents and often not immediately apparent to parents.

Regardless of sex or socioeconomic status, children from Egypt, Japan, the Philippines, Canada, Australia, and the United States agree with each other on what is upsetting even more than do adults and children within the same culture.[31] Loss of a parent is the most stressful event, and parental fights are highly stressful as well. Embarrassing situations—wetting their pants, being caught in a theft, being ridiculed in class—distress children. Although many students like school, it also causes them anxiety, frustration, and unhappiness, with many children worrying about grades, being retained, and making mistakes. Adults may be surprised at children's sensitivity to embarrassing situations and their concern about school.

Daily journals of elementary school students in the United States reveal that boys are more likely to cite external situations and demands, such as school, chores, interruptions, and environmental factors, as sources of stress and girls, disappointments with self and others and failure to live up to responsibilities.[32]

Loneliness

For a long time, social scientists thought that children could not experience loneliness prior to adolescence, when they became more separate from the family. Recent research, however, finds that five- and six-year-old children have conceptions of loneliness as clear as those of adults.[33] They describe feelings of being sad and alone, having no one to play with. Older elementary school children give even more poignant descriptions of loneliness ("Like you're the only one on the moon," "Always in the dark," "Like you have no one that really likes you and you're all alone"). Extreme loneliness is related to lack of friends, shy and submissive behavior, and a tendency to attribute social failure to one's own internal inadequacies. Such loneliness, in turn, prevents the child from interacting with others and intensifies the problem.

Cascading Events

Emotional experiences become part of what may be positive or negative cycles of behavior that affect development for many years. When parents express positive feelings in their interactions with their children, their children show more positive feelings in school, and both peers and teachers rate them as helpful and socially competent over a two-year period of observation.[34]

Children who enter kindergarten with aggressive, confrontational ways of reacting to others experience peer rejection in the early grades.[35] Socially adjusted peers leave them out of activities, and they turn to aggressive peers who encourage greater aggressiveness. By the time they are age twelve, the rejected children have developed externalizing behavioral problems. Similarly, withdrawn children may retreat and be rejected and victimized by peers. By age twelve, they are anxious and depressed. Children's aggressive, noncompliant reactions in elementary school are related to poor academic achievement in adolescence and to worry and internalizing problems in young adulthood.[36]

Coping with Problems

In facing problems children are most likely to strike at the roots of the difficulty when the problem stems from peers or school, where they feel they have more control. Children tend to use distraction strategies to adjust to situations they cannot control, such as doctors' visits.[37] Children also tend to use enjoyable activities to buffer themselves from stress. Athletics, being at home with families, and special treats of food all help children to deal with stressors.[38]

Children often seek help in dealing with stressful situations. They "perceive mothers as being the best multipurpose social provider available, in contrast to friends and teachers, who are relatively specialized in their social value."[39] Friends provide companionship and emotional support second only to parents. Teachers provide information but little companionship. Fathers are excellent providers of information, but are generally less available for direct help. Figure 9-1 illustrates where children of different ages and ethnic groups seek support.[40] Until early adolescence, parents and extended family provide the primary sources of support. Extended family are more important for African American and Latina/o children than for European Americans.

FIGURE 9-1
CONVOYS OF SUPPORT BY AGE AND ETHNICITY

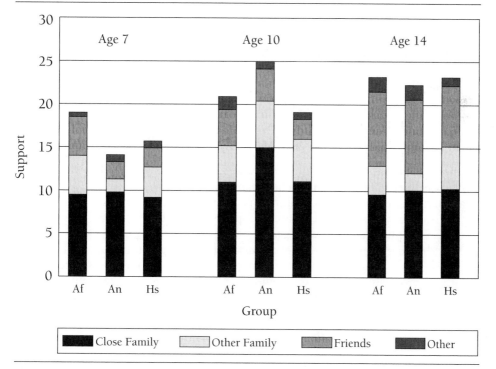

Af = African American, An = Anglo (European) American, Hs = Hispanic

Mary J. Levitt, Nathalie Guacci-Franco, and Jerome L Levitt, "Convoys of Social Support in Childhood and Early Adolescence: Structure and Function," *Developmental Psychology* 29 (1993), p 815. Copyright © 1993 American Psychological Association. Reprinted with permission.

THE DEVELOPMENT OF THE SELF

In elementary school, children think of themselves in more general terms rather than concrete physical traits and specific activities, such as "I am popular" rather than "I play with lots of friends." They become capable of integrating behaviors and forming a more balanced view of themselves that takes into account both positive and negative qualities.[41] Instead of smart or dumb, they think of themselves as smart in some things and not so smart in others.

Children also begin to evaluate their behavior in comparison to their peers. In the early grades, comparisons may be overt and direct—"I can finish the work faster than you"—but as children grow older, comparisons become subtler and less direct—"I have more friends than the other girls in my class." And they evaluate their own behavior, as we take up later.

As we will discuss in greater detail in Chapter 15, adopted children view themselves and their adoptive status in different terms as their thinking becomes more complex during this period.[42] Children become more curious about their biological origins and what led parents to give them up. They also may begin to experience a sense of loss at not knowing their biological family.

Parents provide a supportive family atmosphere and acknowledge that the child's experience of him- or herself is different from that of most children because the child comes from two families. On the other hand, parents must not overemphasize this difference. Ongoing communication can help parents understand the child's experiences and feelings and permit the child to hear the parents' point of view.

Gender Identity

Psychologists used to think that gender development was largely completed in the preschool years. Studies of older children, however, reveal that gender identity continues to develop over a long time; in fact, it never truly ends.[43]

Children in elementary school reason about the constancy of gender identity in more advanced ways than before, and[44] an increasing number of children explain gender constancy in unchangeable, operational terms such as physical characteristics. In these years, children, particularly girls, are more flexible in their preferences for activities and future occupations than they were as preschoolers, and this flexibility increases with age.

While children develop attitudes about what is gender appropriate for their own and the opposite gender, they use their own interests and preferences in determining what is appropriate for them as individuals.[45] For example, six of eight girls who said only men should be doctors expressed an interest in becoming doctors.

The most flexible and tolerant children come from families where parents and same-sex siblings are flexible in their activities. Same-sex peers also play an important role in promoting flexibility and tolerance.

Ethnic Identity

By about age seven, children identify their ethnic group. They learn ethnic consistency and constancy and realize they cannot change their ethnic identity. They construct a sense of ethnic identity much as they construct a sense of gender identity, from experiences at home with parents, at school with peers and teachers, and interactions and observations in the community.[46]

Family routines and activities teach children the distinctive values of their group. Mothers' daily diaries of children's activities in 1997 reveal distinctive activities of four ethnic groups.[47] European American children spend more time playing, more time in sports, and less time studying than the other groups, reflecting the importance of active, social pursuits. They spend more time reading than all but Asian Americans, reflecting the value of general cognitive ability.

African American children differ from other ethic groups in spending more time in church and church activities, reflecting the importance of religion; Latina/o children enjoy more household and family activities, reflecting their group's family orientation; and Asian American children spend more time in educational activities, reflecting a strong drive for academic achievement.

Parents' behavior, verbal messages, and toys and books also shape children's ethnic identity. We discuss African American socialization as more research is available. Homes rich in Afrocentric toys and books stimulate first-graders' cognitive competence and receptive language skills.[48]

Children learn about ethnic identity from peer interactions. Peer acceptance and, thus, self-perceptions are more positive when children attend schools with higher percentages of African American children, perhaps because they are more likely to be socially accepted and viewed as leaders and less likely to be viewed as fighters.[49] When children have African American teachers, they are similarly viewed in a more positive light.

Children also construct views of occupational possibilities from what they see around them.[50] As young as age six, African American children can identify occupations with high percentages of European Americans and high percentages of African Americans, and they believe occupations with many African Americans have lower status. In evaluating novel or made-up occupations, African American children give higher status to jobs when pictures show European Americans performing them and lower status to them when pictures show African Americans doing them.

Although they perceive racial segregation in jobs, they do not endorse it and believe that both European and African Americans can do all jobs. Regardless of social class, young children have high aspirations and prefer to work in high-status jobs. By age twelve, children from higher status families prefer high-status occupations, but children from lower status families no longer aspire to high-status occupations, perhaps because they feel they lack the finances to pursue higher education.

Children not only learn what it means to be part of their group, but they also come to prefer their own group, seeing it quite positively and viewing other groups less favorably.[51] Studies indicate that in-group favoritism develops first in children by about age five. Children initially prefer their own group without looking at the out-group negatively. Attitudes toward out-groups develop gradually in the early elementary school years. Out-group prejudice appears least likely to develop when children attend a multiethnic school where they have interactions with children of different groups and when they can describe negative qualities about the in-group.

Children's ability to recognize negative qualities about their own group seems to enable them to see the positive qualities in other groups. Nevertheless, even when out-group attitudes are not negative, in-group favoritism is so great that out-group children suffer in comparison.

Self-Esteem

Global feelings of self-worth are related to two independent factors: (1) one's feelings of competence in domains of importance and (2) the amount of social support one receives from others.[52] Those highest in self-worth feel good about the abilities they value and also feel that others support and accept them. Those lowest in global self-worth feel they lack competence in domains deemed important and report that they receive little social support.

The areas of competence that contribute most to feelings of self-worth are physical appearance and social acceptance by others—namely, parents and peers. Interestingly, physical appearance and social support continue to be salient across the lifespan for individuals from eight to fifty-five years of age. Elementary school children also evaluate themselves in terms of their scholastic and athletic competence and their conduct.

Although self-esteem depends on the early positive regard given by parents and caregivers, this regard does not fix it for life. Levels of self-esteem can increase over time as competence in areas of importance to them increase or as support from others increases and decreases under the reverse conditions. Times of change and transition, such as entrance into kindergarten or middle school, can trigger changes in self-esteem. Children maintain self-esteem most successfully when they join or create positive social support or when they increase in other areas of competence.

Recall from Chapter 3 that elementary school children of different ethnic groups resemble each other in self-esteem.[53] As they begin to take on culturally valued behaviors, self-esteem scores diverge, depending on the culture's values. When cultural values stress individualism, expressiveness, and self-assertion, then self-esteem scores stay high, as they do in African American and European American groups. When cultural values emphasize respect for tradition, interdependence with others, and critical self-evaluation, then self-esteem scores drop, as they do in Latina/o and Asian American groups.

THE DEVELOPMENT OF SELF-REGULATION

Elementary school children become more self-critical, and their self-esteem is related to their ability to control their feelings and behavior. They feel guilty when they have broken a moral rule, and ashamed when they have committed both moral and social blunders.[54] Since children do not feel good about themselves when they engage in disapproved behaviors,[55] it is important for parents to help children meet approved standards.

Parents' warm and positive expressiveness help children develop effortful control, defined as the ability to observe and plan behavior, inhibiting inappropriate

■ **TABLE 9-1**
PARENTAL QUALITIES ASSOCIATED WITH CHILDREN'S SELF-REGULATION
AND PROSOCIAL BEHAVIOR

1. Being warm and supportive with children

2. Developing mutually responsive relationships with children

3. Helping children understand others' feelings and the effects of their behaviors on others

4. Using reasoning and persuasion to gain children's compliance with rules

5. Including children in family decision making

6. Helping children develop an internal code of rules for behavior

7. Modeling caring and concern for others

Adapted from Nancy Eisenberg and Carlos Valiente, "Parenting and Children's Prosocial and Moral Development," in *Handbook of Parenting,* 2nd ed., ed. Marc H. Bornstein, vol. 5: *Practical Issues in Parenting* (Mahwah, NJ: Erlbaum, 2002), pp. 111–142.

dominant responses and carrying out less dominant, but appropriate responses.[56] Effortful control enables children to regulate their feelings and their behavior. Following children over a four-year period from ages nine to thirteen, researchers found that parents' positive parenting predicted children's effortful control two years later, and that effortful control predicted low levels of externalizing problems at age thirteen. Table 9-1 lists additional parental behaviors associated with children's self-regulation and prosocial behavior.

In the early elementary school years, reasoning about moral and conventional behavior becomes more complex, and children take into account the context of an event. They look at social situations and distinguish certain behaviors as matters of personal choice, other behaviors as matters of social convention, and still others as moral issues.[57] For example, it is morally wrong to deprive a person of a basic right such as access to schooling because of race or gender, but a person has the right of personal choice to choose friends even if someone of another race or gender is not included. Children consider it wrong to violate a moral rule even if an authoritative adult tells them to do it. For example, it is wrong to keep on fighting even if an adult tells you to do so.[58]

PARENT–CHILD RELATIONSHIPS

Children spend more time away from home. While parents and the home remain the center of life activities, friends and extracurricular activities claim more of children's time. Parents spend half as much time with elementary school children and give them less physical affection, compared with preschoolers. Even so, parents enjoy parenting as much as in earlier years, and they report as much caring and regard for children.[59]

Attachment

Children with secure attachments to parents adapt to school demands and perform well academically, and are socially accepted.[60] Secure attachments provide relationships with:

1. open, sensitive, and reciprocal communication
2. collaborative problem solving
3. support for the child's exploration and autonomy

Securely attached children have lower levels of emotional arousal so they can regulate their feelings and their behavior and focus on learning and relating to others. Patterns of open communication, collaborative problem solving, and autonomous behavior promote learning and positive relationships.

Attachment relationships are generally stable from the preschool to elementary school years, with an overall stability rate of 68 percent.[61] In one study children who moved from secure to insecure attachment experienced a decrease in the amount of time and quality of the mother–child communication process while those children who moved from secure to disorganized attachment experienced more severe stress and loss (intense conflict between the parents, parent's death). Children who changed from insecure to secure attachments developed more emotionally supportive and open communication patterns with mothers than those who remained insecure.[62] So, improving communication and availability increase security, and stresses that interfere with sensitivity and availability decrease secure attachment.

Authoritative parenting that combines warmth with firm control of children's behavior with respect for children's individuality and independence helps children manage the transition from home to school.[63] Mothers' and fathers' authoritative parenting of their kindergartners predicted their children's math and reading scores two years later. Mothers' encouragement of autonomy at the end of kindergarten predicted children's achievement and social acceptance at the end of first grade. Children whose mothers consistently encouraged autonomy from the preschool through the early years of school had high scores on academic and social competence and low teacher ratings of externalizing problems.

Parents' Changing Roles

Because parents no longer have exclusive control of children, they permit children to make decisions that parents monitor, supervise, and approve. Sharing control with children, termed coregulation, serves as a bridge to the preadolescent and adolescent years, when children will assume more control.[64]

Conflicts between parents and children center on children's interpersonal behavior with others (fighting, teasing), children's personality characteristics (irritability, stubbornness), and parents' regulating activities, such as rules about TV watching, chores, bedtime, and curfews.[65] Parents justify their point of view in terms of conventionality, practicality, and health issues. Children listen to parents' rules that prevent harm and psychological damage to others. Children report that they have more conflicts with fathers than with mothers. Rather than physical punishment, effective discipline involves removal of privileges.

Mothers' and Fathers' Roles

In the elementary school period, mothers and fathers continue to relate to children in different ways.[66] Mothers take major responsibility for managing family tasks—scheduling homework and baths, for example. Mothers are both more directive with children and more positive in their reactions to them. Both parents are similar in being more demanding of boys than of girls and more disapproving of boys' misbehavior.

Fathers, though more generally neutral in affect, continue to engage in more physical play and give more affection to both boys and girls. When fathers have high-status jobs, they have less time to spend with their children, and so low job salience is related to men's playfulness and caregiving.[67] Men are most likely to be involved as fathers when mothers do not take on all the caregiving. Nevertheless, the more skillful the mothers are with children, the more skillful fathers become.

Though mothers' and fathers' roles differ, children see them as having many qualities in common. Both parents are described as loving, happy, honest, responsible, self-confident individuals.[68] Fathers are more interested in learning and creativity than mothers, and mothers are more concerned about others' feelings than fathers. Children describe themselves less positively than they describe their parents, but still see many similarities with them. Children are loving, happy, and interested in learning and creativity, but they are far below parents in self-confidence, cooperativeness. responsibility, and honesty. Children described "having good family relationships" as the most important family goal of mothers and themselves, but feel fathers value "educational/vocational" goals most.

When parents make demands on the child, social responsibility increases in boys, self-assertiveness in girls. Diana Baumrind suggests that parents actively encourage characteristics outside the usual gender stereotypes.[69] The natural tendencies for both mothers and fathers are to encourage assertiveness in boys and cooperation and a more dependent role in girls, so parents must make special efforts to encourage a broader range of characteristics. Couples attending parenting groups did become less gender-stereotyped in their behaviors, with fathers becoming warmer and mothers becoming more goal- and limit-setting with children.[70]

Socializing Ethnic Identity

Socializing children regarding racial and ethnic issues includes (1) teaching about the group's cultural values, especially taking pride in the group and its achievements (sometimes termed "cultural socialization"); (2) preparation for bias, helping children to deal with bias and discrimination; and (3) promoting skepticism and mistrust of what the majority might do. These aspects of socialization are highly correlated, but they still differ from each other.[71]

Parents' messages regarding racial pride and preparation for bias do not have positive outcomes in the early elementary school years.[72] First-grade girls who heard these messages showed an increase in behavior problems. Parents' messages promoting mistrust of the majority group were related to boys' having more externalizing problems and girls' having more internalizing problems. It may be that first-graders have a greater understanding of what discrimination means than preschoolers but do not yet have coping skills to deal with the implications of the socialization messages thereby becoming emotionally overwhelmed.

When children are ten, parents' racial socialization messages are again related to strong and positive ethnic identity.[73] Mothers tend to do more racial socialization, and their cultural socialization predicts positive ethnic identity. Fathers' racial socialization tends to be directed more to sons than daughters, particularly in the area of preparation for bias, and is related to children's lack of depression. So, when children are older, parents' cultural socialization and preparation for bias appear to have positive effects for children. Parents' messages about bias and mistrust were amplified when children live in neighborhoods with few social supports for families.[74]

In these years, children are more likely to get inaccurate and negative messages from other children, the media, and people outside the home, so it is important for parents to encourage a positive self-image and racial pride. When parents acknowledge social restrictions and barriers but at the same time encourage self-development and ethnic pride and help children develop strategies for dealing with barriers, children, particularly older ones, are happy, high in self-esteem, and successful in school.[75]

RELATIONSHIPS WITH SIBLINGS

Siblings frequently spend more time with each other than they do with parents.[76] Their relationships improve in the elementary school years and become more enjoyable. The degree of satisfaction depends on the emotional climate in the family, because sibling relationships tend to mirror the ways parents treat each other and the ways they relate to children.[77]

When parents are positive and treat children fairly, then siblings have good relationships. Conversely, when mothers and fathers are angry with each other, they are more hostile with their children, who, in turn, show anger at their siblings and their peers.[78] Because conflict in sibling relationships during these years predicts a child's level of anxiety, depression, and acting out in early adolescence, improving these relationships when tension arises is important.[79]

Although most research on sibling relationships has been carried out on European American families, research with rural African American families has yielded similar results.[80] When parents of African American families are positive with each other and their children, older siblings develop good emotional control and are supportive and caring with younger siblings. Even though these parents work long hours and have financial pressures, when parents are caring with them, the older children also show care with younger siblings.

PEER RELATIONSHIPS

In the elementary school years, children spend about 30 percent or more of their time with peers in a wide variety of settings—school, sports, and interest groups—with less adult supervision than before. They spend more time in rough-and-tumble play than in the preschool years and in group games.[81]

Children are attracted to peers whose interests are similar to theirs, but they also look for friends they can trust to be loyal and supportive.[82] Children continue to prefer positive interactions and to work problems out so that everyone's needs are met. Relationships grow when children can express thoughts and feelings clearly. Friendships are likely to endure when partners are kind and sociable and have low levels of conflict.

While some children are identified as popular, what matters in peer relationships is having a quality friendship with sharing, positive interactions, and willingness to work out conflicts. When shy, withdrawn children have such a friendship, they appear to avoid the negative experiences of rejection and victimization.

Aggressive Children

Some children are physically aggressive, hitting and hurting others. Some children are verbally assaultive—taunting, teasing, and humiliating others. These types of aggression are overt, noticeable, and more characteristic of boys than of girls.[83] Another form of aggression, termed "relational aggression," is more subtle, not easily detectable, and more characteristic of girls. It consists of acts designed to deprive children of friends—spreading untrue rumors about a target child, organizing other children to reject the target child, refusing to be a friend unless the target child does favors. These behaviors are considered aggressive because they are meant to hurt or damage another child.

In one study, about 27 percent of boys were described as aggressive, and of those boys 93 percent were overtly aggressive. About 22 percent of girls were described as aggressive, and of those girls 95 percent were engaged in relational aggression.[84] Only about one-quarter of aggressive children used both forms to hurt children; most relied on one or the other. Note that when relational aggression is assessed, girls are almost equal to boys in aggressive behavior.

Bullying

Bullying occurs when an aggressive child targets a single child or a small group and, though unprovoked, pursues the child(ren) and uses force in an unemotional way, divorced from conflict or disagreement. About two-thirds of aggressive children are overt bullies, and 10–15 percent of all children are victims of overt bullying.[85] As noted earlier, almost all aggressive girls engage in relational aggression, and about 8 percent of all girls are victims of relational aggression.[86] Victims of both forms of bullying share certain characteristics. They tend to be quiet, inhibited children with low self-esteem. Some are physically weaker. Some impulsive, disruptive victims evoke negative reactions from peers.

Victims accept the aggression, withdrawing or responding with immature behavior such as crying, thus rewarding the bully's behavior. As victims continue to experience bullying, their self-esteem decreases further, and over time they become depressed and develop behavior problems at home and at school.[87] Some children are both bullies and victims and share the characteristics of both groups.

Research on ways to combat bullying indicate that those children who have confidence in their social skills and resist bullying with self-assertion are able to end the victimization, even if they are initially inhibited or physically weaker children.[88] They need not be physically aggressive, but they do not tolerate the attacks. Parents can help children combat bullying by enrolling children in social skills programs that teach and rehearse self-assertion. While individual efforts are important, in a later section we describe a community effort that is effective in combating bullying.

TASKS AND CONCERNS OF PARENTS

Parenting tasks include new activities as well as previous caregiving behaviors as follows:

- Being attentive, available, and responsive, using authoritative parenting and modeling desired behavior
- Monitoring and guiding children's behavior from a distance
- Structuring the home and daily routines so children have healthy lifestyles
- Encouraging autonomy, new skills and activities, and growing interest in friends
- Maintaining family rituals
- Serving as interpreter of children's experience in the larger world
- Participating in children's activities outside the home in supportive ways (room parent, soccer coach)
- Serving as children's advocate with authorities outside the home
- Sharing leisure activities and fun inside and outside the home

Daily Living That Promotes Growth

Healthy eating, sleeping, and exercise habits affect not only children's physical well-being, but also their intellectual, social, and emotional well-being. These habits are the foundations for positive development, and parents have to establish and monitor them as children lack the self-control to do that.

Parents have no control over what children eat when they are away from home, but they do control the food available at home. Parents can buy healthy foods and model healthy eating habits. If potato chips and soda are available only for parties, children are less likely to beg for them every day.

Parents take an active role in promoting healthy eating, sleeping, and exercise activities that promote overall competence.

Sleep is particularly important. Poor sleep is related to school inattentiveness and restlessness that interfere with learning. A recent study indicates that adding an hour's sleep each night to children's existing schedule increases memory and reaction times on cognitive tests the equivalent of two years of chronological age.[89]

In addition to regular bedtimes and consistent routines, the amount of sleep appears related to emotional warmth and security in the home. Nighttime sleep increases when parents are warm, parents and children eat meals together, and the television is turned off.[90] Disrupted and poor sleep increase for children reporting insecurity about parents' marital relationship.[91]

Parents must attend to sleep problems and their underlying causes because sleep problems affect learning at school, particularly for low-income and African American children.[92] Sleep problems at age four predict problems with short attention span, depression, and anxiety in adolescence.[93]

Parents' and children's busy schedules make it difficult to set aside time for exercise, but it can be a family activity that brings members closer together. Choosing activities and arranging for everyone's participation can be arranged in family meetings, described in Chapter 4.

Two other areas are important for families. It may seem impossible to fit in, but family game times and reading books together bring families closer together and establishes greater feelings of emotional security in children.

In these years, parents talk with children about their moral values and their responses to events that occur in their community. Parents and children can engage together in church or community activities designed to improve, for example, the environment or the school area or solve some other problem. It is a chance to work together and understand each other better and make a positive contribution to solving a problem.

VOICES OF EXPERIENCE

The Joys of Parenting Elementary School Children

"He's nine, and for the last several months, maybe because I'm the dad, he's come and said, 'Now there's this girl who's written me a note, what do I do?' Or, 'I have an interest here, how do I act?' I never heard any of this from my daughters. Then he says, 'What were you doing in the third grade? How did you deal with this when you were in the third grade?'" FATHER

"Being able to see life through their eyes is fun, sharing the way they see things, the questions they ask." MOTHER

"They are very loving kids. They'll give me a kiss good night and say, 'I'll love you forever.' That's a tradition." FATHER

"It was fun to see him learn to read. First, he knew the letters and then he read a little, and by the end of the year, he could read a lot." MOTHER

"I like watching them when they don't know I'm watching. They're playing or taking something apart. That's when you see how well you've transferred your values to them." FATHER

"It's fun to see the children join in with other kids. They went with their cousins to a July 4th celebration. They got right into a game with children they didn't know." MOTHER

"She wrote poems in school this year. It's amazing. She's quiet, and yet when you see the poems, you realize how much goes on in her head, how observant she is." FATHER

"I like seeing how important family is to them. They enjoy seeing their cousins, they like family to visit." MOTHER

"I'm a kid again. I get to do everything I liked to do all over again." FATHER

"It's fun when she says, 'Mommy, smile at me, make me laugh.'" MOTHER

"I enjoy watching their relationship grow. They are nineteen months apart. They play together a lot. She said to me, 'Sometimes, he's fun to play with and I love him, but sometimes he's a rascal.' They do a lot of imaginary play." MOTHER

"Every night we have a talking time just before he goes to bed, either he and his Dad or he and I. He's a real deep thinker, and he likes to get advice or get a response, and he just needs that verbal connection. So a few years ago when he was five, he was talking about being afraid of death and that he might not be married and he might not have children and that would be the worst. I can hear parts of what he might hear at church or other places like school, and he takes it all very seriously; when it collides, he wants to know what the answer is. They are always things we don't know the answer to either." MOTHER

"I can say, as a father of two girls between five and ten, that to be a father to girls is delightful. It's nice being looked on as a combination of God and Robert Redford. They have a little glow in their eyes when they look at Dad, and it's great. The younger one said, 'When I'm ticklish, you know why? Because I love you so much.'" FATHER

Helping Children Regulate Feelings and Behavior

In routine office visits, pediatricians identify a growing number of children aged five to fifteen in need of help for psychological problems.[94] Comparing pediatricians' responses in 1979 with responses in 1996 reveals that in 1979, they identified 6.8 percent of children requiring psychological help, and in 1996, the comparable figure was 18.7 percent. The largest increases were in attention-deficit hyperactivity problems, which went from 1.4 percent of children seen in the 1979 survey to 8.5 percent in 1996, and in emotional problems, which went from 0.2 percent in 1979 to 3.2 percent in 1996.

Anger

Psychologist Tim Murphy has described a program for parents to help their out-of-control children.[95] Describing the angry child, he makes several important points. He defines anger in broad terms: a feeling of displeasure, as a result of a perceived injury, and a desire to retaliate against the source of the injury.

He describes four stages of anger: the buildup, the spark, the explosion, and the aftermath. He also describes what he terms "microbursts" of anger—the sudden, brief outbursts that end almost as soon as they start. He urges parents to attend to these microbursts. Because the child is not extremely upset, parents can often use the episodes to help the child develop a better understanding of feelings and better problem-solving skills.

Murphy describes several important characteristics of the angry child. First, the angry child turns all negative experiences into anger, rather than distinguishing sadness, disappointment, and frustration. Second, the angry child sees the source of the difficulty as someone else's deliberate action against him or her. Frustration is caused by the parent, particularly the mother, not by uncontrollable events or even the child's own difficulty in accomplishing something. Third, and most important, angry children are not clear thinkers or effective problem-solvers. Prone to negative self-talk that immobilizes them, they cannot figure out how to make things better. Sadly, they often equate anger with power and feelings of self-esteem.

According to Murphy, the meaning of anger is related to family patterns of interaction. Anger is a sign of stress in the hurried, busy family. Anger is a sign of pain in the troubled family dealing with problems of addiction, loss, and marital discord. Anger is a sign of power in the angry family. Anger is a sign of desire in the indulging family that has led children to believe they should have what they want so children persist as long and as angrily as necessary to win each battle.

Murphy recommends positive parenting that anticipates and prevents problems. He recommends emotion coaching in calm times, problem-solving skills practice before frustration occurs, and helping children learn enjoyment from the process of doing an activity rather than just the final result. Gerald Patterson's program also deals with children's angry outbursts (see Chapter 2).[96] Problem-Solving Skills Training, described for aggressive children in a later section, is also helpful.

Discouragement

In these years of rapidly developing skills, meeting new friends, and learning in formal settings in comparison with others, discouragement is a common feeling, especially for the more cautious, less confident child. Martin Seligman offers a program quite useful for parents in his book *The Optimistic Child.*[97]

Seligman has documented the nature of pessimistic attitudes that lead to discouragement and withdrawal from challenging tasks. Pessimistic individuals consider difficulty a sign of a pervasive, permanent problem that is one's own fault and is unchangeable. Pessimistic children see a poor math grade as the result of their own stupidity and inability to do math. They sometimes avoid studying because they are discouraged and feel they are no good at the subject.

Parents supply new interpretations of the problem. Perhaps the child did not study enough or needs extra tutoring. Parents can encourage their children to look for solutions to problems and to exert effort to achieve them, as most problems will improve with effort. Parents also must avoid critical personal comments, such as "You never learn at school—you just fool around," which can sap children's confidence.

Lying and Stealing

When parents create a supportive atmosphere in which children can talk about mistakes and misdeeds, and when they offer encouragement rather than criticism, lying and stealing are reduced. Still, almost every child has told a lie at one time, and all parents have concerns about lying and stealing because trust in others is such an important part of close relationships.

Parents express their feelings of concern about dishonesty, accept matter-of-factly that the child has lied or stolen, and problem-solve with the child ways to be more truthful and honest. If a child lies about schoolwork, parents should find out if there are special problems at school. If a child brags about false exploits, parents do well to focus on why he or she needs to do this to feel good. Parents express their belief that their child wants to be honest, and as partners, they need to figure out how to bring this about. Mutual problem solving, as discussed in Chapter 5, is very useful. In this process, the parent becomes an ally and a resource, not an accuser and a judge. The child learns that one can get help when in trouble and that one need not be perfect to be loved.

Promoting Positive Social Relationships

We have seen that parents' secure attachments with children and their use of authoritative parenting predict children's social competence. In contrast, parents of children who are not well liked and/or rejected are reported to use harsh, directive, authoritarian, controlling behaviors with their children. So, positive parenting is a first step in improving children's social behaviors.

When parents believe good social skills are important, model them, and find programs to teach children, social skills improve.[98] Developing new interests and skills such as photography or drawing or getting involved in extracurricular activities are others ways to meet and make friends. Box 9-2 has suggestions many parents can use.

Parents can also seek out behavioral programs for shy and aggressive children. As we have stated, aggressive children benefit from programs meeting the needs of shy children, as aggressive children need to learn how to join groups, how to communicate with peers, and how to validate peers by paying attention to them and helping them. These programs encourage cooperation, develop verbal skills to make requests and suggestions, teach techniques for anger management, and provide opportunities for children to rehearse the skills that increase social competence and peer acceptance. In follow-up studies, children who attended such programs achieved greater peer acceptance and reduced their aggressive responses.[99]

A program designed for aggressive children, Problem-Solving Skills Training, has been carefully researched, and attendance predicts significant reductions in problematic behavior at home and at school.[100] Children attend 20–25 individual sessions that focus on problem-solving skills and ways to settle differences with parents, children, and school authorities. Role-playing, practicing skills, and homework activities help children learn the skills. A parent component, Parent Management Training, consists of 16 individual sessions for parents and a therapist to plan and practice how to change children's behavior at home and at school. Recently a five-session parental stress component has been added and found to further reduce children's problematic behaviors.

Controlling Bullying

In the United States we generally deal with bullying at the individual level—a child complains to a parent, the parent goes to the school, and the school often considers what the individual child can do to handle the bully. In Norway, Dan Olweus designed a highly successful school- and community-based program to decrease bullying.[101] School administrators, teachers, parents, and students have roles in the program. Adults create, at school and at home, an environment in which children experience warm, positive attention and firm limits against negative behaviors. Negative behaviors receive consistent, nonhostile, nonphysical consequences, and monitoring occurs in and out of school.

Interventions occur at the school, class, and individual level and include the formation of a coordinating group, meetings with staff and parents, better supervision during recess, class rules against bullying, and class meetings. At the individual level, parents, teachers, and students meet to discuss specific incidents and to develop strategies to handle them. Emphasis is on developing effective forms of communication and positive behaviors in all students, not just in bullies or victims.

Evaluated by 2,500 students and their teachers, the intervention program reduced bullying by 50 percent and decreased other antisocial acts as well. Moreover, bullying away from the school did not increase. Students expressed greater satisfaction with their schoolwork, and their social relationships with children increased. The benefits were in some instances more marked after two years than after one year.

Box 9-2
RICHARD LAVOIE'S STRATEGIES TO DEVELOP SOCIAL COMPETENCE*

Richard Lavoie has long worked with children who have learning disabilities of many kinds. He observed that social difficulties can be closely linked to difficulties in learning. If a person cannot process auditory material, he may not follow conversations well; if he has expressive language problems, he may be slow and awkward in conversations with a friend.

Lavoie points out that, if you have trouble with academics, you can always enjoy athletic activities and all the social activities away from school. But a child with poor social skills cannot avoid situations that require these skills. "Any and all activities that involve two or more people require the use of social skills." Furthermore, there is no technology to help a child compensate for social difficulties as there are for learning disabilities (e.g., computers and calculators).

Lavoie has developed a system that parents, teachers, and counselors can use to help a child with social difficulties for any reason.

Lavoie believes that children's social missteps are unintentional—children want to have friends, but don't know how to "tune in" to social situations, join groups, make and keep friends, and resolve conflicts. They need help in all these areas, and each area requires many different skills.

To assist the child, parents take several steps. Most important, they remain calm, nonjudgmental helpers who serve as coaches and mutual problem-solvers. As coaches, they help children prepare for difficult situations. If children are going to new classes or new programs, parents and children can go there in advance and become familiar with them. Parents help children rehearse for new social situations such as sleepovers or birthdays. They go over appropriate conversations for upcoming situations, such as meeting new people or giving a gift.

A program used in American schools where bullying was more common than expected—seen 30 times in an hour of playground observation with 20 episodes encouraged by bystanders—is titled Steps to Success.[102] It decreased bullying and bystanders' encouragement of it significantly and increased children's positive social behaviors. Children in the program reported that adults were more responsive, and there was much less tolerance for bullying and aggressive behaviors.

The Partnership of Families and Schools

In the past, people looked on the school as having primary responsibility for educating children. Parents played a secondary role—raising funds, volunteering in the school, and enriching the curriculum with their input and values. Recently, a partnership model for families and schools has been advanced.[103] Acknowledging the powerful impact of parents' involvement and encouragement on children's educational progress, the partnership model seeks to forge a strong link between parents and the schools. This model rests on six kinds of involvement:

When problems arise, the adult and child together, in a calm, nonblaming way, review what happened and carry out what Lavoie calls a "social skills autopsy"—so termed because it is an attempt to determine the cause and effect of a "social error" in order to prevent its happening again. The social skills autopsy consists of five steps:

1. Ask the child to describe what happened.

2. Ask the child to identify what he or she thinks was the social mistake responsible for the difficulty; often, the child fails to identify what went wrong in the situation.

3. Help the child identify the particular social error accurately. Put forward alternative options in the situation, and let the child choose an appropriate one.

4. Create a social scenario with the same basic error or moral and see if the child recognizes the problem. For example, if the child got delayed at home and was late for a birthday party, making everyone wait to go to a movie, a similar scene is created in which the parent is late and delays everyone, and the child is expected to identify the error. If he or she fails, another scenario is made up.

5. The child practices the remedy at least once in the coming week—for example, not being late for social activities or sports.

The adult and child are collaborators; the adult asks questions and leads. The process is ongoing because children advance to new social situations and have to learn new skills. But parents are always there as consultants and coaches.

*Richard Lavoie, *It's So Much Work to Be Your Friend* (New York: Touchstone Books, 2005).

1. Parents establish a home that allows children to (a) be healthy and attend school, (b) be calm and confident enough to pay attention in class and do their work, (c) receive encouragement to perform well, and (d) have home settings that support doing homework and educational projects. Schools provide families with information on effective parenting on school-related issues; they sometimes also provide supportive programs or workshops.

2. Schools keep parents informed of school matters and students' progress and behavior, including notices on students' performance, any difficulties, and any noteworthy behaviors. Schools also provide information on school programs, school needs, and opportunities for parental involvement in projects.

3. Parents, children, and other community members contribute their own special skills to promote children's education, as in cleaning, painting, and giving cultural information of interest.

4. Teachers help parents monitor and help children learn at home. Schools make educational goals and curricula available, show parents how to assist their children, and even give joint assignments that parents and students can carry out together. Teachers are also sensitive to immigrant parents' needs.

5. Parents participate in school organizations and in formal or informal groups that advise educators on school priorities, school improvement programs, and parents' and students' perceptions of problems in the school environment.

6. Finally, parents and schools work with business organizations, local government agencies, and volunteer groups to form partnerships that support school programs.

A PRACTICAL QUESTION: WHAT CAN PARENTS DO WHEN SCHOOL AND PSYCHOLOGICAL DIFFICULTIES INTERFERE WITH ACADEMIC ACHIEVEMENT?

What do parents do when a child's behavior interferes with learning? Space does not permit detailed discussions of the many different problems and conditions—attention problems, learning disabilities, emotional and family problems—that interfere with achievement, but a general plan for dealing with these kinds of problems is described.

School difficulties require accurate diagnosis as the first step in remedying problems. School study teams and school psychologists observe and test the children and provide information to identify the extent and source of the problem. If difficulties do not meet certain criteria or fall in certain categories, schools may refuse to do an assessment. Parents then have to pay privately or seek services in clinics with a sliding scale such as a college clinic.

When specific difficulties are identified, then parents, teachers, and children meet to remedy them. It is important to involve children in the process, as they need to understand specifically what requires changing, and they may have good ideas about how to change. In encouraging new behaviors and skills, parents and teachers identify the specific positive behaviors desired.

The level of work expected must be tailored to children's existing skills and advance as children's skills grow. If assignments are too difficult at the age-appropriate level but are expected nonetheless, then children will grow discouraged and resist doing them.

At the same time that parents help children deal with difficulties, parents also identify children's strengths, inside and outside of school, and help children gain pleasure and satisfaction from them to balance the effort and frustration required by problem areas. For example, sports can channel the energy and frustration of athletic children, and artistic activities such as music or drawing provide outlets for creative children.

Box 9-3
LIVING WITH ADHD[*]

In his last two years of high school, Blake Taylor, now a college student, wrote a book about growing up with ADHD, *ADHD & Me*. Diagnosed at age five, he describes not only his distractible, impulsive, and hyperactive actions, and his use of medications but the inner thoughts and emotional reactions that accompanied them. He provides invaluable insights into the experience of having ADHD that help parents, teachers, and professionals better understand the condition.

In the Acknowledgments and throughout the book, he thanks the many people who have helped and supported him—most particularly his mother and family, and also daily caregivers, some teachers and principals, doctors and counselors, coaches, and friends. Despite considerable support, however, he also describes poignant feelings of exclusion and rejection.

In addition to medications, Blake emphasizes an active, problem-solving approach to ADHD difficulties. Over his desk, he keeps a fortune cookie saying that sums up his approach, "You constantly struggle for self-improvement." While he recognizes that every person with ADHD is different, he still believes people can learn useful strategies from each other. His suggestions go from the general to the specific. In addition to structure, organization, and routines, he advocates getting nine hours of sleep at night and having a regular exercise program. He found swimming on a team gave him exercise and a whole new group of friends who did not care about ADHD, only about how fast he swam.

In addition to taking control of ADHD symptoms, Blake emphasizes developing new skills and reaching out to others. He urges other children with ADHD to develop social skills—talk to others, make conversation (homework and sibling problems are always good topics). Explain to other children that you have ADHD and the behaviors that go with it—he also had to explain tics side effects of medications. He also advises involvement in community activities—he joined a greyhound dog rescue group and made presentations and raised money. He suggests embracing new ways of doing things to overcome rigid thinking

Blake ends the book with a list of the many gifts that he believes ADHD has added to his life—among them, high energy, humor, creativity, an ability to do a lot of things at once, compassion and empathy, an adventurous spirit. To get the benefits, he has to manage the difficulties. This book gives suggestions that may help other children and families as well.

*Blake E. S. Taylor, *ADHD & Me* (Oakland, CA: New Harbinger, 2007).

Siblings may use school difficulties as a means of teasing or for comparisons that enable them to feel better about themselves and their skills. Parents must stop such behavior and teach family members that all children have their own special strengths, and everyone has one or more areas in which they must strive for improvement. Parents can express empathy for children who must spend long hours, year after year, in an atmosphere and activity that brings frustration.

Having fun daily with family members, perhaps after dinner, relaxes everyone and increases good feelings that sustain effort and motivation for work.

PARENTS' EXPERIENCES IN FACING TRANSITIONS

Ellen Galinsky describes this parental stage as the interpretive stage.[104] Parents share facts and information about the world, teach values, and guide children's behavior in certain directions. They decide how they will handle the child's greater independence and involvement with people who may not share similar values.

Parents' behavior at home predicts half the variation in children's adaptation to school.[105] When parents argue with each other, children as young as five years report parents' conflicts, and, sadly, blame themselves.[106] Teachers rate boys and girls as having more behavior problems when marital conflict is covert and expressed as silence or distancing.

Reducing parents' stress from work, marital relationships, and low income improves parenting and children's behavior.[107] Five sessions added to Parent Management Training, described earlier, helped parents identify stresses and find alternative solutions and additional resources that could help (friends, work, community agencies). Possible solutions were tried out as homework. The most common stresses addressed were arranging more time with partner, finding time for oneself, job-related stress, and lack of money. Dealing with parents' stress further reduced parents' and children's problems. Even parents in low-risk, economically stable, two-parent families benefited from talking about their day-to-day relationships with family members in a sixteen-week group, and the quality of children's functioning over a three-year period improved.[108]

Parents also refine their beliefs and values, discarding some and adding others. Children often prompt changes when they discover inconsistencies in what parents say and do. If lying is bad, why do parents tell relatives they are busy when they are not? If parents care about the world and want to make it a safer place, why are they not doing something to make it safe? In the process of answering these questions, parents grow.

SUPPORT FOR PARENTS

Many forms of support exist for parents of elementary school children. Parents work together with teachers and school personnel in parent–teacher associations or local organizations to provide the most effective schools possible. Specialized parent support groups also offer valuable information and resources. For example, Children and Adults with Attention Deficit Disorders (CHADD) provides support for families dealing with ADHD; the Orton Dyslexia Society helps with problems of reading; the Learning Disabilities Association of America, with learning disabilities. In addition, local and state organizations can be helpful.

Parent training programs also provide support, as described earlier. At the Oregon Social Learning Center, Gerald Patterson and his colleagues have worked with married parents, divorced single parents, foster parents, and parent–teacher partnerships to establish structure as well as positive and consistent rewards to help children learn to control aggressive behavior and develop prosocial behaviors at home and at school. These programs are successful and are being refined and expanded.[109]

At all age levels, parents and children find moral support and strength from religious activities. This source of support becomes important at this stage, because children begin to explore moral and ethical issues and are exposed to more ideas about these issues than before. Religious participation provides opportunities for discussing moral principles and applying them to everyday life.

Parents involved in religion can easily include their children. When parents have no affiliation, Joan Beck recommends that parents develop an individual belief system that they share with children as they grow.[110] The process of developing an agreed-upon source of spiritual or secular meaning in life can enrich the entire family.

Religious faith also contributes to feelings of confidence and security. In their study of resilient children who overcame the difficulties of growing up in troubled families, Emmy Werner and Ruth Smith point to the importance of faith:

> A potent protective factor among high-risk individuals who grew into successful adulthood was a faith that life made sense, that the odds could be overcome. This faith was tied to active involvement in church activities, whether Buddhist, Catholic, mainstream Protestant, or fundamentalist.[111]

Children's conception of God adds security to life by providing fallible parents with a backup expert who helps them. "God is my parents' parent and mine, too," said one girl.[112]

MAIN POINTS

As children's competence increases, by the end of this period they have

- acquired all the basic skills in gross and fine motor coordination
- developed more logical thinking abilities so that they can grasp the relations between objects
- learned greater understanding of their own and others' emotional reactions
- gained greater control of their aggressiveness and become less fearful
- learned to remedy situations they control and adjust to situations others control
- come to value themselves for their physical, intellectual, and social competence, developing an overall sense of self-worth

Schools

- are the main socializing force outside the family
- create stress in children's lives because children worry about making mistakes, being ridiculed, and failing
- promote a strong bond with children by encouraging active participation in learning and activities
- promote learning when they provide a calm, controlled environment and when teachers are gentle disciplinarians with high expectations for students
- often do not reward the values of ethnic groups that emphasize cooperation and sharing among their members

- are highly valued by many ethnic group members who wish their children to achieve
- provide opportunities for social experiences

With peers, children

- interact in an egalitarian, give-and-take fashion
- prefer those who are outgoing and supportive of other children
- interact more effectively when parents have been affectionate, warm, and accepting with them and less effectively when there is stress in the family
- can improve relationships when they learn emotional regulatory and social skills

Parenting tasks in this period include

- monitoring and guiding children from a distance as children move into new activities on their own
- interacting in a warm, accepting, yet firm manner when children are present
- strengthening children's abilities to monitor their own behavior and develop new skills
- structuring the home environment so the child can meet school responsibilities
- serving as an advocate for the child in activities outside the home (e.g., with schools, with sports teams, in organized activities)
- providing opportunities for children to develop new skills and positive identities
- becoming active in school and community organizations to provide positive environments for children

In Galinsky's interpretive stage, parents

- have achieved greater understanding of themselves as parents and of their children
- develop strategies for helping children cope with new authorities such as teachers and coaches

Problems discussed center on

- helping children meet school responsibilities
- helping children regulate anger and discouragement
- dealing with social problems such as social isolation, aggression, and bullying
- changing rule-breaking behavior such as lying

Parents' joys include

- observing increasing motor, cognitive, and social skills in children
- reexperiencing their own childhood pleasure through their child's experience

EXERCISES

1. Break into small groups of four or five. Take turns recalling (a) how your parents prepared you for school, (b) the strategies that helped you do well at school. Are there ways parents and teachers could have helped more? Have each group come up with effective strategies for parents and teachers and report them to the class. (c) what your early experiences were, and (d) how confident or shaky you felt about your abilities. Then identify ways parents and teachers could have helped more. Share your group's experiences with the class and come up with recommendations for parents and teachers.

2. In small groups, take turns recalling the pleasurable events you experienced during the years from five to ten. Then come up with a class list of twenty common pleasurable events for that period.

3. Take the list of twenty pleasurable events developed in Exercise 2 and rate each event on a scale of 1 to 7, with 1 being least pleasurable and 7 being most pleasurable, as you would have when you were a child of nine or ten. What are the most pleasurable events? How do parents contribute to them?

4. Recall the first frustrations or stresses you felt in the years from five to ten. Are there gender differences as were reported in the text?

5. In small groups, discuss major activities that built sources of self-esteem in this period for you. Were these athletic activities? Group activities such as Scouts or Brownies? School activities? Come up with recommendations for parents as to the kinds of activities children find the most confidence building.

ADDITIONAL READINGS

Lavoie, Richard. *It's So Much Work to Be Your Friend.* New York: Touchstone Books, 2005.
Murphy, Tim, and Oberlin, Loriann. *The Angry Child.* New York: Three Rivers Press, 2001.
Seligman, Martin E. P. *The Optimistic Child.* New York: Houghton Mifflin, 1995.
Steyer, James. *The Other Parent.* New York: Atria, 2002.
Taylor, Blake E. S. *ADHD & Me.* Oakland, CA: New Harbinger, 2007.

C H A P T E R

10

Parenting Early Adolescents

CHAPTER TOPICS	**IN THE NEWS**
In this chapter, you will learn about:	*New York Times*, November 20[1]: Internet use is an important part of teen socializing. See pages 316–317.
■ Early adolescent development	
■ Relationships with parents, siblings, and peers	
■ Encouraging communication, problem-solving skills, initiative, school success, and peer relationships	
■ Meeting boys' and girls' special needs	

Test Your Knowledge: Fact or Fiction (True/False)

1. Students face a mismatch between their developmental needs and the opportunities offered in the school environment.
2. Brain development is completed in adolescence.
3. Early adolescents are so busy with friends that siblings' behavior has little effect on them.
4. The ways to help aggressive early teens are similar to the ways to help inhibited shy teens.
5. To help children develop, parents are advised to stay less closely connected to boys and more closely connected to girls.

Adolescence is a time of dynamic changes in physical form, in ways of thinking, in time spent away from parents, in school settings, and in the importance of peers. How do parents support children as they adapt to changes? How do parents maintain close relationships while teenagers are becoming more independent? How do parents of different ethnic groups help their teenagers deal with the specific problems youth confront while establishing their identity in a complex world?

Early adolescence is a period of vulnerabilities and opportunities. Children experience the stresses of many changes. Yet, their thinking is maturing, and they engage in exciting activities on their own and with peers. The challenge for parents is to provide the emotional supports and limits necessary for children's growth toward maturity and greater autonomy.

PHYSICAL AND NEUROPHYSIOLOGICAL DEVELOPMENT

Adolescence begins with biological change. The physical changes of puberty, defined as the age at which sexual reproduction is possible, begin at about eight for girls and nine for boys and extend to the end of the second decade.[2]

The brain triggers endocrine organs to release hormones that affect children's physical growth and secondary sexual characteristics (breasts, body and facial hair), resulting in reproductive maturity. Hormonal changes occur before any outward signs of puberty, so parents do not know at first that puberty has begun. For girls, these changes take place from about age eight to seventeen; for boys, on average, from nine to twenty. Although children vary in the age at which changes take place and their rapidity, the sequence remains consistent.

For girls, a spurt in height accompanies the growth of secondary sexual characteristics and the growth of the uterus and vagina. By the time menstruation occurs, on average at twelve and a half, the breasts and body are well developed. Boys' sexual hormonal secretions begin at about nine to ten; the first visible sign of puberty is growth of the testes and the scrotum that holds the testes. The growth spurt begins about a year later along with the growth of the penis and facial and body hair. Boys' voices change later in puberty.

The onset of pubertal changes, studied primarily in girls because of the clear pubertal marker of menstruation, depends on many factors:

- genetic influences—age of mother's menarche is strongest predictor of daughter's[3]
- physical influences—childhood growth in height and weight, nutrition, and percentage of body fat are predictors
- social influences—economic stresses are related to early and late onset
- psychological influences—family constellation, parenting behaviors, life stress are related to timing[4]

Psychological factors playing a role in the early or later onset of sexual development include:

- mothers' and fathers' positive and supportive parenting in the preschool years is related to delays in both boys' and girls' sexual development[5]
- harsh parenting and stress from low family income are related to girls' earlier menarche[6]
- girls' living in homes without a biological father or with stepfathers or mothers' boyfriends are more likely to have earlier menarche[7]

The timing of sexual development—being early, late, or on time—has psychological repercussions for boys and girls.[8] For girls, being on time is related to greater satisfaction with their bodies and their physical appearance than being early or late. For boys being early is related to feeling satisfied with their size and their physical appearance. Both African American boys and girls reported feeling less satisfied with late maturation, and Asian American and European American early adolescents showed little effect of timing on their body image.

Early-maturing girls have greater difficulties than later-maturing girls.[9] They experience more conflicts with parents and with peers—both boys and girls—because their bodies and interests are more advanced, and they are more prone to depression and substance abuse than later-menstruating girls. Early-maturing boys may have an advantage because of increased height and muscular strength but research results are inconsistent.

Puberty also brings changes in emotional intensity.[10] Teens are not a cauldron of raging hormones, but following puberty, both boys' and girls' emotional reactions are more intense. The intensity of their negative affect is related to pubertal status, and their "sensation seeking" and attraction to high-intensity emotional experiences is related not to their age but to their pubertal status.[11] Following puberty, girls have a significantly higher rate of depression than boys, a difference continuing through the adult years, and boys have a higher rate of aggressive and violent behavior, possibly related to increased testosterone.[12] We discuss these changes in Chapter 11.

Pubertal physical changes include changes in sleep patterns.[13] The timing of melatonin secretion changes, and there is later onset of sleep, so adolescents frequently delay going to bed for physical as well as school and social reasons. Parents have to help teens maintain regular sleep schedules to avoid excessive daytime sleepiness.

Scientists have long thought brain development was completed by adolescence,[14] but recent studies with new imaging techniques reveal that brain development continues throughout the second decade of life, especially in the frontal area of the brain, responsible for reasoning, problem solving, planning, and judgment.

In the beginning of early adolescence, there is a spurt in the number of synapses in the frontal and parietal areas of the brain, perhaps triggered by hormones as girls have a spurt about a year before boys do. As in the early years of development, an overproduction of synapses "may herald a critical stage of development when the environment or activities of the teenager may guide selective synapse elimination in adolescence,"[15] thus allowing activities and experience to shape brain functions. "Pruning" or eliminating the least used connections later in adolescence reduces the number of connections and increases the brain's efficiency.

Increasing myelination of nerves (covering the nerves with a sheath of myelin), especially in the prefrontal area, coordinates attention, emotion, and behavior, and increases conductivity and communication between nerve cells, thus contributing to brain efficiency.

Because the brain is developing in areas responsible for reasoning, planning, and problem-solving behavior, parents can expect that teenagers will not be as consistent, organized, and structured as parents might wish. Teens benefit from parents' patience, encouragement, and support in their problem-solving activities, as described on page 320.

VOICES OF EXPERIENCE

What I Wish I Had Known about Early Adolescence

"They seem to get caught up in fads in junior high. They do certain things to the max to be part of the crowd. I wish I'd known how to handle that. At what point are these fads okay, because it's important to identify with your peer group, and at what point do you say no? If they are really dangerous, then it's easy; but with a lot of them, it's a gray area, and I wish I'd known what to do better." FATHER

"I wish I had realized that she needed more structure and control. Because she had always been a good student and done her work, I thought I could trust her to manage school tasks without my checking. But she lost interest in school, and I learned only very gradually that I had to be more of a monitor with her work than I had been in the past." MOTHER

"I wish I had known more about mood swings. When the girls became thirteen, they each got moody for a while, and I stopped taking it personally. I just relaxed. The youngest one said, 'Do I have to go through that? Can't I just skip that?' Sure enough, when she became thirteen, she was moody too." MOTHER

"I wish I'd known how to help the boys get along a little better. They have real fights at times, and while they have a lot of fun together and help each other out, I wish I knew how to cut down on the fighting." FATHER

"I wish I knew what to expect. They are all so different, and they don't necessarily do what the books say. Sometimes, I'm waiting for a stage; now I'm waiting for adolescent rebellion, and there is none." MOTHER

"I wish I had known about their indecisiveness. He wants to do this; no, he doesn't. He gets pressure from peers and from what we think is right, and sometimes he goes back and forth. I am more patient about that now." MOTHER

"I wish I had known that if we had dealt with some behaviors when they were younger, we would not have had a problem from eleven to fourteen. He was always a little stubborn and hardheaded, wanting to do what he wanted. But right now, I wish we had done something about the stubbornness because it is a problem. He does not take responsibility, and it gets him into trouble at school. Looking back it has always been a problem, but we did not deal with it." MOTHER

INTELLECTUAL DEVELOPMENT

Early adolescents' problem solving improves because their working memory and information-processing skills increase, and because they have a broader range of knowledge to use in solving problems. In addition, they gradually become better able to integrate their cognitive functioning with their emotional and social reactions in situations.[16]

Early adolescents between twelve and fourteen enter Piaget's *formal operations period*, when they come to think more abstractly than previously.[17] They reason logically about verbal propositions or hypothetical situations. In this period, adolescents can freely speculate and arrive at solutions by analyzing a problem in their heads. Furthermore, they can enumerate all possible combinations of events and take action to see what possibilities actually exist.

With increased capacity for abstract thought, adolescents turn inward, analyzing their thoughts, feelings, and reactions as well as other people's reactions. They think of the future, what might be happening in the world. They can think of ideal situations or solutions and become impatient with the present because it does not meet the ideal they have pictured. Their introspection, idealism, and impatience with the present all affect parent–child relationships, as we will see.

SCHOOL

At a time of physical and psychological change, many early adolescents go to middle or junior high schools that are typically larger, more demanding, and less supportive in meeting students' needs.[18] Teachers do not know students as well. Assignments demand responsibility and self-direction that many early adolescents do not have, and grading is often based on social comparisons. In addition, friendships may change as children are no longer in the same classes and have little time together. Finally, participation in school activities is more competitive as there are more students to fill leadership roles or team positions.

Often students lose interest in academic subjects, and grades decline. Even when boys and girls achieve good grades, some are reluctant to talk about their interests or their achievements for fear of being thought too smart.[19] Students who have an incremental theory of ability, namely that performance improves with effort, practice, and successful strategies (described in Chapter 9 on page 267), have more positive motivation for schoolwork and their grades are less likely to decline.

Researchers demonstrated the power of an incremental theory of ability with an eight-week workshop given to two groups of seventh-graders who had similar math grades in the spring of their seventh-grade year.[20] Their grades were tracked during the eighth-grade year. One group learned that the brain is like a muscle that changes with experience, and that everything in school is hard at first, but gets easier with practice. These students learned they can choose to practice and, in a sense, get smarter. Students in the other group received general instructions about the brain and processing of memory in the brain.

Prior to the workshops, both groups had decreasing grades, but the students who learned the brain can grow and develop with practice quickly began to improve their grades, whereas the grades of the other group continued to decline. Teachers could see differences in the behaviors of the two groups. Students who thought abilities can grow were more often described as having an interest in learning, asking for extra help, and consistently working hard.

Parents' emphasis on an incremental theory of ability helps children see that no matter what their level of ability in an area, practice and hard work lead to improvement.

EMOTIONAL DEVELOPMENT

Early adolescents' daily reports of their activities and accompanying moods when paged provide a window into the emotional ups and downs of this period. Most studies monitoring moods report that from age ten onward, there is a decline in good feelings and an increase in negative feelings. These changes are relative, however, as early adolescents still have many more good times in a day than negative ones.[21] In one study, negative events rose from 13 percent of all reported events to 20 percent, with 70 percent still being positive.

Early teens generally reported more anxiety and nervousness at school and more positive feelings at home with family members.[22] Those early teens who reported loneliness, low self-esteem, and depression were those who were experiencing unpredictable and upsetting conflicts with friends and family, the people with whom most teens were reporting pleasure. Even so, the lonely teens had more positive than negative moods.

Stressful events reported at home and at school create spillover effects.[23] Ninth-graders who experienced family conflicts showed the effects the next day and for the two following days in their schoolwork—failing to turn in homework, doing poorly on a quiz or exam. Conversely, school problems like not doing well on a test and failing to do homework created stress and increased conflict at home the next day and for the two following days. Daily stresses had long-term consequences as well because home and school stress in the ninth grade predicted stress levels and lower grade point average in the twelfth grade.

There are no sex differences between the daily moods boys and girls report. This contrasts with the lower self-esteem girls report, as we will see in the next section. Ethnic differences have appeared in daily moods. Chinese American early teens reported fewer family stressors than children of European American and Latino backgrounds, but when such stressors did occur they were more disruptive of Chinese American children's schoolwork.[24] In another study of daily moods, high ethnic regard was found to buffer Chinese American and Mexican American early adolescents. When they experienced stressors, they felt anxious, but they were able to maintain high levels of happiness.[25]

Positive experiences can serve as a buffer against the effects of worry and low moods. Such experiences provide an "arena of comfort" in which early teens can escape stress, relax, and feel good. When early adolescents from various ethnic backgrounds were asked about their sources of support, all pointed to the importance of close family relationships and friends.[26] (See Figure 9-1 in Chapter 9.)

Reed Larson, who has conducted several daily mood surveys, reports concern that many, in one study 27 percent of early teens, reported boredom when beeped, much of the time at school and in study activities.[27] Honor students report boredom as often as do acting-out early teens. Early adolescents, Larson writes, "Communicate an ennui of being trapped in the present, waiting for someone to prove to them that life is worth living."[28] He believes that positive development requires that teens develop initiative, defined as a feeling of internal motivation to engage in challenging, effortful activities that are pursued over an extended period of time. Later in this chapter, we discuss how parents promote this quality in children.

THE DEVELOPMENT OF THE SELF

Early adolescents now think more abstractly than before, and they describe themselves in terms of more general traits ("I'm an extrovert with a lot of friends").[29] Though they may think of themselves as stupid because of poor grades and low creativity, they do not yet integrate this negative quality into their overall picture of themselves. The negative and positive qualities remain isolated as separate traits. This separation may serve as a psychological buffer so the negative traits from one sphere do not influence the overall view of the self.

In this period of change, adolescents begin to explore who they are, what they believe, and what they want. They are in the process of forming what Erik Erikson calls a *sense of identity*, a sense of a differentiated and distinct self that is the real inner "me."[30]

James Marcia describes four ways of establishing identity.[31] There are those adolescents, the majority, who explore new experiences and ideas, form new friendships, and make a commitment to values, goals, and behavior. They gain achieved identity through a process of exploration and commitment. On the other hand, some adolescents choose traditional values without even considering for themselves what they want to do with their lives. They face no crisis or conflict, because they do not want to deal with issues. This commitment without exploration is termed *identity foreclosure* to indicate that possibilities have been closed off prematurely.

A different path is taken by adolescents who experience a *moratorium*, or an exploration without commitment. This is essentially a crisis about what they want to do. They have ideas they explore, but they have not yet made a commitment to act. Finally, some adolescents experience *identity diffusion*, in which they can make no choices at all. They drift without direction.

One study found that adolescent boys who rank high in identity exploration come from families in which they can express their own opinions yet receive support from parents even when they disagree with them.[32] Boys are encouraged to be both independent and connected to family members. Adolescent girls who rate high in identity exploration come from families in which they are challenged and receive little support from parents who are contentious with each other. Girls may need this slightly abrasive atmosphere in order to pursue a heightened sense of individuality rather than follow the path of intensifying social relationships. However, these girls do feel connected to at least one parent.

In early to mid-adolescence, gender differences appear in self-esteem—boys have higher levels than girls do. Susan Harter speculates that in these years the ideal good looks that early teens strive for—tall, thin, willowy, large-breasted bodies—are almost impossible to attain so teenage girls devalue themselves for being unattractive.[33] Since girls, on average, do not get satisfaction from physical activity in sports, they are cut off from a major source of esteem when they devalue their bodies. As we will see in the next section, declines in self-esteem may also be related to feelings of pressure for gender conformity.

Level of self-esteem has implications for future adjustment as 57 percent of early adolescents with low self-esteem had multiple psychological and behavioral problems when assessed again in their twenties, and only 17 percent were problem-free.[34] Conversely, 56 percent of early adolescents with high self-esteem were viewed as problem-free, and only 17 percent had multiple problems.

Gender Identity

As teens begin to think more abstractly about their own qualities and wonder what others think of them, they wonder how well they meet society's standards for gender behavior. They may feel satisfied with their behavior or they may feel pressure to conform to others' standards of gender behavior. European American teens who feel satisfied their behavior meets cultural standards report self-esteem and social acceptance, whereas those who feel pressure for gender conformity report worries and lower self-esteem.[35] In African American and Latino early adolescents, the relationship with feelings about gender conformity are not so closely related to positive adjustment.[36] It is possible that these youth may be involved in exploring and forming their ethnic identity, and so are less psychologically involved in gender identity.

Although early adolescents are assessing gender conformity, their attitudes about gender roles, on average, grow more egalitarian and flexible from ages seven to thirteen.[37] At thirteen, they reach a plateau that lasts for two or three years, and at about age sixteen, adolescents become more traditional in their views of gender roles. This picture of average changes obscures different patterns of change, depending on children's own activities. Girls and boys who spend time in cross-gendered activities—sports and math for girls and reading and time alone for boys—have less traditional gender role attitudes and interests.[38]

Changes also depend on gender and parents' attitudes.[39] Boys in families with traditional values never adopt more egalitarian views. Boys whose parents have less traditional views of gender roles become more egalitarian, but at age sixteen, they take a sharp turn in the direction of more traditional values and come close to those boys reared in families with traditional values. At that age, the influence of peers' attitudes and the experience of romantic dating seem to affect their gender role attitudes more than parents' views.

Girls, in general, have more egalitarian and less traditional views of gender roles, perhaps because such attitudes permit them to participate in a wider array of enjoyable activities. Girls resembled their parents with less traditional values and never moved in the direction of adopting more traditional values in later adolescence. Girls with traditional parents become more egalitarian from seven to thirteen and at age seventeen, make only a slight shift in the direction of more traditional values.

Ethnic Identity

Just as early adolescents are exploring their personal qualities to form a sense of identity and evaluating their behavior in terms of gender typicality, many children include their ethnic group in defining who they are. Drawing on Marcia's dimensions of identity, Jean Phinney describes a three-stage model of ethnic identity formation.[40] In the first stage, children do not think about ethnic matters; they have no interest in examining their group's history and traditions. If children remain in this state, they show what is termed "identity diffusion," no exploration and no commitment. If children automatically accept others' views of their ethnic group without questioning, they are thought to show "identity foreclosure," commitment to an identity without exploration.

Most early adolescents enter a second stage, termed "moratorium," in which they explore their ethnic group's history and values. This can be a painful stage for some adolescents as they confront the group's difficulties of the past and the burdens of the present. As a result of active exploration, early adolescents integrate their personal experiences and their ethnic heritage and form a sense of achieved ethnic identity. With achieved identity is thought to come a sense of confidence and self-esteem. Recall the Chinese American and Mexican American early adolescents with positive ethnic identities who were able to maintain happy moods at times of stress.[41]

Longitudinal research has confirmed the four forms of ethnic identity and the general sequence of development from a diffuse state through exploration to achieved identity.[42] The research has indicated there is sometimes movement backward as well as forward. A small number of early adolescents abandon exploration and return to a diffuse state, perhaps because ethnic group status may not be uppermost in their minds. A significant number of those who have achieved identity recycle back for further exploration, perhaps because of new information or an upsetting experience.

The psychological effects of perceived discrimination and prejudice have been tracked in these years.[43] When early teens perceive discrimination, over time they show feelings of anger, aggression, and depression. When teens have nurturing, warm parents, good friends, and are successful in school, they show fewer effects of discrimination.

THE DEVELOPMENT OF SELF-REGULATION

Longitudinal studies that have followed early adolescents into their thirties and forties find adult impulse control is well predicted from behavior during this period.[44] So in this time of multiple changes, children are developing behaviors that predict future functioning. Still, not every impulsive act forebodes a future of impulsivity. Even the most responsible, dependable young teenager will engage in forbidden acts such as taking the car without permission—partly to test the limits, partly to savor the experience, partly to impress friends. How to distinguish an isolated forbidden act from a more serious problem with impulse control is a skill parents must develop.

Early adolescents' moral and prosocial reasoning advances in these years, and they are less likely to justify actions in terms of personal gain and conformity to others, and more likely to justify actions in terms of meeting others' needs and giving care.[45] Their prosocial behaviors increase as they are better able to understand other people and have greater empathy with their experiences. Parents are usually not the recipients of early adolescents' increasing helpfulness. Parents report no change in teens' helping or sharing work at home, and some parents report a decline in these years, perhaps because children spend more time away from home. In these years, helpful, sharing behaviors are often carried out on a regular basis in volunteer activities with youth or church groups.

PARENT–CHILD RELATIONSHIPS

Young adolescents spend about half as much time with parents as they did in the elementary school years.[46] Although there is less time together, parents remain major figures in children's lives.

Parents' Support

Numerous studies document the positive relationship between parents' support and caring and adolescents' cognitive, emotional, and social competence. A recent study included not only younger and older teens in the United States but samples in ten countries in Africa, Asia, the Middle East, Europe, and South America.[47]

In all these countries, teens' reports of parents' support—reflected in comments that parents cared for them, enjoyed spending time with them and talking to them, believed in them and thought they were important—were related to teens' social competence and initiative and to their lack of depression. In many countries it was also related to teens' avoidance of antisocial behavior. In the United States, fathers' support was more predictive of teens' social competence and initiative and mothers' support, more predictive of lack of depression. In most other countries, however, mothers' support was more predictive of both aspects of teens' behavior. Adolescents in other countries listed tangible gifts and financial provisions such as school fees as signs that parents love them, whereas American teens did not.

Studies of parent–teen closeness in ethnic groups within the United States reveal that early teens of European American, Mexican American, and Chinese American backgrounds are equally close to parents, with the exception that European American teens feel closer to fathers than teens in other groups.[48] Closeness, however, is expressed in different ways in each group. In European American families, early adolescents spend more one-on-one time with family members and in leisure time activities with them. Mexican American early teens spend time with parents, working with them and helping them. Chinese American teens spend more time studying each day than helping the family. European American adolescents' time with parents does not interfere with the substantial amount of time spent with peers, which is significantly more than teens from other cultures spend.

Parents' Respect for Early Adolescents' Self-Assertion and Autonomy

While parents' regulation of children's behavior has positive effects, as we discuss in the next section, parents' attempts to control children's private thoughts and feelings are related to early adolescents' feeling dejected and depressed. And not just in the United States. Early adolescents in countries around the world report common reactions of depression and sadness to parents' attempts to control their thoughts and opinions.[49]

With a growing sense of independence, early adolescents assert their desire for choice and self-determination. They argue to get their way about clothes, friends, and when they do chores and homework. They do not challenge parents' moral and social values or their rules about safety issues, but they redefine what parents think are moral and conventional rules for family behavior as matters that should be under their personal control, and they justify their beliefs on the basis of what other teens are doing. While teens disagree openly with parents, the disagreements result in angry relationships with parents in only 5–20 percent of families.[50]

Such behavior is not unique to middle-class, European American teens. Adolescents of Mexican American, Chinese American, and Filipino backgrounds with different beliefs about the authority given to parents and ages for increasing autonomy all report the same level of conflicts at home with parents.[51] The American cultural milieu seems to override families' belief systems so that youth from these ethnic groups behave like European American teens. Furthermore, the European American culture changes the beliefs and expectations with each generation of immigrant families so the beliefs become more like those of European Americans as well.

Parents and children agree that most of the time conflicts end because children follow parents' wishes. In only 18 percent of conflicts do parents follow children's requests, and joint discussion and decisions settle just 13 percent of the disagreements.[52] So in conflicts, children give in, and the relationship between parents and children remains solid.

Judith Smetana, who has investigated parent–teen conflicts for decades in many ethnic groups here and in countries around the world, has this advice for parents:[53]

1. Recognize that children accept parents' basic moral and social values and the need for safety and health rules; having their own beliefs is not a rejection of parents' values

2. Recognize that children's increasing desire for personal choice is part of the process of establishing their own identity and a coherent sense of self

3. Pick your battles and choose to disagree about the most important issues, letting the little things go

4. Give teens opportunities to talk about issues and their reasoning about them with calm and caring parents because such discussions promote decision-making skills; other research suggests that in early adolescence, warm support is most important in stimulating positive behaviors and in later adolescence, engaging in more dialogues about the reasoning process helps.[54]

Regulating and Monitoring Behavior

Research has shown that when parents monitor teens and know where they are, what they are doing, and who they are with, teens are less likely to engage in risk behaviors such as drinking, smoking, and delinquent activity.[55] It was long thought that parental knowledge came from observing and tracking children, but recent studies suggest parents' knowledge comes from adolescents' willingness to tell them what they are doing. This willingness is a part of a reciprocal relationship with parents. When parents behave in a warm, responsive way, children feel accepted and comfortable in sharing information so they are open with parents. When parents have knowledge, they can take effective actions to regulate behavior.

Parents and children agree that teens should share information in areas where parents have authority—namely on moral behavior and other health and safety issues.[56] Both parents and teens agree teens' telling parents how they spend their free time or their money is voluntary because these are personal matters. Early adolescents and their parents believe younger teens have a greater responsibility to disclose what they are doing than older adolescents.

Teens are more likely to disclose when parents are both warm and have clear standards for behavior, and when teens engage in few disapproved activities. Teens feel lying is wrong so they omit details and avoid topics rather than lie outright. Lying more often occurs when parents and teens have poor relationships, when families lack cohesiveness, when teens struggle with impulse control, and families set few rules.

Around the world parental knowledge and monitoring were related to low levels of substance abuse and antisocial activity.[57] It was mothers' knowledge that was particularly predictive of children's behavior. The authors speculate that at times of so many changes in early adolescents' lives, mothers' awareness of what is happening in children's lives is especially important.

Creating Mutually Responsive Dialogues with Early Adolescents

Teens consider parents their first source for information on sexual changes and sexual health. When mothers of fifteen-year-old girls were coached for two ninety-minute sessions to listen more, ask open-ended questions, encourage children to talk, and avoid lecturing, their communication skills increased.[58] Mothers practiced role-playing and applied the skills to discussing issues of sexuality and AIDS with their daughters. Mothers who were coached spoke less, asked more open-ended questions, and were less judgmental than were uncoached mothers. Teens of mothers who were coached did not talk more than teens of mothers who were not coached, but the former teens did feel more comfortable in talking to mothers about sexuality, and they did report more discussion about birth control than did the other teens.

Observing parents and their twelve-year-olds in problem-solving sessions over a two-year period, researchers found that when parents remained supportive and nurturant and persisted in positive parenting, even when dealing with resistant and

INTERVIEW
With Anne C. Petersen

Anne C. Petersen is senior vice president at W. K. Kellogg Foundation in Battle Creek, Michigan.

Her research interests center on adolescence; with John Janeway Conger, she is the author of Adolescence and Youth: Psychological Development in a Changing World.

What do parents of adolescents need to know?

The societal view of adolescents is negative. I collect cartoons, and they portray an extreme view of adolescents as having hormone attacks, being difficult, impossible.

This belief in our country that adolescents are difficult and want to be independent is one of the biggest pitfalls for parents. We know that, although adolescents want to be autonomous, they need parents. We know that young adolescents are argumentative, sometimes obnoxious. Parents throw in the towel, and that is the worst thing they can do. Adolescents need to know that parental support is there. There have been historical changes in the family, increasing the possibility for kids to be independent with cars and to have more time away from home; all these changes have exacerbated the trend toward independence and separation. Too much freedom is detrimental to adolescents' development.

Parents need to know that when you ask adolescents, especially young adolescents, who is most important to them, they say the parents, even if the parents are reporting conflict. We find, then, that parents are less positive about their adolescents than their adolescents are about them. Adolescents' off-putting behavior—telling parents to get lost because the adolescents are mature—is not really the message they want to send. They are asking for a little more space; they are asking for help in becoming autonomous and interdependent rather than independent.

Parents sometimes believe that they need to be their child's buddy, but that's not true. They need to be parents. They need to provide unconditional love, firm guidelines, and strong expectations.

Puberty and all the change that accompanies it is a difficult time for boys and girls, especially when they have to change schools. It seems to work slightly differently for boys than for girls. In general, boys seem less influenced by what is going on with parents, but basic support is pretty important. If parental support is not there, it is

negative teens, their children became more flexible, effective problem-solvers.[59] When parents avoided engaging in teens' negative overtures, teens' behavior eventually changed.

Promoting Gender Identity

Two clinicians urge parents to encourage less traditional attitudes and behavior for both boys and girls.

Mary Pipher, author of *Reviving Ophelia*, believes that, in the teenage years, girls lose their sense of themselves as individuals and become overfocused on the

very bad for girls. Those girls who have a lot of family conflict or lack support are the ones who become the most depressed.

How would you say your own research has influenced the way you rear your children?

I think it has changed a lot of things. That my daughter rebelled was a big shock. I remember vividly the day she refused to do something. There was no door banging, but she said she would not do something I had just assumed she would do. I immediately had the stereotypic reaction, "Oh, my heavens, what is going on here?" All of a sudden I realized that this was what I had been talking about for a long time. Knowing all the data, why should I be surprised that my kid goes through this too?

It helped a lot to know what could be effective in dealing with this. We had a family conference. What she was saying was, "How about taking my needs into account?" She was upset that we just assumed she would be a part of some activity. It is enlightening to realize that we don't treat an adult, a colleague, or a friend like that. It makes sense to change your behavior toward young adolescents. Well, we worked it out. There are still occasional lapses of communication, and that's where the problems really are. Somebody assumes that somebody else is going to do something, and there is either a conflict of schedules or wishes. But at least saying, "Yes, you are right, you ought to have an increasing role in family decision making" and have a forum within which to do it made a lot of difference to her. She did not have to explode. She could put her two cents in.

When there is a good reason, we change our plans to meet her needs. It is important for us to show that we do not need to be controlling things, that we do respect her views, that she does have a voice. I am sure if you were to ask both our children, they would say they do not have as much say as they would like. That is because we still do believe that we are the parents and there are some things that we need to decide.

We believe that it is important to let them see how we are thinking about things and to understand decision-making processes. So, we talk in the family about money and about vacation plans, and we really try to include them—not just out of respect for them to increasingly become a part, but also to let them see how we think about things so they have the benefit of knowing how adults make decisions. That seems to work pretty well.

needs, feelings, and approval of other people.[60] She urges parents to provide homes that offer both protection and challenges to help girls find and sustain a sense of identity. Parents need to listen to daughters and encourage independent thought and rational decision-making skills and to encourage friendships with boys and girls and a wide variety of activities so they develop a sense of identity based on their interests and abilities.

She also encourages altruism to counter the self-absorption that is characteristic of adolescence. Helping others leads to good feelings and to greater maturity.

Clinical psychologist William Pollack believes that boys are socialized from childhood to be strong and tough, aggressive and daring, to achieve status and power and to avoid the expression of feelings such as warmth and empathy. He believes that boys are forced to separate from parents too early and that, if they protest, they are ridiculed and shamed. He writes, "I believe that boys, feeling ashamed of their vulnerability, mask their emotions and ultimately their true selves. This unnecessary disconnection—from family and then from self—causes many boys to feel alone, helpless, and fearful."[61]

Pollack advises parents to get behind the masks that boys develop by (1) becoming aware of signs that sons are hiding their feelings, (2) talking to sons about feelings and listening to what they say, (3) accepting sons' emotional schedules for revealing feelings (boys may be slower than girls), (4) connecting with sons through joint activities that can bring parents and sons closer together, and (5) sharing their own growing-up experiences with their sons. "They need to be convinced, above all, that both their strengths and their vulnerabilities are good, that all sides of them will be celebrated, that we'll love them through and through for being just the boys they really are."[62]

Promoting Ethnic Identity

Parents of different ethnic backgrounds have all the parenting tasks that we have just discussed, and also have a powerful role in helping children develop a positive, affirming sense of ethnic identity.[63]

Parents serve as models for children and as sources of information about ethnic cultures and ethnic identity and ways to cope with discrimination and prejudice. Recall that many children in this age group worry about discrimination for their looks or behavior so even if children do not say anything, the possibility of discrimination is on their minds.

Single mothers of African American children use positive parenting and consistent limit-setting, and their children expressed self-esteem, positive sexual identity, and racial pride.

A program with single mothers of eleven-year-old African American children taught general parenting strategies and also included adaptive ways to develop racial pride by:[64]

- Weaving messages giving children feelings of importance and self-worth into daily interactions
- Teaching children about the difficulties and obstacles that exist for their racial group
- Focusing on ways to manage whatever barriers and discrimination children experience
- Focusing on ways to achieve success in activities

When mothers incorporated these messages in the context of warm, nurturing parent–child relationships and firm limit-setting and monitoring, youth expressed self-esteem, positive sexual identity, and racial pride. When early teens perceived mothers as being both nurturing and vigilant in monitoring behavior, then they were low in substance abuse and early sexual activity.[65]

When parents maintain ethnic traditions at home and encourage early teens to participate in cultural activities, then Latino youth are more likely to explore their ethnic identity.[66] When this socialization occurs in the context of parental involvement, low levels of harsh parenting and low levels of perceived neighborhood risk, then youth affirm that ethnic identity.

Neighborhoods help or hinder racial socialization efforts. Living in communities with strong ethnic identifications can protect children from the negatives effects of discrimination.[67] When neighborhoods are stable and contain a high percentage of people from the same ethnic group, then youth are more likely to affirm their ethnic identity. When neighborhoods are poor and subject to chaotic events, then youth are less likely to affirm their identity.[68]

Family Stressors That Interfere with Effective Parenting and Impact Children's Behavior

When parents cannot get along and disagree, early adolescents experience emotional insecurity that, in turn, impact children's psychological adjustment.[69] They become fearful, sad, angry, and noncompliant in behavior. When parents argue in the context of an otherwise satisfying marriage and stable family life, children's insecurity is reduced.

For some ethnic group parents, the experience of discrimination sets into motion a train of events that impact parenting.[70] In a longitudinal study in Georgia, mothers who experienced discrimination developed health problems and feelings of depression that impacted parenting. They were less warm, less able to avoid repetitious arguing, and were less vigilant in monitoring children. Thus, discrimination, experienced by 67 percent of the mothers, decreased their parenting skills.

Happy family times are important, because they provide a reservoir of good feelings that sustains all family members through times of conflict and crisis. Family life focuses so heavily on routine chores that outings often provide the best means for members to share fun. Family card games, mealtime rituals, and watching certain

VOICES OF EXPERIENCE

The Joys of Parenting Early Adolescents

"Seeing him care for younger children and babies is a great pleasure. He's a great nurturer with small children. He has endless patience." MOTHER

"He is a talented athlete, and his soccer team got to a championship game. He scored the winning goal, and when he took off with the ball down the field, I was very proud of him. It was a unique feeling of being proud that someone I had helped to create was doing that. He had felt a lot of pressure in the game, so to see how incredibly pleased he was gave me great joy." FATHER

"I enjoy the fact that she is very independent and makes up her own mind about things. She is not caught up in fads or with cliques, and I can trust her not to follow other people's ideas. The down side of that is that she resists some of my ideas as well." MOTHER

"I enjoy her sense of humor. She jokes about everyday events, and I laugh a lot around her." MOTHER

"I like that he does things I did, like play the trumpet. He started at the same age I did, and since he took it up, it has rekindled my interest and I started practicing again. This last weekend, we played together. He also brings new interests too. Because he likes sailing, I have started that and really like it." FATHER

"She is in that dreamy preteen state where she writes things. She wrote a poem about the difference between being alone and loneliness. She has a real appreciation of time on her own and how nice being alone can be. I like that because I had that at her age." MOTHER

"It's nice just being able to help them, feeling good because they are being helped out and benefited." FATHER

"It's nice to see her being able to *analyze* situations with friends or with her teachers and come to conclusions. She said about one of her teachers, 'Well, she gets excited

TV programs together can also provide a sense of sharing and solidarity that adolescents report as highly meaningful to them. Making time for fun and games in a busy schedule may save time in the long run as conflicts and arguing decrease.

RELATIONSHIPS WITH SIBLINGS

As in early years, parents' relationships with their early teens influence siblings' relationships. When parents have warm relationships with children, brothers and sisters have warm relationships with each other.[71] Siblings can be especially important as they are on an equal plane, and they can understand each other better than parents sometimes understand children. Thus, siblings can give positive support, offer advice in dealing with problems, and serve as daily companions. When parents are divorced, siblings may be the most constant features in each others' lives.

and she never follows through with what she says, so you know you don't have to take her seriously.'" MOTHER

"I really enjoy being in the Scouts with the boys. Once a month we go on a camping weekend, and I really look forward to that." FATHER

"I was so impressed and pleased that after the earthquake, he and a friend decided to go door to door and offer to sell drawings they made of Teenage Mutant Ninja Turtles. He raised $150 that he gave for earthquake relief. I was very proud that he thought this up all by himself." FATHER

"I was very happy one day when I found this note she left on my desk. It said, 'Hello!!! Have a happy day! Don't worry about home, everyone's fine! Do your work the very best you can. But most important, have a fruitful life!!!' I saved that note because it made me feel so good." MOTHER

"He enjoys life. He has a sense of humor. He's like a butterfly enjoying everything; eventually he'll settle in." MOTHER

"He's very sensitive, and his cousins two years older than he is ask his advice about boys. They may not take it, but they ask him even though he's younger." FATHER

"It's very rewarding to see them in their school activities. My daughter sings in the school chorus, and I enjoy that, and my son is in school plays." FATHER

"I am very pleased that she is less moody now than she used to be. We 'used to refer to her lows as 'Puddles of Frustration,' but she has got past that now." MOTHER

"Well, they have their friends over, and we have ping-pong, pool, cards, and we stressed having these things available. I enjoy playing all these games with them." FATHER

As in earlier years, when parents play favorites, siblings are more likely to have conflicts. Aggression is more likely when unsupervised siblings in stressed families act out their angry feelings with each other. Siblings can also encourage deviant behavior in younger early teens.[72] When younger adolescent boys have warm relationships with their older brothers who engage in delinquent activity, they are likely to join them in these activities. With girls, the quality of the relationship has a different impact. Younger sisters who have warm relationships with their older sisters are less likely to copy their older sisters' delinquent behavior. Brothers and sisters are also likely to emulate older siblings' substance use and sexual behaviors.

Although they may copy negative behaviors, children learn positive skills in sharing and negotiating differences, and these carry over into relationships with peers. Children with positive sibling relationships have positive peer relationships and also do better academically in school.

PEER RELATIONSHIPS

Children continue to choose friends whose interests are similar to their own, and they benefit from the greater intimacy that comes from sharing experiences and feeling understood.[73] Friends have as many conflicts as non-friends but they work out differences in mutually satisfying ways. Best friends are even closer and disclose more to each other. They are supportive and loyal. With all the benefits of friendship, it is not surprising that early adolescents with friends are more socially skilled, more confident, and more academically successful than those who lack friends.[74]

Many teens want to be popular, accepted, and well liked.[75] Research suggests, however, that social success and satisfying friendships do not depend on being broadly popular and sought after. Thirteen-year-olds who considered themselves accepted and liked, even though not rated by schoolmates as popular, had as many friends and were as sought after and socially successful a year later as children designated as popular. The personal feelings of social acceptance may have come from friendships or activities outside school or at church. Whatever the source, children who felt accepted reached out to others and were involved in satisfying relationships. Those early adolescents who had the most difficulties were those

About 80 percent of early teens have access to computers and use them to communicate with peers and to post personal information.

who felt unaccepted and in fact appeared to lack connections with others at age thirteen. They tended to feel angry and retreat from social contact so their problems continued over the next year and intensified.

The Internet now provides ways for teens to relate to peers.[76] Approximately 80 percent of early adolescents have access to computers and use them for e-mail, instant messaging (IM), to enter chat rooms, and to post personal information. Patterns of use vary among teens. When teens communicate with already existing friends via IM, they become closer to their friends. Closeness does not increase for those who are primarily communicating with strangers. While self-disclosure over the Internet was easier for socially anxious teens than face-to-face disclosure, socially anxious teens were less likely to use the Internet than socially confident peers. Those who did use it, communicated more online than non–socially anxious teens.

Parents' worry about their children's friends has some justification.[77] Like siblings, friends can draw a child into deviant behaviors. In addition, with close friends children sometimes engage in what is termed "co-rumination" (dwelling on one's own depressive symptoms over and over); such discussions increase the closeness between friends. While both boys and girls engage in such co-rumination and become closer with friends, girls' co-rumination predicts depressive and anxious feelings whereas it does not predict negative feelings in boys.[78]

In these years, children form cliques, small groups of five to nine members who choose each other as friends.[79] In the beginning of early adolescence, teens spend most of their time in same-sex groups. Girls spend more time than boys talking, and boys more time than girls playing contact sports. Group activities provide sociability and a sense of belonging, promote exploration of the self and achievements, and provide opportunities for learning and instruction. Both self-exploration and learning activities give children the kinds of experiences they need to form a stable sense of identity.

Unfortunately, bullying and harassment continue in these years, and many children fear going to school because of hostile teasing and physical aggression. A longitudinal study analyzed students' reports of being bullied—called names, laughed at, pushed, and robbed—and found that in sixth grade, equal numbers of boys and girls were bullied.[80] More than half the students (57 percent) were sometimes or frequently bullied and only 43 percent, rarely bullied. By the end of eighth grade, boys were the more frequent victims, and bullying had declined to 31 percent being frequently or sometimes bullied.

What did not change over the three years were the emotional reactions to being a victim.[81] Victims and sometimes victims felt unsafe at school, and over time victims developed depression. Witnessing bullying of others impacted students, as those who saw it reported feeling angry and humiliated. Those students who felt only they were being bullied reported the greatest increases in anger and humiliation. They felt like lone targets. We see here that bullying has negative consequences for even those who just witness it.

Unfortunately in our technological society, bullying can reach a wider audience via the Internet. Bullies can use websites and personal pages to spread harmful, hurtful messages and hound early adolescents even when they are not in school. In a survey in 2007, one in three teenagers reported they had experienced some form of harassment via the Internet, and the Centers for Disease Control and Prevention is funding studies on electronic aggression among youth.[82] When children tell parents, parents can help to find solutions to the problem. Unfortunately, some children are so upset they tell no one, and take self-destructive action instead. We discuss later how parents can help teens deal with the problem.

TASKS AND CONCERNS OF PARENTS

Parents' tasks expand as they become not only caregivers and interpreters of the social world but also models for an increasing number of behaviors in the world outside the home. Parenting tasks include the following:

- Continuing to be the single most important influence in the child's life
- Modeling self-controlled, responsible behavior
- Being sensitive to the child's needs and feelings
- Monitoring children's activities and behavior
- Communicating information and values on important but difficult-to-discuss topics such as sexuality, substance use, and discrimination
- Making time, being available for conversation when the child is ready to talk
- Giving children more decision-making power
- Providing support as children undergo many physical changes and social challenges, so home is an understanding place
- Sharing pleasurable time

This section describes how parents use active listening skills and behavioral methods to work effectively with young adolescents. It also emphasizes parenting strategies that help children develop initiative and problem-solving skills so they can resolve intense feelings and engage in activities and peer relations that bring good feelings.

Communicating with the Noncommunicative Early Adolescent

We have talked about how important it is to talk with children, but sometimes children come home, go to their rooms, and shut the door. When they emerge for meals or snacks, they say little, answering any question with only a word or two. They do not talk about what they are doing, thinking, or feeling. Children do not seem unhappy, but parents feel they do not know them anymore. Parents may feel hurt when children say little to them but talk for hours on the phone to their friends.

Parents can do many things to promote conversation. First, they can be good models of communication by talking about their own day, friends, and plans. Second, they can ask for comments: "How's school going?" or "What are you and Jenny doing tonight?" If the child answers with one word or two, parents should drop the conversation and wait for another time. Third, they can comment on nonverbal behavior or body language: "Looks like you had a good day today," or "You look happy." Teens may not follow up with any comments, but parents have made an effort.

Once teens begin to talk, parents can listen and reflect teens' feelings, avoiding criticism, judgments of the child or others, blame, or sarcasm. Reflecting the teenagers' feelings helps teens to continue to talk. If teens talk about problems they are trying to work out and want to discuss them, parents can ask open-ended questions and listen.

There are many "don'ts" to the process of encouraging conversation. Don't force the child to reveal her feelings. Don't give advice once the teen has begun to talk. Don't rush to find the solution. Don't hurry to answer questions; delaying an answer can stimulate thinking.

Adele Faber and Elaine Mazlish describe useful techniques when teens begin to talk about discouragement or frustration.[83,84] They suggest showing respect for the child's struggle with comments such as "That can be hard," "It's not easy," or "Sometimes it helps when . . ." then giving a piece of information: "It helps, when you're rushed, to concentrate on the most important item." Teens are free to use the information or not. Parents have to watch their tone of voice so the information does not sound like advice.

Faber and Mazlish also present interesting alternatives to saying "no." Because teens are sensitive to control and may not like to ask if they often hear "no" in response, having other ways to respond is useful and will encourage greater talkativeness. Suppose a teen wants his mother to take him to the store at 5:30 while she is cooking dinner. Instead of giving a flat "no," she can say, "I'll take you after dinner." If she cannot do it, she can say, "I'd like to be able to help you out, but I have to get dinner on the table and get to that meeting at 7:00." A parent can leave out the "no" and just give information. For example, if a teen asks for an extra, expensive piece of clothing, the parent can say, "The budget just won't take it this month." If there are ways the teen can get the item, the parent can pass that information on: "If you want that as a birthday present at the end of the month, that would be fine."

Using Mutual Problem-Solving to Handle Disputes

In the early adolescent years, conflicts with children over a variety of everyday issues require resolution. When parents use mutual problem solving, listening to children's feelings and sending I-messages, parents respect children's views and their individual needs, and at the same time work with the problem situation so both parents and children feel their needs are met.

Knowing that early teens are most likely to argue about issues they believe should be under their control and most likely to accept parents' requests for safe, healthy, and considerate behavior, parents can explain their requests in terms of these reasons. When parents insist on firm limits on computer and Internet use, requiring that computers be kept in family rooms and monitoring teens' use of them, early adolescents internalize parents' messages and follow their rules.[85]

Health and safety issues should be of paramount importance. In observing how parents both protect children and at the same time find alternative ways to achieve what children want, children learn how to protect their safety and get what they want.

Parents may want to issue orders with the only reason, "Because I said so," but teens need to learn how to reason about these issues, and parents' explanations of their reasoning gives children a model to copy in making decisions. Parents should expect they may have to return to problem behaviors several times, but solutions are more likely to be effective when children have more input.

Encouraging Children's Problem-Solving Skills

We have noted that children's brains are maturing in these years, and planning skills are developing. These skills are important because early teens are often at a great distance from parents and must solve problems on their own.

Problem solving requires the child to define the problem, become aware of his or her feelings and others' feelings and reactions, generate solutions to the problem, choose a solution and carry it out, then evaluate the results, starting over if necessary. Problem solving requires that parents remain calm so that children have opportunities to think and develop their skills. Parents can ask open-ended questions and encourage the child to continue to think of solutions.

Myrna Shure has developed "I Can Problem Solve" programs to teach children from ages four to thirteen to learn to find their own solutions to the problems that bother them.[86] Combining many of the communication skills discussed in this chapter and in Chapter 4 with an emphasis on having children think of alternative actions, these programs help parents avoid highly emotional battles that interfere with good communication and effective solutions.

To solve problems, Shure believes, children must (1) understand others' feelings and underlying motivations, (2) generate new solutions to the problem, (3) anticipate the consequences of each potential solution, and (4) plan behaviors in advance to avoid potential problems. Shure recommends working on only one or two of these skills at a time. Because they are often locked into their own thoughts and feelings of the moment and have trouble seeing different options for action, early adolescents need special help with all of the steps.

If the problem involves them, parents send an I-message that expresses their needs and feelings; otherwise, parents are supportive, refusing to dictate or force solutions. Shure recommends doing this with questions such as "How will the other person feel or react?", "What will happen if you do that?", "What is your plan?", "How will that work?" If children have no answers, parents do not push but instead let children figure the problem out, provided no danger is involved. Where parents have concerns about safety or the necessity of solving the problem now, they engage in mutual problem solving, as described in Chapter 5.

Shure's method helps early adolescents develop the independence and ability to plan that are so necessary for children of this age. Developing initiative has similar aims.

Promoting Initiative

Based on his research with early adolescents and their families, Larson believes that, for positive development in these years, early adolescents must develop initiative, "the ability to be motivated from within to direct attention and effort toward a challenging goal."[87] An important quality in itself, initiative also serves as the foundation for important qualities such as creativity and leadership. Teens, however, experience effort and challenge in activities in which they lack interest, such as schoolwork, and they lack effort and challenge in activities that interest them, such as activities with friends. The task is to find activities that both interest and challenge teens.

Ronald Dahl, who has studied brain and emotional development in adolescence, believes channeling the passions of adolescents into positive activities that engage teens and enable them to use their passions for the benefit of all is an important societal task.[88] Larson believes that structured voluntary activities, pursued over time, are the engaging, stimulating activities adolescents need to develop. The experience of setting goals, organizing activities (often in collaboration with peers), and accomplishing goals leads to the development of independence, decision-making skills, and self-control. These, then, carry over to other activities. For example, participation in voluntary activities in tenth grade predicted an increase in grade point average in later grades. Participants in outdoor adventure programs gained in assertiveness, locus of control, and independence. Furthermore, positive changes continued for as long as two years after the program ended.

Larson speculates that voluntary activities, broadly structured by adults but with direct responsibility given to children for organizing and carrying out the activities, "provided an environment of possibilities for planful action, for initiative."[89] Children develop a language and way of thinking that gives them a sense of agency, of being able to accomplish what they set out to. "Children and adolescents come alive in these activities, they become active agents in ways that rarely happen in other parts of their lives."[90]

Voluntary school activities draw on the problem-solving skills that Shure encourages. Adult leaders in the activities raise open-ended questions that prompt teens to *analyze* and think through the consequences of actions. They are supportive and nonjudgmental. Research shows that when Little League coaches adopt an encouraging attitude, give information on how to improve, provide positive reinforcement for effort as well as for accomplishments, and stress fun and self-improvement rather than winning, players report more enjoyment in playing and greater self-esteem, and they are more likely to sign up for the team the next year than are players whose coaches are not so supportive.[91] Interestingly, positive coaches learned these skills in one three-hour session, and the techniques had the biggest effects on boys with low self-esteem.

Promoting Positive Peer Relationships

Peer acceptance involves both a cognitive understanding of others and oneself and appropriate peer behavior.[92] When children have difficulties—either being too inhibited or too aggressive—problems may exist in how they view people as well as how they behave. Aggressive children, for example, are quick to see others' negative behavior as intentional and therefore worthy of retaliation.[93] Part of the way to help such children is to encourage them to examine their interpretations of others' behavior and adopt more benign views of others' intentions. When they view negative behavior as accidental, children reduce their aggression.

Similarly, shy, inhibited children should be encouraged to review their positive traits and identify the positive contributions they can make to social activities. Peer acceptance requires outgoing behavior that shows respect for others and oneself by listening to others, being open and friendly, having a positive attitude, initiating interactions, and avoiding aggressive, negative behaviors.[94] When children are shy at school and lack friends, parents can encourage friendships away from school— on athletic teams, in artistic activities, or in community or church groups. Parents' highlighting of children's positive behaviors such as kindness and caring with others also increases children's confidence.

On the basis of interviews with adolescents about violence in their schools, James Garbarino and Ellen deLara make many suggestions for parents in combating school bullying and harassment.[95] They advise parents to talk to children about the kinds of negative experiences they have in their school, even if they have not happened to them because many have witnessed them. Talk to other parents about their views about bullying and form a group to talk to school officials, as described in Chapter 9.

The Internet enables bullies to track rather than trail victims into their homes and to spread rumors far and wide. When children report bullying to parents, and many do not want to talk about it, parents encourage them to save whatever record they have that indicates the source of the bullying. Reports can be made to Internet and phone providers who can follow up and take action because such activity usually violates contracts with them. If bullies come from schools, parents can contact the school to determine what they can do. Consider working with other parents to form a Youth Charter, as described at the end of the chapter.

Handling School Problems

Because all the changes of this period sometimes overwhelm early adolescents, parents' support can help teens identify the source of school problems and a constructive plan to remedy it. Active listening and mutual problem-solving sessions are appropriate tactics. Helping teens organize their study area and study schedules, getting tutoring as needed, or arranging for children to attend Homework Clubs can be potentially useful, depending on the particular circumstances. Computer use has helped some children improve reading skills and grade point averages over time so there may be computer programs or games that can help.[96]

Some schools have organized computerized ways parents can get daily information on students' assignments, work turned in, and grades on tests. They can also be useful in helping parents help children keep up.[97] If, however, parents use the information to criticize and berate students or demand immediate changes, the actions are not likely to help children succeed.

Helping children develop an incremental theory of learning can help. Reminding children of previous successes, reminding them that with any area, the more they learn about it, the smarter they get. Encouraging effort and commenting on gains increase confidence. So parents clearly have many ways to help young adolescents deal with various issues. Table 10-1 reflects many of the strategies this section has discussed.

■ **T A B L E 10-1**
TEN STEPS TO HELP CHILDREN DEVELOP THEIR ABILITIES

1. Understand children's special skills and areas of difficulties.
2. Provide appropriate levels of stimulation that neither bore nor overwhelm children.
3. Teach children that their biggest limitations are the ones they place on themselves and what they can do.
4. Help children learn to ask questions and seek answers.
5. Help children identify what really interests and motivates them.
6. Encourage children to take sensible risks even though there is no guarantee of success.
7. Help children take responsibility for their behaviors—both positive and negative.
8. Teach children to tolerate and deal with frustration, delay, and uncertainty.
9. Help children understand other people's feelings and points of view.
10. Remember that, in helping children realize their abilities, what counts is not financial resources, but the way you interact with children and the kinds of experiences children have in everyday life.

Adapted from Wendy M. Williams and Robert J. Sternberg, "How Parents Can Maximize Children's Cognitive Abilities," in *Handbook of Parenting,* 2nd ed., ed. Marc H. Bornstein, vol. 5: *Practical Issues in Parenting* (Mahwah, NJ: Erlbaum, 2002), pp. 169–194.

PARENTS' EXPERIENCES IN FACING TRANSITIONS

Many parents report that they do not feel ready to have teenage children. The childhood years have gone so fast, it seems too soon to have a daughter with a mature figure and sons with bulging muscles and low voices. Parents also find their children's sexual maturity disconcerting. They are surprised to see sons with *Playboy* magazines and hear girls talking about the sexual attractiveness of boys.

Their adolescents' mood swings and desires for greater freedom throw parents back to some of the same conflicts of the toddler and preschool years. The elementary school years were stable because parents could talk and reason with children, but now they are back to dealing with screaming, crying, moody creatures who sometimes act young but at the same time want more freedom. Parents may feel that they themselves have grown and matured as parents, able to handle crises, only to find themselves back at square one, yelling and feeling uncontrolled with their children.

Though it is difficult to give up certain images of themselves and their children, parents must do so. Children are no longer children; they are approaching physical and sexual maturity. They are not psychologically mature, however, so they still need the guidance parents can give. Parents often have to give up images of themselves as the perfect parent of an adolescent. They recall their own adolescence, the ways their parents handled them, and in many cases they want to improve on that. Sometimes they find they are not doing as well as they want and have to step back and see where they went off track.

As they mature, early adolescents gain the physical glow and psychological vitality that comes from feeling the world is a magical place. At the same time, parents are marching to or through middle age. It is hard to live with offspring who present a physical contrast to how parents themselves feel. Furthermore, the world is opening up to adolescents just as some parents feel it is weighing them down. Parents have heavy responsibilities, often taking care of aging parents as well as growing children. Parents feel they have little time and money at their own disposal, yet they live with young people who seem to have a great deal of both.

Thus, parents have to be careful not to let resentment of the freedom and excitement of their teenagers get in the way of being effective parents. As parents develop reasonable expectations of the amount of freedom and responsibilities their children are to have, they must be careful not to restrict or criticize out of envy.

To highlight the greater freedom and control children have, Ellen Galinsky calls this the *interdependent stage* of parenting.[98] Parents have several years to work through these issues before their children are launched. When parents can become more separate from their children—can be available to help them grow yet not stifle them in the process—then parents' and children's relationships take on a new richness.

SUPPORT FOR PARENTS

Parents often feel overwhelmed by cultural forces that do not support their efforts to rear children well. For example, the media bombard teens with messages about sexuality that conform to few families' values. William Damon has developed the Youth Charter program to combat cultural forces that make rearing children more difficult.[99] Parents can initiate this program to organize teachers, clergy, police, and others who care about children to develop community practices and standards that promote children's healthy development. Parents' child-rearing efforts serve as a bridge to connect children to community activities at school, with peers, and in the neighborhood. Communities have to be organized to support parents' goals.

Damon outlines a way of organizing concerned adults to identify children's specific needs and work together to find ways to meet them. Standards and expectations are drawn up for children and for the community so that parents and concerned citizens and youth can control teen drinking, vandalism, and early pregnancy and build a community more supportive of children and families. Damon writes,

> Beneath the sense of isolation that has divided our communities, we all share a deep well of concern for the younger generation. If we can find a way to tap into that well, child rearing can become the secure and fulfilling joy that it should be, rather than the risky and nerve-wracking challenge that it has become for too many parents.[100]

MAIN POINTS

In early adolescence, sexual development
- begins and takes years to complete
- is triggered by biological, social, and psychological factors, and, in turn, triggers psychological reactions in young people
- is related to increases in emotional intensity

Early adolescents
- begin to think more abstractly and analyze themselves and other people
- have daily mood changes related to family interactions and school events
- experience stress that spills over from home to school, and from school to home
- are more involved than previously in peer relationships and cliques

A sense of identity
- depends on exploring a variety of alternatives and making a commitment to values, goals, and behavior
- can be foreclosed if teens make a commitment without exploring their options
- is not achieved when early adolescents experience a moratorium, or explore without making a commitment
- is achieved in youth of racial/ethnic groups when parents are warm and supportive, teach and model racial pride, and discuss ways to deal with mistreatment when that occurs

Peers
- provide positive feelings of acceptance and support, but can also bully and cause negative feelings of victimization
- are sought for different kinds of relationships by boys and girls—with girls wanting to talk and express their feelings and boys wanting to engage in group activities with little self-revelation

In this period, parents
- continue to be sensitive caregivers who connect with children and respect their views
- provide role models of ethical, principled behavior and provide accurate information on topics such as sexual behavior and substance abuse
- monitor children's activities and behavior
- give more decision-making power to adolescents
- use mutual problem solving to resolve conflicts

Problems discussed center on
- developing problem-solving skills and initiative
- controlling emotional reactions and dealing with social difficulties
- failures in communication

Joys include
- observing accomplishments in physical, artistic, and intellectual endeavors
- feeling good because the parent has helped the child in a specific way
- observing the child's capacity to take responsibility for self
- emotional closeness

EXERCISES

1. See the video or DVD of the movie *Akila and the Bee* and compare socializing experiences in the three ethnic groups depicted in the movie. What are the roles of parents and community in the different groups? How do adults and the community socialize children for success in the different groups?

2. In small groups, take a survey of students' school experience in the years when they were eleven to fifteen. What size was the school and what grades were included? Have each student rate that school experience from 1, very dissatisfied, to 7, very satisfied. Tabulate the average ratings for each kind of school setting and note whether students were happier when older students were included.

3. Break into small groups and have students list the kinds of experiences that increased their self-esteem in early adolescent years. With input from the whole class, write suggestions for parents who want to increase the self-esteem of their early teenagers.

4. Divide into pairs. In the first exercise, have one partner take the role of a parent who wants to talk to his or her early adolescent about appropriate sexual behavior for the teenager, while the other partner takes the role of the teen who wants more freedom. Then reverse roles, and have the second "parent" try to convey values about appropriate uses of substances in adolescent years to the second "teen." In doing this, practice active listening and sending I-messages.

5. Discuss with other students the importance of peers in their early adolescent years. Did you experience peer pressure? Did parents let you spend time with your friends? What do you think are reasonable rules with regard to time spent with peers? At what age do you think dating should begin? Why that age?

ADDITIONAL READINGS

Damon, William. *The Youth Charter: How Communities Can Work Together to Raise Standards for All Our Children.* New York: Free Press, 1997.

Elkind, David. *The Hurried Child.* Cambridge, MA: Perseus Books, 2001.

Garbarino, James. *See Jane Hit: Why Girls Are Growing More Violent and What Can Be Done about It.* New York: Penguin, 2006.

Pipher, Mary. *Reviving Ophelia.* New York: Ballantine, 1994.

Pollack, William. *Real Boys.* New York: Holt, 1998.

Shure, Myrna B., with Israeloff, Roberta. *Raising a Thinking Preteen.* New York: Holt, 2000.

Strauch, Barbara. *The Primal Teen.* New York: Random House, 2003.

CHAPTER

11

Parenting Late Adolescents

IN THE NEWS

New York Times, March 15[1]: Schools across the country include immigrant children and provide both education and assimilation into the culture. See pages 337–338.

Test Your Knowledge: Fact or Fiction (True/False)

1. There is no one way for teens of different ethnic groups to harmonize ethnic identity and identity with the larger American culture.
2. Teens' decision making improves when they are in the presence of their peers because they pool their ideas and come up with the best solution.
3. More than half of teens of European American, African American, and Latino/a backgrounds have fears of being discriminated against for some personal quality.
4. Having school success in the early grades reduces the likelihood of substance use in adolescence.
5. Forty-five percent of aggressive boys have symptoms of depression as well.

Late adolescents continue to mature physically, intellectually, emotionally, and socially. They use parents as consultants and coaches as they move farther away from home in activities, schooling, and jobs. How do parents provide support and at the same time help teens develop the skills that enable them to avoid the possible risk behaviors that accompany teens' greater freedom?

Late adolescents are becoming comfortable with all the changes they have experienced and they look to the future. They have after-school jobs and participate in community activities where they make significant contributions. They begin to date and have romantic relationships. They find mentors who join parents as guides to growth. Parents, too, are adjusting to their children's many changes. They sense their child's impending departure from home with mixed feelings.

PHYSICAL DEVELOPMENT

Throughout the adolescent years and into the twenties, brain development continues in the prefrontal cortical area, with increasing connections between cells in that area and between the prefrontal area and other parts of the brain.[2] Executive thinking and planning grow as well.

Boys' physical growth continues, but girls have attained most of their adult height. We describe teens' sexual and substance use behavior here and discuss regulating them in later sections on self-regulation and parents' concerns.

Adolescent Sexual Activity

Adolescents engage in self-stimulating sexual activities such as fantasizing and masturbation before they become sexual with a partner.[3] We know little about these activities, as children are reluctant to talk about them and many feel guilty. Masturbation, which sometimes begins before puberty, is a frequent source of orgasm for boys but not so frequent a source for girls.

Estimating precisely the percentage of adolescents who have same-sex sexual encounters is difficult.[4] Encounters occur prior to adolescence in playful activities or mutual exploration with friends. Of sexually active youth, about 9 percent of boys and 5 percent of girls report same-sex contact, and about half of these contacts are with heterosexual youth. Only about 2 percent of adolescents identify themselves as gay or lesbian in these years.

Sexual activity with a partner of the opposite sex usually proceeds from holding hands to kissing, to touching breasts and genitals with clothes on, then with clothes off, and finally intercourse. A 2001–2002 national sample of fifteen- to seventeen-year olds revealed the following sexual behaviors:[5]

	Boys	Girls
Kissing	89%	82%
Being intimate (activity not specified)	65%	47%
Touching partner's genitals	56%	40%
Having intercourse	42%	33%
Having oral sex	40%	32%

Teens overestimate the number of teens who are having intercourse. About 60 percent of girls and 66 percent of boys agree with the statement, "Waiting to have sex is a nice idea, but nobody really does." Yet about two-thirds of girls and 58 percent of boys were waiting. Of those who had intercourse, only about 40 percent currently had a sexual relationship. As can be seen, boys are more sexually active than girls. Ethnic groups vary in behaviors, with European Americans more likely to report oral sex, and African American and Latino youth having intercourse at younger ages than European Americans.[6]

Of sexually active teens, 85 percent of girls and 65 percent of boys report they are able to talk to their partners about what sexual activities they enjoy. Even though partners talk to each other, about 20 percent of boys and 30 percent of girls report pressure to do sexual things they do not want to do, and a third of sexually active boys and girls say they have been in relationships in which they felt things were moving too fast sexually.

Many fifteen- to seventeen-year-olds report big concerns about sexual health issues—51% about getting pregnant, 46% about getting HIV/AIDS, and 45% about getting a sexually transmitted disease (STD).[7] Almost all girls and boys believe they can discuss birth control with their partners, but they feel less able to discuss STDs with partners. While teens worry about pregnancy, HIV/AIDS, and STDs, they do not always use condoms. Of sexually active teens, 49 percent of girls and 30 percent of boys say they have had intercourse without a condom, and 22 percent of girls and 6 percent of boys said they did not use a condom the last time they had intercourse. Of sexually active girls in this sample, 12 percent say they have been pregnant.

Both teens and parents are so focused on pregnancy as a problem that they ignore other dangers.[8] Forty-seven percent of boys and 30 percent of girls believe that oral sex is safe sex. They underestimate the number of teens who contract STDs and the dangers STDs present in terms of other illnesses and later pregnancy complications.

Eighty percent of teens want more information on sexual health issues, particularly about birth control and about the topic of STDs—how to protect themselves and tell if they have them. And most importantly, they want to know how to talk to doctors about sexual health matters. Almost half said they wanted help to know how to resist pressures they feel to have sex.

Sex education classes are a big source of information, but teens also turn to parents, friends, and the media. Knowing that adolescents want more information, parents can provide accurate written materials for reading at home, raise questions in these areas on the basis of news items, and be alert to any hesitant questions teens may ask. They can also inform doctors that teens may want to talk about these issues. Listening and responding in sensitive ways helps teens ask questions.

Substance Use

Table 11-1 gives the rate of substance use found in a national sample studied longitudinally at the University of Michigan. In early adolescence there are few gender differences in substance use, but by the twelfth grade, boys are much more likely

■ **TABLE 11-1**
SUBSTANCE USE REPORTED IN A NATIONAL
SAMPLE OF ADOLESCENCE IN 2004*

	10th Graders	12th Graders
Cigarettes		
% used in last 30 days	15%	24%
% used daily	8%	15%
Alcohol		
% used last 30 days	33%	47%
% drank heavily in last 2 wks	20%	29%
Marijuana		
% used last 30 days	15%	20%
% used in last year	28%	34%
Cocaine		
% used in last year	3%	4%

* Jerald G. Bachman et al., *The Education–Drug Use Connection: How Successes and Failures in School Relate to Adolescent Smoking, Drinking, Drug Use, and Delinquency* (New York: Erlbaum, 2008).

to use substances.[9] With regard to ethnic differences, Native American teens are found to have the highest rates of substance use and Asian Americans, the lowest. Of the other ethnic groups, European Americans report the highest use, followed by Latinos/as and African Americans.[10]

Eighty percent of parents report concerns about children's drug use, and 74 percent have concerns about alcohol use, the substance teens use most frequently.[11] Alcohol use gradually rises in adolescence, especially among students having academic difficulties. It continues to increase in the college years,[12] gradually decreasing during the twenties.

Alcohol is of concern not only for its role in causing car accidents which are the leading cause of death and injuries in these years, but also because it increases the occurrence of high-risk sexual behaviors.[13] Fifty percent of the boys and girls in the national sample already cited feared they would do more sexually than they planned because of drinking and drugs, and 25 percent of sexually active teens said they had done more than they planned and were afraid they might have gotten pregnant or contracted an STD.[14]

Substance use also decreases learning, with long-term consequences for students.[15] A longitudinal study following African American students from ages six to thirty-three found that, compared to an infrequent/non-user group carefully matched on early demographic and behavioral characteristics, those who used marijuana more than 20 times by the age of seventeen were more likely to drop out of high school, and in their thirties, more likely to continue marijuana use, be unemployed, and parenting a child outside of marriage. While girls were less likely to fall into the category of frequent marijuana use, when they did, the negative outcomes were the same as for boys.

Longitudinal research on substance users reveals that difficulties in elementary school precede substance use in high school.[16] Doing poorly academically in elementary school, being retained, and having deviant behaviors that result in suspension are characteristic of those who will use alcohol and drugs in high school. The inability to meet school demands may increase frustrations already present, whereas meeting school demands may give a sense of competence and confidence that act as protective factors against substance use.

The researchers conclude, "Early academic interventions, additional support for low achieving students, and a focus on personal growth rather than social comparison could be some of the most effective ways to decrease substance use and delinquency when students reach adolescence."[17] This prescription could well apply to decreasing the rate of teen pregnancy, as many girls who go on to have babies as teens perform poorly academically and have few friends in the early elementary grades. (See Chapter 14.)

Qualities of parents and homes contribute significantly to substance avoidance. Teens are less likely to use substances when they come from families in which parents are well educated, compatible with each other, monitor their children's activities, and promote the importance of schoolwork.

INTELLECTUAL DEVELOPMENT

Adolescents' growth in attention, memory, abstract reasoning, and organizational skills enables them to plan activities and make decisions more effectively.[18] Although teens' abstract reasoning and problem solving have improved, they may have individual theories about the material at hand,[19] and the theories often affect their learning and thinking. Increasing knowledge is not accomplished by just feeding new facts into a receptive learner. First, one must dispel inaccurate theories and then present new facts when the person is receptive and ready to absorb the information.

Teens' decision making is effective when teens are calm and not emotionally aroused, and when they are not subject to peer pressure.[20] Laboratory research shows, however, that when adolescents and college students are in the presence of peers and friends, they take significantly more risks in video game playing and make more risky decisions in solving hypothetical dilemmas involving cheating or shoplifting than when alone.[21] Risk-taking and risky decision making decrease as adolescents mature and become young adults whose risk-taking is the same whether they are or are not in the presence of peers. That the laboratory research accurately reflects teens' greater risk-taking is seen in the greater number of auto accidents teens have despite driver education and training.

Researchers believe it is essential for teens to learn to resist peer pressures in decision making, and to recall that the judgments they make on their own may often be better guides to action than group recommendations when the two conflict. Parents can help teens gain confidence in their own assessments and to rely on them first in group activities.

VOICES OF EXPERIENCE

What I Wish I Had Known about Late Adolescence

"I wish that I had got my children involved in more family activities. When they were mostly through adolescence, I heard a talk by a child psychiatrist who said that often when teenagers say they don't want to do something with the family, at times you have to insist because they do go along and enjoy the event. I wish I had known that sooner, because I accepted their first 'No,' when I perhaps should have pushed more." MOTHER

"I had always heard they look for their own independence, their own things to participate in, but until you really experience it with your own, it's hard to deal with it. When you read about independence, it sounds like it's carefully planned out. When it actually happens, all of a sudden they want to do something that they have never done before and which you firmly believe they have no idea how to do. It can be driving for the first time or suddenly announcing they want to go somewhere with friends. I knew it was going to happen, but exactly how to handle it myself and handle it with them so they got a chance to do something new without it being dangerous has been a challenge to me." FATHER

"I wish that I had known that I had to listen more to them in order to understand what they were experiencing. I sort of assumed that I knew what adolescence was about from my own experience, but things had a different meaning to them. What was important to me was not that important to them, and I wish I had realized that in the beginning." MOTHER

"I wish I knew how to raise children in adolescence when you have traditional values and many of the people around you do not. It's very hard to do here in California compared to the South, where we came from. There, everyone reinforces the same values, and it is a lot easier for parents." MOTHER

"I wish I had known to be more attentive, to really listen, because kids have a lot of worthwhile things to say and you come to find out they hold a lot of your viewpoints." FATHER

"I wish I had known it was important to spend time with the children individually. We did things as a family, but the children are so different, and I think I would have understood them better if I had spent time with them alone." MOTHER

SCHOOL

The qualities of schools and teachers are especially important as schools become larger and increasingly impersonal.[22] When schools have a mastery attitude toward learning, helping children find ways to improve their performance, emphasizing diverse goals for students, providing support as well as making demands, students perceive teachers as respectful and friendly, feel attached to schools, and engage in fewer delinquent behaviors than those students in schools emphasizing academic competition and an ability orientation to learning. In the latter schools, more delinquent behaviors are carried out, often, by students who are not performing well.

Schools also contribute to teens' academic performance by having very early start times just when teens have later sleep onsets.[23] Early start times contribute to teens' sleep deprivation that, in turn, leads to poorer school performance. We discuss ways to handle this in the section on parenting tasks.

Adolescents' arguments with authorities and their insistence on more personal choice can complicate teens' adjustment at school.[24] Just as teens want parents to respect their autonomy and give them more freedom, they want schools to respect their rights to dress as they please, have hair in the style they prefer. As with parents, they are often willing to conform to conventional and moral rules that are as necessary at school as they are in society. When teens have conflicts with teachers and rules, they may need parents' help in negotiating ways to gain greater personal choice in the structured school setting.

Because teens want respect, teachers who respect them, engage them in learning, and encourage persistence at times of frustration promote student achievement.[25] Such teachers are especially important for those underachieving students, defined as getting grades significantly below what would be expected on the basis of students' ability tests. Compared with students whose grades are appropriate to their ability, underachieving boys and girls have lower opinions of their abilities, lower feelings of competence, less involvement in academic and extracurricular activities, lower educational and occupational aspirations, and more involvement in heterosexual relationships.[26]

Students of ethnic minority groups often become increasingly frustrated with school because they anticipate a future of limited occupational opportunities due to lack of funds for further schooling.[27] Some students are motivated to increase their grades so they will be able to compete. Some students are further discouraged and alienated from school because of discrimination from teachers and peers. We discuss this topic further in the section on ethnic identity.

Involvement in extracurricular activities and sports can increase students' academic motivation because students derive feelings of self-esteem and confidence from these pursuits, and so persist at frustrating academic tasks.[28]

When parents understand that children's school difficulties can be due to many factors outside their control, parents can problem-solve with children and listen to their concerns and feelings. Parents can work with schools and their child to get the most effective educational plan for that child.

WORKING

Most adolescents work during the school year, even if only occasionally at babysitting. The effects of working depend on the context of the work.[29] Some adolescents make valuable contributions to their families by working and giving money to their parents. They may feel increased self-esteem at being able to help their families.

Some adolescents work to escape the frustrations of school. They work increasingly long hours, and their motivation for school decreases further. These adolescents may earn steady income but they are at risk for developing deviant behaviors such as smoking, drug use, and minor delinquency behavior. Their failure to get further education limits their occupational future. If these students are able to avoid substance use and if they gain motivation to return to school, they may do well in the future.

Work seems most beneficial for those teens who work a few hours a week and still participate fully in school and extracurricular activities. Those who balance school, extracurricular activities, and work were more likely to complete a four-year college than nonworking peers and peers who spent long hours at work.

Parents can serve an important role for teens by monitoring the balance of work and school so teens get the benefit of both acvtivities.

EMOTIONAL DEVELOPMENT

Ronald Dahl has described the strong emotional reactions teens have, and the slower development of the emotional and cognitive skills to manage the feelings.[30] Thus, teens need a strong system of social support while they develop these skills. Teachers, parents, and coaches provide monitoring and are resources as teens integrate feelings and actions.

Extracurricular and community activities bring feelings of competence and confidence.[31] When teens engage in a variety of activities, they develop many different skills that predict success in academic courses and in relationships with peers. Engagement in these activities is also related to lower levels of substance use.

While some have feared that children are overscheduled, a recent review of youth activities finds that extracurricular and community activities do not absorb all children's free time.[32] Those European American and African American teens who engage in these activities are more likely to eat meals with parents and discuss issues with them. Teens report higher self-esteem, academic achievement, and lower substance use.

Self-esteem does increase in these years,[33] and depressed feelings decrease.[34] This greater happiness appears to derive from late adolescents' broader perspectives. They interpret experiences in a new light and as a result become more accepting both of family and of themselves. From grades eight to twelve, girls who express their true thoughts and feelings with friends and feel comfortable being themselves have greater increases in self-esteem than those who are less expressive with peers.[35] Expressing feelings and being authentic in relationships may show similar positive outcomes for boys as well.

THE DEVELOPMENT OF THE SELF

Mid-adolescents speak of the many different "me's"—the self with my mother, the self with my father, the self with my best friend, the self with my boyfriend.[36] Seeing their behavior change with circumstances intensifies mid-adolescents' concerns about "the real me." They feel they express their true selves when they discuss their inner thoughts, feelings, and reactions to events; they express false selves when they put on an act and say what they do not mean. Teens report acting falsely (1) to make a good impression, (2) to experiment with different selves, and (3) to avoid others' low opinions of them. When they believe they have parents' support, adolescents can voice their opinions and express their true selves.

In late adolescence, teens come to terms with contradictory qualities by finding a more general abstraction that explains the contradiction. For example, they explain changes in mood—cheerfulness with friends and discouragement with parents—by describing themselves as moody. They also come to accept the contradictions as normal—"It's normal to be different ways with different people." As they observe their changing behaviors, late adolescents note the situations in which they show the traits they value and in which they feel support, and they come to seek out these situations.

Gender Identity

When teens achieve physical maturity, they often experience increased pressure to meet gender-role expectations, termed "gender intensification."[37] As we saw in the last chapter, boys become more traditional in gender-role interests at age 16, and girls do also, although they remain more egalitarian than boys.

However, looking at boys' and girls' interests and academic performance provides mixed evidence about change.[38] Boys have greater self-rated competence in sports from first grade through high school. In school subjects, boys rate themselves as having greater math competence but by twelfth grade, boys and girls rate themselves as equally competent. In addition, recent research shows that math performance is similar for boys and girls from grades two to eleven; with a concluding statement in *Science*, "Our analysis shows that, for grades 2 to 11, the general population no longer shows a gender difference in math skills."[39]

Behavioral differences in aggression and in depression are found, with boys being higher on aggression and girls higher on depression (discussed later in the chapter). Even within the range of everyday personal qualities, boys' and girls describe themselves differently. Boys' self descriptions emphasize action, and getting ahead in an organized way; they see themselves as more daring, rebellious, and playful in life than girls and, at the same time, more logical, curious, and calm. Girls see themselves as more attuned to people than are boys (more sympathetic, social, considerate, and affectionate) and more emotionally reactive (more worrisome, more easily upset, more needing of approval).[40]

Most girls in junior high and high school, when surveyed, reported at least one experience of sexual harassment (a demeaning joke, touching, comment on one's appearance), academic sexism (negative comments about math, science, or computer abilities), and athletic sexism (negative comments about physical and sports skills).[41] Such experiences occurred usually once or twice.

Boys were the most frequent perpetrators of sexist remarks, but girls also made sexist comments about other girls. Teachers were the most common source of academic sexist comments. Parents too made demeaning comments, with fathers more likely to do so than mothers.

Girls who are unhappy with traditional gender roles are more likely to perceive discrimination than other girls.[42] Latina and Asian American girls reported less sexual harassment than European American or African American girls. The researchers speculate that if boys were surveyed, they, too, would report gender discrimination, particularly if they have less traditional interests.

Gay/Lesbian Identity

Researcher Ritch Savin-Williams describes changes in attitudes about gay, lesbian, and bisexual youth. In the 1970s, they were identified as a distinct group.[43] In the 1980s and 1990s, researchers and the public viewed them as psychologically vulnerable, prone to depression and suicidal thoughts. In the 1990s the public became more understanding and accepting of individuals with same-gender orientations and provided more supports for teens with gay, lesbian, and bisexual orientations, establishing Gay–Straight Alliance support groups, offering counseling in two thousand schools. As a result of greater approval, gay/lesbian teens have increasingly come to think of themselves as like other teens, as adolescents with personal identities who also happen to engage in sexual activities with same-sex partners rather than as having a "gay" or "lesbian" identity.

Failure to arrive at a sexually based identity may also derive from adolescents' having a longer and more fluid process of labeling themselves. In one study following women for ten years, 73 percent of bisexual women, 83 percent of women who gave themselves no sexual label, and 48 percent of lesbians switched their sexual identification during that period, with many bisexual and unlabeled women going back and forth between these two labels.[44]

Around 42 percent of adult men who reported same-sex contact during adolescence did not continue that activity in adulthood, and about half of the gay/bisexual youth report cross-sex sexual experiences in adolescence.[45] Thus, it is not easy to tell who will continue with same-sex activity and incorporate sexual preference into their sense of identity. In general, teens who restrict themselves to same-sex contacts in adolescence are most likely to continue with a preponderance of same-sex activities as adults.

Many adolescents with same-sex attractions get support, but many do not. Members of teen groups in high school report homophobic attitudes and occasional name calling of same-sex attracted peers.[46] Boys are more negative toward same-sex attracted boys than girls are. There is a tendency for attitudes toward lesbians to be less negative. Although some groups have homophobic attitudes, others are supportive of same-sex attracted peers.

Teens also receive criticism from parents and siblings. Teens who have an early awareness of same-sex preferences and whose behavior is gender atypical receive more early criticism from parents, but once they tell parents of their preferences, they gain more support from them than those who do not disclose their preference to parents.[47] Disclosing teens have less internalized self-hatred and less fear of parents' finding out than the one-third of teens who do not tell parents of their sexual preferences because they fear their reactions.

Several factors influence how families respond to the disclosure of same-sex preferences.[48] When parents have had warm relationships with children in the past, have been sensitive to children's needs yet encouraged their autonomy, teens feel high self-esteem and parental support after disclosing. Parents' acceptance of teens' orientation appears a powerful factor in protecting teens from psychological problems. Family members' abilities to discuss emotional feelings, respect each other, and remain a cohesive group influence the whole family's adaptation. Teens with same-sex preferences are most likely to have psychological difficulties and engage in alcohol and drug use when they experience many areas of stress—with peers, parents, and academic problems at school.[49]

Savin-Williams believes we need to understand better the strengths that enable teens to experience psychological tensions and difficulties in adolescence and yet become loving partners and parents as adults.[50]

Cross-Gender Identity

We know less about this group than we would like. A very small group of children and adolescents have a very strong identification with the opposite gender.[51] As children, they dress and play as members of the opposite gender, want to have friends of that gender, and sometimes insist that they are that gender. As adolescents and young adults, they may insist on living as the opposite gender as well and often express a persistent discomfort with the physical characteristics of their assigned gender and a wish to change them.

Those who persistently act and dress like the opposite gender and feel uncomfortable with their assigned gender are diagnosed with gender identity disorder, sometimes termed identity gender dysphoria.[52] Boys more frequently receive the diagnosis than girls. Adult follow-up of twenty-five girls who received this diagnosis at about age eight found that sixteen of the twenty-five were classified as heterosexual, two as bisexual, four as lesbians, and three continued to receive the diagnosis of gender identity disorder. So a child can have marked cross-sex interests and activities, and still have a heterosexual orientation in adulthood.

Ethnic Identity

Adolescents continue to explore their ethnic identities, achieving a sense of identity toward the end of the decade. The process of identity achievement is a fluid one that depends on many factors.

Many teens who have immigrated from another country switch the ethnic labels they apply to themselves from one year to the next in high school, sometimes using a pan-ethnic label such as Chinese or Asian, and sometimes using an American label such as Asian American.[53] Teens were more likely to use pan-ethnic labels such as Chinese or Vietnamese when they were first-generation immigrants who knew their heritage language.

Experiencing discrimination prolongs the exploratory stage for some teens.[54] Teens continue to reflect on the meaning of being a member of their ethnic group.

Teens who report high levels of perceived peer and adult discrimination report lower levels of self-esteem and depressed feelings.[55] Feeling support from large numbers of their ethnic group in the neighborhood and at school encourages identity achievement.[56]

Longitudinal research following Native American adolescents for a three-year period reveals that teens maintain a high level of self-esteem that increases over the adolescent years.[57] When they feel social support from the community around them, Native American teens not only have a high level of personal self-esteem, but also have a strong bicultural identity that reflects both Native American and European American values.

Studies of African American and Mexican American adolescents in schools where they were the major groups and had positive status found that all students formed a positive ethnic identity, but they differed in the degree to which they valued and identified with the broader American culture.[58] *Blended bicultural* students positively identified with both the majority and their own ethnic group. For example, they saw themselves as African and American and saw no conflict between the identities. *Alternating bicultural* students identified with the majority culture when at school or at other places, but primarily identified with their own ethnic group. A third, smaller group were termed *separated* students, as they did not identify at all with the majority culture, which they felt rejected and devalued them. Among African American students, slightly over half were classified as blended biculturals, about a quarter as alternating biculturals, and 17 percent as separated. Among Mexican American students, about one-third were classified as blended biculturals, almost two-thirds as alternating biculturals, and only 2 percent as separated.

Although a positive identification with both cultures is thought to be important for personal adjustment, the three groups of students did not differ on measures of self-concept, academic grades, and level of anxiety. Thus, there appear to be three pathways to integrating the experience of having two cultures, and the pathways all seem equally related to measures of effectiveness.

THE DEVELOPMENT OF SELF-REGULATION

Children's ability to regulate their feelings and behavior continues to foster academic and social competence, but in these years it has health consequences as well. Accidents, assaults, and self-injury are the leading causes of death and injuries, and substance abuse contributes to all three outcomes.

Adolescent self-regulation, however, is based on experiences in past years, and on many factors in the present age period. Teens are most likely to behave impulsively and use substances when they have:

- Been slow to develop behavioral regulation in the years from three to fourteen[59]
- Had academic difficulties in school from the early years[60]

- Low self-esteem[61]
- Lack positive relationships with parents[62]

Factors in the adolescent years that increase high-risk behaviors include:

- Move to a new community with loss of friends and familiar school[63]
- Friends who encourage high-risk behaviors[64]
- Spending long hours at work[65]
- Siblings who engage in high-risk behaviors[66]
- Living in neighborhoods in which there is much deviant behavior[67]

Teens are better able to regulate their behavior when they feel self-esteem from positive activities,[68] spend time with parents,[69] and attend church.[70]

Religious activities are positive factors in teens' lives because they provide a network of relationships with parents, friends, and adults outside the family that are supportive to teens, and they provide a shared vision or goals that increase teens' empathy and altruism.[71]

When all family members participate in religious activities and have warm relationships with each other, teens feel free to think about religion, ask questions, and bring up puzzling issues. Parents listen and give their thoughts on the issues so family members influence each other.[72]

Religious activities have a positive influence in collectivist cultures as well. Indonesian Muslim adolescents' religious involvement positively predicts their academic achievement, social success, self-esteem, emotional regulation, and prosocial development.[73]

PARENT–CHILD RELATIONSHIPS

Although parents see less of their adolescents, the dimensions of parenting that predict competence in the preschool years continue to predict adolescent competence, reflected in self-reliant, independent behavior and in the capacity for meaningful relationships with others.

Attachment

As teens mature and explore more and more of the world, parents remain a secure base to which to return, especially at stressful times. In these years, there is a gradual shift in the balance of power as parents cede teens greater autonomy in actions and decision making. Two qualities are thought to foster a successful parent–teen partnership: (1) the ability to communicate with teens and (2) the ability to allow teens to seek independence while still having a strong relationship with parents.[74]

Parents who are willing to listen to teens have a greater understanding of their children and a greater sensitivity to their needs; teens feel greater support and security. In turn, secure teens are more willing to open up and communicate with parents about their worries and feelings so a very positive process of interaction is established. Teens who have insecure–preoccupied attachments report many symptoms that others close to them do not know. Teens with insecure–dismissive attachments fail to communicate with anyone.

Securely attached teens and their parents are more easily able to engage in problem solving to deal with issues of autonomy, sometimes compromising, sometimes getting one's own way. Anger in these families occurs less often, and when it does, it stimulates discussion to overcome differences and restore harmony.

When teens have insecure–preoccupied attachments with parents, both teens and parents become trapped in angry conflicts, and teens are less successful in establishing autonomy. A negative form of interaction begins in which teens' anger triggers parents' anger, which, in turn, increases teens' anger. While there is some decrease in this pattern at the end of adolescence, these teens take this angry form of interaction into young adult relationships with partners.[75]

Styles of Parenting

Diana Baumrind's typology of parenting styles continues to predict effective functioning in these years. *Authoritative* parents have strong commitments to children and balance demands with responsiveness to children's needs: "Unlike any other pattern, authoritative upbringing *consistently* generated competence and deterred problem behavior in both boys and girls, at *all* stages."[76] Children from authoritarian homes are less skilled, less self-assured and curious, and more dependent. Children from indulgent homes are less mature, less responsible, and more responsive to peer pressure. Those raised in indifferent homes where parents are not understanding, committed, or demanding are most likely to be impulsive and involved in substance abuse.

While research with large groups of adolescents shows that authoritative parenting has positive benefits across all ethnic groups in the United States and in countries around the world, authoritarian parenting has negative outcomes in European American families but is associated with positive features in African American and Asian American families perhaps because these groups combine strict control with warmth and closeness rather than distance that is associated with control in European American families.[77]

After being partners for many years, most parents can work together to parent teenage children. Still, almost 50 percent say that arguments over teens' behavior is the biggest source of their disagreements.[78] When parents disagree with each other and become negative with children, teens are more likely to engage in impulsive and noncompliant behaviors such as cutting school and using substances.[79]

Ethnic Differences in Emotional and Behavioral Autonomy

Cultures and ethnic groups in this country vary in their timetable for granting teens autonomy. European American families have a timetable for independent actions such as "spending own money as he/she wishes," which is earlier than that of Asian Amerian adolescents and their parents.[80]

Furthermore, cultures vary in their expectations of how responsive teens are to families' needs. Teens in Mexican American families are expected to make sacrifices for their families. Asian American and Latin American families express strong values and expectations that they will respect, assist, and support their families, but in everyday life, "Adolescents from all ethnic backgrounds reported fairly similar relationships with their families and friends."[81]

Dealing with Discrimination

About 64 percent of European Americans, 57 percent of African Americans, and 70 percent of Latinos/as have "somewhat" or "very big concerns" about being discriminated against because of their race, ethnicity, or sexual orientation, and these percentages are similar for boys (62 percent) and girls (69 percent).[82] As we saw in identity development, girls, teens in ethnic-racial groups, and teens with sexual minority preferences all experienced discrimination in these years.

What can parents do? Having open relationships with children enables teens to tell parents what is happening in their lives so teens and parents can problem-solve specific upsetting incidents. As we saw with sexual minority youth, parents' acceptance and support was a main protective factor in insulating children from psychological problems because of others' cruelty and can be useful in all situations of discrimination.[83] The program in Chapter 10 is useful in suggesting that parents focus on helping children feel good about themselves and their ethnic group and find ways to manage barriers and discrimination and achieve their goals.[84]

Serving as Consultants

A parent serves as a reliable resource and consultant for children in areas of importance not only by providing factual information and values, as described in Chapter 10, but also by helping teens develop the confidence to carry out effective behaviors. In addition to giving information, parents are available for conversations about sexual behaviors, jobs, career goals, relationships, and anything else teens want to talk about.

RELATIONSHIPS WITH SIBLINGS

Family values and emotional atmosphere influence the quality of sibling relationships. When family values emphasize family closeness, caring, and support, as in Mexican American families, then adolescent siblings spend a lot of time with each other and are daily supports to each other. Relationships are especially close in same-gender pairs, and when children are close in age.[85]

When family relationships are characterized by hostile angry feelings—either parent–parent, parent–child, or sibling–sibling pairs—the hostility seeps through the whole family system, and all members come to resemble each other in negativity.[86] Furthermore, siblings have a tendency for noncompliant, deviant behavior. Older siblings' substance use serves as an example for younger siblings even when economic, social, and family variables are controlled.[87] So there is something very powerful about the sibling example. It can be a protective or risk factor, depending on the older child's example.

PEER RELATIONSHIPS

Teens spend more time with friends, and their relationships with peers differ from those with parents because friends relate to each other on an equal basis; friendships are voluntarily chosen and are often transitory. Teens' peer relationships occur at several levels—there are close and best friends, relationships in small groups or cliques as described in the last chapter, relationships in crowds, and opposite-sex peers in dating and romantic relationships.[88]

Friendships

Adolescents report that their relationships with friends provide intimacy, companionship, and understanding, whereas relationships with parents provide affection, instrumental help, and a sense of reliability.[89] Intimacy increases because friendships involve more self-disclosure, expression of feelings, and support for friends as needed.[90] Friends are expected to tell each other their honest opinions and to express satisfactions and dissatisfactions with the other person. Friends also have to learn to resolve conflicts as they arise. Friendships promote the development of social skills that, in turn, enrich friendships. Intimacy in friendships is related to adolescents' sociability, self-esteem, and overall interpersonal competence.

As teens move into high school, they are likely to join crowds. While crowds can be rigidly structured, inviting only certain people in, then limiting their contact with outsiders, surveys find that two-thirds of teens shift from one group to another between the tenth and twelfth grades. Often the shift is to a similar group—from brains to nerds or druggies to burnouts. Toward the end of high school, teens become less interested in crowds as they form more firm personal identities and pursue their own interests.[91]

In addition to fun and pleasure, peer relationships can include pressure and conflict as well. Cliques and crowds and even best friends can pressure each other to do things that teens feel reluctant to do (e.g., drinking). Conflicts are a daily occurrence in close relationships—an average of eight a day in one survey. In that survey, conflicts were most frequent, in descending order, with mothers, friends, romantic partners, siblings, and fathers.[92] Teens were more likely to negotiate and compromise with friends and romantic partners than with parents and siblings. Conflicts do not sever the relationships with friends.

Dating

Friendships set the stage for dating and romantic relationships.[93] Adolescents learn how to be close to same-sex peers and solve conflicts, then they get to know opposite-sex peers in friendship groups, moving to group and single dating, and finally to romantic relationships. Romantic relationships are usually intense and brief. Because there are almost no studies of same-sex dating, we discuss only heterosexual dating here.

While parent–child attachments have been considered major determiners of the quality of dating and romantic relationships, recent work indicates that the quality of dating relationships is more closely related to the quality of peer friendships. When asked to describe attachment, care received, and affiliation in relationships with parents, friends, and romantic partners, adolescents' perceptions of their relationships with romantic partners were related to their perceptions of their relationships with friends but unrelated to their perceptions of relationships with parents. Parents influence the quality of peer friendships, and the nature of the friendships in turn affects dating and romantic relationships.

By the time teens graduate from high school, most, though not all, have dated. Dating gives practice in developing feelings of trust and enjoyment with the opposite sex and provides the basis for later romantic attachments.[94] Intimacy, support, and companionship are major satisfactions in dating. As with friendships, romantic relationships often involve intense conflicts, which sometimes trigger feelings of sadness and loneliness. Many teens feel that resolving conflicts brings couples closer together, and so conflicts have positive value.

Teens are most likely to postpone sexual activity when they have close relationships with parents and have positive activities they enjoy.[95] About 40–50 percent of teens have their first sexual experiences in these years, often in romantic relationships but sometimes not. When girls have their first sexual experiences earlier than their peers, then they are more likely to suffer from depression, especially if the relationship is dissolved and involved little emotional commitment.[96] Having

"The quality of parental relationships influences teens' relationships with friends, but it is the quality of teens' friendships that reduce their relationships with romantic partners."

first sexual experiences at the normative time or later presents no increased risk of depression for girls. Boys do not appear subject to depression following first sexual experiences.

First sexual experiences change family relationships. Teens' relationships with parents become more distant, and parents and children share less time together in joint activities.[97] Teens also have increased problem-focused interactions with parents. The greater distance between parents and children is related to ongoing sexual activity. When parents remain close to teens and give them room to grow, sexual activity is less likely to continue.

TASKS AND CONCERNS OF PARENTS

In this age period, parents remain supportive caregivers who also grant their teens greater autonomy. Parenting tasks include:

- Being available, responsive caregivers who listen to children
- Serving as models of responsible behavior
- Continuing to monitor and enforce safety rules while supporting and accepting their children's individuality
- Communicating information and values in an atmosphere of open discussion
- Serving as consultant to children as they make important decisions
- Allowing children to separate in an atmosphere of acceptance

The problems encountered during adolescence relate to physical and emotional functioning, social behavior, and family interactions. We now discuss how parents help their children deal with these problems.

Parents worry about health and safety issues because they lack direct control to ensure children's well-being. They must rely on modeling healthy behaviors, having healthy family routines, and monitoring teens so they avoid high-risk behaviors.

In the next few sections, we focus on sleeping and eating problems, early sexual activity, drinking, and anger and depression.

Promoting Healthy Sleep Habits

Many factors contribute to adolescents' getting less sleep in these years. Teens' circadian rhythms change so they fall asleep later. High schools have earlier start times so teens have to get up earlier.[98] High school assignments require more time to complete so teens stay up later. Electronic devices such as TVs, computers, ipods, and cell phones, especially when in the bedroom, encourage teens to stay up later.[99]

Establishing healthy sleep habits are important not only to promote healthy functioning at school and at home, but also to lay down healthy habits because sleep patterns in adolescent years tend to persist into adulthood.[100] For example, when fourteen-year-olds watch TV extensively, they are more likely to have sleep problems at ages sixteen and twenty-two. When they reduce TV watching at age fourteen, they have fewer sleep problems at sixteen and twenty-two.

The emotional atmosphere of the family is an important predictor of teens' sleep. Just as in early years, eating family meals together predicts more sleep each night—each additional hour spent eating together weekly is associated with an additional hour of sleep weekly.[101] Reducing family conflict reduces sleep problems.[102] Those children who live in families with conflict in late childhood and early adolescence are more likely to suffer sleep problems at age eighteen.

Research indicates that when parents supervise and insist teens get a healthy amount of sleep, teens get more sleep.[103] Teens may object that it should be their personal choice when to go to bed, but parents' insistence on health issues is persuasive.

Promoting Healthy Eating Habits

Teens' social life and food preferences combine to reduce the amount of healthy food teens eat. Skipping breakfast to rush to school, eating at fast-food restaurants or buying high-calorie fatty foods at lunch cafeterias, and getting home late for dinner and eating a frozen meal are cause for concern. When the standard teen diet is combined with lack of exercise, it is not surprising that about 30 percent of teens are overweight.[104]

Parents focus on establishing positive habits that ensure good nutrition. They encourage healthy eating by serving nutritious food at family meals, having only healthy food in the house for snacks, and arranging family routines and outings that involve walking, biking, or sports activity. Parents can encourage teens to become cooks or active participants in family meal preparations.[105]

With teens' busy schedules, problem-solving situations may be needed to figure out how families can have four or five dinners together each week, how teens can make healthy choices at fast-food restaurants, and how they can include exercise in their schedules.

Eating Disorders   In these years, three kinds of eating disorders first appear and require immediate medical and psychological help. They are anorexia nervosa (extreme thinness because of calorie restriction or purging; less than 1 percent of the population), bulimia nervosa (engaging in binge eating and then purging; (1–2 percent of a community sample), and eating disorders not otherwise specified that includes binge eating and all other eating behaviors that do not meet the strict requirement of anorexia nervosa and bulimia nervosa (about 3 percent of people).[106]

People with eating disorders are at risk for developing other medical problems such as cardiac and neurological problems as well as depression and substance abuse, so parents should always get professional help. If they have doubts about the needs for treatment, parents can go and explain their concerns and get guidance.[107] Many forms of treatment are available with cognitive-behavioral therapy, family therapy, and medications available to arrive at treatments that will address teens' needs.[108]

VOICES OF EXPERIENCE

The Joys of Parenting Late Adolescents

"It's fun to see them discover things about themselves and their lives. The older ones have boyfriends, and I'm seeing them interact with them." MOTHER

"Sometimes the kids have friends over, and they all talk about things. It's nice to see them get along with their siblings as well as their friends. It gives you a good feeling to see them enjoying themselves." FATHER

"I felt very pleased when my son at sixteen could get a summer job in the city and commute and be responsible for getting there and doing a good job." MOTHER

"I like it when they sit around and reminisce about the things they or the family have done in the past. They all sit around the table, saying 'Remember this?' It's always interesting what they remember. This last summer we took a long sightseeing trip, and what stands out in their minds about it *is* funny. They remember Filene's Basement in Boston, a chicken ranch where we stopped to see friends. One father took the Scouts on a ski trip. They got stuck in the snow on the highway for hours, and the car almost slid off the road. He said, 'Never again.' I said, 'Don't you *realize* that because of those things, the boys will probably remember that trip forever? You have given them wonderful memories.'" MOTHER

"I really enjoy her happiness. She always sees the positive side to a situation. Things might bother her from time to time, but she has a good perspective on things." FATHER

"I really like to see them taking responsibility. Yesterday they had a school holiday, and I was donating some time at an open house fundraiser. They got all dressed up and came along and helped too. The older one coaches a soccer team of

Promoting Later and Protected Sexual Activity

Parents want to prevent all the difficulties that come from unintended pregnancies, STDs, and HIV/AIDS, and they have been succeeding.[109] In 2007, the percentage of teens who have had sex declined 12 percent from 1991. Condom use increased from 1991 to 2007. Still, there are worries. Sexual risk behaviors increased from 2005 to 2007, contributing to the 34 percent increase in HIV/AIDS cases diagnosed in teens from age fifteen to nineteen, and a 6 percent increase in gonorrhea. Since 2005, there has also been a rise in the teen birth rate.

The very parenting behaviors that encourage social and psychological competence in teens also predict postponing sexual activity—namely, a warm, close relationship with mothers and mothers' willingness to talk about their values of postponing sexual activity.[110] As we noted, close relationships and shared activities with parents delay the onset of sexual relations and decrease sexual activity after first encounters.

four-year-olds, and the younger is a patrol leader in the Scouts, so they both have responsibility for children." MOTHER

"I enjoy that she is following in the family tradition of rowing. I rowed in college, and my brothers did, my father and grandfather did, and she saw a city team and signed up. She does it all on her own and has made a nice group of friends through it." FATHER

"I can't believe that she has had her first boyfriend and it worked out so well. They met at a competition, and he lives some distance away, so they talk on the phone. He has a friend who lives here, and he comes for a visit sometimes and does lots of things with the family. We all like him, and it is nice for her to have a boyfriend like that." MOTHER

"The joys are seeing them go from a totally disorganized state to a partially motivated, organized state. You can see their adult characteristics emerging." FATHER

"I enjoy seeing my daughter develop musical ability, seeing her progression from beginning flute to an accomplished player who performs, and seeing how much pleasure she takes in her accomplishment." MOTHER

"I enjoy his maturity. He's so responsible. He tests us, but when we're firm, he accepts that. I'm real proud of him because he looks at the consequences of what he does." FATHER

"I enjoy his honesty and the relationship he has with his friends. He is real open with his feelings, and his friends look up to him. He's a leader." MOTHER

"He's not prejudiced. His best friends are of different ethnic groups. People trust him and like him because he's real concerned about people." FATHER

Most successful sexual education programs have common elements that parents can use as guides for their behavior.[111] Programs include information about pubertal physiological changes, maturation, and sexuality, interpersonal skills so teens can assert their own beliefs, and giving information on contraceptive devices and their availability.

As noted earlier, warm relationships with parents, having available information on safe, responsible sexual activity, and opportunities to talk about it help teens delay sexual activity, and have safe sexual relations when they do engage in it.

Discouraging Substance Use

Earlier in the chapter, we noted that elementary school success and warm relationships with parents serve as protective factors against high school substance use. In addition, parental monitoring discourages use. A large study of Dutch teens and their families finds that teens drink less when parents do not drink and do not make alcohol available in their home, and when parents have specific rules about not drinking and enforce these rules.[112] Conversely, when parents drink, make alcohol available in the home, and are permissive about teens' drinking, then teens drink more.

If parents suspect teens have a drinking problem, they should seek professional help quickly and be included in the treatment, as research does show that parents' behavior affects teens' drinking.

Helping Children Control Aggressive Feelings

James Garbarino, an expert on the impact of violence on children, became concerned about the epidemic of youth killings and determined to discover the causes to help parents and society prevent them. He interviewed young murderers and summarized his conclusions in *Lost Boys: Why Our Sons Turn Violent and How We Can Save Them*.[113] He described all the supports and resources he had in gaining control of his own early temperamental qualities—resources that the young criminals lacked.

He was a difficult, overactive, aggressive toddler and preschooler, and in school, he was impulsive and subject to sudden inner rages. At age twelve, he cruised the neighborhood on his bike, wondering what it would be like to commit the perfect crime, perhaps a murder. By late adolescence, however, he was president of the student council and editor of the yearbook. In 1964, the Lions Club of his city sent him to Washington, D.C., as a model youth.

Garbarino attributes his success to the tremendous help and support he received from his two loving parents, a safe neighborhood, and demanding schools.

> My mother devoted her every minute to me, literally "taming" me as one would a wolf pup. My father was there for me, a positive force in my life. When I started elementary school, I was assigned to strong and effective teachers in the early grades who took charge of me and the rest of their students and made sure we behaved in a civilized manner.[114]

Although he lacked inner controls, Garbarino lived in a world

> filled with people who cared for me, with opportunities to become involved with positive activities at school and in the community, and with cultural messages of stability and moral responsibility. And I believed in God. In other words, while I was still living with a stormy sea inside, I was solidly anchored.[115]

The average aggressive adolescent boy does not murder someone; however, aggressive, rule-breaking boys do continue to have problems through adolescence and into adulthood.[116] They are more apt to abuse substances, to drop out of school, to find getting and keeping a job difficult, and to have driving infractions. Furthermore, they tend to date girls who are also aggressive and to start families early. "It is hard to overemphasize the importance of childhood conduct problems for adjustment failures in young adulthood for males. These failures are pervasive and severe, and the consequences for the young man, his intimate partners, and the children whom he fathers are profound."[117]

What do researchers recommend? As noted in earlier chapters, attentive, fair, supportive, consistent parenting helps boys learn new behaviors to replace the coercive, irritating, negative behaviors learned at home. Social skills programs with age-mates also decrease the aggressive, disruptive behaviors that drive others away.

A third kind of intervention emphasizes learning emotional regulation skills. In one study, aggressive boys who were emotionally volatile—irritating, disruptive, and inattentive to others—had far more problems with peers than did boys who were only aggressive.[118] Thus, these boys must learn to control overreactivity and attend to others' needs. Anger management and communication skills programs can help here.

Treatment for symptoms of depression is important also as rule-breaking boys often suffer depression—45 percent of boys in one longitudinal study—that may well persist into adulthood.[119] The boys who were both angry and depressed were at risk for more severe problems in adulthood than were boys who were either angry or depressed. Thus, help must deal with both sets of problems for a large number of aggressive, rule-breaking boys.

Helping Children Cope with Feelings of Depression

Depression varies along a spectrum. At the one end are depressed moods—feeling down, being unhappy over an upsetting event such as failing a test or fighting with a friend.[120] The feelings may last a brief or an extended time.

In some cases, depression is a normal response to a loss—a parent's death, parents' divorce, moving to a new location. Children may show signs of depression off and on for months following the event, depending on the severity of the loss, but gradually depression lifts. Depression is sometimes expressed in angry, rebellious, acting-out behavior that masks the underlying condition. Children who are serious discipline problems in school and become involved in drugs, alcohol, and risk-taking behavior are often depressed. They lack self-esteem and feel helpless about themselves and helpless to change.[121]

The most serious end of the spectrum, clinical depression or major depressive disorder, involves depressed mood and loss of interest or pleasure in usual pursuits. Disturbances in sleep, eating, and activity patterns may or may not accompany the depressed mood. Energy level drops, and teens move more slowly and accomplish less than they did formerly. Sometimes clinical depression is accompanied by loss of concentration and poor memory, so school performance may drop. Because they feel less interested and withdraw, depressed children may have fewer friends. These are the main markers of clinical depression.[122] Children may also have thoughts or plans to hurt themselves or, less often, someone else.

Studies suggest that between 10 and 15 percent of children and adolescents show some signs of depression.[123] Because this occurs less before puberty, the majority of young people showing depression are teenagers. In any given year, 8.3 percent of adolescents show signs of depression, about 50 percent higher than the adult rate of 5.3 in a given year. Twenty percent of teenagers report having experienced a major depression that was not treated. As noted in the previous chapter, before puberty, boys and girls are equally likely to be depressed, but after puberty, the rate for girls doubles.

INTERVIEW
with Susan Harter

Susan Harter is Professor of Psychology at the University of Denver and has carried out extensive studies on self-esteem. This interview is continued from Chapter 5.

Self-esteem seems very important because it gives the person a kind of confidence to try many new activities. How important is it to have self-esteem?
Self-esteem has powerful implications for mood. The correlation between how much you like yourself as a person and your self-reported mood on a scale from cheerful to depressed is typically about .80.

Low self-esteem is invariably accompanied by depressive affect. We have extended these findings in developing a model that helps us understand suicidal thinking in teenagers. We included Beck's concept of hopelessness and have measured specific hopelessnesses corresponding to the support and self-concept domains. We ask, "How hopeless are you about getting peer support, parent support, about ever looking the way you want in terms of appearance?" "How hopeless are you about your scholastic ability?" There are various separate domains.

The worst consequences occur if you feel inadequate in an area in which support is important and feel hopeless about ever turning that area around. Moreover, if you don't have support and feel there is nothing you can ever do to get that support, this feeds into a depression composite of low self-esteem and low mood, plus general hopelessness. Thus, the worst-case scenario is the feeling that I am not getting support from people whose approval is important, I am not feeling confident in areas in which success is valued, I am hopeless about ever turning things around, I don't like myself as a person, I feel depressed, and my future looks bleak. That, in turn, causes kids to think of suicide as a solution to their problems, as an escape from painful self-perceptions leading to depression.

There is another scenario that may also lead to suicidal thinking, namely, the teen who has done extremely well in all these areas. Then they experience their first failure, for example, scholastically (they get their first B), athletically (they feel they are responsible for a key loss), or socially (they don't get invited to a major party). As a result, they consider suicide as a solution to their humiliation. These teens seem so puzzling, but we think that conditional support plays a role here. We saw kids whose support scores were reasonable, but when we interviewed them, they would say, "Well, my parent only cares about me if I make the varsity team or if I get all As" or whatever the formula is for that family. So conditionality of support is important.

I think it is important to point out that the reason people are spending so much energy and money on studying self-esteem is that low self-esteem has so many consequences, such as depressed mood, lack of energy to get up and do age-appropriate tasks and be productive, and, for some, thoughts of suicide. Most parents want their children to be happy, and self-esteem is an important pathway to happiness and the ability to function in today's world.

Prior to puberty, suicide attempts are rare, but the rate of suicide increases after puberty. Of 451 students followed from eighth to twelfth grade, 32 percent reported suicidal ideation during that period, 14 percent reported having a suicide plan, and 4 percent said they attempted suicide. Parental warmth and support were negatively related to suicidality.[124]

Many factors are related to depressive states:[125]

- Genetic factors reflected in having family members with depression
- Biological factors such as hormonal changes related to puberty
- Stressful life events such as divorce, discrimination, child maltreatment
- Psychological factors such as inability to manage emotions
- Pattern of family interactions such as lack of parental support
- Peer relationships such as rejection and bullying
- Romantic relationships involving rejection and break-ups

When parents notice signs of depression, they should seek qualified professional help. At the present time, there are several forms of help for depression.[126] Family therapy, individual therapy, and group therapy aimed at helping the child change negative self-evaluations are useful. Medications are often used as well. If parents are uncertain whether their concerns are justified, they can consult a therapist by themselves to determine the severity of the depression and the need to bring the child in.

Following the course of depressive feelings in a large sample of twenty thousand teens from seventh to twelfth grade revealed significant ethnic and racial differences.[127] European American boys and girls had the lowest levels of depressed feelings. Latina girls had the highest level of depressed feelings and Asian American girls had almost equally high rates. Among boys, Asian American boys had the highest rates of depressed feelings, followed by Latino boys. African American boys and girls scored higher in depressed feelings than European American boys and girls, but lower than the other two groups.

All groups decreased in depressed feelings over the six years, but European American boys and girls remained significantly lower than the other three groups, which clustered closely together. Immigrant status did not have a significant effect on the rate of decreasing scores. Despite their coping skills, Asian American, Latino/s, and African American boys and girls enter the young adult years with significantly more feelings of depression that may make it harder for them to achieve their goals.

Mothers' support (there was not a measure of fathers' support) was important in reducing depressed feelings in all ethnic groups.

> For both males and females, and among all race-ethnic groups, higher levels of maternal support were found to be related to lower levels of depressive symptoms. In a sense, mothers' support may be a "race-ethnicity equalizer" because its effect is consistent across all groups.[128]

A school-based program designed to prevent the rise of depressed feelings in the junior high years included coping skills training for students and several interventions for parents to improve parenting skills and parent–teen relationships.[129]

The program not only inhibited a rise in depressed feelings in at-risk youth; it also decreased delinquency and substance use.

Promoting Positive Peer Relationships

In the teen years, the quality of parent–child relationships influences teens' orientation to peers.[130] When teens feel they have good relationships with parents and feel that parents allow them a growing role in decision making, teens are better adjusted, less likely to report extreme orientations toward peers, and less likely to seek peers' advice than are teens who feel that parents retain power and control. This latter group of teens seek the egalitarian relationship and mutuality they do not feel with parents. Relationships between fathers and teens are especially predictive of peer relationships, perhaps because fathers and children engage in many recreational activities, and skills learned there transfer to relationships with peers.[131]

Promoting School Success

When adolescents are achieving below their ability levels, studies have found two general approaches helpful.[132] The behavioral technique of regularly monitoring schoolwork by means of a progress report and giving positive consequences such as privileges and rewards helps students raise their performance level. A second strategy is a comprehensive approach to increase teens' study skills, their academic skills (by means of tutoring), and their social skills so they feel more at ease at school. Parents' involvement and use of consequences is also key to such a program. Addressing academic problems alone through tutoring or private therapy has not been as helpful as multifaceted approaches.

Helping Teens Develop a Sense of Purpose

Impressed with the sense of vitality and direction that some young people show, William Damon interviewed 1,200 adolescents and young adults between the ages of twelve and twenty-two to determine how they developed a sense of purpose in life, defined as a commitment to a longer-term goal, an ultimate concern that gives life meaning and guides behavior.

Damon synthesized the parenting actions that encourage a sense of purpose.

> What a parent should do is lead a child toward promising options. A parent can help a child sort through choices and reflect upon how the child's interests match up with the world's opportunities and needs. A parent can support a child's own efforts to explore purposeful directions and open up more potential sources of discovery about possible purposes. These are supporting roles. . . because center stage in the drama belongs to the child. But while the most effective assistance parents can provide is indirect, it is also invaluable.[133]

Specifically, he recommends

- Have conversations about the child's interests and activities and support them
- Listen and pay attention to what arouses your child's interests and support them

Teens develop a sense of purpose when parents lead them toward promising options and help children explore their interests.

- Talk about your own goals and purpose at work
- Talk about the practicalities of accomplishing goals and projects
- Connect your child with mentors in the community
- Support your child's resourceful problem-solving skills and reasonable risk-taking to achieve goals
- Model and support a positive outlook
- Help children develop "a feeling of agency linked to responsibility."

Parents often accomplish these parenting goals in simple conversations while doing an errand or a chore. Being around and available to notice a child's enthusiasm or answer a casual question that triggers more conversation is very important. It is in these little moments that much gets done.

A PRACTICAL QUESTION:
HOW CAN PARENTS TELL WHETHER
THEIR TEEN HAS A SIGNIFICANT PROBLEM?

Parents want to know the signs of a serious problem. Generally, changes or decreases in teens' mood and level of functioning at school, at home, and at work can indicate one or more of several possible problems. When parents have concerns, they need to get professional help because these are all serious problems that rarely disappear with time.

Marcia Herrin outlines the early warning signs of an eating disorder: obvious increases and decreases in weight; a sudden and intense interest in diets, nutrition, and nonfat foods; skipping meals; drinking only noncaloric drinks; a frantic pace of exercise or athletic activity; discomfort around eating and meals; preoccupation with physical appearance; low self-esteem; and depression.[134] These behaviors have more meaning collectively than individually. A professional can help evaluate parents' concerns.

Harold Koplewicz helps parents identify depressed teens.[135] He describes the "moody" teen who has lost a boyfriend and is down for days or weeks but recovers and continues her activities and her relationships with friends and family.

> But if the sadness persists—if [she] has become a different person, if she's lost her sense of humor, if her sleeping and eating habits are disturbed, and if she's becoming socially isolated and is suddenly having trouble keeping up with school-work—it may be that the breakup was the triggering event of an underlying depression that needs to be treated.[136]

In addition to such classical signs of depression, Jane Brody points to tiredness, boredom, irritability, temper outbursts, sudden threats to leave home, physical symptoms such as headaches or stomachaches, and anxiety.[137]

Substance abuse may be harder to detect until it becomes a serious problem, because teens often engage in such behavior away from home with peers, and parents can only detect the consequences of it—coming home drunk, a ticket for driving under the influence, loss of interest in school, cutting classes, a drop in grades, a new group of friends, anger and irritability at parents, a decrease in responsible behaviors such as doing chores, and increasing difficulties with others at school or at work.[138] Changes in eating and sleeping and an increased number of physical complaints may accompany drug use as well.

All these problems share many of the same warning signs. With the help of school and professionals, parents can get the best assessment of what is happening to their child and the form of treatment needed.

As parents identify and seek treatment for their children's problems, they often learn that they themselves have the problem but have not recognized or accepted it. Parents of depressed teens may discover, for example, that they themselves have suffered from depression. Parents of a substance-abusing teen may realize that they are problem drinkers. Parents of children with eating disorders may see they have a problem in this area as well. As parents seek treatment for teens, the whole family benefits.

PARENTS' EXPERIENCES IN FACING TRANSITIONS

To understand how parents react and adapt to the changes and turmoil of their children's adolescence, Laurence Steinberg observed 204 families for three years.[139] He found six aspects of a child's adolescent behavior that trigger parents' emotional reactions: puberty and its associated physical changes, maturing sexuality, dating, increasing independence, emotional detachment, and increasing deidealization of the parent.

Parents with the following risk factors were most likely to experience difficulty: (1) being the same sex as the child making the transition, (2) being divorced or remarried (especially true for women), (3) having fewer sources of satisfaction outside the parental role, and (4) having a negative view of adolescence. Protective factors that eased parents' adjustments to their teens' adolescence were having satisfying jobs, outside interests, and happy marriages. The positive supports buffered parents so that, in times of difficulty with children, they had other sources of satisfaction and self-esteem.

Steinberg found that about 40 percent of parents experienced difficulties, 40 percent responded to children's changes but were not personally affected, and 20 percent enjoyed greater freedom as their children became more independent. Based on his research, Steinberg makes the following suggestions to parents for handling this stage of family development: (1) have genuine and satisfying interests outside of being a parent, (2) do not disengage from the child emotionally, (3) try to adopt a positive outlook about what adolescence is and how the child is changing, and (4) do not be afraid to discuss feelings with partners, friends, or a professional counselor.

SUPPORT FOR PARENTS

Numerous national and local organizations can supply parents with information and resources as well as direct them to professionals in the area. For example, Eating Disorder Awareness and Prevention serves parents in Seattle; Depression and Related Affective Disorders Association helps them in Washington, D.C. Al-Anon and other anonymous family groups are available nationally and locally for families dealing with alcohol and drug problems.

ToughLove is an organization started by parents in the late 1970s to help parents cope with rebellious, out-of-control adolescents. Parents form support groups with other parents and develop communication with agencies and individuals to promote community responses to truancy, drug abuse, running away, and vandalism. Parents seek real consequences for this behavior so adolescents will learn to avoid the disapproved behaviors. Psychiatrist Ron Zodkevitch has updated this method to deal with current issues, such as body piercings and violence, and newer forms of treatment, such as medications. He believes the program has wide applications and is useful for all parents.

The founders of ToughLove, Phyllis and David York, are professionals who had difficulty with their impulsive, acting-out adolescents.[140] They found it hard to set firm, fair limits that they could enforce. Meeting and talking with other parents gave them feelings of support as they set limits and carried them out. In fact, when parents in the group find limit setting difficult, other parents will meet with the family or the teenager and back up the rules. Others offer to go to court hearings or other official meetings. By providing many sets of adults to help parents help children, the group becomes a community effort to establish and maintain a safe environment for all children.

MAIN POINTS

In this period, late adolescents

- reach sexual maturity
- learn about healthy sexual activities, engage in sexual activity, and many have their first sexual intercourse
- think more abstractly but in situations of emotional excitement or under the influence of peers, they can make risky decisions
- get excited at school when permitted active participation and respect
- grow in competence and confidence when they engage in a broad variety of activities
- may become depressed or develop problems such as alcohol abuse if stress is high
- are fearful of experiencing discrimination because of personal or ethnic qualities
- work in large numbers and can gain skills if the work environment is favorable

When late adolescents consider themselves, they

- describe themselves in psychological terms and, through introspection, begin to see patterns in their behavior
- need support from family and community
- reveal gender differences in their self-descriptions, with boys seeing themselves as more daring, logical, and calm than girls, and girls seeing themselves as more attuned to people and more emotionally reactive than boys

Peer Relationships

- provide major sources of support and companionship and are sought out in times of trouble
- include dating relationships that are often intense but short-lived
- provide opportunities to negotiate and resolve problems without ending relationships

Parents

- continue their commitment to children by monitoring, supervising, and enforcing rules, yet at the same time supporting and accepting children's individuality
- serve as consultants and provide factual information on topics of importance to teens
- share more power in decision making with teens so that teens can be more self-governing in the context of warm family relationships and so they can separate with a sense of well-being

Parents' reactions to their children's growth

- stimulate their own psychological growth
- often stimulate parents to find new possibilities in their own lives
- may bring parents closer to each other

Problems discussed center on

- eating problems
- substance use/abuse
- aggression
- school problems
- depression
- peer relationships

Joys include

- observing increasing social maturity and closeness with friends
- enjoying greater personal freedom
- seeing altruistic behavior develop
- watching adult traits emerge

EXERCISES

1. Break into small groups; discuss how parents can help their teenagers get the information that so many teens want about pregnancy, STDs, and contraception availability. List suggestions for parents in short pamphlet.

2. Interview parents about their experience during adolescence: Did they grow up in a city or small town? How much freedom were they allowed? What were the rules for them? What stresses did adolescents at that time face? Whom did they go to for support? How did their parents discipline them? Return to class and break into small groups; discuss the ways that parents' experiences differ from those of adolescents of today and report to the class on four major differences.

3. In small groups, describe the most effective discipline techniques parents used with you and write ten suggestions for parents of adolescents.

4. Describe three ways you found to reduce stress as an adolescent. Work in small groups to compile a list of the ten most popular ways to reduce stress, and come up with a class total.

5. In small groups, discuss ways that adolescent boys and girls can share experiences so they can come to understand how life experiences can differ and what the stresses are for each gender. Share ideas with the whole class.

ADDITIONAL READINGS

Damon, William. *The Path to Purpose: Helping Our Children Find Their Calling in Life.* New York: Free Press, 2008.

Garbarino, James and de Lara, Ellen. *And Words Can Hurt Forever: How to Protect Adolescents from Bullying.* New York: Free Press, 2002.

Lerner, Richard M., with Israeloff, Roberta. *The Good Teen: Rescuing Adolescence from the Myths of the Storm and Stress Years.* New York: Stonesong Press, 2007.

Levine, Madeline. The *Price of Privilege.* New York: HarperCollins, 2006.

Zodkevitch, Ron. *The Toughlove Prescription: How to Create and Enforce Boundaries for Your Teen.* New York: McGraw-Hill, 2006.

CHAPTER

12

Parenting Adults

CHAPTER TOPICS	IN THE NEWS

CHAPTER TOPICS

In this chapter, you will learn about:

- Definitions of adulthood
- Theoretical perspectives
- The influence of historical time
- Many pathways to adulthood
- Parenting children in transition to adulthood
- Parenting independent adult children and dependent adult children
- Parenting the adult parent

IN THE NEWS

USA Today, December 20[1]: College campuses address psychological needs of their students. See page 369.

Test Your Knowledge: Fact or Fiction (True/False)

1. When adolescents leave home at age eighteen, their identities are pretty well formed.
2. Parents do not often give children money once they have obtained schooling and work.
3. Young adults who have developed maladaptive ways of coping have opportunities in their twenties to change and develop competence and resilience.
4. When parents of adults divorce, the divorce has little effect on children's relationships with their parents because they are now independent of them.
5. Aging adults have little opportunity to create better relationships with their adult children because they see little of them.

As all parents know, parenting is a lifelong endeavor. It continues well beyond the years the child lives at home until, finally, as the parent becomes old, the child becomes the parent to the parent. In this chapter, we look at how parents and children relate to each other as they grow older together.

359

Glen Elder and Michael Stranahan emphasize that we live life in a dense social network of shared relationships with family members linked together across generations.[2] We see this clearly in the adult years. Even as children gain increasing independence, they stay connected to parents and rely on them for emotional warmth and material supports in life's ups and downs. Parents too find their own well-being and happiness changing in response to events in their children's lives.

In this chapter, we examine criteria for adulthood and theoretical perspectives on parent–child relationships in the adult years. We look at different patterns of family life and at parenting in the transition to adulthood, parenting independent adult children, parenting dependent adult children, and, finally, parenting the parent.

THEORETICAL PERSPECTIVES

Incorporating Freud's definition of a mature adult as one who loves and works, Erik Erikson described the tasks of adulthood as (1) establishing a productive work life that permits time to relate to partners and families, (2) choosing and committing to a loving partner, and (3) having and rearing children.[3]

John Bowlby's concept of attachment provides insights on parent–child relationships in adulthood. He believes "attachment behavior is held to characterize human beings from the cradle to the grave,"[4] and "availability of the attachment figure is the set-goal of the attachment system in older children and adults."[5]

To Bowlby, availability means three things: open communication with the attachment figure, the attachment figure's physical accessibility, and his or her help as needed. As we will see, communication, physical proximity and contact, and mutual exchange of help are aspects of adult parent–child relationships, and so there is a continuation of the attachment process begun in childhood.

Life-course theory points to the importance of historical time as an influence on parent–child relationships.[6] Social and economic events present successive generations with particular challenges (e.g., the Depression of the 1930s) that shape how adults meet the tasks of adulthood.

Jeffrey Arnett has suggested that the cultural context of our times requires a new stage of psychological development, termed "emerging adulthood."[7] In an information-based economy, most occupations require years of education for jobs, delaying marriage and parenthood, on average, to the mid-to-late twenties.

Emerging adulthood is neither adolescence nor adulthood, but is a time of (1) continued identity exploration, particularly in love and work; (2) instability; (3) feeling caught between adolescence and adulthood; (4) great self-focus; and (5) adulthood optimism about future possibilities.

Research supports Arnett's assertions about a period of change and possibility in the twenties. As we saw in the last chapter, the brain continues to develop in the early twenties and forms new connections in the prefrontal cortex that enable individuals to have greater emotional and behavioral control.[8] Other longitudinal research on coping and resilience finds that the twenties are a period of change, during which resourceful individuals are able to overcome maladaptive behaviors and go on to achieve greater competence and integration in young adulthood than they experienced in their twenties.[9]

Not all young people may experience a period of emerging adulthood. In those developing countries in which adult roles of marriage, settled worker, and parenthood begin at age eighteen or twenty, there is no period of exploration. Within our own industrialized society, this period does not exist for those adolescents who are settled workers and parents at eighteen or nineteen.

CRITERIA FOR ADULTHOOD

No single event marks the arrival at adulthood the way puberty marks the beginning of sexual maturity. The legal system typically defines anyone under age eighteen as a child and everyone over eighteen as an adult.[10] Adolescents can achieve adult status prior to age eighteen if they marry, have a child, enter the military, or petition the court to become emancipated minors who can support themselves.

Adolescents (average age sixteen), twenty-year-olds (average age twenty-four), and adults in their thirties and forties (average age forty-two) agree in their descriptions of behaviors a person must achieve to be considered an adult (see Table 12-1).[11] The items frequently used to define adulthood focus on three areas:

- independence and responsibility for self
- self-control and self-regulation—using contraceptives, not driving while drunk, not shoplifting
- capacity to protect a family and manage a household.

Items used less frequently to describe adulthood are what might be termed "external markers" of the adult role—marriage, having a child, buying a home, avoiding bad language.

Researchers looking at large samples of people in their twenties identify five markers as signs of adulthood: (1) living independently of parents, (2) completing education, (3) having a stable job, (4) marriage, and (5) childbearing.[12]

THE TRANSITION TO ADULTHOOD

Youths' living arrangements vary. Almost 40 percent of youth live at home and go to college, work, or both work and go to college, and 40 percent go away to school and work elsewhere. About 10 percent are married or are single parents and living away from home, and 10 percent are unclassified.[13]

Trends Common to Those Entering Adulthood

Despite the numerous paths to adulthood, common trends are seen for this group as a whole. Psychological well-being improved over the seven years, with increasing levels of self-esteem and decreasing levels of expressed anger and depression

■ **T A B L E 12-1**
ITEMS MOST AND LEAST FREQUENTLY ENDORSED AS DESCRIBING AN ADULT*

Most Frequently Endorsed Items	Percentage Endorsing
Accepts responsibility for consequences of actions	90
Decides own beliefs/values independently of others	80
Establishes relationships with parents as equals	75
Financially independent of parents	71
Avoids committing petty crimes such as vandalism, shoplifting	70
Capable of running a household (women)	64
Uses contraception if sexually active and not trying to have child	63
Avoids drunk driving	63
Capable of keeping family physically safe	62.5
Capable of running a household (men)	61

Least Frequently Endorsed Items	Percentage Endorsing
Has had at least one child	9
Married	13
Committed to long-term love relationship	13
Purchased a home	14
Has had sexual intercourse	16
Not deeply tied to parents emotionally	22
Finished with education	26
Avoids using profanity/vulgar language	26
Avoids becoming drunk	29
Settled in a long-term career	30

For each item, participants were asked whether the behavior must be achieved before a person can be considered an adult; participants checked Yes or No. The percentage given is the average of all participants in the sample who checked Yes.

Have you achieved adulthood? Percentage:	Yes	No	Yes and No
Adolescents (average age 16)	19	33	48
Emerging adults (average age 24)	46	4	50
Young adults (average age 42)	86	2	12

*Adapted from Jeffrey Jensen Arnett, "Conceptions of the Transition to Adulthood: Perspectives from Adolescence through Midlife," *Journal of Adult Development 8* (2001): 133–143.

in a diverse sample followed from ages 18 to 25.[14] In this period, the gap between men's and women's scores on depression and anger gradually narrowed. Youth in families with high parental conflict were more likely to be angry and depressed at the beginning of the period, but their scores decreased sharply over the period. Parents' social support and marriage were related to increases in self-esteem, whereas periods of unemployment were related to higher depression and lower self-esteem scores.[15]

Alcohol and marijuana use increased into the early twenties, and then began to decrease.[16] While overall well-being improved, this is the period in which serious psychological disorders such as schizophrenia became more prevalent.[17]

Young adults' moods are related to past family experiences. A survey of life satisfaction and positive moods in college students in thirty-nine countries found that young adults enter adulthood in good spirits when they come from families in which parents have marriages with good or average agreement between partners.[18] When parents are married and argue or when they divorce and remarry and argue, young adults have lower life satisfaction and more negative moods. When parents argue and divorce, and children grow up in homes with no arguing, their levels of life satisfaction and positive moods resemble those of youth from average marriages.

Parents' Role in Supporting Growth and Development

Parental support takes many forms. Financial or economic support takes the form of paying children's living expenses while they get further training or pay for further education.[19] As children are older, parents offer loans or gifts for cars, deposits for apartments, or down payments on homes. In one large representative sample followed between children's ages of eighteen to thirty four, parents gave an average of $38,000 including support for living at home.[20] They gave more when children were younger, and less as children moved into their thirties. Families with greater resources gave far more in this period, but even those in the lowest quartile of income gave an average of $9,000 over the sixteen-year period.

Social support is divided into emotional, instrumental, and informational benefits.[21] Emotional benefits include feeling cared for, valued, encouraged, understood, and validated as a person. Instrumental benefits include help with certain tasks such as child care or repairing cars. In the study assessing financial giving, parents also gave an average of 380 hours per year in time to help children—that is, an average of 9 weeks of full-time work.[22] Informational benefits include advice about school, referral to resources, or guidance about tasks.

Paths to Adulthood

Researchers following a sample of Midwestern European American middle-class boys (42 percent of the sample) and girls (58 percent of the sample) from ages twelve to twenty-four used five markers to describe adult status at age twenty-four: education status, job status, place of residence, romantic relationships, and parenthood.[23] Using latent class analysis of the data, they identified six pathways to adulthood:

Pathway	% of sample	%M	%F
Fast Starters	12	45	55
Parents without Careers	10	29	71
Educated Partners	19	34	66
Educated Singles	37	47	53
Working Singles	7	53	47
Slow Starters	14	44	56

People in the first three groups live with or are married to partners, and those in the second three groups are single. Three groups—Fast and Slow Starters and Parents without Careers—have children, and the remaining three groups—Educated Partners and Singles and Working Singles—do not. As we can see, more than half of the youth are focused on getting an education, but many are highly focused on work.

Fast Starters are closest to the traditional role of the young adult—having a long-term job, being married, owning a home, caring for children. People in this cluster work longer hours than those in the other groups, and they earn more money, although only a small percentage seeks more education to expand their future opportunities. They have been with their partners and spouses for about two years, and they had known them for three years before that. While they report less dissatisfaction with their spouses than other groups, they also report more instances of physically abusive interactions with partners.

Adults in this group spend most of their time at work or with their family and in household activities. They spend less time in leisure activities such as sports and reading than the sample as a whole. They also have a lower rate of illegal activities such as drug use or vandalism.

Parents without Careers is a group largely made up of women who either do not work at all or work at short-term jobs, resulting in this group's having the fewest hours worked and the lowest income. The men in the group do have full-time jobs and earn more money, but they do not seek more education so advancement may be limited.

The relationships between cohabiting or married partners began earlier than those in the other groups and have lasted longer. Three-quarters of the group, however, feel the relationships have problems and like Fast Starters, there is a history of physical abuse in the relationships.

Both men and women in the group spend most of their time on family activities and spend the least amount of time on leisure activities. Like Fast Starters, they have a low rate of illegal activities.

Educated Partners, like Fast Starters and Parents without Careers, were married or live with romantic partners, but they do not have children. While highly educated, one-quarter continue to seek more education, and as a result, their jobs are less stable and lower paying than those in other groups.

The romantic relationships of this group are shorter-lived than those in the first two groups, but couples dated longer before cohabiting or marrying, and they report the most satisfying partner relationships and fewer problems of all the groups. Because there are no children, their daily activities are more like Educated Singles. Partners report more time in leisure activities and less time in household activities.

Educated Singles are like Educated Partners in many ways, except that they do not live with partners and are more likely to live at home with their parents. Thirty percent are currently reenrolled in college courses, and while their earnings are at the mean, their future prospects are expanding because of education and access to higher status jobs.

Like the other two groups of singles, the happiest individuals are those who are in a steady dating relationship with someone. Like all singles, they spend little time in household activities and much more time in leisure time activities than those living with partners. They are likely to have engaged in some illegal activities such as drug use. Though they have a sociable, less settled lifestyle, they are still as responsible as those in other groups for meeting their own needs.

Working Singles, like Educated Singles, are more likely to live at home and feel more comfortable with a steady, caring relationship. Like Fast Starters, they work long hours, and they earn good money in skilled and technical jobs that are secure. About 16 percent are getting more education.

They spend about the average amount of time in household and family activities and more time in leisure time activities such as sports. Still, they meet all their own needs, with the exception of managing a household. So Working Singles are like Fast Starters in making a significant commitment to work, but like other single groups, they are delayed in making commitments to relationships.

Slow Starters are not settled in a stable job. They hold service and office jobs, working fewer hours and earning less money than those in all other groups except Parents without Careers. However, 21 percent of the group is getting more education so future jobs may be more advanced. Slow Starters are most likely to be living with parents and not involved in romantic relationships. When they do have relationships, they report difficulties. They spend a lot of time in leisure activities, and are the group most likely to violate laws.

Although the group is the most delayed in getting established in jobs, relationships, and independent residence, they are advanced in having children. Almost two-thirds of the group have children. Unlike Fast Starters and Parents without Careers who center much of their time around family and children, Slow Starters devote little time to children.

At age eighteen, several factors predicted the pathways teenagers would take to adulthood. Students' interest and performance in academic courses, their involvement in sports, skill-oriented activities, and community activities all were linked to later membership in Educated Partners and Educated Singles groups. Those who looked forward to marriage and wanted to be married at younger ages were those most likely to be married at age twenty-four. Predicting those who would have children was more difficult. It can be seen, however, that many of those having children early (Parents without Careers and Slow Starters) have fewer financial resources and report more difficulties in partner relationships.

Those eighteen-year-olds whose parents were well educated and had financial resources were those most likely to be in the Educated groups, but lack of money was not a barrier to education. Good students who were poor still got to college and were in the educated groups.

The research did reveal that while Arnett's characteristics of emerging adulthood applied to Educated groups and Slow Starters who are still exploring and making few commitments, still about a third of young people are making significant commitments to work and family at traditional ages.

Those Who Need Special Support in the Transition to Adulthood

Because of physical and psychological problems, learning deficits, and life circumstances, many children received services during childhood and adolescence.[24] As they reach maturity, many of these services decrease or end, and children and their families are left to manage as best they can. Families often do not have resources, and in the cases of children in foster care or the juvenile justice system, family members are often not available.

Although these children have fewer resources than many, they have many needs. Jobs available for high school graduates with no advanced training or skills are few, unstable, and provide few benefits such as health insurance. Furthermore, some of these children have additional problems in learning and in skills for independent living.

Recognizing the needs of these groups, Federal and state agencies take the supportive role of providing transitional services into the early twenties to give vocational training, life skills for independent living, and self-management skills. These programs tend, however, to be inflexible, providing services according to age rather than needs, and failing to provide families with training and support so they can help children effectively.

Even with such programs, significant numbers of these maturing adults suffer from psychological problems and substance use, instability in living arrangements, and early fertility. Those who have been in special education, about 85 percent of this group, fare better, with, for example, only 20 percent experiencing unemployment compared with 50 percent in those exiting foster care or the juvenile justice system. Some people in this group resemble Slow Starters who live at home and have unstable work histories.

Children who have only health problems have fewer difficulties in attaining adult status than those with learning or psychosocial problems. Researchers find that adolescents with chronic health problems such as asthma, diabetes, arthritis, and cerebral palsy "attain levels of education, income, marriage, and self-esteem that are average for their age group."[25] They show differences in rate of employment, with 73 percent of the healthy group and 67 percent of the group with chronic conditions working, as well as a difference of $1,700 in annual income. On years of education, marital status, and self-esteem, no significant differences between the groups appear.

This does not mean that youth with severe physical health conditions, such as youth who are technology dependent on wheelchairs or other equipment, face no obstacles to achieving adult status. Nonetheless, while they or others with severe conditions have added problems, the majority of teens with chronic physical health problems achieve adult status comparable to others in their age group.

Pathways to Adulthood for Youths from Immigrant Groups

Through telephone and face-to-face interviews with children of immigrants living in New York City, researchers identified paths these youths took to adulthood and compared them with those of native-born European and African American youth.[26] The youth, at a median age of twenty-three, came from immigrant families from South American countries (Columbia, Ecuador, and Peru), Caribbean Islands (West Indies, Puerto Rico, and Dominican Republic), Russia, and China. Families, on average, had far fewer resources with which to help their children, but their help was critical.

The same paths to adulthood were found in immigrant groups as those we described in Midwestern youth—working, going to school, working and going to school, doing neither, and having children. However, there were differences among the groups that we illustrate with the marked differences between the Chinese and Puerto Rican youths.

Families from mainland China planned and struggled to get to this country and often came with extended family members. Thus, families often consisted of two parents, and perhaps grandparents with their being a ratio of one adult to each child. Families were very cohesive, and marriages were stable. Families worked in relatives' businesses and got help from the extended family. Both parents often worked, and relatives babysat.

Education was highly valued, and families sought out neighborhoods with the best schools possible, sometimes using false addresses to get into another district. In the high school years, children were encouraged to apply to good schools outside the neighborhood. Education was stressed as the main path to better lives, and youth saw academic success as a way of repaying parents for all the sacrifices they made to give their children improved lives. As a favorably viewed ethnic group, youth reported their rule-breaking was sometimes overlooked, and they were given many opportunities because the group was assumed to be bright.

Even though parents were not highly educated, their children had high levels of academic achievement. Only 1.6 percent of those aged twenty-two to thirty-two were high school dropouts, and 75 percent were enrolled in a four-year college or had a BA degree. Pursuing education was the primary focus, and the group was less likely to form families and have children than any other group so that at age thirty-two, they had the fewest children.

As American citizens, it was easy for Puerto Rican families to come to this country, return home, and come again so there was less focus on organizing support for a difficult change. About half of the Puerto Rican youth grew up in families with two parents, but about 40 percent of the marriages resulted in separation or divorce; almost half grew up in families with a single parent. Because married women often did not work and many parents were single, few Puerto Rican youth had the financial resources of two working parents. Parents experienced severe economic stress and racial and class discrimination that forced them to live in the poorest neighborhoods with the greatest dangers and risks of violence and drugs.

There was no tight and cohesive family to support single mothers who had only themselves and friends for support. Mothers kept children close to them, wanting them to go to neighborhood schools even if they were not adequate. Going to poor schools where they were often stereotyped as poor students, many youth lost interest. Local parochial schools were the usual alternative.

Many Puerto Rican parents had limited educations, and they did not see education as the main path to success. Although Puerto Rican parents had the same educational levels as mainland Chinese parents did, their children had lower aspirations than those of Chinese youth. About 25 percent of Puerto Rican youth dropped out of high school, and even 25 percent of children of college-educated mothers dropped out; only 25 percent were enrolled in four-year colleges.

Children were valued, and Puerto Rican youth tended to start families early. One sixth of the sample were single parents. While it is possible to pursue an education with children, still it is more difficult, and fewer youth get education beyond high school, limiting them to less stable jobs. Early childbearing started a process of unstable, poorly paid jobs that was similar to that of their parents.

In immigrant youths' paths to adulthood, three family factors played a role in children's successful outcomes: (1) more adults to support fewer children; (2) family's having high educational aspirations for children, and encouraging education; and (3) parents' helping children gain access to the best educational opportunities available, seeking out extra services and supportive individuals.

Even if youth have fully formed identities, experiences in educational and job settings can trigger further identity exploration.[27] Experiencing stereotyping or discrimination can stimulate further thoughts about who one is and what being a member of your group means. This process can occur throughout the lifespan.

General Parenting Strategies for the Transition Period

While theory and research have traditionally emphasized the importance of separation from the family, current work indicates that whatever the path to adulthood, positive attachments to parents and parents' warmth, understanding, resources, and all forms of support ease the way.[28]

In addition to providing positive support, the main task of this period is to form a new balance in the parent–child relationship to meet children's growing autonomy.[29] Although they rely on parents' assistance, children want to be treated as independent adults.

Negotiating the Issues of Growing Autonomy

Issues range from small ones, such as whether a college child has a curfew on vacations, to large ones, such as whether children can live at home when they are not going to school or working or whether parents can have access to information about college behavior and problems.

Each issue has to be negotiated on its own merits and on the needs and maturity level of the child as well as parents' needs. As we have seen, some children need additional emotional and family support as they leave high school. Other children eagerly enter independent activities at college, and then become distressed and need additional help. Several universities document increases in the number of students reporting depression, anxiety, learning disabilities, and attention problems.[30] Columbia University reported a 40 percent increase in the number of students coming to the Counseling Center between 1994 and 2002. In addition, alcohol and drug use have increased, with 1,400 college students dying each year from alcohol-related incidents, including alcohol poisoning and car accidents.[31] As in late adolescence, parents provide role models of healthy lifestyle and help college students get professional assistance as needed.

Whatever the issue, parents, as in all previous stages, listen calmly and use mutual problem-solving strategies to give information and work together with children to arrive at mutually agreeable solutions. Children may be surprised that in this stage, parents' needs are consistently given equal weight to children's, when in the past children's needs may have been given greater weight at times because they were still in the process of developing.

Staying Close When Children Are Moving Away from the Family

Even if children continue to live at home while they go to school or work, family relationships are changed, with children having increased involvement in friends and activities outside the home. Parents miss their children, their friends, and the close contact in daily meals, conversations, and activities. With cell phones, text messaging, and e-mail, parents can still stay in touch even when children are thousands of miles away, but new rules apply with independent young adults.

New patterns of connecting are developed. Children may be the prime initiators of contact, and may develop a family routine that if a child has not called home in a week, parents call or initiate conversation. The topics of conversation may shift as children no longer may want parents' advice or approval of what they are doing. The rules of conversation are more like those parents have with friends—one thinks carefully about any negative response or criticism of the child or his or her friends. In many traditional families, parents may resist changes, and they and their children will have to work out solutions.

Siblings and the extended family are also affected when children become more independent.[32] Siblings may feel great loss when brothers or sisters are not there for daily conversations, support, and understanding and are not there to serve as an advocate with parents or as a focus of parents' concerns. Sometimes siblings resent the special privileges or resources given to older brothers and sisters. And sometimes, they enjoy having a room to themselves or the use of the car.

As all the siblings in the family mature, it is important for them to establish a new balance in the relationship in which all are equal in power. Older siblings may continue to feel they should dominate decisions because of their age, but research has shown that those siblings who share equal power in relationships are most likely to have positive relationships over the lifespan.

Grandparents, aunts, and uncles may miss the closeness that has existed, and families have to establish how increasingly independent children share their time with everyone in the family.

PARENTING INDEPENDENT ADULT CHILDREN

Social contexts shape parents' behavior with independent adult children. Some independent adult children live away from home, alone or with their own families; others continue to live with the family or nearby and remain part of all family activities. Whether close by or far away, they relate to parents as equals.

Closeness in Family Life

Vern Bengtson and his colleagues have described the behavioral and emotional ties among parents and adult children who have been followed in the Longitudinal Study of Generations.[33] Looking at families in terms of emotional closeness, patterns of agreement and contact, and ways of giving and receiving help, Bengtson developed a typology of five patterns of family interactions differing in levels of intimacy, closeness, and contact.

Table 12-2 presents five family types based on the patterns of responses on six dimensions of parent–child interactions. In a large, nationally representative sample, Bengtson and his colleagues found that 25 percent of the sample were categorized as tightly knit, 25 percent were sociable, 17 percent were detached, 16 percent were intimate but distant, and 16 percent were obligatory types. While no one type stands out as the most common, two-thirds of the families are described as emotionally close and in agreement on issues, two thirds engage in joint activities

■ **T A B L E 12-2**
CONSTRUCTING A TYPOLOGY OF INTERGENERATIONAL RELATIONSHIPS USING FIVE SOLIDARITY VARIABLES

Types of Relationships	Affect (Close)	Consensus (Agree)	Structure (Proximity)	Association (Contact)	Gives Help	Receives Help
Tight-knit	+	+	+	+	+	+
Sociable	+	+	+	+	−	−
Intimate but distant	+	+	−	−	−	−
Obligatory	−	−	+	+	(+)	(+)
Detached	−	−	−	−		

Reprinted from Vern L. Bengtson, "Beyond the Nuclear Family: The Increasing Importance of Multigenerational Bonds," *Journal of Marriage and the Family 63* (2001): 9. Reprinted with permission.

together, and only 16 percent are detached. Income, age, and gender of children did not affect the distribution of the types.

Gender differences existed for parents with mothers most likely to be closely attached and tightly knit with the next generation and very infrequently (only 5 percent) in the detached category. Fathers were most likely to have sociable and obligatory kinds of relationships with children.

Ethnic groups differed, with European American mothers more likely than African Americans and Latinas/os to have obligatory relationships, and more likely than African Americans to have detached relationships.

Ongoing Nurturance and Support

During this period, children are expected to be self-supporting, independent, and responsible. They need love and emotional support and sometimes information and instrumental support. As noted earlier, demographic changes in economic and family stability have resulted in independent adult children's often requiring more material assistance from parents than did young adults in the past,[34] and at times of trouble such as divorce or economic downturns, they move home with parents.

The majority of parents give some form of help, most often in the form of advice and child care. In one study, however, 25 percent of adult children reported receiving $500 or more from parents in the last year. As we will see, this is significantly more money than parents receive from adult children. See Table 12-3 for a summary of who gives and, in older years, who receives, help.

TABLE 12-3
GIVING AND RECEIVING IN THE FAMILY

Adult parents give to adult children when

- parents have the resources to do so
- parents and children are geographically close
- there is a good relationship between parents and child
- a grandchild arrives
- grandchildren are young
- women are the parents

Older parents who are more likely to receive help from children are

- women who have many children
- women who have been caregivers
- widows

Adapted from Steven H. Zarit and David J. Eggebeen, "Parent–Child Relationships in Adulthood and Later Years," in *Handbook of Parenting*, 2nd ed., ed. Marc H. Bornstein, vol. 1: *Children and Parenting* (Mahwah, NJ: Erlbaum, 2002).

Generational Linkages

Although parents and children are independent of each other at this stage of life, what each does affects the other. For example, parents who report that their adult children are having problems in maintaining independence and responsibility for themselves experience negative affect and unhappiness.[35] Single parents report a general loss of well-being and self-acceptance but do not report a change in the quality of the parent–child relationship; perhaps because it would be too upsetting to see a major relationship as unsatisfying. Married parents confine their negative feelings to the quality of the parent–child relationship. Spouses appear to provide emotional support so that their overall sense of personal well-being and self-acceptance does not decrease.

Conversely, parents' arguing and continuing conflicts in unhappy marriages plague adult children and decrease their well-being.[36] Adult children feel caught in the conflicts and cannot escape them. Adult children whose parents have divorced were no more likely to feel caught between parents than those adults from low-conflict marriages.

Generational closeness decreases when parents divorce and even more when divorced parents remarry.[37] Divorce appears to have a ripple effect across the generations, affecting the relationships between parents and adult children and between grandparents and grandchildren. Grandparents who divorce are more likely to live farther away from children and grandchildren, see them less often, and have weaker ties with grandchildren. The effects of divorce are more pronounced for grandfathers and for paternal grandparents and less pronounced for maternal grandmothers and their grandchildren.

Increasing Closeness with Grandchildren

The birth of grandchildren increases this closeness between generations. As noted earlier, parents are more likely to be giving when a grandchild arrives, as there is more for them to do. They have information about child rearing and information about the new parent as a baby and growing child that is of interest to the new parent as he or she sees the new baby develop. Parents can also provide instrumental help in the form of household help, child care, and general support.

As grandparents, they also have the marvelous opportunity to reexperience the joys of childhood without the responsibilities, unless they become the primary caregivers. As Gail Sheehy writes, "At this stage of our lives, we can let a grandchild take us back to one of the biggest delights of childhood—becoming so absorbed in playing a game or flying a kite or blowing bubbles that time passes and we don't even notice it."[38]

Grandparents serve their grandchildren as storytellers, family supports, playmates, and patient coaches in life.[39] This greatly benefits the grandchildren (see Chapter 4), but it also serves the grandparents. Grandchildren give grandparents a sense of purpose in life, opportunities to pass on values, and sometimes a chance to redo or undo some of the parenting mistakes of the past. Specifically, grandparenting can sometimes help the relationship between parents and adult children and heal

Grandparents serve as coaches in life and a source of positive support and affection.

wounds from the past. The parent can also be more giving and understanding of the adult child, and the adult child can enjoy and benefit from the greater closeness and understanding of the parent. (See the interview with Julie and Leon.)

Sheehy sums it up: "Grandchildren soften our hearts. They loosen the sludge of old resentments and regrets. It's a chance for reconciliation between ourselves and our children."[40] The best gift of all is having the love you feel reflected in your grandchild's smiling response to you.

Sheehy's rules for effective grandparenting include the following: (1) Provide support to your children, not advice; (2) learn to wait your turn for time with grandchildren; and (3) have close relationships by modern means of communication—e-mail, video conferencing by means of a software package, or sending photos from a digital camera.

Conflicts between Parents and Adult Children

Bengtson's research also identified areas of conflict. When parents and adult children in the Longitudinal Study of Generations (LSOG) described areas of conflict, about one-third could not list any conflict, and many made explicit statements about the satisfactory nature of the relationship.[41] About two-thirds described an average of one area of conflict. The most frequent areas accounting for the majority of problems were similar for the two generations:

- Communication/interaction style—about 33 percent complained about communication being critical, indirect, deceptive, and verbally abusive and the amount of time spent in interaction

- Lifestyle habits/personal choices—about 33 percent complained about the other's living arrangements, choice of friends, spending habits, alcohol use

- Child-rearing values and practices—16 percent complained about spacing of children, level of permissiveness and control, acceptance and approval of grandchildren
- Values, religion, politics—about 12 percent reported conflicts in beliefs

Both generations complained about feeling rejected and abandoned because the other family member interacted little with them. Some disagreements here related to divorce and centered on the treatment of one spouse by the other.

An underlying theme of the verbal comments is that both parents and children want to feel close and get along, and both feel disappointed when this does not happen. There may be empty nests, but neither generation wants empty spaces in their hearts.

Ambivalence

We have discussed closeness and conflict in family relationships. *Ambivalence* is a term describing the contradictory feelings parents and adult children have toward each other when they care for each other and are confronted with an ongoing problem that is not easily resolvable with a single conversation or action.[42] For example, parents who love their adult children may feel highly frustrated and upset at their children's failure to maintain an independent adult status. Or adult children may love their parent but feel very frustrated at their parent's unwillingness to limit the intake of food and alcohol that is impairing their health. These are ongoing frustrations that take many small steps to resolve over time, and family members are pulled and pushed with feelings of love and frustration.

While one-third of parents say they are not close with their children, and two-thirds describe having at least one area of conflict, only 8 percent of mothers in one study were able to say that they had mixed feelings about an adult child even though half the mothers of the group could acknowledge some ambivalence about an aspect of the relationship (e.g., children get on their nerves or restrict them).[43]

Social structures also produce ambivalence in parents and children when they have contradictory role expectations that family members can not meet—to be the loyal worker but also to be the loving child caring for a parent.[44]

Promoting Positive Relationships between Parents and Adult Children

From experiences with his wife and nine children, Stephen Covey has developed the seven habits of highly effective families.[45] These habits emphasize positive communication, understanding others' points of view, making plans to improve relationships, taking action to create the kinds of relationships one wants, and doing enjoyable activities with family members, including extended family members. These are the strategies used in earlier years as well.

Covey has always valued intergenerational relationships and activities and has emphasized them in his family life. He believes that such activities provide support to all members. To illustrate the point with his children, he showed them that

INTERVIEW
with Julie and Leon

Julie and Leon are a married couple in their late sixties. They have four children—two sons, ages forty-four and forty-three, and two daughters, ages thirty-eight and thirty-six. All are currently married with children, and one has had a previous divorce. Each family has three children, ranging in age from newborn to eighteen. One daughter lives fifteen minutes from her parents, the sons live about an hour away, and one daughter lives about three hours away. They are a tightly knit family, spending holidays, vacations, and weekend recreational time together. Family members exchange help, with Julie and Leon providing babysitting and emotional support for grandchildren, and the children giving them special recreational opportunities such as an extended two-week vacation. Not only are the children close to the parents, but the children are close to each other and spend time together without the parents.

Julie and Leon became parents in the late 1950s, when families were larger than they are now and when mothers stayed at home. Julie returned to work when her girls were ages ten and twelve, but she had a flexible job that enabled her to be home by three. She continued to work until her retirement two years ago. Leon retired the year before.

What do you think accounts for the fact that you have such a closely knit family and that your children get along with each other so well?

Julie: One of the secrets is, "Keep your mouth shut because so much is different now." Many of the things that we did in raising our children, especially in the first five years, are passe now.

Leon: For example, our children went to bed and stayed in their own beds all night. They could come in early in the morning, but they did not sleep with us at night. It's not right or wrong, but you adjust to differences.

We made sure our kids were active in sports, and when I came home from work, I played with them, practicing kicking for soccer or throwing for baseball. When the boys were in baseball, I was president of the Little League and scheduled all the games for a thousand kids in the league. We were just as active in the girls' sports. We made sure that, when possible, each of the kids attended the other kids' games or tournaments. The girls went to the boys' events, and even when the boys were in college, they attended the girls' games and competitions when they could.

I took time off from work to go to the games, in contrast to my father, who never came to see me play even if he was off work. He said it put too much pressure on me.

Julie: Having come from a divorced family, being involved with the children, being at home for them and not getting divorced were very important to me.

Leon: I wanted our home to be a place where the kids could bring their friends and play. My mother wouldn't let my friends in the house, and if she did, she criticized them so much afterwards that I never wanted her to see them. So I was determined to have the kids and their friends around and to spend a lot of time with them because I enjoyed it. I could relate to them, and it was easier than work. My sons are not having as much time to play with their children as I did.

Julie: We try not to talk about one child to the other. I did not like it when my grandmother came to visit, and she talked about one uncle to us, and then went and talked to another about us. If you do, later you can be quoted.

(continued)

INTERVIEW with Julie and Leon

(continued)

Leon: The kids like to include us in activities because they know we don't make comments, and they can be relaxed around us. I like all my sons- and daughters-in-law. They are all different, and each brings a new dimension to the family. If you don't like them, it comes through, and they don't like you. My sons-in-law are more comfortable around Julie because I am unpredictable, and they don't know what I might say.

Julie: We tried to teach the children to be happy for each other's successes. Sometimes kids are jealous, and they almost don't like to see the other succeed. We tried to say that your successes will come, too, so be happy for this one.

Leon: The kids appreciate each other's strengths and faults. If I ever detect little jealous criticisms in conversations, I put a stop to it right away.

I like to see all the cousins get along with each other. I was disappointed not to be closer to my nieces and nephews and not to have them close with my children, so I was determined that would not happen with my grandchildren. We have activities where all the cousins can be together and have fun.

It is so important that children know you love them. You don't just say it, but you are thoughtful about them and interested in them and ask them questions about what they are doing. Our granddaughter [eighteen] has called Julie a lifesaver. Julie has always been there for her when her divorced parents didn't get along. She came to live with us the last few months of high school and the summer after graduation because her father lived so far away from her friends, and she and her mother were not getting along. My parents were there for me. I could always call my father, get advice. He wrote me insightful letters, and I have continued that with my children. When I became an adult, I felt secure, knowing people cared for me and were cheering for me. We try to do that for our children and our grandchildren.

---

they can easily break one Popsicle stick, but five Popsicle sticks stacked on top of each other are impossible to break. Similarly, family members together are stronger than anyone alone, and joint activities among family members provide energy and strength for all. Covey's principles provide individuals ways to change themselves from the inside out. Over time, others may change in response, and change will be faster if all family members are following the same program. In parenting adult children, one person alone may want the changes but can promote change in others by taking the first step.

PARENTING DEPENDENT ADULT CHILDREN

Some parents will always have parenting responsibilities in some form, because their children have significant disabilities that require active help. Adult children may suffer from severe intellectual delays, congenital or birth injuries, developmental problems such as autism, or serious psychological disorders that have limited their capacity for independence. And some parents will suddenly have responsibilities

Providing care for dependent adult children places demands on parents and family but gives them satisfaction as well.

for dependent children when their sons and daughters return from the Iraq or Afghanistan wars with extensive injuries requiring complete care.

In the last three decades, many changes have increased the numbers of children with special needs living with parents—the closing of institutions that formerly provided residential care for many people, changes in medications that control behaviors, improved care and education of people so there is less need of institutionalization, increased number of community programs providing work and activities, and increased community and government services.[46] All these changes have created a larger role for parents as the ongoing caregiver and advocate for the child.

The new parental responsibilities for lifespan care of children create stress and the need for coping strategies to maintain parents' own well-being. Difficulties are so different, and parents' resources in meeting them so varied, that one can only paint a very broad picture of parenting adult dependent children. The adult parent–child relationship is shaped by cultural context, type of family, nature of the problem, resources of the family, and services the family obtains from outside agencies.[47]

Studies of family caregiving of adults with special needs reveal that in many ways the nature of the difficulty affects caregiving. Severe intellectual delay, for example, appears to involve less stress for caregivers than do severe psychological problems. Diagnosed early in life, severe intellectual delays proceed in generally predictable fashion. There is less stigma attached to it than to psychological problems, as it is no one's "fault." Caregivers often receive sympathy and admiration for providing in-home care. In contrast, severe psychological difficulties often are diagnosed in late adolescence or early adulthood after decades of competent development.[48] Caregivers go through a period of mourning for the time of normal development. The psychological problems take an unpredictable course, and symptoms may appear suddenly. In the minds of many, such problems are the "fault" of parents or family members, and so they feel some shame. As a result, caregivers of these children have a small support network that usually includes someone who also has a child with similar problems.

Siblings are affected differently by the two disorders. Adults whose siblings have serious psychological problems are more affected, in part because they wonder if this could happen to them or their children.[49] Some decide not to have children for fear of the risk of psychological problems.

African American caregivers, and in some studies Latina/o caregivers, cope better with such stresses and consequently feel less burdened. The mutual-aid system that African Americans emphasize reduces stress even when they have fewer financial resources to help than do wealthier European Americans with a more extensive support system. Women of all ages are more likely to be caregivers than are men, who provide less help and experience less strain.[50]

Rachel Simon describes the satisfaction and insights she received from her relationship with her sister, Beth, who was intellectually delayed and lived in a group home.[51]

Rachel began to become a part of Beth's world when she took time to ride the bus with her. Laid off from her job, Beth spent her time riding the bus in Philadelphia from morning to night. She became friends with the drivers, the dispatcher, and the regular riders. On the other hand, Rachel was a hard-driving professional person who was devoted to work. She let friendships lapse and could not make a commitment to a long-time boyfriend when he asked her to marry him.

When Beth had to have eye surgery and became very nervous about the surgery and the recovery that would have to follow, Beth drew on her network of friends, who came to the hospital with her, took her into their homes following the surgery, and cared for her until she recovered. Witnessing the strong, caring bonds Beth had formed with other people changed Rachel, who said,

> I came to want a different life for myself than the one I'd had. And a few months after that, I phoned Sam [the boyfriend to whom she could not make a commitment]. We talked for a long time, and I was no longer scared. From there we began a surprising and wonderful courtship that resulted in our wedding in May 2001.[52]

So, Beth changed Rachel and helped her achieve a major life goal.

The question of out-of-home living, such as in a group home, may arise. Parents may include siblings in the plans and in the ongoing care that will have to continue when parents die. The move to some form of group living may occur naturally as a part of general plans for the dependent adult to become more independent, or because the parent cannot continue the caregiving due to poor health or the dependent adult needs more help. Professionals and support group members can give guidelines and emotional support, but only family members in consultation with the dependent adult can make decisions.

PARENTING ONE'S OWN PARENTS

Parenting one's own parent is a gradual process that actually begins when one is young. The preschooler who points out the location of an item the parent is searching for, the older child who sympathizes with a parent's difficult workload, the college student who gives the parents valuable insight on a problem, all involve supporting and caring for the parent.

Parents today not only have longer lifespans, but they are healthier and wealthier than previous generations as they age. As such, some adult children may give little help or give care for a brief period when a parent has an acute illness. Nonetheless, many adult children will become their parent's parent during these years for a variety of reasons. Increasing divorce means many aging parents do not have care from a spouse and have reduced economic resources as well.[53] Young adult children, however, must often work full time and answer their own children's needs; they are often not geographically available to give care. Furthermore, today's smaller families mean there are fewer children to share the caregiving.

There are many similarities between parenting adult dependent children and parenting an aging parent. Wives and daughters do the primary caregiving, husbands do less, and sons the least.[54]

While they are healthy and well functioning, parents tend to give rather than receive help. When needs arise, though, children do step in to meet parents' needs, especially when relationships are good.[55] Children are most likely to give advice and help with home chores, repairs, shopping, and errands. Financial help is rarer; in one survey, only 3 percent of parents reported receiving $200 or more in five years. The more children one has, the more likely one is to receive help, so having many children continues to ensure help in older age. Those women who have been caregivers for so many years are more likely to receive aid than are men.

As noted earlier, divorce affects relationships through the generations. Parental divorce, which is becoming more frequent, reduces contact between parents and children and decreases the quality of their relationship, so that there is less mutual help between generations.[56] Interestingly, elderly widows receive more assistance than do married parents, perhaps because they have fewer resources.

Most cultures emphasize care of older parents. Both generations prefer parents to live independently when they are healthy and functioning well, but this does not always happen. A major transition occurs when a parent can no longer live alone. This decision is usually made by children, the parents, and the physician. A variety of alternatives exist. Parents may hire live-in help, but the most common arrangement is that the parent comes to live with the child; if needed, hired caregivers can come to or live in the home. Parents may also go to some form of residential living that involves levels of care—independent living, assisted living, and nursing care. There are also nursing homes and board-and-care homes. Even then, children will be involved in visiting, overseeing care, paying bills, and doing other necessary chores for parents. Making the decision for a parent to go into residential care is difficult for children. Parents sometimes spare children this task when they move into places with graded levels of care when healthy and simply move to the next level of care as needed.

Caregivers experience stress from many sources. They become depressed and isolated from others.[57] Conflict with noncaregiving brothers and sisters increases the stress, as does the decision to leave work to meet parents' needs. Caregiving can so take over caregivers' lives that they feel they have lost their personal identities. Social support from friends, siblings, and spouses reduces this stress. Married caregivers feel less strain than do single or divorced caregivers. Sibling support reduces strain as well. Caregivers who are active problem-solvers manage the stress most effectively. Formal support, such as day care programs, can reduce stress as well. Too many caregivers do not have access to them.

PARENTS' EXPERIENCES IN FACING TRANSITIONS

We have seen throughout this chapter the full span of parenting adults, which began when children first left home to be adults. "Empty nest" refers to the sad, empty feelings many parents have as children leave home and make their own lives. Even when children still live at home, parents' roles as caregiver and as primary authority decrease. Although parents welcome children's growing independence and competence, many long nostalgically for the days when everyone was together and all activities outside of work were family activities. Others, however, see these years as times of possibility for themselves.

Barbara Unell and Jerry Wyckoff describe this stage of parenthood as the family remodeling stage.[58] The home is no longer occupied as it once was. Children come and go during the college years or are out and working, so the home needs psychological "remodeling."

With more time and possibly more resources for their needs, parents often look at what they want to do with the rest of their lives. So, while children's leaving brings sadness, it can also spark excitement and renewed energy for the possibilities that greater freedom brings to adults.

The next stage of parenting is the plateau period. Children are grown and independent. Parents have created a satisfying lifestyle and are ready to enjoy grandparenting. Plateau parents have a sense of the circle of life and their role in it. As their children become parents and they grandparents, they move on to mentor another generation. Plateau parents sometimes have to make choices about nurturing and giving, as they are part of the "sandwich generation" that nurtures aging parents as well as adult children.

Unell and Wyckoff describe the final years of parenthood as the rebounding years, when aging parents bounce back from the stresses of illness or other crises

---

INTERVIEW
with Harry

Harry, a Chicago optometrist in his sixties, shared these anecdotes from his own life.

Harry commented, "It's never too late to learn and to change. And you can even be a parent to your parent. When my father was eighty-nine, he had a big birthday party, and I went home for it. There were lots of guests, but my father was sitting off to the side of the garden. He motioned me over to him and said, 'Sit down, I want to talk to you. I want to apologize for all the things I did when you were growing up. I wish I had been a different father.'"

"What did you do?" Harry asked his father.

"You know what I did. Why are you hurting me by making me tell you now?"

"I know that I know, but I want to know what you're apologizing for."

His father stopped, thought, then talked for half an hour about all the things he did. When he was through, he concluded, "I didn't mean to hurt you. I love you."

Harry replied, "I hated you for doing those things, but I want to thank you for apologizing to me. If I had to do it to my children, I would find it very difficult."

His father said, "I want you to know I loved you then, I love you now, and I always will love you."

"Why are you telling me these things now?" Harry asked.

His father explained, "I'm sitting here looking at all these children and how parents behave with them, and I realize I made some terrible mistakes with you."

Harry said, "There was a great release from the anger I carried all those years." His father died a year later.

Harry went on to describe how he changed his mother's behavior. "In all my childhood she never told me she loved me. So when she was about ninety, I thought I would give her what she couldn't give to me. I called every week, and it was usually a superficial conversation, "How are you? What are you doing?" At the end of one phone conversation, I took a deep breath, and said, 'I . . .' It was so hard to say, I almost gave up, but I gritted my teeth and blurted out, 'I love you, Mom.' And she replied she loved me. Each week it was a little easier.

"Then about the sixth week, no sooner had I got into the conversation, she said, 'You know, son, I really love you.'"

"Giving them what they could not give to me has been healing for them and healing for me."

---

and also respond to the overtures of other family members for contact and help. They seek attention and are waiting for family members to interact with them and help as needed. Unell and Wyckoff identify three types of rebounders—the proud independents, the humble submissives, and the aged sages. Proud independents, as the name suggests, want to retain their autonomy as long as possible. They reject any offer of help and worry their children with their independent behaviors. Humble submissives feel apologetic at inconveniencing their children and rarely ask for help directly. As a result, they often do not get the help they want and do not recognize the help that is offered. They tend to feel rejected and complain about their life circumstances. Aged sages try to maintain independence but request help as they need it and express their appreciation for what others do for them. They enjoy others' company and do whatever they can to reciprocate the help they receive:

> When I stopped complaining that my daughter never called or my sons never came to see me, I suddenly became more popular. I had to learn not to push my grandchildren into taking care of me. Instead I asked them about their lives and didn't complain about mine. Like magic, they then started coming to family night at the retirement center where I live, showing off their children's report cards and pictures of their latest vacation. They even remembered to include me on the invitation list for my grandchildren's and great-grandchildren's birthday parties.[59]

Rebounders are in the stage of arriving at what Erik Erikson termed a "sense of integrity" (see Chapter 2), which involves feeling satisfied with one's life and accomplishments.

While parents usually have a greater reliance on children than children have on parents, still many adult children treasure their connection with their aging parent. They rely on being parented with advice and support even when they themselves are giving significant help to their parents.

Reviewing this chapter, we can see that acceptance, nurturing attachment, active listening, and problem solving are the basic strategies of parenting in the adult years, as in all the preceding years.

SUPPORT FOR PARENTS

Support groups provide services for parents across the lifespan. When children have developmental delays or special problems, parents' groups help parents cope with the diagnosis.[60] Support groups also help parents cope with marital and personal issues that arise from dealing with a child with special needs. As noted, such groups are especially important to help caregivers cope with mental illness, as caregivers often feel that only someone who has been in their shoes can understand their situation and feelings. Support groups are equally important for those parenting aging parents. In addition to receiving emotional support, people who attend support groups get information on new treatments, resources in the community and how to access them, and coping strategies that work, as well as establishing a personal network they can rely upon for help.

Certainly, services need to be available for disabled adult children and their caregivers. Such programs need to be designed to counteract some families' tendencies to want to hide the disabled person and to counteract cultural beliefs that caring relatives should not rely on social programs to care for family members.[61]

Although we have focused on the demands of caregiving, benefits also exist. Many parents gain satisfaction from providing care for the adult child who lives with them. As parents age, the adult dependent child with mental illness can sometimes care for the parent. Living with one's own aging parent can bring the joys of intergenerational closeness discussed earlier.

MAIN POINTS

Criteria for adulthood include

- being over age eighteen
- being financially and psychologically self-sustaining
- taking on adult roles of parent and worker

Theoretical perspectives include

- Erikson's lifespan theory emphasizing work, love relationship, and rearing children
- attachment theory, emphasizing communication, availability, and nurturance from attachment figure
- the theory of emerging adulthood

Paths to adulthood

- include some combination of schooling, work, independent living, romantic relationship, and rearing children
- are termed Fast Starters, Parents without Careers, Educated Partners, Educated Singles, Working Singles, and Slow Starters
- are similar in youths from immigrant families
- require more support for youths who have received special services
- achieve similar levels of adult status for youth who have had chronic physical illness
- go more smoothly when parents provide emotional, social, informational, and financial support

When children are adults, families

- differ in closeness, agreement, proximity, contact, and amount of help exchanged
- fall into five typologies—tightly knit, sociable, intimate but distant, obligatory, and detached, with women more likely to be in tightly knit families and men in sociable and obligatory family relationships
- give several types of support—financial, emotional, instrumental, and informational
- are most likely to give help when members are close, see each other frequently, and grandchildren are involved

Positive relationships are promoted

- when grandparents and grandchildren enjoy the grandchildren's childhood together
- when parents emphasize positive communications, win–win solutions, and doing enjoyable activities together to increase family solidarity

Conflicts with adult children center on

- communication/interaction style
- lifestyle habits and personal choices

- child-rearing values and practices

Parenting dependent adults and older parents

- involves caregiving and seeking support
- can be enriching both psychologically and emotionally
- often involves looking for some form of placement outside the home

The stages parents experience as children go through adulthood include

- the family remodeling stage
- the plateau stage
- the rebounding stage

As in other phases of life, parenting in the adult years of life involves

- acceptance, availability, nurturance
- positive support and problem-solving help

EXERCISES

1. If you were a parent of two teenage children, what actions would you take so that your children would have a smooth transition to adulthood?

2. If you were an aging parent, what actions would you take to promote positive relationships with your children and grandchildren?

3. Have the class divide into small groups and discuss their opinions regarding college presidents' call to consider reducing the legal age for drinking alcohol to age eighteen to decrease binge drinking and other drinking problems students experience.

4. Imagine that you are the parent of a dependent adult child with severe intellectual delays or a returning vet with traumatic brain injury or severe physical impairment. What are the services available for people with these problems? Look in the community for the kinds of out-of-home living arrangements available. How would they be paid for?

5. Imagine that you are the child of an aging parent who could not live alone. What living arrangements are possible for such a parent in the community? What is the cost of such arrangements?

ADDITIONAL READINGS

Epstein, Joel. *Sex, Drugs, and Flunking Out*. Center City, MN: Hazelden, 2001.

Isay, Jane. *Walking on Egg Shells*. New York: Flying Dolphin Press, 2007.

Kastner, Laura S., and Wyatt, Jennifer. *The Launching Years*. New York: Three Rivers Press, 2002.

Koplewicz, Harold S. *More Than Moody*. New York: Putnam, 2002.

Peel, Kathy. *Family for Life*. New York: McGraw-Hill, 2003.

Unell, Barbara C., and Wyckoff, Jerry L. *The Eight Seasons of Parenthood*. New York: Times Books, 2000.

III

Parenting in Varying Life Circumstances

C H A P T E R

13

Parenting and Working

IN THE NEWS

New York Times Magazine, June 15[1]:
Parents find many different ways to share working and parenting. See page 396.

Test Your Knowledge: Fact or Fiction (True/False)

1. Children in dual-earner families report lack of time with parents as the source of greatest stress for them.
2. In a survey, children report employed mothers and fathers as equally good at controlling their tempers when children do something wrong.
3. Research shows that, in predicting children's competence, parenting matters much more than day care.
4. Early adolescents are old enough to engage in self-care without negative consequences.
5. The fees for good-quality day care are not very different from fees for mediocre care.

Combining working and parenting is a major challenge for today's men and women. The majority of mothers work from the time their children are infants, and more fathers than ever before are involved in child care. How do parents solve the problems that arise in integrating work and family lives? How do they find child care that promotes children's development? How do they adjust routines to enhance the quality of time they spend with children? How do they adapt to their many responsibilities yet maintain a sense of well-being?

In our present society, most parents work. In 2007, both parents were employed in 59 percent of two-parent families with children under age six and 66 percent of two-parent families with children under age eighteen.[2] The comparable figures for separated and divorced mothers are higher, with 67 percent of those with children under 6 and 78 percent of those with children 6-17 employed. Married fathers' labor participation is very high—95 percent—and single fathers' rate is not listed, although the employment rate for single men of all ages is 70 percent.

In this chapter, we look at how men and women integrate working and parenting, the day care options available when parents work, the impact of day care on children, and ways parents care for themselves as they raise the next generation.

A CONCEPTUAL FRAMEWORK FOR UNDERSTANDING THE IMPACTS OF WORK, FAMILY, AND COMMUNITY ON PARENTS AND CHILDREN

Drawing on Urie Bronfenbrenner's bioecological systems theory (see Chapter 2), Patricia Voydanoff has developed a broad framework for understanding the ways that experiences in the domains of work, family life, and the community influence parents' and children's functioning and well-being.[3]

She describes the microsystem level as the daily, direct interactions parents have in each of these areas—work, family, and community. She also describes the mesosystem level as the interrelationships between the areas—the mesosystems of work–family, work–community, family–community, and work–family–community. We see the interrelationships of the areas in this example: When economic factors change in the community and we shift from a manufacturing economy to a technology-information-based economy requiring workers to have more education, then workers spend more time in school, start stable work later, marry later, and have children later.[4] So community changes impact work and family.

Conversely, family life influences work participation. For example, when injured veterans return home parents or spouses may leave work to care for them. When parents have children, both parents are less likely to be employed in the first three or four years of their children's lives. When people live longer and require more care at the end of life, workers reduce their work hours and community participation to care for aging family members.[5]

Within each domain, demands/strains and resources/supports affect parents' performance in that area and their general feelings of satisfaction and well-being. Boundary-spanning demands and supports in one domain contribute to participation in other domains. Table 13-1 presents Voydanoff's general framework.

The term "fit" describes the relationship between the demands and the resources to carry out the tasks in a domain. The fit is positive when parents have the abilities and resources to manage the demands and perform at work or at home, and feel good about their performance. Stress occurs when the demands overwhelm the person's abilities and resources to function in that area. The fit between two domains (e.g., work–family fit) results from the combination of the demands and

■ **T A B L E 13-1**
CONCEPTUAL FRAMEWORK FOR UNDERSTANDING RELATIONSHIPS
BETWEEN WORK, FAMILY, AND COMMUNITY*

	Work	Family	Community
Time Demands	Scheduled Hours	Child Care Time	Volunteer Time
	Overtime Hours	Spouse Time	Friends
	Nonstandard Work Times	Extended Family Time	
		Household Work	
Strain-Based Demands	Job Demands	Marital Conflict	Neighborhood Problems
	Work Conflicts	Children's Problems	Friend Problems
	Job Insecurity	Caregiver Strain Unfair Housework	
Boundary-Spanning Demands	Overnight Travel	Commuting Time	Hours/Schedules of Services
	Working at Home	Family Activities at Work	
Resources/ Supports	Salary	Spouse Salary	Recreational Programs
	Benefit/Health Care	Positive Spouse Relationship	Safe Neighbor-hoods
	Increasing Skills	Extended Family Help	Friend Help
	Psychological/Social Support		
	Positive Feelings Re Self	Positive Feelings Re Self	Positive Feelings Re Self
Boundary-Spanning Supports	Flexible Work	Benefits from Spouse Work	Child Care After-School Programs
	Dependent Care		

Adapted from Patricia Voydanoff, *Work, Family, Community: Exploring Interconnections* (New York: Psychology Press, 2007).

resources within both domains. Thus, two forms of action are possible to attain a positive fit: decrease the demands or increase the resources to meet the demands. For example, when work demands increase for a period of time, extended relatives can step in and do household chores.

Positive Spillover from Work and Community to Family

Parents' work and community environments benefit them in many ways besides the salary.[6] First, employee benefits provide health care, and dependent care, and disability insurance that aid parents and families. Work also provides paid leave and time in emergencies. Community programs help with child care and elder care programs. Community aid also includes child care subsidies that enable low-income urban mothers to enter the workforce and enable them to comply with employer needs for additional work hours.[7] Mothers have fewer scheduling problems, are able to put in overtime, and earn more money.

In the daily routines of life, flexible work schedules, allowing part-time work and work from home, and establishing work policies that enable parents to have time off during the day to meet family doctor and school appointments increase parents' performance and well-being at home and also at work. Even if parents do not use workplace flexible benefits, the perception of having them increases job and family satisfaction.[8]

About 77 percent of parents report that they often or very often feel successful at work. Success is related to having time to get work done but more importantly to being able to focus on work without interruptions, being able to complete a task before getting another one.[9] Feeling successful at work is related to autonomy in jobs, positive relationships with coworkers, and feeling the job is meaningful.

Work policies that encourage parents' skill development, pay the costs of further education, and offer advancement for the development of new skills promote greater competencies in parents. Work training sometimes includes interpersonal and problem-solving skills that parents use at home. One mother told a psychologist, "My daughter was having trouble going to sleep so 1 decided to handle the problem like we would at work. I asked her what she thought would solve the problem, and she said 'Reading two stories to me.' I did that, and she went to sleep. That cured the problem."[10]

Parents' work behavior affects children's behavior and moods. When fathers are psychologically engaged in work but are available at home, and when mothers have control of their work and feel confident, their children are more likely to be described as socially and academically competent in kindergarten.[11] Adolescents whose single mothers entered the labor force and got and kept a good job that paid a living wage for two years reported feelings of mastery and self-esteem while adolescents whose mothers had unstable unemployment for that period had an increased risk of school dropout and declines in well-being.[12]

Parents who felt positive spillover from work to home (about a third of the parents in one study)[13] were those who (1) were married, (2) had jobs that demanded more days per week, (3) experienced less stress and more autonomy at work, (4) had more supportive supervisors and coworkers, (5) had more parental support from family and friends, and (6) felt they were raising their children as they wanted.

Positive Spillover from Home to Work

About 70 percent of parents with children under age eighteen say that their positive feelings about their children often or very often carry over to work, and about one-third say they often or very often have more energy on the job because of their children.[14] The parents who are more likely to have positive spillover from home to work are those who (1) are fathers, (2) put a higher priority on family life, (3) feel they have support for doing their work—they have day care they trust and parental support at times of difficulty, (4) work more days per week but feel fewer stresses and strains at work, (5) have better-quality jobs with more autonomy and learning opportunities, and (6) have more workplace support from coworkers.

When mothers want to work, when they feel that their children do not suffer from their working, and when they have husbands' support, they feel increased satisfaction with themselves and with life.[15] Like mothers, fathers also experienced increased morale when they were satisfied with child care and children's adjustment to mothers' working.

Negative Spillover from Work to Home

Events and conditions at work can have fleeting and long-term effects on family life. For example, negative interactions at work influence parent–child and marital interactions that day. A study of mothers and preschool children found that when mothers had stressful workdays, they were more withdrawn and less attentive when they picked up their children and less caring and less loving with them.[16] Children tried to please mothers and engage them in activity but sometimes seemed less happy. Job stress was most upsetting to women who already had feelings of anxiety and depression.

When husbands and wives have negative social interactions at work, they both report greater anger in marital interactions and greater withdrawal.[17] Increased workload also predicted wives' increased marital anger and withdrawal.

Several studies have focused on longer-term effects of parents' work hours on parenting and children's behavior. An economy in which businesses operate around the clock creates many jobs outside the standard 9 to 5 hours. When parents work outside the standard hours (working nights and/or weekends), they report greater emotional distress and less effective parenting than parents who work standard hours.[18] Their children, age two to eleven, show greater behavioral difficulties as measured by items from the Children's Behavior Check List. The differences were greatest between families in which both parents worked standard and both parents worked nonstandard hours, but even having one parent working nonstandard hours predicted greater parental distress, less effective parenting, and children's behavioral difficulties.

In a study of primarily low-income, single mothers, nonstandard hours of work predicted concurrent decrease in children's school performance and an increase in their aggressive and noncompliant behaviors.[19] In another study of single mothers, the length of their commute time predicted children's anxiety and nervousness.[20]

Sixty-nine percent of parents in one survey reported that they feel a moderate or large amount of work stress, and 55 percent say they feel a moderate or large amount of frustration at work.[21] Stress appears to be related to job demands—working more hours per day and more days per week, having to take work home, having to travel more, feeling pressured to complete work in short periods of time with little control of how it is done, and feeling that the job is meaningless.

Frustration has similar origins but is more related to the daily work schedule than to the total amount of time worked. Inability to focus, feeling unable to make decisions, and feeling that the job entails no learning also increase frustration.

When parents work unstandard hours, they report greater parental stress and less effective parenting behavior.

Parents who were most likely to experience negative spillover from work to home were those who (1) put a higher priority on work than family, (2) were more likely to be managers or professionals with relatively large responsibilities at work, (3) had demanding jobs that were difficult to complete on time, (4) had jobs that were too stimulating or not stimulating enough, and (5) had less parenting support than did those who did not feel stress.[22]

Negative Spillover from Family to Work

Despite the demands family activities make on parents, parents feel much less stress in caring for children than they do at work.[23] Only 6 percent of parents say they feel a great deal of stress in caring for children, and an additional 36 percent say they feel a moderate amount of stress. By comparison, 24 percent experience a large amount of stress at work, and 45 percent experience a moderate amount.

Both parents felt stress at work when daughters lacked after-school supervision.[24] Parents from the ages of twenty-five to fifty-four reported the same levels of negative spillover from home to work, but the sources of stress changed with age.[25] Younger parents with children under age eighteen, those who were unmarried or divorced and lacked partner support, and older parents who were caring for aging parents all reported negative spillover.

Families with marked stress are the sandwich generation, those caring for dependent children and elder parents and work responsibilities.[26] A national survey revealed that between 10 and 13 percent of families fell into that category, with wives' spending 9.5 hours weekly and husbands' 7.5 on care with elder parents in addition to their child-care responsibilities. The study revealed that it was not the objective factors such as the hours worked or the number of children or elders being cared for that predicted parents' stress at home and at work, but subjective feelings of negative reactivity, the quality of the job role, and for women their satisfaction with their care of children that predicted their feelings of depression and dissatisfaction with their overall role performance.

While women reported more depressive symptoms and greater negative spillover to work than their husbands, they also reported greater positive spillover from family to work and feelings of higher job quality. Wives, as in other studies, were more likely than husbands to adjust work to meet family demands—reduce hours, take paid leave for appointments—and report poorer work performance.[27] Both men and women still reported great satisfaction in being able to care for their elder parents at that stage of life. We will return to this study when we discuss resilience in dealing with negative stress.

Resilience in the Face of Negative Economic Events

Even at times of economic downturns, parents' responses influence marital relationship, effective parenting, and children's well-being. A longitudinal study describing how farm families with two children responded to a severe loss in farm revenues found that two ways of adapting to the stress helped the whole family.[28] When parents were cooperative with each other and provided positive emotional support to each other, they felt self-confident and experienced little distress from the economic pressures. Parents' resilience was also related to their ability to use problem-solving strategies to deal with the specific problems. Couples who used these strategies experienced a sense of mastery. So a supportive marital relationship and the use of problem-solving strategies buffered families from the emotional distress and tension that occur when income disappears.

Since economic pressures affected them less, parents could maintain warm, nurturant parenting that supported children's functioning. Their children reported little emotional distress, and were able to perform well in school, had close friendships, and avoided aggressive and delinquent behaviors. Even if parents were tense with each other and harsh in their parenting, children who had warm relationships with siblings or with adults outside the family still avoided problem behaviors such as drinking. So positive emotional relationships, with parents and with others such as siblings or adults in the community, buffered adolescents' functioning at times of economic stress.

Resilience in Dealing with Stresses at Home

The couples in the sandwich generation used many ways of coping.[29] In general, they decreased the demands in their lives and increased the resources to support them. At work, they drew on benefits such as dependent care, family medical leave that gave them time off, and flexible work schedules to decrease demands on their time. They drew on the support of friends and community programs such as child and elder care or home services to increase resources for handling increased demands on their time.

The key finding of the study was the centrality of spousal support in coping with all the demands and the stress. When wives and husbands were positive and supportive of each other, parents not only felt more life satisfaction and self-satisfaction in their overall role performance, but they adopted the positive parent's coping strategies, felt more comfortable, and were more effective in functioning. A single parent has to build a positive support system with others.

Parents' most frequent emotional and cognitive coping strategies are listed in Table 13-2. Structuring priorities and limiting activities reduce demands. Maintaining positive moods by focusing on the positive aspects of life and seeking outside support increase parental resources. While some couples coped by limiting their social activities, their withdrawal predicted lower work performance and decreased well-being.

PARENTS AND CHILDREN AT HOME

This section focuses on parents and childrens' relationship when parents work.

Children's Ratings of Parents

Ellen Galinsky, president of the Families and Work Institute, has expressed concern that children's opinions have not been included in the discussions of the effects of parents' work on children and family life.[30] Galinsky interviewed a representative sample of 605 employed parents with children under age eighteen and surveyed a representative sample of 1,023 third- to twelfth-grade children. The sample of children varied with respect to the parents' work status—employed or nonemployed—and number of hours worked. Children's attitude toward their mother and their assessment of the parent–child relationship did not depend on the work status of the mother or the number of hours the mother worked.

■ **T A B L E 13-2**
COPING STRATEGIES WHEN CARING FOR CHILDREN AND OLDER PARENTS*

Emotional Strategies Frequently Used by Husbands and Wives

1. I focus on the many good things I have.
2. I try and find humor in the situation.
3. I get moral support and comfort from others.
4. I try to realize that I can't do it all, and it's okay.

Cognitive-Behavioral Strategies Frequently Used by Husbands and Wives

1. I prioritize and do the things that are most necessary.
2. I plan how I'm going to use my time and energy.
3. I take on tasks if no one else is capable or available.
4. I limit my volunteer work.

Adapted from Margaret B. Neal and Leslie B. Hammer, *Working Couples Caring for Children and Aging Parents: Effects on Work and Well Being* (Mahwah, NJ: Erlbaum, 2007), pp. 330–332.

Nonemployed fathers, however, were rated lower than were employed fathers in the areas of (1) making their children feel important and loved and (2) participating in important events in their children's lives. Children tended to give parents higher grades when the family was seen as financially secure.

Seventy-four percent of children felt mothers were very successful in managing work and family life, and 67 percent of children felt fathers were very successful. As shown in Table 13-3, parents received high marks for making children feel important and loved, being understanding, appreciating children, and being there for conversation. Although mothers were overwhelmingly seen as the parent who was there for children at times of sickness, more frequently involved than fathers in school matters, and someone children could go to when upset, the ratings for fathers on other qualities were similar to those given to mothers. Fathers were seen as being appreciative of who the child really was, spending time in conversation, and controlling their temper with the child as well as the mother did.

Parents gave themselves equally high marks in these areas. Children's ratings of parents were higher when they spent more time with parents and when the time with parents was not rushed. About 40 percent of mothers and children and 32 percent of fathers, however, felt that their time together was somewhat or very rushed.

Divergences in Parents' and Children's Perceptions

The survey responses Galinsky obtained from children revealed discrepancies between parents' and children's perceptions. Children were more satisfied with the amount of time parents spent with them than were parents. About 44 percent of mothers and 56 percent of fathers felt they spent too little time with their children, whereas only 28 percent of children felt mothers spent too little time, and

Children gave their relationships with working parents higher ratings when they spent more time with parents that was not rushed.

■ **T A B L E 13-3**
STUDENTS'* LETTER GRADES FOR PARENTS' BEHAVIORS

Letter Grade	A		B		C		D		E	
Parents' Behavior	M*	F*	M	F	M	F	M	F	M	F
Being there for me when I'm sick	85	58	8	20	4	12	2	7	1	3
Appreciating me for who I am	72	69	15	16	6	8	4	5	3	2
Making me feel loved for who I am	72	66	16	18	8	9	4	4	1	2
Attending important events in my life	69	60	18	20	7	12	3	4	3	5
Being someone I can go to when I'm upset	57	48	18	19	11	14	6	8	8	10
Being involved in what's happening to me at school	55	45	22	24	11	15	7	10	5	6
Spending time talking to me	48	47	31	25	12	16	5	8	4	4
Controlling their temper when I do something wrong	28	31	31	28	19	18	11	11	11	12

*Students in third through twelfth grades
*M indicates percentage of students giving mother that grade
*F indicates percentage of students giving father that grade
From Ellen Galinsky, *Ask the Children: What America's Children Really Think about Working Parents* (New York: Morrow, 1999).

35 percent of children felt fathers spent too little time. The survey asked children to name one wish that would change how parents' working affected the family. Parents expected children to say they wanted more time with parents. Children, however, had three more-important wishes. They wished that parents earned more money, returned from work less stressed, and felt less tired.

Also, when asked if they worried about their parents, approximately one-third of children aged eight to eighteen said that they often or very often worried about their parents, and another third said they sometimes worried. So, about two-thirds of children worry about parents at least some of the time. Children said they worried because they were part of a caring family, but they also worried because they felt their parents had a lot of stress from work. Thirty percent of children aged twelve to eighteen said the worst thing about having working parents was that they were stressed out from work. One suspects that children wanted parents to earn more money so they would feel less stressed.

Furthermore, children saw their parents as less emotionally available to them than parents believed they were, and children were more concerned about parents' anger than parents were. Ninety-six percent of mothers and 90 percent of fathers gave themselves As and Bs for being emotionally available when their children were upset, but only 75 percent of children gave mothers As and Bs and 67 percent gave fathers As and Bs. Only 4 percent of mothers and 5.5 percent of fathers gave themselves Ds and Fs for controlling their tempers, whereas 22 percent of children gave mothers Ds and Fs, and 23 percent gave fathers Ds and Fs.

Parents are sometimes not aware of children's wishes and priorities. Children want parents to be happier and less stressed and available for them emotionally without being angry.

Parent–Child Interactions

Parents' levels of satisfaction and stress with work and family rest heavily on how well parents feel they are meeting children's needs.[31] Parents feel good about their parenting when they spend time eating meals together, doing homework, and playing together. Parents' time diaries over a period from 1965 to 2001 reveal mothers are spending as much time with their children as they did in 1965 despite their increasing participation in work.[32] Fathers are now spending more time in routine care with children and have greater knowledge of children's activities than they did earlier.

Parents maintain this high level of involvement both with children and work by increasing their weekly workload. Working mothers have a weekly workload of 71 hours, employed fathers a weekly workload of 64 hours, and unemployed mothers at home with children, a weekly workload of 54 hours.[33]

Employed parents not only spend time with children, but they interact more intensely with them when they are at home.[34] Employed mothers of infants and toddlers play, talk, and stimulate children more than unemployed mothers. Employed fathers play more games and are more involved in educational activities with children.[35] Therefore, children of employed parents have more social interactions with peers at day care and more interactive relationships with parents when home.

Intentional Parenting

Galinsky uses the term *intentional parenting* to refer to the time, energy, and focus that working parents must bring to the process of meeting children's needs.[36] Galinsky believes parents must consider the quality of their interactions with children. Children do not necessarily want more hours with parents. They want parents to be calm, free of anger, and emotionally available to them. Galinsky recommends parents spend time with children by hanging around and being available for conversation and casual play that supports children's interests. Parents improve relationships by communicating their feelings without irritation and anger. Galinsky quotes a twelve-year-old:

> Listen. Listen to what your kids say, because you know, sometimes it's very important. And sometimes a kid can have a great idea and it could even affect you. Because, you know, kids are people. Kids have great ideas, as great as you, as great as ideas that adults have.[37]

Finally, Galinsky recommends that parents talk about their work. Children often do not understand the positive aspects of their parents' work, and so they have a limited view of the meaning of work in people's lives. In part, children may be so concerned about parents' stress because they hear mostly negative things about work. Parents need to discuss what they do, why they like it, and the importance of their work. Children learn many indirect lessons about work from the way parents discuss their own strategies for accomplishing tasks and getting along with others.

Having more time, not feeling rushed, and focusing on children related not only to parents' feelings of satisfaction and success at home, but also to parents' reporting their children had fewer problems with anxiety, depression, and inattention.

Encouraging Family Cooperation in Household Work

Although women usually retain primary responsibility for household management, men's participation in traditionally female household chores serves as a positive example for boys and girls, who do less stereotyping when fathers perform such chores.[38] Furthermore, children who participate routinely in chores that benefit the family tend to show concern for others' welfare.[39]

Although women have traditionally borne the major responsibility for meeting household needs, they are shifting the responsibility to the family as a whole. Jacqueline Goodnow and Jennifer Bowes's interviews with parents and children concerning the distribution of household work reveal that the meanings people attach to particular jobs (men's/women's work, boy's/girl's work, Dad's/Mom's responsibility), the feelings they have about the jobs (like/dislike, feel competence/incompetence), and underlying principles of fairness shape how families distribute work.[40]

Several recommendations emerge from discussions with families. First, a problem-solving approach that focuses on the specific question of "Who does this particular job?" is useful. Second, negotiating chores in an atmosphere of fairness, respect, and open-mindedness increases cooperation. People's preferences are respected and considered. Families can divide household chores into two categories: (1) self-care (making one's bed, picking up clothes or toys) and (2) family care (setting the table, taking out the garbage). Most families assign self-care responsibilities to children as they become able to do them. Performing self-care chores gives children feelings of competence because they can care for themselves. As family chores are distributed among family members, children receive their share to promote feelings of being important participants in family life.

Families often feel dissatisfied with what they are doing and want to alter their patterns. Table 13-4 contains suggestions for handling work responsibilities by staying flexible and focusing on the positive contributions all members make to family life.

Monitoring

Monitoring and supervising children's activities is a major parenting task. Although working parents are often not present after school, they can monitor by phone what school-age children do and make certain children engage in approved activities. Studies have found that parents in dual-earner families monitor as carefully as parents in single-earner families.[41] This is important because less well-monitored boys have

■ **TABLE 13-4**
MOVING TO NEW PATTERNS OF HOUSEHOLD WORK

1. *Take a look at what bothers you.* Ask yourself why you are doing this chore. What specifically bothers you about the chore? What is the worst part of the chore for you?

2. *List the alternatives.* Jobs can be changed in many ways—eliminated, reassigned to someone else in the family, reduced (e.g., iron only some things but not everything), moved outside the family.

3. *Look carefully at the way you frame the problem and at the way you talk and negotiate.* Explain what you want, stick to the point in discussing the problem, and frame the issues in terms of practicality, logic, or benefits to all family members. Avoid name-calling.

4. *Be prepared for difficulties.* The greatest difficulty is dealing with family members' having different standards for completing chores. Children often do not want to do chores because of criticism. Focus on the effort each person puts in and do not insist on perfect completion.

5. *Remember that there is more than one way to express caring and affection in a family.* Men and women have to give up old beliefs that caring must be shown by being a "good provider" or a "good homemaker." Caring for a family is more than doing housework.

6. *Keep in mind the gains as well as the costs.* Although all family members give up time to do household chores, everyone gains. All family members gain in doing chores and contributing to family functioning. They gain self-respect, skills, and the primary benefit of greater closeness to other family members.

Adopted from Jacqueline J. Goodnow and Jennifer M. Bowes, *Men, Women and Household Work* (Melbourne, Australia: Oxford University Press, 1994), pp. 197–201.

lower school grades and less skill in school-related activities, regardless of whether mothers are employed. Girls' behavior is not so clearly related to monitoring.[42]

As we noted in Chapter 10, parents' careful monitoring of their early adolescent boys and girls was related to a lack of externalizing problems such as disobeying and fighting. Careful monitoring counterbalanced the effects of living in an unsafe neighborhood and having a lot of unsupervised activities with peers, two other predictors of externalizing problems.[43]

STRATEGIES FOR NAVIGATING WORK AND FAMILY LIFE

Galinsky makes various specific suggestions for increasing positive feelings and reducing stress.[44] Parents minimize work stress by seeking flextime, prioritizing work, and using problem-solving techniques. Parents improve their focus at work by finding ways to work without interruptions. They improve the quality of their jobs by learning new skills and gaining meaning from their work. They encourage positive relationships with supervisors and coworkers by appreciating support when given and making requests for reasonable modifications to the work environment to meet family needs.

Parents minimize difficulties in making transitions from work to home and from home to work in several ways. Parents do best in transitioning from work to home when they have some act or ritual that separates work from their home life—some do breathing exercises, some listen to music or books on tape or read on the way home. Parents also develop rituals that allow time with children to meet their needs when they first get home and then time to prepare dinner and do other household tasks. If parents have had a bad day at work, they are advised to tell their children and take extra time to reduce their stress. In transitioning from home to work, parents reduce stress by preparing for the next day (laying out clothes, making lunches) and allowing enough time in the morning to avoid rushing.

DAY CARE

As we will see, the context of day care—the child, the family, the setting for care—determines its influence on family life. Adults outside the family have always participated in child care because children require attentive care for an extended time. Thus, Michael Lamb and Lieselotte Ahnert remind us, "Nonparental care is a universal practice with a long history, not a dangerous innovation representing a major deviation from species-typical and species-appropriate patterns of child care."[45]

Patterns of Nonmaternal Care

In the United States where parents receive very limited, if any, paid parental leave at the time of a child's birth, most mothers return to work in the first year, and children enter some form of nonmaternal care. Several forms of care are available:

Relative care—fathers or grandparents living in the home care for the child, or relatives, such as grandparents, care for the child nearby.

Nonrelative family day care—care for infants and children in the home of a nonrelative.

Nonrelative center day care—provides appropriate care and stimulating activities for infants and children and may provide after-school care for children in the elementary grades.

After-school programs—provide supervised care for children in the elementary school years during after-school hours and vacations.

Self-care—care by the child.

Recent data for children under age five with employed mothers reveal that 50 percent are cared for by parents or other relatives, 34 percent in family day care homes, 22 percent in center-based programs, and 3 percent by a sitter at home. Patterns of care vary by the age of the child, with most parents of infants and toddlers preferring care with a relative or in a family day care.[46] As children get older, center-based care becomes the most frequent alternative to relative care.

While most children are in some form of supervised care after they enter school, 15 percent of six- to twelve-year-olds are in self-care on a regular basis, with self-care increasing as children get older—7 percent of children ages six to nine, 26 percent of children ages nine to twelve, and 47 percent of children age fourteen.[47]

Each form of care has advantages and possible drawbacks.[48] Relative care has the advantage that children have special ties to their caregivers and are in a familiar setting. The quality of parental care may be high but can vary if a parent has special stresses or needs, like sleep after working a night shift.

Substitute care at home is expensive but requires that the child adjust to only the new person who is available when the child is sick. As children get older, home care is often supplemented with nursery school attendance or other group activities so the child can be with peers.

Family day care—that is, care in the home of another family with other children—is often cheaper and more flexible than center care and provides the same activities of home care with a stable care provider, but may not be as stimulating. Family day care homes can be, but are not always, licensed. Caregivers who are part of a larger umbrella network can give higher-quality care than can untrained caregivers.

Day care centers provide care and stimulating activities. The parent whose child goes to a day care center is sure of having child care available every day—at some centers from 7:00 A.M. until 7:00 P.M. Many centers have credentialed personnel who have been trained to work with children, and many centers have play equipment and supplies not found in most home-care situations. All centers provide opportunities for contact with same-age children.

Elementary school students receive care in school for three to six hours per day and require special provision only before or after school and over holidays. As noted, an increasing number are in self-care that worries parents.[49] Older, better-educated mothers are more likely to have children in self-care, perhaps because they are more available by phone, live in safe neighborhoods, and children have activities and sports that are supervised.[50] Working-class parents and parents of different ethnic groups prefer to have children supervised.

Availability, Affordability, and Quality of Day Care

We have described the kinds of care possible, but how affordable and available are they?

A national survey revealed that child care costs more than most household expenses.[51] In 2007 in all regions of the country, the average cost of full-time infant care is more than the average two-parent family's cost for food, and the cost of two children of any age is as high or higher than the average monthly mortgage payment. In a single-parent family, the cost of two children was as much as 50 or 102 percent of annual income. In dollar amounts, for full-time, center-based care, parents can pay as much as $14,000 for infants; $10,700, for 4-year-olds; and $8,600 for school-age children; in family day care, $9,600 for infants, $9,100 for 4-year-olds, and $6,600 for school-age children.

Families receive little governmental support in arranging child care.[52] A tax credit, depending on the amount spent for child care, does not cover the full cost of the care and helps primarily middle-class and upper-middle-class families. Single parents and lower-income parents do not pay sufficient taxes to benefit much from the credit. Although federal subsidies provide some block support for child-care expenses of poorer families, only about 10–15 percent of those eligible receive such benefits.

Quality of Care during Infancy and Early Childhood

Quality of care is the major determiner of the effects of nonparental child care on children, and is measured in two ways.[53] *Structural measures* look at the amount of teacher or caregiver training/experience, staff turnover, salaries, and recommended staff ratios. Currently the recommended ratios of adults to children are 1:3 for infants, 1:4 for toddlers, and 1:7 for preschoolers. The number of children recommended for groups is six in infancy, eight in toddlerhood, and fourteen in the preschool years.

Process *measures* examine two aspects of caregiving for children—that is, sensitive, responsive interactions and appropriate activities in a safe, stimulating setting. Observations can focus on the caregiver's sensitive and stimulating behavior in response to all children or on the individual child's experiences of positive care. Since structural and process measures all reflect aspects of good care, they generally are related to each other.

In both center care and family day care, the quality of the interactions with the caregiver—the positive, sensitive responsiveness of the caregiver—is the best measure of the quality of the care.[54] Caregivers' salaries are good measures of caregiver stability; when salaries are high, caregivers stay.

In high-quality day care settings, children build secure attachments to teachers and develop the many positive social qualities associated with early secure attachment to parents.[55] Secure attachment to an available, stable, sensitive, responsive caregiver who provides stimulating activities and monitors the child's behavior to increase self-regulation promotes competent development. The child uses this figure as a safe base for exploring the world, just as he or she uses the secure attachment with the mother or father. In the child's first thirty months, it is important for the teacher to remain the same; but after thirty months, the teacher can change and the child–teacher relationship will still remain stable.

There are, of course, confounding factors. Highly motivated, educated, stable parents seek out high-quality care for children.[56] Those infants who go into low-quality care often have parents who are less organized and use less appropriate socialization practices. A vicious cycle may develop for the infant in low-quality care. Highly stressed families give less attention to the child, and the child goes into a day care setting with few adults to interact with and little to do. These children have less contact with adults and receive less stimulation both at home and in day care than do children of motivated parents. Thus, they have cumulative risks for problems in development.

Federal law requires that states have standards to ensure the health and safety of children in child care, but states vary widely in specific laws and the degree to which they monitor and inspect family day care and child-care centers.[57] Some, but not all, states have set up requirements for staff training and ratios of adults to children. Those states that have stricter standards have fewer centers offering poor-quality care. Insisting on stricter standards for teacher training and adult–child ratios was related to more sensitive caregiving for children.

Availability of Good Quality Care

Most experts agree that shortages exist in services for infants and school-age children. Recent studies have found that, even when available, day care is most often of mediocre quality.[58] Observations of care in centers and family day care found that in centers, 14 percent were of sufficiently high quality to promote development, 74 percent were of mediocre quality, and 12 percent were of such low quality as to be unstimulating and unable to fully meet children's health and safety needs. Forty percent of care for infants and toddlers was described as low quality.

In family day care homes, 9 percent were found to be of good quality, 56 percent of adequate or custodial quality, and 35 percent of inadequate quality. The average family day care provider was described as "nonresponsive or inappropriate in interactions with children close to half the time."[59]

In a national study of the early caregiving experiences of toddlers and preschoolers, positive caregiving was very or somewhat characteristic for 39 percent of children, and somewhat or very uncharacteristic for 61 percent.

While good-quality care is expensive to provide because it requires recommended staffing ratios, as well as educated and trained staff members who stay, the fees charged to parents for good-quality care are not that different from those for mediocre care. Parents need training and awareness to identify quality care. When they compared parents' ratings of quality to their own, researchers found that parents identified as good quality what researchers described as mediocre.[60] Parents of all education and income levels tend to overestimate the quality of the caregiving their children get.

Parents also tend to overestimate their level of communication with caregivers who see themselves as professionals and want parents to consult them for information and skill-building.[61] Caregivers also want family information to understand children, and they want to give information to help parents understand what has happened in the day. But there is little time for conversation. Caregivers often want to talk in the mornings when parents are in a hurry, but they are rushed when parents pick up children and have time to talk.

Nonparental Care during Infancy and Early Childhood

In evaluating research, we must keep in mind first that a selection process related to mothers' education, personality, and interests determines who, in fact, chooses to return to work once children are born. Second, the meaning of maternal employment in a child's life depends on (1) the child's characteristics (age, sex, temperament), (2) family characteristics (education and socioeconomic level, fathers' involvement in the home, mother's satisfaction with working), (3) work characteristics (the number of hours the mother works, the level of her stress at work), and, perhaps most important, (4) the nature of the child's substitute care. Because so many factors influence the effects of day care, our understanding of its effects is more limited than we would like.[62]

Adaptation to Nonmaternal Care

Children enter care early in infancy and the stability and quality of that care can promote positive development. Parents who decided early on the type of care they preferred were more likely to have that type of care and to obtain higher quality care when infants were six months old.[63] Most parents preferred some form of relative care in their own or the relative's home, but family day care and center care were the most stable forms of care.[64]

Studying the stability of child care of infants from six to fifteen months, researchers found that 61 percent of infants had stable care over that period of time, although many infants had more than one kind of care.[65] Two aspects of care predicted the development of positive qualities—quality of day care (at fifteen months and the average quality of care from six to fifteen months) and multiple care arrangements with relatives predicted language comprehension. Poor quality of care negatively predicted language and cognitive performance. Multiple care arrangements with family and nonfamily caregivers predicted poorer language comprehension.

Parents worry that nonmaternal care may interfere with children's secure attachments to mothers. While research in the 1980s suggested this possibility, the findings from the National Institute of Child Health and Human Development Study of Child Care and Youth Development indicated it is mothers' warmth and sensitivity that determined children's attachment security: "Child care by itself constitutes neither a risk nor benefit for the development of the infant–mother attachment."[66]

Currently, there are concerns that day care represents a challenging situation for infants and toddlers.[67] For many infants, cortisol, a stress-sensitive hormone, increases over the course of the day at child care; during the toddler years, 71 percent of children show daytime increases, with declining numbers in the school years. Cortisol increases were not seen when infants and toddlers were observed at home; in fact, cortisol decreases were common across the day.

Peer relationships at day care may play a role. Toddlers who play with peers showed lower cortisol levels, and those who played alone had higher levels. Toddlers whose teachers described them as socially fearful had more elevated levels of cortisol as well. The exact meaning of the elevated cortisol is not clear, but it appears to reflect emotional arousal and challenge.

In Europe where children enter day care after attachments are formed, children became upset at the separations, and both securely and insecurely attached toddlers showed signs of stress, reflected in elevated levels of cortisol.[68] Children were better able to adjust to the prolonged daily separations when mothers remained with them in the day care center for extended periods while toddlers came to know their new caregivers and new settings. Securely attached toddlers had lower levels of cortisol when they were with their mothers in day care.

The cortisol increases in day care settings and the emotional outbursts and demands for attention toddlers show at home suggest that in these early years of day care, parents must help children learn to manage their emotional reactions. Parents must be especially sensitive and responsive to help young children establish emotional balance. "Parents need to be especially attentive to children and their needs, responding sensitively to fusses and cries when they are together, thereby providing the emotion-regulating support that children typically do not obtain from care providers in a group setting."[69]

Cognitive and Social Stimulation

We know that early and continuing intervention programs that stimulate cognitive development promote intellectual growth during the school years and reduce grade retention and the need for special programs in the elementary school years.[70] These programs stimulate intellectual growth in children from economically disadvantaged families. The most successful programs also stimulate social and emotional competence seen in adulthood, as we described in Chapter 7.

Early research raised concerns that early and extensive day care could have negative effects on attachment and children's social-emotional and cognitive functioning.

To respond to concerns about the effects of day care, the National Institute of Child Health and Human Development recruited a network of researchers and, in 1991, a sample of 1,364 newborns and their families to participate in extensive assessments and observations of children at home and at day care and later in school from the age of one month through childhood.

The babies were first seen at one month, then at six, fifteen, twenty-four, thirty-six, and fifty-four months, with phone calls at scheduled intervals as well. The research has focused on the family and day care qualities that predict children's intellectual and social-emotional functioning, and their relationships with peers. Children were tested, then observed at home, at day care, and in the laboratory setting. Ratings were obtained from and about parents and day care workers. The group of researchers presented data about the children's functioning up to the age of fifty-four months. These were the basic findings at that point in the data analysis:[71]

1. Sensitive, responsive parenting consistently and strongly predicted children's competence in all areas at all ages.

2. High-quality day care was defined as day care that provided sensitive, responsive caregiving as well as language and intellectual stimulation. High-quality care predicted intellectual skills and most social-emotional behaviors, as well as some peer ratings to a modest degree.

3. Quantity of child care, or the number of hours children spent in child care, related to children's behavior in different ways. At twenty-four and thirty-six months, a greater number of hours in day care was related to verbal and cognitive skills but to more problem behaviors at thirty-six and fifty-four months and more conflict with the caregiver at fifty-four months. Children

were also observed to show more negative behavior with a peer at fifty-four months as well.

4. The only form of day care related to child outcomes was center care. In early childhood, more time in center care predicted greater language and cognitive skills, but it also predicted more behavior problems. At fifty-four months, more time in center care predicted positive peer relationships.

The researchers discussed the usefulness of these findings for parents of young children. "The primary conclusion is that parenting matters much more than does child care, so parents might make decisions that allow them to have quality time with their children."[72] Some mothers may decide to cut back the number of hours they work so they can spend more quality time with their children, and others may decide that cutting back hours would create such financial stress for the family that parenting would be negatively affected.

The researchers highlighted that "exclusive maternal care was not related to better or worse outcomes for children. There is, thus, no reason for mothers to feel as though they are harming their children if they decide to work."[73] High-quality day care clearly contributes to all children's competence.

When the sample was seen after entrance into elementary school, in the third grade and again at the end of sixth grade, conclusions were similar:[74]

1. Parenting was a stronger and more consistent predictor of development than early child care experiences.

2. Higher quality of care of any kind predicted higher vocabulary scores.

3. More exposure to center-based care predicted teachers' reports of problem behaviors such as noncompliance, aggressiveness, and blaming others for problems.

Nonparental Care during Later Childhood and Adolescence

As in the early years, quality after-school care is related to effective functioning.[75] Contemporaneous after-school day care that is not high quality is also related to children's being rated as noncompliant by teachers and less well liked by peers.

Research found that low-income third-graders in formal after-school programs receive better grades in math, reading, and conduct than do children with other forms of care, including maternal care. From about the fifth grade on, children in self-care behave and perform similarly whether an adult is present or not.

Lack of supervision and monitoring in early adolescence, however, is related to increased use of alcohol, cigarettes, and marijuana. Eighth-graders in self-care for more than eleven hours a week—whether from dual- or single-earner families, from high- or low-income families, with good or poor grades, or active or nonactive in sports—were more likely than those not in self-care to use these substances.[76]

In adolescence, maternal employment is associated with self-confidence and independence.[77] The benefits are more pronounced for girls who obtain good grades and think of careers for themselves, most likely because their mothers serve as role models of competence.

Gender Differences

Boys and girls have more egalitarian views of gender roles when mothers are employed and fathers are more involved in child care.[78] Sons of employed mothers see women as more competent and men as more emotionally expressive and warm. Daughters of employed mothers have more egalitarian gender roles.

RETAIN FAMILIES' SPECIAL NEEDS

The focus thus far has been all families' needs as they integrate work and family. As we have seen, dual-earner families, on average, enjoy greater income and resources that include the benefit of spousal support. But these families must integrate two adults' work lives and careers. Single parents have the daunting challenges of providing income and parenting, often without the support of another adult in the home.

Dual-Earner Families

There is no one way for parents to integrate work and family needs. One study identified three family types in terms of work and parenting characteristics.[79] In *high-status families,* both parents had high levels of education and occupational status, were highly involved in their work, and earned more money than did the other two groups of families. Couples held less traditional ideologies on sex-role activities and shared tasks equally. However, they experienced work overload and stress, and as a result had more marital conflict, less marital satisfaction, and less love between the spouses than did the other two groups. Parents limited tension to the marital relationship, and children in the families were not aware of the marital problems because the stress did not affect the ways parents treated the children.

In *low-stress families,* both parents reported low levels of work overload, high levels of marital satisfaction and love between the spouses, and low levels of conflict. Parents were available to take an active role in monitoring children, and such monitoring improved children's functioning.

In *main-secondary families,* fathers were the primary financial providers and mothers provided a small supplementary income, frequently through employment in lower-status occupations. These families had the lowest incomes of the three types of families and the most traditional ways of organizing family activities. Girls in main-secondary families were more likely to engage in feminine tasks than were girls in other families. Marital satisfaction fell between that of the other two groups, as did their level of conflict.

After interviewing 150 families, Francine Deutsch identified four patterns of working and parenting, which she termed *equal sharers,* 60–40 *couples,* 75–25 *couples,* and *alternating shifters.*[80] Families sometimes moved among these patterns. Families with infants were sometimes unequal sharers, becoming equal sharers over time. Even within the types of families, there were many variations. Equal sharers could be providing all the day care with flexible work hours, or they could have child care and work the same hours outside the home.

Alternating shifters tended to have working-class occupations, as it is these types of occupations that offer daytime and evening shifts. Women's income in alternating-shift families was often very important, and women felt they had power and received appreciation for their contributions.

Patterns of work influenced parents' ways of being with children but not the total amount of time they spent with children. Equal-sharing couples spent the same amount of time with children as did the other three groups of couples, but equal-sharing mothers were alone with children less frequently than were the other mothers. Equal-sharing fathers compensated for this, as they were alone with children more often than were fathers of the other groups. Furthermore, equal-sharing parents were more often together with children than were parents of the other groups.

Couples in the four groups did not differ markedly in politics, education, or class, but they did vary in how they negotiated the everyday issues of child-care and household tasks. Couples who wanted equal sharing of parenting and working made every effort to distribute both kinds of tasks equally and to find friends who supported their decisions.

An interview study of middle-class men and women in dual-earner families looked at families at different points in the life cycle—some before or after having children but most in the child-rearing stages of life.[81] This study focused on middle managers and professionals, as these people not only determine their own fates but also tend to shape the work lives of people they supervise. Sampling couples from upstate New York rather than those from an urban area may have resulted in an overrepresentation of families who have scaled back working demands, however.

In this sample, few participants had dual-career families in which both parents were highly involved in work and both were single-mindedly pursuing work goals. Dual-career couples usually had no children at home, or they hired help to meet many of the family demands. The vast majority of couples relied on one of three strategies for scaling back work demands to carve out time for the family. Although most couples had an egalitarian gender ideology, choices in day-to-day behaviors often resulted in traditionally gendered roles for men and women.

The three work–family strategies were termed *placing limits, job-versus-career,* and *trading-off.* Couples who placed limits (about 30 percent) turned down jobs or promotions that required relocation or traveling, refused overtime hours, and limited the number of hours worked. Women often did this when a child was born, and men sometimes did this when careers became established and parenting involvement grew. Job-versus-career strategies (relied on by about 40 percent) involved one parent's having an absorbing career and the other parent's having a job that produced income but was subordinated to the needs of the family and the parent with the career. In about two-thirds of these families, men had the career and women had the job, but in one-third, the wife had the career and the man the job. Often, chance or early advancement or opportunity determined which parent had the career. In the trading-off group, parents shifted back and forth between jobs and careers, depending on family needs and career opportunities.

The researchers were concerned that couples' scaling-back strategies were private solutions to public workplace problems. They believe that private solutions do not challenge the underlying assumptions that work can make demands on parents—such as 60-hour weeks—while doing little to help them meet family and work needs. The couples appeared to make few demands for formal policies of job-sharing or on-site day care and instead sought informal arrangements to meet family needs. Unfortunately, workers at lower levels in the employment hierarchy might not get such benefits without formal policies.

One can see that there are many ways to meet work and family needs and that families use more than one strategy to meet these needs over time.

Based on her interviews with parents, Deutsch recommends that parents be proactive in making daily choices that enable both parents to have careers and be parents.[82] Couples committed to equal careers and parenting make choices at home and at work that support equality. That means scaling back work—limiting work hours per day, workdays per week, travel, overtime—and "allowing family obligations to intrude on work as a significant part of identity." When both parents make adjustments, neither one has the traditional career.

Mothers also have to be willing to relinquish their identity as primary caregivers and let fathers assume major responsibility for child care and decisions about children. They have to recognize that children benefit when fathers are equal parents, because children can develop closer relationships with them. Marriages benefit as well, because couples share the responsibilities of parenting and work and neither partner feels overburdened.

Single Parents

As discussed further in the next chapter, single parents build a support group of extended family and friends to give the positive emotional support and practical help that benefit dual-earner partners.

Because single parents, on average, earn less income, they actively seek and use every available work, community, and school resource to provide services for their children and themselves.

A PRACTICAL QUESTION: HOW DO WORKING PARENTS TAKE CARE OF THEMSELVES?

Studies we have reviewed suggest ways parents can increase their resources relative to their demands at work and family. Focusing on what is positive in life, using humor, using problem-solving strategies to deal with specific obstacles, reaching out for help from other people, and turning to work and community resources for help are all ways to increase resources to deal with work demands.

Nonprofit organizations help parents as well. For example, the National Association of Child Care Resource and Referral Agencies (www.nccrra.org)[83] provides parents with information (e.g., about child care, parenting, state licensing laws), connects parents with day care in their area, monitors states' activities in licensing and supervising child care, collects data and does research, and advocates policies to ensure quality care for children.

The Families and Work Institute (www.familiesandwork.org)[84] provides parents with information about work policies and laws, and parenting information about integrating work and family life.

Working parents who take care of themselves can take better care of their children. Exercising regularly, eating a balanced diet, making sure they have private time for thinking and pursuing interests, and finding time for pleasurable time with family and friends reduce fatigue and stress. Parents and families have to figure out what works for them.

The life of the working parent is challenging, but increasing resources can reduce demands and make life more enjoyable for all family members.

MAIN POINTS

Work

- has a strong effect on family life and is influenced by what parents experience at home
- develops adults' skills and provides many benefits and emotional resources
- can create stress that disrupts parenting skills

Among the many strategies parents use to navigate the flow of work and family, parents

- place primary importance on spending time with children to meet their needs
- create time for children and family by sharing the workload at home
- maintain control of work demands through problem-solving methods
- build support systems at work and use high-quality child care

Children's nonparental care

- must meet established criteria to be considered high-quality care—specified child–staff ratios that vary according to the age of the child; staff training; safety; structure; sensitive caregiving; organized, stimulating activities
- is not as predictive of children's development as are parental qualities
- in early childhood promotes competence when children have sensitive teachers who provide stimulating activities and monitor them
- in the elementary school years and adolescence is associated with social and intellectual competence if children are supervised
- sometimes includes self-care by older children who enjoy independence but also require monitoring to prevent at-risk behaviors
- promotes development of all children when it is of high quality

Effectively combining working and parenting

- requires that parents make daily decisions to share the workload at home
- involves parents' devoting time to sustaining relationships and their own health and well being

EXERCISES

1. Write a diary entry of a work day for an employed father who has an infant child whose mother is also employed full time. How does he coordinate his work life and his home life on that day, and how does he coordinate his activities with his wife's in the care of their child? Do they spend time with each other? Does he get any time to himself? Or write a diary entry of a weekend day of an employed mother with a teenage son and early adolescent daughter. How does she spend her time with her children and husband? What does she do in the home and outside the home, with family and friends? Does she get any time alone?

2. Imagine you had a child under age five—infant, toddler, or preschooler. Investigate day care options in the community for a child of that age. You might form groups to investigate care for a child of a particular age, with each student visiting at least one center to get information and summarize impressions. One group might investigate family day care in the area and compare the quality and the cost of care with that available in a center (*www.nccrra.org* is a good resource for doing this).

3. Design an ideal day care program for infants or toddlers, specifying the number of caregivers, their qualities, the physical facilities, and the daily routine.

4. Imagine what your family and work life would be like if you were a single parent with a toddler and school-age child. Write diary entries for a day during the week and for a day on the weekend about your life at home and at work.

5. Write a short paper containing advice you could give to a parent of the same sex as you who feels frustrated and pressured trying to care for two teenagers and an aging parent while trying to work full time.

ADDITIONAL READINGS

Drago, Robert W. *Striking a Balance: Work, Family, Life.* Boston: Dollars & Sense, 2007.

Galinsky, Ellen. *Ask the Children: What America's Children Really Think about Working Parents.* New York: Morrow, 1999.

Mason, Linda. *The Working Mother's Guide to Life.* New York: Three Rivers Press, 2002.

Steiner, Leslie Morgan, ed. *Mommy Wars.* New York: Random House, 2006.

Zigler, Edward, Marsland, Katherine, and Lord, Heather. *The Tragedy of Child Care in America.* New Haven, CT: Yale University Press, 2009.

C H A P T E R

14

Single Parenting

IN THE NEWS

New York Times Magazine, February 1[1]: College-educated Single mothers with a support network fear less stress. See page 422.

Test Your Knowledge: Fact or Fiction (True/False)

1. When teen mothers have stable living arrangements and use positive parenting principles, their children function effectively.

2. As long as parents in conflict stay married, their children experience fewer problems than those children whose parents divorce.

3. When families are matched for education and income, children in low-stress single-mother families are indistinguishable from children in two-parent families.

4. As family structures have changed and young couples are more likely to live together, marriage is less valued.

5. A collaborative divorce process offers parents opportunities for arriving at divorce agreements without going through adversarial legal court proceedings.

Biologically speaking, it takes two parents to create a new life. Economic and social changes in the last fifty years, however, have led to an increasing number of children living in family forms other than that of the two-parent biological or adoptive family.

Furthermore, many children experience several forms of family life in their developing years. This chapter focuses on how is life different for children and their parents in single-parent households. We look at how parenting changes when only one parent is there to manage the household and rear children.

In previous chapters we have focused on children's needs and growth patterns. Although we have referred to single parents from time to time, the general assumption has been that there are two parents in the home. And this is generally true. Recall Table 1-1 (page 17) in which 60 percents of children live with two biological or adoptive parents, and another 7 percent live with a biological and a stepparent. Nevertheless, over thirty percent live in other family forms. In the next three chapters we look at how living in different family structures influences children's growth and parents' behavior.

It is important to emphasize that while many children will spend their entire childhood and adolescence in one form of family life, many, perhaps most, will experience many forms of family life. Our recently elected President, Barack Obama, is an example. He was born to a traditional married couple who divorced, lived with a single parent, in a stepfamily, and with grandparents.

This chapter focuses on parenting in homes with one biological parent—teen mothers and fathers, parents who never married, are divorced, or are widows/widowers. Some parents move back and forth between these groups (e.g., starting as teen parents, later marrying, divorcing, and then cohabiting). About one in four children in the United States lives with a single parent—25 percent with a single mother and 4 percent with a single father.[2]

Both numbers and proportions of single-parent families increased in all Western countries and in all ethnic groups in the United States, but have remained level for the last fifteen years.[3] African American families have a higher rate of single-parent families than do other groups; this does not appear to be the result of increased sexual activity among young women but rather of the fact that birthrates have remained the same in this group while rates of marriage have dropped. Thus, more children are born to unmarried mothers.

As in so many areas of parenting, the meaning and effects of single parenting depend on the specific conditions of the child and family.

CHANGING FAMILY STRUCTURES

As noted in Chapter 1, the twentieth century brought many changes in family life. At mid-century, the traditional nuclear family provided the center of people's emotional lives and feelings of closeness for their entire lives. By the 1960s, economic and social changes led to changes in family life. Fewer jobs were available to support families so both parents worked outside the home.[4] The secularization of social values led to a focus on self-interest and self-growth. Marriage and children were postponed, divorces and remarriages increased, and there was a growing acceptance of premarital sex. As couples lived together in growing numbers, the number of children born to unmarried parents grew to its present number of 38 percent of births.[5] In addition, a sizeable number of children (36 percent) are now born to a parent who has a child by a previous partner.[6] In this period, the number of gay/lesbian parents rearing children also increased.

The growing number of children born outside marriage suggests a social change in the value of marriage. Interviews, however, reveal that people of all social groups value marriage and see it as a desired milestone in life.[7] Adolescents anticipate marrying (only 5 percent say they will not), but almost half assume they will cohabit first. They do not consider cohabitation as a substitute for marriage, but a step on the way to marriage.[8] Currently, about half the marriages are preceded by living together, and half the couples living together will marry. Still, many individuals have a series of cohabiting relationships that are seen as an alternative to being single.

In addition to social changes, marriage is related to economic factors. People with education and good incomes marry in large numbers and remain married.[9] They link marriage and children together in that order. People with fewer resources view marriage as a distant goal they hope to achieve some day when they have secure jobs and money for a home, and when they have worked out relationship problems such as domestic violence and substance abuse with partners.[10] These individuals are more likely to remain single or live with partners.

They separate childbearing from marriage. While marriage is looked upon as a distant goal, childbearing can occur in the present, and there is no stigma to having a child outside of marriage. Partners who have relationships or are living together at the time of the often unplanned pregnancy go ahead and have the baby, anticipating marriage as a possibility at a future date.

Single parents face many stresses. In large national surveys, both cohabiters and single parents report less education, less income, more residential moves, and partnership changes than married biological parents.[11] In 2006, the median income for female-headed households was $28,829; for male-headed households, $41,844; and for married-couple families, $69,404.[12] Poverty level is lowest in married-couple families (5 percent) and highest for single-mother households (28 percent), with single-father households falling between at 13 percent.

There is great heterogeneity among subgroups of single parents.[13] Single divorced mothers differ in education and income from teen and unmarried mothers, and divorced fathers are more like married fathers in occupation and income than they are like teen and unmarried fathers. Diversity exists within subgroups as well with, for example, teen parents taking many paths to adulthood.

As we saw in Chapter 13 on working, when stresses are greater than resources, parents feel overwhelmed. Building more resources and supports is a major way to handle stress. In discussing single-parent families—teen, unmarried, divorced, and widows/widowers—we seek to identify those positive factors that provide resources and supports to families to counteract the stresses confronting many single-parent families.

TEEN PARENTS

The United States has the highest rate of babies born to teen mothers of any of the industrialized countries in the world. Although teens engage in similar levels of sexual activity as teens in Western Europe, they do not use contraceptives as effectively.[14] While the teen birthrate declined from 1991 to about 2006, it is now beginning to rise.[15] African American teens tend to be sexually active early and to have more teen births, followed by Latina adolescents, and then European American teens.

Who Are Teen Parents?

Teen parents are those who have children under the age of twenty, and most are single parents (about 80 percent).[16] Several studies suggest caution in concluding it is parents' young age that accounts for the stresses they and their children experience.[17] When the young children of teen parents are compared to the children of mothers' sisters who had their children at older ages, the cousins perform at similar levels on cognitive tests, suggesting it is not young age but parents' family experiences that are important. When similar comparisons are made when children are adolescents, the adolescents of teen mothers are more likely to have been retained in school than their cousins, suggesting mothers' young age may influence that school outcome.

Although only about 19 percent plan their pregnancies, teen mothers are more likely to express a strong desire for children when they lack feelings of independence and self-sufficiency and other sources of satisfaction such as work.[18] About half the pregnant mothers decide to terminate the pregnancy or give the baby up for adoption. Those most likely to terminate pregnancies come from middle-class families; they feel support from family and friends for their decision.[19] Adolescent mothers who release a child for adoption—in one study, 4 percent—come from small, financially stable families. They have had academic success and see other alternatives for themselves. They have positive views of adoption and believe their mothers support their decisions.[20]

Teen parents, especially young ones, are likely to reside with a parent who helps with child care. If grandmothers' behaviors are extreme—becoming the primary caregiver or ignoring the child—mothers do not fare as well as when grandmothers' care supplements mothers' care, and mothers have primary responsibility.[21] Grandmothers can support teens' learning to parent and provide a model of competent behaviors for them while teens complete school and gain skills to be responsible for themselves and their children. When children continue to live with parents into their twenties, they are more likely to have difficulties.

Stresses That Parents Experienced in Their Own Development

The difficulties many teen parents have experienced and bring to parenting start early and fall into four main categories: (1) the teens' social backgrounds, (2) early family relationships with their own parents, (3) their own personality characteristics, and (4) their relationships with peers.[22] The social backgrounds of adolescents who become teen parents contain such risk factors as being the child of an adolescent mother, living in a single-parent home with a parent who has little education, living in poverty, and living in a community with a high level of poverty and welfare assistance. Teen mothers also have experienced more sexual abuse in childhood or early adolescence; in one study, 65 percent had been sexually abused—61 percent by several perpetrators.[23]

The family relationships of adolescent parents often embody change and conflict. Their parents are less involved and less affectionate than parents of teens who do not have teen pregnancies, and they provide less monitoring as well. With parental supervision, teens headed in the direction of deviant behavior tend to stay involved in school and avoid pregnancy.[24]

Teen parents' own personality characteristics in childhood predict later teen pregnancy as early as eight years of age. In longitudinal studies, researchers found that eight-year-old girls who were described by peers as aggressive or aggressive–withdrawn were more likely to be teen mothers than were those girls who were low or average on aggression and withdrawal.[25] In addition, the prospective mothers were more likely to have school and conduct problems in elementary and high school and were more likely to drop out. In grade school, they were more likely to be rejected by peers, and in high school more likely to have deviant friends who broke rules and engaged in high-risk behaviors.

Early maturation and high rates of sexual activity increase girls' chances of becoming pregnant as teens.[26] Studies comparing adolescent mothers with teens who did not have babies have found that adolescent mothers are less independent, less certain of themselves, and less trusting of others.[27] They have a diffuse sense of identity and greater susceptibility to depression.

Most studies of adolescent parents have focused on mothers.[28] Recent work has followed samples of boys to determine the characteristics of those who become adolescent fathers. In many instances, they share the qualities of the mothers.[29] They are from low-income families in which parents often have problems with antisocial behavior. Their parents use ineffective disciplinary techniques and do not monitor the boys well. By early adolescence, these boys begin to engage in deviant, rule-breaking activities. They also have little academic success. Another study identified similar risk factors but concluded that the accumulation of risks, not any one of them, was most predictive of adolescent fatherhood.[30]

Parenting of Teen Parents

The stresses teen parents and their children experience are numerous—limited finances, incomplete education, limited job opportunities, little knowledge or understanding of children, residential and partner instability.[31] So, it is not surprising that teen parents are less sensitive and less responsive caregivers, and are harsher, more demanding, and, at times, abusive parents.

Although they can be as warm as older mothers, adolescent mothers are less realistic in their expectations of children and view their infants as more difficult.[32] They are often out of synch with babies' needs, fostering infants' independence by pushing them to hold their bottles or scramble for toys before they can get them, but restricting toddlers' explorations and choices. Adolescent mothers offer less verbal stimulation and also a less stimulating home with books and activities conducive to learning.

Although adolescent fathers are less involved parents than are older fathers, about 25 percent of adolescent fathers live with their infants, and a national survey suggests that about 57 percent visit weekly in the first two years of life. The percentage of those visiting drops as the children grow older—from 40 percent when the child is between two and four and a half to 27 percent when the child is four and a half to seven.[33] African American fathers continue to be involved with children. Only 12 percent of African American fathers have no contact with their children, whereas 30 percent of European American fathers and 37 percent of Latino fathers have no contact. Adolescent fathers are more likely to be involved when other people in the environment support their involvement. (See the interview in Chapter 6 with James Levine.)

Observed in solving problems and tasks with their two-year old children, fathers were described as more directive and negative, and their behavior stimulated their children's resistance and negativity. Researchers concluded, "Through their fathers' early entry into parenting and their parents' lack of resources and use of negative control, these children may be shaped, like their parents before them, into the next generation of antisocial children."[34]

Children Born to Adolescent Parents

Few differences are found between babies of adolescent parents and older parents at birth. Most infants are healthy, and cognitive measures indicate they are developing well in the first year. In a very detailed study of teen mothers and their children, socioemotional measures indicated some difficulties at six months, when 67 percent of mothers described their babies as irritable, fussy, and more difficult.[35] At one year of age, 63 percent of babies were described as having insecure attachments to mothers. This was a higher percentage than has been found in low-income families.

In the toddler years, language delays are seen, and cognitive delays are noted at age three. In one study, 72 percent of children had at least one area of delay at age 3, and 44 percent had two or more areas of delay.[36] Mothers noted anxious, worried moods and aggressive behaviors by age three. In the school years, children continued to have delays in language, cognitive, and socioemotional skills.

By adolescence, problems with impulse control and emotional regulation were marked, just as had occurred with their parents. Teens of adolescent mothers are more likely than others to become teen parents (in one study, 40 percent of girls and 21 percent of boys)[37]; however, the majority of children of teenage mothers do not themselves become teen parents. Even when they delay childbearing, however, children of teen mothers are not as competent and well adjusted in early adulthood as are the children of those mothers who delayed pregnancy until their twenties.

Teen Parents' Resilient Parenting

Many teen parents and their children experience the problems just described, but many do not. In a longitudinal study in Baltimore, about 75 percent of teen mothers were working in adulthood and not in need of any social services. Delaying a second pregnancy and getting more education predicted greater stability.[38]

A detailed study of Midwestern teen mothers of diverse backgrounds identified characteristics of mothers and children related to children's cognitive, academic, and socioemotional competence as children moved through elementary school. Prior to children's birth, mothers' cognitive readiness to have children, a measure based on mother's knowledge of children and developmental milestones, her expectations of children, her parenting style in response to children's behavior, and attitudes about being mothers predicted children's academic performance on reading achievement and math tests and their ability to cooperate and follow rules in school at age ten.[39] Adding several other measures of mothers' prebirth qualities such as IQ, emotional stability, and social status did not improve prediction of children's behavior based on mothers' cognitive readiness to parent.

A three-item measure of postnatal instability—number of residential moves, school changes, and mothers' romantic partners—also predicted reading scores and children's behavioral problems at age ten with instability related to less effective functioning.[40] Two important factors in predicting outcomes for children of teen mothers are mother's readiness to care for children and her postnatal ability to provide stable living arrangements for them.

Resilient children attained developmental milestones in academic work, emotional stability, and social competence. At age five, 31 percent of children were described as resilient, and at age fourteen, 29 percent. Resilient children came primarily from homes described as "low adversity." Mothers had self-esteem, confidence, gained education, and had job stability. Those resilient children living in adverse environments experienced support from adults outside the immediate family such as fathers or grandparents.

A model describing a process of risk or resilience for children included mothers' prebirth qualities reflecting psychological adjustment, ability to learn, absence of a history of abuse or substance abuse, and the presence of support from fathers, friends, and parents.[41] These qualities helped mothers develop a cognitive readiness for caring for children. Cognitive readiness and infants' characteristics predicted mothers' effective parenting techniques that, in turn, predicted children's competence.

The child's relationship with their mothers was the most important source of support in coping with negative life events, but three other factors combined to yield an overall measure of social support[42]: (1) positive relationships with fathers, (2) family's religious involvement, and (3) children's participation in sports and community activities. Fathers' involvement included financial support, emotional support, caregiving, and other help. When children were age fourteen, 69 percent had some contact with fathers. Although only 8 percent lived with their fathers, fathers were important figures, as 37 percent described fathers as their most important male role model.

Fathers' positive support was related to lower levels of aggressiveness and noncompliance at school and, for sons, to higher levels of reading achievement. Fathers' support was especially important when mothers were considered to have many difficulties functioning. Contact with fathers prevented the increase in children's emotional problems.

The family's involvement in religious activities helped both mothers and children. Compared to mothers low on religious involvement, those mothers involved in church communities had higher self-esteem, more positive and less harsh parenting behaviors, greater educational and occupational success, and their children had fewer behavior problems. Churches may have provided social supports such as job opportunities and child care that enabled mothers to work. A third protective factor was the child's participation in community activities and sports.

Other studies have found that teen mothers of resilient children were more child-centered and more authoritative in their parenting, praising children and communicating rules in a positive way.[43]

In brief, the qualities most likely to stimulate children's development and adaptability are parenting qualities of mothers and fathers—sensitive, responsive, authoritative maternal caregiving, fathers' support and positive relationships with children—children's participation in active community pursuits, having supports from grandparents, a stable lifestyle and involvement in church activities that give a sense of a larger order and meaning to life as well as practical help with the everyday demands of life. These are the same qualities that predict competence in two-parent families. They are just harder to achieve when you are trying to find your own identity and at the same time cope with more than the usual number of stressors.

Programs for Adolescent Parents

Programs can be divided into those aimed at (1) preventing the first teen pregnancy, (2) those aimed at helping teen parents cope with pregnancy, birth, and caregiving of children, and (3) those helping teens successfully negotiate the transition to adulthood so they can complete their educations, get stable jobs, form satisfying relationships with partners, and raise their children.[44]

Pregnancy prevention programs often start in adolescence and focus on sex education, successful use of contraceptives, and social skills to assert opinions with partners. Reviewing all the difficulties teen parents experience early in grade school highlights the need for programs that help children develop competence in early elementary school. If schools stimulate academic and social competence and children have fun with peers, children will be less likely to disengage from school in frustration and engage in impulsive, deviant behaviors such as substance use. Just as substance abuse researchers found a connection between poor school success and later substance use, there appears a similar relationship between poor school performance and early teen parenthood.[45]

Once teens are pregnant, programs to provide information on children's needs and developmental patterns, effective ways to form secure attachments, engaging with infants and providing stimulating activities, and positive parenting strategies for dealing with problem behaviors typical of the age are useful. Many parenting programs also include home visits in the first three years. The most lasting effects are achieved when visits start prenatally and when they help young teens prevent a second pregnancy.

A large national parenting program has as its goal the prevention of child abuse and neglect, which is more frequent among teen parents than older parents.[46] The program provides teens a new mental model of what it means to be a parent. In addition, it teaches parenting skills in a one-on-one relationship, emphasizing positive caregiving and stimulating children's behavior. It teaches parents how to play and attend to children. Parents then teach these skills to one other family member.

A third kind of program helps teen parents make the transition to adulthood, connecting them with educational and community resources so they can complete their education and compete in the job market.[47] Such programs also help teen parents form positive relationships with the other parent. When teen parents are very young and live with grandparents, they may well benefit from being included in parenting programs to learn ways to support their children while still encouraging their autonomy.

Teen fathers have been overlooked in many teen programs, but are more often included now. Charles Ballard, an Ohio social worker, started one of the earliest programs for single teen fathers in 1982.[48] He had been a single teen father and wanted to connect fathers to their children because he felt they could play a powerful role if they had parenting skills and were being responsible and self-controlled in their own lives. The program provides mentors to help young fathers get educations and jobs. Mothers were included in the program so they could form cooperative relationships with fathers and work together to raise children. The program has become a national one with wide recognition.

UNMARRIED PARENTS

Many people think of unmarried mothers as being young teens or economically advantaged professional women. The average unmarried mother is, in fact, a woman in her late twenties or thirties who had her first birth outside of marriage when she was a teenager, and is now having her second or third nonmarital birth.[49] In a sense, many in this group are teen parents grown older, and like teen parents, unmarried mothers experience many stressors such as limited education, lower income, and more residential and partnership changes.

Births to unmarried mothers are twice as likely for African American women and Latina women as for European American women. Cohabiting with the child's father increases intended and unintended pregnancies for all three groups, but Latinas are more likely to plan births with cohabiting husbands than the other two groups, and European American women are more likely to marry the fathers than African American or Latina mothers. African American women are more likely than the other two groups to have births when not cohabiting with fathers.

Almost 40 percent of babies born to unmarried women are born to women living with the baby's father, and almost half of these babies are planned.[50] Although these unions are more unstable than marriages, research shows that within five years, around 60 percent of parents will marry, 12 percent will continue to live together, and 28 percent will separate.[51]

Children of Unmarried Parents

Children born to unmarried mothers take many paths to adulthood; no one outcome characterizes them all. Children in stable living situations generally got more education and were economically self-sufficient and independent in adulthood.[52] Stability could come through adoption to two parents, through living in a stable single-parent family, or living in a three-generational family with single mother and grandparents. Living with grandparents without the mother was related to lower educational attainment and to a higher probability of leaving home by age eighteen.

Many family changes and limited resources create the parental strain and parenting difficulties that are associated with children's behavior problems in the first three years of life. Across all ethnic groups, partner changes that occur significantly more often in single-parent households predict parents' reports of children's anxious and depressed moods and their aggressive behaviors at age three.[53] The greater the number of changes, the greater is the increase in children's problem behaviors. Parents' stress and declining parenting skills independently account for the relationship between partner changes and problem behaviors. The reverse relationships are not statistically significant, indicating that children's problem behaviors and parents' stress do not predict partner changes.

Parents living in single-mother and in cohabiting families report that their children aged six to seventeen have a greater number of school difficulties, peer problems, more worries and anxieties, and, in high school, mood and school problems and noncompliant and less trustworthy behavior than are reported for children living with their married biological parents.[54] When economic and parental resources are controlled, differences between children six to eleven disappear with the exception of school difficulties, but in the adolescent years, differences between children in single- and two-parent homes are found at every economic and social level.

Protective factors in the child, the mother, the parent–child relationship, and the larger social context buttress children from stress and predict positive outcomes for them. Eight protective factors were divided into four categories: the child's characteristics (positive sociability and attentiveness), maternal qualities (efficacy and low risk of depression), parenting qualities (positive parent–child relationship and fathers' involvement), and qualities of the larger social context (social support and few difficult life experiences). In a sample of disadvantaged, never-married mothers, families averaged three out of the eight protective factors, and 20 percent of families had five or more protective factors.

Protective factors assessed when children were eighteen and twenty-one months of age predicted measures of cognitive and social functioning at preschool age.[55] All protective factors except the father's involvement predicted competent psychological functioning, as measured by low aggressive, anxious, depressed, hyperactive, dependent, and withdrawn behaviors.

Only the child's characteristics and positive parent–child relationship predicted cognitive competence, as measured by higher scores on a school-readiness test.

The most important aspect of the parent–child relationship for later well-being was the absence of harsh discipline. Economic disadvantage may have its greatest impact on families by intensifying maternal distress that leads to harsh discipline. The more protective factors in the child's family, the better the child functioned. Nevertheless, even the children with the greatest number of protective factors scored below average, at the 32nd percentile, on the measure of school readiness.

Some suggest that the mood and behavioral problems of children of cohabiting and single parents are due not to economic and psychological stressors but to genetic factors.[56] Parents with irritable temperaments and angry personality traits may find it difficult to get along with other adults so they remain single or get divorced. They pass on these personality traits to their children, who then have problems. Whatever genetic influences affect children of single parents in terms of temperamental dispositions, the behavior of children is improved and problems decreased when their single mothers learn more effective ways of relating to them.

For example, single mothers of young boys aged six to ten received fourteen weeks of training in positive parenting, using consistent rewards for positive behaviors and consistent negative consequences such as time outs for aggressive behaviors.[57] Families were followed for thirty months. Teachers' ratings and test scores revealed children of trained mothers declined in aggressive behaviors and increased in adaptability at school. Children themselves reported they got along better with peers and felt less depressed. Mothers too felt less depressed.

The evidence from many studies, then, suggests that there is no single outcome for children of never-married and single mothers. When children (1) have stable living arrangements and (2) experience positive parenting, they have greater social and cognitive competence.

SINGLE MOTHERS BY CHOICE

An increasing number of women are making the conscious choice to have a child alone through adoption, assisted reproductive technology, or very occasionally through an unplanned pregnancy as a relationship or marriage ended. Strong desires for a child along with the feeling that they have lost the opportunity to do this under the ideal circumstances of marriage to a loved partner spur women to consider this option. This is a relatively homogeneous subgroup of single parents.[58] They are well educated, European American women who are in their mid- to late-thirties. They have good incomes and satisfying jobs, and many have changed lifestyles in advance of having children (e.g., buying a home).

A careful study of single-parent and married-couple families matched for parents' education, income, area of residence, and age and gender of the child observed maternal and child interactions when the child was in the preschool years and a second time when children were ages eight to thirteen.[59]

In the preschool years, single mothers reported more stress than did mothers in two-parent families. Single mothers had to work longer hours and were more worried about finances than were their married counterparts. The greatest difference between these two groups of mothers, however, was that single mothers had fewer social and emotional supports when their children were young. It was precisely this kind of support that predicted optimal parent–child interactions in both single- and two-parent families. When single mothers had socioemotional support, their children's behavior was similar to that of children in two-parent families.

In the preschool years, observations of mothers' and children's behaviors during a mother-directed teaching task revealed few differences between single and married parents, with the exception that single mothers had difficulty managing the behaviors of sons, who were often noncompliant and resistant to mothers' requests. In the years eight to thirteen, however, teachers described children of single mothers as less socially competent, less successful academically, and more problematic in behavior than children of married parents.

Stressful life events in single-mother families had a more direct impact on mothers' parenting and on children's behavior than it did in two-parent families. Single mothers with high stress were less nurturing and less effective in parenting, and children, living in high-stress single-parent homes, independent of parenting, showed more problems. Stressful life events affected children directly and indirectly through mothers' parenting. Teachers and mothers described school-age children living in homes where mothers had high stress levels as having the most problems.

The behavior of children living in single-parent homes with low stress was similar to that of children in two-parent homes. It is the stress level that is critical, perhaps because there are not two parents to manage the stress and care for children. It points to the importance of a strong support system for single mothers even when they have the same educational and income level as two-parent families.

Jane Mattes founded Single Mothers by Choice (SMC), a national organization, to provide information and resources for mothers on the many options for handling the common challenges mothers face as they conceive and rear children.[60]

DIVORCED PARENTS

Mavis Hetherington, who has carried out careful longitudinal studies of intact, divorced, and remarried families for four decades, describes four considerations that underlie all her research: (1) divorce is not a single event but an event that triggers many changes for children and parents over time; (2) changes associated with marital transitions have to be viewed as changes in the entire family system; (3) the entire social milieu—peer group, neighborhood, school, friendship network—influences an individual's response to the transition and (4) there is great diversity in the ways children and parents respond to marital transitions.[61] Most studies of families in transition focus on European American middle-class families, and we do not know how widely we can generalize these findings.

The changes of divorce—new households, changes in finances, changes in parents' and children's moods and behaviors, increased responsibilities in caring for children alone—all create stress for parents. Observing parents and children reveals that it takes around two years to adapt to all the changes and establish new patterns of life.

Two major factors influence how children and their parents fare: parents' abilities' to (1) maintain positive authoritative parenting behaviors and (2) work together cooperatively, putting aside the anger that many parents feel toward the other parent and the divorce.

We have seen that at all ages and in all ethnic groups, parents' ability to be warm and supportive, respectful of children's individuality yet consistent in enforcing appropriate limits, promotes children's competence and well-being. In all the changes and emotional upheaval of divorce, parents' continuing reliance on authoritative techniques helps children to feel secure and cared for.

The anger seen in many divorces is a major predictor of children's mood problems and later behavior problems.[62] Just as in two-parent families, parents' skill in supporting each others' parenting, when living separately, helps parents and children do well. Hetherington estimates that only about 25 percent of parents in her studies were able to put aside their own issues and focus on children's needs, coordinating their efforts to solve problems, to coordinate rules and regulations in the two homes. Sometimes a crisis such as a child's illness or an accident sparked the cooperation.

About 50 percent of parents in Hetherington's samples practiced what she termed "parallel" parenting, in which each parent went his or her own way, ignoring the other parent as much as possible. Each parent had his or her rules; children were expected to adapt to them, and often children did.

About 25 percent of parents engaged in ongoing conflict, sometimes for years. Parents took every opportunity to criticize the other parent's actions. Children have a variety of feelings—anger, sadness, hopelessness—and these feelings are the most frequent predictors of ongoing problems for children.

Children's Immediate Reactions to Divorce

Emotional reactions to divorce, common to children of all ages, include sadness, fear, depression, anger, confusion, and sometimes relief; the predominant emotions vary with the child's age and family circumstances. Even young children verbalize very intense feelings. A three-year-old described divorce: "When Mom and Dad hate each other and your family is dead."[63] And a five-year-old said, "It's when someone signs a paper, someone leaves home, and then kids cry."[64]

Parents can help most by providing emotional support.[65] Parents are urged to (1) communicate with the child about the divorce and the new adjustments, explaining in simple language the reasons for each change that occurs, and (2) reduce the child's suffering, where possible, by giving reassurance that the child's needs will be met. Many children get little information and support as they go through the initial turmoil of divorce. Often, no one talks to them, no one listens to them talk about their feelings or answers their questions, and few relatives give added help and support.

Parents need to say clearly and often, when opportunities arise, that the divorce was *not* caused by the children but was caused by difficulties between the parents. In addition, parents need to remember that children worry about them and how they are doing. Parents cannot always confine their own intense reactions to times when the children are not there, but parents can try to do so.

There are many things divorcing parents should not say. First, they should not burden their children with their own negative views of each other. Second, they should not blame the other parent for all the problems. Third, they should not ask children to take sides—children usually need and want to be loyal to both parents.

Thus far, we have seen the reactions of children who regret their parents' divorce, but about 10 percent of children feel relieved when their parents divorce.[66] Often, these are older children who have witnessed violence or severe psychological suffering on the part of a parent or other family member. These children feel that dissolution of the marriage is the best solution, and progressing from a conflict-ridden home to a more stable environment with one parent helps these children's overall level of adjustment and functioning.

Children's behavioral reactions to the divorce vary, depending on the personal and family characteristics—the level of conflict; the child's age, gender, and temperament; parents' emotional reactions; the amount of time with each parent.[67] Children often feel sad at not living with both parents and become anxious they will lose the parent they live with as well. Young boys frequently express their anger and fearfulness in aggressive, noncompliant behavior that creates even further distance with mothers who feel overwhelmed. Sensitive boys with irritable, reactive temperaments often feel both anxiety and anger, and their behavior drives others away so they do not get the support they need. Young girls get along better with mothers because girls more often are understanding of mothers and compliant, so mothers and daughters grow closer.

Children in divorced families resist mothers' authority. Mothers are more successful and the children have fewer problems when another adult such as a grandparent, reinforces the mother's authority. Adolescents may feel caught between divorced parents whose conflicts intensify adolescents' anxiety, depression, and poor adjustment. Even when parents have high conflict with each other, adolescents can do well, provided parents do not put them in the middle. The feeling of being caught between parents contributes to these children's problems.

Although many children of divorce show aggressive and insecure behaviors in adolescence, others are caring, competent teenagers who cooperate with divorced parents and make significant contributions to family functioning. Still others are caring, responsible teenagers who worry that they will be unable to meet the demands placed on them. The aggressive, insecure children who have many difficulties do not have a single caring adult in their lives. Their parents are neglectful, disengaged, and authoritarian, and the children cannot find support outside the family.

When children have continuing relationships with both parents, they are more likely to adjust well following the divorce process. Fathers are more likely to maintain relationships with their sons than with their daughters. In fact, many mothers relinquish custody of older sons to fathers because they feel sons need a male role model.

Parents' Reactions to Divorce

About thirty-five years ago when much divorce research began, mothers usually had primary legal custody (responsibility for children) and physical custody (place the child lived), and fathers saw children every other weekend. This arrangement paralleled family life in two-parent homes where mothers had primary responsibility for caregiving. As fathers in two-parent families took a more active role in family life and child care, they wanted more time with children when the marriages dissolved. In addition, research was demonstrating that increased contact with fathers was beneficial for boys and girls. Shared physical and legal custody became more accepted in many states unless some particular problem prevented a parent from being responsible for children. Still, mothers often get the larger share of physical custody. In 1998, only 12 percent of fathers received it although more wanted it.[68]

Mothers   In families mothers have had the role of nurturing parent, understanding feelings and communicating them with children. In the first one to two years after the divorce, custodial mothers are preoccupied, sometimes anxious, and depressed. These mood changes are difficult for children because just at the time children are most in need of nurturance, mothers often have less to give.

Mothers are trying to establish independent households with less money and often with the stress of ongoing legal proceedings. Financial pressures increase, and mothers often seek more work and day care. When mothers are financially comfortable, their children show fewer problems than children living with a mother with financial pressures. In response to all the stress, mothers' parenting strategies often change, and mothers become more permissive or harsh or neglectful, and children resist their requests. Mothers often give preadolescents freedom and choices, but are restrictive and limiting with their adolescents. Parenting difficulties are most marked in the first two years following the divorce, but imbalances between freedom and limits may continue.

Over time, mothers' reactions to divorce are diverse. Seventy-five percent of divorced custodial mothers report that at the end of two years, they feel happier than they did in the last year of the marriage. Many of these women go on to develop independent lives and careers that increase their self-esteem. Some divorced women, however, report depression, loneliness, and health problems six to eleven years after the divorce. Still, they do not have as many problems as do nondivorced women in high-conflict marriages, who are more depressed and anxious and have more physical problems.

Fathers   When fathers are custodial parents, they face many of the problems of custodial mothers, feeling overwhelmed as they take full responsibility for children during their time with children. However, they usually have established work schedules, and, on average, they have greater income than divorced mothers so the sources of stress fall mainly in the area of being fully responsible parents.

Fathers differ from mothers in being more comfortable and practiced in setting limits with children and enforcing them in a matter-of-fact way with younger children. Fathers are not so used to understanding children's feelings and emotional needs, especially when children are young and not as logical as fathers might expect. Their parenting experiences with children greatly expand their understanding of others' feelings and their patience, and many fathers report this as a major gain of caring for children, a gain that helps them in all their relationships. With adolescent children, fathers may have the same trouble as mothers, giving too much freedom and not enforcing limits.

Noncustodial fathers have the challenge of maintaining close relationships with children when they see them for briefer periods of time. As a reaction, and especially right after the divorce, noncustodial fathers tend to become either permissive/indulgent or disengaged parents. They are less likely to be disciplinarians and more likely to play the role of recreational companion than are custodial mothers because they do not want the little time they have with children taken up with limit-setting.

And many times noncustodial fathers do not stay involved. Research indicates that increasing numbers of fathers stay involved, and we take this up in a later section. Noncustodial fathers are most likely to stay involved when they feel they play an important role in their children's lives and their long-term development

Hetherington advises parents going through a divorce to take an active role in shaping their lives—get support from others, use resources at work or in the community, plan for long-term goals (e.g., getting more education, different jobs), avoid impulsive decisions, and be aware that cohabiting relationships involve higher rates of relationship breakups before and after marriages. She observes, however, that, "The effects of a new intimate relationship are so profound it is worth repeating my findings: after a divorce, nothing heals as completely as a new love. True for women, this finding is even more true for men, who, being less socially adept and more emotionally isolated, often feel unsupported in the early years without a new partner."[69]

Protective Factors for Children

Protective factors for children as they adjust to divorce include qualities of the child, supportive aspects of the family system, and external social supports.[70] The child's age, sex, and intelligence serve as protection. Younger children appear less affected than elementary school children or early adolescents at the time of the divorce or remarriage. Because they are becoming increasingly independent of the family, late adolescents seem less affected than younger children. Boys appear to suffer more difficulties at the time of the divorce, and girls appear to have more problems at the time of the mother's remarriage. Intelligence can help children cope with the stress.

The child's temperament also influences the process of divorce. An easy, adaptable temperament is a protective factor. In contrast, children with a difficult temperament are more sensitive and less adaptable to change; they can become a focal point for parental anger. On one hand, they elicit the anger with their reactive behavior; on the other, they provide a convenient target for parental anger that may belong elsewhere.

We have already touched on some forms of family interaction that are protective: reduced conflict between the parents, authoritative parenting, structure and organization in daily life. Mothers must be especially firm and fair in establishing limits with boys, as their tendency is to develop a vicious repetitive cycle of complaining and fighting.

Siblings and grandparents are potential supports. When family life is harmonious after divorce, then sibling relationships resemble those in intact families. When conflict between parents arises, siblings fight, with the greatest difficulty occurring between older brothers and younger sisters.

Grandparents can support grandchildren directly with time, attention, and special outings and privileges that help ease the pain of divorce. Many grandchildren credit their grandparents with their own stability and happiness following divorce. Grandparents provide support indirectly by helping one of the parents. In fact, returning to live in the home of one's parents is a solution many young parents choose when they do not have the resources to live on their own. Grandparents can be loving, stable babysitters who enrich children's lives in ways that no one else can. The mother can work and carry on a social life, knowing that her child is well cared for in her absence. This arrangement also usually reduces living expenses. When the mother and grandparents agree on child-rearing techniques and the mother is respected in the household as a mature adult, this solution may be attractive.

School is another major source of support for children. Authoritative, kind teachers and peer friendships give pleasure and a sense of esteem to children. Educational and athletic accomplishments contribute to feelings of competence that stimulate resilience, and many children find mentors in these activities.

Some protective factors lie beyond a parent's control, including age, sex, and temperament of the child, but many lie within it, such as setting aside anger, establishing structure, monitoring behavior, and seeking out external supports for children.

Long-Term Consequences for Children of Divorce

Six years following the divorce, three-quarters of children were doing well in Hetherington's groups, but 25 percent showed difficulties in aggressive/impulsive behaviors and depressed moods (compared to 10 percent in nondivorced families).[71] Other studies too have found that in comparison to children in nondivorced families, children of divorce have an increased risk for problems in cognitive and social competence. The differences are small, and there is much overlap in the functioning of the two groups.

A recent longitudinal study following families with four- to seven-year-old children and observing qualities of divorced families before and after divorce finds that children of divorce have problems years before the divorce.[72] When compared with children whose parents remain together, those children living in families in which parents will later divorce have significantly greater problems with aggressive, noncompliant behaviors and anxious/depressed moods before divorce. After divorce, their aggressive, rule-breaking behaviors decrease, but anxious/depressed moods increase further. These are the same emotions and behaviors Hetherington noted in her samples of children studied twenty years earlier. Despite greater understanding of divorce, and attempts to make things easier for families, children still suffer ongoing anger, depression, and sadness at the dissolution of their families.

When assessed in young adulthood at age twenty-four, 20 percent of Hetherington's sample reported continued problems in the area of impulsive, rule-breaking behavior and in the area of depression. Nevertheless, 80 percent scored within the average range on measures of psychological functioning, and many were doing very well.[73] In comparison, 10 percent of children in two-parent married families showed clinical levels of problems.

Judith Wallerstein, reporting on an adult follow-up of her intensively studied group of divorced children begun in 1971, described the consequences of divorce as serious and pervasive for her adult study members, especially in the area of establishing intimate ties with others.[74] Her statements about serious long-term consequences for children of divorce provoked discussions regarding the exact nature of long-term consequences of divorce.

Paul Amato, analyzing data from adult children of divorce collected in 2000, found that these adults reported high levels of well-being, relatively little discord in their own marriages, and close relationships with fathers in many families.[75] Conversely, some children from nondivorced families reported low levels of well-being, discord in marriages, and distant relationships with fathers. So, like Hetherington, he found diversity of outcomes, with most adults of divorced parents doing well, and some children of intact parents having problems. Amato concluded that although divorce negatively affects some children and is a risk factor for later social and emotional functioning, the majority of children do well.

Amato believes it important to identify the conditions of divorce that lead to negative outcomes and those leading to positive outcomes. He found that children who experienced only one divorce and no other marital transitions reported a sense of well-being similar to that of children who grew up in nondivorced families. Furthermore, when the divorce ended a marriage with intense marital discord, children reported feeling better in adulthood than those adults who continued to live in high-conflict marriages. Stability and limiting conflict are two factors identified as protective factors in other research as well.

Given the negative effects of divorce, many wonder whether it is better for parents to stay together than to divorce. The answer depends on the nature of the conflict in the marriage, the various changes that follow the divorce, the quality of the postdivorce family relationships, and the degree to which the custodial parent relies on authoritative parenting.[76]

When married parents have intense conflicts, children have emotional and behavior problems. Following a divorce, many children have behavior problems for the first two years. If parents of high-conflict marriages divorce and the conflict ends, then children's well-being improves over time, and the turmoil of the divorce is worth it because stability follows and children do well. If parents continue to fight after divorce, then children suffer and parents might as well stay in high-conflict marriages and spare children the problems of the divorce process. It is hard to tell in advance, though, whether parents can end the conflicts after they end the marriage.

Community Resources

The legal system has changed, making it easier for both parents to continue to be involved in the care of children. When parents have difficulty coming to agreement about custody issues, many states now provide court mediation services.

Counselors help parents explore children's and parents' needs and reach agreement on reasonable living arrangements.

Furthermore, laws have been passed to make it easier for single mothers to obtain child support payments decreed by the court. This is imperative because, as noted, mothers who are single heads of household have incomes far below those of other family units.

Court services in many states have organized psychoedeuational programs for divorcing families. Children attend a group with same-age peers while each parent attends a different parent group. The groups last for 6–10 weeks and cover experiences many parents and children have in the process of divorce. In addition to providing information on the psychological experiences common to the divorce process, the groups give family members opportunities to talk without other family members present. These groups also provide coping strategies that children and parents can use and ways for children to raise sensitive topics with parents. Parents and children report they like the program and benefit from it.

A Collaborative Divorce Process

Lawyers and counselors separately recognized the damage and difficulties that an adversarial legal system creates for families, and some joined together to form the International Academy of Collaborative Professionals to offer a different way for parents to bring their marriages to an end. The process helps parents put their anger and intense feelings aside, put children's needs first, and focus on the family's future.[77]

The process includes several professionals working as a team to help the couple work out agreements that reflect their short- and long-term goals. Couples who wish a collaborative divorce agree to keep all the discussions and information gathered confidential; if either parent seeks litigation in the courts, the team does not participate, and all the information gathered remains confidential.

Each parent has both a collaborative lawyer and a divorce coach, and the couple also has a child mental health specialist who advises on the needs of the children, and a financial specialist to give advice on finances. Working with his or her divorce coach, each parent discusses feelings about the marriage, the divorce, and the hoped-for future. Coaches help parents recognize unacknowledged feelings and help them communicate feelings calmly in discussions with the other parent. The child specialist meets with each parent and with the child or children alone and helps parents understand and focus on children's needs in custody arrangements. The financial consultant gives information and options on ways to handle parents' financial needs.

Discussing serious differences in a calm atmosphere helps parents make good decisions at an emotional and challenging time in life. The team meets many times until the divorce agreement is concluded. The team of experts remains available to be reconvened in the future if circumstances change or difficulties arise. Proponents of the process say it is cheaper than the cost of lengthy, expensive litigation that creates bitterness but does not provide consensual solutions.

FATHERS' ROLE IN CHILDREN'S LIVES

We saw in Chapter 13 that fathers' increased role in dual-earner families benefits children as well as mothers who are both working and rearing children. How does diminished contact with fathers affect children?

Fathers' Presence or Absence

Using data from several longitudinal samples, Sara McLanahan and Julien Teitler report the consequences of father presence and absence for children's development, along with the factors underlying those consequences.[78] They report that, compared to children growing up in two-parent families with fathers present, children growing up apart from the fathers have lower grades, achieve less education, are more likely to drop out of school, and are less likely to get and keep a job. Adolescent girls in father-absent homes were more likely to initiate sexual activity at an early age and to have a teen birth or a birth outside of marriage. In one study, 11 percent of adolescent girls in two-parent families had a teen birth, compared with 27 percent of girls in father-absent families. Father absence had a greater effect on the risk for teen births for European American and Latina teens than for African American teens.

The effects of father presence on educational attainment did not vary as a result of gender or racial or ethnic status of the family. Boys and girls of all ethnic groups had increased educational attainment when fathers were present. It did not seem to matter when fathers' absence occurred or how long it lasted. Nor did it matter what family structure the child lived in, with one exception: children in homes with widowed mothers did nearly as well as children in two-parent families. In general, father absence matters more than the circumstances causing it, except in the case of widowhood.

Fathers' Contributions to Children's Lives

McLanahan and Teitler identified three aspects of fathers' contributions: financial, social, and community. Fathers' financial contribution improves the resources available for child rearing. Without the additional resources, families may not have services such as health care and may live in poorer neighborhoods with poorer schools and fewer community services. They estimate that reduced income accounts for approximately 50 percent of the effects of father absence.

These researchers estimate that about half the disadvantage of father-absent homes results from poorer parent–child relationships, poorer relationships with adults, and a loss of resources in the community. As noted, it is extremely difficult for one parent to provide as much time, attention, and balance in parenting as two parents; nevertheless, some single-parent mothers do establish low-conflict homes in which children's functioning improves.

Paul Amato conducted new analyses of data to determine fathers' contributions to children's lives.[79] He looked at both mothers' and fathers' contributions in terms of human, financial, and social capital. *Human capital* refers to parents' skills, abilities, and knowledge that contribute to achievement in our culture. A useful measure of human capital is parents' education. *Financial capital* refers to the economic resources available to the family to purchase needed goods and services. *Social capital* refers to family and social relationships available to promote children's development.

Amato distinguished between the benefits of the coparental relationship and those of the parent–child relationship. In a positive coparental relationship, the child views a model of how two people relate, cooperate, negotiate, and compromise. Children who learn these skills tend to get along better with peers and later partners. In providing a unified authority structure to children, two parents teach that authority is consistent and rational. Amato writes, "Social closure between parents helps children to learn and internalize social norms and moral values. Also, a respect for hierarchical authority, first learned in the family, makes it easier for young people to adjust to social institutions that are hierarchically organized, such as schools and the workplace."[80]

Looking at many studies, Amato demonstrates that children's well-being is positively associated with (1) the father's education, (2) the father's income, (3) the quality of the coparental relationship, and (4) the quality of the parent–child relationship. These relationships hold in two- and one-parent families as well, even in studies where mothers' contributions are controlled for.

In his own longitudinal study, Amato interviewed individuals originally studied as children and followed up to early adulthood. He has found that fathers' education and income are related to children's education and that children's education has positive implications for such areas as friendships, self-esteem, and life satisfaction. Fathers' characteristics appear to account for more variance in children's

Nonresidential fathers play a positive role in children's lives when they provide support, guidance, and monitoring of children.

education, self-esteem, and lack of psychological distress than do mothers' charac-teristics. Mothers' characteristics account for more variance in children's develop-ing kin ties and close friends than do fathers' characteristics. Fathers' and mothers' characteristics account for equal amounts of variance in life satisfaction. Amato summarizes,

> Current research suggests that fathers continue to be important for their contributions of human and financial capital. Current research also suggests, however, that children bene-fit when fathers are involved in socioemotional aspects of family life . . . the current trend for fathers to be less involved in their children's lives (due to shifts in family structure) represents a net decline in the level of resources available for children.[81]

Studies show that nonresidential fathers who confine their activities with children to fun outings play a minimal role in children's development. Amato concludes that fathers matter "to the extent that they are able to provide appropriate support, guidance, and monitoring—especially if this occurs in the context of cooperation between the parents."[82]

Unmarried Fathers

Fathers need not be married and living with children to have a positive impact. As we saw, the children of teen mothers benefited from their relationships with their fathers in the same ways as children living with biological fathers—namely in the areas of school performance and reduced aggressiveness. Boys especially got better grades when fathers were involved.[83]

Fathers also need not be biological fathers to have an impact. Social fathers, defined as men who live with a young child's mother, had a positive impact on children's lives when they were highly engaged with the child.[84] High levels of engagement with children predicted lower levels of aggressive behaviors and better health in children regardless of whether the father was a biological or social father. Social fathers did not diminish the positive relationships children had with their biological nonresident fathers. They seemed to compliment them.

Nonresident unmarried fathers were most likely to stay highly involved over a two-year period when they had positive relationships with mothers, and each par-ent had positive relationships with the other's parents.[85] The extended family, posi-tively supporting both parents, helped fathers to stay involved. The major variable, however, was the parents' romantic involvement. When parents were romantically involved, fathers were engaged. When the romantic relationship ended, fathers decreased their contact. If the romance resumed, fathers became more engaged. One of the policy implications is that if parents get training in relationship and communication skills, they may be better able to continue the romantic relationship that holds the family together.

Children certainly want their fathers involved in their lives. Survey responses of college students whose parents divorced during childhood revealed that 70 percent of men and women believe that equal time with both parents is the best living arrangement after divorce; less than 10 percent of students wanted less time with fathers.[86]

Encouraging Fathers' Participation

James Levine has written extensively on the advantages for children of fathers' increased involvement regardless of whether fathers are married to mothers.[87] He identifies three lessons he has learned over the years.

The first important ingredient in successfully involving fathers is the recognition that fathers want to be involved and can be effective parents with preparation and help. Second, single fathers need a support network that guides their behavior. Third, women play a key role in supporting men as fathers.

Fathers who confine their activities with children to fun outings play a minimal role in children's lives. Fathers matter when they provide appropriate support, guidance, and monitoring with children.

Figure 14-1 describes the "on-ramps" that facilitate men's connections with their children and families. Such on-ramps come from those in the community who interact with fathers—at the hospital, at doctors' visits, at schools. Levine writes,

> Our model does not absolve any man from primary responsibility; indeed, it holds that all fathers—whether unmarried, married, or divorced—are responsible for establishing and maintaining connection to their children. But it broadens that responsibility so it is also shared appropriately by all those in the community who, in their everyday work, have the opportunity and the capacity to build—or influence the building of—the on-ramps to connection.[88]

As Levine mentioned in his interview in Chapter 6, the context of interactions with fathers can help involve them. One example is the Hospital Paternity Establishment Program in West Virginia, which has increased the number of

◼ **F I G U R E 14-1**
CONNECTION: A SHARED RESPONSIBILITY

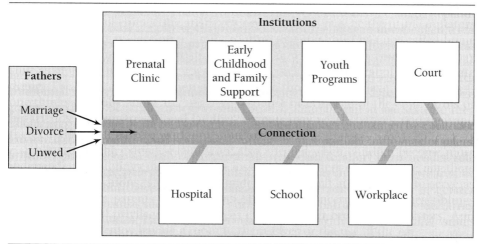

James A. Levine with Edward W. Pitt, New *Expectations: Community Strategies for Responsible Fatherhood* (New York: Families and Work Institute, 1995), p. 41. Reprinted with permission of the Families and Work Institute.

unwed fathers who establish paternity from 600 per year to 3,000 per year. Recall that changing expectations emphasize that new fathers need education about establishing paternity and that they need to be approached in terms of the benefits to the father and the child rather than to the state. Hospital staff were educated to involve fathers when they visited their newborns. Fathers then met with professionals, such as a child psychologist, who could explain the psychological importance of the father to the child; a doctor, who could explain the medical importance; and a lawyer, who could discuss the legal benefits to the child of having a father who is known. "Public education is the key," says Gary Kreps, who designed the program.[89]

DEATH IN THE FAMILY

When a parent dies, nothing is the same. Earl Grollman writes, "Never again will the world be as secure a place as it was before. The familiar design of family life is completely disrupted."[90] While there are differences in the ways that children and parents grieve, there are also many similarities, and we touch on them first and then move to what is unique for children and parents.

For the child the death of a parent is "the worst loss."[91] The child has lost the figure he or she depended on for security in life, and the parent has lost his or her life companion. John Bowlby described four phases of the grief process: (1) a period of numbing lasting for hours or weeks in which the person has taken in the fact of the death but has not registered it emotionally because the pain is so great; (2) a period of protest and yearning in which the person refuses to accept the fact of the death and searches for the parent; (3) a period of sadness and despair in which the reality of the death has sunk in emotionally and life without that person seems unbearable; and (4) a period of reorganization of life to go on without that person.[92]

Bowlby did not think of these as clear-cut stages but rather as a "succession of phases." It is possible to move back and forth between two phases while moving in the direction of adapting to and accepting the fact of the person's death.[93] Thus, a person can move from feeling sad to being engaged in reorganization and then back to feeling sad again. Bowlby also believed it is not necessary to detach completely from the memory of the person; it is possible to reorganize your life in a meaningful way and still have a continuing sense of the dead person's presence in your life.

There is no specific length of time for grieving. Children may proceed through the phases of grief more rapidly than adults. It used to be thought that about a year was the usual length of mourning, and to be sad and grieving after a year indicated problems. Now, we realize it may take two or more years before people have reorganized their lives and are on a steady emotional keel most of the time. Still, there will always be reminders and sudden experiences of intense grief. Psychological consultation is often recommended when the usual reactions to grief persist in intense ways that disrupt daily functioning. However, sometimes getting immediate professional advice eases the process of mourning and prevents the development of problems.

Children's Special Needs

A child's developmental level and temperament will guide what is said to the child about death. At the Dougy Center for Grieving Children, counselors have four guiding principles:

- Grief is a natural and expectable response to loss.
- Each individual carries within him or her an innate capacity to heal.
- The duration and intensity of grief is unique for each individual.
- Caring and acceptance are helpful to a person in resolving grief.[94]

Talking to Children   One has to give as much accurate information as possible to children in words that they can understand.[95] Young children think of death as a reversible condition, and it is not until they are age five to seven that they understand it is irreversible. So little children may ask when the parent is returning. Regardless of their initial understanding, as they get older and their thinking becomes more mature, they may have new questions and new reactions they want to discuss. So, the initial explanation of the death is the beginning of conversations that will extend over the years.

Parents are sometimes told to wait for children to ask questions, but children may not know enough to ask questions at the time, and only later may have the words or thoughts they need answers to.[96] For example, a preschooler refused to go to bed after her infant sister died of SIDS because she thought she too would die in her sleep. She did not volunteer this information until her mother asked her what was upsetting her at bedtime.

Parents have to be aware that children are prone to feel guilt and to blame themselves for the death of a loved one. One family was surprised to learn that their daughter blamed herself for a family death. She was not present, but blamed herself because she thought the death was God's punishment for not saying her prayers at night.

Ways Children's Reactions Differ from Adults   The Dougy Center lists several ways in which children's grief differs from adults.[97] First, children are more physical in their expressions of grief. They may want to ride a bike, shoot baskets, or run as a way of dealing with grief. They also may have more physical complaints of stomachaches or headaches. Second, children are less verbal, and sometimes parents think they are not grieving because they are not talking about it. They may use imaginative play or actions rather than words to express grief. Third, children express their anger about the death more directly and may do more quarreling or arguing or simply express anger at everyone and life in general.

Fourth, children may be more attuned to parents' needs and feelings than parents realize. As a result, they may behave in ways that they think will please or help their parents. For example, if they see that their questions upset a parent, they may stop asking them even though they are still confused about the death. Fifth, children need breaks from grieving; parents may find it hard to understand that they can become immersed in an activity and not grieve. Parents misinterpret that as not caring for the dead person, but children do have the ability to live in the moment. They can grieve intensely and then happily be with friends.

Helping Children Grieve   Joan Huff, program director at the Dougy Center, believes that parents create a supportive emotional climate in which children feel safe to go through the process of grieving.[98] To create such a climate, she advises:

- In age-appropriate terms, give accurate, detailed information about the death and answer all questions; be prepared to continue discussions in the future.

- Reassure children that the remaining parent will continue to nurture and care for them, and although the grief process may last an extended period of time, they will always be taken care of.

- "Keep your children with you, and include them in family and religious observances: viewings, funerals, burials, wakes, and the like. The question of at what age children should attend funerals comes up frequently. Talking with children, I hardly ever heard a child complain he was forced to attend a funeral against his will. Much more often, children complained that they had been sent away, excluded from this profoundly important event in their family's life."[99] If children are babies or toddlers, other relatives can hold them or supervise them. In the future, it is valuable for them to know that they were there with the rest of the family even though they do not remember it.

- Talk to children about what they want to do with their parent's possessions; parents make the final decision but get input from children.

- Express your grief in front of your children so they receive permission to grieve as well; parents may worry that their grief may overwhelm children; certainly in extreme form, wailing or sobbing can overwhelm them, so it is wise to try to strike a balance between expressing your feelings so children feel free to grieve also and expressing them so intensely that children are overwhelmed and afraid.

- Structure observances of the death so that all close family members are included and have a role, such as lighting a candle on anniversaries or making a donation in the name of the person.

Parents' Special Needs

We all live with the assumption that we will grow up, marry, raise children, live for many years after children are grown, and then die when we are old and infirm. The untimely death of a young parent violates our sense of the order of life events and arouses fear that other frightening events or another untimely death can occur as well. Parents' expectations about life are dashed and they have many of the emotional reactions children have—anger, guilt, fear, insecurity. One father said, "When you lose a child, you lose a piece of yourself. You lose your illusions. You lose reason and predictability; all the order falls out of the universe. And you lose your future."[100] The same feelings exist when you lose your husband or wife.

Parents need as much support and nurturance as their young children at this devastating time, and yet they also have the responsibility for providing and looking after other family members. So what helps them cope? Living in an emotionally safe environment with people who respect that they will grieve in their own individual way and who give them support as they find their way enables adults to get through the process of grieving.

Helpful strategies include:[101]

- Talking to other people, sometimes in a group of people who have suffered a similar loss such as Compassionate Friends; talking to other family members and staying connected; expect to have to educate them about the grief process as you experience it.

- Knowing that life will not always be this painful; you will get through this experience, that however painful it is, how many ups and downs you experience, you will survive.

- Striving for balance in your life with physical exercise, healthy eating, and little pleasures to offset the pain that you are experiencing.

- Seeking a spiritual or broader connection to provide meaning in life; many people find help in a religious or spiritual understanding of the event; others seek meaning by becoming involved in groups to prevent the kind of tragedy that happened to them; still others find meaning and vitality to their lives by providing services to others (e.g., bringing pets or plants or services to people in nursing homes).

- Valuing what they do have rather than focusing on what they have lost.

In all forms of single parent life we have seen that children function competently when parents use positive, authoritative parenting, maintain stable family lives with low stress, work cooperatively with the other parent if available, find ways to deal with anger and stress so they are not directed at others in front of children, and build support groups that provide resources a second parent ordinarily contributes. People and agencies in the community can organize the support activities families may need but do not ask for, such as babysitting or household cleaning.

MAIN POINTS

Family structures have changed over the last forty years with

- parents marrying later
- an increase in unmarried couples living together
- increasing number of babies born to unmarried parents many of whom have a child by a previous partner
- increase in single women having children alone by choice
- teen parents

When compared to children in two-parent families, children in single-parent and unmarried families are at greater risk for

- aggressive, noncompliant behaviors at age three
- school problems, peer problems, and anxiety and worry when in the elementary school years
- school and mood problems as well as noncompliant aggressive behaviors in high school

Teen parents

- come to parenting having experienced many difficulties and less parental support
- often have unrealistic expectations and are more directive and harsh in their discipline
- are more effective parents when the understand children's development and their needs are able to respond sensitively to children
- are helped by programs that support parents' caregiving and their transition to adulthood

Children of teen parents

- are at greater risk for insecure attachments with mothers
- are at greater risk for delays in language, cognitive, and socio-emotional skills
- are more likely to show effective behaviors when mothers are stable and sensitive parents, fathers are positive and involved, family receives support from religious involvement, and children are involved in athletic and community activities

The process of divorce

- is often preceded by marital conflict, which upsets children and arouses their feelings of self-blame
- is a major disruption for all family members
- involves many changes for children that can include fewer economic resources as well as a new neighborhood, a new school, and new friends
- places stress on children and parents, which can be reversed if parents establish low-conflict divorced homes and use authoritative parenting

Protective factors for children at the time of divorce include

- a child's age, sex, intelligence, and temperament
- manageable amounts of stress and appropriate support from grandparents and other relatives
- educational and athletic accomplishments that contribute to children's feelings of competence and stimulate resilience

Children's behavior

- becomes more problematic at the time of divorce but improves as time passes

- is less carefully monitored in single-parent than in dual-parent homes in early adolescence
- improves when parents resolve their anger and use authoritative parenting

Men make positive contributions to children's development when

- they provide their human, financial, and social capital to the family
- the social context encourages their involvement

When a parent dies

- children feel many emotions, which they are more likely to express in physical, motoric activity when they are young
- children need parents' help and encouragement in talking about feelings
- children worry about the remaining parent
- the remaining parent needs to get support and people with whom to talk
- takes individual amounts of time before people are able to reorganize their lives

EXERCISES

1. Explore what programs are available in your community for teen mothers and teen fathers. How do teen parents meet requirements for high school graduation in the local high schools? Are there programs that care for infants at school while mothers attend classes?

2. Imagine that your married brother, sister, or friend came to you and said that he or she was getting a divorce and wanted help in making arrangements so his or her eight-year-old daughter and six-year-old son would experience the fewest negative effects. What guidelines would you give him or her?

3. If possible, attend divorce court for a morning and summarize the cases presented there. What issues do parents argue about? What issues about children arise? Describe whether you agree with the judge's ruling, and state why.

4. Read Roger Rosenblatt's *New Yorker* article, "Making Toast" (December 15, 2008, pp. 44–49), about caring for his grandchildren after their mother's sudden death from a heart defect. Describe how their father and grandparents provided a supportive atmosphere for the children to grieve for their mother.

5. Look in the community to determine what training is available for unmarried parents in relationships and communication skills so they can improve and maintain their relationships.

ADDITIONAL READINGS

Borkowski, John G. et al., eds. *Risk and Resilience: Adolescent Mothers and Their Children Grow Up.* Mahwah, NJ: Erlbaum, 2007.

Connor, Michael E., and White, Joseph L., eds. *Black Fathers: An Invisible Presence in America.* Mahwah, NJ: Erlbaum, 2006.

Hetherington, E. Mavis, and Kelly, John. *For Better or For Worse: Divorce Reconsidered.* New York: Norton, 2002.

Mattes, Jane. *Single Mothers By Choice: A Guidebook for Single Women Who Are Considering or Have Chosen Motherhood.*, 2nd ed. New York: Times Books, 1997.

Tesler, Pauline H. and Thompson, Peggy. *Collaborative Divorce.* New York: HarperCollins, 2006.

15

Parenting in Complex Family Structures

IN THE NEWS

New York Times, May 27[1]: Study finds adoptive parents need preparation for adopting a child of a different race. See page 457.

Test Your Knowledge: Fact or Fiction (True/False)

1. Most adults are so traumatized and financially burdened by divorce that only a minority remarry and form new families.

2. Teenagers report more psychological problems when they live in stepfamilies and have both involved stepfathers and involved biological fathers because they feel divided loyalties.

3. Most lesbian partners who are awaiting the adoption of a child, believe it is important for their children to have interactions with men and make a deliberate plan for how to include male relatives and friends in their children's lives.

4. All adopted children at one time or another plan to search for their biological parents and family members.

5. The same principles of authoritative parenting that have positive effects in intact families, also provide benefits in families with complex structures, illustrating that it is the nature of the parent-child interactions, not the form of the family structure, that matters in the development of psychosocial competence.

In this chapter we focus on parenting in complex family structures that include many individuals who are intimately connected to family members but live outside the immediate family. Parents have the task of incorporating individuals' sometimes conflicting points of view and promoting positive relationships among all the individuals.

In this chapter we focus on parents and children in complex family structures. The word *complex* has many meanings, but the first is something woven together of many parts.[2] We use the word complex to refer to families that consist of many individuals who do not live within the basic unit of parents and children but who play an important roles as parent figures in children's lives and must be incorporated as intimate family members. This is easiest to see in stepfamilies in which each parent may have a previous spouse and their new partners who care for children in their own home and influence children's growth and development, as well as stepbrothers and stepsisters who reside in other homes but come for specific periods of time and require care. All the adults' and children's needs must be addressed in the family unit.

Lesbian/gay families are complex because many children were conceived in heterosexual marriages that ended in divorce, so there are ex-spouses and new partners. Lesbian/gay parents must consider the legal aspects of parenthood since one parent may have biological ties to the child and the other does not. Legal procedures are required for both partners to have legally recognized ties to children. Lesbian/gay adoptions of children can also include birth parents.

Adoptive parents may have the simplest arrangement of adopting a child and having no contact with the birth parents, but this is becoming less common as open adoption becomes more frequent. With open adoption, you may have not only the birth parents but the birth grandparents and extended family involved. In addition, adoption sometimes involves adopting children from another country or another culture, and then one has the task of including another culture in the family. Many families who adopt children from abroad, for example, keep some of the customs of that country, and travel there so children have a connection with their country of origin.

The word *complex* comes from the Latin and means "entwined or braided together," and that is the task of families in this chapter—to weave together the many individuals who play a parenting role in children's lives. In this chapter, we focus on stepfamilies, gay/lesbian families, and adoptive families as examples of complex family structures.

Before proceeding, it is important to point out that while society codifies family relationships strictly on the basis of biological and legal ties among members, adults today have differing opinions of family and are more flexible, incorporating relationship status in addition to biological and legal ties as criteria.[3] For example, when asked to describe the family status of cohabiting, married, past, and present stepparents, adults used the relationship status of the person to the parent, in addition to legal status. If a person was living with the parent currently, he or she was part of the family, although a married stepparent was seen as more a part of the family. If the stepparent had lived with the adult as a stepparent in the past, he or she retained some status in the family, even though no longer involved with the parent. Therefore, adults construct a view of family members based on relationship experience as well as legal ties.

STEPFAMILIES

About 65 percent of divorced women and 75 percent of divorced men marry again, and half of the adults have children.[4] Remarriage provides many benefits to parents. First, it provides emotional closeness, intimacy, and sexual satisfaction.

In caring relationships, parents feel greater self-esteem, contentment, and happiness.[5] Second, parents have someone with whom they can share both the financial and caregiving responsibilities. We know most about remarried families that consist of the custodial mother, her children, and the stepfather, who may or may not have children, but there are an increasing number of studies of families with resident fathers and stepmothers. Few studies focus on marriages of single mothers who have children, even though these may have many characteristics of stepfamilies.

Challenges of Stepfamilies

Stepparenting is more demanding than parenting in intact families for several reasons. First, a stepparent does not have long-standing emotional bonds with the children to help all of them overcome the feelings of frustration and stress that occur as a result of remarriage.[6]

Second, a stepfamily includes more people than does a nuclear family, so it has different needs and interests to consider. There are husbands and wives, their biological children, ex-spouses and their new partners, stepbrothers and stepsisters, half-brothers and half-sisters, and stepgrandparents. Parents have the multiple tasks of solidifying and maintaining marital ties while sustaining relationships with their biological children and promoting positive sibling relationships.

Third, members of stepfamilies have memories of the earlier marriage and may feel sadness at its loss and ambivalence about the present family, where there is less time for each member. Children may feel that the new marriage is depriving them of their parent. Parents must accept those feelings as realistic—there is less time for each child. Conversely, the parents may feel that the children are intruding on the marriage.

Fourth, anger and frustration with former spouses and relatives may present the stepfamily with ongoing irritations and problems that dampen the mood in the stepfamily. Fifth, there are no clear guidelines for being a stepparent. There are few enough for biological parents, but the role of stepparent remains even vaguer. The stepparent must create his or her role according to his or her individual personality, the ages and sexes of the children, and the family's living arrangements. Stepparents who are forewarned about the problems of stepparenting and who think and talk in advance about how to cope with these problems can find their new roles rewarding and exciting.

Mavis Hetherington identifies four myths that create unrealistic expectations for parents as they enter stepfamilies:[7]

The nuclear family myth—that family members will love and be close to each other, and children will respect both parents in the home

The compensatory myth—the new spouse and family will be everything that the first family and marriage were not

Instant love expectations—the stepparent and children will form instant, close, loving bonds

Rescue fantasy—the new parent will solve all the child-rearing and financial problems in the family and everything will be fine.

If parents can be realistic about their own contributions to difficulties and family problems, and work through problems as they arise in the stepfamily, then remarried couples are as happy as nondivorced couples after five or six years. Not everyone works through problems, and about 60 percent of remarriages end in divorce, often in the first few years.

Types of Mother and Stepfather Families

From his ten-year study of 100 stepfamilies made up of custodial mothers, stepfathers, and young children and a controlled sample of 100 nondivorced families, James Bray has provided a basic understanding of developmental issues facing stepfamilies.[8] His major findings include the following:

1. A stepfamily has a natural cycle of changes and transition points.
2. A stepfamily takes many years to form a basic family unit.
3. The greatest risk to the stepfamily occurs in the first two years, when about 25 percent of remarriages fail.
4. In a stepfamily, there is no honeymoon period of high satisfaction followed by a gradual decrease, as there is in a first marriage; in a stepfamily, marital satisfaction starts at a moderate level and builds up from there or decreases to the point of divorce.
5. A stepfamily has four basic tasks to achieve cohesion:
   a. Integrating the stepfather into the family
   b. Creating a satisfying second marriage
   c. Separating from the ghosts of the past
   d. Managing all the changes
6. A stepfamily eventually takes one of three forms: *neotraditional, matriarchal,* or *romantic*. Neotraditionals almost always succeed, matriarchals succeed much of the time, and romantics face great risk of divorce.

The neotraditional family is described as a "contemporary version of the 1950s, 'white-picket fence family' it is close-knit, loving, and works very well for a couple with compatible values."[9] The matriarchal family is one in which the wife-mother is a highly competent woman who directs and manages all the family activities. The romantic family seeks everything the neotraditional family does but wants it all immediately, as soon as the marriage occurs. The romantic family is at great risk for not surviving the conflicts and changes of the first two years. The three types of families do not differ in the crises and turning points they face, but they do differ in their expectations and their willingness to change their expectations and their behaviors to solve the problems they confront.

The first cycle of change that stepfamilies experience in the process of their formation occurs in the first two years of the remarriage. In this stressful period, all members of the family try to find ways to live together, deal with ex-spouses and noncustodial parents, and form a stable unit that brings *everyone* happiness. By the end of two years, the second cycle begins; family members find mutually satisfying ways of getting along, and a family unit is established. Tensions are reduced, and happy stepfamilies resemble nondivorced families. A third cycle of change occurs when children move into adolescence and become more insistent on independence and individuality.

Neotraditional families successfully navigate the changes because they give up unrealistic expectations and because they communicate feelings and solve problems.

Bray describes the neotraditional family as having the ability to (1) identify and express feelings clearly; (2) identify and understand other family members' thoughts, feelings, and values so differences are bridged; (3) resolve conflicts; (4) state a complaint so the other person feels empathy; (5) establish new rituals that help define the family as a unit; and (6) accept other family members. Romantic families seek the same cohesiveness and close ties that neotraditional families do, but they find it very difficult to give up unrealistic expectations and solve the problems at hand.

Bray reports that despite the crises and difficulties of remarriage, many stepfamilies succeed and form stable, cohesive family units that give all members a sense of warmth and accomplishment. A significant number of stepfamilies do not succeed, however, and dissolve the marriages because the parents do not have the commitment to work through the problems to reach a joint resolution. A third group of families stay together and seem happy enough, but they lack a sense of vitality and seem to "just get by." These families do not want open communication or to really understand each other and instead choose habitual ways of relating to each other. Bray asked successful families what got them through all the stressful periods. "The consistent answer was commitment. Commitment to a life together, not just getting by but living and loving fully, communicating about issues, building a stable family, and enjoying a good life together."[10]

Types of Father and Stepmother Families

In a study of fathers rearing children with stepmothers, stepmothers had many of the same difficulties as stepfathers—uncertainty about their role in the family, uncertainty about how to establish relationships with stepchildren and whether to discipline.[11] The majority of stepmothers relied on one of three role models: the nuclear, the extended, or the couple. In the nuclear model, stepmothers expected to take the same role as the biological mother and to focus energy on the family unit, disciplining children and expecting children would distance themselves from the other parent and family, and look to her as the primary caregiving person. These mothers were disappointed and frustrated when children rejected them as the primary parent.

In the extended model, stepmothers were similar to nuclear mothers in wanting to be important figures in their stepchildren's lives but mainly as coparent with the biological parent. They also saw the family as an extended unit and wanted their own family to be very involved with stepchildren and the whole family unit.

About a third of stepmothers used a couple model and focused on forming a strong marital relationship with the biological father, believing that a strong marriage would benefit everyone. They believe that the biological parents should have primary responsibility for raising the children. While these stepmothers are warm and friendly with stepchildren, they leave discipline to the biological parent.

INTERVIEW

with the late Emily Visher and the late John Visher

Emily Visher, a clinical psychologist, and John Visher, a psychiatrist, were founders of the Stepfamily Association and authors of such books as Stepfamilies: Myths and Realities *and* Old Loyalties, New Ties: Therapeutic Strategies with Stepfamilies.

You have worked with stepparents and stepfamilies for many years, so I want to talk to you about what you feel are the important things for parents to do in order to ease the difficulties that can arise in stepfamilies.

E. Visher: We talk about a parenting coalition that is the joining of all the adults in the child's life. For example, you see, there could be three or four parenting adults—if both parents have remarried, there will be four. If those adults can somehow develop a working relationship around raising the children, the loyalty conflicts of the children will be much less. The adults will get a lot out of it, too, because there is less tension, and better relationships develop between stepparent and stepchild.

We chose the word *coalition* because it means a temporary alliance of separate entities for accomplishing a task. The households and couples are separate, and it is a temporary alliance among all the adults. The task they are working on together is raising the children. Families can flounder on the basis of the stepparent's trying to be a parent and the children saying basically, "I've got a mother or a father." We have moderated panels of teenagers in stepfamilies, and we always ask them, "What do you want your stepparents to be? What is their role?" I don't think we have ever heard anyone say anything other than "a friend." The difficulty is that by "friend," they mean something very different. They don't mean a pal; it's closer than that.

They are able to talk to the stepparent in a meaningful way that is different from the way they would talk to a parent. They are freer to talk to a stepparent because they are not so involved. One teenager on a panel said she wanted her stepfather to be her friend, and then later she said, "I love my stepfather, and I've never told him." She's saying she wants a friend, but she has very deep feelings for him. He was in the back of the room and heard her.

It is important to take a role that is satisfying to the adult and to the child, and that may be different for children living in the same household and for children in different households. The relationship is different depending on the age of the child—a six-year-old needs something different from a sixteen-year-old. For the young child, the stepparent may well become a parent.

J. Visher: The only power the stepparent has as a parent is delegated from the remarried parent.

E. Visher: The adults need to be supportive of one another. Together they need to decide what the house rules are, and the parent of the children takes care of enforcing the rules until a relationship is set up.

J. Visher: Another major tip is to develop realistic expectations about what it is going to take to make everything work. So many people feel that they have failed after a few weeks or months, that the remarriage has faltered because things are chaotic. It takes four or five years for things to settle down and for people really to get satisfaction out of the whole family relationship.

One of the keys is for people to inform themselves by reading or talking to other people who also are in stepfamilies. They learn that making the stepfamily work takes time and that you shouldn't expect close family relationships quickly.

The most common pattern now is for children to move back and forth and feel part of two households. If all the adults form a parenting coalition, then children are most likely to feel they belong in both places.

Working out the parenting coalition so that it is at least civil makes an enormous difference to everybody. The children can go through the remarriage smoothly if there is no constant warfare. Sometimes parents who divorce or separate are tied together in bonds of anger. The anger can reflect an inadequate separation between the biological parents. They keep together by fighting.

E. Visher: Truman Capote said, "It's easy to lose a good friend, but it's hard to lose a good enemy." The anger ties you together. Hostility eats you up, and you are not free to go on.

J. Visher: Most people don't understand how much damage they are doing to themselves and to the children. Sometimes people say, "How can I work with that S.O.B. when I couldn't even stay married to him?" We say maybe you can split off the part that does not want to be married to him and share the parenting experience.

E. Visher: What the children need from that parent is different from what the spouse needed.

What can you do to decrease the hostility?

J. Visher: One thing is to trade assurances between the households that you are not trying to take the child away from them or trying to get the child to like you better. Often, in a single-parent household, the parent is afraid of further loss, afraid that the ex-spouse and his or her new spouse will encourage the child to stay there and the child will want to because it is a more attractive place or there is more money. This fear fuels the anger and makes the parent cling to the child more and try to influence the child to turn against the other parent.

E. Visher: So we think that sometimes the anger is not left over from the former marriage but has to do with the fear that builds up between the two households, the fear of more loss. The other household becomes a threat, and the ex-spouses become like enemies rather than like people trying to raise a child. The parents are afraid of each other, and they are not aware that the anger substitutes for fear. If they are more aware of it, they can deal with it.

Also important is the guilt the remarried parent feels. He or she feels guilty that the children have been unhappy through the death or divorce and then the remarriage. That parent has a real investment in its being a big, happy family right away. Yet they have difficulty setting limits for the children who live there or visit. The stepparent goes up the wall.

Sometimes they feel that to form a good couple relationship and make that primary is a betrayal of their relationship with their child. The parent–child relationship is different from the relationship with the spouse.

(continued)

INTERVIEW with the late Emily Visher and the late John Visher

(continued)

J. Visher: There may be an unusually strong bond between parent and child; perhaps it has lasted for many years, and the new spouse is a rival. It becomes a power struggle between spouse and child for the loyalty of the biological parent. The child is sometimes suddenly out of a job as confidant.

E. Visher: I don't think people realize the change for the children, that now they have to share. One mother described that she and her daughter had lived together for five years. When she came home from work, she talked to her daughter. Now that she is remarried, she talks to her husband. That one little thing is not so little, as the daughter has to share her mother.

If people are aware of the losses for the children in the new structure, they can acknowledge those changes with the children and do things differently—sit down with the children alone and talk. When children sense their feelings are accepted, they will talk about them. One stepmother commented to her stepson that when the father talked to the son, she felt left out, and she wondered if he felt left out when the father talked to her. He agreed he did, and they talked about it. There was not a lot they could change, but after they had the talk, they got along better.

J. Visher: We hope that as people are more informed, they will be able to deal more effectively with the situation.

Research suggests that the couple model may be most effective as stepmothers are less stressed and stepchildren have fewer pressures on them.

Parents' Behaviors over Time

There are no differences in how biological parents parent their own children in nondivorced and remarried families. Regardless of family status, mothers and fathers are warmer, more supportive, and closer to their biological children than to their stepchildren, and their children are more often closer to them.[12]

No matter what the age of a child at a parent's remarriage, stepfathers initially feel less close to their stepchildren than to their biological children, and they do not monitor behavior as well as fathers do in intact families. When children are relatively young at the time of the remarriage, stepfathers may be able to build relationships with stepchildren by taking on the role of a warm and supportive figure and forgoing the role of disciplinarian until a relationship is established. Young boys have an easier time building relationships, while young girls often feel angry at the loss of the close relationship with mothers. Girls resist stepfathers and direct angry, negative behavior to the custodial mother.[13]

When children are early adolescents at the time of the remarriage, there appears to be little adaptation to the new family over a two-year period.[14] Children are negative and resistant and, as a result, stepfathers remain disengaged, critical, and distanced from the day-to-day monitoring of children. When, however, stepparents can be authoritative parenting figures—warm, positive, appropriate in monitoring—then children's adjustment improves. With adolescents, stepparents fare better when they are authoritative from the start.

Adolescents at the time of the remarriage are often unwilling to become involved with stepparents, and they frequently retreat from the families and establish strong relationships with families of friends. At the same time, they become more argumentative with the biological parents, both custodial and noncustodial. Adolescents feel closer to noncustodial mothers than to noncustodial fathers.[15]

In stepfamilies, marital happiness has a different relation to children's behavior than it has in intact families.[16] In nondivorced families, marital happiness is related to children's competent functioning and positive relationships with parents. In stepfamilies, marital happiness is related to children's negative and resistant behavior with parents. Girls may especially resent the loss of the close relationship with their custodial mother.

Relationships with siblings are less positive and more negative in remarried families than in nondivorced families.[17] Although girls tend to be warmer and more empathetic than boys, they are almost equally aggressive. As siblings become adolescents, they become more separated from each other. Interestingly, relationships with their stepsiblings appear less negative than relationships with their own siblings.

Children's Behavior over Time

Children's adjustment in stepfamilies varies. Often, initial declines in cognitive and social competence follow the remarriage, but when boys are young and stepparents are warm and authoritative, problem behaviors improve, and boys in these stepfamilies show levels of adjustment similar to those of boys in nondivorced families. Young girls continue to have more acting-out and defiant behavior problems than do girls in intact or divorced families.[18] Most gender differences in adjustment disappear at early adolescence, when both boys and girls have more problems.

Still, large-scale surveys of teens living with biological parents and stepparents find that many adolescents feel close to stepparents when relationships were formed early. In a study of 1,100 teens living with mothers and stepfathers, but still seeing nonresidential fathers, 91 percent of teens felt close to mothers, 61 percent felt close to stepfathers, and 41 percent felt close to nonresidential fathers.[19] About 25 percent of teens reported feeling close to both fathers and 24 percent felt close to neither.

When teens reported close relationships to stepfathers and fathers, or even to stepfathers alone, teens had better grades, more positive moods, and less aggressive, noncompliant behaviors. Close relations with the two fathers were part of a generally close family in which parents got along with each other, and the teen felt close to both. Those adolescents who felt close to neither parent tended to be girls, were older, and were more likely to have been born outside of marriage. Parents in the home did not get along well, and these teens reported the more anxious or depressed moods, more aggressive behaviors, and poor grades.

Close relationships between teens and both fathers may occur, in part, because stepfathers go out of their way to include fathers in the child's life.[20] One study found that about 40 percent of stepfathers went out of their way to encourage nonresidential fathers' phone calls, visiting, and participation in children's lives because they saw children were happier and because stepfathers too had children in other households that they wanted more time with.

When teens live with biological fathers and stepmothers and still see non-residential mothers, 92 percent reported having close relationships with fathers, 67 percent had close relationships with stepmothers, and 60 percent had close relationships with biological mothers.[21] In these families, it was teens who had close relationships with biological fathers and mothers who had the more positive moods, less aggressive behaviors, and less substance use. Closeness with stepmothers did not predict teens' well-being.

At all ages, a small subsample of children in remarried families, like children in divorced families, have poorer school performance, more problems in social responsibility, and more rule-breaking behaviors than do children in intact families. Still, the majority do well. Between two-thirds and three-quarters of children in remarried families score within the average range on assessment instruments. Although this falls below the comparable figure of 90 percent for children of nondivorced parents, it indicates that most children in remarried families are doing well.[22]

As with children of divorced families, children of remarried families are at a disadvantage in early adulthood.[23] Compared with children of nondivorced parents, they are more likely to leave home at an early age, less likely to continue in school, and more likely to leave home as a result of conflict. As adults, they feel they can rely less on their families. Still, responses vary and many of these children feel close to and supported in stepfamilies.

Many of the difficulties stepfamilies encounter can be avoided or lessened if they are anticipated and prepared for. Stepfamilies can strengthen their ties in many ways, such as nurturing relationships, finding personal space and time, building trust and using authoritative parenting.[24]

LESBIAN AND GAY PARENTS

Lesbian and gay parents are a heterogeneous group.[25] In early studies, most lesbian and gay parents had children in the context of heterosexual marriages and then divorced and adopted a lesbian or gay identity, rearing their children with partners of the same sex. These families faced not only all the stresses of remarried families but also the pressure of prejudice against lesbian and gay parents. Much of the initial research done on lesbian and gay parents and their children was conducted in order to prevent parents' being denied custody of and visitation with their children.

More and more lesbian and gay parents are choosing parenthood after proclaiming a lesbian or gay identity. Parents are usually living with partners and choose to have a child through adoption, assisted reproductive technology, or surrogate parenthood. The child may have a biological relationship with one parent, with the other parent becoming a coparent through legal adoption of the child, or the child may have no biological relationship with either parent. A single lesbian or gay person may have a child in the same way.

Divorced Lesbian and Gay Parents

The largest group studied has been divorced lesbian mothers.[26] Concerns have focused on their mental health and on their sex-role behavior and its effects on children. Most studies have compared lesbian and heterosexual mothers and find no differences between them on self-concept, overall psychological adjustment, psychiatric status, sex-role behavior, or interest in children and child rearing. Divorced lesbian mothers are more likely to be living with partners and more worried about custody issues than are divorced heterosexual mothers.

Studies reveal no differences between the biological fathers of children of lesbian mothers and fathers divorced from heterosexual mothers in terms of paying child support, but fathers in the former group may have more frequent visitation.

Research is just beginning on such topics as when and how lesbian mothers should reveal their sexual identity to children. Although there is no firm agreement, it is thought best to avoid doing this during the child's adolescence so that the child's own sexual identity and identity formation can occur without distraction.

Much less is known about divorced gay fathers. There is no research comparing the psychological stability of gay and heterosexual divorced fathers, perhaps because men do not often seek physical custody. Research comparing their parenting behaviors suggests that gay fathers are more responsive, more careful about monitoring, and more likely to rely on authoritative parenting strategies than are heterosexual divorced fathers. Studies of the family lives of gay fathers, teen sons, and fathers' partners indicate greater family happiness when the partner has a good relationship with the adolescent boy.

Comparisons of divorced lesbian mothers and gay divorced fathers reveal that gay fathers report more income and more frequent sex-stereotypical toy play by their children.[27]

Lesbian and Gay Couples' Transition to Parenthood

In the 1990s, many lesbian and gay individuals in committed partnerships chose to have children either through assisted reproductive technology or through adoption. One study of gay men who chose to become fathers found that fathers were older and more likely to be European American men with good incomes and higher social status than men who had not chosen fatherhood. Fathers reported that they thought when they identified themselves as gay men they had renounced the possibility of being fathers.[28]

Over time, as adoptions and assisted reproductive technology gave new options to gay men, they found themselves thinking about becoming fathers. Interacting with children and caring for them (e.g., nieces and nephews or friends' children) awakened desires to rear their own children, and they decided to pursue the option even though they might face barriers. With determination, they found adoption agencies or identified egg donors and surrogate mothers to participate in the process of having a biological child. For some men, the biological connection was an important one, but for others, it was not. With time, the men achieved their goals.

In the transition period, lesbian partners' experiences are similar to those of heterosexual couples. A study of lesbian partners and heterosexual couples seeking adoption found that both groups of parents reported similar levels of psychological well-being.[29] All prospective parents experienced some anxiety and tension about the adoption process. A subsample of both lesbian and heterosexual parents reported feelings of depression related to their unsuccessful efforts to conceive a child. Both groups of parents sought support for their decision to adopt from their families and friends. Women, both lesbian and heterosexual, were more likely to receive family and friend support than were men. Lesbian women, however, received less family support than heterosexual women did, particularly if they had been with their partner a short time. Partners who had been together a longer time received more family support. Friend support was sufficiently strong that lesbian partners did not suffer any loss of overall well-being.

Interviews in the last trimester with lesbian partners about to have their first child by means of donor insemination found that all women, both the biological mothers and their co-mother partners, considered that men would play a role in their child's life.[30] They were not looking for a traditional father figure, but they were thinking about men who would interact with their children and would be a good model of what it means to be a man. All the women knew men—fathers, brothers, gay and straight friends—who could take on this role.

The women could be grouped in three categories. The largest group, forty of the sixty lesbian women, termed "deliberate," made very definite plans about how to include men. A group of fifteen, termed "flexible," thought they would let circumstances dictate how men were included. A final group of five, termed "ambivalent," were uncertain how important it was to include men.

These women's views were subject to change once the baby arrived. At the interview when babies were three months old, three flexible mothers had become very deliberate about including men because they saw that their babies responded differently to men. Mothers' thinking about including men in their children's lives appeared part of being a sensitive parent who wanted to provide their child with the best possible experiences as children.

Lesbian women's transition to parenthood appeared much like that reported for heterosexual couples.[31] Like heterosexual couples, lesbian parents reported a decline in feelings of love in the partnership and an increase in conflict from the last trimester to three months after the birth. New demands on time and less time available for the partner relationship seemed to account for some of the changes, but personality characteristics, relationship qualities, as well as family support played a role in minimizing or increasing the changes.

In lesbian partnerships, the biological mother takes primary care of the child in the earliest months, but nonbiological co-mothers often report an immediate attachment to the child and take a larger role when the child is twelve months or older.[32] There was more equal sharing of child care and household work in lesbian partnerships than in heterosexual marriages. Lesbian partners also report a high level of relationship satisfaction and greater satisfaction with the division of labor. Co-mothers were seen as more knowledgeable about child care and more willing to assume equal care of the child than were heterosexual fathers.

A study comparing single and coupled lesbian mothers with single and coupled heterosexual mothers found that (1) single heterosexual and lesbian mothers were warmer and more positive with their children than were coupled heterosexual mothers, and all lesbian mothers were more interactive with their children than were single heterosexual mothers, and (2) single heterosexual and lesbian mothers reported more serious, though not more frequent, disputes with children than did coupled heterosexual mothers.[33]

Children of Lesbian and Gay Parents

Research has focused on three questions: the nature of children's gender identity, their psychological stability, and their social relationships with other children. With respect to gender identity, there is no evidence that children of lesbian and gay parents have an increased likelihood of having a lesbian/gay gender identity or same-sex sexual orientation.[34]

Children living with lesbian and gay parents are as well adjusted and socially competent as children living with heterosexual parents. Children of lesbian parents show no special problems with self-concept. The results of research indicate that family process variables operate in much the same way in lesbian and gay families as in heterosexual families—that is, when parents are warm and involved, as many lesbian and gay parents are, their children do well.

The most detailed research has been carried out with data from the National Longitudinal Study of Adolescent Health, a national sample of children from grades 7 to 12 in eighty different schools.[35] Adolescents filled out questionnaires at school, and a subsample of 12,105 were interviewed at home. One parent, preferably the resident mother, was interviewed and filled out questionnaires regarding characteristics of the home, the parents, and the parent–teen relationship. In addition, peers also rated the teens on social relationships, and schools provided grades.

Children whose parent reported being in a same-sex marriage or marriage-like relationship were identified and matched with teens from families headed by a heterosexual couple. Forty-four children of lesbian partners were found. Because only six teens lived in homes headed by a gay couple, the study was restricted to 44 living with lesbian parents.

Reports from adolescents and their parents, peers, and school provided a picture of adolescents' functioning in a variety of areas—psychological stability, relationships with parents, academic success, dating and romantic relationships,[36] social friendships and peer acceptance,[37] and substance use and delinquent activities.[38] In all these areas of behavior, adolescents of lesbian couples were functioning as well as teens from families headed by heterosexual couples. Their dating and romantic attachments were similar, and both teens and peers reported they were well accepted socially.

Although gender identity of parents did not predict differences in teens' behavior, the quality of parent–teen relationships did predict teens' behavior. Regardless of sexual orientation of parents, parents' reports of close relationships with their teens predicted adolescents' competence in school and social relations and less substance use and delinquent activity.

Many single women are now approved for adoption and their children function as well as children adopted by couples.

This study, with carefully collected data on a national sample that included 38 percent non-white teens, provides strong evidence that children living in lesbian couple families are doing as well as children in traditional families.

WHEN PARENTS ADOPT

Like many aspects of parenting, adoption has undergone changes in the last two or three decades. Between 2 and 4 percent of children in the United States are adopted, about half are adopted by biological relatives and other kin such as stepparents, and about half by adults not biologically related to them. This section focuses on those children adopted by people not related to them.[39]

Changes in the Nature of Adoption

Historically, adopted children were the offspring of single women, but in the last three decades, fewer babies were available for adoption because abortions decreased births to single women, and more single women kept their babies.

Parents wanting to adopt a child looked to other sources for children. They looked at transracial adoptions within the United States (discouraged in the 1970s and 1980s but less so in the 1990s); they considered adopting children with special needs, defined as older children or children with special physical or emotional needs. Adopting parents also began to look to orphanages in Europe, Latin America, and Asia. The number of visas issued for immigrant orphans rose from 8,000 in 1989 to 23,000 in 2004.[40] Asia and Latin America are the areas from which adopted children most often come today.

Adults previously excluded from adoption—older, single, gay or lesbian, disabled, or poor adults—are now approved for adoption. Preliminary research indicates that these adoptive parents experience great satisfaction in their roles as parents and have good placement outcomes. Children adopted by single parents do as well as those adopted by young couples, even though single people tend to adopt more difficult children. In addition, legislation has enabled foster parents to adopt children in their care.

Open Adoption

In the past, adopting parents had limited or no information or contact with biological or birth parents. Currently, adoptive and birth parents have been allowed greater access to information about and more contact with each other. In some instances, the birth mother selects the adopting parents and maintains ongoing contact with the child and the family; this is referred to as open adoption. The adopted child is sometimes included in the birth mother's family and activities as well. More-open adoption has helped remove the element of secrecy from the adoption process. *All* the child's parents can know what is happening to the child, and the child can know them all as well (see Box 15.1). Children learn that birth parents have love for them even though they cannot provide for them.

Research on open adoptions suggests that the birth mothers show better adjustment after placement than birth mothers who do not maintain contact.[41] Adoptive parents also seem to feel better because they are less fearful of losing children and they have a better understanding of birth parents so they can answer children's questions more completely. As rated by adoptive parents, children in open adoptions appear to have fewer problems than do other adopted children, although this is not always a consistent finding. Sometimes there are no differences. Teens who experienced contact with birth mothers and other birth family members such as grandparents and birth fathers reported fewer problems with angry feelings and noncompliant behaviors.[42]

Transracial and International Adoptions

Studies of children adopted in the United States and growing up with parents of racial and ethnic backgrounds different from their own find that many children function well, but some report identity confusion.[43] This is greatly reduced when parents provide experiences that enable children to develop a positive racial identity, as parents adopting children from other countries are required to do.

Box 15-1
EXTENDED FAMILIES

Because families are created in many ways, we now have new family members. Open adoption is one in which birth parent or parents hve shared knowledge and some form of continuing contact with their child and the adoptive parents. It creates ties that can meet everyone's needs and removes many of the mysteries of adoption to the benefit of all. Birth parents know what is happening in the child's life, the child knows who the biological parent is, how he or she resembles that parent and why the parent chose adoption for the child. The adoptive parents can answer children's questions about their family history. They also gain a clearer understanding of their own role in their child's life and less fear that the biological parent wants to come and take the child away. In many ways adoptive parents gain confidence in their own importance to their child.

A major advantage is that birth parents emerge from the shadows and become real individuals who had difficulties and made the best choice they could to give their child a happy, healthy life. Adam Pertman, who adopted two children and wrote the book, *Adoption Nation,* described his family's experiences with two open adoptions:

> "The kids are delighted and so are Judy and I. We now have a way of getting answers to medical and genealogical questions (among others), and most wonderfully, we all care about one another and feel we're members of an extended family. Counterintuitive as it may seem—and true to the research into open adoption—there's no role confusion, no divided loyalty, or any of those sorts of concerns. Some parents may have different experiences, but I'm deeply grateful for this transformation in our lives."*

Even if birth parents remain unknown, adoptive parents may include them in their mental pictures of family. Christina Frank describes her many thoughts about the birth mother of her Vietnamese daughter, Lucy. When her birth mother left the child at a clinic, she left only a short note giving her birth date, and the brief explanation, "A family situation."**

As Mrs. Frank walked the streets of Hanoi, she looked at every woman, wondering if she were the one. When she returned to the United States with the baby, and people commented, "How could a mother give up her child?" Mrs. Frank felt fiercely protective of the mother, thinking Americans could not understand the poverty and desperate circumstances in some countries that would lead a mother to give up her child. While she said nothing the first time anyone made that remark, she later would reply that only a "fool would question the reasons behind *my* daughter's birth mother's decision." She wrote, "By then, Lucy was not the only new member of my family. I had come to think of her birth mother and all her biological relatives as family too."***

*Adam Pertman, "And Then Everything Changed," in *Like No Other Love,* eds. Pamela Kruger and Jill Smolowe (New York: Riverhead, 2005), pp. 213–214.
**Christina Frank, "She Is Among Us," in *Like No Other Love,* eds. Kruger and Smolowe, p. 15.
***Ibid., p.19.

When parents adopt children from other countries, they must meet all the criteria for adoption in that country as well as those of the state in which they live. Currently the Hague Convention on International Adoption is seeking an internationally agreed-upon set of criteria to safeguard children's rights.

A major concern of adopting parents centers on the emotional trauma children may have experienced in orphanages or other settings prior to adoption and the effects of such trauma on attachment and later psychological development.[44] Research shows that the longer the children have spent in institutional care, the more likely children will have intellectual and emotional problems; nonetheless, with major support from parents and professional help, these children improve substantially over time.

In families with transracial or international adoption, children's adjustment is eased when parents form a new family ethnic identity.[45] Parents provide experiences that connect not just the child but the whole family to the child's ethnic group of origin. This may mean learning a new language or new customs, celebrating new holidays, or living in new areas where there are more families of the child's origin. Such a child needs models of the culture and opportunities to have friends of his or her group of origin. Currently, organizations form tours to countries where children were adopted, in order to acquaint children with the geographical regions and, in some instances, with birth families, although this is rare because usually records do not exist.

Since many of the adoptive American parents tend to be European American, middle- and upper-middle-class people, parents need preparation to help children cope with experiences of bias they themselves have never had.

Parents who are aware of the differential treatment of racial and ethnic groups in this country are more likely to give their children cultural information about their country of origin, involve them in cultural activities related to their countries, and to participate themselves in post-adoption groups. They also think it important to prepare children for bias.[46]

Mothers of adopted Asian children were more likely to provide cultural socialization for children when they themselves felt connected to Asian culture.[47] They got their children involved in activities and taught them about Asian culture. They started cultural socialization early in the preschool years and continued consistently through adolescence. They also prepared children for experiencing bias, helping children counteract difficult experiences. Mothers did not start this until children were around age eight and reached a peak in the years from twelve to fourteen, dropping off in later adolescence.

While cultural socialization was related to mothers' reports of lower levels of aggressive, noncompliant problem behaviors, preparation for bias was related to older children's higher levels of aggressive, oppositional behaviors.

We deal with the special issues of adoption as they arise in the course of development—for example, the transition to parenting in Chapter 6, and forming positive identities in Chapters 9.

Talking about Adoption and Children's Understanding of It

When parents feel secure, they neither overemphasize the fact of adoption nor do they deny that adoptive families have certain differences.[48] They acknowledge certain differences and are open to talk to children about their reactions and their views. They can explain the different ways to form a family, and they accept that their child has links to two families—to them and to biological parents. Much of the information in this section pertains to children who do not have open adoptions, either because parents chose not to or because it was impossible, as in many international adoptions, to know who the biological parents were.

The general advice is to tell children they are adopted sometime in the toddler and preschool years.[49] Adoption, however, is not something you explain once or twice when the child is young and then forget about. Recent research suggests that most preschoolers may not understand what adoption is even when parents have explained it to them and they refer to themselves as adopted. While many preschoolers confuse adoption and birth, making no distinction between the two ways of having children, still others grasp the basic facts. By the age of six, most children can understand that there are two paths to parenthood—birth and adoption—and they understand that adoption makes the child a permanent member of the family.

In the toddler and preschool years, children focus on the happy experiences of adoption—parents having children they want and children coming to live with people who love them. Between ages seven to eleven, children begin to think about adoption in new ways. They understand that adoption is not the usual way families grow. They understand families are usually made up of blood or biological relations and they are not biologically related to their adoptive family. They learn that out in the world somewhere, they have biological parents, grandparents, and perhaps brothers and sisters. And they begin to wonder about them, and why they gave the child up for adoption.

Children become more preoccupied with questions about why they were given up for adoption. Because parents felt there was something wrong with them?[50] Because parents thought they were bad or ugly? Why couldn't their parents fix things so the child could live with them? Children have a variety of feelings, some intense anger and fear and some vague, lingering doubts about themselves. They may feel intense anger at their biological parents for abandoning them or angry at the adoptive parents for taking them away. They may have vague feelings of being different, not like other children; they may feel sad at not knowing who or where their biological parents are. Children may begin to have intense worries that adoptive parents will give them up, and there will be no one to care for them. Some may develop feelings they are too much to handle. All these intense feelings may account for the fact that adopted children on average begin to show psychological and mood problems in the elementary school years.

In the case of open adoptions, children may know much more about their biological parents but still have some questions about the need for adoption and still retain feelings of being different from other children.

When children become teenagers, their questions about adoption may focus on identity issues. "What are my roots in this world?" "How am I like my biological parents?" As sexual interest increases in adolescence, children's interest in their own conception and birth may also increase. They fantasize about their biological parents. Though the fantasies start in early childhood, teens may think about searching.

A careful longitudinal study of internationally adopted young adults in the Netherlands found four different patterns regarding searching.[51] About one-third of the sample were uninterested and not searching for parents, another third were interested in finding their biological parents but were not searching for them, and about one-third were searching. Almost half of the searching group (14 percent of the sample) had reunited with their birth parents and the remainder of the group (18 percent of the sample) was still searching.

Personal and social data on the adopted sample were available at three time periods: early adolescence, late adolescence, and young adulthood, ages twenty-four to thirty. In adulthood, the members of the four groups resembled each other in their school success, levels of education and professional status, and their rates of marriage and having children. So in the major markers of adulthood, the four groups were alike.

However, the adults differed in their experience of adoption, with the greatest contrasts occurring between those still searching for their biological parents and those who were not interested and were not searching. The searchers were preoccupied with adoption and they felt less positive about their adoption experience, feeling they were intellectually and psychologically different from their adoptive parents.

Searchers were older at the time of placement. As a group overall, they had not experienced more abuse, but boys had experienced greater early abuses than boys in other groups and girls less than girls in other groups. Even as teenagers they were interested in searching for biological parents and wanted to have close relationships with them. More than the other three groups, they had worries and problem behaviors in adolescence, and they continued to describe themselves as nervous and depressed in young adulthood.

Those who were not interested in finding their biological parents felt positive about their adoptive experiences, and even in adolescence, they had been uninterested in finding their biological parents. As adults, they felt they were similar to their adoptive parents both psychologically and intellectually, and they had more contact with them. As teens and adults, they reported the fewest worries and problems of the four groups.

Searchers who had reunited with their biological parents reported that as teens they had a great interest in searching, but now in adulthood, they were no longer preoccupied with adoption issues. Reunited searchers reported fewer worries and problems in adolescence and young adulthood than continuing searchers but more than uninterested nonsearchers. Reuniting with biological parents brought them satisfaction, but their worries remained at the same childhood level. Worries and preoccupations did not appear to spur the search, and worries did not decrease after reuniting with biological parents.

Gender differences were found as girls were more interested and preoccupied with searching, as was also found in other studies, but they did not necessarily do more searching.

In other studies most searchers were pleased to have reunited with their parents and maintained the contact over a period of years.[52] Many who established contact reported decreases in feelings of loss and rejection. A small number, about one in three, thought of the biological parent as a parent, but half thought of the parent as a friend or relative, and about 18 percent continued to feel distant from the parent. The reunion brought some adopted children closer to their adoptive parents, but about one in six felt it had led to a decline in their relationships with adoptive parents.

Even though it is difficult, adoptive parents must listen and be receptive to questions about biological parents and teens' interest in finding them without being hurt or personally threatened. The Netherlands data suggested that searching interest reflected a natural curiosity that was sometimes intensified by feelings of distance from adoptive parents or by an event such as adoptive parents' divorce.

Parenting Behaviors of Adopting Parents

Many adopting parents come to parenthood with feelings of sadness at not having a biological child and anxiety from the intense scrutiny they have undergone to determine their suitability as parents. One can imagine their feeling self-conscious and uncertain in their parenting behaviors.[53]

However, a study comparing the parenting strategies of parents who adopted a child at birth, parents who relied on donor insemination and ART, and parents who conceived a child naturally found few differences among the parenting behaviors of the three groups.[54] When children were between ages four and eight, adopting mothers did not differ from mothers of naturally conceived children in warmth, sensitivity, or attachment to their children. Mothers using donor insemination and ART were warmer and more involved than were the other two groups. Teachers and psychiatric evaluation judged children in the three groups as functioning equally well, with no problems.

Parents who adopt a child at birth show similar parenting behaviors as those parents who have naturally conceived a child.

When these children were age twelve, the adopting parents continued to have warmth and control similar to that of parents of naturally conceived children. Again, psychiatric evaluation and teachers' assessments indicated that children, too, continued to function well in all three groups, with no significant differences among them. Mothers of adopted children, however, described their children as having problems of rule-breaking and aggressiveness, but a more objective assessment did not present such a picture. Thus, the parenting behaviors of parents who adopted a child at birth seem quite similar to those of parents who have naturally conceived a child.

And the behavioral effects of their parental actions with children are the same as they are in biologically related families. For example, even though mothers do not share any genetic relationship with children, their sensitive responses with babies and secure attachments they form with babies uniquely predicted children's social and intellectual competence at age seven.[55]

Family communication patterns can create a shared reality and sense of solidarity that is important in adoptive families. Greater communication might well, for example, have helped the searching teens and young adults in the Dutch study to feel similar to their adoptive parents from whom they felt so different. Observing the communication patterns of teens and their family members in adoptive and biologically related two-parent families, researchers identified four patterns with similar proportions of adoptive and nonadoptive families in each.[56]

These types of communication intensified or reduced problem behaviors:

Consensual pattern—parents and children were warm and open, expressing their views and listening to others, and each family member tried to influence others' attitudes and behavior to support family rules and structure (7 percent of adoptive and 4 percent of nonadoptive families fell in this pattern).

Pluralistic pattern—parents and children were cool and distant and spoke about their thoughts and feelings, but did little to persuade others to adopt their standards of behavior (30 percent of adoptive and 30 percent of nonadoptive families fell in this pattern).

Protective pattern—parents did not encourage open expression of views but insisted that children meet their standards and do what they considered appropriate (20 percent of adoptive and 26 percent of nonadoptive families fell here).

Laissez faire—nobody in the family spoke or listened or tried to influence each other so there was neither conversation nor pressure to agree to family standards (41 percent of adoptive and 40 percent of nonadoptive families fell here).

Researchers then looked at the rates of angry, externalizing behavior problems (as measured by self and others' reports) for adoptive and nonadoptive teens in the four communication groups. In general, adoptive teens were more sensitive to difficulties in family communication patterns, as seen in their having more problems than nonadoptive teens did. For example, adoptive children had the most problems in families using *laissez faire* patterns (27 percent of adoptive teens had problems compared to 8 percent of nonadoptive) and protective patterns

(18 percent of adoptive teens had problems compared to 4 percent of nonadoptive). Adoptive children appear more sensitive to the neglect of *laissez faire* parents and to the overcontrol of protective parents. These two groups incorporate between 60 and 66 percent of the families in the two samples.

In families using consensual forms of communication, both adoptive and non-adoptive teens had low rates of problems (3 percent for adoptive teens and 0 percent for nonadoptive teens). Combining an emphasis on individual expression with conformance to parents' standards, this style of communication incorporates the basic principles of authoritative parenting. About the same percentages of teens developed problems in families using pluralistic forms of communication—17 percent for adoptive and 12 percent for nonadoptive. Communication without parental control and standards appeared to produce the most problems for nonadoptive teens.

Overall, the study indicates that just as in biological families, the same principles of respect for individuality, open communication, and structured standards for children are related to competent functioning and the reduction of problems.

A major parenting task with adopted children then is to help them feel comfortable in the family so they can express their vague or intense feelings to their parents without worrying about hurting or upsetting them. Parents can help children by accepting and acknowledging all feelings and using problem-solving strategies to raise potential solutions. If parents feel they are not helpful, they can obtain counseling for children. Talking over the typical problems adoptive children experience with a neutral third party can be very useful.

A major set of feelings that require resolution, according to those who counsel adopted children, are the numerous feelings of loss—loss of their biological family and extended relatives, of their ethnic background, of their medical history, of the feelings of a secure place in the world with people who will not abandon you.[57]

As infants, they may feel a sense of loss when they are separated from their biological family, their culture, and language that has surrounded them. Those feelings may be reflected in passivity and mild withdrawal for a period of time. But it is often not until the school years and adolescence that such feelings are felt strongly. They may continue to exist in adulthood as well, and are often intensified by the birth of their own children. Parents' sensitive and responsive interactions with children can help them accept and acknowledge them.

Children's Behaviors

There are suggestions, as we noted, that adopted children may have more problems in the school years, with teachers seeing them as less socially and emotionally mature and their being seen in mental health clinics for psychological problems such as aggressiveness and academic problems.[58] They represent 5 percent of clinic populations when they are 2 percent of the general population. Several possible factors may account for these statistics. Children may be more vulnerable because of genetic predispositions of biological parents and prenatal and immediate postnatal environments, and adoptive parents may be more alert to difficulties and want to see them addressed.

Studies of adult functioning of adopted children reveal that by early and middle adulthood, they resemble adults reared in biological families.[59] In a study comparing adopted adults with friends, the two groups were similar with respect to life satisfaction, purpose in life, intimacy, and substance use.[60] The adopted adults, however, reported lower self-esteem than did friends, although the difference of 1.5 points was small, and greater depression. More of the adopted sample (30 percent) fell in the clinical range of depression than did the sample of friends (19 percent), but 70 percent of the adopted adults fell within the normal range when the figure for the average sample was 80–85 percent. A factor in the findings was the greater variability among the adopted sample, in part related to whether the adult was seeking his or her biological family. Adopted adults seeking their biological families reported lower self-esteem and greater depression than did other adopted adults. Still, all adopted adults expressed insecurity about adult attachments. They formed relationships with peers but expressed greater discomfort in the relationships than did their friends.

A meta-analysis of 101 studies on behavior problems and mental health referrals for internationally adopted children and teens included a total of 25,000 adopted children and 80,000 controls.[61] The conclusion was that most adopted children were doing well despite the medical and psychological adversities many experienced prior to their adoption. While they received more mental health services, the difference in adjustment with controls was modest.

David Brodzinsky and Ellen Pinderhughes caution that focusing on the problems of adopted children obscures the real benefits of adoption for children.[62] Recall from Chapter 1 that the biological children of parents at risk for petty criminality adopted early in life and reared by adopted parents not at risk for petty criminality had less than one-third the risk of these behaviors in adulthood as did children reared by their at-risk biological parents.

Other studies comparing adopted children with children who were reared by parents who had considered giving them up for adoption or were ambivalent about keeping them found that adopted children functioned better. Adopted children also functioned more effectively than children in institutions, long-term foster care, or poverty.

Adoption clearly provides benefits to children even though children will have to manage feelings of loss, deal with whatever mysteries exist about biological parents, and have a more complex path to identity formation.

A PRACTICAL QUESTION: CAN A THREE-SESSION INTERVENTION ENHANCE ADOPTIVE PARENTS' SENSITIVITY TO PROMOTE SECURE ATTACHMENT?

In the Netherlands, babies are adopted primarily from foreign countries and many of them come to adoptive homes after stressful experiences of separation from the biological mother and deficient care in institutional or foster placements. Their neuroendocrine systems may respond to the stress by shutting down so babies are initially less responsive.[63] Their responses and signals to parents may be more subdued and difficult to interpret, making it harder for parents to respond in sensitive ways. Many of these babies had been noted to develop disorganized attachments to mothers at twelve months.[64]

In Chapters 2 and 7, we described the use of video-feedback interventions to increase parents' positive, sensitive caregiving with their children. This method was also used with adoptive parents in the Netherlands to increase their responsive interactions with their babies and promote secure attachments with infants. Babies were adopted from Sri Lanka, South Korea, and Colombia. The intervention with mothers consisted of four home visits with video feedback and a book on sensitive caregiving when babies were five, six, nine, and twelve months.[65] Mother–child interactions were observed in the laboratory in the Strange Situation procedure at twelve and eighteen months.

On the first visit, the home visitor videotaped mother–child interactions and assessed sensitivity of interactions prior to the intervention. On the second visit, mothers were shown excerpts from the videotape, illustrating mothers' positive, sensitive interactions. Home visitors talked about babies' needs for warm, close relationships with mothers and their needs for opportunities to explore. They also described babies' signals of gestures and vocalizations that tell mothers what they need. In reviewing the videotaped excerpts, home visitors "spoke" for the babies and interpreted their signals.

On two more visits, home visitors followed the same procedures, reviewing mothers' sensitive responses. At twelve months, mother–child interactions were observed in free play, and level of attachment was observed in the Strange Situation procedure. At twelve months, mothers who received video feedback were significantly more sensitive than mothers in two control groups, one that received no intervention and one that received only a book about sensitive caregiving.

In adoptive families without birth children, children whose mothers received video-feedback intervention had significantly higher rates of secure attachments—at twelve months, 90 percent in the intervention group and 70 percent in the control group, and at eighteen months, 90 percent with secure attachments in the intervention group and 73 percent in the control group. In a second subsample of adoptive parents with birth children, the intervention was not so successful initially. Only 53 percent of attachments were secure in the intervention group, and 80 percent in the control group. However, by eighteen months, 79 percent of the video-feedback group had secure attachments compared to 75 percent in the control group. The intervention also reduced disorganized attachments to 6 percent in the intervention group as compared to 22 percent in the control group.

The three-session intervention also had long-term effects for children in adoptive families with birth children. Those girls whose mothers received the feedback intervention in infancy had greater ego resiliency and ego control at age seven, and both boys and girls whose mothers received the intervention had fewer internalizing problems than children in the control group. The video-feedback system may have taught parents to respond empathically and sensitively to children's sad and anxious feelings, thus reducing children's worries. The fact that the intervention did not predict long-term functioning for children in families without birth children may be that those families without birth children had more stressful events in their lives such as illnesses, and one would expect greater discontinuity in children's behavior. Furthermore, the ratings in that group had less variation, and so statistical properties may have made a difference in predictive power.

Based on the positive results of the study, all new adoptive families in the Netherlands are permitted to apply for four video-feedback sessions at a low fee in the first two and a half years after the adoption.

We have seen then that in complex families made up biologically and nonbiologically related individuals, in heterosexual two-parent families and in families headed by same-sex partners, and in families incorporating different cultures and ethnic groups, children do well when parents have warm, sensitive relationships with children, establish open communication that builds shared understandings among family members, and enforce structured guidelines for children. It is the quality of the interactions that matters not the particular constellation of family members.

MAIN POINTS

Families with complex structures

- are families that must find ways to include many figures outside the immediate family as important parenting figures in children's lives
- include stepfamilies, lesbian/gay families, and adoptive families

When parents remarry, children

- differ in their reactions, with girls having more difficulty in adjusting to parents' remarriage than do boys
- show initial declines in social and cognitive competence
- show improvements in behavior, following an initial decline, when parenting figures are warm and authoritative

Stepfamilies

- often have unrealistic expectations about how quickly closeness and cohesiveness of family members will develop
- need empathy and communication skills to work through the crises and conflicts that occur in the first two years

Parenting tasks at times of partner and marital transition include

- maintaining positive emotional relationships with children and including nonresidential parents
- learning effective conflict resolution skills
- relying on authoritative parenting strategies
- modeling positive relationships with the extended family
- encouraging children to have positive experiences in their own social world

Lesbian/gay parents

- are as psychologically competent and effective caregivers as biological two-parent families
- share child care and household tasks more equally than heterosexual parents

- make the transition to parenthood much as heterosexual partnered parents do
- have children whose functioning in all areas assessed is comparable to the functioning of children in biological two-parent families

Adoptive parents

- are a diverse group of adults who adopt an increasingly diverse group of children in terms of age, ethnic background, and special needs
- increasingly include contact with biological parents and relatives in open adoptions
- are as effective as biological parents in caregiving

Adoptive children

- confront additional issues in development
- must deal with issues of having two families and what it means to the individual child
- are by and large well adjusted and the differences in functioning in a small group are modest
- function well when parents encourage open communication and provide guidelines for behavior
- often overcome early deficits in preadoption care with the care and support of parents and growth-enhancing services

EXERCISES

1. Suppose your brother told you he was going to marry a woman who had two children from a previous marriage, and he had one child from a previous marriage. What advice could you offer him to ease adjustments for all in the new marriage? In a class discussion, share your ideas on how to advise your brother.

2. Imagine that your remarried brother, sister, or friend was experiencing increased conflict with his or her stepson who is now a teenager. What questions would you ask about conflicts and what advice might you give in helping them to decrease conflicts? What guidelines would you give your relative or friend?

3. In small groups, imagine that you are the parent of a preschool child. How would you tell the child he or she is adopted and how would you explain what adoption is?

4. Have small groups consider the possible reasons that the children of lesbian partners function so well. While children of divorced, remarried, and single-parent families all have a subgroup of children who have significantly more problems than children living in biological two-parent families, this does not seem to be true with the children of lesbian partners. In all areas of functioning, children of lesbian partners function well.

5. If you were the adoptive parent of a six-year-old child from China, how would you provide this child with cultural socialization? What resources are available in your area?

ADDITIONAL READINGS

Bray, James H., and Kelly, John. *Stepfamilies: Love, Marriage, and Parenting in the First Decade.* New York: Broadway Books, 1998.

Hetherington, E. Mavis, and Kelly, John. *For Better or Worse: Divorce Reconsidered.* New York: Norton, 2002.

Johnson, Suzanne M., and O'Connor, Elizabeth. *For Lesbian Parents: Your Guide to Helping Your Family Grow Up Happy, Healthy, and Proud.* New York: Guilford Press, 2001.

Kruger, Pamela, and Smolowe, Jill, eds. *Like No Other Love.* New York: Riverhead, 2005.

Pertman, Adam. *Adoption Nation.* New York: Basic Books, 2000.

CHAPTER

16

Parenting in Challenging Times

CHAPTER TOPICS	IN THE NEWS
In this chapter you will learn about:	*New York Times,* June 8[1]: Foster parents need special training to help children with psychological and behavioral problems. See page 484.
■ Ways parents and children cope with stresses of illness	
■ Forms of child maltreatment, risk factors, ways of preventing and intervening when maltreatment occurs	
■ Challenges foster parents and foster children meet and manage	
■ Dealing with national disasters and potential disasters	
■ Stresses military families face and manage	
■ Challenge model of intervention	

Test Your Knowledge: Fact or Fiction (True/False)

1. Childhood is a time of health and energy, and physical problems in the family concern parents' and grandparents' health.
2. Children who experience one form of maltreatment often experience several others.
3. In foster homes, children are able to deal with the problems that brought them there, and so they have fewer problems when they leave.
4. Disasters and national violence are so overwhelming that families can do little to minimize their effects.
5. Most families of deployed service members cope with the numerous stresses involved in having a parent in harm's way.

When traumatic events occur, parents face difficult challenges. What reactions can parents expect from children? What can parents do to manage their own reactions and help children cope? What can parents do to protect children from violence and enable them to feel secure in a world that is sometimes unsafe? How can they help children develop resilience in challenging times?

In previous chapters, we have talked about the moderately stressful events of life such as school and peer problems. Life also includes major losses, traumas, and violence. In Chapters 14 and 15 we talked about the losses and sadness of divorce, death of a parent, and separations from biological parents. Here, in this chapter, we talk about many other major traumatic events: illness, abuse, neglect, and violence in the home, the community, and the nation. We also look at foster parenting and parenting when one or both parents are in the military. Sadly, some people experience several major losses and traumas, and ironically and unfairly, experience all the moderately stressful life events as well. (See Box 16-1.)

Sometimes we experience these in our personal lives, and sometimes, in an increasingly interconnected world, in the lives of others whom we know or learn about through the media. As we noted in Chapter 2, motor neurons in the brain enable us to be especially sensitive to what we witness. This chapter focuses on how parents help themselves and their children cope with the challenges of illness, neglect, abuse, community and national disaster, and violence and the parenting that takes place around these events.

SYSTEMS PERSPECTIVE

A systems perspective emphasizes that all family members are affected by the stressful life event of one family member. One person may have physical illness with pain and treatment, but everyone in the family feels pain at that person's illness. If it is the child who is ill, parents rearrange their own and their other children's lives so they can provide physical care for the one who is ill. Others have to care for brothers and sisters or drive them to their activities. Everyone worries and sympathizes with the one who is sick, and the one who is sick usually worries about all the extra demands he or she is making on the family. If it is the parent who is ill, the child worries and wants to help even if there is little he or she can do. The whole extended family is on alert, and grandparents may take leaves from jobs to come and help out.

A systems perspective also highlights that a person's difficulty in one area of development can trigger difficulties in other areas as well. For example, when children with asthma have many flareups, they miss school, begin to fall behind academically, and so they often develop school problems. They may be unable to participate in certain sports or attend parties at homes with pets, and they feel left out of social activities. As a result of increased difficulties at school and feelings of loneliness, children become angry and irritable and resist parents' requests at home, alienating the support that they need from parents.

A system of social support for parents and children is what enables everyone to cope well in the face of loss or trauma. Feeling loved and cared for helps people deal with all the extra stresses. Usually, immediate and extended family members offer

Box 16-1
THE MANY STRESSES THAT CAN COME YOUR WAY*

In the book *Conquering Your Child's Chronic Pain*, Dr. Lonnie Zeltzer describes the case of Damien, whom she treated for pain related to his sickle cell disease. Up to the age of eleven or twelve, he rarely came to the hospital with complaints of pain. He was a happy boy, doing well at school, and having fun with his brothers.

When he entered middle school, however, he began to have school difficulties and his grades started to drop; in retrospect he seemed to have a learning disability with math. At thirteen, he experienced a traumatic event, but said nothing to the doctors who were overseeing his medical care.

When Dr. Zeltzer met him, he was a quiet thirteen-year-old boy who said little about himself or his life when he came for medical visits to control the pain that was causing him increasing difficulties. Gradually, over a two-year period he told Dr. Zeltzer details of the trauma. His older brother had joined a gang and was killed in a gang-related shooting. Damien had worshipped him and blamed himself for his brother's death. Damien had telephoned his brother and asked him to come home and help him repair his bicycle. They were walking to the store to get parts for the bike when a car came by and someone shot his brother.

Damien blamed himself because if he had not called, his brother would not have been on the street that day. Following the death, Damien began to have symptoms of anxiety and flashbacks of the shooting. He felt on alert, startled easily, and he could not sleep at night. Tired during the day, he had even greater difficulty with schoolwork, and his grades dropped further. Furthermore, the adrenaline that was racing through his system was making the pain of the sickle cell disease worse.

He was also having problems with peers. Sickle cell disease stunted his growth, and bullies at school began to tease him for his shortness. To escape the teasing, he began to cut school with his friends. His parents, caught up in their own grief, tried to handle Damien's problems by yelling and predicting that Damien would meet the same fate as his brother.

At this time, Damien's pain became unmanageable because he stopped taking his medications regularly, refused help from his parents, skipped his regular doctors' appointments, and began to show up in the Emergency Room at irregular intervals for pain-killing medications. Medical staff became concerned he was using street drugs and gave him only minimal pain medications in the Emergency Room. As a result, Damien ended up screaming for pain medications.

One can see how a combination of physical illness, his particular age, and most of all the trauma of his brother's death put Damien on a downhill course. Had he and his parents been able to talk about his brother's death and Damien received psychological help for his symptoms of posttraumatic stress disorder at the time they began, he and his parents might have been spared much psychological pain.

*From Lonnie K. Zeltzer and Christina Blackett Schlank, *Conquering Your Child's Chronic Pain* (New York: HarperCollins, 2005).

the most extensive help, with emotional support and extra caregiving of children as needed. Friends often serve the same role as family members. Groups at the family's work and church often provide enormous help in times of trouble. One couple grieving for the loss of their infant son described how grateful they were to their church members who brought them dinner every night for a month.[2]

While special support is needed at challenging times, the basic skills important in all parenting activities—positive interactions with others, effective communication of information and feelings and problem-solving skills—are still important in dealing with traumatic situations as well.

ILLNESS

We think of childhood as a time of health and energy. Yet, over 10 percent of children have serious or chronic illnesses.[3] The most common chronic illnesses are asthma, which affects from 4 to 9 percent of children, diabetes, cerebral palsy, human immunodeficiency virus (HIV), cystic fibrosis (a genetic disorder involving many symptoms and daily treatments), cancer, sickle cell disorder, juvenile rheumatoid arthritis, and hemophilia. In addition, up to 20 percent of children between the ages of 5 and 17 suffer from chronic headaches, and many others from bowel and stomach pains.[4]

Illnesses differ in their symptoms, treatments, pain involved, and life-threatening potential, but all create stress and worry and require interventions. They interrupt family's daily schedules and activities. We discuss special sources of stress for children and parents and special strategies for maintaining family closeness and effectiveness.

Sources of Stress for Children

When illness strikes, children experience discomfort and are often forced to undergo procedures and follow routines that restrict their activities and often cause great pain. Stress comes from lack of knowledge and misinformation about illnesses, from anxiety and fear of what may happen, from pain, from guilt, and from irritability at restrictions and routines that must be followed.

Children's Understanding of Their Bodies and Illness

Children do not have clear conceptions of their bodies and illness, and so they may not understand what is happening or they may have upsetting misconceptions of what is or has happened and their role in causing the illness.

Young children get their ideas about their bodies from colloquial expressions, their own bodily sensations, and from time devoted to that part of the body.[5] For example, they think "nerves" give you courage. One little girl thought hair was the most important part of the body because her mother spent so much time brushing it. It is wise to remember that children may hear parts of conversations about their illness and misinterpret what they hear. With increasing age, children's concepts of the body become more accurate, but their notions of how the body works remain rudimentary even in early adolescence. For example, one thirteen-year-old girl thought lungs were in the throat and one was for breathing and one was for eating.

Their thoughts about illness also expand and become more detailed with age.[6] In the preschool years, children think of illness as a single symptom caused by a vague distant event like the sun. In these years, children sometimes think illness is caused by an immoral act—you are bad and you get punished. As children move into elementary school years, they see illness as several symptoms that are caused by germs, dirt, and—still—bad behavior. Direct contact with germs or dirt causes illness and it can be avoided if you stay away from direct contact with the cause.

Parents and health professionals must explore with children all their ideas about their physical functioning and what they think is the cause of their illness. When given accurate information in words they can understand, children, even in preschool years, can develop scripts about what they must do and why in order to get over the illness or to control symptoms.

Anxiety and Fear of the Unknown

Children get anxious about shots and blood tests with which they have had experience, and procedures they do not understand. Parents give accurate information about whether a shot will be given and reassure the child that the pain will be brief and helps keep the child well, so despite the pain, it serves a good purpose. When a child starts to cry, the parent can sympathetically comment that when things hurt, people cry, and it is okay to cry.

A parent can reduce a child's anxiety by encouraging the child to talk about feelings, clarifying any misconceptions, and giving the child strategies to reduce the nervousness by slowing down breathing or focusing on other thoughts. If the child is very young, it is helpful for the child to have a favorite toy or object to bring along. If a parent cannot reduce the child's anxiety, then consultation with a pediatric or clinical psychologist can be useful because elevated anxiety can increase symptoms and obstruct healing.

Guilt

As noted, children often think that illness is a punishment for something they have done or have not done, and so they feel guilty, making the illness experience even worse because they believe they caused it themselves. Parents can be alert for any indication of such feelings and even raise the topic in a casual way, saying, "Sometimes children believe they caused their illnesses. Do you ever feel this way?" Even if the child's behavior played a part in an accident or an injury, parents can reassure the child that everyone makes a mistake from time to time, and, most often there is not such a heavy penalty. Or the parent can say he or she knows the child did not intend to get injured. Sometimes parents are at a loss for words, as they never would have imagined the way in which their child felt responsible for the illness.

Pain

Pain is a common element of many illnesses, and is stressful for children and parents. In the past, medical personnel minimized the pain that children felt, believing that it was different from that of adults, and so they often failed to treat it effectively with medication. Since pain is a subjective experience and very young children and some children with developmental disabilities do not have language to express pain, it is difficult to determine how much pain a child has.

Dr. Lonnie Zeltzer, Director of the University of California at Los Angeles Pediatric Pain Program, writes in her book for parents, "I believe that if a child complains of pain, the pain is real and the child is suffering. The job of parents and physicians is to figure out what might have started the pain and, more importantly, what is keeping the pain going. Typically the pain is continuing not because of one single thing such as torn cartilage but more commonly from an array of factors."[7] Parents work with medical personnel to plan a comprehensive pain relief program that includes medication, relaxation exercises, physical exercises, and a generally healthy lifestyle.

Anger and Irritability over Restrictions and Demands

Most illnesses limit the activities of children for varying amounts of time. Children may not be able to play certain games because grasses trigger asthma flareups or eat foods that contain sugar that all their friends eat. At the same time, they often have the frustrating demands of daily treatments or regimes. Children with asthma must measure oxygen flow each day and do breathing treatments. Children with diabetes must test their blood sugar and adjust insulin accordingly. Sometimes the procedures are painful, and all cut into time that children would rather spend elsewhere.

Parents must cope with children's resistance and also insist calmly that treatments be completed. It requires parents' organization to allow enough time for children to carry out the tasks and for monitoring to ensure completion. Parents must also keep their own emotions under control when children complain and direct their anger at the illness to parents who are there and can respond. Listening to children's feelings and accepting them while staying problem-focused is difficult, but when parents do that, children usually comply after their feelings have been heard. Adolescents may have the most difficulties even after years of compliance because they want very much to do what their peers are doing and because they want their independence, and illness limits it.

Engaging the child in problem solving to eliminate the most irritating aspects of the treatments helps, but parents must convey that although they understand the child's reasons for anger, the restrictions must be followed and treatments must still be completed. When everyone in the family follows the restrictions of the ill child—if that is feasible and healthy—then the child feels less alone and less limited. For example, it is possible for everyone in the family to follow a diet very similar to that of the child with diabetes with no refined sugars, limited carbohydrates such as bread, including many vegetables, and several smaller meals during the day at home. No candy is eaten at home. Brothers and sisters can have some sugary treats at school or with friends, but at home, everyone eats a diet very similar to that of the person who is restricted. Furthermore, healthy lifestyles advised for all children with illnesses are followed by all family members. Everyone in the family joins with the ill child to the degree that is possible.

Sources of Stress for Parents and Strategies for Successful Coping

Parents' distress comes from many sources:[8]

1. Worries and uncertainties about what the illness and treatments involve and the possible lasting effects of the illness

2. Feelings of guilt that they did not prevent and cannot cure the illness, and such guilt may be intensified if the illness is a genetic one

3. Feelings of helplessness at not having control over what is happening to their child and not being able to fix it

4. Financial burdens from the cost of the illness and treatment

5. Feelings of inadequacy at meeting everyone's needs—the child's, their other children's, their spouse's, their own, their extended family members', the needs of the workplace

6. Disruption of work life, needing time off, diminished work performance

7. Disruption of social ties to extended family and friends

Parents cope with all these stresses by clear and effective communication with everyone involved, expressing feelings and concerns and listening to others. They help sick children ask their questions and express their worries, and they find time to talk with other children in the family and their partner and relatives. They try to keep pace with work demands if they can. Research indicates that it is the mother who is often the linch pin in this situation.[9] If she gets information and accepts the diagnosis, family stress is reduced. Fathers feel greater marital satisfaction, and are more helpful and supportive. Children also feel more secure attachments to mothers when mothers accept the diagnosis.

Effective problem solving and organization also help parents with the many extra activities involved with illness. Scheduling relatives and friends to help out with chores and provide support reduces stress. Parents must also take some time to unwind even if it is only a few minutes at the end of the day.

Other strategies to reduce the stress of illness include:[10]

1. Forming a collaborative partnership with health-care providers, working as a team, sharing information and concerns, presenting the child's point of view

2. Balancing the needs of all family members, especially siblings, so that their needs are not ignored

3. Focusing on the positive aspects of the situation—help and support given, seeing the cooperation and caring of brothers and sisters, working together as a family

4. Emphasizing the commitment all family members feel toward the family and helping everyone in it do well

5. Maintain ties to friends and extended family members

6. Be flexible with family roles and let others take on new roles to get things done

7. Separating the illness from the child; and treating the sick child as nearly as possible like a healthy child, even if the child is dying; they have chores within their capacities, go to school, and receive discipline like other children

CHILD MALTREATMENT

Family violence and child maltreatment are traumatic to children, more traumatic than community and national disaster and violence because it is personal and most often occurs at the hands of the very individuals who were expected to protect the child. In addition to the pain or damage of the abuse itself, the child experiences a great loss of trust in parents and authority in general that cannot be easily restored.

We look at a bioecological view of abuse, then at the definitions, incidence, and prevalence of maltreatment, factors that place families at high risk for maltreatment, the problems children experience as a result of such experiences, and finally forms of intervention and prevention.

Bioecological View of Maltreatment

Using Urie Bronfenbrenner's ecological model presented in Chapter 2, researchers describe risk and protective factors for maltreatment at the cultural, community, family, and individual levels of experience.[11] Cultural beliefs that physical force is an acceptable way to settle differences, that children are property and one can spank them if one wishes, and that sexual prowess is a sign of masculinity are macrosystemic cultural beliefs that contribute to abuse.

At the exosystemic level, community factors, such as the absence of supervised play areas and recreational activities for children and the social isolation of poor neighborhoods, contribute to increased risk for abuse. Factors at the community level can interact with factors at the family level. For example, a neighborhood with high unemployment and drug addiction may in turn add to the distress of an unemployed father, who then becomes more physically punishing with his son.

Children experience violence at the *microsystemic level* in daily interactions with siblings, parents, peers, and teachers. Both parents and children bring their individual characteristics to these interactions. Parents who mistreat children have their own difficult pasts, as we will see. They interact with children in many negative ways besides the actual abuse. Children's individual characteristics such as health also can influence the likelihood of abuse.

Finally, children experience violence at the *ontogenic level*—that is, in how they develop as individuals—in their attachment relationship with the parent, their regulation of emotion, self-concept, peer relationships, and adaptation to school and learning.

The model also has implications for interventions that can help families and provide protective factors for them. First, there are interventions at the micro-systemic level, with the individual and the family—helping them deal with the situation, the feelings that arise from it, and the problems that ensue.

Then there are interventions at the exosystemic level—helping parents and children reach out to social agencies and social structures such as schools and community organizations to get support to enable the family to cope. Community agencies also identify high-risk parents and provide, often in the home, train-ing and modeling in appropriate caregiving and help parents adopt effective problem-solving skills.

Finally, there are interventions at the macrosystemic level—changing the societal views of violence and sexuality that permit victimization of children. Although this is a complicated process, giving all parents training in effective caregiving and child-rearing strategies also makes abuse less likely.[12]

Incidence and Definitions of Maltreatment

Table 16-1 presents the number of maltreatment reports made to government agen-cies and the number of substantiated victims of abuse in 2006, along with the forms of maltreatment and the ages and sexes of children who were maltreated. In the year 2000, 2,000 children died as a result of maltreatment.[13] It is estimated 90 percent of abusers are parents.[14] This is not surprising since 80 percent of the cases involve physical abuse and neglect, and parents are the primary providers of daily care.

From 1990 to 2004, social scientists have documented significant decreases in physical and sexual abuse cases.[15] However, the overall number of cases increased 26 percent during that time, and neglect became the most frequent form of mal-treatment, increasing from 49 to 62 percent of cases.[16] It is not clear what has caused the declines in physical and sexual abuse and what has led to the increase in neglect and overall number of cases. Perhaps there have been cultural changes in beliefs that led to decreases in these two areas.

Definitions of maltreatment are difficult because we do not have an agreed-upon code of what is acceptable parental care and discipline, so it is hard to define when a parent's behavior is unacceptable. In addition, we have cultural and ethnic dif-ferences within our country as to what is acceptable discipline. Immigrants from other countries have cultural traditions that include more severe hitting and hitting with objects, and parents who cannot give up these traditions are more likely to be reported as abusive when they would not be considered such in their countries of origin. Furthermore, what is appropriate for a child of one age may be abusive at another age (e.g., it is neglect to leave a four-year-old at home alone, but not a fourteen-year-old).

There are ethnic differences in the number of maltreatment reports made to Child Welfare Services.[17] Since maltreatment is more likely to occur in poor fami-lies of low socioeconomic status, and more Native American, African American, and Latinos/as are living below the poverty level, these groups may well have higher

■ **TABLE 16-1**
VICTIMS OF CHILD MALTREATMENT IN 2006*

Total Number of Reports: Investigated	1,907,264
Victims of Substantiated Abuse:	885,245
Neglect	64%
Physical abuse	16%
Sexual abuse	9%
Emotional abuse	7%
Medical neglect	2%
Other and unknown**	16%
Sex of Victims:	
Boys:	48%
Girls	52%
Age of Victims:	
One and Under	18%
2 to 5	25%
6 to 9	22%
10 to 13	19%
14 to 18	16%

*U.S. Bureau of the Census, *Statistical Abstract of the United States: 2009,* 128th ed. (Washington, DC: U.S. Government Printing Office, 2008).

**Total is greater than 100 percent as some children experience more than one type of abuse.

reports of child maltreatment because of poverty. Racial bias may play a role, however, as one study found that substance-abusing, pregnant African American women were ten times more likely to be reported to authorities than European American women despite the fact that the rates of pregnancy drug tests were the same for the two groups.[18] Once infants were in foster care, agency caseworkers had less contact and made fewer case plans for African American families.

Broader government surveys of maltreatment, drawing on hospitals, community agencies, and health professionals, do not find significant ethnic differences in the rates of maltreatment.[19] So it is still important to have a clearer understanding about the ethnic differences in the number of reports made.

Dante Cicchetti and Sheree Toth define four major areas of abuse as follows:[20]

Physical abuse: the infliction of bodily injury on a child by other than accidental means.

Sexual abuse: sexual contact or attempted sexual contact between a caregiver or other responsible adult and a child for purposes of the caregiver's gratification.

Neglect: The failure to provide minimum care and the lack of appropriate
supervision.

Emotional maltreatment: Persistent and extreme thwarting of a child's basic
emotional needs.

Other forms of abuse to the child are *moral–legal–educational* maltreatment that
involves failure to help the child develop appropriate moral and social values (e.g.,
involving the child in selling drugs)[21] and exposure to domestic or family violence.
Exposure to family violence is included as a form of abuse because, although
the violence is directed to another person, it traumatizes children and negatively
affects their behavior.[22] Furthermore, a review of several studies reveals that 40–70
percent of children living in violent homes were physically abused, and 40 percent
of physically abused children live in violent homes. The term *exposure* (to domestic
or family violence) is used rather than witness to include children who hear the
violence, see the effects of the violence, or are involved in interrupting the violence
by calling the police.

Some consider *community violence* a form of maltreatment because children
are threatened, robbed, assaulted, stabbed, or shot, or witness these acts directed
against others, and they suffer from it in the same ways that they do when they
experience neglect or physical abuse.[23] Community violence is repetitive, inescapable, personal, and traumatic and so shares more with maltreatment than it does
with external trauma such as car accidents or natural disasters. At the end of this
section we discuss victimization, which is a broader category than maltreatment,
and community violence falls within that broad category.

Prevalence

Incidence figures reported in Table 16-1 are reports of the cases investigated in
a year. Prevalence figures report the total number of people who have had such
experiences. There are no statistics on the prevalence of family violence, but it is
estimated that between three and ten million children are exposed to it, beginning
in utero.[24] Sixteen percent of women questioned in prenatal clinics reported spousal
abuse, and half of them reported several incidents.

Determining the incidence and prevalence of sexual abuse in childhood is
extremely difficult, as the acts are taboo, secret, and most are not reported. Estimates
are that one in four girls and one in six boys has experienced some form of sexual
abuse by age eighteen.[25]

While two million reports regarding all forms of abuse are investigated each
year, parents' self-reports of physical abuse are higher. In a 1985 national telephone
survey, the caregivers for 10 percent of children reported one or more instances of
physical abuse or severe violence, consisting of kicking, biting, hitting with a fist
or object, or burning. Had the caregivers of 10 percent of children been reported,
there would be seven million physically abused children in this country.[26]

Twenty to 50 percent of children are thought to witness or experience community violence.[27] While neglect is the most frequent form of abuse, accurate
statistics on its prevalence are lacking. Similar figures are lacking for emotional and

moral–legal–educational maltreatment. Emotional abuse is thought, however, to accompany most other forms of abuse.

Factors That Place Families at High Risk for Maltreatment

In looking at family risks for maltreatment, it is important to recall that some abuse is experienced outside the home with strangers, and the child's family may have taken all possible protective actions to prevent maltreatment, yet it occurred— perhaps at a reliable babysitter's or on the school grounds. In that case there are no family risk factors.

When research was first carried out on families and children who were abused, the search was for single factors that led to each kind of abuse, and the specific problem that resulted from the abuse. While we distinguish the major forms of abuse listed above, they are not so much separate problems as several different ways children experience violence and trauma in a family setting. In fact, children often experience two or more different forms of abuse or two or more different episodes of the same form of abuse. In a study of 160 adolescents who had been sexually abused, 20 percent experienced four other forms of abuse as well; 36 percent experienced three other kinds of abuse in addition to the sexual abuse; and only 6 percent of the sample had only sexual abuse.[28]

In general, three general kinds of risk factors are identified for child maltreatment. First is the social context in which the family lives. Maltreatment, as noted, is more likely to be reported in poor families of low socioeconomic status. The majority of poor people do not abuse their children, but lack of resources for essential goods and services and living in neighborhoods with higher rates of crime and violence and fewer services increase parents' stress, which, in turn, can make them more likely to act impulsively. It is important to note that physical abuse is more than living in a poor neighborhood and having family stress. A recent study statistically disentangled the contributions of physical abuse, low income, and life stress, and physical abuse made a significant contribution to children's behavior problems beyond that related to economic disadvantage and stress as a result of negative life events.[29]

A second set of predisposing factors include the stresses of everyday life— difficulties or layoffs at work, conflicts with spouse or neighbors—that increase parental stress and make it harder to be patient and calm in dealing with the demands that the average child makes. When you are worried about how you are going to buy groceries for dinner, it is hard to be patient and supportive when a child spills a quart of milk.

A third set of predisposing factors is the personal qualities parents bring to parenting. Recall the "optimal parenting environment" described in Chapter 6— parents' self-esteem and self-confidence, their positive relationships with partners and their extended family, and their problem-solving skills.[30] Parents in homes where maltreatment occurs have fewer of these resources.

Between 25 and 40 percent of abusing parents were themselves abused, so they come to parenting with fewer models of positive parent–child interactions.[31] Their self-confidence, network of positive relationships, and problem-solving skills are diminished. They have many of the problems we describe as responses to abuse. They are often angry, depressed, and worried, and often form partnerships with people like themselves. Most parents who have been abused do not abuse their children, and we will look at what prevents this in the section on prevention, but a subgroup continues a vicious cycle of experience of maltreatment and violence, and hostile, depressive reactions that result in repetition of the maltreatment with their own children.

People who maltreat their children often have unrealistic expectations of them and what is required to meet their needs, and they often misinterpret the meanings of children's behavior.[32] For example, one mother of a toddler thought he was clingy and dependent because he kept approaching her to show her his discoveries and see her reactions. She kept urging him to get away and play on his own. Contrast that with the responses of professional parents described in Chapter 2 who gave excited, positive verbal feedback to their toddlers every other minute, encouraging them to explore, to talk, to engage.

Because of their high and unrealistic expectations, parents express less satisfaction with their children, and they use more disciplinary techniques than do nonmaltreating parents. Because they are often inconsistent, children learn to resist their directives and get involved in the coercive cycle that Patterson and his workers described in Chapter 2. When parents meet problems with children, they have fewer problem-solving skills for dealing with them, perhaps because they are depressed and withdrawn, and perhaps because of substance abuse issues.

Substance abuse issues are a major contributor to all forms of abuse.[33] In a review of studies, substance and alcohol abuse figured in 80–90 percent of the cases of physical abuse and neglect. It is considered to be a major risk factor for sexual abuse. And it is also a major reason for having children removed from the home.

The social network of maltreating parents is smaller, and they feel more isolated. They often have marital problems or are single parents, and so they cannot turn to partners for support. They have less group support. They are not connected to organizations or social groups, and so they do not have friends who can help them or at the very least, give them a few encouraging words, to get a parent through the day.

A final set of risk factors for maltreatment concerns the child's qualities. Children who, because of prematurity, medical problems, disability, or difficult, overactive temperament require highly skilled parenting, put a highly stressed family at risk for neglect or abuse. The family does not have the resources, either financial or emotional, to deal with yet another source of stress and demand. In fact, even a colicky baby can tax the patience of highly educated parents with many resources, and many professionals report that one of the eye-opening experiences of parenthood has been how angry, frustrated, and helpless they can feel when confronted for hours with a crying baby.

It is important to emphasize as we move to children's reactions and problems in response to abuse that most poor people and most parents who have been abused do not maltreat their children. As we look at ways to intervene and prevent maltreatment, we describe how parents exit the vicious cycle of abuse and repetition of abuse.

Children's Neurobiological Responses to Maltreatment

Parents can understand children's reactions better when they are aware of the many neurobiological changes associated with abuse in childhood.[34] Maltreatment creates fear that activates the brain to produce hormones that, in turn, trigger the adrenal glands to produce cortisol as well as other hormones. High levels of cortisol help the body respond to stress. Cortisol triggers the brain to shut down the stress response system and return to normal levels of arousal when stress has passed.

Cortisol not only helps the body respond to stress, it also regulates the daily pattern of arousal, alertness, and attention.[35] In human beings, cortisol is elevated in the morning and gradually declines during the day and early evening as individuals get ready to sleep. Ongoing stress disrupts the usual patterns of cortisol release and children show atypical patterns, with some children showing low levels in the morning and throughout the day, and some high. When continuously low, children may be less responsive and alert and attentive.

When fear is ongoing as it sometimes is in maltreatment, and the body maintains high levels of cortisol, there can be changes in the immune system and changes in the memory area of the brain.[36] Some children who have symptoms of ongoing hyper-arousal show declines in intellectual functioning, attention, and memory. Not all children show these changes, and they are often reversible when stress subsides. Still, they are of concern, and a major reason for prompt attention to these symptoms. As we will see, infants experience symptoms of hyperarousal, and interventions can calm their stress response systems.

Children's Psychological Responses to Maltreatment

Children often respond to maltreatment with symptoms of posttraumatic stress disorder (PTSD).[37] The symptoms have been described in terms of adults' reactions to stress and adults' ability to verbalize their reactions, and have to be translated to fit children's level of development and their reactions. PTSD refers to a cluster of reactions that follow exposure to an unusual, threatening stress that arouses fear, helplessness, and horror in the person. The person suffers from repetitive recollections of the event or dreams about it or relives it—in children, the repetitive themes can occur in play. There is also a cluster of symptoms around feeling numb, uninterested in usual activities, avoidance of activities or thoughts that serve as reminders of the stress, feeling dissociated and detached from the events yet at the same time, feeling a sense of a shortened future. The person also experiences heightened emotional arousal, with difficulties sleeping, concentrating, being startled easily, and feeling irritable and on alert for another disaster. A diagnosis is not made until the person has had such symptoms for more than a month.

Traumatic events often trigger children's self-blame, and it may play a role in the continuing existence of difficulties.[38] The more adolescents blame themselves, the more serious the behavior changes. Even though adolescents, and probably children as well, give the perpetrator primary responsibility for the abuse, the majority of victims of all kinds of abuse consider that they too deserve blame because they did not prevent or avoid the abuse. Blaming oneself and feeling ashamed intensify feelings of depression and withdrawal that can continue on into adulthood.

Changes in behavior are associated with the severity of the abuse and the age at which it occurred as well as the identity of the perpetrator. Some research suggests that the earlier the abuse occurred and the longer it lasted, the more behavioral effects are seen.[39] Those who experienced abuse in infancy and the toddler years still showed differences in behavior from nonmaltreated children in the school years, and those abused in preschool were especially prone to developing aggressive and bullying behavior in the school years. The speculation is that ongoing stress is more disorganizing to the individual in periods in which the person is developing an understanding of the world and refining basic ways of relating to people. Still, abuse in childhood and adolescence is associated with many behavior changes as well.

Parental maltreatment very often results in a disorganized/disoriented form of attachment in which the child happily approaches the parent on some occasions, and then at other times avoids the parent. Such attachments occur in as many as 80 percent of maltreated children and do not provide a secure base for exploration or a positive inner working model of relationships.[40]

When maltreatment occurs early in life and continues, children have great difficulty in understanding others' reactions and ways of thinking, and they find it hard to understand others' points of view.[41] As preschoolers, they have a more negative view of themselves and their relationships with their mothers, and they begin to become aggressive.[42]

Physical abuse has been associated with peer problems.[43] The abusive experience in the family appears to lead to distortions in how people relate to each other and what is required to get along. As noted earlier, this is especially sad because children then lose a major source of support in coping with their problems. Abuse and violence damage children's trust in their parents and their peers and decrease their capacity for positive relationships, thus removing an important resource for such children.

Maltreated children also may have difficulties with emotional control, in part because their feelings are intense and in part because they do not have appropriate ways of expressing them verbally.[44] They may express their feelings in aggressive, demanding behaviors or in silent retreats from others. In either way, they are more likely to have peer problems because they do not have good control of their feelings. Because of their intense feelings, it will also be harder for them to focus and concentrate on schoolwork so they may develop academic problems.

The impact of sexual abuse depends very much on the child and the specific circumstances of the abuse. Even in a fairly narrowly defined form of abuse, children's responses can differ widely depending on the frequency of the event and the perpetrator, and the actions that followed disclosure.[45] For example, girls aged six to sixteen who experienced sexual abuse of genital contact or penetration within the family responded differently depending on the frequency of the abuse and whether the family member was the biological father or a nonbiological father-figure such as a stepfather or mother's boyfriend. Parents have to always pay attention to how their child experienced and reacted to the event.

Victimization

David Finkelhor and his coworkers have focused on a broader range of childhood victimizations, many of them acts in the community, such as peer assaults, because they believe that victims of one form of abuse often experience other victimizations that do not fall in the categories of the major forms of maltreatment.[46] They believe that numerous victimizations in part account for the severity of the problems children experience.

The Juvenile Victimization Survey consists of 34 questions covering five areas:

Conventional crime—personal theft, robbery,

Child maltreatment—physical/emotional abuse, neglect

Peer/sibling victimization—peer or sibling assault, peer or sibling bullying

Sexual assault—by adult, peer, or stranger

Witnessing victimization—school/neighborhood assaults, stabbings, shootings

Two telephone interviews carried out one year apart with parents of children ages two to nine, and with children ten to seventeen, supplied information on the number of victimizations a nationally representative sample of children experienced in a year and the emotional reactions to the victimizations.

Seventy percent of the 1,400 children had experienced one or more victimizations, with the mean number of different kinds being 2.8 victimizations in the course of a year. Eighteen percent of the children had four or more victimizations and were termed *polyvictims*. The percentage of polyvictims increased with age, from 12 percent of children two to five, 14 percent of children six to nine, 22 percent of children ten to thirteen, and 24 percent of children fourteen to seventeen. Polyvictims did not differ in gender, ethnicity, place of residence, or socioeconomic status. They did tend to be older and to live in single-parent families or in stepfamilies. Correlations between prior symptoms the year before and current year victimization were significant, indicating that children who have symptoms of trauma are more likely to be victimized in the coming year.

Polyvictimized children who had more serious forms of victimization such as sexual abuse or physical abuse, were most likely to have psychological symptoms of trauma such as anxiety and depression, and more general adversities such as illnesses, accidents, and family stresses. Even controlling for past polyvictimization and for trauma symptoms at the beginning of the year, polyvictimization in the current year still predicted an increase in trauma symptoms. When only one form of victimization was related to psychological symptoms, the relationship between victimization and psychological symptoms was reduced, suggesting that people with the greatest number of symptoms may be individuals who have experienced many forms of victimization over time rather than people who have been traumatized by one event and been unable to recover.

This research also points to the importance of inquiring about a whole range of victimizations that may have occurred for individuals when a report of abuse is made rather than focus just on the one area of initial complaint. Clinicians make the same suggestion.[47] They believe understanding the broad range of victimizations many children experience will permit a better matching of treatment program to the child's needs.

While treatment programs provide significant help, children who experience many adversities in the course of life often get help from their own daily activities. Data from two longitudinal studies indicate that adverse experiences such as a parent's psychological problems or divorce predict increases in children's problem behaviors. As adversities grow in number, problem behaviors increase. When, however, children are able to engage positively in school activities, that activity serves to buffer the child from the increase in problem behaviors that would ordinarily occur.[48] Engaging in valued activity appears to give the child a sense of self-worth, control, and social connection. Programs that encourage such strengths as school engagement and volunteer activities can have particular benefits for those who have known many adversities and victimizations in life.

Intervention and Prevention

The first step in intervention is to ensure the safety of the mistreated child. This can take several forms. In violent families at risk for imminent harm, it may mean getting the safe parent and children to a shelter. In physically and sexually abusive families, it may mean removing the abusive family member from the home, or it may mean out-of-home placement for the child in the event there is no other parent or relative to care for the child. Out-of-home placement can be with relatives or family friends known to the child or it can be in foster care with strangers. The out-of-home care can last for weeks, months, or years, and may be episodic throughout childhood for some children.

While studies reveal that foster care has potential benefit for the children it serves[49] (a more detailed discussion follows), a small, but carefully controlled study suggests that out-of-home placement with strangers may place an extra layer of stress for children already under emotional siege.[50] A recently developed intervention for infants and toddlers and their foster care parents has helped to reduce the hyperarousal and behavioral difficulties that often follow when children are removed from their parents and placed with strangers.[51] A ten-hour manualized program carried out in the foster home with an experienced professional teaches foster care parents of infants and toddlers to (1) follow the child's lead, (2) touch and cuddle infants to soothe them, and (3) allow the child to express emotions so he or she can learn to regulate them. Hyperarousal, as measured by atypical patterns of cortisol production, decreased following this program and resembled those of children not in foster care. The cortisol pattern of a control group receiving a psychoeducational program remained significantly different from the group not in foster care.

Once safety is established for family members, then other forms of intervention can occur. Interventions for young children: Home visitation programs, parenting programs, and psychotherapy can be instituted to prevent abuse or help children and families cope with the many effects of maltreatment.[52] Home visitation programs can help young mothers with few resources to provide adequate care for children. One program following families at high risk from pregnancy to the child's fifteenth birthday found that regular nurse visits during pregnancy and the first two years of life resulted in less maltreatment in these homes, and when maltreatment occurred, fewer problem behaviors in children. The nurse was able to form a relationship with the mother, give information on early child development and care, and connect the mother to other resources.

Recall the intervention with mothers in Chapter 7 (see page 229) that empowered mothers to examine their own beliefs about children's behaviors and take action to solve problems. That intervention, added to a home visiting program, dramatically reduced the incidence of physical maltreatment in the group.[53]

The relationship the home visitor formed with the mothers seems critical. In two studies of treatment for abusing mothers—mothers of infants and mothers of preschool children—mothers received home visits and counseling that focused on either (1) the transmission of parenting information and skill-building or (2) helping mothers build positive mother–child attachments by means of infant–or preschool–mother psychotherapy. In the latter form of visit, the focus was on helping mothers see connections between their past and present relationships with others and their way of relating to their children in the present. The therapists were supportive and respectful with mothers, hoping to give them new experiences in ways of relating to others. Therapists also focused on expanding mothers' sensitivity, responsiveness, and their skills in granting autonomy to children.

Both kinds of visits, lasting about an hour and a half and occurring each week for a year, had significant impacts. In the study of infants, infants in the infant–mother psychotherapy group went from 3.6 percent with secure attachments at 12 months to 61 percent secure attachments at 24 months; in the psychoeducational group, there was a similar increase, from 0 percent secure attachments to 54 percent secure attachments.[54] The control maltreated group who received community services went from 0 percent secure attachments to 1.9 percent. The study indicated that attachment did not need to be the focus of the home visits in order for attachment classification to change. Furthermore, the study showed interventions could reverse the effects of maltreatment and perhaps interrupt the persistent course of problems that could be expected without intervention.

When mothers of preschoolers received the intensive parent psychotherapy sessions for a year, their preschoolers decreased their negative views of themselves and their parents, and increased their positive views of themselves.[55] While those preschoolers whose mothers received parenting information, skill-building, and self-care strategies made similar kinds of changes, they were not so marked as those seen in the families that received the psychotherapy sessions. Interventions based on attachment theory were more effective than those based on a didactic model of intervention.

Interventions with Older Children   Improving mothers' parenting skills decreased aggressive, noncompliant behaviors of children living with domestic violence. Children who made the transition from shelters to new living situations benefited when mothers participated in a supportive program that not only helped mothers develop problem-solving skills, but also taught them new strategies for rearing children—focusing on nurturing skills and positive parenting strategies, giving attention to approved behaviors, increasing communication skills, giving negative nonphysical consequences for disapproved behaviors, and problem solving at times of conflict.[56]

Therapists came to the home and worked with mothers during an eight-month period, after they left the shelters, for an average number of twenty-three one-and-a-half-hour visits. Students offered support and served as models for children during the visits. Mothers were not the source of the aggressive problems, but different child management styles, particularly the avoidance of physical punishment, significantly helped children.

Two years after the intervention, children's behaviors were compared to those children in a control group whose mothers received community services and one contact a month with the researchers. Children whose mothers had received training had far fewer problems with aggressive, noncompliant behavior (15 percent of children compared to the control's 53 percent). Mothers reported their children were happier and had better social relationships with others. Furthermore, mothers were less likely to have used physical discipline than mothers in the control group and less likely to have returned to the abusive partner.

A form of cognitive-behavioral therapy first used to help traumatized sexually abused children, Trauma-Focused Cognitive-Behavioral Therapy (TF-CBT), has been adapted and proved successful with many other forms of maltreatment—physical abuse, school violence, and community violence.[57] The program includes both children and parents and draws on strategies from many sources. Psycho-education gives children and parents knowledge about trauma or abuse, common reactions to it, and effective ways of coping and preventing it in the future. It uses cognitive-behavioral therapy strategies to manage intrusive thoughts and feelings and to desensitize the child and family to upsetting thoughts and places, family therapy to help children and parents deal with the maltreatment, relaxation and stress management training to deal with symptoms of hyperarousal, and problem-solving skills to achieve future goals. The program has been used with individual children and their families and with groups and varies from twelve to twenty sessions. Many well-controlled studies have documented its effectiveness in reducing symptoms of trauma and abuse and increasing children's and parents' well-being.

All forms of intervention involve increasing parents' skills with children. If parents have been the source of abuse, then they learn new patterns of relationships. Even when parents are not the source of the maltreatment, increasing their skills in helping children regulate feelings, cope with stresses, develop problem-solving strategies helps children overcome problems. Supporting activities that give children feelings of self-worth and control also reduce problems.

Interrupting the Cycle of Abuse

Positive relationships appear to be critical to breaking the cycle of maltreatment and ongoing socioemotional problems. In a longitudinal study in Minnesota, children were followed into adulthood, and it was possible to compare adults abused as children who did not continue this pattern to determine what helped them avoid it.[58] Researchers looked at the 30 percent of the sample who provided good care to their infants and compared them with the 40 percent who abused their children (30 percent of abused children provided borderline care). Three kinds of positive relationships helped young adults escape the cycle of abuse. Mothers who, in childhood had emotionally supportive relationships with an adult outside the family or received emotional support in psychotherapy did not abuse their infants. The third form of positive relationship was with a partner in adulthood. None of these factors were found in the lives of mothers who continued the abuse. Nonabusing mothers also tended to have come to terms with their childhood experiences of abuse and been able to form an integrated sense of self.

FOSTER FAMILIES

Foster parents care for children whose parents cannot care for them, for a variety of reasons. Parents may have died and left no relatives or friends to care for the child. Parents may have been incarcerated or hospitalized for psychiatric or medical reasons, and no relatives or friends could step in to provide care. But most often, children live in foster families because parents' care has been found to be neglectful or abusive.

Approximately 300,000[59] children are taken into foster care each year, and approximately 500,000[60] children live in foster care, some with biological relatives but a half or more with nonrelatives. At present, the average length of stay in foster care is twenty-two months. About 20–25 percent of children will not return to their biological parents to live. Children of ethnic groups with high rates of poverty such as Native American, African American, and Latina/o families are overrepresented among children going into foster care.

Foster parents provide care for children whose parents are unable to do so, and they feel strongly protective of children.

The major law governing foster care is the Adoption and Safe Family Act (ASFA), passed by Congress in 1997.[62] Its main thrust is to provide services for families at high risk of abuse so children can remain with biological parents. These services include, for example, parenting programs, anger management programs, and therapy. If, however, children are removed from the home, the second main thrust of the program is to motivate parents to make changes in their behavior within about eighteen months. Agencies and parents set up plans for change, with periodic checks to note progress. If changes are not made, and if the child cannot be returned to the biological parents within about eighteen months, then parental rights are terminated. This is to maximize the possibility that the child can be adopted and have a permanent home. Before the time frame was established, some children were in foster care for years, waiting for parents to change, and by the time parents' rights were terminated, children were considered hard to adopt because they were older.

Foster Parents

There is no national registry of foster parents, and our knowledge about them is based on small surveys. They are generally married (60 percent), with an average education of high school level; about half are of middle-class background, 15 percent are of upper-middle-class background, and 35 percent are of working-class background. Still, 40 percent are single parents, and many have limited financial resources.[63]

Adults who become foster parents give several reasons: (1) to have children, (2) to be altruistic, and (3) to help deprived children. People who foster for these reasons receive higher ratings as parents than adults who become parents to nurture children. The latter group of parents may feel disappointed when children do not respond to their nurturance.[64]

Foster parents undertake a daunting challenge.[65] They have all the stresses and strains that any parent experiences, plus several others. The children who come into their homes arrive with a history of difficult life experiences—the death of a parent, physical or sexual abuse, neglect—and they are often dealing with strong emotional reactions to those experiences. In addition, they have the stress of being separated from their parents, brothers and sisters, and often friends as well. Finally, there is the stress of living with a new family, adjusting to new rules and expectations. Children may express their anger, disappointment, or sadness in their interactions with their foster parents, and resist efforts to follow the family routines. Foster parents, like stepparents, have had no previous attachment relationship with children, and it is such ties that often motivate children to cooperate. Building such relationships at times of crisis is difficult. A further difficulty for foster parents is that they have to relinquish the ties when children leave their care.

Because of the numerous sources of difficulties, foster parents need to be trained to understand what children have been through, to be patient, sensitive, and warm yet firm and supportive in helping children meet age-appropriate demands at home and at school. One study found that, when foster parents learned ways to stimulate verbal and cognitive development of preschoolers, the children had fewer emotional and behavioral problems, perhaps because they felt more competent.

The Web of Foster Care Relationships

In carrying out their caregiving responsibilities, foster parents are enmeshed in a web of what can be competing responsibilities.[66] First, they are to provide good care to the children, and they often feel strongly protective of them. Second, they are to work with the agency workers, helping to implement reunification programs with biological parents. Third, they work with biological parents, helping them and their children to establish effective patterns of interaction, sometimes arranging or supervising visits, sometimes helping parents' understand children's feelings. Looming over the system are the judge and court, which make final decisions about what will happen with children.

When there is clear communication and everyone is working together for the child's best interests, such a system can work well. But competing interests can easily surface. Foster parents may feel critical of parents and the protective agencies if they feel not enough is being done to safeguard the child. Birth parents may feel angry that children were taken, because parents had little help and support to do well, and frustrated that they are competing for their children with foster parents who have more resources. Agency workers may feel frustrated with many cases and many demands on them.

Foster Children

There is less research than we would like on contemporary foster children. In the earlier days of foster care, older children typically came to these homes from stable families because of the death or absence of a parent. As child maltreatment cases have increased, children come to foster care with many emotional and behavioral problems. As drug abuse has increased among young women, infants have been sent to foster care from the hospital, and they make up a growing percentage of children in foster care.[67] Little is known about their attachment experiences and how foster care will affect their development over time, because there can be many moves within the foster-care system.

A small, well-controlled study provides information on children's experiences in foster care.[68] Following a sample of high-risk families (at risk because of young age of mothers, parents' low levels of education, poverty income, unstable environments) as children progressed through childhood to adulthood, University of Minnesota researchers were able to select three groups of maltreated children: (1) those who remained with the maltreating parent, (2) children who were removed from the home but lived with relatives or family friends, and (3) children who went into foster care with strangers. In 70 percent of the cases, removal from the home was for parental maltreatment or neglect, and in 30 percent, it was because of the death of a parent, homelessness, or a parent's being incarcerated. The remainder of the high-risk sample served as a control group of children who were not maltreated or placed in foster care.

There was detailed information on these children prior to the abuse and the removal from the family as well as after they left foster care. Prior to placement, maltreated children at home and those going into out-of-home placement showed more behavior problems than the control group, and those who stayed at home and those who were in out-of-home care did not differ from each other. Age at entry and length of time out of the home did not predict later functioning.

As soon as placement occurred, behavior problems of foster children sharply increased. Those who remained at home had no such spike. At the time of release from foster care, those leaving foster care had slightly higher levels of emotional and behavioral problems than those who had remained at home. Both groups of maltreated children continued to have more problems than those in the control group who did not experience maltreatment. Assessments of all groups of children in adolescence up to age seventeen and a half revealed that those who stayed at home with the maltreating parent had slightly fewer problems than those who went into foster care. Going into foster care may well place an extra layer of stress on children and increase the behavior problems children have even after they leave foster care. Those who went into homes with familiar adults were less anxious, depressed, and withdrawn than those who went into foster care with strangers. Although this study is small, there were many controls for the social status of the groups and for the children's behavior ratings, as they were done by teachers, not by social workers or parents, who might have been less objective.

Support for the stressfulness of foster care with strangers comes from the fact that those children who go into foster homes of working-class and lower socio-economic-status families, which are more like the families children lived in before foster care, have greater success, perhaps because the child feels more familiar with the routines and values expressed there.[69]

Sadly, children in foster care are at increased risk for abuse.[70] More reports of abuse are made about children in foster families than those in families in the general community, but the rate of substantiation is much lower for children in foster families. Existing studies indicate that, although the abuse rate may be higher in foster families than in community families, the rate is lower in foster families than is the rate of repeated abuse when children remain with biological parents. Furthermore, foster parents may not always be the abusers; it may be the biological parent on a visit or someone else living in the foster home. Abuse is more likely to be reported in foster families with a younger mother, lower income, poorer health of the foster parents, and a crowded situation where foster children slept together.

The largest study of children leaving foster care provided some good news and some bad news about their experiences.[71] The good news is that, at age seventeen, 90 percent of the group of 732 young people leaving foster care in Illinois, Wisconsin, and Iowa felt optimistic about the future. More than half felt "lucky" to have been placed in foster care, and an even larger percentage felt "mostly satisfied" with their foster-care experience.

The bad news is that this sample of youth experienced more difficulties in their growing-up years than a national sample of young people their age, and they faced the future with fewer skills. In comparison to the national group, the foster-care group was more likely to have been held back a year in school, twice as likely to have been suspended, and four times as likely to have been expelled. Though most at age seventeen were in the last grades of high school, they were reading, on average, at the seventh-grade level.

The foster-care sample was much more likely to have received counseling and medication for psychological problems, and a large number had had conflict with the law—one-fifth reported conviction for a crime, and more than half had been arrested.

When followed up at age nineteen, the group still "wrestled" with worse problems than the national sample of nineteen-year-olds.[72] More than a third had no high school diploma—the comparable figure for the national sample was 10 percent—and they were more likely to be unemployed, pregnant, unable to pay rent, and sometimes hungry and homeless. Those who remained in foster care beyond their eighteenth birthdays were more likely to be in school or a training program to prepare for the future.

It is important to point out that the appropriate comparison group may not be a broad national sample of same-aged youths but a sample of poorer youths who have known many difficulties as well, or a group of children who were maltreated and did not go to foster care, as in the Minnesota study. The children exiting foster care have suffered many negative experiences, including poverty and traumatic events of abuse. Studies of mistreated children suggest that they had many emotional problems when they entered foster care, and it even with counseling, has not remedied them.

Richard Wexler, executive director of the National Coalition for Child Protection Reform, says, "What these results should tell us is that we've got to stop throwing so many children into foster care in the first place. What you can see is, regardless of what the problems were going in, foster care surely didn't fix them."[73] Despite all the problems, it is important to recall that half the children felt that they were lucky to have been in foster care. Box 16-2 describes innovations in foster care that may make it more effective.

Kinship Foster Care and Nonrelative Foster Care

As suggested in the Minnesota study, kinship foster care has some advantages. It appears to provide more stability.[74] Children are less likely to be moved from it, and biological parents appear to keep in closer contact with children, with 56 percent visiting at least once a month and 19 percent visiting four or more times a month; the comparable figures in nonrelative foster care are 32 percent once a month and 3 percent four or more times a month. In addition, abuse is less likely to be reported in kinship foster families than in nonrelative foster families. Some foster-care professionals have expressed concern that, in kinship foster homes, children may receive fewer services and may be exposed to the influences that created difficulties for the parent, but kinship foster homes do appear to provide greater stability, and children seem to have fewer problems there.

Termination of Parental Rights

In our country, the tie between biological parent and child is considered so important that it is severed only because the parent cannot meet his or her responsibilities to provide adequate care for the child for an extended period of time. Even if a child

Box 16-2
INNOVATIVE FOSTER CARE PROGRAMS

Two innovative programs seek to build a more effective, supportive foster care system for everyone involved.

In 1998, New York City established the family-to-family program* to create an open family system in which biological and foster parents meet with each other, plan the care of the children, and have ongoing contact as parents work toward having children live at home again. Meetings are initially held in agency offices where biological parents can meet the foster parents, give information about their child's routines and habits, and can express their preferences for things like church attendance, dress rules, and hairstyles.

When visiting starts, parents sometimes come to the foster homes a number of times before they start unsupervised visits. Parents frequently maintain relationships with each other and children go back to visit after they return to their biological parents. Foster parents become part of the extended family system. In many ways, foster parents and biological parents form the kind of relationship we referred to in Chapter 4 as coparenting, even though foster parents are more like mentors to parents in the beginning.

The program in New York is a voluntary one unless court prohibition forbids it, and about 60 percent of parents have had some contact with foster parents. The program requires special training for agency workers and for foster parents who frequently feel critical of parents because of their child maltreatment. The program has resulted in children's returning to their biological families about three months sooner than under the older system. The rate at which parental rights are terminated remains the same, but the parent has better understanding that he or she can not provide an effective level of care.

In the midwest, Brenda Eheart, an Illinois sociologist concerned that many foster children were not able to return to their biological parents, started a program she called "Generations of Hope," to recreate for foster children the kind of close and caring social ties she had had growing up in a small town.** She was able to negotiate the purchase of part of a decommissioned Air Force Base and organized a community to live there. She advertised for adults who would become foster parents with the goal of adopting the children. She also advertised for older adults who would live there, volunteer services to care for children, tutoring them, and teaching them skills in exchange for reduced rent of comfortable homes. And she contacted the Illinois Department of Children and Family Services for hard-to-place children.

Her program provides therapy, tutoring, and respite services for children and families. Eheart compares her program with state programs of residential centers. In those programs, which are expensive, children have to leave at age eighteen. She summarizes her program, "We give children a childhood, a sense of permanence." Older adults as well as children have gained from the program because they have important, useful jobs, and they too have community connections.

*Leslie Kaufman, "Birth Parents Retaining a Voice in New York Foster Care Model," *New York Times,* June 3, 2004, p. A1.
**Lou Ann Walker, "A Place Called Hope," *Parade Magazine,* July 7, 2002, pp. 10–12.

has been placed for adoption and has lived happily for two or three years with adoptive parents as the only parents he or she has known, the courts will return the child to a competent biological father who did not know of the child's existence before adoption and who seeks the child out as soon as he learns he has one.[75] Parents' rights can be relinquished voluntarily, as when young parents give up a baby for adoption. Parents' rights are terminated when they have demonstrated to a court that they are unable to care for the child or children for an extended period of time. These decisions are not easy, for there can be mitigating circumstances that make it hard to meet the time limit—loss of a job or place to live, time in jail. Still, the court is concerned about the child's right to permanent placement with parents who can care for him or her. The child's interest will be considered only if the parent has proved unable or unwilling to make changes to become a competent parent.

DISASTERS

In this section, we discuss local and national disasters, and fear of terrorist attack.

Natural Disasters

We have seen the devastating effects of powerful hurricanes on the southern coast of the United States, and there is reason to think that we are in a phase of weather cycles or changes that will produce a continuation of such disasters.[76] Hurricane Katrina damaged large sections of several southern states, killed thousands of people, and upended the lives of hundreds of thousands of individuals and their families. Survivors are scattered around the country, and while many will get their lives back together, it will take individuals, communities, and state agencies years to rebuild the structure of life as they knew it there.

Natural disasters vary in their predictability, and unpredictability increases stress. Hurricanes can be anticipated and sometimes escaped, but earthquakes and tornados are sudden and unpredictable. Even when predicted, the unprecedented damage of Hurricane Katrina was not planned for, and the country saw the anguished faces of families seeking safety or seeking loved ones whose whereabouts were unknown.

The effects of a natural disaster depend on its duration, which is usually short-lived in comparison to abuse or community violence that may be ongoing, and on the amount of damage it wreaks. In general, in the first year after the disaster, moderate to severe symptoms of PTSD are found in 30–50 percent of children who experience the effects of the disaster. PTSD symptoms experienced after disasters more often include reexperiencing the event and having intrusive thoughts and less often include numbing and avoidance of the topic. Long-term follow-ups of children are few, but generally, symptoms decrease after the first year. Children who had problems prior to the disaster are more likely to have more serious problems after the disaster or to have their own difficulties intensified by the disaster.

TF-CBT therapy, as noted, has proven useful with traumatized children. Other useful interventions for reactions following disasters include school programs that help children process events, normalize their reactions of immediate distress, and give creative outlets for expression of feelings are useful. If schools are not in session, then such programs can be carried out at community centers.

However, having to seek aid in community agencies may have the effect of making teens feel more helpless because families cannot cope on their own.[77] A sample of teens displaced after Hurricane Katrina and living in relocation camps reported lower levels of self-esteem and higher levels of depression and distress than a matched control group not affected by Hurricane Katrina. In both the samples of victims and controls, teens whose families relied on community agencies for help reported lower self-esteem and more distress than teens whose families used less community aid. Teens may be especially senitive to feelings of social stigmatization and vulnerable to feelings of helplessness when family members do not have resources for managing. Also, talking to community workers may remind teens of the disaster.

Massage therapy was found to be helpful in reducing elementary school children's feelings of anxiety and depression following Hurricane Andrew in Florida.[78] Children who reported many symptoms of PTSD were assigned to receive back massages twice-weekly for thirty minutes or to a control group who watched a video while sitting on the lap of a research assistant for the same amount of time. Children who received massages had lower levels of anxiety and depression, and reduced levels of cortisol, indicating less stress after the massages. Parents were taught to give their children back massages.

As in all cases of trauma and disaster, returning to normal routines as soon as possible helps children and adults feel more secure. Even if not living at home, reviving daily routines and activities helps people feel less stressed.

Managing Fears of National Violence

On September 11, 2001, Americans across the country and people around the world witnessed via television the tragic and violent deaths of three thousand people killed in the terrorist attacks in New York, Washington, D.C., and Pennsylvania. All joined with their families and communities in mourning their deaths. Americans have since lived with the fears of possible terrorist killings through bombs, bio-chemical agents released in the air or in the mail, and shootings. These fears have been heightened as the nation has engaged in war overseas. At the national level, we are now experiencing the ongoing fears people in inner cities have experienced for years, and the research on handling fear and stress in that situation can be applied to our present national tragedy.

Research after the Oklahoma City bombing revealed that symptoms following a terrorist attack can be long-lived. School-age children who lived a hundred miles away from Oklahoma City and suffered no physical or direct contact with the bombing were studied two years after the bombing. Almost a third of the children indicated knowing a friend who knew someone who had been injured or killed. Twenty percent of the children described bomb-related symptoms that decreased their level of functioning at home or in school.[79]

In studies of children's worries following the September 11 bombings, researchers found that children had fewer worries after the September bombings than they had in June 2000.[80] Parents made a great effort to talk to children about their fears and concerns, and children felt reassured. Children who were panel members to discuss these studies stated they wanted parents to talk to them about their everyday concerns such as bullying and television violence like they talked to them after September 11. They recommend that parents push at times to get information even if children say they are not worried because children will not talk spontaneously about their worries for fear of burdening their parents. One researcher commented, "When things are 'normal,' children seem to feel most alone and helpless in their fear, and unlike Code Orange times, parents can be clueless about kids' anxiety, and kids know that."

Parents want to know what to do to help their children in these scary times. Parents, as we have learned, are the most important figures in helping children cope with trauma and stress of all kinds, and their most important role is to talk to children. Here, as well as at the chapter's end, are suggestions parents can use.[81]

1. Examine and manage their own fears, because children model their responses on their parents' behavior.

2. Turn off the television and radio when their children are awake, to reduce the stress of repeated exposure to visual images and discussion of the tragedies.

3. Listen and observe children to determine their level of stress, as reflected in eating, sleeping, and level of energy. Parents should respond to children's questions and concerns in a supportive way.

4. Give honest statements of reassurance—saying they and the government are working to keep children safe, not promising that nothing bad will happen.

5. Respond in age-appropriate ways when talking to children. Preschoolers do not need the level of information and discussion useful for older children.

6. Maintain daily activities and routines, as familiar patterns of behavior provide reassurance and feelings of security.

7. Have a friend's phone number outside the community whom all family members can call to report safety and whereabouts in the event of a community disaster.

8. Appreciate and comment on the good things in life today—for example, the family's being together, the closeness with friends. Feelings of enjoyment provide a reserve of strength to deal with stress when it comes.

9. Read stories about the country's history that inspire and give confidence that we can survive and flourish in times of struggle and adversity (e.g., getting to the Pacific coast from St. Louis, getting to the moon, surviving the battles of the Revolution and of the War of 1812, when the White House and many government buildings were burned down by the British).

10.   Volunteer with children in some activity to make a part of the world a better place. We cannot directly influence those who might wish to hurt us now, but we can increase the pleasure and joy some people get out of life.

In all these difficult situations, the family remains the main source of support for children. Agencies and therapies can help, but it is individuals who are close and have a sense of the child's individuality who are truly helpful. If parents cannot do this, other relatives or family friends, teachers, or day care workers can step in.

MILITARY FAMILIES

Of all the families discussed in this book, these families face the greatest challenges because family members are participating in military conflicts abroad where one or both parents face injury or death on a regular basis. That most families cope with the numerous stresses involved is a testament to their strength, especially when other families around them are living lives without these stresses.

In the United States at the present time, there are 1.4 million active duty service members and their families include 1.2 million children.[82] The National Guard and Reserves include another 900,000 service members with 700,000 children, so almost two million children live in military families, with 25 percent under the age of 5.[83] At any one time, about 700,000 children experience the deployment of a parent to a war zone.

In the best of times, children in these families experience added stresses of multiple moves, separations from loved ones on duty, and the influence of strict military culture.[84] Often children and families have the resources of living on military bases with many other families who share similar challenges and can provide support to each other. In times of war, there are longer separations and the risk of injury and death for loved ones. Injuries, when they occur, may influence family life and all family members for decades.

Military families are very diverse and include single-parent families, dual-parent families in which both parents are in service, regular military service members, and National Guard and Reservists who live in communities with less support and less understanding and quick orders for deployment with marked drops in income during deployment.

Families cope best when they accept the military lifestyle and see meaning in the sacrifices they make. When spouses are self-reliant and active in coping with problems, have a strong support system, and have an optimistic view of the future, families do well. When families have additional stresses to those of military life—young children, low pay, no support system, added psychological problems—they do less well.

Deployment Cycle

Deployment is the most stressful experience for military families because the service member is at risk of death. It consists of four stages: pre-deployment (notification to actual departure), deployment (time away from family in war zone), reunion (return to family), and post-deployment (period of adjustment in the family, with many facing future deployments). Children's responses depend on the child's age, the specific family context, the child's temperament, and personal qualities.[85]

Pre-Deployment   About 15 percent of families rate this period as the most stressful time in the cycle. Service members are doing their regular jobs and are also preparing to leave. Their family members have many emotional reactions. Even young infants can sense changes in the family and become more irritable, not eating or not sleeping well. Preschoolers may be confused, unhappy, or crying at the impending departure. Older children may have a clearer understanding of the dangers involved, and many feel sad and angry at the impending separation. Teens may retreat from their feelings and deny they are concerned.

Deployment   Families have to reorganize to take on the tasks that the service member did. The remaining spouse has all the burdens of a single parent in addition to the worry about the safety and welfare of the absent parent. The caregiving parent's stable mood and ability to maintain the usual family routines help children cope. However, their eating and sleeping can be disrupted, especially at times of anxiety. Older schoolchildren may be more aware of the dangers for the absent parent and have physical complaints, moodiness, and trouble completing schoolwork. They may resist the usual rules. Teens may try to take the place of the absent parent and help with chores and enjoy their greater role in the family. Some feel worried and depressed and have school problems. It is easier for family members when they live in a community of other families who face the same challenges. Family members can feel understood and share solutions. Twenty-nine percent of families find the mid-point of deployment the most stressful time.

A primary task in this period is maintaining contact with the absent parent. This can be done in many ways—phone, cell phone, e-mail, video calls, and letters. Families can stay close, and the absent parent can be involved in daily events when contact is frequent, but there may have to be ground rules about what is shared. If all the details of everyday life are shared, an absent parent may worry about what is happening at home and feel helpless to solve problems. Distracting worries may interfere with work and cause mistakes or injuries. Knowing certain details of a parent's surroundings can also increase the family's worries.

The family gradually becomes adjusted to the parent's absence. Sometimes, there is great pride in expanding responsibilities—mothers may feel great at fixing a faucet or changing the tire on a car—and children may feel pleased at their valued contributions. Everyone looks forward to the return of the parent in idealistic ways, thinking things will be perfect.

Reunion   Everyone is happy, and expectations are high for the reunion. However, everyone in the family has changed. Everyone is older, and their experiences have led to new skills and abilities and new feelings. It is easiest to see with babies who are toddlers and talkers when their parent returns. Caregiving parents have taken on many new jobs and feel independent and pleased at their skills. The returning service member has perhaps experienced the biggest changes in war. Everyone has to get reacquainted and get back in the family routines. If contact has been close, this is much easier.

Post-Deployment   This is a period of readjustment for the family. The absent parent is incorporated back in the family, and roles change. Spouses may find it hard to give up making all the decisions. Service members may find it hard to forget their wartime experiences, or they may miss the friends and close relationships of their military unit. Many live with the certainty that they will have to redeploy and go through the same cycle again in six to twelve months, so happiness is short-lived.

There is limited help given to families in this readjustment period, as little is known about the processes involved, especially about the process for single parents and for dual-parent military families. Some service members settle back into routine family life with minimal difficulties. Others find it hard to be around young children and feel irritable at the noise and chaos. Some may suffer from depression or PTSD that was not diagnosed at the time of return. When families are close to a base, there are more services available to help with the readjustment process. Those in the Guard or Reserves have to seek help in the private community where professionals are less likely to have experience in military problems.

A major problem is also the military's past history of minimizing psychological difficulties and encouraging a "tough it out" attitude that delays getting needed help. Because of the traumatic nature of their experiences, returning service members are more emotionally vulnerable, and, as has been found, at greater risk for domestic violence and child abuse. So, if problems do not subside, help must be sought quickly. Outside agencies such as Head Start have partnered with military bases and installations to give training to their staffs to help them be sensitive to children's reactions in the deployment cycle.[86] Teachers have been able to refer families for needed services, and have been active in helping community agencies understand the needs of military families. Schools for older children have also provided group programs when there are a sizeable number of children to participate.

There are a great many problems if a parent suffers serious injuries, as more than 30,000 returning veterans have. Because of the nature of the wounds, many service members return without limbs and with closed-head injuries that may be difficult to diagnose. The caregiving parent has many new responsibilities and less time for child care. All family members are under stress, and all resources must be mobilized. The death of the parent is most feared. Military counseling may be available and helpful, and the support of other military families can help.

In dealing with all these stresses, mobilizing family support so the remaining parent gets help in carrying out all these responsibilities is important because the parent is the person that helps each child function and develop. Connecting to military and community resources is essential. A main rule in dealing with all the stress is to pay attention to each family member's feelings, as each person may perceive the situation differently and have different needs. Accepting and responding sensitively to each person's feelings is the most important thing one can do.

THE CHALLENGE MODEL

Therapy can help children deal with the effects of certain traumatic events and troubled family situations. Some therapists have become concerned, however, that certain forms of intervention so emphasize the pain and damaging effects of these difficulties that children and adults believe they are doomed to emotionally impoverished lives as a result of the trauma.

Steven Wolin and Sybil Wolin term this the *damage model* of human development, in that it focuses on the harmful effects produced by traumas; therapy in this model can only help individuals understand the damage and how it occurred. Drawing on clinical insights and on the research of such people as Ruth Smith and Emmy Werner (see the interview with Emmy Werner in Chapter 4), Wolin and Wolin have developed a *challenge model* of development.[87] Although adversity brings stress, harm, and vulnerability to the individual, Wolin and Wolin believe it also stimulates the person to branch out, to take measures to protect him- or herself, and find other sources of strength that promote development. So, the individual experiences pain but develops resiliencies that can limit the pain and promote accomplishment and satisfaction.

In their book *The Resilient Self,* Wolin and Wolin identify seven resiliencies that help individuals rebound in the face of difficult circumstances:

1. *Insight*—[developing] the habit of asking tough questions and giving honest answers

2. *Independence*—drawing boundaries between yourself and the troubled people around you; keeping emotional and physical distance while satisfying the demands of your conscience

Children cope best with community disasters when family members are supportive.

3. *Relationships*—[building] intimate and fulfilling ties to other people that balance a mature regard for your own needs with empathy and the capacity to give to someone else

4. *Initiative*—taking charge of problems; exerting control; [acquiring] a taste for stretching and testing yourself in demanding tasks

5. *Creativity*—imposing order, beauty, and purpose on the chaos of your troubling experiences and painful feelings

6. *Humor*—finding the comic in the tragic

7. *Morality*—[developing] an informed conscience that extends your wish for a good personal life to all of humankind.[88]

Their book describes the many ways resiliencies grow in childhood, adolescence, and adulthood and offers an optimistic approach that encourages survivors of traumas and difficult childhood experiences to review their lives in terms of the strengths they have developed. As a result, people experience pride in their ability to overcome hardships—whether as a result of violence or abuse or natural disasters such as floods and earthquakes—and confidence in their capacity to make further changes as needed. In focusing on pain and the sources of pain in the past, the damage model tends to discourage individuals, because the past cannot be changed and the pain undone. In contrast, the challenge model asserts that life can be satisfying, joyful, and productive even with the pain and scars of the past.

MAIN POINTS

Chronic illness
- affects 4–9 percent of children
- changes child's and family's routines
- brings feelings of worry, helplessness
- makes great demands on child and family
- requires parents build an alliance with health-care providers
- requires building and maintaining a positive support system

An ecological/transactional model of community violence and child maltreatment
- describes characteristics of the child, parent, and environment that increase the risk of violence
- describes violence at several ecological levels: the macrosystem, the exosystem, the microsystem, and the ontogenic, or personal, level
- has implications for types of intervention at the various ecological levels

Child maltreatment
- includes many forms—individual (physical/emotional abuse, neglect), family (domestic violence), and school/community (assaults, shootings)
- includes a broader array of victimizations that increase the level of symptoms children have

- includes 18 percent of children who have had four or more victimizations in a year
- requires organized community interventions to prevent family violence

Risks for maltreatment include

- social characteristics of family (e. g., poverty status, neighborhood violence)
- parents' personal characteristics (history of abuse, substance use, psychological stability)
- child's characteristics (medical problems, overreactive temperament)

Children's response to maltreatment include

- neurobiological hyperarousal
- posttraumatic stress disorder
- disorganized/disoriented attachment to parent
- poor peer relations
- poor emotional regulation and feelings of self-blame

Interventions take many forms that include

- separating child from abuser
- training parents so they can help children cope
- therapy to help children manage feelings
- activities that promote feelings of self-worth, control, and social connections
- interrupting cycle of abuse by providing a supportive adult outside the family, therapist, or supportive partner in adulthood

Foster parenting

- involves the satisfactions and challenges of providing care for children who are dealing with difficult life experiences
- involves many other people and agencies and the ongoing supervision of parents
- has difficulty helping children overcome problems they enter with, but innovative programs provide useful interventions

Military families

- include 1.2 million children
- have more stresses than most families because of separations from loved ones and increased risk of harm
- experience stages in deployment process
- by and large cope well with the many difficulties involved

The challenge model

- focuses on strengths people develop to cope with negative family experiences or other traumas
- identifies seven resiliencies: insight, independence, relationships, initiative, creativity, humor, and morality
- presents an optimistic view of people's capacity to create satisfying lives despite the scars of painful experiences

EXERCISES

1.   Imagine that a close friend told you that her four-year-old twin boys fought so hard each day that they often inflicted injuries so she had to take them to the Emergency Room for treatment. What would you say to her about sibling victimization and what would you advise her to do?

2.   Divide into groups of four and describe the general information you would choose to include in an eight-session parenting course for men and women who have physically abused their children. Share your group's results with the entire class. What elements were chosen by only one or two groups? Combine the best information from all groups and come up with one eight-session program. If possible, compare it with a program offered in your area, such as Parental Stress.

3.   Divide into groups of four and describe a 6-session parenting program for foster parents who will care for elementary school-aged children.

4.   Imagine that you had unlimited money to go into a low-income housing project in a high-crime area. What kinds of programs would you devise to help children cope with the violence they witness around them?

5.   What would you tell a nine-year-old brother or sister who is afraid of experiencing an earthquake or hurricane or flood?

ADDITIONAL READINGS

Cozolino, Louis. *The Neuroscience of Human Relationships.* New York: W. W. Norton, 2006.

Darcy, John S., and Fiore, Lisa B. *The Safe Child Handbook: How to Protect Your Family and Cope with Anxiety in a Threat-Filled World.* San Francisco: Jossey-Bass, 2006.

Osofsky, Joy D., ed. *Young Children and Trauma.* New York: Guildford Press, 2004.

Pipe, Margaret-Ellen et al., eds. *Child Sexual Abuse: Disclosure, Delay, and Denial.* Mahwah, NJ: Erlbaum, 2007.

Zelter, Lonnie K., and Schlank, Christinne Blackett. *Conquering Your Child's Chronic Pain.* New York: HarperCollins, 2005.

EPILOGUE

We have looked at parenting behaviors in many different circumstances. We have discussed parenting children of all ages living in families of diverse values and goals and in diverse family structures with one or two parents, who are sometimes of the same sex. We have looked at parenting in ordinary times and in times of special stress such as divorce or trauma. No matter what the age of the child; no matter whether the child is a biological or an adopted child, a child with special gifts or special needs, or a child with the usual gifts and needs; no matter whether parents are married, single, or remarried—four basic principles stand out.

The four basic principles are straightforward. First, parents give children positive attention. Positive attention does not mean accepting and approving all behaviors. It does mean that parents view children in terms of their special qualities and strengths, and that parents maintain their positive view of children while helping them make needed changes in behavior.

Second, parents provide support for the growth of children's competence by modeling positive behavior, guiding children's behavior, and teaching them problem-solving skills to deal with challenges. Third, parents talk about what is happening, listen to children's feelings, and answer children's questions so children have a clear understanding of situations and a chance to express their concerns. Fourth, parents deal with unresolved anger and hostility directed at the child or expressed to or about others in the child's presence. The persistence of such feelings destroys children's good feelings and their effectiveness in the world.

Relying on these four principles, parents can help children grow and realize their potential. No matter how strong the desire, parents cannot guarantee children a problem-free life, especially in these historical times, but they can guarantee children a lifetime attachment that provides the support and help necessary to grow and to meet life's challenges.

Throughout the book, we have seen that parents benefit from support as they go about rearing the next generation. In our individualistic society, this support usually comes from individuals and voluntary organizations. Government programs do not give much help to the vast array of parents, though such programs are effective in providing services—for example, home visiting programs for parents of infants or early childhood stimulation programs for children with special needs.

In most parents' lives, support comes primarily from marital partners, extended family members such as grandparents, friends, coworkers, and organizations like CHADD (Children and Adults with Attention Deficit Disorder) designed to help special groups of parents and children. More recently, organizations like the National Parenting Association have addressed the broader needs of all parents. Further, parents themselves have followed the Youth Charter plan of William Damon to organize the entire community to address the needs of all youth. This is vitally important for all of us, because children are the future of our society.

If you are not a parent or grandparent, you may wonder what you can do to help parents. First, every one of us can give parents the respect and acknowledgment for their hard work and sacrifice that our society generally withholds from parents.

Second, with whatever your special skills, you may be able to take actions in your everyday life to support parents and parenting. A single individual has tremendous power, as the actions of Barbara Barlow illustrate.[1] A pediatric surgeon at Harlem Hospital in New York, she became concerned at the growing number of preventable injuries she was treating. Children fell from open windows, were hit by automobiles while playing in the street, and were victims of violence.

In 1988, Barlow started Harlem Hospital's Injury Prevention Project (IPP) with a grant from the Robert Wood Johnson Foundation. With a staff of three, she worked to rebuild playgrounds and parks in the community, making them safe places to play. She photographed all the parks and playgrounds and took the information to the Parks Department and the Board of Education. The Parks Department has since made nearly all the parks in the area safe. Private funding was obtained, and with the suggestions of teachers and students, eight new parks were built.

The Injury Prevention Program has expanded to include activities that foster children's competence. For example, an in-hospital art program allows patients to express their feelings about illness and hospitalization. Children have exhibited and sold their work, with half of the profits going to the children and half to the art program. The IPP also sponsors baseball teams, a soccer team, a dance program serving 200 children, and a greening program in which children can grow vegetables and flowers.

Since the implementation of this program, major injuries to children in Harlem have decreased by 37 percent. Motor vehicle accidents have decreased by 50 percent, and fewer children fall from windows. In addition, dancers, athletes, artists, and gardeners have developed skills they would not have been able to develop without the programs.

An increase in violent injuries led Barlow to start the Anti-Violence Project, which contains several specific programs for (1) teaching children how to stay safe, (2) helping children deal with violence after they experience it, and (3) teaching the children, their parents, and educators, conflict resolution techniques and other ways to avoid violence.

Funding for all these programs comes from individuals, corporations, foundations, and fees from Barlow's speaking engagements. Barlow concludes,

> You have to give to get in this world, and we give a lot. We put in lots of hard work, but *it's* immensely satisfying. There is no such thing as not being able to make things better. In any community, every individual can make a tremendous difference if they truly care, if they look around to see what needs to be done.[2]

NOTES

CHAPTER ONE

1. Robert Lee Hotz, "Some Scientists Argue We Are Built to Coo at the Sight of a Baby," *Wall Street Journal,* April 4, 2008, Cl.
2. U.S. Bureau, *Statistical Abstract of the United States: 2009,* 128th ed. (Washington, DC: U.S. Government Printing Office, 2008).
3. Morten L. Kringelbach et al., "A Specific and Rapid Neural Signature for Parental Instinct," *PLoSONE* 2008 3 (2), p. e1664 (www.plosone.org); Eckhard H. Hess, "Ethology and Developmental Psychology," in *Carmichael's Manual of Child Psychology,* ed. Paul H. Mussen, vol. 1 (New York: Wiley, 1970), pp. 1–38.
4. Lois Wladis Hoffman and Jean Denby Manis, "The Value of Children in the United States: A New Approach to the Study of Fertility," *Journal of Marriage and the Family* 41 (1979): 583–596.
5. Donald G. McNeil, Jr., "Demographic 'Bomb' May Only Go Pop!," *New York Times,* August 29, 2004, Section 4, p. 1.
6. Personal communication, July 10, 1989.
7. Hoffman and Manis, "The Value of Children."
8. Gerald Y. Michaels, "Motivational Factors in the Decision and Timing of Pregnancy," in *The Transition to Parenthood,* eds. Gerald Y. Michaels and Wendy Goldberg (New York: Cambridge University Press, 1988), pp. 23–61.
9. Arthur T. Jersild et al., *The Joys and Problems of Child Rearing* (New York: Bureau of Publications, Teachers College, Columbia University, 1949).
10. William Morris, ed., *The American Heritage Dictionary of the English Language* (Boston: American Heritage Publishing and Houghton Mifflin, 1969).
11. Diana Baumrind and Ross A. Thompson, "The Ethics of Parenting," in *Handboook of Parenting,* 2nd ed., ed. Marc H. Bornstein, vol. 5: *Practice Issues in Parenting* (Mahwah, NJ: Erlbaum, 2002), p. 3.
12. Marc H. Bornstein, "Parenting Science and Practice," in *Handbook of Child Psychology,* 6th ed., eds. William Damon and Richard M. Lerner, vol. 4: *Child Psychology in Practice,* eds. K. Ann Renninger and Irving E. Sigel (Hoboken, NJ: Wiley, 2006), pp. 893–949.
13. Jay Belsky, "The Determinants of Parenting: A Process Model," *Child Development* 55 (1984): 83–96.
14. Urie Bronfenbrenner and Pamela A. Morris., "The Bioecological Model of Human Development," in *Handbook of Child Psychology,* 6th ed., eds. William Damon and Richard M. Lerner, vol. 1: *Theoretical Models of Human Development,* ed. Richard Lerner (Hoboken, NJ: Wiley, 2006), pp. 793–828.
15. Belsky, "Determinants of Parenting."
16. Richard M. Lerner, Elizabeth E. Sparks, and Laurie D. McCubbin, "Family Diversity and Family Policy," in *Handbook of Family Diversity,* eds. David H. Demo, Katherine R. Allen, and Mark A. Fine (New York: Oxford University Press, 2000), p. 391.
17. Baumrind and Thompson, "The Ethics of Parenting."
18. Belsky, "Determinants of Parenting."
19. Ibid.
20. Pauline M. Pagliocca et al., "Parenting and the Law," in *Handbook of Parenting,* 2nd ed., ed. Bornstein, vol. 5, pp. 463–485.
21. Baumrind and Thompson, "The Ethics of Parenting."
22. Laura Landro, "Parents Barred From Teen Health Files," *Wall Street Journal,* August 8, 2005, p. Dl.
23. Pagliocca et al., "Parenting and the Law."
24. Baumrind and Thompson, "The Ethics of Parenting."
25. Margaret B. Neal and Leslie B. Hammer, *Working Couples Caring for Children and Aging Parents: Effects on Work and Well-Being* (Mahwah, NJ: Erlbaum, 2007).
26. Elizabeth Olson, "U.N. Surveys Paid Leave for Mothers," *New York Times,* February 16, 1998, p. A1.
27. Mark K. Rank, "As American as Apple Pie: Poverty and Welfare," in *Shifting the Center: Understanding Contemporary Families,* 3rd ed., ed. Susan J. Ferguson (New York: McGraw-Hill, 2007), pp. 739–745.
28. U. S. Bureau of the Census, *Statistical Abstract of the United States: 2009.*

29. Gerald Nadler, "Not Much Change in Children's Death Rate," *San Francisco Chronicle,* October 8, 2004, p. A13.

30. Vern Bengston, "Beyond the Nuclear Family: The Increasing Importance of Multigenerational Bonds," *Journal of Marriage and Family 63* (2001): 1–16.

31. Ibid., p. 5.

32. Steven H. Zarit and David J. Eggebeen, "Parent–Child Relationships in Adulthood and Later Years," in *Handbook of Parenting,* 2nd ed, ed. Marc H. Bornstein, vol. 1: *Children and Parenting* (Mahwah, NJ: Erlbaum, 2002), pp. 135–161.

33. Bengston, "Beyond the Nuclear Family," p. 7.

34. Ibid.

35. Carol C. Gohm et al., "Culture, Parental Conflict, Parental Marital Status, and the Subjective Well-Being of Young Adults," *Journal of Marriage and the Family 60* (1998): 319–334.

36. U.S. Bureau of the Census, *Statistical Abstract of the United States: 2009.*

37. Julia Preston, "U.S. Immigrant Population Is Highest Since the 1920s," *New York Times,* November, 29, 2007, A15.

38. U.S. Bureau of the Census, *Statistical Abstract of the United States: 2009.*

39. Rand D. Conger and Katherine J. Conger, "Resilience in Midwestern Families: Selected Findings from the First Decade of a Prospective Longitudinal Study," *Journal of Marriage and Family 64* (2002): 361–373.

40. Sylvia Hewlett and Cornel West, *War Against Parents* (Boston: Houghton Mifflin, 1998).

41. Steve Farkas et al., *A Lot Easier Said Than Done: Parents Talk about Raising Children in Today's America* (New York: Public Agenda, 2002).

42. Ibid.

43. Urie Bronfenbrenner, "Growing Chaos in the Lives of Children: How Can We turn It Around," in *Parenthood in America,* ed. Jack C. Westman (Madison: University of Wisconsin Press, 2001), pp. 197–210.

44. James Garbarino, "Supporting Parents in a Socially Toxic Environment," in *Parenthood in America,* ed. Jack C. Westman (Madison: University of Wisconsin Press, 2001), pp. 220–231.

45. Kelly J. Kelleher et al., "Increasing Identification of Psychosocial Problems: 1979–1996," *Pediatrics 105* (2000): 1313–1321.

46. Judith Rich Harris, *The Nature Assumption: Why Children Turn Out the Way They Do* (New York: Free Press, 1998), p. 351.

47. Jay Belsky, Elliot Robins, and Wendy Gamble, "The Determinants of Parental Competence: Toward a Contextual Theory," in *Beyond the Dyad,* ed. Michael Lewis (New York: Plenum Press, 1984), pp. 251–280.

48. Lynn Singer et al., "Relationship of Prenatal Cocaine Exposure and Maternal Postpartum Psychological Distress to Child Development Outcome," *Development and Psychopathology 9* (1997): 473–489.

49. Gurney Williams III, "Toxic Dads," *Parenting* (October 1998): p. 94.

50. W. Andrew Collins et al., "Contemporary Research on Parenting: The Case for Nature and Nurture," *American Psychologist 55* (2000): 218–232.

51. Arnold Sameroff et al., "Family and Social Influences on the Development of Child Competence," in *Families, Risk, and Competence,* eds. Michael Lewis and Candice Feiring (Mahwah, NJ: Erlbaum, 1998), pp. 161–185.

52. Ronald Seifer et al., "Child and Family Factors That Ameliorate Risk between 4 and 13 Years of Age," *Journal of the American Academy of Child and Adolescent Psychiatry 31* (1992): 893–903.

53. Sameroff et al., "Family and Social Influences," pp. 178–179.

54. Arnold Sameroff, "Democratic and Republican Models of Development Paradigms or Perspectives," *APA Division 7 Newsletter* (Fall 1996): 8.

55. Gary W. Evans et al., "Cumulative Risk, Maternal Responsiveness, and Allostatic Load among Young Adolescents," *Developmental Psychology 43* (2007): 341–351.

56. Collins et al., "Contemporary Research on Parenting."

57. Stephen J. Suomi, "Attachment in Rhesus Monkeys," in *Handbook of Attachment: Theory, Research, and Clinical Applications,* 2nd ed., eds. Jude Cassidy and Phillip R. Shaver (New York: Guilford Press, 2008), pp. 173–191.

58. Stephen J. Suomi, "Risk, Resilience, and Gene–environment (G × E) Interactions in Primates," Master Lecture Delivered at Head Start's Ninth National Research Conference, Washington, DC, June 25, 2008.

59. Eleanor E. Maccoby, "Parenting and Its Effects on Children: On Reading and Misreading Behavior Genetics," *Annual Review of Psychology* 51 (2000): 1–27.

60. C. Robert Cloninger et al., "Predispositions to Petty Criminality in Swedish Adoptees. II. Cross-Fostering Analysis of Gene–Environment Interaction," *Archives of General Psychiatry* 39 (1982): 1242–1247.

61. Laraine Masters Glidden, "Parenting Children with Developmental Disabilities: A Ladder of Influence," in *Parenting and the Child's World: Influences in Academic, Intellectual and Socio-Emotional Development* eds. John G. Borkowski, Sharon Landesman Ramey, and Marie Bristol-Power (Mahwah, NJ: Erlbaum, 2002), pp. 329–344.

62. Ibid., p. 336.

63. Benjamin S. Bloom, ed., *Developing Talent in Young People* (New York: Ballantine, 1985).

64. Matthew Purdy, Andrew Jacobs, and Richard Lezin Jones, "Life Behind Basement Doors: Family and System Fail Boys," *New York Times,* January 12, 2003, p. Al.

65. David Kocieniewski, "State Admits Losing Track of Children," *New York Times,* January 11, 2003, p. Al5.

66. Richard Lezin Jones and Leslie Kauftnan, "Gaps in Children's Safety Net Are Seen in New Jersey Case," *New York Times,* March 14, 2003, p. A25.

67. Robert Pear, "US Finds Fault in All 50 States' Child Welfare Programs and Penalties May Follow," *New York Times,* April 26, 2004, p. A17.

68. Farkas et al., *A Lot Easier Said Than Done.*

69. Steve Farkas et al., *Kids These Days: What Americans Really Think about the Next Generation* (New York: Public Agenda, 1997).

70. Ibid.

71. Ellen Galinsky, *Ask the Children: What American Children Really Think about Working Parents* (New York: Morrow, 1999).

72. Jay Belsky and John Kelly, *The Transition to Parenthood* (New York: Delacorte, 1994), p. 23.

73. Marian J. Bakermans-Kranenburg et al., "Experiential Evidence for Differential Susceptibility: Dopamine D4 Receptor Polymorphism (DRD4 VNTR) Moderates Intervention Effects on Toddlers' Externalizing Behavior in a Randomized Controlled Trial," *Developmental Psychology* 44 (2008): 293–300.

74. Adele Diamond et al., "Preschool Program Improves Cognitive Control," *Science 318* (2007): 1387–1388.

75. Michael I. Posner and Mary K. Rothbart, *Educating the Human Brain* (Washington, DC: American Psychological Association, 2007).

76. Susan Saulny, "They Stand When Called Upon and When Not," *New York Times,* February 25, 2009, p. A1.

77. Ibid., p. A15.

78. Katherine Ellison, *The Mommy Brain: How Motherhood Makes Us Smarter* (New York: Basic Books, 2005).

79. Ibid., p. 7.

80. James J. Dillon, "The Role of the Child in Adult Development," *Journal of Adult Development 9* (2002): 267–275.

81. Ibid., p. 271.

82. Ibid., p. 272.

83. Jersild et al., *The Joys and Problems of Child Rearing,* p. 122.

84. Sandra T. Azar, "Parenting and Child Maltreatment" in *Handbook of Parenting,* 2nd ed., ed. Marc H. Bornstein, vol. 4: *Social Conditions and Applied Parenting* (Mahwah, NJ: Erlbaum, 2002), pp. 361–388.

85. Interview with Steven Wolin in Jane B. Brooks, *Process of Parenting.* 5th ed. (Mountain View, CA: Mayfield, 1999), 458–459.

86. Ibid.

87. Ibid.

88. June Lichtenstein Phelps, Jay Belsky, and Keith Crnic, "Earned Security, Daily Stress, and Parenting: A Comparison of Five Alternative Models," *Development and Psychopathology 10* (1998): 21–38.

89. Daniel J. Siegel and Mary Hartzell, *Parenting from the Inside Out: How a Deeper Self-Understanding Can Help You Raise Children Who Thrive* (New York: Penguin, 2003), p. 4.

90. Ibid., p. 248.

91. Carolyn Pape Cowan and Philip A. Cowan, *When Partners Become Parents* (New York: Basic Books, 1992).

CHAPTER TWO

1. Benedict Carey, "After Abuse, Changes in the Brain," New York Times, February 24, 2009, D5.

2. Valerie French, "History of Parenting: The Ancient Mediterranean World" in *Handbook of Parenting,* 2nd ed., ed Marc

H. Bornstein, vol 2: *Biology and Ecology of Parenting* (Mahwah, NJ: Erlbaum, 2002), pp. 345–376.

3. Linda A. Pollock, *Forgotten Childhood: Parent–Child Relations from 1500 to 1900* (New York: Cambridge University Press, 1983).

4. Ibid., p. 268.

5. Ibid., p. 270.

6. International Human Genome Sequencing Consortium, "Finishing the Euchromatic Sequence of the Genome," *Nature 431* (2004): 931–945.

7. Charles A. Nelson, Kathleen M. Thomas, and Michelle DeHaan, "Neural Bases of Cognitive Development," in *Handbook of Child Psychology*, 6th ed., eds, William Damon and Richard M. Lerner, vol.2: *Cognition, Perception, and Language,* eds. Deanna Kuhn and Robert S. Siegler (Hoboken, NJ: Wiley, 2006), pp. 3–57.

8. Peter Huttenlocher, *Neural Plasticity: The Effects of Environment on the Development of the Brain* (Cambridge, MA: Harvard University Press, 2002).

9. Avshalom Caspi et al., "Role of Genotype in the Cycle of Violence in Maltreated Children," *Science 297* (2002): 851–854.

10. Patrick O. McGowan et al., "Epigenetic Regulation of the Glucocorticoid Receptor in Human Brain Associates with Childhood Abuse," *Nature Neuroscience 12* (2009): 342–348.

11. Marian J. Bakermans-Kranenburg et al., "Effects of an Attachment-Based Intervention on Daily Cortisol Moderated by Dopamine Receptor D4: A Randomized Control Trial on 1- to 3-Year-Olds Screened for Externalizing Behavior," *Development and Psychopathology 20* (2008): 805–820.

12. Marian J. Bakermans-Kranenburg et al., "Experiential Evidence for Differential Susceptibility: Dopamine D4 Receptor Polymorphism (DRD4 VNTR) Moderates Intervention Effects on Toddlers' Externalizing Behavior in a Randomized Controlled Trial," *Developmental Psychology 44* (2008): 293–300.

13. Huttenlocher, *Neural Plasticity.*

14. Ibid.

15. Ibid.

16. Louis Cozolino, *The Neuroscience of Human Relationships: Attachment and the Developing Social Brain* (New York:

Norton, 2006); Sandra Blakeslee, "Cells That Read Minds," *New York Times,* January 10, 2006, p. D1.

17. Bruce D. Perry, "Incubated in Terror: Neurodevelopmental Factors in the Cycle of Violence," in *Children in a Violent Society,* ed. Joy D. Osofsky (New York: Guilford Press, 1997), pp. 124–149.

18. Blakeslee, "Cells that Read Minds."

19. Nelson, Thomas, and DeHaan, "Neural Bases of Cognitive Development."

20. Huttenlocher, *Neural Plasticity.*

21. Jay N. Giedd et al., "Brain Development during Childhood and Adolescence: A Longitudinal MRI Study," *Nature Neuroscience 2* (1999): 861–863.

22. Huttenlocher, *Neural Plasticity.*

23. Ibid.

24. Ibid., p. 215.

25. Clancy Blair, Douglas Granger, and Rachel Peters Razza, "Cortisol Reactivity Is Positively Related to Executive Function in Preschool Children Attending Head Start," *Child Development 76* (2005): 554–567.

26. Hermann Englert, "Sussing Out Stress," *Scientific American Mind 14*(1) (2004): 56–61.

27. Mary Dozier et al., "Foster Children's Diurnal Production of Cortisol: An Exploratory Study," *Child Maltreatment 11* (2006): 189–197.

28. Gary W. Evans and Michelle A. Shamberg, "Childhood Poverty, Chronic Stress, and Adult Working Memory," *Proceedings of the National Academy of Sciences 106* (2009): 6545–6549.

29. Adele Diamond et al., "Preschool Program Improves Cognitive Control," *Science 318* (2007): 1387–1388.

30. Michael I. Posner and Mary K. Rothbart, *Educating the Human Brain* (Washington, DC: American Psychological Association, 2007).

31. Diamond et al., "Preschool Program Improves Cognitive Control,"; Elena Bodrova and Deborah J. Leong, Tools of the Mind: The Vygotskian Approach to Early Childhood Education, 2nd ed. (Upper Saddle River, NJ: Pearson Prentice-Hall, 2007).

32. Posner and Rothbart, *Educating the Human Brain.*

33. John E. Bates, Christine A. Maslin, and Karen H. Frankel, "Attachment Security, Mother-Child Interaction and Temperament as Predictors of Behavior Problem Ratings at Age Three Years," in

Growing Points of Attachment Theory and Research, eds. Inge Bretherton and Everett Waters, *Monographs of the Society for Research in Child Development,* 50 (Serial no. 109) (1985): 167–193.

34. Avshalom Caspi and Phil A. Silva, "Temperamental Qualities at Age 3 Predict Personality Traits in Young Adulthood: Longitudinal Evidence from a Birth Cohort," *Child Development* 66 (1995): 486–498.

35. Jerome Kagan et al., The Preservation of Two Infant Temperaments into Adolescence, *Monographs of the Society for Research in Child Development,* 72 (Serial no. 287) (2007).

36. Mary K. Rothbart and John E. Bates, "Temperament," in *Handbook of Child Psychology,* 6th ed., eds. William Damon and Richard M. Lerner, vol. 3: *Social, Emotional, and Personality Development,* ed. Nancy Eisenberg (Hoboken, NJ: Wiley, 2006), p. 100.

37. Ibid.

38. Kagan et al., *The Preservation of Two Infant Temperaments into Adolescence.*

39. Ibid.

40. Rothbart and Bates, "Temperament."

41. Bates, Maslin, and Frankel, "Attachment Security, Mother-Child Interaction and Temperament as Predictors of Behavior Problem Ratings at Age Three Years."

42. Dymphna C. van den Boom, "The Influence of Temperament and Mothering on Attachment and Exploration: An Experimental Manipulation of Sensitive Responsiveness among Lower-Class Mothers," *Child Development* 65 (1994): 1457–1477; Dymphna van den Boom, "Do First-Year Intervention Effects Endure? Follow-up During Toddlerhood of a Sample of Dutch Irritable Infants," *Child Development* 66 (1995): 1798–1816.

43. Denise L. Newman et al., "Antecedents of Adult Interpersonal Functioning: Effects of Individual Differences in Age 3 Temperament," *Developmental Psychology* 33 (1997): 206–217.

44. Daniel Hart, Robert Atkins, and Suzanne Fegley, Personality and Development in Childhood: A Person-Centered Approach, *Monographs of the Society for Research in Child Development,* 68 (Serial no. 271) (2003).

45. Rothbart and Bates, "Temperament."

46. Ibid.

47. Michael Cole, Sheila R. Cole, and Cynthia Lightfoot, *The Development of Children,* 5th ed. (New York: Worth, 2005).

48. Albert Bandura, *Self-Efficacy: The Exercise of Control* (New York: Freeman, 1997).

49. Laura E. Berk, *Awakening Children's Minds: How Parents and Teachers Can Make a Difference* (New York: Oxford University Press, 2001).

50. Herbert Ginsburg and Sylvia Opper, *Piaget's Theory of Intellectual Development* (Englewood Cliffs, NJ: Prentice-Hall, 1969); Jean Piaget and Barbel Inhelder, *The Psychology of the Child* (New York: Basic Books, 1969).

51. Jean Piaget, *The Child's Conception of the World* (Paterson, NJ: Littlefield, Adams & Co., 1963).

52. E. Mark Cummings and Jennifer S. Cummings, "Parenting and Attachment," in *Handbook of Parenting,* 2nd ed., ed. Marc H. Bornstein, vol. 5: *Practical Issues in Parenting* (Mahwah, NJ: Erlbaum, 2002), pp. 35–58.

53. Erik H. Erikson, *Childhood and Society,* 2nd ed. (New York: Norton, 1963).

54. Erik H. Erikson, "Human Strength and the Cycle of Generations," in *Insight and Responsibility* (New York: Norton, 1964), 109–157.

55. Ross A. Thompson, "The Development of the Person: Social Understanding, Relationships, Conscience, Self," in *Handbook of Child Psychology,* 6th ed., eds. Damon and Lerner, vol. 3, p. 43.

56. Cummings and Cummings, "Parenting and Attachment."

57. Thompson, "The Development of the Self."

58. Ibid.

59. Karlen Lyons-Ruth et al., "Infants at Social Risk Maternal Depressions and Family Support Services as Moderators of Infant Development and Security of Attachment," *Child Development* 61 (1990): 85–98.

60. Thompson, "The Development of the Self."

61. L. Alan Sroufe et al., *The Development of the Person: The Minnesota Study of Risk and Adaptation from Birth to Adulthood* (New York: Guilford Press, 2005).

62. Jay Belsky et al., "Instability of Infant–Parent Attachment Security," *Developmental Psychology* 32 (1996): 921–924.

63. Claire E. Hamilton, "Continuity and Discontinuity of Attachment from Infancy through Adolescence," *Child Development*

71 (2000): 690–694; Everett Waters et al., "Attachment Security in Infancy and Early Adulthood: A Twenty-Year Longitudinal Study," *Child Development* 71 (2000): 684–689.

64. Michael Lewis, Candace Feiring, and Saul Rosenthal, "Attachment over Time," *Child Development* 71 (2000): 707–727; L. Alan Sroufe and Byron Egeland, "Attachment from Infancy to Early Adulthood in a High-Risk Sample: Continuity, Discontinuity, and Their Correlates," *Child Development* 71 (2000): 695–702.

65. Sroufe et al., *The Development of the Person*.

66. Gilbert Gottlieb, Douglas Wahlsten, and Robert Lickliter, "The Significance of Biology for Human Development. A Developmental Psychobiological Biological Systems View," in *Handbook of Child Psychology*, 6th ed., eds. William Damon and Richard M. Lerner, vol. 1: *Theoretical Models of Human Development*, ed. Richard M. Lerner (Hoboken, NJ: Wiley, 2006), pp. 210–257.

67. Urie Bronfenbrenner and Pamela A. Morris, "The Bioecological Model of Human Development," in *Handbook of Child Psychology*, 6th ed., eds. Damon and Lerner, vol. 1, pp. 793–828.

68. David F. Bjorklund and Anthony D. Pellegrini, "Child Development and Evolutionary Psychology," *Child Development* 71 (2000): 1687–1708; David F. Bjorklund, Jennifer L. Yunger, and Anthony D. Pellegrini, "The Evolution of Parenting and Evolutionary Approaches to Childrearing," in *Handbook of Parenting*, 2nd ed., ed. Bornstein, vol. 2, pp. 3–30.

69. Bjorklund and Pellegrini, "Child Development and Evolutionary Psychology."

70. Bronfenbrenner and Morris, "The Bioecological Model of Human Development."

71. Urie Bronfenbrenner, "Growing Chaos in the Lives of Children: How Can We Turn It Around?" in *Parenthood in America*, ed. Jack C. Westman (Madison: University of Wisconsin Press, 2001), pp. 197–210.

72. Bronfenbrenner and Morris, "The Bioecological Model of Human Development."

73. Ibid.

74. Bronfenbrenner, "Growing Chaos in the Lives of Children."

75. Haim G. Ginott, *Between Parent and Child* (New York: Avon, 1969).

76. Thomas Gordon, *P.E.T.: Parent Effectiveness Training* (New York: New American Library, 1975).

77. Rudolf Dreikurs with Vicki Soltz, *Children: The Challenge* (New York: Hawthorn, 1964).

78. Ann Hulbert, *Raising America* (New York: Alfred A. Knopf, 2003).

79. T. Berry Brazelton and Stanley I. Greenspan, *The Irreducible Needs of Children* (Cambridge, MA: Perseus, 2000).

80. Dr. Phil McGraw, *Family First: Your Step by Step Plan for Creating a Phenomenal Family* (New York: Free Press, 2004).

81. Deborah Carroll and Stella Reid, *Nanny 911: Expert Advice for All Your Emergencies* (New York: HarperCollins, 2005).

82. Ibid., p. xvii.

83. Ibid., p. xviii.

84. McGraw, *Family First*, p. xiv.

85. Ibid.

86. Diana Baumrind, "The Development of Instrumental Competence through Socialization," in *Minnesota Symposium on Child Psychology*, ed. Ann D. Pick, vol. 7 (Minneapolis University of Minnesota Press, 1973), pp. 3–46.

87. Ibid., pp. 42–43.

88. Ibid., p. 3.

89. Gerald R. Patterson et al., *A Social Learning Approach to Family Intervention*, vol. 1: *Families with Aggressive Children* (Eugene, OR: Castalia, 1975).

90. Gerald R. Patterson and Philip A. Fisher, "Recent Developments in Our Understanding of Parenting: Bidirectional Effects, Causal Models, and the Search for Parsimony," in *Handbook of Parenting*, 2nd ed., ed. Bornstein, vol. 5, pp. 59–88.

91. Gerald R. Patterson, "The Early Development of the Coercive Family Process," in *Antisocial Behavior in Children and Adolescents*, eds. John B. Reid, Gerald R. Patterson, and James Snyder (Washington, DC: American Psychological Association, 2002), pp. 25–44.

92. Femmie Juffer, Marian J. Bakermans-Kranenburg, and Marinus van IJzendoorn, "Methods of Video-Feedback Programs to Promote Positive Parenting Alone with Sensitive Discipline and with Representational Attachment Discussion," in *Positive Parenting: An Attachment-Based*

Intervention, eds. Femmie Juffer, Marian J. Bakermans-Kranenburg, and Marinus van IJzendoorn (New York: Erlbaum, 2008), pp. 11–23.

93. Marinus van IJzendoorn, Marian J. Bakermans-Kranenburg, Femmie Juffer, "Video-Feedback Intervention to Promote Positive Parenting: Evidence-Based Intervention for Enhancing Sensitivity and Security," in *Positive Parenting,* eds. Juffer, Bakermans-Kranenburg, and van IJzendoorn, pp. 193–202.

94. Karli Treyvaud et al., "Parenting Behavior Is Associated with the Early Neuro-behavioral Development of Very Preterm Children," *Pediatrics* 123 (2009): 555–561.

CHAPTER THREE

1. Susan Saulny, "In Obama Era, Voices Reflect Rising Sense of Racial Optimism," *New York Times,* May 3, 2009, pA1.

2. Joseph E. Illick, *American Childhoods* (Philadelphia: University of Pennsylvania Press, 2002).

3. William Morris, ed., *The American Heritage Dictionary of the English Language* (Boston: American Heritage Publishing Co., 1969).

4. Sara Harkness and Charles Super, "Culture and Parenting," in *Handbook of Parenting,* 2nd ed., ed. Marc H. Bornstein, vol. 2: *Biology and Ecology of Parenting* (Mahwah, NJ: Erlbaum, 2002), pp. 253–280.

5. Rebecca I. New and Amy L. Richman, "Maternal Beliefs and Infant Care Practices in Italy and the United States," in *Parents' Cultural Belief Systems: Their Origins, Expressions, and Consequences,* eds. Sara Harkness and Charles M. Super (New York: Guilford Press, 1996), pp. 385–404.

6. Daphne Blunt Bugental and Joan E. Grusec, "Socialization Processes," in *Handbook of Child Psychology,* 6th ed., eds. William Damon and Richard M. Lerner, vol. 3: *Social, Emotional, and Personality Development,* ed. Nancy Eisenberg (Hoboken, NJ: Wiley, 2006), pp. 366–428.

7. Rogers Brubaker, *Ethnicity without Groups* (Cambridge, MA: Harvard University Press, 2004).

8. William A Corsaro and Katherine Brown Rosier, "Documenting Productive-Reproductive Processes in Children's Lives: Transition Narratives of a Black Family Living in Poverty," in *Interpretive Approaches to Children's Socialization,* eds. William A. Corsaro and Peggy J. Miller, New Directions for Child Development, no. 66 (San Francisco: Jossey Bass, 1992), pp. 67–91.

9. Bugental and Grusec, "Socialization Processes."

10. Meagan M. Patterson and Rebecca S. Bigler, "Preschool Children's Attention to Environmental Messages About Groups," *Child Development* 77 (2006): 847–860.

11. Velma McBride Murry, Emilie Phillips Smith, and Nancy E. Hill, "Race, Ethnicity, and Culture in Studies of Families in Context," *Journal of Marriage and Family* 63 (2001): 912.

12. Nicholas Wade, "Race is Seen As Real Guide to Track the Roots of Disease," *New York Times,* July 30, 2002, p. D1.

13. Ross D. Parke and Raymond Buriel, "Socialization in the Family: Ethnic and Ecological Perspectives," in *Handbook of Child Psychology,* 6th ed., eds. Damon and Lerner, vol. 3: p. 465.

14. Robert H. Bradley et al., "The Home Environments of Children in the United States: Part II: Relations with Behavioral Development through Age Thirteen," *Child Development* 72 (2001): 1868–1886.

15. Annette Lareau, *Unequal Childhoods: Class, Race, and Family Life* (Berkeley: University of California Press, 2003), p. 274.

16. William E. Cross, Jr., "A Two-Factor Theory of Black Identity: Implications for the Study of Identity Development in Minority," in *Children's Ethnic Socialization: Pluralism and Development,* eds. Jean S. Phinney and Mary Jane Rotheram (Beverly Hills, CA: Sage, 1987), pp. 117–133.

17. Michael J. Chandler et al., "Personal Persistence, Identity Development, and Suicide," *Monographs of the Society for Research in Child Development* 68, (Serial no. 273) (2003).

18. Patricia M. Greenfield, Lalita K. Suzuki, and Carrie Rothstein-Fisch, "Cultural Pathways through Human Development," in *Handbook of Child Psychology,* 6th ed., eds. William Damon and Richard M. Lerner, vol. 4: *Child Psychology in Practice,* eds. K. Ann Renninger and Irving E. Sigel (Hoboken, NJ: Wiley, 2006), pp. 655–699.

19. Ruth Feldman and Shafiq Masalha, "The Role of Culture in Moderating the Links Between Early Ecological Risk and Young

Children's Adaptation," *Development and Psychopathology* 19 (2007): 1–21.

20. Daniel J. Hernandez, Nancy A. Denton, and Suzanne E. Macartney, "Children in Immigrant Families: Looking to America's Future," *Social Policy Report* 22 (3) (2008): 1–22.

21. Ibid.

22. Cynthia Garcia Coll and Laura A. Szalacha, "The Multiple Contexts of Middle Childhood," *The Future of Children* 14 (2) (2004): 81–97.

23. Ibid., p. 89.

24. Cynthia Garcia Coll and Lee M. Pachter, "Ethnic and Minority Parenting," in *Handbook of Parenting,* 2nd ed., ed. Marc H. Bornstein, vol. 4: *Social Conditions and Applied Parenting* (Mahwah, NJ: Erlbaum, 2002), p. 7.

25. Ibid.

26. Parke and Buriel, "Socialization in the Family."

27. "California Seeks to Stop the Use of Child Medical Interpreters," *New York Times,* October 30, 2005, p. A 17.

28. Tina Hoff, Liberty Greene, and Julia Davis, *National Survey of Adolescents and Young Adults: Sexual Health and Knowledge, Attitudes and Experiences* (Menlo Park, CA: Kaiser Family Foundation, 2003).

29. John W. Berry, "Acculteration," in *Handbook of Socialization: Theory and Research,* eds. Joan E. Grusec and Paul D. Hastings (New York: Guilford Press, (2007), pp. 543–558.

30. Gene H. Brody et al., "Perceived Discrimination and the Adjustment of African American Youths: A Five-Year Longitudinal Analysis with Contextual Moderation Effects," *Child Development* 77 (2006): 1170–1189.

31. Gene H. Brody et al., "Linking Perceived Discrimination to Longitudinal Changes in African American Mothers' Parenting Practices," *Journal of Marriage and Family* 70 (2008): 319–331.

32. Steven R. Beach et al., "Change in Caregiver Depression as a Function of the Strong African American Families Program," *Journal of Family Psychology* 22 (2008): 241–252.

33. Frances E. Aboud, "The Formation of In-Group Favoritism and Out-Group Prejudice in Young Children: Are They Distinct Attitudes?" *Developmental Psychology* 39 (2003): 48–60.

34. Jennifer H. Pfeifer, Christa Spears Brown, and Jaana Juvonen, "Teaching Tolerance in Schools: Lessons Learned Since *Brown v. Board of Education* about the Development and Reduction of Children's Prejudice," *Social Policy Report* 21 (2) (2007): 1–23.

35. Jean M. Twenge and Jennifer Crocker, "Race and Self-Esteem: Meta-Analyses Comparing Whites, Blacks, Hispanics, Asians, and American Indians and Comment on Gray-Little and Haldahl (2000)," *Psychological Bulletin* 64 (2002): 703–716.

36. Paul R. Amato and Frieda Fowler, "Parenting Practices, Child Adjustment, and Family Diversity," *Journal of Marriage and Family* 64 (2002): 703–716.

37. Marjory R. Gray and Laurence Steinberg, "Unpacking Authoritative Parenting: Reassessing a Multidimensional Construct," *Journal of Marriage and the Family* 61 (1999): 574–587.

38. Vonnie C. McLoyd and Julia Smith, "Physical Discipline and Behavior Problems in African American, European American, and Hispanic Children: Emotional Support as Moderator," *Journal of Marriage and Family* 64 (2002): 40–53.

39. Mary Kay DeGenova, "Introduction," in *Families in Cultural Context: Strengths and Challenges to Diversity,* ed. Mary Kay DeGenova (Mountain View, CA: Mayfield, 1997), p. 6.

40. Erika Hoff, Brett Laursen, and Twila Tardif, "Socioeconomic Status and Parenting," in *Handbook of Parenting,* 2nd ed., ed. Marc H. Bornstein, vol. 2, pp. 231–252.

41. Betty Hart and Todd R. Risley, *Meaningful Differences in the Everyday Experiences of Young American Children* (Baltimore: Brookes, 1995).

42. Lareau, *Unequal Childhoods.*

43. Sandra L. Hofferth, "Linking Social Class to Concerted Cultivation, Natural Growth and School Readiness," in *Disparities in School Readiness: How Families Contribute to Transitions into School,* eds. Alan Booth and Ann C. Crouter (New York: Erlbaum, 2008), pp. 199–205.

44. Robert Serpell et al., "Intimate Culture of Families in the Early Socialization of Literacy," *Journal of Family Psychology* 16 (2002): 391–405.

45. Joseph A. Buckhalt, Mona El-Sheikh, and Peggy Keller, "Children's Sleep and Cognitive Functioning: Race and Socioeconomic Status as Moderators of Effects," *Child Development* 78 (2007): 213–231.

46. Rand D. Conger and Katherine J. Conger, "Resilience in Midwestern Families: Selected Findings from the First Decade of a Prospective Longitudinal Study," *Journal of Marriage and Family 64* (2002): 361–373.

47. Leslie Morrison Gutman and Jacquelynne S. Eccles, "Financial Strain, Parenting Behaviors, and Adolescent Achievement Testing Model Equivalence between African American and European American Single- and Two-Parent Families," *Child Development 70* (1999): 1464–1476.

48. Nancy E. Hill, Kevin R. Bush, and Mark W. Roosa, "Parenting and Family Socialization Strategies and Children's Mental Health: Low-Income Mexican-American and Euro-American Mothers and Children," *Child Development 74* (2003): 189–204.

49. Conger and Conger, "Resilience in Midwestern Families."

50. Vonnie C. McLoyd, Nikki L. Aikens, and Linda M. Burton, "Childhood Poverty, Policy, and Practice," in *Handbook of Child Psychology,* 6th ed., eds. Damon and Lerner, vol. 4, pp. 700–775.

51. U.S. Bureau of the Census, *Statistical Abstract of the United States: 2009,* 128th ed. (Washington, DC: Government Printing Office, 2008).

52. Mary E. Corcoran and Ajay Chaudry, "The Dynamics of Childhood Poverty," *Future of Children 7*(2) (1997): 40–54.

53. McLoyd, Aikens, and Burton, "Childhood Poverty, Policy, and Practice."

54. Jeanne Brooks-Gunn and Greg J. Duncan, "The Effects of Poverty on Children," *The Future of Children 7*(2) (1997): 55–71.

55. Gary W. Evans, The Environment of Childhood Poverty," *American Psychologist 59* (2004): 77–92.

56. Ibid.

57. Romina M. Barros, Ellen Silver, and Ruth E. K. Stein, "School Recess and Group Classroom Behavior," *Pediatrics 123* (2009): 431–436.

58. Gary W. Evans, "A Multimethodological Analysis of Cumulative Risk and Allostatic Load Among Rural Children," *Developmental Psychology 39* (2003): 924–933.

59. Eric Dearing, Kathleen McCartney, and Beck A. Taylor, "Within-Child Associations Between Family Income and Externalizing and Internalizing Problems," *Developmental Psychology 42* (2006): 237–252.

60. National Institute of Child Health and Human Development Early Child Care Network, "Duration and Developmental Timing of Poverty and Children's Cognitive and Social Development from Birth Through Third Grade," *Child Development 76* (2005): 795–810.

61. Dearing, McCartney, and Taylor, "Within-Child Associations Between Family Income and Externalizing and Internalizing Problems."

62. Suniya S. Luthar and Shawn Latendresse, "Comparable 'Risks' at the Socioeconomic Status Extremes: Preadolescents Perceptions of Parenting," *Development and Psychopathology 14* (2005): 2–30.

63. Richard Rothstein, "Rx for Good Health and Good Grades," *New York Times,* September 11, 2002, p. A30.

64. McLoyd, Aikens, and Burton, "Childhood Poverty, Policy, and Practice."

65. John M. Love et al., "The Effectiveness of Early Head Start for Three-Year-Old Children and Their Parents: Lessons for Policy and Programs," *Developmental Psychology 41* (2005): 885–901.

66. Aletha C. Huston et al., "Impacts on Children of a Policy to Promote Employment and Reduce Poverty for Low Income Parents: New Hope After 5 Years," *Developmental Psychology 41* (2005): 902–918.

67. David L. Kirp, "Life Way After Head Start," *New York Times Magazine,* November 21, 2004, pp. 32–38.

68. Tammy L. Mann, "Findings from the Parent-Child Project and the Impact of Values on Parenting Reflections in a Scientific Age," *Zero to Three 20* (December 1999–January 2000): 3–8.

69. Ibid., p. 8.

70. Ibid.

71. Vivian J. Carlson and Robin L. Harwood, "Understanding and Negotiating Cultural Differences Concerning Early Development Competence: The Six Raisin Solution," *Zero to Three 20* (December 1999–January 2000): 19–24.

72. Ibid., p. 24.

CHAPTER FOUR

1. Sue Shellenbarger, "Life Stories: Children Find Meaning in Old Family Tales," *Wall Street Journal*, March 11, 2009, p. D1.

2. Lois Wladis Hoffman and Jean Denby Manis, "The Values of Children in the United States: A new Approach to the Study of Fertility," *Journal of Marriage and the Family 41* (1979): 583–596.

3. Steven Farkas et al., *A Lot Easier Said Than Done: Parents Talk About Raising Children* (New York: Public Agenda, 2002).

4. Philip A. Cowan, Douglas Powell, and Carolyn Pape Cowan, "Parenting Interventions: A Family Systems Perspective," in *Handbook of Child Psychology*, 5th ed., ed. William Damon, vol. 4: *Child Psychology in Practice*, eds. Irving E. Sigel and K. Anne Renninger (New York: Wiley, 1998), pp. 3–72.

5. John H. Grych, "Marital Relationships and Parenting," in *Handbook of Parenting*, 2nd ed., ed. Marc H. Bornstein, vol. 4: *Social Conditions and Applied Parenting* (Mahwah, NJ: Erlbaum, 2002), pp. 203–225.

6. Marcie C. Goeke-Morey, E. Mark Cummings, and Lauren M. Papp, "Children and Marital Conflict Resolution: Implications for Emotional Security and Adjustment," *Journal of Family Psychology 21* (2007): 744–753.

7. E. Mark Cummings et al., "Interparental Discord and Child Adjustment: Prospective Investigations of Emotional Security as an Explanatory Mechanism," *Child Development 77* (2006): 132–152.

8. Jay Belsky and R. M. Pasco Fearon, "Exploring Marriage–Parenting Typologies and Their Contextual Antecedents and Developmental Sequelae," *Development and Psychopathology 16* (2004): 501–523.

9. James McHale et al., "Coparenting in Diverse Family Systems," in *Handbook of Parenting*, 2nd ed., ed. Marc H. Bornstein, vol. 3: *Being and Becoming a Parent* (Mahwah, NJ: Erlbaum, 2002), pp. 75–107.

10. Ibid., p. 76.

11. Ibid.

12. Jennifer M. Jenkins et al., "Change in Maternal Perception of Sibling Negativity: Within- and Between-Family Influences," *Journal of Family Psychology 19* (2005): 533–541.

13. Melissa K. Richmond, Clare M. Stocker, and Shauna L. Rienks, "Longitudinal Associations Between Sibling Relationship Quality, Parental Differential Treatment, and Children's Adjustment," *Journal of Family Psychology 19* (2005): 550–559.

14. Barbara Shebloski, Katherine J. Conger, and Keith F. Widaman, "Reciprocal Links Among Differential Parenting, Perceived Partiality and Self-Worth: A Three-Wave Longitudinal Study," *Journal of Family Psychology 19* (2005): 633–641.

15. Laurie Kramer and Amanda K. Kowal, "Sibling Relationship Quality from Birth to Adolescence: The Enduring Contributions of Friends," *Journal of Family Psychology 19* (2005): 503–511.

16. Suzanne M. Bianchi, John P. Robinson, and Melissa A. Milkie, *Changing Rhythms of American Family Life* (New York: Russell Sage, 2006).

17. Victoria Rideout, Donald E. Roberts, and Ulla G. Foehr, "Generation M: Media in the Lives of 8–18-Year-Olds," Kaiser Family Foundation Report No. 7250, March 2005, www.kff.org.

18. Ellen Galinsky, *Ask the Children: What America's Children Really Think About Working Parents* (New York: Morrow, 1999).

19. Bianchi, Robinson, and Milkie, *Changing Rhythms of American Family Life*.

20. Reed W. Larson and Suman Verma, "How Children and Adolescents Spend Time Across the World: Work, Play, and Developmental Activities," *Psychological Bulletin 125* (1999): 701–736.

21. Suniya S. Luthar, Karen A Shoum, and Pamela J. Brown, "Extracurricular Involvement Among Affluent Youth: A Scapegoat for 'Ubiquitous Achievement Pressures?'" *Developmental Psychology 42* (2006): 583–597.

22. Ibid., p. 595.

23. W. Andrew Collins and Brett Laursen, "Parent–Adolescent Relationships and Influences," in *Handbook of Adolescence*, 2nd ed., eds. Richard M. Lerner and Laurence Steinberg (Hoboken, NJ: Wiley, 2004), pp. 331–361.

24. Peter Huttenlocher, *Neural Plasticity: The Effects of Environment on the Development of the Brain* (Cambridge, MA: Harvard University Press, 2002).

25. E. Mavis Hetherington and John Kelly, *For Better or Worse: Divorce Reconsidered* (New York: Norton, 2002).

26. Rebecca M. Ryan, Ariel Kalil, and Kathleen M. Ziol-Guest, "Longitudinal Patterns of Nonresident Fathers' Involvement: The Role of Resources and Relations," *Journal of Marriage and Family 70* (2008): 962–977.

27. Scott M. Stanley et al., "Premarital Education, Marital Quality, and Marital Stability: Findings from a Large, Random Household Survey," *Journal of Family Psychology 20* (2006): 117–126; W. Kim Halford, Howard J. Markman, and Scott Stanley, "Strengthening Couples' Relationships with Education: Social Policy and Public health Perspectives," *Journal of Family Psychology 22* (2008): 497–505.

28. Barbara L. Fredrickson, "The Role of Positive Emotions in Positive Psychology: The Broaden-and-Build Theory of Positive Emotions," *American Psychologist 56* (2001): 218–226.

29. Ann S. Masten, "Ordinary Magic: Resilience Processes in Development," *American Psychologist 56* (2001): 227–238.

30. Charles C. Carlson and John C. Masters, "Inoculation by Emotion: Effects of Positive Emotional States on Children's Reactions to Social Comparison," *Developmental Psychology 22* (1986): 760–765.

31. Ashley Montague, *Touching*, 2nd ed. (New York: Harper & Row, 1978).

32. Tiffany Field, "Infant Massage Therapy," in *Handbook of Infant Mental Health*, 2nd ed., ed. Charles H. Zeanah (New York: Guilford press, 2000): pp. 494–500.

33. Lane Strathearn et al., "Does Breastfeeding Protect Against Substantiated Child Abuse and Neglect? A Fifteen-Year Cohort Study," *Pediatrics 123* (2009): 483–493.

34. Urs A. Hunziker and Ronald G. Barr, "Increased Carrying Reduces Crying: A Randomized Controlled Trial," *Pediatrics 77* (1986): 641–647.

35. Tiffany Field, "The Effects of Mother's Physical and Emotional Availability on Emotion Regulation," in Development of Emotion Regulation: Biological and Behavioral Considerations, ed. Nathan A. Fox, *Monographs of the Society for Research in Child Development 59*, (Serial no. 240) (1994): 208–227.

36. Field, "Infant Massage Therapy."

37. Benedict Carey, "Holding Loved One's Hand Can Calm Jittery Nerves," *New York Times* January 31, 2006, p. D7.

38. Field, "The Effects of Mother's Physical and Emotional Availability on Emotion Regulation."

39. Dorothy C. Briggs, *Your Child's Self-Esteem* (Garden City, NY: Doubleday, 1970), pp. 61–62.

40. John M. Gottman, Lynn Fainsilber Katz, and Carole Hooven, "Parental Meta-Emotion Philosophy and the Emotional Life of Families: Theoretical Models and Preliminary Data," *Journal of Family Psychology 10* (1996): 243–268.

41. John Gottman with Joan DeClaire, *The Heart of Parenting: Raising an Emotionally Intelligent Child* (New York: Simon & Schuster, 1997).

42. Ibid.

43. Beverly J. Wilson and John M. Gottman, "Marital Conflict, Repair, and Parenting," in *Handbook of Parenting*, 2nd ed., ed. Bornstein, vol. 4, pp. 227–258.

44. Thomas Gordon with Judith G. Sands, *P.E.T. in Action* (New York: Bantam Books, 1978); Thomas Gordon, *Teaching Children Self-Discipline* (New York: Random House, 1989).

45. Gordon with Sands, *P.E.T. in Action*, p. 47.

46. Judy Dunn, Jane Brown, and Lynn Beardsall, "Family Talk about Feeling States and Children's Later Understanding of Others' Emotions," *Developmental Psychology 27* (1991): 448–455.

47. Adele Faber and Elaine Mazlish, *Liberated Parents/Liberated Children* (New York: Avon Books, 1975).

48. John A. Clausen, Paul H. Mussen, and Joseph Kuypers, "Involvement, Warmth, and Parent-Child Resemblance in Three Generations," in *Present and Past in Middle Life*, eds. Dorothy H. Eichorn et al. (New York: Academic Press, 1981), pp. 299–319.

49. Steven J. Wolin and Linda A. Bennett, "Family Rituals," *Family Process 23* (1984): 401–420.

50. Linda A. Bennett et al., "Couples at Risk for Transmission of Alcoholism: Protective Influences," *Family Process 26* (1987): 111–129.

51. Barbara Fiese et al., "A Review of 50 Years of Research on Naturally Occurring Family Routines and Rituals: Cause for

Celebration?" *Journal of Family Psychology* 16 (2002): 381–390.

52. Ibid.

53. Robert Serpell et al., "Intimate Culture of Families in the Early Socialization of Literacy," *Journal of Family Psychology* 16 (2002): 391–405.

54. Fiese et al., "A Review of 50 Years of History."

55. William J. Doherty, *The Intentional Family* (New York: Avon, 1997).

56. Susan Engel, *The Stories Children Tell* (New York: Freeman, 1999), p. 184.

57. Ibid., p. 4.

58. Ibid.

59. Ibid., p. 207.

60. Ibid.

61. Barbara H. Fiese and Kathleen A. T. Marjinsky, "Dinnertime Stories: Connecting Family Practices with Relationship Beliefs and Child Adjustment," in The Stories That Families Tell: Narrative Coherence, Narrative Interaction and Relationship Beliefs, eds. Barbara H. Fiese et al., *Monographs of the Society for Research in Child Development* 64 (2, Serial no. 257) (1999): 52–68.

62. Arnold J. Sameroff and Barbara H. Fiese, "Narrative Connections in the Family Context: Summary and Conclusions," in The Stories That Families Tell," eds. Barbara H. Fiese et al., p. 122.

63. Bianchi, Robinson, and Milkie, *Changing Rhythms of American Family Life.*

64. John P. Robinson and Geoffrey Godbey, *Time for Life* (University Park: Pennsylvania State University Press, 1997), pp. 48–49.

65. Ibid.

66. Ibid., p. 316.

67. Keith Crnic and Christine Low, "Everyday Stresses and Parenting," in *Handbook of Parenting,* 2nd ed., ed. Marc H. Bornstein, vol. 5: *Practical Issues in Parenting* (Mahwah, NJ: Erlbaum, 2002), pp. 243–267; Theodore Dix, "The Affective Organization of Parenting: Adaptive and Maladaptive Processes," *Psychological Bulletin 110* (1991): 3–25.

68. Ernest N. Jouriles, Christopher M. Murphy, and K. Daniel O'Leary, "Effects of Maternal Mood on Mother–Son Interaction Patterns," *Journal of Abnormal Child Psychology* 17 (1989): 513–525.

69. John U. Zussman, "Situational Determinants of Parenting Behavior: Effects of Competing Cognitive Activity," *Child Development* 51 (1980): 772–780.

70. Crnic and Low, "Everyday Stresses and Parenting."

71. Crnic and Low, "Everyday Stresses and Parenting"; Jay Belsky, Keith Crnic, and Sharon Woodworth, "Personality and Parenting: Exploring the Mediating Role of Transient Mood and Daily Hassles," *Journal of Personality* 63 (1995): 905–929.

72. Katherine Covell and Rona Abramovitch, "Understanding Emotion in the Family: Children's and Parents' Attributions of Happiness, Sadness, and Anger," *Child Development* 57 (1987): 985–991.

73. Sarah J. Schoppe-Sullivan, Alice C. Schermerhorn, and E. Mark Cummings, "Marital Conflict and Children's Adjustment: Evaluation of the Parenting Process Model," *Journal of Marriage and Family* 69 (2007): 1118–1134.

74. Mona El-Sheikh and Stephanie A. Whitson, "Longitudinal Relations Between Marital Conflict and Child Adjustment: Vagal Regulation as a Protective Factor," *Journal of Family Psychology* 20 (2006): 30–39; Cummings et al., "Interparental Discord and Child Adjustment."

75. Alice Schermerhorn et al., "Children's Influence in Marital Relationship," *Journal of Family Psychology* 21 (2007): 259–269.

76. Goecke-Morey, Cummings, and Popp, "Children and Marital Conflict Resolution."

77. Nancy Samalin with Catherine Whitney, *Love and Anger: The Parental Dilemma* (New York: Penguin Books, 1992).

78. Jane Nelson, *Positive Discipline* (New York: Ballantine Books, 1981).

79. Rudolf Dreikurs with Vicki Soltz, *Children: The Challenge* (New York: Hawthorne, 1964), pp. 55–56.

80. Jane L. Pearson et al., "Black Grandmothers in Multigenerational Households: Diversity in Family Structures on Parenting in the Woodlawn Community," *Child Development* 61 (1990): 434–442.

81. Peter K. Smith and Linda M. Drew, "Grandparenthood," in *Handbook of Parenting,* 2nd ed., ed. Marc H. Bornstein, vol. 3: *Being and Becoming a Parent* (Mahwah, NJ: Erlbaum, 2002), pp. 141–172.

82. Ibid., p. 147.

83. Ibid.

84. Ibid.

85. Natalie Angier, "Weighing the Grandma Factor," *New York Times,* November 5, 2002, p. D1.

86. Smith and Drew, "Grandparenthood."

87. Peter C. Scales, Peter L. Benson, and Eugene C. Roehlkepartain, *Grading Grownups: American Adults Report on Their Real Relationships with Kids* (Minneapolis MN: Lutheran Brotherhood and Search Institute, 2001).

88. Anita Weiner, Haggai Kuppermintz, and David Guttmann, "Video Home Training (The Orion Project): A Short-Term Preventive and Treatment Intervention for Families of Young Children," *Family Process 33* (1994): 441–453.

89. Jay D. Schvaneveldt, Marguerite Fryer, and Renee Ostler, "Concepts of 'Badness' and 'Goodness' of Parents As Perceived by Nursery School Children," *The Family Coordinator 19* (1970): 98–103.

90. John R. Weisz, "Autonomy, Control and Other Reasons Why 'Mom Is the Greatest': A Content Analysis of Children's Mother's Day Letters," *Child Development 51* (1980): 801–807.

CHAPTER FIVE

1. Julian Guthrie, "New iPhone Roles— Educator, Babysitter," *San Francisco Chronicle,* May 2, 2009, p. C1.

2. Steve Farkas et al., *A Lot Easier Said Than Done: Parents Talk about Raising Children in Today's America* (New York: Public Agenda, 2002).

3. Lynn Okagaki and Diana Johnson Divecha, "Development of Parental Beliefs," in *Parenting: An Ecological Perspective,* eds. Tom Luster and Lynn Okagaki (Hillsdale, NJ: Erlbaum, 1993), pp. 35–67.

4. Kees Keizer, Siegwart Lindenberg, and Linda Steg, "The Spreading of Disorder," *Science 322* (2008): 1681–1685.

5. Elizabeth L. Pollard and Mark L. Rosenberg, "The Strengths-Based Approach to Child Well-Being: Let's Begin with the End in Mind," in *Well-Being: Positive Development Across the Life Course,* eds. Marc H. Bornstein et al. (Mahwah, NJ: Erlbaum, 2003), pp. 131–21.

6. Farkas et al., *A Lot Easier Said than Done.*

7. David A. Sleet and James A. Mercy, "Promotion of Safety, Security, and Well-Being," in *Well-Being,* eds. Bornstein et al., pp. 81–97.

8. Wanda M. Hunter et al., "Injury Prevention Advice in Top-Selling Parenting Books," *Pediatrics 116* (2005): 1080–1088.

9. Linda C. Mayes and Sean D. Truman, "Substance Abuse and Parenting," in *Handbook of Parenting,* 2nd ed., ed. Marc H. Bornstein, vol. 4: *Special Conditions and Applied Parenting* (Mahwah, NJ: Erlbaum, 2002), pp. 329–359.

10. Caroline H. Leavitt, Thomas F. Tonniges, and Martha F. Rogers, "Good Nutrition— The Imperative for Positive Development," in *Well-Being,* ed. Bornstein, 35–49.

11. Gina Kolata, "Thinning the Milk Does Not Mean Thinning the Child," *New York Times,* February 12, 2006, section 4, p. 3.

12. Leavitt, Tonniges, and Rogers, "Good Nutrition."

13. Kaiser Family Foundation Report, "Role of Media on Childhood Obesity," February 2006. *www.kff.org.*

14. Tara Parker-Pope, "How to Give Your Child A Longer Life," *Wall Street Journal,* December 9, 2003, p. R1.

15. Kolata, "Thinning the Milk Does Not Mean Thinning the Child."

16. Jeanette M. Connor, "Physical Activity and Well Being," in *Well-Being,* ed. Bornstein, pp. 65–79.

17. Kim Severson, "Politicians Prodded on Child Obesity," *San Francisco Chronicle,* December 12, 2002, p. A1.

18. Jane E. Brody, "Time to Get Out, for the Body and the Mind," *New York Times,* February 14, 2006, p. D7.

19. Connor, "Physical Activity and Well Being."

20. Beth Azar, "Wild Findings in Animal Sleep," *Monitor on Psychology* (January 2006): 54–55.

21. David Tuller, "Poll Finds Even Babies Don't Get Enough Rest," *New York Times,* March 30, 2004, p. D5.

22. James C. Sillbury et al., "Sleep Behavior in an Urban U.S. Sample of School-Age Children," *Archives of Pediatric and Adolescent Medicine 158* (2004): 988–994.

23. Ronald E. Dahl and Mona El-Sheikh, "Considering Sleep in a Family Context: Introduction to the Special Issue," *Journal of Family Psychology 21* (2007): 1–3.

24. Avi Sadeh, Reut Gruber, and Amiram Raviv, "The Effects of Sleep Restriction and Extension on School-Age Children: What a Difference an Hour Makes," *Child Development* 74 (2003): 444–455.

25. Joseph A. Buckhalt, Mona El-Sheikh, and Peggy Keller, "Children's Sleep and Cognitive Functioning: Race and Socioeconomic Status as Moderators of Effects," *Child Development* 78 (2007): 213–231.

26. Marc Weissbluth, *Healthy Sleep Habits, Happy Child* (New York: Fawcett, 1999).

27. Alice M. Gregory and Thomas G. O'Connor, "Sleep Problems in Childhood: A Longitudinal Study of Developmental Change and Association with Behavioral Problems," *Journal of the American Academy of Child and Adolescent Psychiatry* 41 (2000): 964–971.

28. Emma K. Adam, Emily K. Snell, and Patricia Pendry, "Sleep Timing and Quantity in Ecological and Family Context: A Nationally Representative Time-Diary Study," *Journal of Family Psychology* 21 (2007): 4–19.

29. Mona El-Sheikh et al., "Child Emotional Insecurity and Academic Achievement: The Role of Sleep Disruptions," *Journal of Family Psychology* 21 (2007): 29–38.

30. Rebecca A. Bernert et al., "Family Life Stress and Insomnia Symptoms in a Prospective Evaluation of Young Adults," *Journal of Family Psychology* 21 (2007): 58–66.

31. Robert H. Bradley and Robert F. Corwyn, "Productive Activity and the Prevention of Behavior Problems," *Developmental Psychology* 41 (2005): 89–98.

32. Victoria Rideout, Donald F. Roberts, and Ulla G. Foehr, "Generation M: Media in the Lives of 8–18 Year Olds," Kaiser Family Foundation Report No. 7251, March 2005. www.kff.org.

33. Victoria Rideout and Elizabeth Hamel, "The Media Family: Electronic Media in the Lives of Infants, Toddlers, Pre-schoolers, and Their Parents," Kaiser Family Foundation Report No. 7500, May 2006. www.kff.org.

34. Ibid.

35. American Academy of Pediatrics, "Children, Adolescents, and Television," *Pediatrics* 107 (2001): 423–426

36. Rideout, Roberts, and Foehr, "Generation M."

37. Ibid.

38. Aimee Dorr, Beth E. Rabin, and Sandra Irlen, "Parenting in a Multimedia Society," in *Handbook of Parenting*, 2nd ed., ed. Marc H. Bornstein, vol. 5: *Practical Issues in Parenting* (Mahwah, NJ: Erlbaum, 2002), pp. 349–373.

39. Ulla G. Foehr, "Media Multitasking Among American Youth: Prevalence, Predictors, and Pairings," Kaiser Family Foundation Report No. 7592, December 2006. www.kff.org.

40. Patricia M. Greenfield, "Technology and Informal Education: What Is Taught, What Is Learned," *Science* 323 (2009): 69–71.

41. Rideout and Hamel, "The Media Family."

42. Ibid.

43. Ibid.

44. Dorr, Rabin, and Irlen, "Parenting in a Multimedia Society."

45. Donna L. Mumme and Anne Fernald, "The Infant as Onlooker: Learning from Emotional Reactions Observed in a Television Scenario," *Child Development* 74 (2003): 221–237.

46. Daniel R. Anderson et al., "Early Childhood Television Viewing and Adolescent Behavior," *Monographs of the Society for Research in Child Development* 66 (Serial no. 264) (2001): 1.

47. Greenfield, "Technology and Informal Education," p. 71.

48. Michael I. Posner and Mary K. Rothbart, *Educating the Human Brain* (Washington, DC: American Psychological Association, 2006).

49. Pamela J. Hines, Barbara R. Jasny, and Jeffrey Mervis, "Adding a T to the Three R's," *Science* 323 (2009): 53.

50. Darcy A. Thompson and Dimitri A. Christakis, "The Association between Television Viewing and Irregular Sleep Schedules Among Children Less Than Three Years of Age," *Pediatrics* 116 (2005): 851–856.

51. Dimitri Christakis et al., "Early Television Exposure and Subsequent Attentional Problems in Children," *Pediatrics* 113 (2004): 708–713.

52. Frederick J. Zimmerman and Dimitri A. Christakis, "Children's Television Viewing and Cognitive Outcomes: A Longitudinal Analysis of National Data," *Archives of Pediatric and Adolescent Medicine* 159 (2005): 619–625.

53. Dina L. G. Borzekowski and Thomas N. Robinson, "The Remote, the Mouse, and the No. 2 Pencil," *Archives of Pediatric and Adolescent Medicine 159* (2005): 607–613.

54. Thomas N. Robinson, "Reducing Children's Television to Prevent Obesity: A Randomized Controlled Trial," *Journal of the American Medical Association 282* (1999): 1561–1567.

55. John D. Coie, Donald Lynam, and Kenneth A. Dodge, "Aggression and Antisocial Behavior in Youth," in *Handbook of Child Psychology*, 6th ed., eds. William Damon and Richard M. Lerner, vol. 3: *Social, Emotional, and Personality Development,* ed. Nancy Eisenberg (Hoboken, NJ: Wiley, 2006), p. 746.

56. L. Rowell Huesmann et al., "Longitudinal Relations between Children's Exposure to TV Violence and Their Aggressive and Violent Behavior in Young Adulthood: 1977–1992," *Developmental Psychology 39* (2003): 201–221.

57. Brian H. Bornstein and Monica K. Miller, "Just a Game? Psychologists Play a Critical Role in Video Game Controversy," *Monitor on Psychology* (May 2006): 99.

58. Liliana Escobar-Chaves, "Impact of the Media on Adolescent Sexual Behavior," *Pediatrics 116* (2005): 297–331.

59. Rebecca L. Collins et al., "Watching Sex on Television Predicts Adolescent Initiation of Sexual Behavior," *Pediatrics 114* (2004): 280–289.

60. Jane D. Brown et al., "Sexy Media: Exposure to Sexual Content in Music, Movies, Television, and Magazines Predicts Black and White Adolescents' Sexual Behavior," *Pediatrics 117* (2006): 1018–1027.

61. Escobar-Chaves, "Impact of Media on Adolescent Sexual Behavior."

62. Rideout and Hamel, "The Media Family."

63. Rideout, Roberts, and Foehr, "Generation M."

64. Ibid.

65. Dorr, Rabin, and Irlen, "Parenting in a Multimedia Society."

66. Robinson, "Reducing Children's Television Viewing to Prevent Obesity;"Thomas N. Robinson et al., "Effects of Reducing Children's Television and Video Game Use on Aggressive Behavior: A Randomized Controlled Trial," *Archives of Pediatric and Adolescent Medicine 155* (2001): 17–23.

67. American Academy of Pediatrics, "Children, Adolescents, and Television."

68. Greenfield, "Technology and Informal Education," p. 71.

69. Ross A. Thompson, Sara Meyer, Meredith McGinley, "Understanding Values in Relationships: The Development of Conscience," in *Handbook of Moral Development*, eds. Melanie Killen and Judith Smetana (Mahwah, NJ: Erlbaum, 2006), pp. 267–297.

70. Grazyna Kochanska et al., "Maternal Parenting and Children's Conscience: Early Security as Moderator," *Child Development 75* (2004): 1229–1242.

71. Gerald R. Patterson and Philip A. Fisher, "Recent Developments in Our Understanding of Parenting: Bidirectional Effects, Causal Models, and the Search for Parsimony," in *Handbook of Parenting*, 2nd ed., ed. Marc H. Bornstein, vol. 5: *Practical Issues in Parenting* (Mahwah, NJ: Erlbaum, 2002), pp. 59–88.

72. Barbara Rogoff, "Cognition as Collaborative Process," in *Handbook of Child Psychology*, 5th ed., ed. William Damon, vol. 2: *Cognition, Perception, and Language,* eds. Deanna Kuhn and Robert S. Siegler (New York: Wiley, 1998), pp. 679–744.

73. Ibid.

74. Ibid.

75. Watty Piper, *The Little Engine That Could* (New York: Platt & Monk, 1930).

76. Rudolf Dreikurs with Vicki Soltz, *Children: The Challenge* (New York: Hawthorn, 1964).

77. Ibid., p. 39.

78. Ibid., p.108.

79. Femmie Juffer, Marian J. Bakermans-Kranenburg, and Marinus van IJzendoorn, "Methods of Video-Feedback Programs to Promote Positive Parenting Alone with Sensitive Discipline and with Representational Attachment Discussion," in *Positive Parenting: An Attachment-Based Intervention*, eds. Femmie Juffer, Marian J. Bakermans-Kranenburg, and Marinus van IJzendoorn (New York: Erlbaum, 2008), pp. 11–23.

80. Farkas et al., "Easier Said Than Done."

81. Nancy Eisenberg, Richard A. Fabes, and Tracy L. Spinrad, "Prosocial Development," in *Handbook of Child Psychology*, 6th ed., eds. Damon and Lerner, vol. 3, p. 646.

82. Ibid.

83. Daniel K. Lapsley, "Moral Stage Theory," in *Handbook of Moral Development*, eds. Killen and Smetana, pp. 37–66.

84. Eisenberg, Fabes, and Spinrad, "Prosocial Development."

85. Lashley, "Moral Stage Theory."

86. Ibid.

87. Elliot Turiel, "The Development of Morality," in *Handbook of Child Psychology*, 6th ed., eds. Damon and Lerner, vol. 3, pp. 789–857.

88. Lashley, "Moral Stage Theory."

89. Turiel, "The Development of Morality."

90. Eisenberg, Fabes, and Spinrad, "Prosocial Development."

91. Ibid.

92. Ibid.

93. Turiel, "The Development of Morality."

94. Ibid., p. 845.

95. Dreikurs with Soltz, *Children: The Challenge.*

96. Thomas Gordon, *P.E.T.: Parent Effectiveness Training* (New York: New American Library, 1975).

97. Patricia Chamberlain and Gerald R. Patterson, "Discipline and Child Compliance in Parenting," in *Handbook of Parenting,* ed. Marc H. Bornstein, vol. 4: *Applied and Practical Parenting* (Mahwah, NJ: Erlbaum, 1995), pp. 205–225.

98. Lawrence S. Wissow, "What Clinicians Want to Know about Teaching Families New Disciplinary Tools," *Pediatrics 98* (1996): 815–817.

99. Thomas F. Caltron and John C. Masters, "Mothers' and Children's Conceptualizations of Corporal Punishment," *Child Development 64* (1993): 1815–1828.

100. Murray A. Straus, "Spanking and the Making of a Violent Society," *Pediatrics 98* (1996): 837–844.

101. Farkas et al., "Easier Said Than Done."

102. Diana Baumrind, "Necessary Distinctions," *Psychological Inquiry 8* (1997): 176–182.

103. Vonnie C. McLoyd and Julia Smith, "Physical Discipline and Behavior Problems in African American, European American, and Hispanic Children: Emotional Support As a Moderator," *Journal of Marriage and Family 64* (2002): 40–53.

104. Elizabeth Thompson Gershoff, "Corporal Punishment by Parents and Associated Child Behaviors and Experiences: A Meta-Analysis and Theoretical Review," *Psychological Bulletin 128* (2002): 539–579; Ray Guarendi with David Eich, *Back to the Family* (New York: Simon & Schuster, 1991).

105. Anthony M. Graziano, Jessica L. Hamblen, and Wendy A. Plante, "Subabusive Violence in Child-Rearing in Middle-Class Families," *Pediatrics 98* (1996): 845–848.

106. Randal D. Day, Gary W. Peterson, and Coleen McCracken, "Predicting Spanking of Younger and Older Children by Mothers and Fathers," *Journal of Marriage and the Family 60* (1998): 79–94; Jean Giles-Sims, Murray A. Straus, and David B. Sugarman, "Child, Maternal, and Family Characteristics Associated with Spanking," *Family Relations 44* (1994): 170–176.

107. Glenn D. Wolfner and Richard J. Gelles, "A Profile of Violence toward Children: A National Study," *Child Abuse and Neglect 17* (1993): 199–214.

108. Day, Peterson, and McCracken, "Predicting Spanking."

109. Giles-Sims, Straus, and Sugarman, "Child, Maternal, and Family Characteristics."

110. Day, Peterson, and McCracken, "Predicting Spanking"; Gershoff, "Corporal Punishment"; Giles-Sims, Straus, and Sugarman, "Child, Maternal, and Family Characteristics."

111. Diana Baumrind, "The Development of Instrumental Competence through Socialization," in *Minnesota Symposium on Child Psychology,* Vol. 7, ed. Ann D. Pick (Minneapolis: University of Minnesota Press, 1973), pp: 3–46. Peterson, and McCracken, "Predicting Spanking."

112. Day, Peterson, and McCracken, "Predicting Spanking."

113. McLoyd and Smith, "Physical Discipline and Behavior Problems."

114. Giles-Sims, Straus, and Sugarman, "Child, Maternal, and Family Characteristics."

115. Day, Peterson, and McCracken, "Predicting Spanking."

116. Giles-Sims, Straus, and Sugarman, "Child, Maternal, and Family Characteristics."

117. Ibid.

118. Wissow, "What Clinicians Want to Know about Teaching Families New Disciplinary Tools."

119. Baumrind, "Discipline Controversy Revisited."

120. McLoyd and Smith, "Physical Discipline and Behavior Problems."

121. Ibid., p. 50.
122. Gershoff, "Corporal Punishment."
123. Straus, "Spanking and the Making of a Violent Society."
124. Baumrind, "The Disciplinary Controversy Revisited," p. 413.
125. Patterson and Fisher, "Recent Developments."
126. Robert W. Chamberlin, "It Takes a Whole Village: Working with Community Coalitions to Promote Positive Parenting and Strengthen Families," *Pediatrics 98* (1996): 805.
127. Baumrind, "The Discipline Controversy Revisited," p. 413.
128. Grace Hechinger, *How to Raise a Street-Smart Child* (New York: Ballantine, 1984).
129. Marc H. Bornstein, "Parenting Science and Practice," in *Handbook of Child Psychology*, 6th ed., eds. William Damon and Richard M. Lerner, vol. 4: *Child Psychology in Practice*, eds. K. Ann Renninger and Irving E. Sigel (Hoboken, NJ: Wiley, 2006), pp. 893–949.
130. Carolyn Pape Cowan and Philip A. Cowan, *When Partners Become Parents* (New York: Basic Books, 1992).
131. Carolyn Pape Cowan, Philip A. Cowan, and Gertrude Heming, "Two Variations of a Preventive Intervention for Couples: Effects on Parents and Children During the Transition to School," in *The Family Context of Parenting in Children's Adaptation to Elementary School*, eds. Philip A. Cowan et al. (Mahwah, NJ" Erlbaum, 2005), pp. 277–312.
132. Gene H. Brody et al., "The Strong African-American Families Program: Translating Research into Prevention Programming," *Child Development 75* (2004): 900–917.
133. Camille Smith, Ruth Perou, and Catherine Lesesne, "Parent Education," in *Handbook of Parenting*, 2nd ed., ed. Marc H. Bornstein, vol. 4: *Social Conditions and Applied Parenting*, p. 405.
134. Arnold Gesell and Frances L. Ilg, *The Child from Five to Ten* (New York: Harper & Row, 1946), p. 308.

CHAPTER SIX

1. Peggy Orenstein, "Your Gamete, Myself," New York Times Magazine, July 15, 2007. P. 34.
2. David Lykken, "Parental Licensure," *American Psychologist 56* (2001): 885–894.
3. Christoph Heinicke, "The Transition to Parenting," in *Handbook of Parenting*, 2nd ed., ed. Marc H. Bornstein, vol. 3: *Being and Becoming a Parent* (Mahwah, NJ: Erlbaum, 2002), pp. 363–388.
4. John G. Borkowski, Thomas I. Whitman, and Jaelyn R. Farris, "Adolescent Mothers and Their Children: Risks, Resilience, and Development," in *Risk and Resilience: Adolescent Mothers and Their Children Grow Up*, eds. John G, Borkowski et al. (Mahwah, NJ: Erlbaum, 2007), pp. 1–34.
5. Jeanette M. Connor and James E. Dewey, "Reproductive Health," in *Well Being: A Positive Development Across the Life Course*, eds. Marc H. Bornstein et al. (Mahwah, NJ: Erlbaum, 2003), pp. 99–107.
6. Kelly Musick, "Planned and Unplanned Childbearing Among Unmarried Women," *Journal of Marriage and Family 64* (2002): 915–929.
7. Ibid.
8. Paul R. Amato et al., "Precursors of Young Women's Family Formation Pathways," *Journal of Marriage and Family 70* (2008): 1271–1286.
9. Ibid.
10. D. Wayne Osgood et al., "Six Paths to Adulthood: Fast Starters, Parents without Careers, Educated Partners, Educated Singles, Working Singles, and Slow Starters," in *On the Frontier of Adulthood: Theory, Research, and Public Policy*, eds. Richard A. Settersten, Jr., Frank F. Furstenberg, Jr., and Ruben C. Rumbaut (Chicago: University of Chicago Press, 2005), pp. 320–355.
11. Amato et al., "Precursors of Young Women's Family Formation Pathways"; Robert Schoen and Paula Tufis, "Precursors of Nonmarital Fertility in the United States," *Journal of Marriage and Family 65* (2003): 1030–1040.
12. Osgood et al., "Six Pathways to Adulthood."
13. Katie Zezima, "More Women Than Ever Are Childless, Census Finds," *New York Times,* August 19, 2008, p. A12.
14. Tanya Koropeckorj-Cox and Gretchen Pendell, "The Gender Gap in Attitudes About Childlessness in the United States," *Journal of Marriage and Family 69* (2007): 899–915.
15. Joyce C. Abma and Gladys M. Martinez, "Childlessness Among Older Women in

the United States: Trends and Profiles," *Journal of Marriage and Family* 68 (2006): 1045–1056.

16. Elizabeth Fussell and Frank F. Furstenberg, Jr., "The Transition to Adulthood During the Twentieth Century: Race, Nativity, and Gender," in *On the Frontier of Adulthood.* eds. Settersten Jr., Furstenberg, Jr., and Rumbaut, pp. 29–75.

17. Carolyn Pape Cowan and Philip A. Cowan, *When Partners Become Parents* (New York: Basic Books, 1992).

18. Jacinta Bronte-Tinkew et al., "Resident Fathers' Pregnancy Intentions, Prenatal Behaviors, and Links to Involvement with Infants," *Journal of Marriage Family* 69 (2007): 977–990.

19. Musick, "Planned and Unplanned Childbearing."

20. Conner and Dewey, "Reproductive Health."

21. Jennifer S. Barber, William G. Axinn, and Arland Thornton, "Unwanted Childbearing, Health, and Mother–Child Relationships," *Journal of Health and Social Behavior* 40 (1999): 231–257.

22. Henry P. David, Zdenek Dytrych, and Zdenek Matejcek, "Born Unwanted," *American Psychologist* 58 (2003): 224–229.

23. Adam Pertman, *Adoption Nation* (New York: Perseus, 2000), pp. 47–48.

24. Julia McQuillan et al., "Frustrated Fertility: Infertility and Psychological Distress Among Women," *Journal of Marriage and Family* 65 (2003): 1007–1018.

25. U.S. Census Bureau, *Statistical Abstract of the United States: 2009,* 128th ed. (Washington, DC: Government Printing Office, 2008).

26. Carol Harkness, *The Infertility Book,* 2nd ed. (Berkeley, CA: Celestial Arts, 1992).

27. Andrew Yarrow, *Latecomers: Children of Parents over 35* (New York: Free Press, 1991).

28. Xi-Kuan Chen et al., "Paternal Age and Adverse Birth Outcomes: Teenager or 40 +, Who Is at Risk?" *Human Reproduction* 23 (2008): 1290–1296.

29. Stephanie Belloc, "Father's Age a Factor in Infertility," Paper presented at the European Society of Human Reproduction and Embryology, Barcelona, Spain, July 6, 2008.

30. Emma Frans et al., "Advancing Paternal Age and Bipolar Disorder," *Archives of General Psychiatry* 65 (2008): 1034–1040.

31. Susan Golombok, "Parenting and Contemporary Reproductive Technologies," in *Handbook of Parenting,* 2nd ed., ed, Bornstein, vol. 3, pp. 339–360.

32. J. Reefhuis et al., "Assisted Reproductive Technology and Major Structural Birth Defects in the United States," *Human Reproduction* 24 (2008): 360–366.

33. Debora Spar, *The Baby Business: How Money, Science, and Politics Drive the Commerce of Conception* (Boston: Harvard University Press, 2006).

34. National Center on Birth Defects and Developmental Delays, "Assisted Reproductive Technology and Major Structural Birth Defects United States."

35. Golombok, "Parenting and Contemporary Reproductive Technologies."

36. Pam Belluck, "From Stem Cell Opponents, an Embryo Crusade," *New York Times,* June 2, 2005, p. A1.

37. Pam Belluck, "It's Not So Easy to Adopt an Embryo," *New York Times,* June 12, 2005, section 4, p. 5.

38. Belluck, "From Stem Cell Opponents."

39. Spar, *The Baby Business.*

40. Lori B. Andrews, "Designer Babies," *Reader's Digest,* July 2001, p. 72.

41. Golombok, "Parenting and Contemporary Reproductive Technologies."

42. Susan Golombok et al., "Parenting Infants Conceived by Gamete Donations," *Journal of Family Psychology* 18 (2004): 443–452.

43. Susan Golombok et al., "Families Created Through Surogacy Arrangements: Parent–Child Relationships in the 1st Year of Life," *Developmental Psychology* 40 (2004): 400–411.

44. Golombok, "Parenting and Contemporary Reproductive Technologies."

45. David Plotz, "Who's Your Daddy?" *New York Times,* May 19, 2005, p. A35.

46. Peggy Orenstein, "Looking for a Donor to Call Dad," *New York Times Magazine,* June 18, 1995, p. 28.

47. David M. Brodzinsky and Ellen Pinderhughes, "Parenting and Child Development in Adoptive Families," in *Handbook of Parenting,* 2nd ed., ed. Marc H. Bornstein, vol. 1: *Children and Parenting* (Mahwah, NJ: Erlbaum, 2002), pp. 279–311.

48. Spar, *Baby Business.*

49. Ibid.

50. Edward Zigler et al., *The First Three Years & Beyond* (New Haven CT: Yale University Press, 2002).

51. Ibid.

52. Janet A. DiPietro et al., "Maternal Stress and Affect Influence Fetal Neurobehavioral Development," *Developmental Psychology* 38 (2002): 659–668.

53. Stacey Rosenkrantz Aronson and Aletha C. Huston, "The Mother–Infant Relationship in Single, Cohabiting, and Married Families: A Case for Marriage?" *Journal of Family Psychology* 18 (2004): 5–18.

54. Ellen Galinsky, *Between Generations: The Six Stages of Parenthood* (New York: Times, 1981).

55. Tamar Lewin, "Unwed Fathers Fight for Babies Placed for Adoption by Mothers," *New York Times*, March 19, 2006, p. A1.

56. Ronald Mincy, Irwin Garfinkel, and Lenna Nepomnyaschy, "In-Hospital Paternity Establishment and Father Involvement in Fragile Families," *Journal of Marriage and Family* 67 (2005): 611–626.

57. Melissa Curran et al., "Representations of Early Family Relationships Predict Marital Maintenance During Transition to Parenthood," *Journal of Family Psychology* 19 (2005): 189–197.

58. Ross D. Parke and Barbara J. Tinsley, "Family Interaction in Infancy," in *Handbook of Infant Development*, 2nd ed., ed. Joy Doniger Osofsky (New York: Wiley, 1987), pp. 579–641.

59. Jay Belsky and John Kelly, *The Transition to Parenthood* (New York: Delacorte Press, 1994).

60. Galinsky, *Between Generations*.

61. Myra Leifer, "Psychological Changes Accompanying Pregnancy and Motherhood, *Genetic Psychology Monographs* 95 (1977): 55–96.

62. Cowan and Cowan, *When Partners Become Parents*.

63. Belsky and Kelly, *Transition to Parenthood*.

64. James McHale, *Charting the Bumpy Road of Coparenthood: Understanding the Challenges of Family Life* (Washington, DC: Zero to Three, 2007).

65. Susan Goldberg and Barbara DiVitto, "Parenting Children Born Preterm," in *Handbook of Parenting*, 2nd ed., ed. Bornstein, vol. 1, pp. 329–354.

66. Ruth Feldman et al., "Testing a Family Intervention Hypothesis: The Contribution of Mother–Infant Skin-to-Skin Contact (Kangaroo Care) to Family Interaction Proximity and Touch," *Journal of Family Psychology* 17 (2003): 94–107.

67. Saria Goldstein Ferber and Imad R. Makhoul, "The Effect of Skin-to-Skin Contact (Kangaroo Care) Shortly After Birth on the Neurobehavioral Responses of the Term Newborn: A Randomized, Controlled Trial," *Pediatrics* 113 (2004): 858–865.

68. Galinsky, *Between Generations*.

69. Ibid., p. 317.

70. Kathryn E. Barnard, Colleen E. Morisett, and Susan Spieker, "Preventive Interventions: Enhancing Parent–Infant Relationships," in *Handbook of Infant Mental Health*, ed. Zeanah, pp. 386–401.

71. Amy Wolfson, Patricia Lacks, and Andrew Futterman, "Effects of Parent Training on Infant Sleeping Patterns, Parents' Stress, and Perceived Parental Competence," *Journal of Consulting and Clinical Psychology* 60 (1992): 41–48.

72. Cowan and Cowan, *When Partners Become Parents*.

CHAPTER SEVEN

1. Tara Parker-Pope, "Coping with the Caveman in the Crib," *New York Times*, February 5, 2008, p. 5.

2. Thomas Anders, Beth Goodlin-Jones, and Avi Sadeh, "Sleep Disorders," in *Handbook of Infant Mental Health*, 2nd ed., ed. Charles H. Zeanah, Jr. (New York: Guildford, 2000), pp. 326–338.

3. Marc Weissbluth, *Crybabies* (New York: Arbor House, 1984).

4. Ibid.

5. Ross Thompson, "The Development of the Person: Social Understanding, Relationships, Conscience, Self," in *Handbook of Child Psychology*, 6th ed., eds. William Damon and Richard M. Lerner, vol. 3: *Social, Emotional and Personality Development*, ed. Nancy Eisenberg (Hoboken, NJ: Wiley, 2006), pp. 24–98.

6. Ibid.

7. Tiffany Field, "The Effects of Mother's Physical and Emotional Availability on Emotion Regulation," in Development of Emotion Regulation: Biological and Behavioral Considerations, ed. Nathan A. Fox, *Monographs of the Society for*

Research in Child Development 59, (Serial no. 240) (1994): 208–227.

8. Jayne Standley, "Music Therapy in the NICU: Promoting Growth and Development of Premature Infants," Zero to Three 23, no. 1 (2002): 23–30.

9. Thompson, "The Development of the Person."

10. Ruth Feldman, Charles W. Greenbaum, and Nurit Yirmiya, "Mother–Infant Affect as an Antecedent of the Emergence of Self-Control," Developmental Psychology 35 (1999): 223–231.

11. Thompson, "The Development of the Person."

12. Gabriela Markova and Maria Legerstee, "Contingency, Imitation, and Affect Sharing: Foundations of Infants' Social Awareness," Developmental Psychology 42 (2006): 132–141.

13. Robin Hornick, Nancy Eisenhoover, and Megan Gunnar, "The Effects of Maternal Positive, Neutral, and Negative Affect Communication on Infant Responses to New Toys," Child Development 58 (1987): 936–944.

14. James P. McHale, Charting the Bumpy Road of Coparenthood: Understanding the Challenges of Family Life (Washington, DC: Zero to Three, 2007).

15. Susan Goldberg and Barbara DiVitto, "Parenting Children Born Preterm," in Handbook of Parenting, 2nd ed., ed. Marc H Bornstein, vol. 1: Children and Parenting (Mahwah, NJ: Erlbaum, 2002), pp. 329–354.

16. Ibid.

17. Ibid.

18. Mark T. Greeenberg and Kenneth Crnic, "Longitudinal Predictors of Developmental Status and Social Interaction in Premature and Full-Term Infants at Age Two," Child Development 59 (1988): 544–553.

19. Goldberg and DiVitto, "Parenting Children Born Preterm."

20. Marilyn Stern and Katherine A. Hildebrandt, "Prematurity and Stereotyping: Effects on Mother–Infant Interaction," Child Development 57 (1986): 308–315.

21. Cynthia I. Zarling, Barton J. Hirsch, and Susan Landry, "Maternal Social Networks and Mother–Infant Interactions in Full-Term and Very Low Birthweight, Preterm Infants, Child Development 59 (1988): 178–185.

22. Glenn Affleck et al., "Effects of Formal Support on Mothers' Adaptation to the Hospital-to-Home Transition of High-Risk Infants," Child Development 60 (1989): 488–501.

23. Thompson, "The Development of the Person."

24. Susan Crockenberg and Esther Leerkes, "Infant Social and Emotional Development in Family Context," in Handbook of Infant Mental Health, 2nd ed., ed. Zeanah Jr., pp. 60–90.

25. Herbert Ginsburg and Sylvia Opper, Piaget's Theory of Intellectual Development (Englewood Cliffs, NJ: Prentice-Hall, 1969); Jean Piaget and Barbel Inhelder, The Psychology of the Child (New York: Basic Books, 1969).

26. James V. Wertsch and Peeter Tulviste, "L.S. Vygotsky and Contemporary Developmental Psychology," Developmental Psychology 28 (1992): 548–557.

27. Lois Bloom, "Language Acquisition in Its Developmental Context," in Handbook of Child Psychology, 5th ed., ed. William Damon, vol. 2: Cognition, Perception, and Language, eds. Deanna Kuhn and Robert S. Siegler (New York: Wiley, 1998), pp. 309–370.

28. Shannon M. Pruden et al., "The Birth of Words: Ten-Month-Olds Learn Words Through Perceptual Salience," Child Development 77 (2006): 266–280.

29. Betty Hart and Todd R. Risley, Meaningful Differences in the Everyday Experiences of Young American Children (Baltimore, Brookes, 1995).

30. Elaine Reese and Rhiannon Newcombe, "Training Mothers in Elaborative Reminiscing Enhances Children's Autobiographical Memory and Narrative," Child Development 78 (2007): 1153–1170.

31. Hart and Risley, Meaningful Differences.

32. Michael Cole, Sheila R. Cole, and Cynthia Lightfoot, The Development of Children, 5th ed. (New York: Worth, 2005).

33. Michael Lewis, "The Emergence of Human Emotions," in Handbook of Emotions, 2nd ed., eds. Michael Lewis and Jeannette M. Haviland-Jones (New York: Guilford Press, 2000), pp. 265–280.

34. Theodore Dix et al., "Autonomy and Children's Reactions to Being Controlled: Evidence that Both Compliance and Defiance May Be Positive Markers in Early

Development," *Child Development* 78
(2007): 1204–1221.

35. Lenneke R.A. Alink et al., "The
Early Childhood Aggression Curve:
Development of Physical Aggression in
10- to 50-Month Old Children," *Child
Development* 77 (2006): 954–966.

36. Florence L. Goodenough, *Anger in Young
Children* (Minneapolis: University of
Minnesota Press, 1931).

37. Claire B. Kopp, "Regulation of Distress
and Negative Emotions: A Developmental
View," *Developmental Psychology* 25
(1989): 343–354.

38. Marion Radke-Yarrow et al., "Learning
Concern for Others," *Developmental
Psychology* 8 (1973): 240–260; Herbert
Wray, *Emotions in the Lives of Young
Children,* Department of Health, Education,
and Welfare Publication no. 78-644
(Rockville, MD, 1978); Carolyn Zahn-
Waxler et al., "Development of Concern
for Others," *Developmental Psychology* 28
(1992): 126–136.

39. Thompson, "The Development of the
Person."

40. Deborah Stipek, Susan Recchia, and Susan
McClintic, Self-Evaluation in Young
Children, *Monographs of the Society for
Research in Child Development* 57 (Serial
no. 226) (1992).

41. Harriet L. Rheingold, Kay V. Cook, and
Vicki Kolowitz, "Commands Cultivate
the Behavioral Pleasure of Two-Year-Old
Children," *Developmental Psychology* 23
(1987): 146–151.

42. Susan Harter, "The Self," in *Handbook of
Child Psychology,* 6th ed., eds. William
Damon and Richard M. Lerner, vol.
3: *Social, Emotional, and Personality
Development,* ed. Nancy Eisenberg
(Hoboken, NJ: Wiley, 2006), pp. 505–571.

43. Claire B. Kopp, "Antecedents of Self-
Regulation: A Developmental Perspective,"
Developmental Psychology 18 (1982):
199–214; Susan D. Calkins, "Early
Attachment Processes and the Develop-
ment of Emotional Self-Regulation," in
Handbook of Self-Regulation, eds. Roy
F. Baumeister and Kathleen D. Vohs
(New York: Guilford Press, 2004),
pp. 324–339.

44. Donelda J. Stayton, Robert Hogan,
and Mary D. Salter Ainsworth, "Infant
Obedience and Maternal; Behavior: The

Origins of Socialization Reconsidered,"
Child Development 42 (1971): 1057–1069.

45. Kopp, "Antecedents of Self-Regulation."

46. Brian E. Vaughn et al., "Process Analysis
of the Behavior of Very Young Children in
Daily Tasks," *Developmental Psychology* 22
(1986): 752–759.

47. Kenneth H. Rubin, William M. Bukowski,
and Jeffrey G. Parker, "Peer Interactions,
Relationships, and Groups," in *Handbook
of Child Psychology,* 6th ed., eds. Damon
and Lerner, vol. 3, pp. 571–645.

48. Marianne S. De Wolff and Marinus van
IJzendoorn, "Sensitivity and Attachment:
A Meta-Analysis on Parental Antecedents
of Infant Attachment," *Child Development*
68 (1997): 571–591.

49. Jutta Heckhausen, "Balancing
for Weaknesses and Challenging
Developmental Potential: A Longitudinal
Study of Mother-Infant Dyads
in Apprenticeship Interactions,"
Developmental Psychology 23 (1987):
762–770.

50. Ross D. Parke, "Fathers and Families," in
Handbook of Parenting, 2nd ed., ed. Marc
H. Bornstein, vol. 3: *Being and Becoming
a Parent* (Mahwah, NJ: Erlbaum, 2002),
pp. 27–73.

51. W. Jean Yeung et al., "Children's Time
with Fathers in Intact Families," *Journal of
Marriage and Family* 63 (2001): 136–154.

52. Ibid.

53. Parke, "Fathers and Families."

54. Kathryn E. Barnard and JoAnne E.
Solchany, "Mothering," in *Handbook of
Parenting,* 2nd ed., ed. Bornstein, vol. 3,
pp. 3–25.

55. Parke, "Fathers and Families."

56. Jay Belsky, Bonnie Gilstrap, and Michael
Rovine, "The Pennsylvania Infant and
Family Development Project I: Stability
and Change in Mother–Infant and Father–
Infant Interaction in a Family Setting at
One, Three, and Nine Months," *Child
Development* 55 (1984): 692–705.

57. Marc H. Bornstein, "Parenting Infants,"
in *Handbook of Parenting,* 2nd ed, ed.
Bornstein, vol. 1, pp. 3–43.

58. T. Berry Brazelton and Stanley I.
Greenspan, *The Irreducible Needs of
Children* (Cambridge, MA: Perseus, 2000).

59. Patricia M. Greenfield, Lalita K. Suzuki,
and Carrie Rothstein-Fisch, "Cultural
Pathways Through Human Development,"

in *Handbook of Child Psychology*, 6th ed., eds. William Damon and Richard M. Lerner, vol. 4: *Child Psychology in Practice*, eds. K. Ann Renninger and Irving E. Sigel (Hoboken, NJ: Wiley, 2006), pp. 665–775.

60. Sylvia M. Bell and Mary D. Salter Ainsworth, "Infant Crying and Maternal Responsiveness," *Child Development 43* (1972): 1171–1190.

61. Judy Dunn, *Distress and Comfort* (Cambridge, MA: Harvard University Press, 1977), p. 23.

62. Urs A. Hunziker and Ronald G. Barr, "Increased Carrying Reduces Crying: A Randomized Controlled Trial," *Pediatrics* 77 (1986).

63. Elizabeth Anisfeld et al., "Does Infant Carrying Promote Attachment?: An Experimental Study of the Effects of Increased Physical Contact on the Development of Attachment," *Child Development 61* (1990): 1617–1627.

64. Suzi Tortora, "Studying the Infant's Multisensory Environment: A Bridge Between Biology and Psychology," *Zero to Three 24* (May 2004): 13–24.

65. Jodi A. Mindell, *Sleeping Through the Night*, rev. ed. (New York: HarperCollins, 2005).

66. William A. H. Sammons, *The Self-Calmed Baby* (Boston: Little, Brown, 1989).

67. Gilda Morelli et al., "Cultural Variations in Infants' Sleeping Arrangements: Questions of Independence," *Developmental Psychology 28* (1992): 604–613.

68. Richard Ferber, *Solve Your Child's Sleep Problems*, rev. ed. (New York: Simon & Schuster, 2006).

69. Mindell, *Sleeping Through the Night*.

70. Ibid.

71. Ibid.

72. Task Force on Sudden Infant Death Syndrome, "The Changing Concept of Sudden Infant Death Syndrome: Diagnostic Coding Shifts, Controversies Regarding the Sleeping Environment, and New Variables to Consider in Reducing Risk," *Pediatrics 116* (2005): 1245–1255.

73. Ibid.

74. Ibid.; Ferber, *Solve Your Child's Sleep Problems*; Mindell, *Sleeping Through the Night*.

75. William Sears, introduction to *Attachment Parenting* by Katie Allison Granju with Betsy Kennedy (New York: Pocket Books, 1999).

76. Katie Allison Granju with Betsy Kennedy, *Attachment Parenting* (New York: Pocket Books, 1999).

77. Ibid., p. 9.

78. Ibid., p. 10.

79. Kate Harwood, Neil McLean, and Kevin Durkin, "First-Time Mothers' Expectations of Parenthood: What Happens When Optimistic Expectations Are Not Matched by Later Experiences?" *Developmental Psychology 43* (2007): 1–12.

80. Linda Gilkerson, Larry Gray, and Nancy Mark, "Fussy Babies, Worried Families, and a New Service Network," *Zero to Three 25* (Januaary 2005): 34–41.

81. Ibid.

82. Deborah Laible and Ross A. Thompson, "Early Socialization: A Relationship Perspective," in *Handbook of Socialization: Theory and Research*, eds. Joan E. Grusec and Paul D. Hastings (New York: Guilford Press, 2007), pp. 181–207.

83. Laible and Thompson, "Early Socialization."

84. J. Heidi Gralinski and Claire B. Kopp, "Everyday Rules for Behavior: Mothers' Requests to Young Children," *Developmental Psychology 29* (1993): 573–584.

85. Cheryl Minton, Jerome Kagan, and Janet A. Levine, "Maternal Control and Obedience in the Two-Year-Old," *Child Development 42* (1971): 1873–1894.

86. Marja C. Paulussen-Hoogeboom et al., "Child Negative Emotionality and Parenting from Infancy to Preschool: A Meta-Analytic Review," *Developmental Psychology 43* (2007): 438–453.

87. Thompson, "The Development of the Person."

88. Grazyna Kochanska, Nazam Aksan, and Mary E. Joy, "Children's Fearfulness as a Moderator of Parenting in Early Socialization: Two Longitudinal Studies," *Developmental Psychology 43* (2007): 222–237.

89. Ibid.

90. Marc H. Bornstein, "On the Significance of Social Relationships in the Development of Children's Earliest Symbolic Play: An Ecological Perspective," in *Play and Development: Evolutionary, Sociocultural, and Functional Perspectives*, eds. Artin Goncu and Suzanne Gaskins (Mahwah, NJ: Erlbaum, 2007), pp. 101–129.

91. Robert H. Bradley and Robert F. Corwyn, "Productive Activity and the Prevention

of Behavior Problems," *Developmental Psychology 41* (2005): 89–98.

92. Robert H. Bradley and Robert F. Corwyn, "Externalizing Problems in Fifth Grade: Relations With Productive Activity, Maternal Sensitivity, and Harsh Parenting From Infancy Through Middle Childhood," *Developmental Psychology 43* (2007): 1390–1401.

93. Helen Raikes et al., "Mother–Child Bookreading in Low-Income Families; Correlates and Outcomes During the First Three Years of Life," *Child Development 77* (2006): 924–953.

94. Ellen Galinsky, *Between Generations: The Six Stages of Parenthood* (New York: Basic Books, 1981).

95. McHale, *The Bumpy Road of Coparenthood.*

96. Tiffany Field, "Psychologically Depressed Parents," in *Handbook of Parenting,* ed. Marc H. Boorstein, vol. 4: *Applied and Practical Parenting* (Mahwah, NJ: Erlbaum, 1995), pp. 85–99.

97. Ibid.

98. Sharon B. Ashman, Geraldine Dawson, and Heracles Panagiotides, "Trajectories of Maternal Depression over 7 Years: Relations with Child Psychophysiology and Behavior and Role of Contextual Risks," *Development and Psychopathology 20* (2008): 55–77.

99. Carolyn Zahn-Waxler et al., "Antecedents of Problem Behaviors in Children of Depressed Mothers," *Development and Psychopathology 2* (1990): 271–291.

100. Field, "Psychologically Depressed Parents."

101. Daphne Blunt Bugental et al., "A Cognitive Approach to Child Abuse Prevention," *Journal of Family Psychology 16* (2002): 243–258.

102. *Zero to Three 28* (November 2007): 48.

103. Claire Lerner and Amy Laura Dombro, *What's Best for My Baby and Me?* (Washington, DC: Zero to Three Press, 2006).

104. Patricia K. Coleman and Katherine H. Karraker, "Self-Efficacy and Parenting Quality: Findings and Future Applications," *Developmental Review 18* (1997): 47–85.

CHAPTER EIGHT

1. Robin Morantz Henig, "Taking Play Seriously." *New York Times Magazine,* February 17, 2008, p. 38.

2. Allison Gopnik, Andrew N. Meltzer, and Patricia K. Kuhl, *The Scientist in the Crib* (New York: Morrow, 1999).

3. Jean Piaget and Barbel Inhelder, *The Psychology of the Child* (New York: Basic Books, 1969).

4. Rebecca A. Williamson, Andrew N. Meltzoff, and Ellen Markman, "Prior Experiences and Perceived Efficacy Influence 3-Year-Olds' Imitation," *Developmental Psychology 44* (2008): 275–285.

5. Melissa A. Koenig and Paul L. Harris, "Preschoolers Mistrust Ignorant and Inaccurate Speakers," *Child Development 76* (2005): 1261–1277.

6. Ross A. Thompson, "The Development of the Person: Social Understanding, Relationships, Conscience, Self," in *Handbook of Child Psychology,* 6th ed. eds. William Damon and Richard M. Lerner, vol. 3: *Social, Emotional, and Personality Development,* ed. Nancy Eisenberg (Hoboken, NJ: Wiley, 2006), pp. 24–98.

7. Clancy Blair, Douglas Granger, and Rachel Peters Razza, "Cortisol Reactivity Is Positively Related to Executive Function in Preschool Children Attending Head Start," *Child Development 76* (2005): 554–567.

8. Lisa A. Turner and Burke Johnson, "A Model of Mastery Motivation for At-Risk Preschoolers," *Journal of Educational Psychology 95* (2003): 495–505.

9. Lois Bloom, "Language Acquisition in Its Developmental Context," in *Handbook of Child Psychology,* 5th ed., ed. William Damon, vol. 2: *Cognition, Perception, and Language,* eds. Deanna Kuhn and Robert S. Siegler (New York: Wiley, 1998), pp. 309–370.

10. Betty Hart and Todd R. Risley, *Meaningful Differences in the Everyday Experiences of American Children* (Baltimore: Brookes, 1995).

11. Ibid.

12. NICHD Early Child Care Research Network, "Pathways to Reading: The Role of Oral Language in the Transition to Reading," *Developmental Psychology 41* (2005): 428–442.

13. William Roberts and Janet Strayer, "Parents' Responses to the Emotional Distress of Their Children: Relations with Children's Competence," *Developmental Psychology 23* (1987): 415–422.

14. Thompson, "The Development of the Person."

15. Inge Bretherton et al., "Learning to Talk about Emotions: A Functionalist Perspective," *Child Development* 57 (1986): 529–548.

16. Thompson, "The Development of the Person.".

17. Michael Lewis and Margaret Wolan Sullivan, "The Development of Self-Conscious Emotions," in *Handbook of Competence and Motivation*, eds. Andrew J. Elliott and Carol S. Dweck (New York: Guilford Press, 2005), pp. 185–201.

18. Ibid.

19. NICHD Early Child Care Research Network, Trajectories of Physical Aggression from Toddlerhood to Middle Childhood, *Monographs of the Society for Research in Child Development*, 69 (Serial no. 278) (2004).

20. Carolyn Webster-Stratton, M. Jamila Reid, and Mary Hammond, "Preventing Conduct Problems, Promoting Social Competence: A Parent and Teacher Training Partnership in Head Start," *Journal of Child Clinical Psychology* 30 (2001): 283–302.

21. Jerome Kagan and Nancy Snidman, "Temperamental Factors in Human Development," *American Psychologist* 46 (1991): 856–862.

22. Kenneth H. Rubin et al., "Parenting Beliefs and Behaviors: Initial Findings from the International Consortium for the Study of Emotional Development (ICSSED)," in *Parenting Beliefs, Behaviors, and Parent–Child Relations: A Cross-Cultural Perspective,* eds. Kenneth H. Rubin and Ock Boon Chung (New York: Psychology Press, 2006), pp. 81–103.

23. Richard A. Fabes et al., "Preschoolers Attributions of the Situational Determinants of Others' Naturally Occurring Emotions," *Developmental Psychology* 24 (1988): 376–385.

24. Nancy Eisenberg, Richard A. Fabes, and Tracy L. Spinrad, "Prosocial Development," in *Handbook of Child Psychology*, 6th ed, eds. Damon and Lerner, vol. 3: pp. 646–718.

25. Susan Harter, "The Self," in *Handbook of Child Psychology*, 6th ed., eds. Damon and Lerner, vol. 3: pp. 505–570.

26. Jeffrey R. Measelle, "Children's Self-Perceptions As a Link Between Family Relationship Quality and Social Adaptation to School," in *The Family Context of Parenting in Children's Adaptation to Elementary School,* eds. Philip A. Cowan et al. (Mahwah, NJ: Erlbaum, 2005), pp. 163–187.

27. Harter, "The Self."

28. Diane N. Ruble, Carol Lynn Martin, and Sheri A. Berenbaum, "Gender Development," in *Handbook of Child Psychology*, 6th ed., eds. Damon and Lerner, vol. 3, pp. 858–932.

29. Susan Golombok and Robyn Fivush, *Gender Development* (New York: Cambridge University Press, 1994), p. 111.

30. Diane N. Ruble et al., "The Role of Gender Constancy in Early Gender Development," *Child Development* 78 (2007): 1121–1136.

31. Susan A. Gelman, Marianne G. Taylor, and Simone P. Nguyen, Mother–Child Conversations about Gender, *Monographs of the Society for Research in Child Development,* 69 (Serial no. 275) (2004).

32. Ruble, Martin and Berenbaum, "Gender Development."

33. Carolyn Zahn-Waxler, "Warriors and Worriers: Gender and Psychopathology," *Development and Psychopathology* 5 (1993): 79–89.

34. Ross D. Parke and Raymond Buriel, "Socialization in the Family: Ethnic and Ecological Perspectives," in *Handbook of Child Psychology,* 6th ed., eds. Damon and Lerner, vol. 3, p. 465.

35. Brett Laursen and Vickie Williams, "The Role of Ethnic Identity in Personality Development," in *Pathways to Successful Development: Personality in the Life Course,* eds. Lea Pulkkinen and Avshalom Caspi (New York: Cambridge University Press, 2002), pp. 203–226.

36. Margaret O'Brien Caughey et al., "The Influence of Racial Socialization Practices on the Cognitive and Behavioral Competence of African American Preschoolers," *Child Development* 73 (2002): 1611–1625.

37. Judith G. Smetana, "Social-Cognitive Domain Theory: Consistencies and Variations in Children's Moral and Social Judgments," in *Handbook of Moral Development*, eds. Melanie Killen and Judith G. Smetana (Mahwah, NJ: Erlbaum, 2006): pp. 119–153.

38. Charles W. Kalish and Rebecca Cornelius, "What Is to Be Done?: Children's

Ascriptions of Conventional Obligations," *Child Development* 78 (2007): 859–878.

39. Smetana, "Social-Cognitive Domain Theory."

40. Kristin Hansen Lagattuta, "When You Shouldn't Do What You Want to Do: Young Children's Understanding of Desires, Rules, and Emotions," *Child Development* 78 (2005): 713–733.

41. Daniel Hart, Robert Atkins, and Suzanne Fegley, "Personality Development in Childhood: A Person-Centered Approach," *Monographs of the Society for Research in Child Development, 68,* (Serial no. 272) (2003).

42. Parke and Buriel, "Socialization in the Family."

43. Thompson, "The Development of the Person."

44. Femmie Juffer, Marian J. Bakermans-Kranenburg, and Marinus H. van IJzendoorn, *Promoting Positive Parenting: An Attachment-Based Intervention* (New York: Erlbaum, 2007); Judi Mesman et al., "Extending the Video-Feedback Intervention to Sensitive Discipline: The Early Intervention of Anitsocial Behavior," in *Promoting Positive Parenting,* eds. Juffer, Bakermans-Kranenburg, and van IJzendoorn, pp. 171–191.

45. James P. McHale, *Charting the Bumpy Road of Coparenthood* (Washington, DC: Zero to Three, 2007).

46. Laura E. Berk, *Awakening Children's Minds* (New York: Oxford, University Press 2001).

47. Parke and Buriel, "Socialization in the Family."

48. Philip A. Cowan, Isabel Bradburn, and Carolyn Pape Cowan, "Parents' Working Models of Attachment: The Intergenerational Context of Parenting and Children's Adaptation to School," in *The Family Context of Parenting in Children's Adaptation to Elementary School,* eds. Cowan et al., pp. 209–235.

49. Ibid.

50. Campbell Leaper, "Parenting Boys and Girls," in *Handbook of Parenting,* 2nd ed., ed. Marc H. Bornstein, vol. 1: *Children and Parenting* (Mahwah, NJ: Erlbaum, 2002), pp. 189–225; Ruble, Martin, and Berenbaum, "Gender Development."

51. Campbell Leaper, "Gender Affiliation, Assertion, and the Interactive Context of Parent-Child Play," *Developmental Psychology* 36 (2000), 381–393.

52. Beverly I. Fagot, "Parenting Boys and Girls," in *Handbook of Parenting,* ed. Marc H. Bornstein, vol. 1: *Children and Parenting* (Mahwah, NJ: Erlbaum, 1995), pp. 163–183.

53. Leaper, "Parenting Boys and Girls."

54. Gelman, Taylor, and Nguyen, *Mother–Child Conversations.*

55. Meagan M. Patterson and Rebecca S. Bigler, "Preschool Children's Attention to Environmental Messages About Groups," *Child Development* 77 (2006): 847–860.

56. Gelman, Taylolr, and Nguyen, "Mother–Child Conversations."

57. Ruble, Martin, and Berenbaum, "Gender Development."

58. Jeanette Hsu, "Marital, Quality, Sex-Typed Parenting, and Girls' and Boys' Expression of Problems Behaviors," in *The Family Context of Parenting in Children's Adaptation to Elementary School,* eds. Cowan et al., pp. 139–162.

59. Caughey et al., "The Influence of Racial Socialization Practices."

60. Peggy J. Miller, "Personal Storytelling as a Medium of Socialization in Chinese and American Families," *Child Development* 68 (1997): 557–568.

61. Robert Serpell et al., "Intimate Culture of Families in the Early Socialization of Literacy," *Journal of Family Psychology* 16 (2002): 391–405.

62. Geetha B. Ramani and Robert S. Siegler, "Promoting Broad and Stable Improvements in Low-Income Children's Numerical Knowledge Through Playing Number Board Games," *Child Development* 79 (2008): 375–394.

63. Catherine S. Tamis-LaMonda, Ina C. Uzgiris, and Marc H. Bornstein, "Play in Parent-Child Interaction," in *Handbook of Parenting,* 2nd ed., ed. Marc H. Bornstein, vol. 5: *Practical Issues in Parenting* (Mahwah, NJ: Erlbaum, 2002), pp. 221–241.

64. McHale, *Charting the Bumpy Road of Coparenthood.*

65. Nazli Baydar, April Geek, and Jeanne Brooks-Gunn, "A Longitudinal Study of the Effects of the Birth of a Sibling During the First 6 Years of Life," *Journal of Marriage and the Family* 59 (1997): 939–956; Nazli Baydar, Patricia Hyle, and Jeanne Brooks-Gunn, "A Longitudinal Study of the Effects of the Birth of Sibling During Preschool and Early Grade School

Years," *Journal of Marriage and the Family* 59 (1997): 957–965.

66. Robert B. Stewart et al., "The Firstborn's Adjustment to the Birth of a Sibling: A Longitudinal Assessment," *Child Development* 58 (1987): 341–355.

67. Judy Dunn, "Siblings and Socialization," in *Handbook of Socialization: Theory and Research,* eds. Joan E. Grusec and Paul D. Hastings (New York: Guilford Press, 2007), pp. 309–327.

68. Judith F. Dunn, Robert Plomin, and Denise Daniels, "Consistency and Change in Mothers' Behavior Toward Young Siblings," *Child Development* 57 (1986): 348–356; Judith F. Dunn, Robert Plomin, and Margaret Nettles, "Consistency of Mothers' Behavior Toward Infant Siblings," *Developmental Psychology* 21 (1985): 1188–1195.

69. Dunn, "Siblings and Socialization."

70. Carollee Howes, Peer Interaction of Young Children, *Monographs of the Society for Research in Child Development,* 53 (Serial no. 217) (1987).

71. Kenneth H. Rubin, William M. Bukowski, and Jeffrey G. Parker, "Peer Interactions, Relationships, and Groups," in *Handbook of Child Psychology,* 6th ed., eds. Damon and Lerner, vol. 3, pp. 571–645.

72. Ibid.

73. Ibid.

74. Ibid.

75. Richard Ferber, *Solve Your Child's Sleep Problems,* rev. ed. (New York: Simon & Schuster, 2006).

76. Patty Rhule, "Sleep Trouble in School-Aged Kids," *USA Weekend,* November 15–17, 2002, p. 16.

77. Ferber, *Solve Your Child's Sleep Problems.*

78. Ibid., p. 163.

79. Ibid.

80. Jodi Mindell, *Sleeping Through the Night,* rev. ed.(New York: HarperCollins, 2005).

81. Ross A. Thompson and Sara Meyer, "Socialization of Emotion Regulation in the Family," in *Handbook of Emotion Regulation,* ed. James J. Gross (New York: Guilford Press, 2007), pp. 249–268.

82. Thomas Gordon with Judith Gordon Sands, *P.E.T. in Action* (New York: Bantam, 1978).

83. John D. Krumboltz and Helen B. Krumboltz, *Changing Children's Behavior* (Englewood Cliffs, NJ: Prentice-Hall, 1972).

84. Stanley Turecki and Leslie Tonner, *The Difficult Child* (New York: Bantam, 1972).

85. Dunn, "Siblings and Socialization."

86. Gordon with Sands, *P.E.T. in Action.*

87. Rudolf Dreikurs with Vicki Soltz, *Children the Challenge* (New York: Hawthorn, 1964).

88. David M. Buss, Jeanne H. Block and Jack Block, "Preschool Activity Level: Personality Correlates and Developmental Implications," *Child Development* 51 (1980): 401–408.

89. David M. Buss, "Predicting Parent–Child Interaction from Children's Activity Level," *Developmental Psychology* 17 (1981): 59–65.

90. Marinus H. van IJzendoorn, Marian J. Bakermans-Kranenburg, and Femmie Juffer, "Video Feedback Intervention to Promote Positive Parenting: Evidence-Based Intervention for Enhancing Sensitivity and Security," in *Promoting Positive Parenting,* eds. Juffer, Bakermans-Kranenburg, and van IJzendoorn, pp. 193–202.

91. Berk, *Awakening Children's Minds.*

92. Robert Eimers and Robert Aitchison, *Effective Parents/Responsible Children* (New York: McGraw-Hill, 1977).

93. Kenneth H. Rubin and Kim B. Burgess, "Parents of Aggressive and Withdrawn Children," in *Handbook of Parenting,* 2nd ed., ed. Bornstein, vol. 1, pp. 383–418.

94. Webster-Stratton, Reid, and Hammond, "Preventing Conduct Problems, Promoting Social Competence."

95. Paul D. Hastings et al., "The Development of Concerns for Others in Children with Behavior Problems," *Developmental Psychology* 36 (2000): 531–546.

96. Rubin and Burgess, "Parents of Aggressive and Withdrawn Children."

97. National Center for Birth Defects and Developmental Disabilities, "Autistic Spectrum Disorders Overview," www.cdc.gov/ncbddd/autism/overview.htm, 4/7/2008.

98. Linda Gilkerson and Frances Stott, "Parent–Child Relationships in Early Intervention with Infants and Toddlers with Disabilities and Their Families," in *Handbook of Infant Mental Health,* 2nd ed., ed. Charles H. Zeanah, Jr. (New York: Guilford Press, 2000), p. 460.

99. Penny Hauser-Cram et al., Children with Disabilities, *Monographs of the Society for*

Research in Child Development 66, (Serial no. 266) (2001).

100. Berk, *Awakening Children's Minds,* p. 180.
101. Ellen Galinsky, *Between Generations: The Six Stages of Parenthood* (New York: Times Books, 1981).
102. McHale, *Charting the Bumpy Road of Coparenthood,* p. 252.
103. Measelle, "Children's Self-Perceptions."
104. Carolyn Pape Cowan, Philip A. Cowan, and Gertrude Heming, "Two Variations of a Preventive Intervention for Couples: Effects on Parents and Children During the Transition to School," in *The Family Context of Parenting in Children's Adaptation to Elementary School,* eds. Cowan et al., pp. 163–187.

CHAPTER NINE

1. Perri Klass, "At Last, Facing Down Bullies (and Their Enablers)," *New York Times,* June 9, 2009, D 5.
2. Clancy Blair, "School Readiness: Integrating Cognition and Emotion in a Neurobiological Conceptualization of Children's Functioning at School Entry," *American Psychologist 57* (2002): 111–127.
3. W. Andrew Collins, Stephanie D. Madsen, and Amy Susman-Stillman, "Parenting during Middle Childhood," in *Handbook of Parenting,* 2nd ed., ed. Marc H. Bornstein, vol. 1: *Children and Parenting* (Mahwah, NJ: Erlbaum, 2002), pp. 73–101.
4. Robert S. Siegler, "Microgenetic Analyses of Learning," in *Handbook of Child Psychology,* 6th ed., eds. William Damon and Richard M. Lerner, vol. 2: *Cognition, Perception, and Language,* eds. Deanna Kuhn and Robert S. Siegler (Hoboken, NJ: Wiley, 2006), pp. 464–510.
5. Emilie Phillips Smith et al., "Opportunities for Schools to Promote Resilience in Children and Youth," in *Investing in Children, Youth, Families, and Communities: Strength-Based Research and Policy,* eds. Kenneth I. Maton et al. (Washington, DC: American Psychological Association, 2004), pp. 213–231.
6. Allan Wigfield et al., "Development of Achievement Motivation," in *Handbook of Child Psychology,* 6th ed., eds. William Damon and Richard M. Lerner, vol. 3: *Social, Emotional, and Personality Development,* ed. Nancy Eisenberg (Hoboken, NJ: Wiley, 2006), pp. 933–1002.

7. Ibid.
8. Ibid.
9. Jennifer A. Fredricks and Jacquelynne S. Eccles, "Children's Competence and Value Beliefs from Childhood through Adolescence: Growth Trajectories in Two Male-Typed Domains," *Developmental Psychology 38* (2002): 519–533.
10. Jennifer A. Fredricks, Sandra Simpkins, and Jacquelynne S. Eccles, "Family Socialization, Gender, and Participation in Sports and Instrumental Music," in *Developmental Pathways Through Middle Childhood: Rethinking Contexts and Diversity as Resources,* eds. Catherine R. Cooper et al. (Mahwah, NJ: Erlbaum, 2005), pp 41–62.
11. Eva M. Pomerantz, Wendy S. Grolnick, and Carrie E. Price, "The Role of Parents in How Children Approach Achievement: A Dynamic Process Perspective," in *Handbook of Competence and Motivation,* eds. Andrew J. Elliot and Carol S. Dweck (New York: Guilford Press, 2005), pp. 259–278.
12. Eva M. Pomerantz, Qian Wang, and Florrie Fei-Yin Ng, "Mothers' Affect in the Homework Context: The Importance of Staying Positive," *Developmental Psychology 41* (2005): 414–427.
13. Pomerantz, Grolnick, and Price, "The Role of Parents in How Children Approach Achievement."
14. Smith et al., "Opportunities for Schools to Promote Resilience in Children and Youth."
15. Bridget K. Hamre and Robert C. Pianta, "Can Instructional and Emotional Support in the First-Grade Classroom Make a Difference for Children at Risk of School Failure?", *Child Development 76* (2005): 949–967.
16. Heidi Gazelle, "Class Climate Moderates Peer Relations and Emotional Adjustment in Children With an Early History of Anxious Solitude: A Child X Environment Model," *Developmental Psychology 42* (2006): 1179–1192.
17. Karin S. Frey and Diane Ruble, "What Children Say about Classroom Performance: Sex and Grade Differences in Perceived Competence: Sex and Grade Differences in Perceived Competence," *Child Development 58* (1987): 1066–1078.
18. Wigfield et al., "Development of Achievement Motivation."

19. Deborah Stipek, "Children As Unwitting Agents in Their Developmental Pathways," in *Developmental Pathways Through Middle Childhood,* eds. Catherine R. Cooper et al. (Mahwah, NJ: Erlbaum, 2005), pp. 99–120.

20. NICHD Early Child Care Research Network, Trajectories of Physical Aggression from Toddlerhood to Childhood, *Monographs of the Society for Research in Child Development 69,* (Serial no. 278), (2004).

21. Mona El Sheikh et al., "Child Emotional Insecurity and Academic Achievement: The Role of Sleep Disruptions," *Journal of Family Psychology 21* (2007): 29–38.

22. Wigfield et al., "Development of Academic Motivation."

23. Patricia M. Greenfield, Lalita K. Sazuki, and Carrie Rothstein-Fisch, "Cultural Pathways Through Human Development," in *Handbook of Child Psychology,* 6th ed., eds. William Damon and Richard M. Lerner, vol. 4: *Child Psychology in Practice,* eds. K. Ann Renninger and Irving E. Sigel (Hoboken, NJ: Wiley, 2006), pp. 655–699.

24. Laura T. Zionts, "Examining Relationships between Students and Teachers: A Potential Extension of Attachment Theory," in *Attachment in Middle Childhood,* eds. Kathryn A. Kerns and Rhonda H. Richardson (New York: Guilford Press, 2005), pp. 231–254.

25. Cynthia T. Garcia Coll, Laura Szalacha, and Natalia Palacios, "Children of Dominican, Portuguese, and Cambodian Immigrant Families: Academic Attitudes and Pathways During Middle Childhood," in *Developmental Pathways Through Middle Childhood,* eds. Cooper et al., pp. 207–233.

26. Andrew J. Fuligni et al., "Family Obligation and the Academic Motivation of Young Children from Immigrant Families," in *Developmental Pathways Through Middle Childhood,* eds. Cooper et al., pp. 261–282.

27. Greenfield, Suzuki, and Rothstein-Fisch, "Cultural Pathways Through Human Development."

28. Carolyn Saarni et al., "Emotional Development: Action, Communication, and Understanding," in *Handbook of Child Psychology* , 6th ed., eds. Damon and Lerner, vol. 3, pp. 226–299.

29. Dayna Fuchs and Mark H. Thelen, "Children's Expected Interpersonal Consequences of Communicating Their Affective State and Reported Likelihood of Expression," *Child Development 59* (1988): 1314–1322.

30. Saarni et al., "Emotional Development."

31. Kaoru Yamamoto et al., "Voices in Unison: Stressful Events in the Lives of Children in Six Countries," *Journal of Child Psychology and Psychiatry 28* (1987): 855–864.

32. Elaine Shaw Sorensen, *Children's Stress and Coping* (New York: Guildford Press, 1993).

33. Steven R. Asher et al., "Peer Rejection and Loneliness in Childhood," in *Peer Rejection in Childhood,* eds. Steven R. Asher and John D. Coie (Cambridge, UK: Cambridge University Press, 1990), pp. 253–273.

34. Susan L. Isley et al., "Parent and Child Expressed Affect and Children's Social Competence: Modeling Direct and Indirect Pathways," *Developmental Psychology 35,* (1999): 547–560.

35. Gary W. Ladd, "Peer Rejection, Aggressive or Withdrawn Behavior and Psychological Maladjustment from Ages 5 to 12: An Examination of Four Predictive Models," *Child Development 77* (2006): 822–846.

36. Ann S. Masten et al., "Developmental Cascades: Linking Academic Achievement and Externalizing and Internalizing Symptoms over 20 Years," *Developmental Psychology 41* (2005): 733–746.

37. Jennifer L. Altshuler and Diane N. Ruble, "Developmental Changes in Children's Awareness of Strategies for Coping with Uncontrollable Stress," *Child Development 60* (1989): 1337–1349.

38. Sorensen, *Children's Stress and Coping.*

39. Molly Reid et al., "My Family and Friends: Six to Twelve-Year-Old Children's Perceptions of Social Support," *Child Development 60* (1989): 896–910.

40. Mary J. Levitt, Nathalie Guacci-Franco, and Jerome L. Levitt, "Convoys of Social Support in Childhood and Early Adolescence," *Developmental Psychology 29* (1993): 811–818.

41. Susan Harter, "The Self," in *Handbook of Child Psychology,* 6th ed., eds. Damon and Lerner, vol. 3, pp. 505–570.

42. David M. Brodzinsky and Ellen Pinderhughes, "Parenting and Child Development in Adoptive Families," in *Handbook of Parenting,* 2nd ed., ed. Bornstein, vol. 1, pp. 279–311.

43. Diane N. Ruble, Carol Lynn Martin, and Sheri A. Berenbaum, "Gender Development," in *Handbook of Child Psychology*, 6th ed., eds. Damon and Lerner, vol. 3, pp. 858–932.

44. Joel Szkrybalo and Diane N. Ruble, "God Made Me a Girl: Sex-Category Constancy Judgments and Explanations Revisited," *Developmental Psychology* 35 (1999): 392–402.

45. Lynn S. Liben and Rebecca S. Bigler, The Developmental Course of Gender Differentiation, *Monographs of the Society for Research in Child Development,* 67 (Serial no. 269) (2002); Diane N. Ruble and Carol Lynn Martin, Commentary: The Developmental Course of Gender Differentiation, *Monographs of the Society for Research in Child Development,* 67 (Serial no. 269) (2002).

46. Frances E. Aboud, "The Development of Ethnic Self-Identification and Attitudes," in *Children's Ethnic Socialization*, eds. Jean S. Phinney and Mary Jane Rotheram (Beverly Hills, CA: Sage, 1987), pp. 32–55.

47. Sandra L. Hofferth and John F. Sandberg, "How American Children Spend Their Time," *Journal of Marriage and Family* 63 (2001): 295–308.

48. Margaret O'Brien Caughey et al., "Neighborhood Matters: Racial Socialization of African American Children," *Child Development* 77 (2006): 1220–1236.

49. Melissa Faye Jackson et al., "Classroom Contextual Effects of Race on Children's Peer Nominations," *Child Development* 77 (2006): 1325–1337.

50. Rebecca S. Bigler, Cara J. Averhart, and Lynn S. Liben, "Race and the Workforce: Occupational Status, Aspirations, and Stereotyping Among African American Children," *Developmental Psychology* 39 (2003): 572–580.

51. Frances E. Aboud, "The Formation of In-Group Favoritism and Out-Group Prejudice in Young Children: Are They Distinct Attitudes?" *Developmental Psychology* 39 (2003): 48–60.

52. Susan Harter, "Causes, Correlates, and the Functional Role of Global Self-Worth: A Life-Span Perspective," in *Competence Considered*, eds. J. Kolligian and Robert Sternberg (New Haven: CT Yale University Press, 1990), pp. 67–97.

53. Jean M. Twenge and Jennifer Crocker, "Race and Self-Esteem: Meta-Analysis Comparing Whites, Blacks, Hispanics, Asians, and American Indians and Comment on Gray-Little and Hofdahl (2000)," *Psychological Bulletin* 128 (2002): 371–408.

54. Tamara J. Ferguson, Hedy Stegge, and Ilse Damhuis, "Children's Understanding of Guilt and Shame," *Child Development* 62 (1992): 827–839.

55. Hazel J. Marcus and Paula S. Nurius, "Self-Understanding and Self-Regulation in Middle Childhood," in *Development During Middle Childhood*, ed. W. Andrew Collins (Washington, DC: National Academy Press, 1984), pp. 147–183.

56. Nancy Eisenberg et al., "Relations Among Positive Parenting, Children's Effortful Control and Externalizing Problems: A Three-Wave Longitudinal Study," *Child Development* 76 (2005): p. 1055–1071.

57. Melanie Killen et al., How Children and Adolescents Evaluate Gender and Racial Exclusions, *Monographs of the Society for Research in Child Development* 67, (Serial no. 271) (2002).

58. Eliot Turiel, "The Development of Morality," in *Handbook of Child Psychology*, 6th ed., eds. Damon and Lerner, vol. 3, pp. 789–857.

59. Collins, Madsen, and Susman-Stillman, "Parenting during Middle Childhood."

60. Cathryn Booth-LaForce et al., "Attachment and Friendship Predictors of Psychosocial Functioning in Middle Childhood and the Mediating Roles of Social Support and Self-Worth," in *Attachment in Middle Childhood,* eds. Kerns and Richardson, pp. 161–188.

61. Ellen Moss at al., "Stability of Attachment During the Preschool Period," *Developmental Psychology* 41 (2005): 773–783.

62. Ellen Moss et al., "Quality of Attachment at School Age: Relations Between Child Attachment Behavior, Psychosocial Functioning and School Performance," in *Attachment in Middle Childhood,* eds. Kerns and Richardson, pp. 189–211.

63. Jonathan F. Mattanah, "Authoritative Parenting and the Encouragement of Children's Autonomy," in *The Family Context of Parenting in Children's Adaptation to Elementary School,* eds. Philip A. Cowan et al. (Mahwah, NJ: Erlbaum, 2005), pp. 119–138.

64. Collins, Madsen, and Susman-Stillman, "Parenting during Middle Childhood."

65. Judith G. Smetana, "Adolescents and Parents' Reasoning about Actual Family Conflict," *Child Development 60* (1989): 1052–1067.

66. Graeme Russell and Alan Russell, "Mother–Child and Father–Child in Middle Childhood," *Child Development 58* (1987): 1753–1585.

67. Frances K. Grossman, William S. Pollack, and Ellen Golding, "Fathers and Children: Predicting the Quality and Quantity of Fathering," *Developmental Psychology 24* (1988): 822–891.

68. Molly Reid, Sharon Landesman Ramey, and Margaret Burchinal, "Dialogues with Children about Their Families," in *Children's Perspectives on the Family,* eds. Inge Bretherton and Malcolm W. Watson, New Directions for Child Development, no. 48 (San Francisco: Jossey-Bass, 1990), pp. 5–28.

69. Eleanor E. Maccoby, "Middle Childhood in the Context of the Family," in *Development during Middle Childhood,* pp. 184–239.

70. Carolyn Pape Cowan, Philip A. Cowan, and Gertrude Heming, "Two Variations of a Preventive Intervention for Couples: Effects on Parents and Children During the Transition to School," in *The Family Context of Parenting,* eds. Philip A. Cowan et al. (Mahwah NJ: Erlbaum, 2005) pp. 277–312.

71. Caughey et al., "Neighborhood Matters: Racial Socialization of African American Children."

72. Ibid.

73. Susan M. McHale et al., "Mothers' and Fathers' Racial Socialization in African American Families: Implications for Youth," *Child Development 77* (2006): 1387–1402.

74. Caughey et al., "Neighborhood Matters: Racial Socialization of African American Children."

75. Carolyn Bennett Murray and Jelani Mandara, "Racial Identity Development in African American Children: Cognitive and Experiential Antecedents," in *Black Children,* 2nd ed., ed. Harriette Pipes McAdoo (Thousand Oaks, CA: Sage, 2002), pp. 73–96.

76. Collins, Madsen, and Susman-Stillman, "Parenting during Middle Childhood;"

77. Wyndol Furman and Richard Lanthier, "Parenting Siblings," in *Handbook of Parenting,* 2nd ed., ed. Bornstein, vol. 1, pp. 165–188.

77. Ibid.

78. Clare M. Stocker and Lise Youngblade, "Marital Conflict and Hostility Links with Children's Siblings and Peer Relationships," *Journal of Family Psychology 13* (1999): 598–609.

79. Clare M. Stocker, Rebecca A. Burwell, and Megan L. Briggs, "Sibling Conflict in Middle Childhood Predicts Children's Adjustment in Early Adolescence," *Journal of Family Psychology 16* (2002): 50–57.

80. Gene H. Brody et al., "Sibling Relationships in Rural African American Families," *Journal of Marriage and the Family 61* (1999): 1046–1057.

81. Kenneth H. Rubin, William M. Bukowski, and Jeffrey G. Parker, "Peer Interactions, Relationships and Groups," in *Handbook of Child Psychology,* 6th ed., eds. Damon and Lerner, vol. 3, pp. 571–645.

82. Ibid.

83. Nicki R. Crick and Jennifer Grotpeter, "Relational Aggression, Gender, and Social-Psychological Adjustment," *Child Development 66* (1995): 710–722.

84. Ibid.

85. Dan Olweus, "Annotation: Bullying at School: Basic Facts and Effects of a School Based Intervention Program," *Journal of Child Psychology and Psychiatry 35* (1994): 1171–1190.

86. Nicki R. Crick and Jennifer K. Grotpeter, "Children's Treatment of Peers: Victims of Relational and Overt Aggression," *Development and Psychopathology 8* (1996): 367–380.

87. David Schwartz et al., "Peer Group Victimization As a Predictor of Children's Behavior Problems at Home and in School," *Development and Psychopathology 10* (1998): 87–99.

88. Susan K. Egan and David G. Perry, "Does Low Self-Regard Invite Victimization?" *Developmental Psychology 34* (1998): 299–309.

89. Avi Sadeh, Reut Gruber, and Amiram Raviv, "The Effects of Sleep Restriction and Extension in School-Age Children: What a Difference an Hour Makes," *Child Development 74* (2003): 444–455.

90. Emma K. Adam, Emily K. Snell, and Patricia Pendry, "Sleep Timing and Quantity in Ecological and Family Context: A Nationally Representative Time-Diary Study," *Journal of Family Psychology 21* (2007): 4–19.

91. El-Sheikh et al., "Child Emotional Insecurity and Academic Achievement."

92. Ibid.

93. Alice M. Gregory and Thomas G. O'Connor, "Sleep Problems in Childhood: A Longitudinal Study of Developmental Change and Association with Behavioral Problems," *The Journal of Academy of Child and Adolescent Psychiatry 41* (2002): 964–971.

94. Kelly J. Kelleher, "Increasing Identification of Psychosocial Problems: 1979–1996," *Pediatrics 105* (2000): 1313–1321.

95. Tim Murphy and Loriann Hoff Oberlin, *The Angry Child* (New York: Three Rivers, Press, 2001).

96. Gerald R. Patterson, "The Early Development of the Coercive Family Process," in *Antisocial Behavior in Children and Adolescents,* eds. John B. Reid, Gerald R. Patterson and James Snyder (Washington, DC: American Psychological Association, 2002), pp. 25–44.

97. Martin E. P. Seligman, *The Optimistic Child* (Boston: Houghton Mifflkin, 1995).

98. Marlene Jacobs Sandstrom and John D. Coie, "A Developmental Perspective on Peer Rejection: Mechanisms of Stability and Change," *Child Development 70* (1999): 955–966.

99. Sherri Oden and Steven R. Asher, "Coaching Children in Social Skills for Friendship Making," *Child Development 48* (1977): 495–506.

100. Alan E. Kazdin and Moira K. Whitley, "Treatment of Parental Stress to Enhance Therapeutic Change among Children Referred for Aggressive and Antisocial Behavior," *Journal of Consulting and Clinical Psychology 71* (2003): 504–515.

101. Olweus, "Annotation: Bullying at School."

102. Karin S. Frey et al., "Reducing Playground Bullying and Supporting Beliefs: An Experimental Trial of the Steps to Respect Program," *Developmental Psychology 41* (2005): 479–491.

103. Joyce L. Epstein and Mavis G. Sanders, "Family, School, and Community Partnerships," in *Handbook of Parenting,* 2nd ed., Marc H. Bornstein, vol. 5, *Practical Issues in Parenting* (Mahwah, NJ: Erlbaum, 2002), pp. 407–437.

104. Ellen Galinsky, *Between Generations: The Six Stages of Parenthood* (New York: Times Books, 1981).

105. Cowan, Cowan, and Heming, "Two Variations of a Prevention Program for Couples."

106. Jennifer C. Ablow, "When Parents Conflict or Disengage: Children's Perceptions of Parents' Marital Distress Predict School Adaptation," in *The Family Context of Parenting in Children's Adaptation to Elementary School,* eds. Philip A. Cowan et al. (Mahwah, NJ: Erlbaum, 2005) pp. 189–208.

107. Kazdin and Whitley,, "Treatment of Parental Stress to Enhance Therapeutic Change."

108. Cowan, Cowan, and Heming, "Two Variations of a Prevention Program for Couples."

109. Reid, Patterson, and Snyder, eds., *Antisocial Behavior in Children and Adolescents.*

110. Joan Beck, *Effective Parenting* (New York: Simon & Schuster, 1976).

111. Emmy E. Werner and Ruth S. Smith, *Overcoming the Odds* (Ithaca, NY: Cornell University Press, 1992), p. 177.

112. Robert Coles, *The Spiritual Life of Children* (Boston: Houghton Mifflin, 1990), p.127.

CHAPTER TEN

1. Tamar Lewin, "Study Finds Teenagers' Internet Socializing Isn't Such a Bad Thing," New York Times, November 20, 2008, p. A20.

2. Elizabeth J. Susman and Alan Rogol, "Puberty and Psychological Development," in *Handbook of Adolescent Development,* 2nd ed., eds. Richard M. Lerner and Laurence Steinberg (New York: Wiley, 2004), pp. 15–44.

3. Bruce J. Ellis and Marilyn J. Essex, "Family Environments, Adrenarche, and Sexual Maturation: A Longitudinal Test of a Life History Model," *Child Development 78* (2007): 1799–1817.

4. Jay Belsky et al., "Family Rearing Antecedents of Pubertal Timing," *Child Development 78* (2007): 1302–1321.

5. Ellis and Essex, "Family Environments, Adrenarche, and Sexual Maturation."

6. Belsky et al., "Family Rearing Antecedents of Pubertal Timing."

7. Ibid.

8. Susman and Rogol, "Puberty and Psychological Development."

9. Ibid.

10. W. Andrew Collins and Laurence Steinberg, "Adolescent Development in Interpersonal Context," in *Handbook of Child Psychology,* 6th ed., eds. William Damon and Richard M. Lerner, vol. 3: *Social, Emotional, and Personality Development,* ed. Nancy Eisenberg (Hoboken, NJ: Wiley, 2006), pp. 1003–1067.

11. Ronald E. Dahl, "Adolescent Brain Development: Vulnerabilities and Opportunities," *Annals of the New York Academy of Sciences 1021* (2004): 1–22.

12. Susman and Rogol, "Puberty and Psychological Development."

13. L. LaBerge et al., "Development of Sleep Patterns in Early Adolescence," *Journal of Sleep Research 10* (2001): 59–67.

14. Jay N. Giedd et al., "Brain Development During Childhood and Adolescence: A Longitudinal MRI Study," *Nature Neuroscience 2* (1999): 861–863.

15. Ibid., p. 863.

16. Collins and Steinberg, "Adolescent Development in Interpersonal Context."

17. Herbert Ginsberg and Sylvia Opper, *Piaget's Theory of Intellectual Development* (Englewood Cliffs, NJ: Prentice-Hall, 1969); Jean Piaget and Baarbel Inhelder, *The Psychology of the Child* (New York: Basic Books, 1969).

18. Allan Wigfield et al., "Development of Achievement Motivation," in *Handbook of Child Psychology,* 6th ed., eds. Damon and Lerner, vol. 3, pp. 933–1002.

19. Allan Wigfield and A. Laurel Wagner, "Competence Motivation and Identity Development during Adolescence," in *Handbook of Competence and Motivation,* eds. Andrew J. Elliott and Carol S. Dweck (New York: Guilford Press, 2005), pp. 222–239.

20. Lisa S. Blackwell, Kali Trzesniewski, and Carol S.Dweck, "Implicit Theories of Intelligence Predict Achievement Across an Adolescent Transition: A Longitudinal Study and an Intervention," *Child Development 78* (2007): 246–263.

21. Reed W. Larson et al., "Continuity, Stability, and Change in Daily Emotional Experiences across Adolescence," *Child Development 73* (2002): 1151–1165.

22. Josien Schneiders et al., "Mood Reactivity to Daily Negative Events in Early Adolescence: Relationship to Risk for Psychopathology," *Developmental Psychology 42* (2006): 543–554.

23. Lisa Flook and Andrew J. Fuligni, "Family and School Spillover in Adolescents' Daily Lives," *Child Development 79* (2008): 776–787.

24. Ibid.

25. Lisa Kiang et al., "Ethnic Identity and the Daily Psychological Well-Being of Adolescents from Mexican and Chinese Backgrounds," *Child Development 77* (2006): 1338–1350.

26. Mary J. Leavitt, Nathalie Guacci-Franco, and Jerome L. Levitt, "Convoys of Social Support in Childhood and Early Adolescence: Structure and Function," *Developmental Psychology 29* (1993): 811–818.

27. Reed W. Larson, "Toward a Psychology of Positive Youth Development," *American Psychologist 55* (2000): 170–183.

28. Ibid., p. 170.

29. Susan Harter, "The Self," in *Handbook of Child Psychology,* 6th ed., eds. Damon and Lerner, vol. 3, pp. 505–570.

30. Erik H. Erikson, *Childhood and Society,* 2nd ed. (New York: Norton, 1963).

31. James F. Marcia, "Identity in Adolescence," in *Handbook of Adolescent Psychology,* ed. Joseph Adelson (New York: Wiley, 1980), pp. 159–187.

32. Harold D. Grotevant, "Adolescent Development in Family Contexts," in *Handbook of Child Psychology,* 5th ed., ed. William Damon, vol. 3: *Social, Emotional, and Personality Development,* ed. Nancy Eisenberg (New York: Wiley, 1998), pp. 1097–1149.

33. Harter, "The Self."

34. Kali H. Trzesniewski et al., "Low Self-Esteem During Adolescence Predicts Poor Health, Criminal Behavior, and Limited Economic Prospects During Adulthood," *Developmental Psychology 42* (2006): 381–390.

35. Jennifer L. Yunger, Priscilla R. Carver, and David G. Perry, "Does Gender Identity Influence Children's Psychological Well-Being?" *Developmental Psychology 40* (2004): 572–582.

36. Brooke C. Corby, Ernest V. E. Hodges, and David G. Perry, "Gender Identity and

Adjustment in Black, Hispanic, and White Preadolescents," *Developmental Psychology* 43 (2007): 261–266.

37. Ann C. Crouter et al., "Development of Gender Attitude Traditionality Across Middle Childhood and Adolescence," *Child Development 78* (2007): 911–926.

38. Susan McHale et al., "Links Between Sex-Typed Time Use in Middle Childhood and Gender Development in Early Adolescence," *Developmental Psychology 40* (2004): 868–881.

39. Crouter et al., "Development of Gender Attitude Traditionality."

40. Jean S. Phinney, "Stages of Ethnic Identity Development in Minority Group Adolescents," *Journal of Early Adolescence 9* (1989): 34–49.

41. Kiang et al., "Ethnic Identity and the Daily Psychological Well-Being of Adolescents from Mexican a nd Chinese Backgrounds."

42. Eleanor K. Seaton, Krista Maywalt Scottham, and Robert M. Sellers, "The Status Model of Racial Identity Development in African American Adolescents: Evidence of Structure, Trajectories, and Well Being," *Child Development 77* (2006): 1416–1426.

43. Gene H. Brody et al., "Perceived Discrimination and the Adjustment of African American Youths: A Five-Year Longitudinal Analysis with Contextual Moderation Effects," *Child Development 77* (2006): 1170–1189.

44. Jane B. Brooks, "Social Maturity in Middle Age and Its Developmental Antecedents," in *Present and Past in Middle Life,* eds. Dorothy H. Eichorn et al. (New York: Academic Press, 1981), pp. 243–265.

45. Nancy Eisenberg and Amanda Sheffield Morris, "Moral Cognition and Prosocial Responding in Adolescence," in *Handbook of Adolescent Development,* 2nd ed., eds. Richard M. Lerner and Laurence Steinberg (New York: Wiley, 2004), pp. 155–188.

46. Reed Larson and Maryse H. Richards, "Daily Companionship in Late Childhood and Early Adolescence: Changing Developmental Contexts," *Child Development 62* (1991): 284–300.

47. Brian K. Barber, Heidi E. Stolz, and Joseph A Olsen, Parental Support, Psychological Control, and Behavioral Control: Assessing Relevance Across Time, Culture, and

Method, *Monographs of the Society for Research in Child Development, 70* (Serial no. 282) (2005).

48. Christina Hardway and Andrew J. Fuligni, "Dimensions of Family Connectedness Among Adolescents with Mexican, Chinese, and European Backgrounds," *Developmental Psychology 42* (2006): 1246–1258.

49. Barber, Stolz, and Olsen, *Parental Support, Psychological Control, and Behavioral Control.*

50. Judith G. Smetana, "Adolescent–Parent Conflict: Resistance and Subversion as Developmental Process," in *Conflict, Contradiction, and Contrarian Elements in Moral Development and Education,* ed. Larry Nucci (Mahwah, NJ: Erlbaum, 2005), pp. 69–91.

51. Andrew J. Fuligni, "Authority, Autonomy, and Parent–Adolescent Conflict and Cohesion: A Study of Adolescents from Mexican, Chinese, Filipino, and European Backgrounds," *Developmental Psychology 34* (1998): 782–792.

52. Judith G. Smetana, "Concepts of Self and Social Convention: Adolescents' and Parents' Reasoning about Hypothetical and Actual Family Conflicts," in *Development during the Transition to Adolescence: Minnesota Symposium on Child Psychology,* vol. 21, eds. Megan R. Gunnar and W. Andrew Collins (Hillsdale, NJ: Erlbaum, 1988), pp. 79–122.

53. Smetana, "Adolescent–Parent Conflict."

54. Eisenberg and Morris, "Moral Cognition and Prosocial Responding in Adolescence."

55. Judith G. Smetana, "It's 10 O'Clock: Do You Know Where Your Children Are?: Recent Advances in Understanding Parental Monitoring and Adolescents' Information Management," *Child Development Perspectives 2* (2008): 19–25.

56. Judith G. Smetana et al., "Disclosure and Secrecy in Adolescent–Parent Relationships," *Child Development 77* (2006): 201–217.

57. Barber, Stolz, and Olsen, *Parental Support, Psychological Control, and Behavioral Control.*

58. Eva S. Lefkowitz, Marian Sigman, and Terry Kit-fong Au, "Helping Mothers Discuss Sexuality and AIDS with Adolescents," *Child Development 71* (2000): 1383–1394.

59. Martha A. Rueter and Rand D. Conger, "Reciprocal Influences between Parenting and Adolescent Problem-Solving Behavior," *Developmental Psychology 34* (1998): 1470–1482.

60. Mary Pipher, *Reviving Ophelia* (New York: Ballantine, 1994), p. 283.

61. William Pollack, *Real Boys* (New York: Henry Holt, 1998), p. xxiv.

62. Ibid., p. 398.

63. Susan M. McHale et al., "Mothers' and Fathers' Racial Socialization in African American Families: Implications for Youth," *Child Development 77* (2006): 1387–1402.

64. Velma McBride Murry et al., "Parental Involvement Promotes Rural African American Youths' Self-Pride and Sexual Self-Concepts," *Journal of Marriage and Family 67* (2005): 627–642.

65. Gene H. Brody et al., "The Strong African American Families Program: Prevention of Youths' High-Risk Behavior and a Test of a Model of Change," *Journal of Family Psychology 20* (2006): 1–11.

66. Andrew J. Supple et al., "Contextual Influences on Latino Adolescent Ethnic Identity and Academic Outcomes," *Child Developmental 77* (2006): 1427–1433.

67. Ronald L. Simons et al., "Discrimination, Crime, Ethnic Identity, and Parenting as Correlates of Depressive Symptoms Among African American Children: A Multilevel Analysis," *Development and Psychopathology 14* (2002): 371–393.

68. Supple et al., "Contextual Influences on Latino Adolescent Ethnic Identity and Academic Outcomes."

69. Patrick T. Davies et al., Child Emotional Security and Interparental Conflict, *Monographs of the Society for Research in Child Development,* 67 (Serial no. 270) (2002).

70. Gene H. Brody et al., "Linking Perceived Discrimination to Longitudinal Changes in African American Mothers' Parenting Practices," *Journal of Marriage and Family 70* (2008): 319–331.

71. Judy Dunn, "Siblings and Socialization," in *Handboook of Socialization: Theory and Research,* eds. Joan E. Grusec and Paul D. Hastings (New York: Guilford Press, 2007), pp. 309–327.

72. Cheryl Slomkowski et al., "Sisters, Brothers, and Delinquency: Evaluating Social Influence during Early and Middle Adolescence," *Child Development 72* (2001): 271–283.

73. Kenneth H. Rubin, William M. Bukowski, and Jeffrey G. Parker, "Peer Interactions, Relationships and Groups," in *Handbook of Child Psychology,* 6th ed., eds. Damon and Lerner, vol. 3, pp. 571–645.

74. Kathleen Mullan Harris and Shannon E. Cavenagh, "Indicators of the Peer Environment in Adolescence," in *Key Indicators of Child and Youth Well-Being,* ed. Brett V. Brown (Mahwah, NJ: Erlbaum, 2008), pp. 259–278.

75. Kathleen B. McElhaney, Jill Antonishak, and Joseph P. Allen, "'They Like Me, They Like Me Not': Popularity and Adolescents' Perceptions of Acceptance Predicting Social Functioning Over Time," *Child Development 79* (2008): 720–731.

76. Patti M. Valkenburg and Jochen Peter, "Preadolescents' and Adolescents' Online Communication and Their Closeness to Friends," *Developmental Psychology 43* (2007): 267–277.

77. Rubin, Bukowski, and Parker, "Peer Interactions, Relationships, and Groups."

78. Amanda J. Rose, Wendy Carlson, and Erika M. Waller, "Prospective Associations of Co-Rumination with Friendship and Emotional Adjustment: Considering the Socioemotional Trade-Offs of Co-Rumination," *Developmental Psychology 43* (2007): 1019–1031.

79. Rubin, Bukowski, and Parker, "Peer Interactions, Relationships, and Groups."

80. Karen Nylund et al., "Subtypes, Severity, and Structural Stability of Peer Victimization: What Does Latent Class Analysis Say?" *Child Development 78* (2007): 1706–1722.

81. Adrienne Nishina and Jaana Juvonen, "Daily Reports of Witnessing and Experiencing Peer Harassment in Middle School," *Child Development 76* (2005): 435–450.

82. Victoria Kim, "Free Speech, Schools, and Cyber-Bullying," *Los Angeles Times,* August 3, 2008, p. A1.

83. Don Dinkmeyer and Gary D. McKay, *STEP/TEEN Systematic Training for Effective Parenting of Teens* (Circle Pines, MN: American Guidance Service, 1983).

84. Adele Faber and Elaine Mazlish, *How to Talk So Kids Will Listen and Listen So*

Kids Will Talk (New York: Rawson Wade, 1980).

85. Tori DeAngelis, "Web Pornography's Effects on Children," *Monitor on Psychology* (November 2007): 50–52.

86. Myrna B. Shure with Robert Israeloff, *Raising a Thinking Preteen* (New York: Henry Holt, 2000).

87. Larson, "Toward a Psychology of Positive Youth Development," p. 170.

88. Dahl, "Adolescent Brain Development."

89. Larson, "Toward a Psychology of Positive Youth Development," p. 177.

90. Ibid., p. 179.

91. Ibid.

92. Rubin, Bukowski, and Parker, "Peer Interactions, Relationships, and Groups."

93. Ibid.

94. Ibid.

95. James Garbarino and Ellen deLara, *And Words Can Hurt Forever* (New York: Free Press, 2002).

96. Linda A. Jackson et al., "Does Home Internet Use Influence the Academic Performance of Low Income Children?" *Developmental Psychology* 42 (2006): 429–435.

97. Jan Hoffman, "I Know What You Did Last Math Class," *New York Times*, May 4, 2008, Sunday Styles, p. 1.

98. Ellen Galinsky, *Between Generations: The Six Stages of Parenthood* (New York: Times Books, 1981).

99. William Damon, *The Youth Charter: How Communities Can Work Together to Raise Standards for All Children* (New York: Free Press, 1997).

100. Ibid., p. ix.

CHAPTER ELEVEN

1. Ginger Thompson, "Where Education and Assimilation Collide," *New York Times*, March 15, 2009, p. A1.

2. Ronald E. Dahl, "Adolescent Brain Development: A Period of Vulnerabilities and Opportunities," *Annals of the New York Academy of Science 1021* (2004): 1–22.

3. Ritch C. Savin-Williams and Lisa M. Diamond, "Sex," in *Handbook of Adolescent Development*, 2nd ed., eds. Richard M. Lerner and Laurence Steinberg (Hoboken, NJ: Wiley, 2004), pp. 189–231.

4. Ibid.

5. Tina Hoff, Liberty Greene, and Julia Davis, *National Survey of Adolescents and Young Adults: Sexual Health and Knowledge, Attitudes and Experiences* (Menlo Park, CA: Kaiser Family Foundation, 2003).

6. Ibid.

7. Ibid.

8. Ibid.

9. Jerald G. Bachman et al., *The Education–Drug Use Connection: How Successes and Failures in School Relate to Adolescent Smoking, Drinking, Drug Use, and Delinquency* (New York: Erlbaum, 2008).

10. Laurie Chassin et al., "Adolescent Substance Use," in *Handbook of Adolescent Psychology*, 2nd ed., eds. Lerner and Steinberg, pp. 665–696.

11. Hoff, Greene, and Davis, *National Survey of Adolescents and Young Adults*.

12. Bachman et al., *The Education–Drug Use Connection*.

13. Joyce A. Martin et al., "Annual Summary of Vital Statistics: 2006," *Pediatrics 121* (2008): 788–801.

14. Hoff, Greene, and Davis, *National Survey of Adolescents and Young Adults*.

15. Kerry M. Green and Margaret E. Ensminger, "Adult Social Behavioral Effects of Heavy Adolescent Marijuana Use Among African Americans," *Developmental Psychology* 42 (2006): 1168–1178.

16. Bachman et al., *The Education–Drug Use Connection*.

17. Ibid., p.30.

18. Dahl, "Adolescent Brain Development."

19. Karen Bartsch, "Adolescents' Theoretical Thinking," in *Early Adolescent Perspectives on Research, Policy, and Intervention*, eds. Richard M. Lerner (Hillsdale, NJ: Erlbaum, 1993), pp. 143–157.

20. Dahl, "Adolescent Brain Development."

21. Margo Gardner and Laurence Steinberg, "Peer Influence on Risk Taking, Risk Preference, and Risky Decision Making in Adolescence and Adulthood: An Experimental Study," *Developmental Psychology 41* (2005): 625–635.

22. Jacquelynne S. Eccles, "Schools, Academic Motivation, and Stage-Environment Fit," in *Handbook of Adolescent Development*, 2nd ed., eds. Lerner and Steinberg, pp. 125–153.

23. Martha Hansen et al., "The Impact of School Daily Schedule on Adolescent Sleep," *Pediatrics 115* (2005): 1555–1561.

24. Judith G. Smetana, "Adolescent–Parent Conflict: Resistance and Subversion as

Developmental Processes," in *Conflict, Contradiction, and Contrarian Elements in Moral Development and Education,* ed. Larry Nucci (Mahwah, NJ: Erlbaum, 2005), pp. 69–91.

25. Eccles, "Schools, Academic Motivation, and Stage-Environment Fit."

26. Robert B. McCall, Cynthia Evahn, and Lynn Kratzer, *High School Underachievers* (Newbury Park, CA: Sage, 1992).

27. Eccles, "Schools, Academic Motivation, and Stage–Environment Fit."

28. Ibid.

29. W. Andrew Collins and Laurence Steinberg, "Adolescent Development in Interpersonal Context," in *Handbook of Child Psychology*, 6th ed., eds. William Damon and Richard M. Lerner, vol. 3: *Social, Emotional, and Personality Development,* ed. Nancy Eisenberg (Hoboken, NJ: Wiley, 2006), pp. 1003–1067.

30. Dahl, "Adolescent Brain Development."

31. Michael A. Busseri et al., "A Longitudinal Examination of Breadth and Intensity of Youth Activity Involvement and Successful Development," *Developmental Psychology* 42 (2006): 1313–1326.

32. Joseph L. Mahoney, Angela L. Harris, and Jacquelynne S. Eccles, "Organized Activity Participation, Positive Youth Development, and the Overscheduling Hypothesis," *Society for Research in Child Development Social Policy Report 20*(4) (2006): 1–30.

33. Susan Harter, "The Self," in *Handbook of Child Psychology*, 6th ed., eds. Damon and Lerner, vol. 3, pp. 505–570.

34. J. Scott Brown, Sarah O. Meadows, and Glen H. Elder, Jr., "Race–Ethnic Inequality and Psychological Distress: Depressive Symptoms from Adolescence to Young Adulthood," *Developmental Psychology 43* (2007): 1295–1311.

35. Emily A. Impett et al., "Girls' Relationship Authenticity and Self-Esteem Across Adolescence," *Developmental Psychology 44* (2008): 722–733.

36. Harter, "The Self."

37. Nancy L. Galambos, "Gender and Gender Role in Adolescence," in *Handbook of Adolescent Development,* 2nd ed., eds. Lerner and Steinberg, pp. 233–262.

38. Ibid.

39. Janet S. Hyde et al., "Gender Similarities Characterize Math Performers," *Science 321* (2008): 495.

40. Jack Block, "Some Relationships Regarding the Self from the Block and Block Longitudinal Study," paper presented at the Social Science Research Council conference on Selfhood, Stanford, CA, October 1985.

41. Campbell Leaper and Christia Spears Brown, "Perceived Experiences with Sexism Among Adolescent Girls," *Child Development 79* (2008): 685–704.

42. Ibid.

43. Ritch C. Savin-Williams, *The New Gay Teenager* (Cambridge, MA: Harvard University Press, 2005).

44. Lisa M. Diamond, "Female Bisexuality From Adolescence to Adulthood: Results From a 10-Year Longitudinal Study," *Developmental Psychology 44* (2008): 5–14.

45. Savin-Williams and Diamond, "Sex."

46. V. Paul Poteat, "Peer Group Socialization of Homophobic Attitudes and Behavior During Adolescence," *Child Development 78* (2007): 1830–1842.

47. Anthony R. D'Augelli, Arnold H. Grossman, and Michael T. Starks, "Parents' Awareness of Lesbian, Gay, and Bisexual Youths' Sexual Orientations," *Journal of Marriage and Family 67* (2005): 474–482.

48. Laurie Hetherington and Justin A. Lavner, "Coming to Terms With Coming Out : Review and Recommendations for Family Systems–Focused Research," *Journal of Family Psychology 22* (2008): 329–343.

49. Michael A. Busseri et al., "On the Association Between Sexual Attraction and Adolescent Risk Behavior Involvement: Examining Mediation and Moderation," *Developmental Psychology 44 (2008):* 69–80.

50. Savin-Williams, *The New Gay Teenager.*

51. Kenneth J. Zucker, "Gender Identity Development and Issues," *Child and Adolescent Psychiatric Clinics of North America 13* (2004): 551–568.

52. Kelly D. Drummond et al., "A Follow-Up Study of Girls with Gender Identity Disorder," *Developmental Psychology 44* (2008): 34–45.

53. Andrew J. Fuligni et al., "Stability and Change in Ethnic Labeling Among Adolescents from Asian and Latin American Immigrant Families," *Child Development 79* (2008): 944–956.

54. Kerstin Pahl and Niobe Way, "Longitudinal Trajectories of Ethnic Identity Among Urban Black and Latino

Adolescents," *Child Development* 77 (2006): 1403–1415.

55. Melissa L. Greene, Niobe Way, and Kerstin Pahl, "Trajectories of Perceived Adult and Peer Discrimination Among Black, Latino/a, and Asian American Adolescents: Patterns and Psychological Correlates," *Developmental Psychology* 42 (2006): 218–236.

56. Pahl and Way, "Longitudinal Trajectories of Ethnic Identity Among Urban Black and Latino Adolescents."

57. Nancy Rumbaugh Whitesell et al., "Developmental Trajectories of Personal and Collective Self-Concept Among American Indian Adolescents," *Child Development* 77 (2006): 1487–1503.

58. Jean S. Phinney and Mona Devitch-Navarro, "Variations in Bicultural Identification among African-American and Mexican-American Adolescents," *Journal of Research on Adolescence* 7 (1997): 3–32.

59. Maria Wong et al., "Behavioral Control and Resiliency in the Onset of Alcohol and Illicit Drug Use: A Prospective Study from Preschool to Adolescence," *Child Development* 77 (2006): 1016–1033; Lisa J. Crockett et al., "Psychological Profiles and Adolescent Adjustment: A Person-Centered Approach," *Development and Psychopathology* 18 (2006): 195–214.

60. Bachman et al., *The Education–Drug Connection.*

61. Wong, "Behavioral Control and Resiliency in the Onset of Alcohol and Illicit Drug Use", Crockett, "Psychological Profiles and Adolescent Adjustment: A Person-Centered Approach."

62. Crockett, "Psychological Profiles and Adolescent Adjustment: A Person-Centered Approach."

63. Scott J. South, Dana L. Haynie, and Sunita Bose, "Residential Mobility and the Onset of Adolescent Sexual Activity," *Journal of Marriage and Family* 67 (2005): 499–514.

64. David B. Henry et al., "Peer Selection and Socialization Effects on Adolescent Intercourse Without a Condom and Attitudes About the Costs of Sex," *Child Development* 78 (2007): 825–838.

65. Bachman et al., *The Education–Drug Use Connection.*

66. Elizabeth A. Pomery et al., "Families and Risk: Prospective Analyses of Familial and Social Influences on Adolescent Substance Use," *Journal of Family Psychology* 19 (2005): 560–570.

67. Ibid.

68. Steinunn Gestsdottir and Richard M. Lerner, "Intentional Self-Regulation and Positive Youth Development in Early Adolescence: Findings from the 4-H Study of Positive Youth Development," *Developmental Psychology* 43 (2007): 508–521.

69. Bachman et al., *The Education–Drug Use Connection.*

70. Michael D. Resnick et al., "Protecting Adolescents from Harm," *Journal of the American Medical Association* 278 (1997): 823–832.

71. Pamela Ebstyne King and James L. Furrow, "Religion as a Resource for Positive Youth Development: Religion, Social Capital, and Moral Outcomes," *Developmental Psychology* 40 (2004): 703–713.

72. Fritz K. Oser, W. George Scarlett, and Anton Bucher, "Religious and Spiritual Development throughout the Life Span," in *Handbook of Child Psychology,* 6th ed., eds. William Damon and Richard M. Lerner, vol 1: *Theoretical Models of Human Development,* ed. Richard M. Lerner (Hoboken, NJ: Wiley, 2006), pp. 942–998.

73. Doran C. French et al., "Religious Involvement and the Social Competence and Adjustment of Indonesian Muslim Adolescents," *Developmental Psychology* 44 (2008): 597–611.

74. Joseph P. Allen, "The Attachment System in Adolescence," in *Handbook of Attachment,* 2nd ed., eds. Jude Cassidy and Phillip K. Shaver (New York: Guilford press, 2008), p. 424.

75. Kee Jeong Kim et al., "Parent–Adolescent Reciprocity in Negative Affect and Its Relation to Early Adult Social Development," *Developmental Psychology* 37 (2001): 775–790.

76. Diana Baumrind, "The Influence of Parenting Style on Adolescent Competence, and Problem Behavior," paper presented the American Psychological Association meetings, New Orleans, LA, August 1989, p. 16.

77. Collins and Steinberg, "Adolescent Development in Interpersonal Context."

78. Mark E. Feinberg, Marni L. Kan, and E. Mavis Hetherington, "The Longitudinal Influence of Coparenting Conflict on Parental Negativity and Adolescent

Maladjustment," *Journal of Marriage and Family* 69 (2007): 687–702.

79. Feinberg, Kan, and Hetherington, "The Longitudinal Influence of Coparenting Conflict on Parental Negativity and Adolescent Maladjustment"; Megan E. Baril, Ann C. Crouter, and Susan M. McHale, "Processes Linking Adolescent Well Being, Marital Love, and Coparenting," *Journal of Family Psychology* 21 (2007): 645–654.

80. Collins and Steinberg, "Adolescent Development in Interpersonal Context."

81. Andrew J. Fuligni, Vivian Tseng, and May Lam, "Attitudes toward Family Obligations among American Adolescents with Asian, Latin American, and European Backgrounds," *Child Development* 70 (1999): 1039.

82. Hoff, Greene, and Davis, *National Survey of Adolescents and Young Adults.*

83. Hetherington and Lavner, "Coming to Terms With 'Coming Out'."

84. Velma McBride Murry et al., "Parental Involvement Promotes Rural African American Youths' Self-Pride and Sexual Self-Concepts," *Journal of Marriage and Family* 67 (2005): 627–642.

85. Kimberly A. Updegraff et al., "Adolescent Sibling Relationships in Mexican American Families: Exploring the Role of Familism," *Journal of Family Psychology* 19 (2005): 512–522.

86. Mark E. Feinberg et al., "Differential Association of Family Subsystem Negativity on Siblings' Maladjustment: Using Behavior Genetic Methods to Test Process Theory," *Journal of Family Psychology* 19 (2005): 601–610.

87. Pomery et al., "Families and Risk."

88. Collins and Steinberg, "Adolescent Development in Interpersonal Context."

89. Wyndol Furman, "Friends and Lovers: The Role of Peer Relationships in Adolescent Romantic Relationships," in *Relationships as Developmental Contexts: The 30th Minnesota Symposium on Child Development*, eds. W. Andrew Collins and Brett Laursen (Hillsdale, NJ: Erlbaum, 1999), pp. 133–154.

90. Duane Buhrmester, "Intimacy and Friendship, Interpersonal Competence, and Adjustment during Preadolescence and Adolescence," *Child Development* 61 (1990): 1101–1111.

91. B. Bradford Brown, "Adolescents' Relationships with Peers," in *Handbook of Adolescent Psychology*, 2nd ed., eds. Lerner and Steinberg, pp. 363–394.

92. Ibid.

93. Ibid.

94. Ibid.

95. Geoffrey L. Ream and Ritch C. Savin-Williams, "Reciprocal Associations Between Adolescent Sexual Activity and Quality of Youth–Parent Interactions," *Journal of Family Psychology* 19 (2005): 171–179.

96. Ann M. Meier, "Adolescent First Sex and Subsequent Mental Health," *American Journal of Sociology* 112 (2007): 1811–1847.

97. Ream and Savin-Williams, "Reciprocal Associations Between Adolescent Sexual Activity and Quality of Youth–Parent Interactions."

98. Hansen et al., "The Impact of School Daily Schedule on Adolescent Sleep."

99. Jan Van den Bulck, "Television Viewing, Computer Game Playing, and Internet Use and Self-Reported Time Out of Bed in Secondary School Children," *Sleep* 27 (2004): 101–104.

100. Frederick J. Zimmerman, "Children's Media Use and Sleep Problems: Issues and Unanswerable Questions," Kaiser Family Foundation Report No. 7674, June 2008. www.kff.org.

101. Emma K. Adam, Emily K. Snell, and Patricia Pendry, "Sleep Timing and Quantity in Ecological and Family Context: A Nationally Representative Time-Diary Study," *Journal of Family Psychology* 21 (2007): 4–19.

102. Alice M. Gregory et al., Family Conflict in Childhood: A Predictor of Later Insomnia," *Sleep* 29 (2006): 1063–1067.

103. Adam, Snell, and Pendry, "Sleep Timing and Quantity in Ecological and Family Context."

104. David Ludwig with Suzanne Rostler, *Ending the Food Fight* (New York: Houghton Mifflin, 2007).

105. Ibid.

106. G. Terence Wilson, Carlos M. Grilo, and Kelly M. Vitousek, "Psychological Treatment of Eating Disorders," *American Psychologist* 62 (2007): 199–216.

107. Mark Chavez and Thomas R. Insel, "Eating Disorders: National Institute of

108. Wilson, Grilo, and Vitousek, "Psychological Treatment of Eating Disorders."

Mental Health's Perspective," *American Psychologist 62* (2007): 159–166.

109. "Teenagers Changing Sexual Behaviors," *New York Times,* August 26, 2008, p. D7.

110. Erin Calhoun Davis and Lisa V. Friel, "Adolescent Sexuality: Disentangling the Effects of Family Structure and Family Context," *Journal of Marriage and Family 63* (2001): 669–681.

111. Jonathan D. Klein and the Committee on Adolescence, "Adolescent Pregnancy: Current Trends and Issues," *Pediatrics 116* (2005): 281–286.

112. Rinka M. P. Van Zundert et al., "Pathways to Alcohol Use Among Dutch Students in Regular Education and Education for Adolescents with Behavioral Problems: The Role of Parental Alcohol Use, General Parenting Practices, and Alcohol-Specific Parenting Practices," *Journal of Family Psychology 20* (2006): 456–467.

113. James Garbarino, *Lost Boys: Why Our Sons Turn Violent and How We Can Save Them* (New York: Free Press, 1999).

114. Ibid., p. 75.

115. Ibid., p. 149.

116. Deborah M. Capaldi and Mike Stoolmiller, "Co-occurrence of Conduct Problems and Depressive Symptoms in Early Adolescent Boys: III. Prediction to Young Adult Adjustment." *Development and Psychopathology 11* (1999): 335–346.

117. Ibid., p. 78.

118. Alice W. Pope and Karen L. Bierman, "Predicting Adolescent Peer Problems and Antisocial Activities: The Relative Roles of Aggression and Dysregulation," *Developmental Psychology 35* (1999): 335–346.

119. Capaldi and Stoolmiller, "Co-occurrence of Conduct Problems and Depressive Symptoms in Early Adolescent Boys."

120. Dante Cicchetti and Sheree L. Toth, "The Development of Depression in Children and Adolescents," *American Psychologist 53* (1998): 221–241.

121. Laurie Chassin et al., "Adolescent Substance Abuse," *Handbook of Adolescent Development,* 2nd ed., eds. Lerner and Steinberg, pp. 665–696.

122. Cicchetti and Toth, "The Development of Depression in Children and Adolescents."

123. Harold S. Koplewicz, *More Than Moody: Recognizing and Treating Adolescent Depression* (New York: Putnam, 2002).

124. Jennifer J. Connor and Martha A Rueter, "Parent–Child Relationships as Systems of Support or Risk for Adolescent Suicidality," *Journal of Family Psychology 20* (2006): 143–155.

125. Julia A. Graber, "Internalizing Problems During Adolescence," in *Handbook of Adolescent Psychology,* ed. Lerner and Steinberg, pp. 587–626.

126. Anne C. Petersen et al., "Depression in Adolescence," *American Psychologist 48* (1993): 135–168.

127. Brown, Meadows, Elder, Jr., "Race–Ethnic Inequality and Psychological Distress."

128. Ibid., p. 308.

129. Arin M. Connell and Thomas J. Dishion, "Reducing Depression Among At-Risk Early Adolescents: Three-Year Effects of a Family-Centered Intervention Embedded Within Schools," *Journal of Family Psychology 22* (2008): 574–585.

130. Collins and Steinberg, "Adolescent Development in Interpersonal Context."

131. W. Andrew Collins et al., "Conflict Processes and Transitions in Parent and Peer Relationships," *Journal of Adolescent Research 12* (1997): 179–198.

132. McCall, Evahn, and and Kratzer, *High School Underachievers.*

133. William Damon, *The Path to Purpose: Helping Our Children Find Their Calling in Life* (New York: Free Press, 2008), p. 131.

134. Marcia Herrin and Nancy Matsumoto, *The Parent's Guide to Childhood Eating Disorders* (New York: Holt, 2002).

135. Koplewicz, *More Than Moody.*

136. Harold J. Koplewicz, "More than Moody: Recognizing and Treating Adolescent Depression," *Brown University Child and Adolescent Newsletter 18* (December 2002): 7.

137. Jane E. Brody, "Adolescent Angst or a Deeper Disorder?: Tips for Spotting Serious Symptoms," *New York Times,* December 24, 2002 , p. D5.

138. Nikki Babbit, *Adolescent Drug and Alcohol Abuse: How to Stop It and Get Help for Your Family* (Sebastopol, CA: O'Reilly, 2000).

139. Laurence Steinberg and Wendy Steinberg, *Crossing Paths: How Your Children's Adolescence Triggers Your Own Crisis* (New York: Simon & Schuster, 1994).

140. Ron Zodkevitch, *The Tough Love Prescription: How to Create and Enforce Boundaries for Your Teen* (New York: McGraw-Hill, 2006).

CHAPTER TWELVE

1. Marvin Krislov, "Mental Illness on Campus: A Quiet Danger No Longer," *USA Today*, December 20, 2007, p. 13A.

2. Glen H. Elder Jr. and Michael J. Shanahan, "The Life Course and Human Development," in *Handbook of Child Psychology*, 6th ed., eds. William Damon and Richard M. Lerner, vol. 1: *Theoretical Models of Human Development*, ed. Richard M. Lerner (Hoboken, NJ: Wiley, 2006), pp. 665–715.

3. Erik H. Erikson, *Childhood and Society*, 2nd ed. (New York: Norton, 1963).

4. John Bowlby, *The Making and Breaking of Affectional Bonds* (London: Tavistock, 1979,) p. 129.

5. Mary D. Salter Ainsworth, "Some Considerations Regarding Theory and Assessment Relevant to Attachments beyond Infancy," in *Attachment in the Preschool Period: Theory, Research, and Intervention*, eds. Mark T. Greenberg, Dante Cicchetti, and E. Mark Cummings (Chicago: University of Chicago Press, 1990), p. 474.

6. Elder and Shanahan, "The Life Course of Human Development."

7. Jeffrey Jensen Arnett, "Emerging Adulthood: Understanding the New Way of Coming of Age," in *Emerging Adults in America: Coming of Age in the 21st Century*, eds. Jeffrey Jensen Arnett and Jennifer Lynn Tanner (Washington, DC: American Psychological Association, 2006), pp. 3–19.

8. Ronald E. Dahl, "Adolescent Brain Development: A Period of Vulnerabilities and Opportunities," *Annals of the New York Academy of Science 1021* (2004): 1–22.

9. Ann S. Masten et al., "Resources and Resilience in the Transition to Adulthood: Continuity and Change," *Development and Psychopathology 16* (2004): 1071–1094.

10. Gail S. Goodman, Robert E. Emery, and Jeffrey J. Haugaard, "Developmental Psychology and the Law: Divorce, Child Maltreatment, Foster Care, and Adoption," in *Handbook of Child Psychology*, 5th ed., ed. William Damon, vol. 4: *Child Psychology in Practice*, eds. Irving E. Sigel and K. Anne Renninger (New York: Wiley, 1998), pp. 775–784.

11. Jeffrey Jensen Arnett, "Conceptions of the Transition to Adulthood: Perspectives from Adolescence through Midlife," *Journal of Adult Development 8* (2001): 133–143.

12. D. Wayne Osgood et al., "Six Paths to Adulthood: Fast Starters, Parents without Careers, Educated Partners, Educated Singles, Working Singles, and Slow Starters," in *On the Frontier of Adulthood: Theory, Research, and Public Policy*. eds. Richard A. Settersten, Jr., Frank F. Furstenberg, Jr., and Ruben C. Rumbaut (Chicago: University of Chicago Press, 2005), pp. 320–355.

13. John Schulenberg et al., "Early Adult Transitions and Their Relation to Well Being and Substance Use," in *On the Frontier of Adulthood*, eds. Settersen, Furstenberg, and Rumbaut, pp. 417–453.

14. Nancy L. Galambos, Erin T. Barker, and Harvey J. Krahn, "Depression, Self-Esteem, and Anger in Emerging Adulthood: Seven-Year Trajectories," *Developmental Psychology 42* (2006): 350–365.

15. Ibid.

16. Schulenberg, et al., "Early Adult Transitions and Their Relation to Well Being and Substance Use."

17. John E. Schulenberg and Nicole R. Zarrett, "Mental Health During Emerging Adulthood: Continuity and Discontinuity in Courses, Causes, and Functions," in *Emerging Adults in America*, eds. Arnett and Tanner, pp. 135–172.

18. Carol L. Gohm et al., "Culture, Parental Conflict, Parental Marital Status, and the Subjective Well Being of Young Adults," *Journal of Marriage and the Family 60* (1998): 319–344.

19. Moncrieff Cochran, "Parenting and Personal Social Networks," in *Parenting: An Ecological Perspective*, eds. Tom Luster and Lynn Okagaki (Hillsdale, NJ: Erlbaum, 1993), pp. 149–178.

20. Robert F. Shoeni and Karen E. Ross, "Material Assistance from Families during the Transition to Adulthood," in *On the Frontier of Adulthood*, eds. Settersten, Furstenberg, and Rumbaut, pp. 396–416.

21. Cochran, "Parenting and Personal Social Networks."

22. Shoeni and Ross, "Material Assistance from Families During the Transition to Adulthood."

23. Osgood et al., "Six Paths to Adulthood."

24. E. Michael Foster and Elizabeth J. Gifford, "The Transition to Adulthood for Youth Leaving Public Systems: Challenges to Policies and Research," in *On the Frontier of Adulthood,* eds. Settersten, Furstenberg, and Rumbaut, pp. 501–533.

25. Steven L. Gortmaker et al., "An Unexpected Success Story: Transition to Adulthood in Youth with Chronic Physical Health Conditions," *Journal of Research on Adolescence 3* (1993): 333.

26. John Mollenkopf et al., "The Ever Winding Path: Ethnic and Racial Diversity in the Transition to Adulthood," in *On the Frontier of Adulthood,* eds. Settersten, Furstenberg, and Rumbaut, pp. 454–500.

27. Jean S. Phinney, "Ethnic Identity Exploration in Emerging Adulthood," in *Emerging Adults in America,* eds. Arnett and Tanner, pp. 117–134.

28. William S. Aquilino, "Family Relationships and Support Systems in Emerging Adulthood,' in *Emerging Adults in America,* eds. Arnett and Tanner, pp. 193–217.

29. Ibid.

30. Erica Goode, "Students' Emotional Health Worsens," *San Francisco Chronicle,* February 3, 2003, p. A9.

31. Ray Delgado, "Report on College Drinking's Toll Shows Health Crisis, Experts Say," *San Francisco Chronicle,* April 10, 2002, p. A7.

32. Aquilino, "Family Relationships and Support Systems in Emerging Adulthood."

33. Vern Bengtson, "Beyond the Nuclear Family: The Increasing Importance of Multigenerational Bonds," *Journal of Marriage and Family 63* (2001): 1–16.

34. Steven H. Zarit and David J. Eggebeen, "Parent-Child Relationships in Adulthood and Later Years," in *Handbook of Parenting,* 2nd ed., ed. Marc H. Bornstein, vol. 1: *Children and Parenting* (Mahwah, NJ Erlbaum, 2002), pp. 135–161.

35. Emily A. Greenfield and Nadine F. Marks, "Linked Lives: Adult Children's Problems and Their Parents' Psychological and Relational Well Being," *Journal of Marriage and Family 68* (2006): 442–454.

36. Paul R. Amato and Tamara D. Afifi, "Feeling Caught Between Parents: Adult Children's Relations with Parents and Subjective Well Being," *Journal of Marriage and Family 68* (2006): 222–235.

37. Valarie King, "The Legacy of Grandparents' Divorce: Consequences for Ties Between Grandparents and Grandchildren," *Journal of Marriage and Family 65* (2003): 170–183.

38. Gail Sheehy, "It's About Pure Love," *Parade Magazine,* May 12, 2002, p. 8.

39. Ibid.

40. Ibid., p. 7.

41. Edward J. Clarke et al., "Types of Conflicts and Tensions between Older Parents and Adult Children," *Gerontologist 39* (1999): 261–270.

42. Vern Bengston, "Solidarity, Conflict, and Ambivalence: Complementary or Competing Perspectives on Intergenerational Relationships?," *Journal of Marriage and Family 64* (2002): 568–576.

43. Karl Pillemer and J. Jill Suitor, "Explaining Mothers' Ambivalence Toward Their Adult Children," *Journal of Marriage and Family 64* (2002): 602–613.

44. Ingrid Arnet Connidis and Julie Ann McMullon, "Sociological Ambivalence and Family Ties: A Critical Perspective," *Journal of Marriage and Family 64* (2002): 558–567.

45. Stephen R. Covey, *The Seven Habits of Highly Effective Families* (New York: Golden Books, 1997).

46. Marsha Mailick Seltzer and Tamar Heller, "Families and Caregiving across the Life Course: Research Advances on the Influence of Context," *Family Relations 46* (1997): 321–323.

47. Ibid.

48. Jan S. Greenberg et al., "The Differential Effects of Social Support on the Psychological Well-Being of Aging Mothers of Adults with Mental Illness or Mental Retardation," *Family Relations 46* (1997): 383–394.

49. Marsha Mailick Seltzer et al., "Siblings of Adults with Mental Retardation or Mental Illness: Effects on Lifestyle and Psychological Well-Being," *Family Relations 46* (1997): 395–405.

50. Harriet P. Lefley, "Synthesizing the Family Caregiving Studies: Implications for Service Planning, Social Policy, and

Further Research," *Family Relations 46* (1997): 443–450.

51. Rachel Simon, "Riding the Bus with Beth," *Reader's Digest,* September 2002, pp. 140–145.

52. Ibid., p. 145.

53. Zarit and Eggebeen, "Parent–Child Relationships."

54. Ibid.

55. Ibid.

56. Ibid.

57. Ibid.

58. Barbara G. Unell and Jerry L. Wyckoff, *The Eight Seasons of Parenthood* (New York: Times, 2000).

59. Ibid., p. 270.

60. Lefley, "Synthesizing."

61. Ibid.

CHAPTER THIRTEEN

1. Lisa Belkin, "When Mom and Dad Share It All," *New York Times Magazine,* June 15 2008, 44-49

2. U.S. Census Bureau, *Statistical Abstract of the United States: 2009,* 128th ed., (Washington, DC: U.S. Government Printing Office, 2008).

3. Patricia Voydanoff, *Work, Family, and Community: Exploring Interconnections* (New York: Psychology Press, 2007).

4. Jeffrey Jensen Arnett, "Emerging Adulthood: Understanding the New Way of Coming of Age," in *Emerging Adults in America,* eds. Jeffrey Jensen Arnett and Jennifer Lynn Tanner (Washington, DC: American Psychological Association, 2006), pp. 3–19.

5. Sara B. Raley, Marybeth J. Mattingly, and Suzanne M. Bianchi, "How Dual Are Dual-Income Couples?: Documenting Change from 1970 to 2001," *Journal of Marriage and Family 68* (2006): 11–28.

6. Voydanoff, *Work, Family, and Community.*

7. Julie E. Press, Jay Fagan, and Lynda Laughlin, "Taking Pressure Off Families: Child Care Subsidies Lessen Mothers' Work-Hour Problems," *Journal of Marriage and Family 68* (2006): 155–171.

8. Blake L. Jones et al., "Perceived Versus Used Workplace Flexibility in Singapore: Predicting Work–Family Fit," *Journal of Family Psychology 22* (20008): 774–783.

9. Ellen Galinsky, *Ask the Children: What America's Children Really Think about Working Parents* (New York: Morrow, 1999).

10. Personal communication to author.

11. Marc S. Schulz, "Parents' Work Experiences and Children's Adaptation to School," in *The Family Context of Parenting in Children's Adaptation to Elementary School,* eds. Philip A. Cowan et al. (Mahwah, NJ: Erlbaum, 2005), pp. 237–253.

12. Ariel Kalil and Kathleen M. Ziol-Guest, "Single Mothers' Employment Dynamics and Adolescent Well Being," *Child Development 76* (2005): 196–211.

13. Galinsky, *Ask the Children.*

14. Ibid.

15. Ellen Greenberger and Robin O'Neil, "Parents' Concerns about Their Child's Development: Implications for Fathers' and Mothers' Well Being and Attitudes toward Work," *Journal of Marriage and the Family 52* (1990): 621–635; Ellen Greenberger and Robin O'Neil, "Spouse, Parent, Worker: Role Commitments and Role-Related Experiences in the Construction of Adults' Well Being," *Developmental Psychology 29* (1993): 181–197.

16. Rena L. Repetti and Jennifer Wood, "Effects of Daily Stress at Work on Mothers' Interactions with Preschoolers," *Journal of Family Psychology 11* (1997): 90–108.

17. Lisa B. Story and Rena Repetti, "Daily Occupational Stressors and Marital Behavior," *Journal of Family Psychology 20* (2006): 690–700.

18. Lyndall Strazdins et al., "Unsociable Work? Nonstandard Work Schedules, Family Relationships, and Children's Well-Being," *Journal of Marriage and Family 68* (2006): 394–410.

19. JoAnn Hsueh and Hirokazu Yoshikawa, "Working Nonstandard Schedules and Variable Shifts in Low-Income Families: Associations with Parental Psychological Well-Being, Family Functioning, and Child Well-Being," *Developmental Psychology 43* (2007): 620–632.

20. Rachel Dunifon, Ariel Kalil, and Ashish Bajracharya, "Maternal Working Conditions and Child Well-Being in Welfare Leaving Families," *Developmental Psychology 41* (2005): 851–859.

21. Galinsky, *Ask the Children.*

22. Ibid.

23. Ibid.

24. Rosalind Chait Barnett and Karen C. Gareis, "Parental After-School Stress

and Psychological Well Being," *Journal of Marriage and Family 68* (2006): 101–108.

25. Joseph G. Grzywacz, David M. Almeida, and Daniel A. McDonald, "Work–Family Spillover and Daily Reports of Work and Family Stress in the Adult Labor Force," *Family Relations 51* (2002): 28–36.

26. Margaret B. Neal and Leslie B. Hammer, *Working Couples Caring for Children and Aging Parents: Effects on Work and Well Being* (New York: Erlbaum, 2007).

27. David J. Maume, "Gender Differences in Restricting Work Efforts Because of Family Responsibilities," *Journal of Marriage and Family 68* (2006): 859–869.

28. Rand D. Conger and Katherine J. Conger, "Resilience in Midwestern Families: Selected Findings from the First Decade of a Prospective Longitudinal Study," *Journal of Marriage and Family 64* (2002): 361–373.

29. Neal and Hammer, *Working Couples Caring for Children and Aging Parents.*

30. Galinsky, *Ask the Children.*

31. Ibid.

32. Suzanne M. Bianchi, John P. Robinson, and Melissa A. Milkie, *Changing Rhythms of American Family Life* (New York: Russell Sage, 2006).

33. Sarah Damaske, Book Review of *Changing Rhythms of American Life, Journal of Marriage and Family 69* (2007): 545–546.

34. Michael E. Lamb and Lieselotte Ahnert, "Nonparental Child Care: Context, Concepts, Correlates, and Consequences," in *Handbook of Child Psychology*, 6th ed., eds. William Damon and Richard M. Lerner, vol. 4: *Child Psychology in Practice*, eds. K. Ann Renninger and Irving E. Sigel (Hoboken, NJ: Wiley, 2006), pp. 950–1016.

35. Ann C. Crouter and Susan M. McHale, "The Long Arm of the Job Revisited: Parenting in Dual-Earner Families," in *Parenting: An Ecological Perspective*, 2nd ed., eds. Tom Luster and Lynn Okgaki (Mahwah, NJ: Erlbaum, 2005), pp. 275–296.

36. Galinsky, *Ask the Children.*

37. Ibid., p. 232.

38. Grace G. Baruch and Rosalind C. Barnett, "Fathers' Participation in Family Work and Children's Sex-Role Attitudes," *Child Development 57* (1986): 1210–1223.

39. Joan E. Grusec, Jacqueline J. Goodnow, and Lorenzo Cohen, "Household Work and the Development of Concern for Others," *Developmental Psychology 32* (1996): 999–1007.

40. Jacqueline J. Goodnow and Jennifer M. Bowes, *Men, Women, and Household Work* (Melbourn, Australia: Oxford University Press, 1994).

41. Crouter and McHale, "The Long Arm of the Job Revisited."

42. Gregory Petit, "After-School Experience and Social Adjustment in Early Adolescence: Individual, Family, and Neighborhood Risk Factors," paper presented at the meetings of the Society for Research in Child Development in Washington, D.C., April 11, 1997.

43. Jean L. Richardson et al., "Substance Use among Eighth-Grade Students Who Take Care of Themselves After School," *Pediatrics 84* (1989): 556–566.

44. Galinsky, *Ask the Children.*

45. Lamb and Ahnert, "Nonparental Care," p. 951.

46. Ibid.

47. Ibid.

48. Edward F. Zigler, Matia Finn-Stevenson, and Nancy W, Hall, *The First Three Years of Life and Beyond* (New Haven, CT: Yale University Press, 2002).

49. Barnett and Gareis, "Parental After-School Stress and Psychological Well Being."

50. Lamb and Ahnert, "Nonparental Care."

51. National Association of Child Care Resources and Referrals Agencies, *Parents and the High Price of Child Care: 2008 Update* (Arlington, VA: 2008).

52. Zigler, Finn-Stevenson, and Hall, *The First Three Years of Life and Beyond.*

53. Lamb and Ahnert, "Nonparental Care."

54. Carollee Howes, Deborah A. Phillips, and Marcy Whitebook, "Thresholds of Quality Implications for the Social Development of Children in Center-Based Child Care," *Child Development 63* (1992): 449–460.

55. Cheryl D. Hayes, John L. Palmer, and Martha Zaslow, eds., *Who Cares for America's Children* (Washington, DC: National Academy Press, 1990).

56. Carollee Howes, Catherine C. Matheson, and Claire B. Hamilton, "Maternal, Teacher, and Child Care History Correlates of Children's Relationships with Peers," *Child Development 65* (1994): 264–273.

57. National Association of Child Care Resource and Referral Agencies, *We Can*

Do Better: NACCRRA Ranking of State Child Care Center Standards and Oversight (Arlington, VA, 2007).

58. Suzanne W. Helburn and Carollee Howes, "Child Care Cost and Quality," *The Future of Children* 6(2) (1996): 62–82.

59. Ibid., p. 69.

60. Ibid.

61. Lamb and Ahnert, "Nonparental Care."

62. Ibid.

63. Rachel A. Gordon and Robin S. Hognas, "The Best Laid Plans: Expectations, Preferences, and Stability of Child Care Arrangements," *Journal of Marriage and Family* 68 (2006): 373–393.

64. Henry Tran and Marsha Weinraub, "Child Care Effects in Context: Quality, Stability, and Multiplicity in Nonmaternal Child Care Arrangements During the First 15 Months of Life," *Developmental Psychology* 42 (2006): 566–582.

65. Ibid.

66. NICHD Early Child Care Research Network, "The Effects of Infant Child Care on Infant–Mother Attachment Security: Results of the NICHD Study of Early Child Care," *Child Development* 68 (1997): 876.

67. Sarah E. Watamura et al., "Morning to Afternoon Increases in Cortisol Concentrations for Infants and Toddlers at Child Care: Age Differences and Behavioral Correlates," *Child Development* 74 (2003): 1006–1020.

68. Lieselotte Ahnert, Martin Pinquart, and Michael E. Lamb, "Security of Children's Relationships with Nonparental Care Providers: A Meta-Analysis," *Child Development* 77 (2006): 664–679.

69. Lamb and Ahnert, "Nonparental Care," p. 975.

70. Ibid.

71. NICHD Early Child Care Research Network, "Child Care Effect Sizes for the NICHD Study of Early Child Care and Youth Development," *American Psychologist* 61 (2006): 99–116.

72. Ibid., p. 111.

73. Ibid., p. 111.

74. Jay Belsky et al., "Are There Long-Term Effects of Early Child Care?" *Child Development* 78 (2007): 681–701.

75. Lamb and Ahnert, "Nonparental Care."

76. Richardson et al., "Substance Use among Eighth Grade Students."

77. Lois Wladis Hoffman, "Effects of Maternal Employment in the Two-Parent Family," *American Psychologist* 44 (1989): 283–292.

78. Ross D. Parke and Raymond Buriel, "Socialization in the Family: Ethnic and Ecological Perspectives," in *Handbook of Child Psychology*, 6th ed., eds. William Damon and Richard M. Lerner, vol. 3: *Social, Emotional, and Personality Development*, ed. Nancy Eisenberg (Hoboken, NJ: Wiley, 2006), pp. 429–504.

79. Ann C. Crouter and Beth Manke, "Development of a Typology of Dual-Earner Families: A Window into Differences between and within Families in Relationships, Roles, and Activities," *Journal of Family Psychology* 11 (1997): 62–75.

80. Francine M. Deutsch, *Having It All: How Equally Shared Parenting Works* (Cambridge, MA: Harvard University Press, 1999).

81. Penny Edgell Becker and Phyllis Moen, "Scaling Back: Dual-Earner Couples' Working Family Strategies," *Journal of Marriage and the Family* 61 (1999): 995–1007.

82. Deutsch, *Having It All*.

83. The National Association of Child Care Resource and Referral Agencies (www.naccrra.org).

84. Families and Work Institute (www.familiesandwork.org).

CHAPTER FOURTEEN

1. Emily Bazelon, "Two Kids, Ø Husband Family," *New York Times Magazine*, February 1, 2009. 30–35.

2. www.childstats.gov/americaschildren/famsocl.asp. Table Family 1.B "Family Structure and Children's Living Arrangements."

3. Marsha Weinraub, Danielle L. Horvath, and Mary B. Gringlas, "Single Parenthood," in *Handbook of Parenting*, 2nd ed., ed. Marc H. Bornstein, vol. 3: *Being and Becoming a Parent* (Mahwah, NJ: Erlbaum, 2002), pp. 109–140.

4. Andrew J. Cherlin, "The Deinstitutionalization of American Marriage," *Journal of Marriage and Family* 66 (2004): 848–861.

5. United States Bureau of the Census, *Statistical Abstract of the United States:*

2009, 128th ed. (Washington, DC: U.S. Government Printing Office, 2008).

6. Kristen Harknett and Jean Krab, "More Kin, Less Support: Multipartnered Fertility and Perceived Support Among Mothers," *Journal of Marriage and Family* 69 (2007): 237–253.

7. Andrew Cherlin et al., "Promises They Can Keep: Low-Income Women's Attitudes Toward Motherhood, Marriage, and Divorce," *Journal of Marriage and Family* 70 (2008): 919–933.

8. Wendy D. Manning, Monica A. Longmore, and Peggy C. Giordano, "The Changing Institution of Marriage: Adolescents' Expectations to Cohabit and to Marry," *Journal of Marriage and Family* 69 (2007): 559–575.

9. Pamela J. Smock, "The Wax and Wane of Marriage: Prospects for Marriage in the 21st Century," *Journal of Marriage and Family* 66 (2004): 966–973.

10. Kathryn Edin and Joanna M. Reed, "Why Don't They Just Get Married: Barriers to Marriage among the Disadvantaged," *Future of Children* 15(2) (2005): 117–137.

11. Kelly Musick, "Planned and Unplanned Childbearing Among Unmarried Women," *Journal of Marriage and Family* 64 (2002): 915–929.

12. U.S. Bureau of the Census, *Statistical Abstract of the United States: 2009.*

13. Weinraub, Horvath, and Gringlas, "Single Parenthood."

14. Charles M. Blow, "Let's Talk About Sex," *New York Times* September 6, 2008, p. A23.

15. "Teenagers Changing Sexual Behavior," *New York Times* August 28, 2008, p. D7.

16. Mignon R. Moore and Jeanne Brooks-Gunn, "Adolescent Parenthood," in *Handbook of Parenting,* 2nd ed., ed. Marc H. Bornstein, vol. 3, pp. 173–214.

17. Judith A. Levine, Clifton R. Emery, and Harold Pollack, "The Well-Being of Children Born to Teen Mothers," *Journal of Marriage and Family* 69 (2007): 105–122.

18. Gerald Y. Michaels, "Motivational Factors in the Decision and Timing of Pregnancy," in *The Transition to Parenthood* eds. Gerald Y. Michaels and Wendy A. Goldberg (New York: Cambridge University Press, 1988), pp. 23–61.

19. Nancy J. Cobb, *Adolescence* (Mountain View, CA: Mayfield, 1992).

20. Brenda W. Donnelly and Patricia Voydanoff, "Factors Associated with Releasing for Adoption among Adolescent Mothers," *Family Relations* 40 (1990): 404–410.

21. Moore and Brooks-Gunn, "Adolescent Parenthood."

22. Lianne Woodward, David M. Fergusson, and L. John Horwood, "Risk Factors and Life Processes Associated with Teenage Pregnancy Results of a Prospective Study from Birth to Twenty Years," *Journal of Marriage and the Family* 63 (2001): 1170–1184.

23. Judith Musick, "The Special Role of Parenting in the Context of Poverty: The Case of Adolescent Motherhood," in *Threats to Optimal Developmental: Integrating Biological Psychological and Social Risk Factors,* ed. Charles A. Nelson (Hillsdale, NJ: Erlbaum, 1994), pp. 179–216.

24. Laura V. Scaramella et al., "Predicting Risk for Pregnanacy by Late Adolescence: A Social Contextual Perspective," *Developmental Psychology* 34 (1998): 1233–1245.

25. Lisa A. Serbin et al., "Intergenerational Transfer of Psychosocial Risk in Women with Childhood Histories of Aggression, Withdrawal, or Aggression and Withdrawal," *Developmental Psychology* 34 (1998): 1242–1262.

26. Woodward, Fergusson, and Horwood, "Risk Factors and Life Processes."

27. Joy D. Osofsky, Della M. Hann, and Claire Peebles, "Adolescent Parenthood: Risks and Opportunities for Mothers and Infants," in *Handbook of Infant Mental Health,* ed. Charles H. Zeanah, Jr. (New York: Guilford Press, 1993), pp. 106–119.

28. Ibid.

29. Ibid.

30. Terrence P. Thornberry, Carolyn A. Smith, and Gregory J. Howard, "Risk Factors for Teenage Fatherhood," *Journal of Marriage and the Family* 59 (1997): 505–522.

31. Tom Luster and Julie Laser Haddow, "Adolescent Mothers and Their Children," in *Parenting: An Ecological Perspective,* 2nd eds. Tom Luster and Lynn Okagaki (Mahwah, NJ: Erlbaum, 2005), pp. 73–101.

32. Moore and Brooks-Gunn, "Adolescent Parenthood."

33. Ross D. Parke and Raymond Buriel, "Socialization in the Family: Ethnic and Ecological Perspectives, in *Handbook of Child Psychology,* 5th ed. ed. William Damon, vol. 3: *Social, Emotional, and Personality Development,* ed. Nancy Eisenberg (New York: Wiley, 1998), pp. 463–552.

34. Beverly I. Fagot et al., "Becoming an Adolescent Father: Precursors and Parenting," *Developmental Psychology 34* (1998): 1217.

35. John G. Borkowski, Thomas I. Whitman, and Jaelyn R. Farris, "Adolescent Mothers and Their Children: Risks, Resilience, and Development," in *Risk and Resilience: Adolescent Mothers and Their Children Grow Up,* ed. John G. Borkowski et al. (Mahwah, NJ: Erlbaum, 2007), pp. 1–34.

36. Ibid.

37. Moore and Brooks-Gunn, "Adolescent Parenthood."

38. Frank F. Furstenberg, Jr., J. Brooks-Gunn, and S. Philip Morgan, *Adolescent Mothers in Later Life* (Cambridge, UK: Cambridge University Press, 1990.

39. Borkowski, Whitman, and Farris, "Adolescent Mothers and Their Children;" Jaelyn R. Farris, Leann E. Smith, and Keri Weed, "Resilience and Vulnerability in the Context of Multiple Risks," in *Risks and Resilience,* eds. Borkowski et al., pp. 179–204.

40. Farris, Smith, and Weed, "Resilience and Vulnerability in the Context of Multiple Risks."

41. Borkowski, Whitman, and Farris, "Adolescent Mothers and Their Children."

42. Kimberly S. Howard et al., "Overcoming the Odds: Protective Factors in the Lives of Children," in *Risk and Resilience,* eds. Borkowski et al., pp. 205–232.

43. Luster and Haddow, "Adolescent Mothers and Their Children."

44. Cynthia J. Schellenbach, Bonnie J. Leadbeater, and Kristen Anderson Moore, "Enhancing the Developmental Outcomes of Adolescent Parents and Their Children," in *Investing in Children, Youth, Families, and Communities: Strengths-Based Research and Policy,* eds. Kenneth I. Maton et al. (Washington, DC: American Psychological Association, 2004), pp. 117–136

45. Jerald G. Bachman et al., *The Education–Drug Use Connection: How Success and Failures in School Relate to Adolescent Smoking, Drinking, Drug Use, and Delinquency* (Mahwah, NJ: Erlbaum, 2008).

46. John G. Borkowski, Jaelyn R. Farris, and Keri Weed, "Toward Resilience: Designing Effective Prevention Programs," in *Risk and Resilience,* eds. John G. Borkowski et al. (Mahwah, NJ: Erlbaum, 2007), pp. 259–278.

47. Shellenbach, Leadbeater, and Moore, "Enhancing the Developmental Outcomes of Adolescent Parents and Their Children."

48. Michael E. Connor, "Walking the Walk: Community Programs That Work," in *Black Fathers: An Invisible Presence in America,* eds. Michael E. Connor and Joseph L. White (Mahwah, NJ: Erlbaum, 2006), pp. 257–267.

49. Musick, "Planned and Unplanned Childbearing Among Unmarried Women."

50. Ibid.

51. Wendy D. Manning, "The Implications of Cohabitation for Children's Well-Being," in *Just Living Together,* eds. Alan Booth and Ann C. Crouter (Mahwah, NJ: Erlbaum, 2002), pp. 121–152.

52. William S. Aquilino, "The Life Course of Children Born to Unmarried Mothers: Child Living Arrangements and Young Adult Outcomes," *Journal of Marriage and Family 58* (1996): 293–310.

53. Cynthia Osborne and Sara McLanahan, "Partnership Instability and Child Well Being," *Journal of Marriage and Family 69* (2007): 1065–1083.

54. Susan L. Brown, "Child Well-Being in Co-habiting Families," in *Just Living Together,* eds. Booth and Crouter, pp. 173–187; Susan L. Brown, "Family Structure and Child Well-Being: The Significance of Parental Cohabitation," *Journal of Marriage and Family 66* (2004): 351–367.

55. Martha J. Zaslow et al., "Protective Factors in the Development of Preschool-Age Children of Young Mothers Receiving Welfare," in *Coping with Divorce, Single Parenting, and Remarriage,* ed. E. Mavis Hetherington (Mahwah, NJ: Erlbaum, 1999), pp. 193–223.

56. Paul R. Amato, "The Impact of Family Formation Change on the Cognitive, Social, and Emotional Well-Being of the

Next Generation," *Future of Children 15* Fall (2005): 75–96.

57. Charles R. Martinez, Jr. and Marion Forgatch, "Preventing Problems with Boys' Concompliance: Effects of a Parent Training Intervention for Divorcing Mothers," *Journal of Consulting and Clinical Psychology 69* (2001): 416–428.

58. Weinraub, Horvath, and Gringlas, "Single Parenthood."

59. Ibid.

60. Jane Mattes, *Single Mothers by Choice,* 2nd ed. (New York: Times Books, 1997).

61. E. Mavis Hetherington, "An Overview of the Virginia Longitudinal Study of Divorce and Remarriage with a Focus on Early Adolescence," *Journal of Family Psychology 7* (1993): 39–56.

62. E. Mavis Hetherington and John Kelly, *For Better or For Worse: Divorce Reconsidered* (New York: Norton, 2002).

63. Pauline H. Tessler and Peggy Thompson, *Collaborative Divorce* (New York: HarperColllins, 2006), p. 130

64. Ibid.

65. Hetherington and Kelly, *For Better or For Worse.*

66. Judith S. Wallerstein and Joan B. Kelly, *Surviving the Breakup* (New York: Basic Books, 1980).

67. E. Mavis Hetherington and Margaret Stanley-Hagan, "Parenting in Divorced and Remarried Families," in *Handbook of Parenting,* 2nd ed., ed. Bornstein, vol. 3, pp. 287–315.

68. Ibid.

69. Hetherington and Kelly, *For Better or For Worse,* p. 80.

70. Ibid.

71. Ibid.

72. Lisa Strohschein, "Parental Divorce and Child Mental Health Trajectories," *Journal of Marriage and Family 67* (2005): 1286–1300.

73. Hetherington and Kelly, *For Better or For Worse.*

74. Judith S. Wallerstein, Julia M. Lewis, and Sandra Blakeslee, *The Unexpected Legacy of Divorce* (New York: Hyperion, 2000).

75. Paul R. Amato, "Reconciling Divergent Perspectives: Judith Wallerstein, Quantitative Family Research, and Children of Divorce," *Family Relations 52* (2003): 332–339.

76. Hetherington and Kelly, *For Better or For Worse.*

77. Tessler and Thompson, *Collaborative Divorce.*

78. Sara McLanahan and Julien Teitler, "The Consequence of Father Absence," in *Parenting and Child Development in Nontraditional Families,* ed. Michael E. Lamb (Mahwah, NJ: Erlbaum, 1999), pp. 83–102.

79. Paul R. Amato, "More Than Money: Men's Contributions to Their Children's Lives," in *Men in Families: When Do They Get Involved? What Difference Does It Make?* eds. Alan Booth and Ann C. Crouter (Mahwah, NJ: Erlbaum, 1998), pp. 241–278.

80. Ibid., p. 244.

81. Ibid., pp. 271–272.

82. Ibid., p. 257.

83. Howard et al., "Overcoming the Odds."

84. Sharon H. Bzostek, "Social Fathers and Child Well-Being," *Journal of Marriage and Family 70* (2008): 950–961.

85. Rebecca M. Ryan, Ariel Kalil, and Kathleen M. Ziol-Guest, "Longitudinal Patterns of Nonresident Fathers' Involvement: The Role of Resources and Relations," *Journal of Marriage and Family 70* (2008): 962–977.

86. William V. Fabricius, "Listening to Children of Divorce: New Findings that Diverge from Wallerstein, Lewis, and Blakeslee," *Family Relations 52* (2003): 385–396.

87. James A. Levine with Edward W. Pitt, *New Expectations: Community Strategies for Responsible Fatherhood* (New York: Families and Work Institute, 1995).

88. Ibid., p. 41.

89. Ibid., p. 108.

90. Earl Grollman, "Prologue," in *Explaining Death to Children,* ed. Earl Grollman (Boston: Beacon, 1967), p. 15.

91. Barbara D. Rosoff, *The Worst Loss* (New York: Henry Holt, 1994).

92. John Bowlby, *Attachment and Loss,* vol. 3: *Loss, Sadness, and Depression* (New York: Basic Books, 1980.

93. Ibid.

94. Rosoff, *The Worst Loss,* p. 108.

95. Ibid.

96. Ibid.

97. Ibid.

98. Ibid.

99. Ibid., p. 128.

100. Ibid., p. 14.

101. Ibid.

CHAPTER FIFTEEN

1. Ron Nixon, "De-emphasis on Race in Adoption is criticized, *New York Times,* May 27, 2008, p. A15.
2. William Morris, ed., *The American Heritage Dictionary of the English Language* (Boston: American Heritage Publishing Company and Houghton Mifflin, 1969).
3. Maria Schmeeckle et al., "What Makes Someone Family?: Adult Children's Perceptions of Current and Former Stepparents," *Journal of Marriage and Family* 68 (2006): 595–610.
4. E. Mavis Hetherington and Margaret Stanley-Hagan, "Parenting in Divorced and Remarried Families," in *Handbook of Parenting,* 2nd ed., ed. Marc H. Bornstein, vol. 3: *Being and Becoming a Parent* (Mahwah, NJ: Erlbaum, 2002), pp. 287–315.
5. Judith Wallerstein and Sandra Blakeslee, *Second Chances* (New York: Ticknor & Fields, 1989).
6. Fitzhugh Dodson, *How to Discipline with Love* (New York: Rawson Associates, 1977).
7. E. Mavis Hetherington and John Kelly, *For Better or Worse: Divorce Reconsidered* (New York: Norton, 2002).
8. James H. Bray and John Kelly, *Stepfamilies: Love, Marriage, and Parenting in the First Decade* (New York: Broadway Books, 1998).
9. Ibid., p. 16.
10. Ibid., p. 265.
11. Hetherington and Kelly, *For Better or Worse.*
12. E. Mavis Hetherington and Kathleen M. Jodl, "Stepfamilies As Settings for Child Development," in *Stepfamilies: Who Benefits? Who Does Not?* eds. Alan Booth and Judy Dunn (Hillsdale, NJ: Erlbaum, 1994), pp. 55–79.
13. Ibid.
14. E. Mavis Hetherington, "An Overview of the Virginia Longitudinal Study of Divorce and Remarriage with a Focus on Early Adolescence," *Journal of Family Psychology 1* (1993): 39–56.
15. Hetherington and Stanley-Hagan, "Parenting Divorced and Remarried Families."
16. Ibid.
17. Ibid.
18. Ibid.
19. Valarie King, "The Antecedents and Consequences of Adolescents' Relationships With Stepfathers and Nonresident Fathers," *Journal of Marriage and Family* 68 (2006): 910–928.
20. William Marsiglio and Ramon Hinojosa, "Managing the Multifather Family: Stepfathers as Father Allies," *Journal of Marriage and Family* 69 (2007): 845–862.
21. Valarie King, "When Children Have Two Mothers: Relationships with Nonresident Mothers, Stepmothers, and Fathers," *Journal of Marriage and Family* 69 (2007): 1178–1193.
22. Hetherington and Kelly, *For Better or Worse.*
23. Lynn White, "Stepfamilies over the Life Course: Social Support," in *Stepfamilies,* eds. Booth and Dunn, pp. 109–137.
24. Emily Visher, "The Stepping Ahead Program," in *Stepfamilies Stepping Ahead,* ed. Mala Burt (Baltimore: Stepfamilies Press, 1989), pp. 57–89.
25. Charlotte J. Patterson, "Lesbian and Gay Parenthood," in *Handbook of Parenting,* 2nd ed., ed. Bornstein, vol. 3, pp. 317–338.
26. Ibid.
27. Charlotte J. Patterson and Raymond W. Chan, "Families Headed by Lesbian and Gay Parents," in *Parenting and Child Development in Nontraditional Families,* ed. Michael E. Lamb (Mahwah, NJ: Erlbaum, 1999), pp. 191–219.
28. Dana Berkowitz and William Marsiglio, "Gay Men: Negotiating Procreative, Father, and Family Identities," *Journal of Marriage and Family* 69 (2007): 366–381.
29. Abbie E. Goldberg and JuliAnna Z. Smith, "Social Support and Psychological Well-Being in Lesbian and Heterosexual Preadoptive Couples," *Family Relations 57* (2008): 281–294.
30. Abbie E. Goldberg and Katherine R. Allen, "Imagining Men: Lesbian Mothers' Perceptions of Male Involvement During the Transition for Parenthood," *Journal of Marriage and Family* 69 (2007): 352–365.
31. Abbie E. Goldberg and Aline Sayer, "Lesbian Couples Relationship Quality Across the Transition to Parenthood," *Journal of Marriage and Family* 68 (2006): 87–100.
32. Patterson, "Lesbian and Gay Parenthood."

33. Patterson and Chan, "Families Headed by Lesbian and Gay Parents."

34. Patterson, "Lesbian and Gay Parenthood."

35. Jennifer L. Wainwright, Stephen T. Russell, and Charlotte J. Patterson, "Psychosocial Adjustment, School Outcomes, and Romantic Relationships of Adolescents with Same-Sex Parents," *Child Development 75* (2004): 1886–1898.

36. Ibid.

37. Jennifer L. Wainwright and Charlotte J. Patterson, "Peer Relations Among Adolescents with Female Same-Sex Parents," *Developmental Psychology 44* (2008): 117–126.

38. Jennifer L. Wainwright and Charlotte J. Patterson, "Delinquency, Victimization, and Substance Use Among Adolescents with Female Same-Sex Parents," *Journal of Family Psychology 20* (2006): 526–250.

39. David M. Brodzinsky and Ellen Pinderhughes, "Parenting and Child Development in Adoptive Families," in *Handbook of Parenting,* 2nd ed., ed. Marc H. Bornstein, vol. 1: *Children and Parenting* (Mahwah, NJ: Erlbaum, 2002), pp. 279–311.

40. Femmie Juffer and Marinus H. van IJzendoorn, "Behavior Problems and Mental Health Referrals of International Adoptees," *Journal of the American Medical Association 293* (2005): 2501–2515.

41. Brodzinsky and Pinderhughes, "Parenting and Child Development in Adoptive Families."

42. Lynn Von Korff, Harold D. Grotevant, and Ruth G. McRoy, "Openness Arrangements and Psychological Adjustment in Adolescent Adoptees," *Journal of Family Psychology 20* (2006): 531–534.

43. Brodzinsky and Pinderhughes, "Parenting and Child Development in Adoptive Families."

44. Ibid.

45. Ibid.

46. Richard M. Lee et al., "Cultural Socialization in Families with Internationally Adopted Children," *Journal of Family Psychology 20* (2006): 571–580.

47. Kristen E. Johnston et al., "Mothers' Racial, Ethnic, and Cultural Socialization of Transracially Adopted Asian Children," *Family Relations 56* (2007): 390–402.

48. Brodzinsky and Pinderhughes, "Parenting and Child Development in Adoptive Families."

49. Ibid.

50. David M. Brodzinsky, Marshall D. Schechter, and Robin Marantz Henig, *Being Adopted: The Lifelong Search for Self* (New York: Anchor Books, 1992).

51. Wendy Tieman, Jan van der Ende, and Frank C. Verhulst, "Young Adult International Adoptees Search for Birth Parents," *Journal of Family Psychology 22* (2008): 678–687.

52. Mary Dozier and Michael Rutter, "Challenges to the Development of Attachment Relationships Faced by Young Children in Foster and Adoptive Care," in *Handbook of Attachment: Theory, Research, and Clinical Applications,* 2nd ed., eds. Jude Cassidy and Phillip R. Shaver (New York: Guilford Press, 2008), pp. 698–717.

53. Brodzinsky and Pinderhughes, "Parenting and Child Development in Adoptive Families."

54. Susan Golombok, "Parenting and Contemporary Reproductive Technologies," in *Handbook of Parenting,* 2nd ed., ed. Bornstein, vol. 3, pp. 339–360.

55. Geert-Jan J. M. Stams et al., "Maternal Sensitivity, Infant Attachment, and Temperament in Early Childhood Predict Adjustment in Middle Childhood: The Case of Adopted Children and Their Biologically Unrelated Parents," *Developmental Psychology 38* (2002): 806–821.

56. Martha A. Rueter and Ascan F. Koerner, "The Effect of Family Communication Pattern on Adopted Adolescent Adjustment," *Journal of Marriage and Family 70* (2008): 715–727.

57. Brodzinsky, Schecter, and Henig, *Being Adopted.*

58. Brodzinsky and Pinderhughes, "Parenting and Child Development in Adoptive Families."

59. Gail S. Goodman, Robert E. Emery, and Jeffrey J. Haugaard, "Developmental Psychology and Law: Divorce, Child Maltreatment, Foster Care, and Adoption," in *Handbook of Child Psychology,* 5th ed., ed. William Damon, vol. 4: *Child Psychology in Practice,* eds. Irving E. Sigel and K. Anne Renninger (New York: Wiley, 1998), pp. 775–874.

60. Dianne Borders, Judith M. Penny, and Francine Portnoy, "Adult Adoptees and Their Friends: Current Functioning and Psychosocial Well Being," *Family Relations* 49 (2000): 407–418.

61. Juffer and van IJzendoorn, "Behavior Problems and Mental Health Referrals of International Adoptees."

62. Brodzinsky and Pinderhughes, "Parenting and Child Development in Adoptive Families."

63. Dozier and Rutter, "Challenges to the Development of Attachment Relationships."

64. Femmie Juffer, Marinus H. van IJzendoorn, and Marian J. Bakermans-Kranenburg, "Supporting Adoptive Families with Video-Feedback Intervention," in *Promoting Positive Parenting: An Attachment-Based Intervention,* eds. Femmie Juffer, Marian J. Bakermans-Kranenburg, and Marinus H. van IJzendoorn (New York: Erlbaum, 2008), pp. 139–153.

65. Ibid.

CHAPTER SIXTEEN

1. Lisa W. Foderaro, "As Teenagers Leave Group Homes, a Challenge Placing Those Who Remain," *New York Times,* June 8, 2008, p. A31.

2. Barbara D. Rosoff, *The Worst Loss* (New York: Henry Holt, 1994).

3. Barbara G. Melamed, "Parenting the Ill Child," in *Handbook of Parenting,* 2nd ed., ed. Marc H. Bornstein, vol. 5: *Practical Issues of Parenting* (Mahwah, NJ: Erlbaum, 2002), pp. 329–348.

4. Lonnie K. Zeltzer and Christine Blackett Schlank, *Conquering Your Child's Chronic Pain* (New York: HarperCollins, 2005).

5. Elizabeth Gellert, "Children's Conceptions of the Content and Functions of the Human Body," *Genetic Psychology Monographs* 65 (1962): 293–405.

6. Roger Bibace and Mary E. Walsh, "Developmental States of Children's Conceptions of Illness," in *Health Psychology,* eds. George C. Stone, Frances Cohen, and Nancy E. Adler (San Francisco: Jossey-Bass, 1979), pp. 285–301.

7. Zeltzer and Schlank, *Conquering Your Child's Chronic Pain,* p. 32.

8. Melamed, "Parenting the Ill Child."

9. Ibid.

10. Ibid.

11. Dante Cicchetti and Michael Lynch, "Toward an Ecological/Transactional Model of Community Violence and Child Maltreatment: Consequences for Child Development," *Psychiatry* 56 (1993): 96–118.

12. Sandra T. Azar, "Parenting and Maltreatment," in *Handbook of Parenting,* 2nd ed., ed. Marc H. Bornstein, vol. 4: *Social Conditions and Applied Parenting* (Mahwah, NJ: Erlbaum, 2002), pp. 361–388.

13. Ibid.

14. Edward F. Zigler, Matia Finn-Stevenson, and Nancy W. Hall, *The First Three Years & Beyond* (New Haven, CT: Yale University Press, 2002.

15. David Finkelhor and Lisa Jones, "Why Have Maltreatment and Child Victimization Declined?" *Journal of Social Issues* 62 (2006): 685–716.

16. U.S. Bureau of the Census, *Statistical Abstract of the United States:* 2009, 128th ed. (Washington, DC: U.S. Government Printing Office, 2008).

17. Katherine Elliott and Anthony Urquiza, "Ethnicity, Culture, and Maltreatment," *Journal of Social Issues* 62 (2006): 787–809.

18. Gregory K. Fritz, "The Foster Care System: Can't Live With It and Can't Live Without It," *Brown University Child and Adolescent Behavior Newsletter* (March 2004) p. 7.

19. Elliott and Urquiza, "Ethnicity, Culture, and Maltreatment."

20. Dante Cicchetti and Sheree L. Toth, "Developmental Psychopathology and Preventive Intervention, " in *Handbook of Child Psychology,* 6th ed., eds. William Damon and Richard M. Lerner, vol. 4: *Child Psychology in Practice,* eds. K. Ann Renninger and Irving E. Sigel (Hoboken, NJ: Wiley, 2006), pp. 497–547.

21. Gail S. Goodman, Robert E. Emery, and Jeffrey J. Haugaard, "Developmental Psychology and Law: Divorce, Child Maltreatment, Foster Care, and Adoption," in *Handbook of Child Psychology,* 5th ed., ed. William Damon, vol. 4: *Child Psychology in Practice,* eds. Irving E. Sigel and K. Ann Renninger (New York: Wiley, 1998), pp. 775–874.

22. John W. Fantuzzo and Wanda K. Mohr, "Prevalence and Effects of Child Exposure to Domestic Violence," *The Future of Children* 9 (3) (1999): 21–32.

23. Judith A. Cohen et al., "Psychosocial Interventions for Maltreated and Violence-Exposed Children," *Journal of Social Issues* 62 (2006): 737–766.

24. Lucy Salcido Custer, Lois A. Weithorn, and Richard E. Berman, "Domestic Violence and Children: Analysis and Recommendations," *The Future of Children 9* (3) (1999): 4–20.

25. Sally Zierler, "Studies Confirm Long-Term Consequences of Childhood Sexual Abuse," *Brown University Child and Adolescent Newsletter 8* (1992): 3.

26. Glenn D. Wolfner and Richard J. Gelles, "A Profile of Violence toward Children: A National Study," *Child Abuse and Neglect 17* (1993): 199–214.

27. Cohen, "Psychosocial Interventions for Maltreated and Violence-Exposed Children."

28. Robin McGee, David Wolfe, and James Olson, "Multiple Maltreatment, Attribution of Blame, and Adjustment among Adolescents," *Development and Psychopathology 13* (2001): 827–846.

29. Azar, "Parenting and Maltreatment," Alexandra Okun, Jeffrey G. Parker, and Alytia Levendosky, "Distinct and Interactive Contributions of Physical Abuse, Socioeconomic Disadvantage and Negative Life Events to Children's Social, Cognitive, and Affective Adjustment," *Development and Psychopathology 6* (1994): 77–98.

30. Christoph Heinicke, "The Transition to Parenthood," in *Handbook of Parenting,* 2nd ed., ed. Marc H. Bornstein, vol. 3: *Being and Becoming a Parent* (Mahwah, NJ: Erlbaum, 2002), pp. 363–388.

31. Azar, "Parenting and Maltreatment"; L. Alan Sroufe et al., *The Development of the Person* (New York: Guilford Press, 2005).

32. Azar, "Parenting and Maltreatment."

33. Ibid.

34. Tiffany Watts-English et al., "The Psychobiology of Maltreatment in Childhood," *Journal of Social Issues 62* (2006): 717–736.

35. Mary Dozier et. al., "Developing Evidence-Based Interventions for Foster Children: An Example of a Randomized Clinical Trial with Infants and Toddlers," *Journal of Social Issues 62* (2006): 767–785.

36. Watts-English et al., "The Psychobiology of Maltreatment in Childhood."

37. American Psychiatric Association, *Diagnostic and Statistical Manual of Mental Disorders,* 4th ed. (Washington, DC: American Psychiatric Association, 1994).

38. McGee, Wolfe, and Olson, "Multiple Maltreatment."

39. Jody Todd Manly et al., "Dimensions of Child Maltreatment and Children's Adjustment: Contributions of Developmental Timing and Subtype," *Development and Psychopathology 13* (2001): 759–782.

40. Robert E. Emery and Lisa Laumann-Billings, "An Overview of the Nature, Causes, and Consequences of Abusive Family Relationships: Toward Differentiating Maltreatment and Violence," *American Psychologist 53* (1998): 121–135.

41. Dante Cicchetti et al., "False Belief Understanding in Maltreated Children," *Development and Psychopathology 15* (2003): 1067–1091.

42. Sheree L. Toth et al., "The Relative Efficacy of Two Interventions in Altering Maltreated Preschool Children's Representational Models: Implications for Attachment Theory," *Development and Psychopathology 14* (2002): 877–908.

43. Dante Cicchetti, "An Odyssey of Discovery: Lessons Learned Through Three Decades of Research on Child Maltreatment," *American Psychologist 59* (2004): 731–741.

44. Manly et al., "Dimensions of Child Maltreament."

45. Penelope K. Trickett et al., "Variants of Intrafamilial Sexual Abuse Experience: Implications for Short- and Long-Term Development," *Development and Psychopathology 13* (2001): 1001–1019.

46. David Finkelhor, Richard K. Ormrod, and Heather A. Turner, "Polyvictimization and Trauma in a National Longitudinal Cohort," *Development and Psychopathology 19* (2007): 149–166.

47. Cohen, "Psychosocial Interventions for Maltreated and Violence-Exposed Children."

48. Irwin N. Sandler et al., "Adversities and Public Policy," in *Investing in Children, Youth, Families, and Communities,* eds. Kenneth I. Maton et al., (Washington, DC: American Psychological Association, 2004), pp. 31–49.

49. Goodman, Emery, and Haugaard, "Development, Psychology, and the Law."

50. Catherine R. Lawrence, Elizabeth A. Carlson, and Byron Egeland, "The Impact of Foster Care on Development," *Development and Psychopathology 18* (2006): 57–76.

51. Dozier et al., "Developing Evidence-Based Interventions for Foster Children."

52. John Eckenrode et al., "Child Maltreatment and the Early Onset of Problem Behaviors: Can a Program of Nurse Home Visitation Break the Link?" *Development and Psychopathology 13* (2001): 873–890.

53. Daphne Blunt Bugental et al., "A Cognitive Approach to Child Abuse Prevention," *Journal of Family Psychology 16* (2002): 243–258.

54. Cicchetti and Toth, "Developmental Psychopathology and Preventive Intervention."

55. Toth et al., "The Relative Efficacy of Two Interventions in Altering Maltreated Preschool Children's Representational Models."

56. Renee McDonald, Ernest N. Jouriles, and Nancy A. Skopp, "Reducing Conduct Problems Among Children Brought To Women's Shelters: Intervention Effects 24 Months Following Termination of Services," *Journal of Family Psychology 20* (2006): 127–136.

57. Cohen, "Psychosocial Interventions for Maltreated and Violence-Exposed Children."

58. Sroufe et al., *The Development of the Person.*

59. Fritz, "The Foster Care System."

60. Jeffrey Haugaard and Cindy Hazan, "Foster Parenting," in *Handbook of Parenting,* 2nd ed., ed. Marc H. Bornstein, vol. 1: *Children and Parenting* (Mahwah, NJ:Erlbaum, 2002), pp. 313–327.

61. Fritz, "The Foster Care System."

62. Haugaard and Hazan, "Foster Parenting."

63. Ibid.

64. Ibid.

65. Ibid.

66. Ibid.

67. Ibid.

68. Lawrence, Carlson, and Egeland, "The Impact of Foster Care on Development."

69. Haugaard and Hazan, "Foster Parenting."

70. Goodman, Emery, and Haugaard, "Develeopment, Psychology, and the Law."

71. Monica Davey, "Youths Leaving Foster Care Are Found Facing Obstacles," *New York Times,* February 24, 2004, p. A10.

72. Monica Davey, "Those Who Outgrow Foster Care Struggle, Study Finds," *New York Times,* May 19, 2005, p. A14.

73. Ibid.

74. Goodman, Emery, and Haugaard, "Development, Psychology, and the Law."

75. Ibid.

76. Annette M. LaGreca and Mitchell J. Prinstein, "Hurricanes and Earthquakes," in *Helping Children Cope with Disasters and Terrorism,* eds. Annette M. LaGreca et al., (Washington DC: American Psychological Association, 2002), pp. 107–138.

77. Jacob M. Vigil and David C. Geary, "A Preliminary Investigation of Family Coping Styles and Well-Being Among Adolescent Survivors of Hurricane Katrina," *Journal of Family Psychology 22* (2008): 176–180.

78. LaGreca and Prinstein, "Hurricanes and Earthquakes."

79. Robin H. Gurwitch et al., "The Aftermath of Terrorism," in *Helping Children Cope with Disasters and Terrorism,* eds. LaGreca et al., pp. 327–357.

80. Deborah Smith, "Everyday Fears Trump Worries about Terrorism," *Monitor on Psychology* (May 2003): 22–23.

81. Joshunda Sanders, "What to Tell Kids about War," *San Francisco Chronicle,* March 19, 2003, p. A21.

82. American Psychological Association, "The Psychological Needs of U.S. Military Service Members and Their Families: A Preliminary Report," 2007, Retrieved January 2009 from www.apa.org/releases/MilitaryDeploymentTaskForceReport.pdf.

83. Julia Yeary, "Operation Parenting Edge: Promoting Resiliency through Prevention," *Zero to Three 27* (July 2007): 7–12.

84. American Psychological Association, "The Psychological Needs of U.S. Military Service Members and Their Families."

85. Ibid.

86. Yeary, "Operation Parenting Edge."

87. Steven J. Wolin and Sybil Wolin, *The Resilient Self* (New York: Villard, Books, 1993).

88. Ibid., pp. 5–6.

CREDITS

Text Credits

Figure 1-1, from "Beyond the Nuclear Family: The Increasing Importance of Multi-generational Bonds," by Vern L. Bengston, *Journal of Marriage and Family,* 63. Copyright © 2001 by the National Council on Family Relations, 3989 Central Ave. ME, Suite 550, Minneapolis, MN 55421. **Figure 3-1**, reprinted with Permission from William J. Cross, Jr., "A Two-Factor Theory of Black Identity," in *Children's Ethnic Socialization,* ed. Jean S. Phinney and Mary Jane Rotheram (Newbury Park, CA: Sage, 1987), p. 122. Reprinted by permission of Sage Publications. **Table 3-1**, from Patricia Greenfield, Lalita K. Sazuki, and Carrie Rothstein-Fisch, "Contrasting Cultural Models of Parent-Child Relations," *Handbook of Child Psychology,* 6th ed., eds. William Lerner and Richard M. Lerner, vol. 4: *Child Psychology in Practice,* eds. K. Ann Renninger and Irving E Sigel (Hoboken, NJ: Wiley, 2006), p. 676. Reprinted with permission of John Wiley and Sons, Inc. **Figure 3-2**, "An Integrative Model of Child Development," from Cynthia Garcia Coll and Laura A. Szalacha, "The Multiple Contexts of Middle Childhood," *The Future of Children* 14 (2) 2004: 83. Reprinted with permission of the David and Lucile Packard Foundation. **Table 3-4**, "Typology of Differences in Children Rearing," from Annette Lareau, *Unequal Childhoods: Class, Race, and Family Life* (Berkeley. University of California Press, 2003), p. 31. Reprinted by permission from the University of California Press. **Table 5-1**, "Developmental Challenges Faced by Children and Caregivers from Infancy through Adolescence," from E. Mark Cummings, Patrick T. Davies, and Susan B. Campbell, *Developmental Psychopathology and Family Process* (New York: Guildford Press, 2000), p. 207. Reprinted with permission from Guilford Press. **Table 5-2 and Table 5-3**, "Time Spent with the Media" and "Time Spent in Non-Media Activities" from *Generation M: Media in the Lives of 8–18 Year Olds* (#7251), The Henry J. Kaiser Family Foundation, March 2005, www.kff.org, pp. 7 and 8. The Kaiser Family Foundation, based in Menlo Park California, is a non-profit, private operating foundation focusing on the major health care issues facing the nation and is not associated with Kaiser Permanente or Kaiser Industries. New York. All rights reserved. **Figure 9-1**, Mary J. Levitt, Nathalie Guacci Franco, and Jerome L. Levitt, "Convoys of Social Support in Childhood and Early Adolescence: Structure and Function," *Developmental Psychology* 29 (1993): p. 815. Reprinted with permission from the American Psychological Association. **Figure 12-1**, table adapted from Jeffrey Jensen Amett, "Conceptions of the Transition to Adulthood: Perspectives from Adolescence to Midlife," *Journal of Adult Development* 8 (2001): p. 127. Reprinted with kind permission from. Springer Science and Business Media. **Table 12-2**, Vern L. Bengston, "Beyond the Nuclear Family: The Increasing Importance of Multigenerational Bonds." Copyright © 2001 by the National Council on Family Relations. Reprinted by permission. **Figure 14-2**, from *New Expectations: Community Strategies for Responsible Fatherhood* by James Levine and Edward

W. Pitt, (New York: Families and Work Institute, 1995), p. 41. Reprinted with permission of the Families and Work Institute.

Photo Credits

Page 4: Stockbyte/Getty Images; 16: Jack Hollingsworth/Getty Images; 57: image100/PunchStock; 63: Digital Vision/Getty Images; 85: Image Source/Alamy; 107: Big Cheese Photo LLC/Alamy; 113: Brand X Pictures; 146: Brand X Pictures/PunchStock; 153: Ariel Skelley/Getty Images; 192: BananaStock/Punchstock; 201: Brand X Pictures/PunchStock; 207: Bananastock/JupiterImages; 217: Photodisc/Getty Images; 238: Rubberball/Getty Images; 239: David De Lossy/Getty Images; 268: Buccina Studios/Getty Images; 285: Ronnie Kaufman/Getty Images; 312: Royalty-Free/Corbis; 316: Thinkstock/JupiterImages; 343: Purestock/PunchStock; 353: Image Source/Punchstock; 373: Comstock/Corbis; 377: Richard Hutching/PhotoEdit; 391: BananaStock/PunchStock; 394: Photodisc/PunchStock; 431: Thinkstock/Corbis; 454: Amos Morgan/Getty Images; 460: Blend Images/Getty Images; 487: Digital Vision/PunchStock; 499: Mike Okoniewski/The Image Works.

INDEX